Annotated Model Code of Judicial Conduct

Third Edition

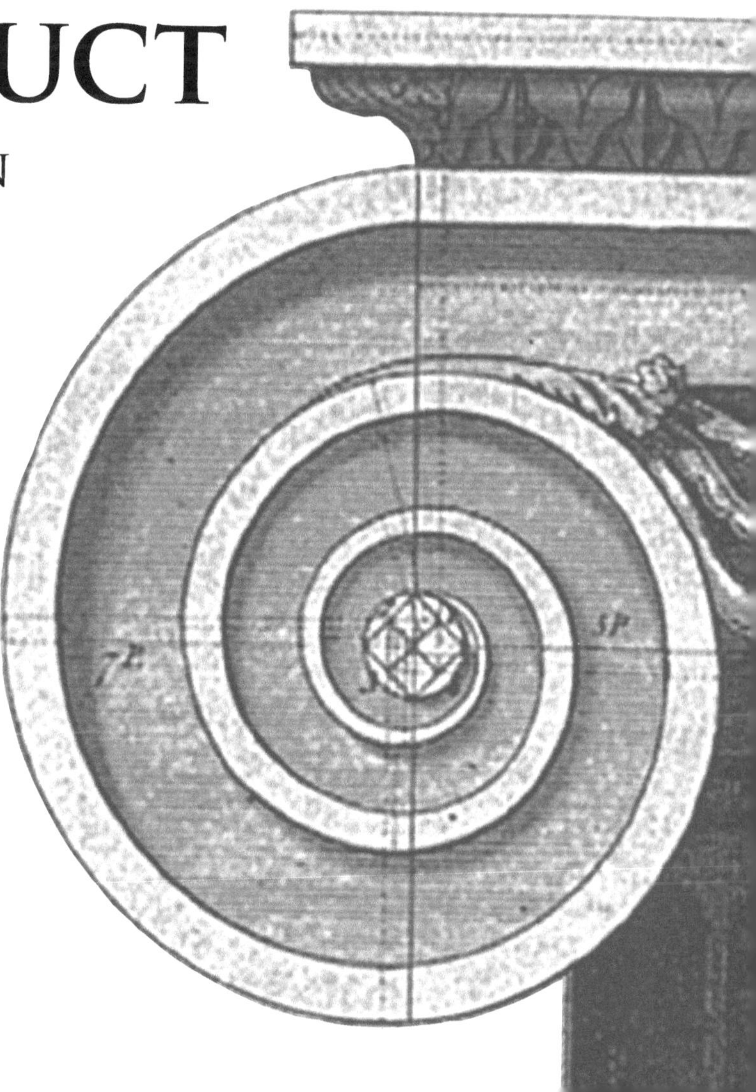

Arthur H. Garwin
Mary McDermott
Dennis A. Rendleman

American Bar Association
Center for Professional Responsibility

Cover design by Betsy Kulak/ABA Design

Printed in the United States of America.

25 24 23 5 4 3

Library of Congress Cataloging-in-Publication Data

Names: Garwin, Arthur, 1949- author. | Rendleman, Dennis A., author. | McDermott, Mary author.
Title: Annotated model code of judicial conduct / Arthur H. Garwin, Dennis Alan Rendleman, and Mary McDermott.
Description: Third edition. | [Chicago] : American Bar Association, [2016] | Includes bibliographical references and index.
Identifiers: LCCN 2016047228 (print) | LCCN 2016047332 (ebook) | ISBN 9781634256551 (text : alk. paper) | ISBN 9781634256568 (epub)
Subjects: LCSH: Judicial ethics—United States.
Classification: LCC KF8779 .A96 2016 (print) | LCC KF8779 (ebook) | DDC 347.73/14—dc23
LC record available at https://lccn.loc.gov/2016047228

Discounts are available for books ordered in bulk. Special consideration is given to state bars, CLE programs, and other bar-related organizations. Inquire at Book Publishing, ABA Publishing, American Bar Association, 321 N. Clark Street, Chicago, Illinois 60654-7598.

www.ShopABA.org

Contents

Dedicated to the memory of
Jeanne P. Gray
Director, ABA Center for Professional Responsibility,
1982–2013

Acknowledgments

In the six years between the publication of the first and second editions of the *Annotated Model Code of Judicial Conduct*, the Model Code of Judicial Conduct underwent a comprehensive review by the Joint Commission to Evaluate the Model Code of Judicial Conduct. The revised Model Code was adopted by the ABA House of Delegates in February 2007. At the time of publication of this third edition, 35 jurisdictions had approved revisions of their judicial codes in line with the Model Code, 10 had established committees to review their codes, one had proposed final revisions to its code, and only five had yet to establish committees to review their codes. As a result of the adoptions, many new cases, citing to the rules in their current structure, have been added to this edition. The older cited cases remain instructive since the majority of the new rules derive directly from the earlier Canons. This book provides a comparision to the former standards, along with the authority that flowed from them.

This publication presents an authoritative and practical analysis of the judicial ethics rules and the cases, ethics opinions, and other legal authorities essential to understanding them. The book follows the successful style of the *Annotated Model Rules of Professional Conduct*, and builds upon the historical work presented in the *Reporter's Notes to Code of Judicial Conduct* by E. Wayne Thode in 1973, *The Development of the ABA Judicial Code* by Lisa L. Milord in 1992, the *Reporters' Notes to the Model Code of Judicial Conduct* by Charles G. Geyh and W. William Hodes in 2009, and the first two editions of this book.

Special appreciation is in order to Mary McDermott for her work on this edition, and to Dennis Rendleman for his work on this and the previous edition. Appreciation also goes to Kathleen Maher and Eileen Libby, much of whose work on the previous edition is still evident in this publication.

The Center for Professional Responsibility also acknowledges the West Publishing Company for its generous gift of the West Professional Responsibility Law Library, the resource for much of the research that is reflected in this work.

Arthur Garwin, Director
ABA Center for Professional Responsibility

Preface

In 1924, the American Bar Association (ABA) adopted the Canons of Judicial Ethics, which, according to Chief Justice William Howard Taft, who chaired the ABA Committee on Judicial Ethics, were intended to be a "guide and reminder to the judiciary."[1] The 1924 Canons of Judicial Ethics consisted of 36 provisions that included both generalized, hortatory admonitions and specific rules of proscribed conduct. The 1924 Canons were not intended to be a basis for disciplinary action. Many states, however, adopted this "guide" as a set of substantive rules, giving the Canons in those states the force of law, with the added persuasion of sanctions for violations.[2]

Answering criticism that the 1924 Canons engaged in "moral posturing," which was more "hortatory than helpful in providing firm guidance for the solution of difficult questions,"[3] the ABA appointed a Special Committee on Standards of Judicial Conduct in 1969 to develop new ethics rules for judges. California Supreme Court Justice Roger J. Traynor chaired the Special Committee. After three years' work by the Special Committee, the Code of Judicial Conduct was adopted by unanimous vote of the ABA House of Delegates on August 16, 1972.[4] The 1972 Code was designed to be enforceable, and was intended to preserve the integrity and independence of the judiciary.[5]

In 1986, the ABA Standing Committee on Ethics and Professional Responsibility, with jurisdiction over the Code, conducted a survey that led to the conclusion that the Code, in general, was serving its purposes well, but a comprehensive review of the Code was desirable. That review was conducted from 1987 to 1990 by the Standing Committee on Ethics and Professional Responsibility, and its Judicial Code Subcommittee composed of several

1. *See* Randall T. Shepard, *Campaign Speech: Restraint and Liberty in Judicial Ethics*, 9 Geo. J. Legal Ethics 1059, 1065 n. 26 (1996) (citing the *Final Report and Proposed Canons of Judicial Ethics*, 9 A.B.A.J. 449, 449 (1923)).

2. *Id.* (citing Robert Martineau, *Enforcement of the Code of Judicial Conduct*, 1972 Utah L. Rev. 410, 410).

3. Robert McKay, *Judges, the Code of Judicial Conduct, and Nonjudicial Activities*, 1972 Utah L. Rev. 391, 391.

4. American Bar Association, *Report of the Special Committee on Standards of Judicial Conduct*, 96 Rep. of the A.B.A. 733–34 (1971).

5. *See* E. Wayne Thode, Reporter's Notes to the Code of Judicial Conduct (1973).

current and former members of the Ethics Committee, and several members of the judiciary. This national effort was funded by the Josephson Institute for the Advancement of Ethics, the State Justice Institute, and the ABA.

In the revision process, the ABA sought and considered the views of members of the judiciary, the bar, and the general public. The Committee was aware that the 1972 Canons, apart from their subsections, were used widely as a basis for discipline. Therefore, the Committee declined to replace the black letter language with descriptive headings and determined that the Code, consisting of statements of norms denominated Canons, specific Sections, and explanatory Commentary, stated the appropriate ethical obligations of judges.[6]

On August 7, 1990, the ABA House of Delegates adopted the Model Code of Judicial Conduct. In the 1990 Code, a Preamble and a Terminology section were added, and an Application section followed the Canons. The 1990 Code was amended three times: on August 6, 1997, August 10, 1999, and August 12, 2003.

In September 2003, with a grant from The Joyce Foundation of Chicago, Illinois, the ABA announced the appointment of the Joint Commission to Evaluate the Model Code of Judicial Conduct under the auspices of the ABA Standing Committee on Ethics and Professional Responsibility and the ABA Standing Committee on Judicial Independence. The mandate of the Commission was to review the 1990 Code and to recommend revisions for possible adoption. The 11-member Commission was composed of judges, experts in the field of judicial and legal ethics, and a public member, and was supported by two reporters, ten advisors, and counsel from the ABA.

Over the course of three and one half years, the Commission conducted a comprehensive examination of the standards for the ethical conduct of judges and judicial candidates that promote the independence, integrity, and impartiality of the judiciary. This examination was prompted, in part, by the collective experience of judges and judicial regulators who had worked with the 1990 Code for more than a decade, and by the emergence of new types of courts and courts processes, the increasing frequency of pro se representation, and the utilization of diverse methods in the judicial selection process. This national effort culminated in the adoption of the revised Model Code of Judicial Conduct by the ABA House of Delegates on February 12, 2007.

The 2007 Code proposed both format and substantive changes to the 1990 Code. Following a format similar to the ABA Model Rules of Professional Conduct, the 2007 Code preserved the Canons, which state overarching principles of judicial conduct, followed by enforceable black letter Rules, as well as Comments that provide both aspirational statements and guidance in interpreting and

6. *See* LISA L. MILORD, THE DEVELOPMENT OF THE ABA JUDICIAL CODE at 8 (1992).

applying the Rules. The four Canons and their numbered Rules and Comments were reorganized to provide topics under a functional arrangement. Canon 1 addresses the paramount obligations of judges to uphold the independence, integrity, and impartiality of the judiciary, and to avoid impropriety and its appearance; Canon 2 solely addresses the judge's professional duties as a judge; Canon 3 addresses extrajudicial and personal conduct; and Canon 4 addresses the political conduct of judges and judicial candidates. Also included are four sections that precede the Canons: a Preamble, which states the objectives of the Model Code; a Scope section, which describes the manner in which the Canons and their Rules and Comments are to be interpreted, used for guidance, and enforced; a Terminology section, which provides definitional guidance; and an Application section, which establishes when the various Rules apply to a judge or judicial candidate.

Two appendixes, which are not intended to be adopted as part of the Code, are presented. One appendix provides information on establishing judicial ethics advisory committees, and the second contains two Correlation Tables to the ABA Model Code of Judicial Conduct that compare the provisions between the 2007 Code and the 1990 Code.

The ABA continues to pursue its goal of ensuring the highest standards of professional competence and ethical conduct. The Standing Committee on Ethics and Professional Responsibility, entrusted with interpreting the professional standards of the ABA and recommending appropriate amendments and clarifications, issues opinions interpreting the Model Rules of Professional Conduct and the Model Code of Judicial Conduct. The opinions of the Committee are published by the ABA.

ABA Joint Commission to Evaluate the Model Code of Judicial Conduct (2003–2007)

Mark I. Harrison
Phoenix, AZ, *Chair*

James J. Alfini
Houston, TX

Loretta C. Argrett
Washington, DC

Jan Witold Baran
Washington, DC

Dianne Cleaver
Kansas City, MO

Thomas M. Fitzpatrick
Tukwila, WA

Donald B. Hilliker
Chicago, IL

Hon. M. Margaret McKeown
San Diego, CA

Hon. Cara Lee T. Neville
Minneapolis, MN

Hon. Harriet L. Turney
Phoenix, AZ

Hon. James A. Wynn
Raleigh, NC

Reporters

Charles G. Geyh
Bloomington, IN

W. William Hodes
Indianapolis, IN

Advisors

Hon. Carol Bagley Amon
Judicial Conference of the United States

Hon. Peter W. Bowie
Judicial Conference of the United States

Robert P. Cummins
American Judicature Society

Marvin L. Karp
Standing Committee on Ethics and Professional Responsibility

M. Peter Moser
1990 Model Code Revision Project

D. Dudley Oldham
Standing Committee on Judicial Independence

Hon. Ellen F. Rosenblum
National Judicial College

Seth Rosner
Center for Professional Responsibility Coordinating Council

Chief Justice Randall T. Shepard
Conference of Chief Justices

Robert H. Tembeckjian
Association of Judicial Disciplinary Counsel

AMERICAN BAR ASSOCIATION CENTER FOR PROFESSIONAL RESPONSIBILITY

Jeanne P. Gray
Director

Marcia L. Kladder
Program Director

George A. Kuhlman
Ethics Counsel

Susan M. Campbell
Paralegal

Eileen Libby
Associate Ethics Counsel

Benjamin Woodson
Project Manager

AMERICAN BAR ASSOCIATION JUSTICE CENTER

Aimee Skrzekut-Torres
Director

Eileen C. Gallagher
Justice Center Counsel (2003–2005)

Joint Commission to Evaluate the Model Code of Judicial Conduct Chair's Introduction

On September 23, 2003, American Bar Association President Dennis W. Archer, Jr., announced the appointment of a Joint Commission to Evaluate the Model Code of Judicial Conduct under the auspices of the Standing Committee on Ethics and Professional Responsibility and the Standing Committee on Judicial Independence. The last Model Code revision occurred in 1990 and, although specific provisions of the Model Code were amended in the intervening years, there was a need for a comprehensive evaluation and revision in light of societal changes, as well as changes in the role of judges. The Model Code revision project was funded almost entirely by the Joyce Foundation, which provides resources for countless projects that contribute to the betterment of our society.

The unanimous approval of the revised Model Code of Judicial Conduct by the ABA House of Delegates on February 12, 2007, culminated a three and one-half year effort by a group comprised of distinguished judges, lawyers, academicians and a public member. The work of the Joint Commission was significantly enhanced by the active participation of an advisory group comprised of representatives of the organizations principally involved in the work of the judiciary and in the enforcement of the rules governing judicial conduct, and the invaluable assistance of two able Reporters and Center for Professional Responsibility counsel and professional staff.

The revised Model Code is the product of a transparent process during which the Joint Commission held nine public hearings, met in-person twenty times, had more than thirty teleconferences, and regularly posted its work on its website with requests for feedback and comment. Although the Commission set out to preserve as much of the 1990 Code as it could, consistent with the process of overall evaluation, it carefully considered all submitted suggestions and criticism and incorporated many of the suggested changes into the revised Model Code that was adopted by the House of Delegates.

At the time of its adoption, the revised Model Code had the support of the Conference of Chief Justices and the co-sponsorship of the Judicial Division of the ABA, the ABA Standing Committees on Ethics and Professional Responsibility; Professional Discipline and on Judicial Independence, the ABA Sections of Litigation and Dispute Resolution, and the American Judicature Society. In light of this significant support from the judiciary and the profession, the Joint Commission expects that the highest court in each state will adopt the revised

Model Code, thereby improving and clarifying the standards of conduct for the judiciary throughout the nation and creating national uniformity.

An independent, impartial judiciary is indispensable to our system of justice. Equally important is the confidence of the public in the independence, integrity and impartiality of our judiciary as an institution. In fulfilling its mission, the Joint Commission took great care to adhere to those principles as it worked to provide sound, clear, and reasoned guidance to judges faced with difficult issues involving their conduct. The end result is a Model Code that should serve both judges and the public well for many years to come.

Mark I. Harrison
April 2007

About the Authors

Art Garwin is Director of the American Bar Association (ABA) Center for Professional Responsibility. He has served as Staff Counsel to the ABA Task Force on the Future of Legal Education, ABA Standing Committee on Professionalism, ABA Commission on Multidisciplinary Practice, and ABA Task Force on the Model Definition of the Practice of Law. He has written numerous articles on professional responsibility for the *ABA Journal* and a chapter on *Confidentiality and Its Relationship to the Attorney-Client Privilege* in multiple editions of the ABA book *The Attorney-Client Privilege in Civil Litigation.* He is the author of *The Paralegal's Guide to Professional Responsibility (4th edition),* co-author and editor of the *Annotated Model Code of Judicial Conduct (2nd and 3rd editions),* editor of *A Legislative History of the Model Rules of Professional Conduct, 1982–2013,* and co-editor of *Annotated Standards for Imposing Lawyer Sanctions.* Mr. Garwin is a member of the Advisory Board of the Miller-Becker Center for Professional Responsibility at the University of Akron School of Law. He has B.S. and J.D. degrees from the University of Illinois and an M.B.A. from Northwestern University. He practiced law before coming to the ABA in 1990.

Dennis A. Rendleman is the Ethics Counsel at the ABA Center for Professional Responsibility, where he provides expertise and research on legal and judicial ethics and professional responsibility law and professionalism. He is counsel to the ABA Standing Committee on Ethics and Professional Responsibility. Before joining the ABA, Rendleman was Assistant Professor of Legal Studies at the University of Illinois at Springfield, and spent 23 years at the Illinois State Bar Association, leaving in 2003 as General Counsel. Mr. Rendleman has engaged in private practice as a consultant and expert witness in professional responsibility and discipline matters. He is a former member of, and current liaison to, the Illinois Supreme Court's Committee on Professional Responsibility, and has been a member of the Illinois Judicial Ethics Committee since its founding in 1998. He is a graduate of the University of Illinois College of Law.

Mary McDermott is the Associate Ethics Counsel at the ABA, where she provides research and writing support to the Standing Committee on Ethics and Professional Responsibility. Mary has more than 25 years of experience working with lawyers and judges who seek answers to ethics questions. Prior to joining the ABA, Ms. McDermott's focus was on Illinois law when she worked for the Illinois State Bar Association and the Administrative Office of the Illinois Courts.

Preamble

[1] An independent, fair and impartial judiciary is indispensable to our system of justice. The United States legal system is based upon the principle that an independent, impartial, and competent judiciary, composed of men and women of integrity, will interpret and apply the law that governs our society. Thus, the judiciary plays a central role in preserving the principles of justice and the rule of law. Inherent in all the Rules contained in this Code are the precepts that judges, individually and collectively, must respect and honor the judicial office as a public trust and strive to maintain and enhance confidence in the legal system.

[2] Judges should maintain the dignity of judicial office at all times, and avoid both impropriety and the appearance of impropriety in their professional and personal lives. They should aspire at all times to conduct that ensures the greatest possible public confidence in their independence, impartiality, integrity, and competence.

[3] The Model Code of Judicial Conduct establishes standards for the ethical conduct of judges and judicial candidates. It is not intended as an exhaustive guide for the conduct of judges and judicial candidates, who are governed in their judicial and personal conduct by general ethical standards as well as by the Code. The Code is intended, however, to provide guidance and assist judges in maintaining the highest standards of judicial and personal conduct, and to provide a basis for regulating their conduct through disciplinary agencies.

1990 Code Comparison

The 1990 Preamble has been essentially dissected, with the objective of describing the general purpose and rationale of the Code in the Preamble, and moving to a new "Scope" section the specific explanation of how the Rules are intended to operate. Charles G. Geyh & W. William Hodes, *Reporters' Notes to the Model Code of Judicial Conduct* 1–2 (2009).

The 1990 Code Preamble language discussing the "degree of discipline to be imposed" in the course of enforcing the Code's provisions has been deleted. New language has been added to emphasize that, at all times, judges should aspire to conduct that ensures the greatest possible public confidence in their independence, integrity, impartiality, and competence. *Id.*

The language from former Canon 1A, which stated that a judge "should participate in establishing, maintaining, and enforcing high standards of conduct," has been revised and moved to the Preamble. The Commission concluded that such hortatory language should not be confused with enforceable standards and to avoid such confusion, it should not appear in black letter Rules. *Id.* at 19–20.

ANNOTATION

INTRODUCTION

In 1924, the American Bar Association (ABA) House of Delegates adopted the first judicial code of ethics, titled the Canons of Judicial Ethics. The Canons remained unchanged until 1972 when, after undergoing comprehensive review, the ABA House of Delegates replaced them with the Code of Judicial Conduct. In 1990, that Code was again revised significantly and renamed the Model Code of Judicial Conduct. In July 2003, the Joint Commission to Evaluate the Model Code of Judicial Conduct ("Joint Commission" or "Commission") was formed to undertake a comprehensive review of the ABA's judicial ethics policies. In February 2007, the ABA House of Delegates adopted a revised Model Code of Judicial Conduct, which made both formative and substantive changes to the 1990 Code.

GUIDANCE FOR JUDGES

The Model Code of Judicial Conduct is designed to provide guidance to judges and candidates for judicial office, and to provide a structure for regulating conduct through disciplinary agencies. The ABA does not enforce the Judicial Code or discipline judges for violating it. Instead, the ABA offers its Code as a model for jurisdictions to adopt, and those that do are responsible for creating a mechanism to enforce it. Ronald D. Rotunda & John S. Dzienkowski, *Legal Ethics: The Lawyer's Deskbook on Professional Responsibility* 1387 (2015).

The Code requires judges, in their professional and personal lives, to adhere to a high ethical standard that will evoke public confidence in the integrity and impartiality of the judiciary. It should not be applied in a manner that impinges on judicial independence, nor should it be utilized in an effort to gain a mere tactical advantage in a proceeding. As stated in the Preamble, the Model Code of Judicial Conduct is not intended to be an exhaustive guide for the conduct of judges or judicial candidates, who should also adhere to general ethical standards. Instead, the Code is intended to state basic standards to govern the conduct of all judges, to provide guidance to judges and assist them in maintaining the highest standards of judicial and personal conduct, and to provide a basis for regulating their conduct through disciplinary agencies.

PROMOTE PUBLIC CONFIDENCE IN THE INTEGRITY OF THE JUDICIARY

One objective of the Code of Judicial Conduct is to require judges, in their professional and personal lives, to adhere to a high ethical standard that evokes public confidence in the integrity and impartiality of the judiciary. *McDonald v. Ethics Committee*, 3 S.W.3d 740 (Ky. 1999); *In re Justice of Peace Cook*, 906 So.2d 420 (La. 2005) (justice of the peace who fails to attend mandatory training courses cannot be said to be participating in establishing, maintaining, and enforcing, or personally observing, high standards of conduct so that the integrity and independence of the judiciary may be preserved); *In re Williams*, 987 S.W.2d 837 (Tenn. 1998) ("Public confidence in the performance and impartiality of the judiciary is maintained only when judges rigorously adhere to the Code of Conduct. Violations of the Code, if left unaddressed, diminish public confidence and injure the entire judicial system."); *In re Starcher*, 501 S.E.2d 772 (W. Va. 1998) ("[T]he integrity of the judiciary is of paramount importance."). *See also, Reedy v. Wright*, 2002 WL 598434 (Va. Cir. Ct. 2002) ("The signal importance of public confidence in the judiciary is noted in the Preamble and in Canons 1 and 2."). Even though adherence to a code of conduct limits judges' freedom of action to a degree, the advantages of such limits in encouraging public respect outweigh any disadvantage created by them. *Hayden v. City of Port Townsend*, 622 P.2d 1291 (Wash. Ct. App. 1981). *See generally* Gregory C. Pingree, *Where Lies the Emperor's Robe? An Inquiry into the Problem of Judicial Legitimacy*, 86 Or. L. Rev. 1095 (2007).

The U.S. Supreme Court has recognized that there is "vital state interest" in safeguarding "public confidence in the fairness and integrity" of the judiciary. *Caperton v. A. T. Massey Coal Co.*, 556 U. S. 868, 889 (2009); *Williams–Yulee v. Fla. Bar*, 575 U.S. ____, 135 S. Ct. 1656, 1666, 191 L. Ed. 2d 570 (2015) ("The judiciary's authority therefore depends in large measure on the public's willingness to respect and follow its decisions.").

AVOID IMPROPRIETY AND THE APPEARANCE OF IMPROPRIETY

The Preamble stresses that judges should maintain the dignity of judicial office at all times and avoid impropriety and the appearance of impropriety in both their personal and professional lives. *See generally* Cynthia Gray, *Avoiding the Appearance of Impropriety: With Great Power Comes Great Responsibility*, 28 U. Ark. Little Rock L. Rev. 63 (2005).

PROTECT JUDICIAL INDEPENDENCE AND IMPARTIALITY

The Preamble underscores the importance of an independent and impartial judiciary. The U.S. Supreme Court has emphasized this in *Caperton v. A.T. Massey Coal Co.*, 556 U.S. 868 (2009), wherein the majority states, under the circumstances, "a realistic appraisal of psychological tendencies and human weakness," regardless of whether a judge is actually biased, presents "a risk of actual bias" that exists if the judge has a "direct, personal, substantial, pecuniary interest," such that the judge should recuse himself. The Court concluded that, under the U.S. Constitution, judicial impartiality has due process underpinnings.

The intent of the Code is to preserve, and not to undermine, judicial independence. *In re Arrigan*, 678 A.2d 446 (R.I. 1996). Judicial independence is necessary to ensure public confidence in the fairness of judicial decisions. *McDonald v. Ethics Committee*, 3 S.W.3d 740 (Ky. 1999). The Code helps maintain judicial independence through its guarantee that judges will generally not be disciplined for mere errors of law in their decisions. *In re Barr*, 13 S.W.3d 525 (Tex. Special Review Tribunal 1998) ("There can be no greater threat to a free society than judicial anarchy, which would certainly be realized through the continued erosion of judicial independence. It is that constant quest for independence that should prohibit the imposition of disciplinary action upon a judge for an incorrect ruling. The potential impact on the independence of the judiciary . . . cannot be overstated, for the preservation of an independent judiciary requires that judges not be exposed to personal discipline on the basis of case outcomes or particular rulings.").

SCOPE

[1] The Model Code of Judicial Conduct consists of four Canons, numbered Rules under each Canon, and Comments that generally follow and explain each Rule. Scope and Terminology sections provide additional guidance in interpreting and applying the Code. An Application section establishes when the various Rules apply to a judge or judicial candidate.

[2] The Canons state overarching principles of judicial ethics that all judges must observe. Although a judge may be disciplined only for violating a Rule, the Canons provide important guidance in interpreting the Rules. Where a Rule contains a permissive term, such as "may" or "should," the conduct being addressed is committed to the personal and professional discretion of the judge or candidate in question, and no disciplinary action should be taken for action or inaction within the bounds of such discretion.

[3] The Comments that accompany the Rules serve two functions. First, they provide guidance regarding the purpose, meaning, and proper application of the Rules. They contain explanatory material and, in some instances, provide examples of permitted or prohibited conduct. Comments neither add to nor subtract from the binding obligations set forth in the Rules. Therefore, when a Comment contains the term "must," it does not mean that the Comment itself is binding or enforceable; it signifies that the Rule in question, properly understood, is obligatory as to the conduct at issue.

[4] Second, the Comments identify aspirational goals for judges. To implement fully the principles of this Code as articulated in the Canons, judges should strive to exceed the standards of conduct established by the Rules, holding themselves to the highest ethical standards and seeking to achieve those aspirational goals, thereby enhancing the dignity of the judicial office.

[5] The Rules of the Model Code of Judicial Conduct are rules of reason that should be applied consistent with constitutional requirements, statutes, other court rules, and decisional law, and with due regard for all relevant circumstances. The Rules should not be interpreted to impinge upon the essential independence of judges in making judicial decisions.

[6] Although the black letter of the Rules is binding and enforceable, it is not contemplated that every transgression will result in the imposition of discipline. Whether discipline should be imposed should be determined through a reasonable and reasoned application of the Rules, and should depend upon factors such as the seriousness of the transgression, the facts and circumstances that existed at the time of the transgression, the extent of any pattern of improper activity, whether there have been previous violations, and the effect of the improper activity upon the judicial system or others.

[7] The Code is not designed or intended as a basis for civil or criminal liability. Neither is it intended to be the basis for litigants to seek collateral remedies against each other or to obtain tactical advantages in proceedings before a court.

1990 Code Comparison

This new Scope section contains the concepts in the 1990 Preamble that explain how the various parts of the Rules are intended to operate. The section states that judges may be disciplined only for violating a Rule. The Scope section also explains that the Canons are overarching principles that provide important guidance in interpreting the rules. Charles G. Geyh & W. William Hodes, *Reporters' Notes to the Model Code of Judicial Conduct* 3–4 (2009).

Annotation

Introduction

As noted in paragraph [1] of the Scope, the Model Code consists of four Canons, numbered Rules under each Canon, and Comments that follow and explain each Rule. The presentation of black letter Rules that follow each of the "Canons," or statements of overarching principles of judicial conduct, is a notable difference from the 1990 Code. In the 1990 Code, each Canon was followed by "sections" that established the parameters of permissible and prohibited conduct. A consensus was reached by the Commission that a structure similar to that of the ABA Model Rules of Professional Conduct, which address permitted and prohibited conduct for lawyers, would be more straightforward and user-friendly. Similar to the organization of the Model Rules of Professional Conduct, the Rules here are usually followed by Comments that provide both aspirational statements and guidance in interpreting and applying the Rules. These Comments neither add to nor subtract substantively from the force of the Rules themselves.

The Commission considered the Canons to be "overarching principles" with the exception of the direction to avoid the "appearance of impropriety." This was a particular problem as it was a part of the 1990 Code in a Canon, but not in an underlying section. However, it was frequently utilized in disciplinary actions and was repeatedly favored in presentations to the Commission. Consequently, it was placed in both Canon 1 and in Rule 1.2. Charles G. Geyh & W. William Hodes, *Reporters' Notes to the Model Code of Judicial Conduct* 3–4 (2009). *See* Peter L. Ostermiller, *The New ABA Judicial Code as a Basis for Discipline: Defending a Judge* 28 Just. Sys. J. 309 (2007).

The material treated under each Canon has been reorganized to provide a more logical, functional, and helpful arrangement of topics. Canon 1 and its Rules combine most of the subject matter of Canons 1 and 2 in the 1990 Code, addressing the obligations of judges to uphold the independence, integrity, and impartiality of the judiciary, to avoid impropriety and its appearance, and to avoid abusing the prestige of judicial office. Canon 2 and its Rules solely address the judge's professional duties as a judge, which constituted most of Canon 3 in the 1990 Code. Canon 3 and its Rules address specific types of personal conduct, including involvement in extrajudicial activities and in business or financial activities, most of which previously had been addressed in Canon 4. Finally, Canon 4 and its Rules address, as did Canon 5 of the previous Code, acceptable political conduct of judges and judicial candidates. The 1990 Preamble has been divided into two parts: a new Preamble stating the objectives of the Model Rules, and a Scope section describing the manner in which they are to be interpreted, used for guidance, and enforced. The Terminology section provides additional guidance and the Application section establishes when particular Rules apply to other than full-time judges.

MANDATORY AND PERMISSIVE STANDARDS

The Preface to the 1972 Code stated that "The black-letter canons and the text establish mandatory standards, unless otherwise indicated." ABA *Code of Judicial Conduct*, Preface (1972). Despite this adjuration, the text of the 1972 Code expressed its commands primarily with the word "should," instead of the word "shall." In contrast, the 1990 Model Code primarily used the word "shall" to express a mandatory obligation and "should" to express a desirable, though not mandatory, standard of conduct. *Joachim v. Chambers*, 815 S.W.2d 234, n.9 (Tex. 1991); *In re Kroger*, 702 A.2d 64 (Vt. 1997); *In re Starcher*, 501 S.E.2d 772 (W. Va. 1998). In fact, the Louisiana Supreme Court, commenting on this significant language change from the 1972 Code to the 1990 Model Code observed that, "The original 1976 Louisiana Code of Judicial Conduct used the word 'should' 58 times and the word 'shall' zero times, in its ethical standards. In contrast, after the July 8, 1996 amendments, the amended Code uses 'should' a mere 14 times and 'shall' 69 times in its ethical standards." *In re Lemoine*, 686 So. 2d 837, n.8 (La. 1997).

The revised Model Code has Canons, which state overarching principles of judicial ethics that all judges must observe, and Rules, which are enforceable. Although a judge may be disciplined only for violating a Rule, the Canons provide guidance in interpreting the Rules. According to the Scope, where a Rule contains a permissive term, such as "may" or "should," the conduct being addressed is committed to the personal and professional discretion of the judge or candidate, and "no disciplinary action should be taken for action or inaction within the bounds of such discretion." Additionally, not every transgression of the Rules will result in discipline. Paragraph [6] of the Scope section explains that determination of whether discipline should be imposed will be based on a "reasonable and reasoned" application of the Rules, and should depend on factors such as "the seriousness of the transgression, the facts and circumstances that existed at the time of the transgression, the extent of any pattern of improper activity, whether there have been previous violations, and the effect of improper activity upon the judicial system or others."

NOT A BASIS FOR CIVIL LIABILITY

The Scope provides that, although a violation of the Code's ethical standards may be the basis of judicial discipline, it is not a separate basis for civil or criminal liability. *Lofton v. State*, 944 S.W.2d 131 (Ark. Ct. App. 1997). Nor may lawyers and litigants use alleged violations of the Code to attempt to gain a tactical advantage over a judge by suing or threatening to sue the judge in his or her private capacity. *Seto v. McMahon*, 862 F. Supp. 255 (C.D. Calif. 1994); *Terrazas v. Slagle*, 142 F.R.D. 136 (W.D. Tex. 1992); *Franklin Design Associates, Inc. v. Toupin*, 1998 WL 182625 (R.I. Super. 1998). Litigants and their lawyers may not use the disqualification provision of the Code to conduct fishing expeditions to find a basis of disqualification. *Hogan v. Warden*, 916 P.2d 805 (Nev. 1996). However, failure to properly disqualify or recuse may result in reversal of an opinion in which the disqualified judge participated as a member of a panel. *See, e.g., PETA v. Bobby Berosini, Ltd.*, 894 P.2d 337 (Nev. 1995).

TERMINOLOGY

The first time any term listed below is used in a Rule in its defined sense, it is followed by an asterisk (*).

"Aggregate," in relation to contributions for a candidate, means not only contributions in cash or in kind made directly to a candidate's campaign committee, but also all contributions made indirectly with the understanding that they will be used to support the election of a candidate or to oppose the election of the candidate's opponent. See Rules 2.11 and 4.4.

"Appropriate authority" means the authority having responsibility for initiation of disciplinary process in connection with the violation to be reported. See Rules 2.14 and 2.15.

"Contribution" means both financial and in-kind contributions, such as goods, professional or volunteer services, advertising, and other types of assistance, which, if obtained by the recipient otherwise, would require a financial expenditure. See Rules 2.11, 2.13, 3.7, 4.1, and 4.4.

"De minimis," in the context of interests pertaining to disqualification of a judge, means an insignificant interest that could not raise a reasonable question regarding the judge's impartiality. See Rule 2.11.

"Domestic partner" means a person with whom another person maintains a household and an intimate relationship, other than a person to whom he or she is legally married. See Rules 2.11, 2.13, 3.13, and 3.14.

"Economic interest" means ownership of more than a de minimis legal or equitable interest. Except for situations in which the judge participates in the management of such a legal or equitable interest, or the interest could be substantially affected by the outcome of a proceeding before a judge, it does not include:

(1) an interest in the individual holdings within a mutual or common investment fund;
(2) an interest in securities held by an educational, religious, charitable, fraternal, or civic organization in which the judge or the judge's spouse, domestic partner, parent, or child serves as a director, an officer, an advisor, or other participant;
(3) a deposit in a financial institution or deposits or proprietary interests the judge may maintain as a member of a mutual savings association or credit union, or similar proprietary interests; or
(4) an interest in the issuer of government securities held by the judge.

See Rules 1.3 and 2.11.

"Fiduciary" includes relationships such as executor, administrator, trustee, or guardian. See Rules 2.11, 3.2, and 3.8.

"Impartial," "impartiality," and **"impartially"** mean absence of bias or prejudice in favor of, or against, particular parties or classes of parties, as well as maintenance of an open mind in considering issues that may come before a judge. See Canons 1, 2, and 4, and Rules 1.2, 2.2, 2.10, 2.11, 2.13, 3.1, 3.12, 3.13, 4.1, and 4.2.

"Impending matter" is a matter that is imminent or expected to occur in the near future. See Rules 2.9, 2.10, 3.13, and 4.1.

"Impropriety" includes conduct that violates the law, court rules, or provisions of this Code, and conduct that undermines a judge's independence, integrity, or impartiality. See Canon 1 and Rule 1.2.

"Independence" means a judge's freedom from influence or controls other than those established by law. See Canons 1 and 4, and Rules 1.2, 3.1, 3.12, 3.13, and 4.2.

"Integrity" means probity, fairness, honesty, uprightness, and soundness of character. See Canons 1 and 4, and Rules 1.2, 3.1, 3.12, 3.13, and 4.2.

"Judicial candidate" means any person, including a sitting judge, who is seeking selection for or retention in judicial office by election or appointment. A person becomes a candidate for judicial office as soon as he or she makes a public announcement of candidacy, declares or files as a candidate with the election or appointment authority, authorizes or, where permitted, engages in solicitation or acceptance of contributions or support, or is nominated for election or appointment to office. See Rules 2.11, 4.1, 4.2, and 4.4.

"Knowingly," "knowledge," "known," and **"knows"** mean actual knowledge of the fact in question. A person's knowledge may be inferred from circumstances. See Rules 2.11, 2.13, 2.15, 2.16, 3.6, and 4.1.

"Law" encompasses court rules as well as statutes, constitutional provisions, and decisional law. See Rules 1.1, 2.1, 2.2, 2.6, 2.7, 2.9, 3.1, 3.4, 3.9, 3.12, 3.13, 3.14, 3.15, 4.1, 4.2, 4.4, and 4.5.

"Member of the candidate's family" means a spouse, domestic partner, child, grandchild, parent, grandparent, or other relative or person with whom the candidate maintains a close familial relationship.

"Member of the judge's family" means a spouse, domestic partner, child, grandchild, parent, grandparent, or other relative or person with whom the judge maintains a close familial relationship. See Rules 3.7, 3.8, 3.10, and 3.11.

"Member of a judge's family residing in the judge's household" means any relative of a judge by blood or marriage, or a person treated by a judge as a member of the judge's family, who resides in the judge's household. See Rules 2.11 and 3.13.

"Nonpublic information" means information that is not available to the public. Nonpublic information may include, but is not limited to, information that is sealed by statute or court order or impounded or communicated in camera, and information offered in grand jury proceedings, presentencing reports, dependency cases, or psychiatric reports. See Rule 3.5.

"Pending matter" is a matter that has commenced. A matter continues to be pending through any appellate process until final disposition. See Rules 2.9, 2.10, 3.13, and 4.1.

"Personally solicit" means a direct request made by a judge or a judicial candidate for financial support or in-kind services, whether made by letter, telephone, or any other means of communication. See Rule 4.1.

"Political organization" means a political party or other group sponsored by or affiliated with a political party or candidate, the principal purpose of which is to further the election or appointment of candidates for political office. For purposes of this Code, the term does not include a judicial candidate's campaign committee created as authorized by Rule 4.4. See Rules 4.1 and 4.2.

"Public election" includes primary and general elections, partisan elections, nonpartisan elections, and retention elections. See Rules 4.2 and 4.4.

"Third degree of relationship" includes the following persons: great-grandparent, grandparent, parent, uncle, aunt, brother, sister, child, grandchild, great-grandchild, nephew, and niece. See Rule 2.11.

1990 Code Comparison

The Commission changed the use of asterisks to indicate defined terms, employing them only where the term is used for the first time in any particular Rule. Several commentators observed that the use of asterisks each time a frequently-appearing defined term occurred in a Rule was more interruptive than useful to the reader.

Apart from the addition of "domestic partner" to the definitions of "Member of the candidate's family" and "Member of the judge's family," the following terms are defined in a manner essentially identical to the way they are defined in the 1990 Code (any differences are intended to be purely stylistic):

Aggregate
Appropriate authority
Economic interest
Fiduciary
Knowingly, knowledge, known, or knows
Law
Member of the candidate's family
Member of the judge's family
Member of the judge's family residing in the judge's household
Nonpublic information
Public election
Third degree of relationship

The following terms are no longer contained in the Terminology Section:

"Continuing part-time judge," on the theory that the provision applicable to continuing part-time judges in the Application Section provides a definition already.
"Court personnel," which in the 1990 Code was not, in fact, a definition, but a statement that the term did not include lawyers in a proceeding before the judge. The Commission believed this was too evident to need statement, and otherwise believed that the term "court personnel" is clear enough that it does not need definition. The term "court personnel' has been replaced with "court staff, court officials, and others subject to the judge's direction and control."
"Periodic part-time judge" (on the same theory as applied to "continuing part-time judge"; see above).
"Pro tempore part-time judge" (same reason as above).
"Require," which the Commission believed is easily understood.

The following definitions have been modified in the 2007 Code:

"De minimis" is defined specifically in the context of "interests pertaining to the disqualification of a judge," because it is only in Rule 2.11 ("Disqualification") that the Commission believes a precise definition of the term need be applied.
"Judicial candidate" is similar to the 1990 Code's term "candidate." The phrase "including a sitting judge" has been added for clarification.

The language stating that the term "candidate" applies to a judge who is seeking a non-judicial office has been deleted, consistent with the reformulation of the term being defined.

"Political organization" has been expanded to include the qualifying language "sponsored by or affiliated with a political party or candidate," the principal purpose of which is to further the election or appointment of candidates for political office. In addition, language has been added to clarify that the term is not meant to include a judicial candidate's own campaign committee.

The following new defined terms have been added:

"Domestic partner," on the theory that now commonplace "non-traditional" relationships that exist outside marriage are deserving of treatment equal to that afforded marital relationships in evaluating their potential conflict-of-interest implications under the Rules.

"Impartiality," because it is a fundamental goal of the judicial system, and additionally because it has become a defined term in recent decisional law with respect to political activity of judges.

"Impending matter," in order to set temporal limits on the phrase.

"Impropriety," because of its fundamental importance as a concept underlying the importance of appearances created by judges.

"Independence," as a fundamental concept underlying the justice system.

"Integrity," for the same reason as above.

"Pending matter," so as to set temporal limits on the phrase and create greater certainty in the application of the Code's restrictions on judicial speech.

See Charles G. Geyh & W. William Hodes, *Reporters' Notes to the Model Code of Judicial Conduct* 7–10 (2009).

Application

The Application section establishes when the various Rules apply to a judge or judicial candidate.

I. Applicability of This Code

(A) The provisions of the Code apply to all full-time judges. Parts II through V of this section identify provisions that apply to four categories of part-time judges only while they are serving as judges, and provisions that do not apply to part-time judges at any time. All other Rules are therefore applicable to part-time judges at all times. The four categories of judicial service in other than a full-time capacity are necessarily defined in general terms because of the widely varying forms of judicial service. Canon 4 applies to judicial candidates.

(B) A judge, within the meaning of this Code, is anyone who is authorized to perform judicial functions, including an officer such as a justice of the peace, magistrate, court commissioner, special master, referee, or member of the administrative law judiciary.[1]

Comment

[1] The Rules in this Code have been formulated to address the ethical obligations of any person who serves a judicial function, and are premised upon the supposition that a uniform system of ethical principles should apply to all those authorized to perform judicial functions.

---

1. Each jurisdiction should consider the characteristics of particular positions within the administrative law judiciary in adopting, adapting, applying, and enforcing the Code for the administrative law judiciary. *See, e.g.*, Model Code of Judicial Conduct for Federal Administrative Law Judges (1989) and Model Code of Judicial Conduct for State Administrative Law Judges (1995). Both Model Codes are endorsed by the ABA National Conference of Administrative Law Judiciary.

[2] The determination of which category and, accordingly, which specific Rules apply to an individual judicial officer, depends upon the facts of the particular judicial service.

[3] In recent years many jurisdictions have created what are often called "problem solving" courts, in which judges are authorized by court rules to act in nontraditional ways. For example, judges presiding in drug courts and monitoring the progress of participants in those courts' programs may be authorized and even encouraged to communicate directly with social workers, probation officers, and others outside the context of their usual judicial role as independent decision makers on issues of fact and law. When local rules specifically authorize conduct not otherwise permitted under these Rules, they take precedence over the provisions set forth in the Code. Nevertheless, judges serving on "problem solving" courts shall comply with this Code except to the extent local rules provide and permit otherwise.

II. RETIRED JUDGE SUBJECT TO RECALL

A retired judge subject to recall for service, who by law is not permitted to practice law, is not required to comply:

(A) with Rule 3.9 (Service as Arbitrator or Mediator), except while serving as a judge.

(B) at any time with Rule 3.8(A) (Appointments to Fiduciary Positions).

COMMENT

[1] For the purposes of this section, as long as a retired judge is subject to being recalled for service, the judge is considered to "perform judicial functions."

III. CONTINUING PART-TIME JUDGE

A judge who serves repeatedly on a part-time basis by election or under a continuing appointment, including a retired judge subject to recall who is permitted to practice law ("continuing part-time judge"),

(A) is not required to comply:

(1) with Rule 4.1 (Political and Campaign Activities of Judges and Judicial Candidates in General) (A)(1) through (7), except while serving as a judge; or

(2) at any time with Rules 3.4 (Appointments to Governmental Positions), 3.8(A) (Appointments to Fiduciary Positions), 3.9 (Service as Arbitrator or Mediator), 3.10 (Practice of Law), and 3.11(B) (Financial, Business, or Remunerative Activities); and

(B) shall not practice law in the court on which the judge serves or in any court subject to the appellate jurisdiction of the court on which the judge serves, and shall not act as a lawyer in a proceeding in which the judge has served as a judge or in any other proceeding related thereto.

Comment

[1] When a person who has been a continuing part-time judge is no longer a continuing part-time judge, including a retired judge no longer subject to recall, that person may act as a lawyer in a proceeding in which he or she has served as a judge or in any other proceeding related thereto only with the informed consent of all parties, and pursuant to any applicable Model Rules of Professional Conduct. An adopting jurisdiction should substitute a reference to its applicable rule.

IV. Periodic Part-Time Judge

A periodic part-time judge who serves or expects to serve repeatedly on a part-time basis, but under a separate appointment for each limited period of service or for each matter,

(A) is not required to comply:

(1) with Rule 4.1 (Political and Campaign Activities of Judges and Judicial Candidates in General) (A)(1) through (7), except while serving as a judge; or

(2) at any time with Rules 3.4 (Appointments to Governmental Positions), 3.8(A) (Appointments to Fiduciary Positions), 3.9 (Service as Arbitrator or Mediator), 3.10 (Practice of Law), and 3.11(B) (Financial, Business, or Remunerative Activities); and

(B) shall not practice law in the court on which the judge serves or in any court subject to the appellate jurisdiction of the court on which the judge serves, and shall not act as a lawyer in a proceeding in which the judge has served as a judge or in any other proceeding related thereto.

V. Pro Tempore Part-Time Judge

A pro tempore part-time judge who serves or expects to serve once or only sporadically on a part-time basis under a separate appointment for each period of service or for each case heard is not required to comply:

(A) except while serving as a judge, with Rules 2.4 (External Influences on Judicial Conduct), 3.2 (Appearances before Governmental Bodies and Consultation with Government Officials), and 4.1 (Political and Campaign Activities of Judges and Judicial Candidates in General) (A)(1) through (7); or

(B) at any time with Rules 3.4 (Appointments to Governmental Positions), 3.8(A) (Appointments to Fiduciary Positions), 3.9 (Service as Arbitrator or Mediator), 3.10 (Practice of Law), and 3.11(B) (Financial, Business, or Remunerative Activities).

VI. TIME FOR COMPLIANCE

A person to whom this Code becomes applicable shall comply immediately with its provisions, except that those judges to whom Rules 3.8 (Appointments to Fiduciary Positions) and 3.11 (Financial, Business, or Remunerative Activities) apply shall comply with those Rules as soon as reasonably possible, but in no event later than one year after the Code becomes applicable to the judge.

COMMENT

[1] If serving as a fiduciary when selected as judge, a new judge may, notwithstanding the prohibitions in Rule 3.8, continue to serve as fiduciary, but only for that period of time necessary to avoid serious adverse consequences to the beneficiaries of the fiduciary relationship and in no event longer than one year. Similarly, if engaged at the time of judicial selection in a business activity, a new judge may, notwithstanding the prohibitions in Rule 3.11, continue in that activity for a reasonable period but in no event longer than one year.

1990 CODE COMPARISON

Section A of the 1990 Code was revised in Section I, Paragraph (A) to clarify which provisions of the Code apply to each different category of judges or judicial candidates. Charles G. Geyh & W. William Hodes, *Reporters' Notes to the Model Code of Judicial Conduct* 15 (2009). Section I, Paragraph (B) includes justices of the peace and the administrative law judiciary within the term "judges" in the Code. This is consistent with prior policy adopted by ABA. Definitions of other types of part-time judges are contained in Sections III, IV, and V and have been deleted from the Terminology section. *Id.* at 15–16.

Sections (D)(2) and (E)(2) of the 1990 Code, which had addressed periodic and part-time judges acting as lawyers in matters they had earlier judged, were deleted because they were properly addressed by the Model Rules of Professional Conduct, Rule 1.12(a), not by the Judicial Code. *Id.* at 16.

ANNOTATION

The Application section of the Model Code of Judicial Conduct defines who is a judge and excuses some types of judges from compliance with some provisions of the Code. In general, anyone who is an officer of a judicial system and performs judicial functions is a judge, regardless of whether he or she is a lawyer. *See Miss. Jud. Performance Comm'n v. Thomas*, 549 So.2d 962 (Miss. 1989) (court holds that mayor was a "judge" under the Code because he was performing judicial function in his role as judge pro tempore of municipal court).

The Application section was intended to be more user-friendly than the 1990 Code. Lisa L. Milord, *The Development of the ABA Judicial Code*, 56–57 (1992). The ABA House of Delegates adopted additional amendments relating to "part-time" judges at the 2010 Annual Meeting. These changes strengthen this goal.

Several of the amendments originated from state study committees, while others came either from the ABA Standing Committee on Ethics and Professional Responsibility or as a result of input from other ABA entities and other parties in the judicial process. Standing Committee on Ethics and Professional Responsibility, *Report 113 to ABA House of Delegates* 6 (August 2010).

The 2010 amendments identify specific provisions from which part-time judges are either sometimes or always exempt. *Id.* at 6.

Canon 1

A judge shall uphold and promote the independence, integrity, and impartiality of the judiciary, and shall avoid impropriety and the appearance of impropriety.

1990 Code Comparison

Canon 1 includes the majority of Canons 1 and 2 from the 1990 Model Code of Judicial Conduct, addressing both the obligation of judges to uphold the independence, integrity, and impartiality of the judiciary, and the obligation to avoid impropriety and its appearance. The decision to combine Canons 1 and 2 of the 1990 Code into a single Canon was based on the premise that they are essentially directed toward the same end—to articulate a limited number of general, overarching principles that should govern a judge's conduct. The former Canons 1 and 2 were inextricably linked; avoiding "impropriety and the appearance of impropriety" in former Canon 2 was instrumental to upholding "the independence and integrity of the judiciary" in former Canon 1. Moreover, the former Code blurred the distinction between its Canons 1 and 2 by including in Canon 2A a duty to act in a manner that "promotes public confidence in the integrity and impartiality of the judiciary," which essentially paraphrased Canon 1's directive to "uphold the integrity and independence of the judiciary." In the Commission's view, the overlap between the Canons was so great that preserving the two as discrete Canons was unnecessarily confusing, and combining them added coherence to the overall structure of the Code. Charles G. Geyh & W. William Hodes, *Reporters' Notes to the Model Code of Judicial Conduct* 17 (2009).

The "appearance of impropriety" was at the core of the debate over the philosophy and black letter of Canon 1. The discussions reflected competing perspectives. The main purpose of the Code is to advise judges and inspire them to adhere to the highest standards of ethical conduct. To preserve public confidence in the courts, judges must avoid both actual improprieties and the appearance of impropriety. The "black letter" Rules, however, also serve as the basis for discipline. To discipline judges for appearing to act improperly—even when they did not act improperly in fact—is considered by many to raise due process issues because of the vagueness of the term "impropriety." *Id.* at 17–18.

The Commission's preliminary draft included a Comment, which noted that historically, judges have not been disciplined solely for violating their duty to avoid the appearance of impropriety. Rather, it is in combination with other, more specific rule violations that the appearance problem has been cited. When the preliminary draft was circulated for public comment in June 2005, it was criticized for diluting the "appearance of impropriety" standard. Further, deletion of former Canon 2A's directive that "a judge shall . . . act at all times in a manner that promotes public confidence in the integrity and impartiality of the judiciary" (the "act at all times" clause), which had been a rule through which the appearance of impropriety was commonly enforced, prompted discussion. In response, the Commission deleted the draft Comment and restored the "act at all times" clause. The Commission had considered an alternative position of retaining the appearance of impropriety language only in the Canon in order to prevent it from being used as a disciplinary standard and for including a statement in the Scope Section that the Canons could be enforced only in conjunction with a Rule violation. However, legal organizations and the judiciary strongly argued for reinstatement of the obligation of a judge to avoid impropriety and the appearance of impropriety as black letter Rule 1.2. With an enforceable rule "on the books," any objections to the non-enforceability of the Canons were withdrawn, and the Scope provision was retained. *Id.* at 18.

Other changes to Canon 1 included the addition of the word "promote" because the Commission deemed it desirable to speak in terms of an ethical duty to promote as well as uphold judicial independence, integrity, and impartiality. Also, in the previous Code, "impartiality" did not appear in the titles of Canons 1 or 2, even though it appeared in underlying sections, such as Canon 2A. In the Commission's view, independence, integrity, and impartiality are overarching, fundamental values that the Rules promote, warranting mention in the title of Canon 1. The term "impartiality" has been added to integrity and independence throughout the Rules, and the Rules have been revised throughout to preserve consistency. The importance of judicial independence, integrity, and impartiality is underscored by the recurrence of the phrase throughout the Rules. *Id.* at 19.

RULE 1.1 COMPLIANCE WITH THE LAW

A judge shall comply with the law,* including the Code of Judicial Conduct.

1990 CODE COMPARISON

Rule 1.1 is the first clause of Canon 2A in the 1990 Code, combined with a statement from the Commentary to Canon 1A. The former Canon associated the duty to respect and comply with the law to the duty to act at all times in a manner that promoted public confidence in the independence, integrity, and impartiality of the judiciary. The Commission regarded these as distinct and discrete concepts. To be sure, the judge who does not comply with the law diminishes public confidence in judges, but the "act at all times" clause encompasses a far broader range of conduct that deserved to be highlighted and articulated at the beginning of the Canon. The reference to a judge's duty to "respect" the law was deleted because it was believed to be both unnecessary and impossible to define. Charles G. Geyh & W. William Hodes, *Reporters' Notes to the Model Code of Judicial Conduct* 19 (2009).

The Commission decided to add the phrase "including the Code of Judicial Conduct" in order to leave no doubt that the scope of "law" within the meaning of this Rule applies to the Rules themselves. *Id.*

The Commission deleted the Commentary to Canon 1A because integrity and independence, which were discussed in that comment, are defined terms in the revised Terminology section. And, because former Canon 1's statement that a judge "should participate in establishing, maintaining, and enforcing high standards of conduct" is hortatory, the Commission determined that in order to avoid confusion, it should not appear in the black letter rules. Consequently, it was revised and moved to the Preamble. *Id.* at 19–20.

ANNOTATION

COMPLYING WITH THE LAW

Rule 1.1 demands that a judge comply with the law, which is defined in the Terminology section as "court rules as well as statutes, constitutional provisions, and decisional law." ABA Model Code of Judicial Conduct, Terminology (2007). A judge who does not comply with the law diminishes public confidence in the judiciary. *See, e.g., In re Coffey*, JD-2007-003 (N.H. 2008) (court stated that "when one whose job is to enforce the law, instead interferes with and disregards the law to her own benefit, the public rightfully questions whether the judicial system itself is worthy of respect"). Courts have asserted that a judge has a higher duty than an ordinary citizen's to comply with the law. *Disc. Counsel v. Connor*, 822 N.E.2d 1235 (Ohio 2004). As noted in the Rule, the "law" also includes other provisions of the Code of Judicial Conduct. Courts have imposed discipline of varying degrees upon judges who have engaged in violations of the law. Courts have rejected the argument that the illegal conduct must have a connection to the judicial-decision making process. *See In re Carney*, 79 A.3d 490 (Pa. 2013). The cases are myriad and varied.

Violations of Law

No doubt exists that a judge who has engaged in illegal conduct has failed to "comply with the law." *See, e.g., In re Koch*, 890 P.2d 1137 (Ariz. 1995) (judge removed from office after being convicted of solicitation of prostitution and implicated in three assaults upon his ex-girlfriend and her boyfriend); *In the Matter Concerning Brehmer* (Cal. Comm'n on Jud. Performance 2012) (judge violated California's Political Reform Act while a candidate and after successful election); *In re Hawkins*, 151 So. 3d 1200 (Fl. 2014) (judge removed from office, in part, for failing to pay state sales taxes on merchandise sold through personal business that judge operated from courthouse); *In re Gatewood*, CJD 2007-089 (Md. Comm'n on Jud. Disabilities 2009) (judge received private reprimand following conviction of filling in state wetlands without license and other crimes related to activities on protected properties); *In re Adams*, 833 N.W.2d 897 (Mich. 2013) (judge removed for perjury and forgery committed while litigant in divorce proceeding and lying to state judicial discipline agency); *In re Walker*, 172 So. 3d 1165, 1168 (Miss. 2015) (judge removed from office after pleading guilty to "attempting to influence a witness subpoenaed to appear before a Federal Grand Jury proceeding and attempting to impede the provision of documents by the witness to the Federal Grand Jury with the intent to influence the outcome of the proceeding"); *In re Abbatangelo* (Nev. Comm'n on Jud. Disc. 2011) (judge publicly censured and prohibited from seeking judicial office for four years after misdemeanor conviction of domestic battery); *In re Sherrill*, 403 S.E.2d 255 (N.C. 1991) (judge's conviction on felony and misdemeanor drug possession charges warranted removal); *Disc. Counsel v. Russo*, No. 2010-Ohio-605, slip op. (judge convicted of "disorderly conduct-persistent" resulting from domestic violence with girlfriend given one-year suspension from practice of law, stayed on condition respondent completes lawyer's assistance contract regarding alcohol abuse and other conditions); *Disc. Counsel v. Ault*, 852 N.E.2d 727 (Ohio 2006) (municipal court judge, who deceived several doctors into over-prescribing painkilling drugs for his use and who was convicted of attempting to obtain a dangerous drug by deception, violated Code of Judicial Conduct); *Off. of Disc. Counsel v. Gallagher*, 693 N.E.2d 1078 (Ohio 1998) (holding that former judge's plea of guilty to federal charges of distribution of cocaine warranted permanent disbarment); *In re Ferguson*, 762 S.E.2d 385 (S.C. 2014) (judge publicly reprimanded and barred from seeking or accepting a judicial office without the permission of Court after conviction for giving two women "money and/or other benefits for the handling and disposition of legal matters" before the judge in return for women allowing judge to have sexual contact with them); *In re Rutland*, 618 S.E.2d 897 (S.C. 2005) (judge publicly reprimanded after conviction for loitering to engage in criminal activity); *In re Densen*, No. CJC 09-0948-RT (Tex. Comm'n on Jud. Conduct 2010) (judge publically warned after conviction of criminal mischief for keying neighbor's car); *In re Steed*, 131 P.3d 231 (Utah 2006) (judge's conduct in maintaining multiple marriage relationships with three wives for more than 20 years violated bigamy statute, thus warranting judge's removal from bench); *In re Hecht*, CJC No. 5863-F-142 (Wash. Comm'n on Jud.

Conduct 2010) (judge who resigned after conviction for patronizing a prostitute and felony harassment was censured and not allowed to seek judicial office in the future); *but see In re Hunter*, 715 So. 2d 1188 (La. 1998) (no discipline of judge who, prior to her election, had purchased two run-down properties with the hopes of renovating them for profit and failed to cure deficiencies in violation of municipal ordinances relating to the properties' condition; court reasoned that judge had made significant efforts to maintain the properties, was not a member of the judiciary during most of her period of ownership and, upon taking office, did everything possible to sell the properties).

Conviction of Crime Not Necessary

Pursuant to Canon 2A, which was superseded by Rule 1.1, a conviction was not necessary to establish a Code violation. Some courts allowed that a judge could be sanctioned for an ethics violation, whether or not that judge was criminally convicted, when the alleged conduct was serious and could damage public confidence in the judiciary. *See, e.g., In re Shenberg*, 632 So. 2d 42 (Fla. 1992) (seriousness of grand jury indictment alleging racketeering and extortion warranted suspension of judges prior to evidentiary finding of misconduct; suspensions without compensation do not violate presumption of innocence as they are "based on allegations with an indicia of reliability" and are necessary to protect public confidence in judiciary"); *In re King*, 857 So. 2d 432 (La. 2003) (rejecting argument that a conviction is necessary for a judge's possible criminal conduct to fall under the category of behavior for which removal is appropriate); *In re Halloran*, 647 N.W.2d 505 (Mich. 2002) (disciplining judge whose conduct could constitute offense of indecent exposure, though the prosecuting attorney filed no criminal charges arising out of the incident in question); *In re Jenkins*, 465 N.W.2d 317 (Mich. 1991) (judge disciplined for fixing tickets and accepting bribes, though judge had been partially acquitted on certain criminal bribery charges in a previous federal trial); *Miss. Comm'n on Jud. Performance v. Hartzog*, 822 So. 2d 941 (Miss. 2002) (suspension with pay for judge who was under two-count felony indictment for false pretense and attempted false pretense, pending resolution of criminal charges; court reasoned that because the judge sits in judgment of defendants charged with crimes based on the issuance of bad checks and in civil cases involving collection matters "[t]he appearance of impropriety or prejudice cannot be overcome"; in this case of first impression in the jurisdiction, the court surveys cases from other states in which an indictment for a felony, by itself, was enough to warrant temporary suspension); *In re Hensley* (N.Y. Comm'n on Jud. Conduct 2012) (judge censured for lawful participation as a player in unlawfully run, for-profit card games as his participation "made it possible for crimes to occur"); *In re Cruickshanks*, 648 S.E.2d 19 (W. Va. 2007) (holding that a judge may be suspended without having been charged criminally, let alone convicted, because the court has duty to promote and protect the honor, integrity, dignity, and efficiency of the judiciary and the justice system); *In re Toler*, 613 S.E.2d 604 (W. Va. 2005) (magistrate who was suspended without pay following his indictment was not entitled to immediate reinstatement upon being acquitted of all criminal charges; other aspects of the case must be considered, such as the public's confidence in the honor, integrity, dignity, and efficiency of the judicial system); *cf. In re Larsen*, 655 A.2d 239 (Pa. Ct. Jud. Disc. 1994) (rejecting per se rule that suspension with pay be entered upon felony indictment and that suspension be automatically converted to suspension without pay upon finding of guilt; totality of the circumstances is more appropriate test, with each case decided on its own facts).

Courts are careful to state that imposition of a suspension does not reflect on the judge's guilt or innocence in the underlying matter. *In re Shenberg*, 632 So. 2d 42 (Fla. 1992) (court "acutely mindful" that judges were only indicted and "there abides with them a presumption of innocence until the final resolution of the charges."); *In re Brennan*, 483 N.E. 2d 484 (N.Y. 1985) (issue before the court suspending without pay judge under federal indictment for attempted murder, assault, criminal possession of weapon and sale of controlled substance was not question of judge's guilt or innocence but "cloud" created by number and seriousness of charges).

Theft

Judges who are guilty of theft may be disciplined under Rule 1.1 in addition to being criminally liable. *See, e.g., In re Garrett*, 613 So. 2d 463 (Fla. 1993) (judge disciplined for knowingly shoplifting a VCR); *In re Imbriani*, 652 A.2d 1222 (N.J. 1995) (judge stole money from a corporation whose affairs the judge managed and in which the judge was a shareholder); *In re Singleton*, 584 S.E.2d 365 (S.C. 2003) (magistrate failed to turn over to county proceeds from sales of abandoned vehicles); *In re Brown*, 540 S.E.2d 452 (S.C. 2000) (judge co-mingled personal and public funds and kept incorrect records); *cf. In re Greenville County Mag. Hensley*, 627 S.E.2d 716 (S.C. 2006) (magistrate's failure to supervise office manager who embezzled money from criminal deposits warranted public reprimand).

Drug Use

A judge's illegal use of drugs while off the bench violates the Code of Judicial Conduct and is grounds for discipline. *See, e.g., In re Peters*, 715 S.E.2d 56 (Ga. 2011) (judge who obtained and used marijuana at least once a week for two months violated Code); *Starnes v. Jud. Ret. & Removal Comm'n*, 680 S.W.2d 922 (Ky. 1984) (judge who engaged in illegal drug activity violated Code of Judicial Conduct); *In re Garza*, 161 P.3d 876 (N.M. 2007) (judge removed from office for misconduct including cocaine use); *Disc. Counsel v. Cox*, 862 N.E.2d 514 (Ohio 2007) (municipal court judge's conduct that led to pleading guilty to attempted possession of drugs violated Code of Judicial Conduct); *In re Toczydlowski*, 853 A.2d 24 (Pa. Ct. Jud. Disc. 2004) (judge publicly reprimanded after admission of possession of small amounts of marijuana on two occasions); *In re Curtis*, 583 S.E.2d 754 (S.C. 2003) (public reprimand of magistrate based on his guilty plea to two counts of possession of cocaine); *In re Ward*, No. 20130797-SC, Utah Sup. Ct. (2013) (resigned judge censured for possession with intent to distribute oxycodone); *cf. Disc. Counsel v. Ault*, 852 N.E.2d 727 (Ohio 2006) (municipal court judge, who deceived several doctors into overprescribing pain-killing drugs for his use and who was convicted of attempting to obtain a dangerous drug by deception, violated Code of Judicial Conduct).

Driving Under the Influence (DUI) or While Intoxicated (DWI)

Judges arrested for or convicted of driving under the influence or other alcohol-related offenses while off the bench also violate the Code of Judicial Conduct. In censuring a judge for driving under the influence of alcohol and leaving the scene of an accident, the New Jersey Supreme Court summed up the prevailing attitude toward this conduct: "We do not view offenses arising from the driving of an automobile while intoxicated with benign indulgence. They are serious and deeply affect the safety and welfare of the public." *In re Connor*, 589 A.2d 1347 (N.J. 1991). Other jurisdictions are in accord. *See, e.g., In re Harper*, No. 11-207 (Ark. Jud. Disc. & Disability Comm'n 2011) (judge reprimanded for DUI); *In re Doyle* (Cal. Comm'n on Jud. Performance 2010) (judge admonished for DUI conviction); *In re Nelson*, 95 So. 3d 122 (Fla. 2012) (public reprimand of judge who drove while impaired, crashed her car in a bridge, identified herself as judge to responding officer, and refused field sobriety test); *Inquiry Concerning a Judge re Fletcher*, 664 So. 2d 934 (Fla. 1995), supplemental opinion at 666 So. 2d 137 (Fla. 1996) (reprimanding judge who, under the influence of alcohol, drove his boat into a dock, left the scene of the accident and falsely denied striking the dock when stopped by a marine patrol officer); *In re Smith*, 2011-84 (Ga. Jud. Qualifications Comm'n 2011) (judge reprimanded after DWI and pleading guilty to reduced charge of reckless driving); *In re Purham*, 09 CC 2 (Ill. Cts. Comm'n 2010) (judge reprimanded for DUI); *In re Hughes*, 947 N.E.2d 418 (Ind. 2011) (judge disciplined for driving under the influence); *In re Hanley*, 867 N.E.2d 157 (Ind. 2007) (judge reprimanded after pleading guilty to DUI); *In re Block*, 816 N.W.2d 362 (Iowa 2012) (judge reprimanded for DWI, having open containers of alcoholic beverages in vehicle, speeding, and driving erratically); *In re Boone*, 2009-117 (Md. Comm'n on Jud. Disabilities 2011) (judge disciplined for DUI); *In re McEvoy*, 2009-45 (Mass. Comm'n on Jud. Conduct 2010) (judge reprimanded for DUI); *In re Nebel*, 777 N.W. 132 (Mich. 2010) (judge censured and suspended for 90 days for DUI and speeding); *In re D'Ambrosio*, 723 A.2d 943 (N.J. 1999) (reprimanding ex-judge who had been arrested for DUI); *In re Apple* (N.Y. Comm'n on Jud. Conduct 2012) (judge reprimanded for DUI); *In re Martineck* (N.Y. Comm'n on Jud. Standards 2010) (judge censured for DUI); *In re Carraway* (N.C. Jud. Standards Comm'n 2012) (judge was driving under the influence of impairing substances); *In re Compl. Against Resnick*, 842 N.E.2d 31 (Ohio 2005) (Supreme Court justice convicted of the offense of driving a motor vehicle while under the influence of alcohol violated Code of Judicial Conduct); *In re Lyman*, CJC No. 6527-F-152 (Wash. Comm'n on Jud. Conduct 2011) (judge reprimanded for driving under the influence of alcohol and leaving the scene of an accident); *In re Binkoski*, 515 S.E.2d 828 (W. Va. 1999) (magistrate's admission to DUI and possessing marijuana warranted public censure); *In re Baran*, 2007 WL 6180185 (FM2007-002 Conn. Jud. Rev. Council July 3, 2007) (judge who was arrested for driving under the influence of alcohol, evading responsibility, risk of injury to a minor and failure to drive right, failed to respect and comply with the law and act in a manner promoting public confidence in the integrity and impartiality of the judiciary and was suspended for 60 days without pay); *but cf. In re Walters*, 697 A.2d 320 (Pa. Ct. Jud. Disc. 1997) (judge violated constitutional provision barring judges from engaging in activities prohibited by law when he was found operating automobile with blood-alcohol level in excess of 0.19 percent by weight, but did not violate Rules 1, 2A, or 13, of Governing Standards of Conduct for District Judges by engaging in that conduct).

In some instances, however, a court may temper a sanction "when illegal acts emanate from alcohol or chemical addictions and [the court] believe[s] that the judge or attorney is committed to recovery and no longer poses a threat to the public or the judicial system." *Disc. Counsel v. Connor*, 822 N.E. 2d 1235 (Ohio 2004).

Tax Evasion

Tax evasion is another example of a violation of law that may result in a Rule 1.1 violation. *See, e.g., Jud. Disc. & Disability Comm'n v. Thompson*, 16 S.W.3d 212 (Ark. 2000) (newly elected judge removed from office for committing a host of legal and ethical violations including writing 59 checks drawn on insufficient funds without overdraft protection and failing to pay federal income taxes in the amount of $86,936.91); *In re Williams*, 701 A.2d 825 (Del. Jud. 1997) (judge failed to pay employee withholding taxes and parking tickets); *In re Hawkins*, 151 So. 3d 1200 (Fla. 2014) (judge removed from office, in part, for failing to pay state sales taxes for sale of merchandise through an unregistered business judge operated from courthouse); *In re Huckaby*, 656 So. 2d 292 (La. 1995) (after taking office, judge pled guilty to a charge of failure to file a federal tax return several years before being elected to the bench and was sentenced to one year in prison; judge violated Code of Judicial Conduct because, although the ethical violation involved behavior taking place several years before the judge took office, the judge failed to correct the problem); *In re Ballance*, 643 S.E.2d 584 (N.C. 2007) (judge removed from office after conviction for failing to file federal tax return); *In re Ballentine*, 7 JD 13 (Penn. Ct. of Jud. Disc. 2015) (judge removed from office for failure to file income taxes and failure to pay business taxes while on probation for dismissing several of her own traffic citations); *In re Hamer*, 537 S.E.2d 552 (S.C. 2000) (judge who was indicted for filing false federal income tax returns, mail fraud, and money laundering publicly reprimanded); *In re Henderson*, 387 S.E.2d 264 (S.C. 1990) (judge publicly reprimanded for, among other things, filing an affidavit misstating his residence so as to avoid taxes and fees on truck purchased in state). A judge may also be disciplined for failing to file a timely income tax return. *See, e.g., In re Doherty*, 2006 WL 6219554 (J2006-015-002 Conn. Jud. Rev. Council, July 14, 2006) (judge suspended without pay for failing to timely file state and federal income tax returns).

Violations of Court Rules

Since the Terminology section of the Code defines law as including court rules, judges can be disciplined under Rule 1.1 for violating court rules and procedures. *See, e.g., In re Mapp*, No. 13-203 (Ariz. Comm'n on Jud. Conduct 2013) (judge reprimanded for court "standing policy" to disregard the statutory requirements for waiver of service); *In re Sims*, 09-325 (Ark. Jud. Disc. & Disability Comm'n 2010) (judge admonished for issuing writ of coram nobis in violation of what Arkansas Supreme Court described as "clear precedent"); *In re Alford*, (Ark. Jud. Disc. & Disability Comm'n, Nov. 29, 2004) (judge violated Supreme Court rules by failing to pay annual attorneys' licensing fee); *In re O'Flaherty*, 50 Cal.4th CJP Supp. 1 (2010) (judge censured, in part, for not allowing defendants to be heard prior to issuing a restraining order); *In re Reinholtzen* (Cal. Comm'n on Jud. Performance 2015) (judge admonished for falsifying salary affidavits required by court rule); *In re Fowler*, 696 S.E.2d 644 (Ga. 2010) (judge removed from bench in part for failure "to grasp the basic tenets of criminal procedure", routinely telling defendants they must prove their innocence and hearing matters outside the judge's jurisdiction); *Crawford v. State*, 770 N.E.2d 775 (Ind. 2002) (judge ignored mandated witness order in attempt to accommodate witnesses' schedules; the court noted, "[a] court's indifference to clearly stated rules breeds disrespect for and discontent with our justice system. Government cannot demand respect of the laws by its citizens when its tribunals ignore those very same laws."); *In re Jacobi*, 715 N.E.2d 873 (Ind. 1999) (judge suspended for failing to follow proper procedures required to grant a TRO); *Alred v. Jud. Conduct Comm'n*, 395 S.W.3d 417 (Ky. 2012) (judge who changed defendant's bond conditions without notice or hearing violated law and called into question judicial integrity and independence); *In re Broussard*, 900 So. 2d 814 (La. 2005) (nonlawyer justice of the peace's unauthorized practice of law, by preparing, notarizing, and filing or processing divorce pleadings in eight cases, violated the Code of Judicial Conduct, Supreme Court rules and state law); *In re Justin*, 809 N.W.2d 126 (Mich. 2012) (judge removed from bench for improperly dismissing cases, some after defendants had pled guilty, and not ordering costs when part of plea); *Miss. Comm'n on Jud. Performance v. Buffington*, 55 So. 3d 167 (Miss. 2011) (judge reprimanded for improperly issuing subpoenas to county commissioners and stating publicly that he did not care that the subpoenas did not comply with the law); *Miss. Comm'n on Jud. Performance v. Wells*, 794 So. 2d 1030 (Miss. 2001) (judge found defendant guilty of disturbing the peace and simple assault based solely on affidavits, without affording the defendant the opportunity to defend herself); *In re Fenster*, 649 A.2d 393 (N.J. 1994) (judge allowed mayor to make speech during a quasi-criminal proceeding, though mayor was not properly called as a witness by either party, and defense counsel strenuously objected); *In re Rael*, No. 2011-040 (N.M. Jud. Std. Comm'n 2012) (judge disciplined for issuing temporary restraining order without jurisdiction); *In re Curtis* (N.Y. Comm'n on Jud. Conduct 2012) (judge censured for issuing four protection orders with no pending criminal action filed); *In re Halstead* (N.Y. Comm'n on Jud. Conduct 2011) (judge removed from bench, in part, for failing to deposit court funds and timely file accurate reports with the state comptroller, resulting in deficiencies in the court's bank account); *In re Riordan* (N.Y. Comm'n on Jud. Conduct 2011) (judge disciplined for holding court in his small, crowded chambers instead of in the courtroom that was accessible to the public); *In re Ammons*, 11-020 (N.C. Jud. Stand. Comm'n 2011) (judge improperly granted five motions that were late, not certified, without notice to the opposing party, not filed with the clerk, and not supported by an affidavit); *In re Gaul*, 936 N.E.2d 28 (Ohio 2010) (judge failed to comply with the law when making findings of fact not based on evidence presented); *In re Love*, 702 S.E.2d 115 (S.C. 2010) (judge used a procedure for handling fines and bond services for certain defendants that was not in accordance with the orders of the Chief Justice of the Supreme Court of South Carolina); *In re Holmes*, 692 S.E.2d 905 (S.C. 2010) (judge disciplined for proceeding to trial and finding defendant guilty in absentia when neither party was present); *In re Moon*, No. 11-441 (Tenn. Court of the Judiciary 2012) (judge reprimanded for failure to appoint counsel for indigents and failing to appoint counsel in probation revocation hearings); *In re Perez*, No. 10-0516-JP (Tex. Comm'n on Jud. Conduct 2011) (judge issued public warning after directing court staff to issue an arrest warrant when no case was pending and no criminal charges were filed); *In re Jones*, 55 S.W.3d 243 (Tex. Spec. Ct.

Rev. 2000) (justice of the peace willfully violated Code of Judicial Conduct by issuing writs of attachment in lieu of appropriate summons or arrest warrants in peace bond proceedings, issuing writs of attachment on the basis of oral testimony alone, and ordering defendant and victim to mediation as part of a peace bond application process); *In re Lowery*, 999 S.W.2d 639 (Tex. 1998) (misconduct by justice of the peace included commencing impromptu hearing at automobile repair shop in attempt to personally enforce prior order); *In re Poyfair*, CJC No. 6691-F-153 (Wash. Comm'n on Jud. Conduct 2012) (judge refused to recognize biological parent's right to revoke consent to adoption, right to return of the child, right to counsel, and injected immigration status to intimidate litigant); *In re Hille*, CJC No. 6392-F-150 (Wash. Comm'n on Jud. Conduct 2010) (judge reprimanded for "dispensing with mitigation hearings in favor of automatic" fine reductions based on petition alone); *cf. In re Tucker*, 501 S.E.2d 67 (N.C. 1998) (court rejected recommended censure of judge who disposed of two DWI cases ex parte based upon shorthand system used by judge, defense attorneys, and assistant DA for quickly handling weak DWI cases; judge disposed of the cases based upon a misrepresentation by a defense attorney that the state would not present evidence in the DWI cases).

Ignoring or Interfering with the Orders of Other Courts

When a judge ignores the orders of other courts, or tries to circumvent another judge's authority, a Rule 1.1 violation may be found. *See, e.g., In re Edwards* (Cal. Comm'n on Jud. Performance 2012) (presiding judge admonished for cancelling a court reporter assignment issued by another judge; management of the court "does not extend to intruding on another judge's case-related authority by countermanding that judge's case-related orders"); *In re Johnson*, 715 N.E.2d 370 (Ind. 1999) (judge granted habeas corpus petition raising issues of law relating to another court's order, with knowledge that petitioner was incarcerated pursuant to that court's order and that prosecutor before other court had not been notified); *In re Cahill*, 13-32, 13-41, 13-42 (Minn. Bd. on Jud. Standards 2014) (judge reprimanded in part for disregarding appellate precedent and issuing memorandum stating "This court is well aware of two Court of Appeals cases, which have held that potential immigration consequences are not to be taken into consideration for sentencing purposes. . . . This court respectfully suggests that the Court of Appeals went astray in those cases"); *Miss Comm'n on Jud. Performance v. Thompson*, 80 So. 3d 86 (Miss. 2012) (judge suspended for 30 days after reducing defendant's bond in case not assigned to judge); *Miss Comm'n on Jud. Performance v. Blakeney*, 848 So. 2d 824 (Miss. 2003) (judge advocated, in ex parte communication, that an officer not appear in court on a case assigned to another judge as a means of securing a dismissal of charges); *In re Complaint Against White*, 651 N.W.2d 551 (Neb.

2002) (suspending judge who, after the district court had vacated her sentence, brought motion for appointment of special prosecutor to appeal resentencing by another judge); *In re Reardon*, 596 S.E.2d 915 (S.C. 2004) (judge suspended for six months for misconduct including willful violation of valid court order to report returned check to court administration and Office of Disciplinary Counsel); *In re Atherton*, B15-6256 and B15-6265 (Tenn. Bd. of Jud. Conduct 2015) (judge reprimanded for dismissing divorce case for lack of subject matter jurisdiction based on finding that Tennessee state courts could no longer hear divorce matters after the U.S. Supreme Court's decision in Obergefell v. Hodges, 135 S. Ct. 2584 (2015)); *In re Bell*, 11-4565 (Tenn. Ct. of the Judiciary 2012) (judge on military leave and stationed in Germany "gave instructions" that the judge would continue to hear matters despite the existence of Supreme Court order appointing substitute judges); *In re Bales*, 11-4440 (Tenn. Ct. of the Judiciary 2011) (judge reprimanded for raising bond set by appeals court despite lack of jurisdiction to do so); *Jud. Inquiry & Rev. Comm'n v. Lewis*, 568 S.E.2d 687 (Va. 2002) (while serving as judge of juvenile and domestic relations district court, judge enforced an order he knew had been stayed by the circuit court); *In re Crawford*, 629 N.W.2d 1 (Wis. 2001) (judge attempted to coerce chief judge to change administrative order by threatening to "go public" with "influence peddling" and misconduct allegations against chief judge, members of the chief judge's family, and district court administrator).

Personal Observation of Standards

The judge's obligations to be independent, as discussed in Canon 1 and Rule 1.2, and to comply with the law are not inconsistent duties. As the Maine Supreme Court has explained, the failure of a judge to follow the rules poses a real danger to judicial independence. *In re Ross*, 428 A.2d 858 (Me. 1981) ("Independence of the judiciary is not inconsistent with accountability for judicial conduct. Lawless judicial conduct—the administration, in disregard of the law, of a personal brand of justice in which the judge becomes a law unto himself—is as threatening to the concept of government under law as is the loss of judicial independence. We see no conflict between judicial independence and judicial accountability. Indeed, a lack of judicial accountability may itself be the greatest danger to judicial independence.").

When judges "become a law unto themselves," courts have found a Code violation. *See, e.g., Harris v. Smartt*, 57 P.3d 58 (Mont. 2002) (justice of the peace violated Canon requiring judges to "administer justice according to law," by accessing sexually explicit website at work on county-owned computer and exposing co-workers to images); *In re Davis*, 946 P.2d 1033 (Nev. 1997) (judge's misconduct included failing to comply with zoning law even after he had been advised of zoning violations); *In re Eagen*, 814 A.2d 304

(Pa. Ct. Jud. Disc. 2002) (judge's misdemeanor conviction of obstruction of administration of law violated Code provision that states that "[j]udges should respect and comply with the law"); *cf. Off. of Disc. Counsel v. Gallagher*, 693 N.E.2d 1078 (Ohio 1998) (permanent disbarment of lawyer who held judicial office at time of his guilty plea to federal charges of distribution of cocaine); *cf. In re Hughes*, 640 N.E.2d. 1065 (Ind. 1994) (lawyer disbarred following felony convictions for submitting false reimbursement claims for attending conferences and seminars while serving as city court judge; "Where those whose job it is to enforce the law break it instead, the public rightfully questions whether the system itself is worthy of respect" (citing *In re Oliver*, 493 N.E.2d 1237 (Ind. 1986))).

RULE 1.2 PROMOTING CONFIDENCE IN THE JUDICIARY

A judge shall act at all times in a manner that promotes public confidence in the independence,* integrity,* and impartiality* of the judiciary, and avoid impropriety* and the appearance of impropriety.

COMMENT

[1] Public confidence in the judiciary is eroded by improper conduct and conduct that creates the appearance of impropriety. This principle applies to both the professional and personal conduct of a judge.

[2] A judge should expect to be the subject of public scrutiny that might be viewed as burdensome, if applied to other citizens, and must accept the restrictions imposed by the Code.

[3] Conduct that compromises or appears to compromise the independence, integrity, and impartiality of a judge undermines public confidence in the judiciary. Because it is not practicable to list all such conduct, the Rule is necessarily cast in general terms.

[4] Judges should participate in activities that promote ethical conduct among judges and lawyers, support professionalism within the judiciary and the legal profession, and promote access to justice for all.

[5] Actual improprieties include violations of law, court rules, or other specific provisions of this Code. The test for appearance of impropriety is whether the conduct would create, in reasonable minds, a perception that the judge violated this Code or engaged in other conduct that reflects adversely on the judge's honesty, impartiality, temperament, or fitness to serve as a judge.

[6] A judge should initiate and participate in community outreach activities for the purpose of promoting public understanding of and confidence in the administration of justice. In conducting such activities, the judge must act in a manner consistent with this Code.

1990 CODE COMPARISON

The first clause of Rule 1.2 is taken from Canon 2, which was previously a part of Canon 2A. As explained in the general discussion of Canon 1, it is now a free-standing rule. The second clause establishing an "appearance of impropriety" as an independent basis for discipline was added at the urging of the judiciary and others. Charles G. Geyh & W. William Hodes, *Reporters' Notes to the Model Code of Judicial Conduct* 20–21 (2009).

The substance of Comments [1], [2], [3], and [5] is derived from the Commentary to former Canon 2A. Language that was deemed self-evident, redundant, or otherwise unnecessary was deleted. Comment [4] is new to the Code. Although it was never suggested that judges be subject to discipline for failing to participate in such activities, the Commission agreed that judges should promote professionalism and access to justice, and that these aspirational objectives of the Code were well-served by including this Comment. Comment [6], which is also new, is designed to encourage judges to participate in community outreach activities. Existing ABA policy encourages judges to engage in such activities as a means to promote public confidence in the courts. *Id.* at 21.

ANNOTATION
"AT ALL TIMES": GOOD CONDUCT EXPECTED ON AND OFF BENCH

The language of Rule 1.2, that a judge must act "at all times" in a manner that promotes public confidence in the independence, integrity, and impartiality of the judiciary, is an exacting standard that presents a judge with the prospect of living life in a fishbowl. As the Commentary explains, a judge must expect to be subjected to "public scrutiny." Model Code of Judicial Conduct Rule 1.2 cmt. [2]. The duty to avoid improper conduct and conduct that creates the appearance of improper conduct applies both to a judge's professional and personal life. Further, a judge must accept restrictions on behavior that would be considered burdensome if applied to other citizens. *Id.*

Case law has recognized this need for extraordinary scruples in both personal and professional conduct. *See, e.g., Miss. Comm'n on Jud. Performance v. Milling*, 651 So. 2d 531 (Miss. 1995) (judge pursued romantic relationship and openly lived with a fugitive from another state who was charged with several drug felonies; the court noted that "[t]he Canon makes clear that judges have responsibilities with regard to their personal conduct that greatly exceed those of ordinary citizens"); *In re Ramirez*, 135 P.3d 230 (N.M. 2006) ("the behavior of a judge should be as circumspect off the bench as it is on the bench"); *In re Reese*, 495 S.E.2d 548 (W. Va. 1997) ("[a] judge whether on or off the bench, is bound to strive toward creating and preserving the image of the justice system as an independent, impartial source of reasoned actions and decisions. Achievement of this goal demands that a judge, in a sense, behave as though he is always on the bench." (citations omitted)).

Improper Conduct While Acting on Official Judicial Business

Judges are sworn to uphold and apply the law in their official capacity as judges. When they fail to do so, they violate Rule 1.2's requirement of promoting the independence, integrity, and impartiality of the judiciary, among other Code provisions. *See, e.g., Matter of Inquiry Concerning a Judge No. 94-70*, 454 S.E.2d 780 (Ga. 1995) (judge violated provisions of rule by issuing orders and using contempt powers to intimidate other elected officials); *In re Inquiry Concerning Holien*, 612 N.W.2d 789 (Iowa 2000) (judge refused to abide by statute and rules regarding public access to courtroom and accepted procedures); *Miss. Comm'n on Jud. Performance v. Perdue*, 853 So. 2d 85 (Miss. 2003) (judge violated provisions of code of judicial conduct regarding integrity and independence of judiciary, avoidance of appearance of impropriety, and performance of adjudicative and administrative duties by entering ex parte temporary custody order without notice or hearing); *Miss. Comm'n on Jud. Performance v. Wells*, 794 So. 2d 1030 (Miss. 2001) (finding defendant guilty of disturbing the peace and simple assault based only on affidavits without permitting her to defend herself amounted to an attack on integrity and independence of the judicial office); *In re Blackburne*, 851 N.E.2d 1175 (N.Y. 2006) (judge who prevented a defendant's arrest by having defendant escorted out of court's back entrance to avoid detective who had come to court to arrest defendant on felony charge failed to act in a manner that promotes public confidence in the integrity and impartiality of the judiciary); *Disc. Counsel v. Elum*, 979 N.E.2d 289 (Ohio 2012) (judge, who conducted probation review outside presence of either prosecutor or defense counsel and, in a separate matter, threatened to hold prosecutor in contempt for failing to turn over information about an alleged cover-up of police officer's misconduct when all proceedings on the underlying matter were resolved and an internal investigation had commenced, sanctioned for violating Rule 1.2); *Disc. Counsel v. Karto*, 760 N.E.2d 412 (Ohio 2001) (judge conducted contempt proceedings without proper formalities as a means of intimidating individuals; court stated the judge's conduct "not only throws doubts on [his] impartiality, but also weakens the public's perception of the integrity of the judiciary."); *In re Dixon*, 559 S.E.2d 576 (S.C. 2002) (judge signed bench warrant without a summons, contempt hearing or formal imposition of sentence, resulting in the improper arrest, incarceration, and fine of an assault victim who appeared before the judge); *In re Hey*, 457 S.E.2d 509 (W. Va. 1995) (judge sexually harassed court employees and appeared on bench while intoxicated).

In addition to following applicable laws, judges must behave respectfully while on the bench. Failure to do so can diminish public confidence in the judiciary and result in discipline. For example, Rule 2.8(B) mandates that "A judge shall be patient, dignified, and courteous to litigants, jurors, witnesses, lawyers, court staff, court officials, and others with whom the judge deals in an official capacity, and shall require similar conduct of lawyers, and of staff, court officials, and others subject to the judge's direction and control." For cases discussing this standard, see Rule 2.8(B) and accompanying text.

Disrespectful Conduct

Judges have been disciplined for behaving disrespectfully while on the bench, including the use of profanity or other inappropriate language in court. *See, e.g., In re Goodfarb*, 880 P.2d. 620 (Ariz. 1994) (judge suspended for using racially inflammatory language and profanity in an official court proceeding); *In re Bowers*, 721 So. 2d 875 (La. 1998) (judge's pattern of inappropriate language and discourteous treatment of individuals appearing in his courtroom had negative impact on integrity and respect for judiciary, particularly because appearance in that court may have been litigant's and witness's only exposure to the system; court stated "[i]t is a presiding judge's duty to rise above the chaos that may surround him in order to ensure professionalism and civility on the part of all persons involved. . . . While a judge may be forceful and stern, he or she must remain respectful and in control of his or her temper—hostile, demeaning or humiliating language is never warranted.").

Judges have also been sanctioned for disrespectful conduct toward individuals appearing in their courtrooms. *See, e.g., In re Lamdin*, 948 A.2d 54 (Md. 2008) (judge suspended for lack of courtesy and use of vulgar language in speaking to defendants); *In re Hocking*, 546 N.W.2d 234 (Mich. 1996) (judge suspended for making scathing attack on female lawyer); *Miss. Comm'n on Jud. Performance v. Guest*, 717 So. 2d 325 (Miss. 1998) (judge disciplined for assaulting litigant in crowded courtroom); *In re Troisi*, 504 S.E.2d 625 (W. Va. 1998) (resignation and sanctions against judge's law license accepted as settlement agreement with judge who initiated physical confrontation with criminal defendant in courtroom). For additional discussion of judicial discipline for disrespectful conduct, see Rule 2.8(B) and accompanying text.

Similarly, Rule 1.2 may be violated when a judge impugns the integrity of other members of the bench. *See, e.g., Moran v. Clarke*, 309 F.3d 516 (8th Cir. 2002) (district court's factually unfounded innuendo that U.S. Court of Appeals decided recusal motion on basis of race undermined public's confidence in federal courts); *In re Lamdin*, 948 A.2d 54 (Md. 2008) (judge suspended for inappropriate language on the bench including comments that disparaged and undermined fellow members of the judicial system).

For an extreme example of judicial disrespect toward another judge, see *In re Jones*, 581 N.W2d. 876 (Neb. 1998), wherein a judge sent a death threat to another judge. *See also In re Jones*, 800 So. 2d 828 (La. 2001) (judge engaged in a physical altercation with another judge); *In re Assini*, 720 N.E.2d 882 (N.Y. 1999) (town court justice's "truly egregious" conduct included disparaging judicial colleague in vile terms); *see generally* William G. Ross, *Civility Among Judges: Charting the Bounds of Proper Criticism by Judges of Other Judges*, 51 Fla. L. Rev. 957 (1999) (discussing "bilious" acerbic written opinions; canvassing case law on judges' public and private comments about fellow judges; suggesting that though some judges defend such criticism as free speech, First Amendment should not provide a shield and judges should refrain from intemperate remarks about colleagues).

Disrespect toward subordinates is also grounds for discipline, particularly when the judge engages in harassing or demeaning conduct. *See, e.g., Fitch v. Comm'n on Jud. Performance*, 887 P.2d 937 (Cal. 1995) (judge's misconduct included offensive remarks to female court reporters and clerks and inappropriate non-consensual touching of women working under his supervision); *In re Disc. Action Against McGuire*, 685 N.W.2d 748 (N.D. 2004) (judge's inappropriate comments to, and physical contacts with, female courthouse employees violated provisions of Code of Judicial Conduct regarding upholding integrity of judiciary, avoiding impropriety and appearance of impropriety, and being patient, dignified, and courteous toward people subject to judge's direction and control); *Disc. Counsel v. Campbell*, 623 N.E.2d 24 (Ohio 1993) (judge's law license suspended for unwelcome and offensive sexual remarks and physical contact directed toward female employee while judge was judicial candidate and female lawyers appearing in judge's courtroom; court stated "such conduct would be unacceptable by any member of society. We, however, find it particularly intolerable by an attorney and abhorrent for a member of the judiciary"); *In re Nelson*, 532 S.E.2d 609 (S.C. 2000) (magistrate acted in loud, disorderly and vulgar manner in county detention center and made sexually oriented and inappropriate remarks to female deputy, among other infractions). *See generally Disciplinary action against judge on ground of abusive or intemperate language or conduct toward attorneys, court personnel, or parties to or witnesses in actions, and the like*, 89 A.L.R. 4th 278 (1991). For additional discussion of sexual harassment and other inappropriate behavior toward court employees, see Rule 2.8(B) and accompanying text.

Improper Off-Bench Conduct

Because of the very public nature of the role of judge, a judge's "off-bench" behavior is also subject to scrutiny. Although such scrutiny may be unpleasant, it is a price of enjoying the privileges of judicial office and is necessary for maintaining public confidence in the judiciary. *See generally* Howard T. Markey, *The Delicate Dichotomies of Judicial Ethics*, 101 F.R.D. 373 (1984) (explaining that judging is not merely a "job" but the privilege of dealing with "society's most precious asset, justice" and that the public does not perceive justice is being done if observation of judicial performance is limited to that of "judge qua judge"; offering as an example that "a judge might do an outstanding 'job' on the Bench, while appearing drunk in a public bar three nights a week, but few if any of the public would believe it – and the few who might would still prefer that their judges, however good their judicial performance, not be chosen from drunkards"); Charles Gardner Geyh, James J. Alfini, Steven Lubet, & Jeffrey M. Shaman, *Judicial Conduct and Ethics* § 10.03 at 10–3 (5th ed. 2013) (policy reasons for regulating off-bench conduct of judges include avoiding the appearance of partiality, favoritism or misuse of office, maintaining public confidence in judiciary and ensuring that judges will not be distracted by non-judicial activities); *see also In re Disc. Proc. Against Anderson*, 981 P.2d 426 (Wash. 1999) ("The Canons apply equally to judicial and extra-judicial behavior of judges"; judge disciplined for involvement as personal representative of a deceased client's estate after being sworn in, including participation in sale of client's business, failure to disclose vehicle loan payments made by a friend, and continuing to serve as president of three corporations).

Courts considering the relative significance of off-bench versus on-bench misconduct of judges have generally found that official misconduct is more significant. *See, e.g., In re Peck*, 867 P.2d 853 (Ariz. 1994) ("[w]e must treat official conduct even more strictly than improprieties in a judge's private life because it goes to the very integrity of our judicial system."); *In re Brown*, 625 N.W.2d 744 (Mich. 1999) ("everything else being equal . . . misconduct on the bench is usually more serious than the same misconduct off the bench").

Nonetheless, a wide variety of off-bench conduct has been found sanctionable. *See, e.g., In re Gunnels*, 12-261 (Ariz. Comm'n on Jud. Conduct 2013) (judge reprimanded for being profane and disrespectful to emergency personnel and officers called to scene of motorcycle accident involving judge); *In re Pope*, 12-763 (Ark. Sup. Ct. 2012) (judge suspended for 30 days without pay for physical altercation with male companion of estranged wife); *In re Saucedo* (Cal. Comm'n on Jud. Performance 2015) (judge removed from bench for duping courtroom clerk into believing someone was sending letter accusing clerk of having an affair with a court bailiff to pressure clerk into a "special friend" relationship with judge, giving clerk $26,000 in gifts, and providing legal advice to her son); *In re Dean*, 717 A.2d 176 (Conn. 1998) (judge failed to make court-ordered installment payments in satisfaction of judgment against him; court noted "although the conduct of the respondent in this case is private, as opposed to official or judicial conduct, it relates directly to the system of justice in which he, in his official capacity, plays a central role."); *In re Adams*, 932 So. 2d 1025 (Fla. 2006) (a judge who has a romantic relationship with a lawyer who has several cases before the judge fails "to act in a manner promoting public confidence in the judiciary"); *In re Popejoy*, 10-CC-1 (Ill. Courts Comm. 2012) (judge suspended for not stopping after accident, but instead driving faster, and keeping police waiting at door while charging cell phone and placing calls); *In re McClain*, 662 N.E.2d 935 (Ind. 1996) (judge's participation in harassment of employee and her family violated judicial Canons requiring judge to participate in and preserve integrity of judiciary and to act at all times in manner that promoted public confidence in integrity of judiciary and constituted willful misconduct); *In re Gerard*, 631 N.W.2d 271 (Iowa 2001) (judge engaged in two-month secret sexual affair in various rooms of the courthouse with married assistant county attorney who appeared before him on daily basis; court stated, "A judge is simply held to a higher standard of conduct by virtue of his office. This standard may make what the judge does in private a public concern"); *In re Ellender*, 889 So. 2d 225 (La. 2004) (judge suspended for one year after appearing in public, at Halloween party, in costume with afro wig, blackface makeup, and prison jumpsuit; judge's conduct caused the public to question his integrity and ability to be fair to African-Americans and diminished the integrity and respect citizens hold for Louisiana's judiciary); *In re Halloran*, 647 N.W.2d 505 (Mich. 2002) (judge's conduct in exposing himself to undercover police officer in men's room at airport constitutes failure to observe high standards of conduct so that the integrity and independence of the judiciary is preserved); *Miss. Comm'n on Jud. Performance v. Whitten*, 687 So. 2d 744 (Miss. 1997) (judge reprimanded for detaining trespassers at gun point, shooting at tires of trespassers' vehicle and threatening trespassers with bodily harm; court stressed that although the judge was not acting in his judicial capacity, judges must always maintain the integrity of the judiciary through their conduct); *In re Williams*, 777 A.2d 323 (N.J. 2001) (judge gave false information to police after confrontations with her former boyfriend and his female companion; court noted that "although her actions were related only to her private life, they took place in public where others, knowing of her status as a judge, could lose confidence in the integrity and impartiality of the judiciary"); *In re Tamsen*, 789 N.E.2d 613 (N.Y. 2003) (town court justice removed for misappropriation of funds and related subterfuge resulting in his disbarment as an attorney while he was sitting as judge; sanction was warranted even though wrongdoing was unrelated to his judicial office and predated his ascension to the bench); *In re Smith*, N.C. Jud. Standards Comm'n No. 09-138 (2010) (judge reprimanded for off-bench behavior toward counsel opposing judge's lawyer/spouse in court case and allowing a family relationship to interfere with duty to act at all times in a manner that promotes integrity of judiciary); *Disc. Counsel v. Spicer*, 834 N.E.2d 332 (Ohio 2005) (judge's role in creating and airing negative television ads attacking his opponent in re-election campaign violated Canons of judicial conduct requiring judges to act at all times in a manner that promotes public confidence in the integrity and impartiality of the judiciary); *In re Norblad*, 39 P.3d 860 (Or. 2002) (judge charged with driving under the influence of alcohol; court cited the state disciplinary commission's determination that the judge's "lack of judgment reflects badly, not just on his own character, but also on the judiciary as a whole" and that though his errors occurred off the bench, they "were of such a magnitude as to engender concern about the [j]udge's on-the-bench judgment"); *In re McKenzie*, Tenn. Bd. of Jud. Conduct Complaint Nos. B12-5167, B13-5219, and B13-5220 (April 11, 2013) (judge reprimanded for approaching the spouse of a court employee in courthouse hallway and using inappropriate language to question the spouse about employee's "personal issue" with the judge); *In re Disc. Proc. Against Sanders*, 145 P.3d 1208 (Wash. 2006) (Supreme Court Justice who visited facility for sexually violent predators, where he had conversations with residents concerning reasons for their confinement, and where one or more of residents had matters pending before the Supreme Court, failed to enforce high standards of judicial conduct and to promote public confidence in the integrity and impartiality of the judiciary); *In re Disc. Proc. Against Turco*, 970 P.2d 731 (Wash. 1999) (extrajudicial conduct of judge in allegedly pushing his wife to ground at public affair was subject to discipline under Canons of Judicial Conduct); *In re McCourt*, 633 S.E.2d 17 (W. Va. 2006) (judge who was presiding over petitioner's request for domestic violence protection order suspended without pay after calling petitioner at her motel to tell her of her husband's arrest, going to petitioner's motel room, asking to see petitioner's bruises, and touching bruises on petitioner's breast).

In some instances, however, the fact that certain conduct occurred out of court has insulated judges. *See, e.g., Panitch v. Panitch*, 770 A.2d 1237 (N.J. Super. 2001) (judge refused to recuse himself though plaintiffs claimed that during the discovery process in a divorce proceeding, judge told counsel "I'll put the [expletive deleted] [plaintiff] in jail" and used other obscenities; appellate court affirmed trial court decision because, though the judge's comments may have constituted a violation of the Code, they did not necessarily constitute bias; court noted "[t]his incident was *not* in Court, but on the *telephone* with attorneys and was an expression of frustration at having the discovery process again delayed after over 2 1/2 years of litigation.").

Additionally, a judge's out of court conduct may be protected on First Amendment grounds. *See Miss. Comm'n on Jud. Performance v. Wilkerson*, 876 So. 2d 1006 (Miss. 2004) (holding that judge could not be sanctioned under Code of Judicial Conduct for statements in letter to newspaper and on radio network proclaiming that homosexuals were mentally ill; such speech constituted speech regarding matter of political/public importance and private religious speech and could only be sanctioned if doing so would serve compelling state interest); but see *Miss. Comm'n on Jud. Performance v. Boland*, 975 So. 2d 882 (Miss. 2008) (comments by judge at national drug court seminar break-out session, that members of board of supervisors in county in which she served were ignorant, that fellow seminar participant should "get the hell out" of the room, and that African-Americans in her community could "go to hell," did not involve a matter of legitimate public concern, and thus were not protected by the First Amendment in judicial disciplinary proceeding); *Miss. Comm'n on Jud. Performance v. Osborne*, 687 So. 2d 744 (Miss. 2009) (judge suspended for one year for improper membership in political organization and racially inflammatory speech at organization's meeting. Court followed *Boland* finding speech not protected by First Amendment).

Conduct That Occurred before Taking the Bench

A judge may be disciplined under Rule 1.2 for conduct that occurred prior to the time that he or she took the bench. For instance, in *In re Inquiry Concerning Judge Robertson*, 596 S.E.2d 2 (Ga. 2004), the court held that a judge's false swearing that he had not been convicted of a felony involving moral turpitude on candidate affidavit amounted to conduct eroding public confidence in judiciary and putting at risk the integrity of judicial system. *See also In re Huckaby*, 656 So. 2d 292 (La. 1995) (after taking office, judge pleaded guilty to a charge of failure to file a federal tax return several years before being elected to the bench and was sentenced to one year in prison; judge violated Code of Judicial Conduct because although the ethical violation involved behavior taking place several years before the judge took office, the judge failed to correct the problem); *In re Hedges*, 20 N.Y.3d 677 (2013) (judge's admitted sexual contact with a minor, although occurring 40 years earlier and 13 years before judge was elevated to the bench, warranted removal).

PROMOTING PUBLIC CONFIDENCE IN THE INDEPENDENCE OF THE JUDICIARY

Pursuant to Rule 1.2, judges must make decisions independent of inappropriate outside influences. *See generally* Michael Traynor, *Judicial Independence: A Cornerstone of Liberty*, 37 Golden Gate U. L. Rev. 487 (2007); Rebecca Love Kourlis, *Judicial Independence and Independent Judges*, 80 Denv. U. L. Rev. 746 (2003); Vincent R. Johnson, *The Ethical Foundations of American Judicial Independence*, 29 Fordham Urb. L. Rev. 1007 (2002). Judges who advocate on behalf of one party or engage in improper campaign conduct may jeopardize public confidence in their independence and impartiality.

Advocacy

When a judge "steps off the bench" in a controversy, that is, abandons the judicial role to become an advocate for one party or another, the judge's impartiality is subject to question. Such conduct may violate Rule 1.2, in addition to other provisions of the Code. *See, e.g., In re Frankel, Karp*, 12-118 (Ariz. Comm'n on Jud. Conduct 2012) (two judges disciplined for filing amicus brief in appeal of cases they heard because such action "failed to promote public confidence that judges are to be neutral and impartial and not advocates for particular legal results"); *Fletcher v. Comm'n on Jud. Performance*, 968 P.2d 958 (Cal. 1998) (judge, in denying prosecution's motion to dismiss charges against defendant and then directing clerk to subpoena all prosecution witnesses, "took it upon himself to do the district attorney's job" and thus deprived defendant of impartial judge); *In re Graham*, 09-31 (Ga. Jud. Qualifications Comm'n 2010) (judge reprimanded for calling into chambers FBI agents investigating drug case and attacking their credibility and character in matter not assigned to judge and holding a hearing in chambers regarding a matter not before the judge); *In re Fuselier*, 837 So. 2d 1257 (La. 2003) (judge's institution of worthless check collection program inappropriately sent message that judge can assume function of advocate for one party and then adjudicate the dispute between those for whom he advocated and their opponents); *In re Moore*, 626 N.W.2d 374 (Mich. 2001) (disciplining judge who "frequently has failed to distinguish his role as an impartial arbitrator with that of a quasi-social worker and partisan advocate"; judge excessively interjected and interfered in trial proceedings, assumed prosecutorial role, expressed pro-prosecutorial and anti-defense sentiment, and prejudiced juries, among other violations); *Miss. Comm'n on Jud. Performance v. Justice Court Judge S.S.*, 834 So. 2d 31 (Miss. 2003) (judge failed to uphold the integrity and independence of judicial office by participating in a petition procedure against an officer who regularly presented cases in his court and "cautioning" sheriff with petition); *In re Compl. Against White*, 651 N.W.2d 551 (Neb. 2002) (judge's communications with deputy county attorney providing advice to aid attorney in appealing reversal of sentence judge had imposed violated Code of Judicial Conduct provisions regarding integrity and independence of judiciary and regarding avoidance of impropriety and appearance of impropriety; the judge abandoned the judicial role to become an advocate for her own ruling); *Disc. Counsel v. Campbell*, 931 N.E.2d 558 (Ohio 2010) (judge became a participant in two investigations when he encouraged police to follow up on an issue, questioned defendants, and reviewed a prosecutor's file); *Disc. Counsel v. Karto*, 760 N.E.2d 412 (Ohio 2001) (judge's misconduct included initiating contempt proceeding, stepping off bench, discarding robe, serving as witness and prosecutor in testifying and making closing statement, and then issuing the ruling in the case); *In re Larsen*, 616 A.2d. 529 (Pa. 1992) ("A judge plainly violates Canon

1 [requiring judges to uphold the integrity and independence of the judiciary] if he ignores the separation of powers and becomes excessively entangled in the prosecutorial functions of the police and district attorney.").

Campaign Conduct

A judge's improper campaign conduct may result in a Rule 1.2 violation. *See, e.g., In re Buckson*, 610 A.2d 203 (Del. 1992) (judge's attending and speaking at political gatherings and publicly endorsing himself as a "candidate" for office of governor, without first resigning judicial office, warrants censure and removal from office; court adopted Board's finding that "A judge who actively seeks the nomination of a political party as its candidate necessarily jeopardizes the independence and integrity of the judiciary"; court also found that judge's unofficial retirement from all judicial activities while drawing judicial salary diminished public confidence in the integrity of the judiciary.); *In re Rodriguez*, 829 So. 2d 857 (Fla. 2002) (judge's knowingly accepting campaign contribution made for the purpose of influencing the results of her judicial contest and filing misleading campaign reports violated Canons providing that judge shall uphold integrity and independence of the judiciary and shall avoid impropriety); *In re McMillan*, 797 So. 2d 560 (Fla. 2001) (making explicit campaign promises to favor state and police in court proceedings and making unfounded attacks on incumbent county judge and local court officials, among other offenses warranted removal); *In re Bass*, 2013-31 (Ga. Jud. Qualifications Comm'n 2013) (judge solicited votes from courtroom audience, questioned court officials about their support of his opponent, and threatened court contractors who did not publicly support judge's campaign); *In re Trudel*, 638 N.W.2d 405 (Mich. 2002) (chief district court judge disciplined for improper behavior, both in and out of the courtroom, including improper use of court equipment, supplies, and personnel for his campaign to retain judicial office); *Miss. Comm'n on Jud. Performance v. Osborne*, 11 So. 3d 107 (Miss. 2009) (judge suspended for one year for improper membership in political organization and racially inflammatory speech at organization's meeting during campaign); *In re Anderson*, 2013 Annual Report 11 (N.Y. Comm'n on Jud. Conduct 2013) (omitting information on financial disclosure forms created an appearance of impropriety); *In re Stephenson*, 552 S.E.2d 137 (N.C. 2001) (judge solicited re-election votes from defendants and attorneys appearing before him); *cf. In re Hopewell*, 507 N.W.2d 911 (S.D. 1993) (lawyer's unprofessional attacks against opponent in judicial election campaign warrant suspension from practice of law; "During a judicial campaign, a candidate may in an appropriate manner accurately criticize a sitting judge, but may not impugn the integrity of the judicial system."); *but see In re Stoker*, 827 P.2d 986 (Wash. 1992) (dismissing decision of Commission on Judicial Conduct that judge violated Code of Judicial Conduct by engaging in campaign activities at booths for major political parties at county fair; county fair was not "political gathering" for purposes of Code; court stated "While we must hold judges and judicial candidates to the highest standards of conduct, we must, at the same time, avoid, without a clear factual basis, reading into proper conduct 'implied' results, which constitute violations of the Code of Judicial Conduct").

Political conduct of judges, on behalf of others, also may result in a violation of Rule 1.2. *In re Shea*, 815 So. 2d 813 (La. 2002) (judge censured for making contributions to other candidates from judge's excess campaign funds); *In re Curcio*, 216 N.J. 335, 80 A.3d 373 (2013) (judge who acted as "Host Committee Chairman" and drafted and signed fund-raising letters did not act with integrity or independence).

PROMOTING PUBLIC CONFIDENCE IN THE INTEGRITY OF THE JUDICIARY

The Terminology section of the Code defines integrity as "probity, fairness, honesty, uprightness, and soundness of character." A lack of these attributes may result in discipline for judges under Rule 1.2 for failure to promote public confidence in the independence, integrity, and impartiality of the judiciary.

Probity and Uprightness

Judges have been disciplined for a lack of "probity," defined in the dictionary as "tried virtue or integrity; complete honesty; uprightness in one's dealings" and uprightness, defined as "marked by strong moral rectitude." *In re Seaman*, 627 A.2d 106 (N.J. 1993) (judge sexually harassed judicial clerk; clear and convincing evidence showed a "lack of uprightness" and compromised the integrity of the judiciary); *In re Case of Snow*, 674 A.2d 573 (N.H. 1996) (judge violated Code by contacting police officer regarding speeding ticket issued to judge's brother; court stated "judges are the most visible symbol of the rule of law in our society; without judges who are perceived and trusted by members of the public as impartial, the authority of the rule of law is compromised").

Imposing One's Moral Views on Others

While judges should always strive to act in an upright manner, they may be disciplined for imposing their own moral views upon litigants and court personnel. When judges do so, they overstep the boundaries of their office. *See, e.g., In re Singbush*, 93 So. 3d 188 (Fla. 2012) (judge reprimanded for habitual tardiness and inappropriate statement regarding religion in which judge professed a belief in God); *Miss. Comm'n on Jud. Performance v. A Mun. Ct. J.*, 755 So. 2d 1062 (Miss. 2000) (judge ordered probationers to marry because "he did not want [probationer] who was living in adultery to be placed immediately in jeopardy of being revoked based on their living arrangement in violation of [unlawful cohabitation statute]"); *State v. Pattno*, 579 N.W.2d 503 (Neb. 1998) (sentencing judge's interjecting his own religious views immediately prior to sentencing and reading of Bible passage disparaging defendant's homosexual lifestyle could cause a reasonable person to question the impartiality of the judge); *In re Empson*, 562 N.W.2d 817 (Neb. 1997) (judge committed ethical violation by disseminating religious materials in courthouse to jurors; giving spiritual advice and a Bible to distraught litigant outside of court who sought judge's advice, however, was not an ethical violation); *Off. of Disc. Counsel v. Mestemaker*, 676 N.E.2d 870 (Ohio 1997) (judge's misconduct included ordering marriage as condition of probation in three cases); *but see In re Quirk*, 705 So. 2d 172 (La. 1997) (judge's use of church attendance as condition of probation was not misconduct where defendants could attend a religious institution of their choosing, were not required to profess any belief, and where the law on the Establishment Clause was "rife with confusion" and subject to various interpretations). For additional information, *see generally* Mark C. Modak-Truran, *Reenchanting the Law: The Religious Dimension of Judicial Decision Making*, 53 Cath. U. L. Rev. 709 (2004); Rebekah L. Osborn, Note, *Beliefs on the Bench: Recusal for Religious Reasons and the Model Code of Judicial Conduct*, 19 Geo. J. Legal Ethics 895 (2006); Sanja Zgonjanin, *Quoting the Bible: The Use of Religious References in Judicial Decision-Making*, 9 N.Y. City L. Rev. 31 (2005).

Fairness

Judges who have failed to demonstrate fairness by making decisions in an apparently arbitrary manner have been subject to discipline. *See, e.g., In re Brown*, 662 N.W.2d 733 (Mich. 2003) (judge used a coin flip in custody dispute to decide where children would spend holiday); *In re Rainville*, 13.001 (Vt. Jud. Conduct Board 2014) (judge arbitrarily refused to admit self-authenticating documents); *but see Galloway v. Thompson*, 2001 WL 102356 (S.D. Ala. 2001) (dismissing as frivolous defendant's claim that judges "rubber stamp" certain district court decisions because of bias and prejudice in favor of the government).

Judicial unfairness based on racism, sexism, or other improper consideration of class meets with particular disapproval. *See In re Brown*, 625 N.W.2d 744 (Mich. 1999) (articulating standard that judicial misconduct involving unequal application of justice on the basis of race, color, ethnic background, gender, or religion is more serious than breaches of justice that do not disparage the integrity of the system on the basis of a class of citizenship). *See also In re Ferrara*, 582 N.W.2d 817 (Mich. 1998) (judge made untruthful statements and attempted to fabricate evidence regarding her racist statements; court noted "whatever [the judge's] right to her own private opinion, a person harboring and communicating such revolting [racist] views is unworthy of holding the privileges and responsibilities of public office. Indeed, the mean-spirited, crude, and biased nature and tone of the statements that were made public are inexcusable and unacceptable from a judge").

Dishonesty and Deception as Grounds for Discipline

Case laws offer examples of judges who have been disciplined for dishonesty and deception, usually in conjunction with several provisions of the Code of Judicial Conduct. *See, e.g., In re DeForest*, 12-266 and 12-275 (Ariz. Comm'n on Jud. Conduct 2012) (justice of the peace reprimanded for inflating experience and training in online biography and on resume); *In re Reinholtzen* (Cal. Comm'n on Jud. Performance 2015) (judge admonished for falsifying salary affidavits claiming judge had no cases pending for decision longer than 90 days); *In re Recksiedler*, 161 So. 3d 398 (Fla. 2015) (judge reprimanded for incomplete and inaccurate responses to nominating commission); *In re Frank*, 753 So. 2d 1228 (Fla. 2000) (making false statement in attorney grievance proceeding against daughter's then-husband and failing to disclose connection to counsel representing daughter in divorce proceeding warranted public reprimand); *In re Inquiry Concerning McCormick*, 639 N.W.2d 12 (Iowa 2002) (truth and honesty lie at the heart of the judicial system, and judges who conduct themselves in an untruthful manner contradict this most basic ideal; consequently, a judge who misrepresents the truth tarnishes the dignity and honor of his or her office); *In re Milhouse*, 605 N.W.2d 15 (Mich. 2000) (judge executed a judgment of sentence that falsely stated defendant had knowingly waived right to counsel and pleaded guilty); *In re Krepela*, 628 N.W.2d 262 (Neb. 2001) (judge falsified copy of police report and asked police officer to alter original report); *In re Coffey's Case*, 949 A.2d 102 (N.H. 2008) (suspending judge for three years after finding she created a trust to hide her and her husband's assets from creditors; court said, "A judge has the duty to be honest."); *In re Inquiry Concerning a Judge Renfer*, 493 S.E.2d 434 (N.C. 1997) (judge falsified official court documents by false entry of guilty pleas without knowledge of the defendants); *Disc. Counsel v. Ault*, 852 N.E.2d 727 (Ohio 2006) (judge who deceived several doctors into overprescribing painkilling drugs for his use and who was convicted of attempting to obtain a dangerous drug by deception failed to uphold the integrity of the judiciary); *Disc. Counsel v. O'Neill*, 815 N.E.2d 286 (Ohio 2004) (conduct of judge in engaging in a pattern of misrepresentation in her interactions with judges, litigants, attorneys, and court personnel violated Code of Judicial Conduct); *In re Augustus*, 626 S.E.2d 346 (S.C. 2006) (magistrate made false statements regarding his attendance at continuing legal education seminar); *In re White*, 499 S.E.2d 813 (S.C. 1998) (magistrate's lying about his education on his magistrate application warrants reprimand; the court stressed the importance to the integrity of the judiciary of a judicial candidate's truthful representation of credentials; because the public's trust in the judiciary is founded upon the presumption that every judge has met minimum education requirements, the magistrate's conduct threatened public confidence in the judiciary); *In re Riffle*, 558 S.E.2d 590 (W. Va. 2001) (judge made false statements, filed untrue reports with the Department of Public Safety, and fraudulently attempted to collect workers' compensation benefits).

Lying to disciplinary authorities about an underlying matter of misconduct can also compromise the integrity of the system the judge was sworn to uphold. *See, e.g., In re McCormick*, 639 N.W.2d 12 (Iowa 2002) (judge's false statement in letter to Judicial Qualifications Commission in which he asserted that his wife authorized placement of campaign sign in his front yard warranted public reprimand); *Thomas v. Jud. Conduct Comm'n*, 77 S.W.3d 578 (Ky. 2002) (judge's misconduct included misrepresenting to Judicial Conduct Commission a material fact regarding judge's personal relationship with criminal defendant's ex-wife); *In re King*, 857 So. 2d 432 (La. 2003) (lying to the Judiciary Commission in a sworn statement taken as part of an investigation into judicial misconduct is simply conduct which Supreme Court cannot and will not tolerate); *In re Ferrara*, 582 N.W.2d 817 (Mich. 1998) (after publication of tapes in which judge had uttered racial slur, judge publicly misrepresented the tapes as fake and tried to introduce a fraudulent letter into evidence; misstatements compromised the public's confidence in the judiciary's integrity); *Miss. Comm'n on Jud. Performance v. Willard*, 788 So. 2d 736 (Miss. 2001) (during disciplinary proceedings, judge concocted evidence and demonstrated disdain for the process by openly displaying a tape recorder during witness testimony, producing and displaying a knife during witness testimony, and attempting to send messages to some members of the Commission panel by facsimile); *In re Collazo*, 691 N.E. 2d 1021 (N.Y. 1998) (judge disciplined for passing a note to his court attorney concerning physical attributes of female law intern, suggesting intern remove part of her apparel in his presence, and subsequently engaging in pattern of evasive, deceitful, and untruthful behavior in an attempt to conceal pending investigation while seeking appointment to Supreme Court).

However, judges likely do not violate the Code when they unintentionally make false or misleading statements. *See, e.g., In re Inquiry Concerning Davey*, 645 So. 2d 398 (Fla. 1994) (to constitute judicial misconduct, lack of candor must be knowing and willful; giving inaccurate or false statement under oath not misconduct unless when making statement judge did not believe it to be true); *In re Rainville*, 13.001 (Vt. Jud. Conduct Board 2014) (to violate Canon, judge must have intentionally made incorrect amendment to entry order); *In re Kroger*, 702 A.2d 64 (Vt. 1997) (judge made false statements under oath at a meeting of the Vermont Association of County Judges; court stressed that only knowingly made false statements are punishable, not unintentionally false or misleading statements). Intent can be inferred from the evidence. For instance, "if the evidence shows that a judge had personal knowledge of facts contrary to the judge's statement, the judge's intent to deceive may be inferred." *In re Kroger*, 702 A.2d 64, 68, n.2; *see, e.g., In re Matter of Jud. Disc. Proc. Against Carver*, 531 N.W.2d 62 (Wis. 1995) (judge disciplined for denying that defendant had contacted court or asked for special treatment, when in fact, defendant had written to judge and asked for his assistance; judge's claim that he had forgotten was unreasonable given that he had received two letters from defendant one day earlier).

Soundness of Character

Cases wherein the soundness of a judge's character comes into question often involve judges who have exhibited a pattern of poor behavior, which, in many cases, warrants removal from office. *See, e.g., In re Carpenter*, 17 P.3d 91 (Ariz. 2001) (removal of judge who committed 14 infractions of the Code of Judicial Conduct in first year in office; removal was necessary because actions were undertaken in judge's official capacity and, therefore, directly harmful to the judicial system itself); *In re Jefferson*, 753 So. 2d 181 (La. 2000) (judge removed for persistent pattern of reckless, disrespectful, and injudicious behavior, including exceeding contempt power and banning city prosecutor from courtroom and thereafter dismissing 41 criminal cases when no prosecutor was present to proceed); *In re Seitz*, 495 N.W.2d 559 (Mich. 1993) (removal of judge for hostile attitude toward employees, abuse of contempt power, and other acts that "demonstrated an attitude, a mind-set, that leaves us firmly convinced that he is woefully unfit for judicial office. He not only exhibited a lack of the qualities from which judicial temperament springs, but he has exhibited a distinct pattern of injudicious temperament and conduct"); *Miss. Comm'n on Jud. Performance v. Spencer*, 725 So. 2d 171 (Miss. 1998) (removal warranted for, among other violations, a continuing pattern of offensive sexual comments to members of the court staff, constituting gross personal conduct).

Charges of Criminal Conduct as Affecting Integrity

While a criminal activity is also grounds for discipline under Rule 1.1, conduct that does not result in a conviction may violate Rule 1.2. *See* Conviction of Crime Not Necessary.

Courts are careful to state that imposition of a suspension does not reflect on the judge's guilt or innocence in the underlying matter. *In re Shenberg*, 632 So. 2d 42 (Fla. 1992) (court "acutely mindful" that judges were only indicted and "there abides with them a presumption of innocence until the final resolution of the charges"); *In re Brennan*, 483 N.E. 2d 484 (N.Y. 1985) (issue before the court suspending without pay judge under federal indictment for attempted murder, assault, criminal possession of weapon, and sale of controlled substance was not question of judge's guilt or innocence but "cloud" created by number and seriousness of charges).

CONDUCT THAT ADVERSELY AFFECTS PUBLIC CONFIDENCE IN INDEPENDENCE, INTEGRITY, AND IMPARTIALITY OF JUDICIARY

The Commentary to Rule 1.2 acknowledges that Rule 1.2's proscription against conduct that compromises or appears to compromise the independence, integrity, and impartiality of a judge is cast in general terms. The Commentary, however, defends this language as necessary, noting it is not "practicable" to list all prohibited acts. Model Code of Judicial Conduct Rule 1.2 cmt. [3]. Some examples of conduct that are frequently grounds for discipline are discussed in the following sections.

Sexual Misconduct

Sexual misconduct is not compatible with the high standards of conduct imposed upon members of the judiciary, and is a frequent reason for finding a violation of the provisions of Rule 1.2. *See e.g., People v. Biddle*, 180 P.3d 461 (Colo. 2007) (in case of first impression, attorney suspended for three years for engaging in sexual relationship with deputy district attorney assigned to his court while he served first as magistrate and then judge); *In re Downey*, 937 So. 2d 643 (Fla. 2006) (judge's admission to repeated viewing of pornography from computer in his chambers and exposing court personnel to pornographic images on several occasions supported stipulation to public reprimand; judge also stipulated to retire at the end of his current term of office and to be permanently barred from serving as a judge in Florida based upon other allegations regarding improper contact and communication with female attorneys); *In re Associate Judge Polito*, 12-CC-1 (Ill. Cts. Comm. 2013) (associate judge and admitted pornography addict under treatment suspended for viewing pornographic images on court computer during work hours); *In re Robertson*, 120 P.3d 790 (Kan. 2005) (removal of judge from office was proper and just sanction for judge's misconduct, which consisted of using county-owned computer located in his office to access and display sexually explicit images, messages, and materials); *In re Alvord*, 847 P.2d 1310 (Kan. 1993) (judge publicly censured for unwanted advances toward 21-year-old clerk); *In re Empson*, 562 N.W.2d 817 (Neb. 1997) (making repeated offensive and unwelcome sexual inquiries into private and personal lives of various female court personnel, student interns, and women having business in the court violated requirement that judge avoid impropriety and appearance of impropriety); *In re Seaman*, 627 A.2d 106 (N.J. 1993) (judge who sexually harassed a judicial clerk by repeated lewd comments and inappropriate touching suspended for 60 days); *In re Cioppa*, No. 4 JD 12, Penn. Ct. of Jud. Discipline (2012) (judge removed from office after pleading guilty to indecent assault and official oppression based on allegations judge bargained away his impartiality, "trading it for a little sexual *quid pro quo*" when the judge told two tenants facing eviction that he could make their cases go away in exchange for sexual favors); *In re Gravely*, 467 S.E.2d 924 (S.C. 1996) (magistrate reprimanded for having intercourse in the magistrate's office with a pro se defendant in an eviction proceeding); *In re Hatcher*, 748 S.E.2d 220 (S.C. 2013) (lawyer, who resigned from bench, publicly reprimanded for kissing bond court clerk on the forehead); *In re Canales*, 113 S.W.3d 56 (Tex. Rev. Trib. 2003) (judge engaged in inappropriate, unsolicited, and sexually suggestive conduct in chambers, including sexual assault and battery against court secretary, a part-time employee of the district attorney's office, and the daughter of his court bailiff); *In re Hare*, 11-4JC-015 (Utah Jud. Conduct Comm'n 2011) (judge censured for exposing himself in a public restroom to a police officer); *In re Toler*, 625 S.E.2d 731 (W. Va. 2005) (magistrate's acts of sexual misconduct with women who sought assistance from his court warranted censure, one-year suspension without pay, $5,000 fine, and assessment of costs of disciplinary proceedings); *but see In re Subryan*, 900 A.2d 809 (N.J. 2006) (comments and jokes about gender and sex made in judge's chambers by judge and others were inappropriate, but they did not violate code of judicial conduct where record suggested that people who participated in the banter believed it to be harmless; however, judge's unwanted advance to his law clerk by kissing her against her will violated Code).

Rude and Insensitive Behavior

Rude or insensitive behavior also diminishes public confidence in the integrity or impartiality of the judiciary, and has thus been found sanctionable. *See, e.g., In re Gibson* (Cal. Comm'n on Jud. Performance 2010) (judge admonished for making rude, inappropriate, and insensitive remarks while on the bench, in chambers, and in courthouse hallway); *In re Wright*, 694 So. 2d 734 (Fla. 1997) (judge adopted rude, abusive, and inappropriate manner in addressing two assistant state attorneys and one crime victim during two separate incidents while on bench); *In re Inquiry Concerning Golden*, 645 So. 2d 970 (Fla. 1994) (judge disciplined for engaging in numerous instances of unprofessional behavior, including making racially insensitive, sexist, and rude comments in court); *Matter of Jenkins*, 503 N.W.2d 425 (Iowa 1993) (judge repeatedly made degrading attacks of a personal nature about parties before him, such as referring to an individual as a "beer-bellied, full-bearded, unemployed, seedy, coverall-clad lout."); *In re Marko*, 595 So. 2d 46 (Fla. 1992) (judge exhibited rude and inappropriate behavior at marriage dissolution hearing, telling the wife to "go out and get another guy … the single bars are full of them … there are all kinds of bimbos in those places, and there are all kinds of guys running around in open shirts with eagles on their chests. There are great guys out there … you go find a brain surgeon.");

In re Council, 076315 (N.J. 2015) (judge suspended without pay for one month for inappropriately pushing court employee out of a courthouse social event and back to work and pulling employee by the ear leaving employee demeaned and humiliated); *In re Romano*, 712 N.E.2d 1216 (N.Y. 1999) (judge disciplined for twice making inappropriate comments in court).

Racial Slurs

Courts show great intolerance for judges who use racial slurs, or otherwise indicate prejudice toward particular groups, disciplining such conduct under the language of Rule 1.2 and other Code provisions. *See, e.g., In re Judicial Misconduct (Cebull)*, 751 F.3d 611 (U.S. Jud. Conf. Comm. on Jud. Conduct and Disability 2014) (judge publicly reprimanded for sending "hundreds" of disrespectful emails lambasting politicians, racial minorities, religions, gays, and women); *In re Pet. for Removal of a Chief Judge*, 592 So. 2d 671 (Fla. 1992) (chief judge's impartiality questioned due to judge's endorsement, in newspaper interview, of discriminatory stereotypes); *In re Inquiry Concerning Carr*, 593 So. 2d 1044 (Fla. 1992) (judge lessened public confidence in the dignity, integrity, and impartiality of the judiciary by making the following statement in a hearing in his courtroom: "Now, you can throw your Italian temper around in the bars but you don't throw them around in my courtroom. Do you understand, Mr. Orsello? I'm just as Irish as you are Dago. Do you understand? The only trouble is I'm the boss here and I've got two cops who do anything I tell them to, including taking you to jail."); *In re Moore*, 626 N.W.2d 374 (Mich. 2001) (judge disciplined for misconduct, including making stereotypical comments on basis of race); *Miss. Jud. Performance Comm'n v. Walker*, 565 So. 2d 1117 (Miss. 1990) (judge held an unsuccessful litigant in contempt and made a racial slur to him; when an African-American prosecutor failed to win against an African-American defendant, judge suggested collusion due to race); *In re Mulroy*, 731 N.E.2d 120 (N.Y. 2000) (judge violated Canon by using profanity while court was in session and making a number of offensive racial slurs); *In re Schiff*, 635 N.E.2d 286 (N.Y. 1994) (justice stated that he recalled a time when it was safe for young women to walk the streets "before the blacks and Puerto Ricans moved here" and later remarked that he did so because he knew an attorney present was Hispanic; court noted that "[a] deliberate and calculated remark of this nature, even if isolated, 'casts doubt on [petitioner's] ability to fairly judge all cases before him,' and seriously violated the governing rules related to his duty to uphold the integrity and impartiality of the judiciary and to avoid even the appearance of impropriety"); *In re Gosnell*, 621 S.E.2d 659 (S.C. 2006) (county magistrate's use of racial remark made toward a defendant appearing before the magistrate, violated Canons regarding preservation of integrity and independence of the judiciary and performance of duties with impartiality). *See generally* Frank M. McClellan, *Judicial Impartiality & Recusal: Reflection on the Vexing Issue of Racial Bias*, 78 Temp. L. Rev. 351 (2005).

Bias

A judge can be disciplined for creating an impression of bias by his words or conduct. *See, e.g., In the Matter Concerning Commissioner Alan Friedenthal* (Cal. Comm'n. on Jud. Performance 2012) (judge publicly admonished for appearance of bias for repeatedly mentioning litigant's parent and parent's complaints against judge and attempt to remove judge from case; judge's remark that complaints are "going nowhere" undermines public confidence in integrity of the judicial system); *In re Goodman*, 649 N.E.2d 115 (Ind. 1995) (judge created appearance that "the court's business was based upon the exchange of favors" where judge had hired a corporation run by a close friend of the court administrator to provide services for a court program, corporation hired a relative of the court administrator to run the program, and judge subsequently became engaged to a corporation accountant); *In re Cresap*, 940 So. 2d 624 (La. 2006) (judge's conduct during recusal hearing exhibited an unethical bias in favor of plaintiff's counsel and a prejudice against defense counsel); *In re Brown*, 691 N.E.2d 573 (Mass. 1998) (judge violated Canon by making comments expressing strong disfavor against a non-party union and its leadership, including description of union as, "an outfit that's always in trouble" and a "union gone amok"); *State v. Simmons*, 646 N.W.2d 564 (Minn. App. 2002) (remarks by district court judge during sentencing demonstrated bias, including the following: "You are immoral. Completely, unequivocally immoral. And the Board is wrong when they say judges can't use that term and they've told me that to my face. But I'm a free American and I can say what I please. You are immoral. Your record reflects that you are immoral and that is the correct term. Although that belittles people, I'm told, you need to be belittled, because you are. ... you're no different than the people who took down the World Trade Center. ... I hope the feds have the time to carry out their prosecution against you."); *People v. Conyers*, 487 N.W.2d 787 (Mich. Ct. App. 1992) (judge's lack of neutrality in criminal trial, including excessive interference in witness examination, disparaging remarks to defense counsel, and impatience in front of jury showed "attitude of partisanship" and deprived defendant of fair trial); *Miss. Comm'n on Jud. Performance v. Osborne*, 11 So. 3d 107 (Miss. 2009) (judge suspended for one year for improper membership in political organization and racially inflammatory speech disdaining local Caucasian officials at organization's meeting during campaign); *In re Newberry County Mag. English*, 625 S.E.2d 919 (S.C. 2006) (magistrate's conduct suggested bias in favor of the state in DUI trial when after the arresting officer, defendant and defense attorney failed to appear, magistrate directed that the officer be located, trial was delayed and the officer was given the opportunity to appear but no similar effort was made to locate the defendant or to give the defendant an opportunity to be present); *In re Burns* CJC No. 4118-F-111 (Wash. Comm'n on Jud. Conduct 2004) (judge who wrote "NTG," which was believed to mean "Nail This Guy" on the bottom of some defendants' judgments and sentence forms created appearance that judge was biased against those defendants and undermined public confidence in integrity and impartiality of judiciary).

Hostility toward Parties, Witnesses, and Jurors

A judge's treatment of members of the public who come into the courtroom has a direct effect on either building or destroying public confidence in the judiciary. Thus, judges who have mistreated witnesses or parties in the courtroom have been disciplined pursuant to the language of Rule 1.2. *See, e.g., In re Steensland* (Ala. Ct. of the Judiciary 2011) (judge publicly censured for demeaning, mocking, and humiliating litigants); *In re Johnson* (Cal. Comm'n on Jud. Performance 2012) (judge publicly admonished for comments regarding rape victim and lack of serious bodily injury, explaining the comments did not promote confidence in the judiciary); *In re Sloop*, 946 So. 2d 1046 (Fla. 2006) (judge removed from office after failing to seek prompt release of eleven citizens whom he had ordered arrested after they were directed to the wrong courtroom for traffic citation proceedings, resulting in citizens' being confined for nine hours and subjected to jail intake procedures including strip search); *Inquiry Concerning a Judge re Graziano*, 661 So. 2d 819 (Fla. 1995) (judge allowed an attorney to subpoena a physician-witness by fax one day before physician was scheduled to speak at a professional conference and take a family vacation to Europe; upon the judge's order, the physician was handcuffed and arrested at the conference and returned to the United States); *In re Inquiry Concerning Perry*, 641 So. 2d 366 (Fla. 1994) (judge admonished and berated an army recruiter for wearing his uniform into court; court said "[j]udges are expected to be temperate, attentive, patient and impartial, diligent in ascertaining facts, and prompt in the performance of a judge's duties. Common courtesy and considerate treatment of [others] are traits properly expected of judges."); *In re Fleet*, 610 So. 2d 1282 (Fla. 1992) (while on bench, judge displayed a handgun, loaded it, and began questioning an unruly witness); *Matter of Inquiry Concerning a Judge No. 1496*, 407 S.E.2d 743 (Ga. 1991) (judge's conduct warranted permanent bar from active service where, during divorce proceeding, he interrupted and refused to listen to witnesses, made remarks about a female witness's physical appearance, used biblical verse to support his judgment, and announced at the beginning of the proceeding that he would rule against the complainant as long as she was living with a man to whom she was not married); *State v. Miller*, 49 P.3d 458 (Kan. 2002) (defendant's conviction reversed and remanded for a new trial because of repeated improper comments by the judge questioning the truthfulness of a witness); *In re Moore*, 626 N.W.2d 374 (Mich. 2001) (judge disciplined for pattern of persistent interference in and frequent interruption of trial of cases, impatient, discourteous, critical, and sometimes severe attitudes toward jurors, witnesses, counsel, and others present in courtroom, and use of controversial tone and manner in addressing litigants, jurors, witnesses, and counsel); *In re Aldrich*, 08-104, 08-105, 09-110, and 09-111 (Minn. Bd. on Jud. Standards 2010) (judge reprimanded for belittling witnesses and making disrespectful remarks to lawyer); *In re Baker*, No. 2010-151 (New Jersey Adv. Comm. on Jud. Conduct 2011) (judge reprimanded for using inappropriate language when speaking to litigant in courtroom including telling litigant to "shut your mouth" and "When I talk, you listen."); *In re Popeo* (N.Y. Comm'n on Jud. Conduct 2015) (judge's remarks "were not only discourteous but impugned the lawyers' integrity and undermined their role in the eyes of defendants and the public, which is inconsistent with established ethical standards requiring judges to act in a manner that promotes public confidence in the integrity and impartiality of the judiciary"); *In re Greene*, 403 S.E.2d 257 (N.C. 1991) (judge censured for making comments in domestic battery case in which he indicated that battered women deserved to be hit, that the battered-woman's advocacy agency that accompanied the battered woman in court were "she-dogs," and that the judge himself had beat his wife); *In re Lindner*, 710 N.W.2d 866 (Neb. 2006) (judge reprimanded for making derogatory remark in apparent reference to defendant); *In re Mathesius*, 910 A.2d 594 (N.J. 2006) (judge who entered jury room and asked jury "what the hell" they were thinking, violated Canons, which required judges to uphold integrity and independence of judiciary); *Disc Counsel v. McCormack*, 977 N.E.2d 598 (Ohio 2012) (judge who "treated the litigants and their counsel with disdain," terminated hearings before all evidence presented, and "acted on his own whims" violated Rule 1.2); *Disc. Counsel v. Campbell*, 931 N.E.2d 558 (Ohio 2010) (judge went to defendant's holding cell and yelled that he would not accept the defendant's plea); *Disc. Counsel v. Hoague*, 725 N.E.2d 1108 (Ohio 2000) (judge suspended for (1) making statements on court letterhead to intimidate persons he believed to be guilty of reckless driving into appearing before him so that he could personally reprimand them and (2) interrogating persons he believed were guilty of reckless driving, without informing them of their right to counsel, and indicating his intent to contact their employers concerning their driving habits; although judge explained that he held reckless driving in particular contempt, court responded that "strong feelings do not excuse a judge from complying with the judicial Canons"); *State v. Bayer*, 656 N.E.2d 1314 (Ohio App. 1995) (judge's conduct failed "to evince an aura of pure impartiality"; judge refused to allow defendant in criminal menacing case to question the integrity of an attorney-witness and stated in open court that "[h]is credibility is not an issue with this Court anyway. I've known [the attorney-witness] for 20 years, and I've never known his credibility to be anything"; judge further stated that defendant "was going to be convicted no matter what"); *In re Barnack*, 299 P.3d 525 (Or. 2013) (judge censured for calling child sex abuse defendant a "piece of shit" during trial, and other similar comments); *In re Martin*, 734 S.E.2d 165 (S.C. 2012) (judge publicly reprimanded for telling defendant, "I'll beat your ass if you call me a liar"); *In re Glynn*, 389 S.E.2d 868 (S.C. 1990) (judge made offensive and intemperate remarks to a defendant's family); *In re Watkins*, 757 S.E.2d 594 (W. Va. 2013) (judge suspended for four years for pattern of abusive behavior toward litigants that demonstrated lack of impartiality). *See also* Rule 2.8(B), which requires judges to be patient, dignified, and courteous to litigants, jurors, witnesses, and others with whom the judge deals in an official capacity.

Hostility toward Lawyers

Threatening or offensive conduct toward attorneys who appear before a judge is also unacceptable behavior under the language of Rule 1.2. *See, e.g., In re Cohen*, 99 So. 3d 926 (Fla. 2012) (judge reprimanded for using power of office to create hostile courtroom environment for lawyer who filed motion to disqualify); *In re Schapiro*, 845 So. 2d 170 (Fla. 2003) (judge belittled, embarrassed, and screamed at attorneys who appeared before him and exhibited a long-term pattern of rude and intemperate behavior; court said "[t]o undermine public confidence and respect by such serious violations strikes at the very roots of an effective judiciary, for those who are served by the courts will not have confidence in and respect for the courts' judgments if judges engage in this egregious conduct."); *Inquiry Concerning a Judge McAllister*, 646 So. 2d 173 (Fla. 1994) (judge removed from office for, among other reasons, abusive conduct toward attorneys in Public Defender's Office); *Inquiry Concerning a Judge re Carnesoltas*, 563 So. 2d 83 (Fla. 1990) (judge used obscene language while appearing as counsel in case before district court judge and falsely accused district court judge of personal animosity; while presiding as a judge, the judge demeaned an attorney appearing in her court by having the attorney removed from the courtroom); *In re McDowell*, CJD 2011-013 and 2011-014 (Maryland Comm'n on Jud. Disabilities 2011) (judge reprimanded for lying to lawyers when judge told lawyers that case would be set for jury trial the following day, directed clerk to public and posted false docket sheet supporting lie, and caused parties to appear in court all with knowledge that no jurors were to be called in for the case); *In re Hocking*, 546 N.W.2d 234 (Mich. 1996) (judge instigated a personal attack against attorney in court, making caustic comments and using an abusive tone; Michigan Supreme Court noted that while rules do not prevent a judge from expressing "strong displeasure or even anger," judicial comments must not be "clearly prejudicial to the administration of justice"; no Code violation found when same judge filed grievance with the Attorney Grievance Commission against lawyer who had requested investigation of the judge by the Judicial Tenure Commission, absent showing that grievance was filed for retaliatory purposes or "patently frivolous"); *In re Duckman*, 699 N.E.2d 872 (N.Y 1998) (judge disciplined for misconduct, including personally attacking assistant district attorneys and displaying obvious bias against the prosecution); *In re Mogil*, 673 N.E.2d 896 (N.Y. 1996) (misconduct included publicly disseminating offensive and threatening remarks regarding attorney complaints against judges—promising that retaliation would follow unless "your first figurative blow is so credible, powerful, and based upon indelible truth as to put [the judge] 'down for the count.' If not, and your target can arise after your most potent broadside, *you've had it!*"); *In re Scarlett*, No. 10-209 (N. C. Jud. Standards Comm'n 2011) (judge reprimanded for conducting hearing in courtroom at which judge provided lawyer, with whom judge had a personal disagreement, with behavioral directives. Proceeding did not meet basic due process requirements and judge dragged other court personnel into the disagreement); *In re LaSalata*, CJC No. 6279-F-149 (Wash. Comm'n on Jud. Conduct 2010) (judge admonished for telling deputy prosecutor that he would "rip her head off" if she interrupted him again). *See also* Rule 2.8(B), which requires judges to be patient, dignified, and courteous to lawyers and others with whom the judge deals in an official capacity.

Hostility toward Other Judges

Discourteous comments or conduct directed toward other judges may also be grounds for discipline. *See, e.g., Moran v. Clarke*, 309 F.3d 516 (8th Cir. 2002) (chiding district judge for making factually unfounded innuendo that appellate court decided recusal motion on basis of race; court noted, "[i]t is one thing for a district judge to disagree on a legal basis with a judgment of this court. It is quite another to openly challenge the court's ruling and attempt to discredit the integrity of the judgment in the eyes of the public," quoting *Reserve Mining Co. v. Lord*, 529 F. 2d 181 (8th Cir. 1976)); *In re Inquiry Concerning a Judge*, 832 So. 2d 716 (Fla. 2002) (judge disciplined for a number of indiscretions, including angrily engaging in an ex parte discussion with another judge in that judge's hearing room); *In re Diaz*, 908 So. 2d 334 (Fla. 2005) (judge disciplined for sending anonymous email messages to another judge that could be construed as implied threat of organized group retaliation against recipient judge because of his alleged practice of reporting illegal immigrants to federal authorities when he became aware of their status during hearings); *In re Danikolas*, 838 N.E.2d 422 (Ind. 2005) (judge's discharge of magistrate from employment in retaliation for testimony she provided during a previous disciplinary matter brought against judge violated Canons requiring judge to personally observe high standards of conduct in order to preserve the integrity and independence of the judiciary, and to act in a manner that promotes public confidence in the integrity and impartiality of the judiciary); *In re Sauce*, 561 N.E.2d 751 (Ind. 1990) (judge engaged in ex parte communications with the judge handling his dissolution case and making off-color and outrageous comments implying retaliation against his wife's attorney); *In re Jones*, 800 So. 2d 828 (La. 2001) (judge referred to Fourth Circuit Court of Appeal judge as a "son of a bitch" in the presence of other judges and had a verbal confrontation that escalated into a physical altercation with another judge, where judges engaged in a "pushing/shoving" match and grappled with each other); *Miss. Comm'n on Jud. Performance v. Thompson*, 972 So. 2d 582 (Miss. 2008) (judge publicly reprimanded for interjecting himself into case assigned to other judge after he had recused himself); *In re Jones*, 581 N.W.2d 876 (Neb. 1998) (judge consistently used intemperate and threatening language and sent a death threat to a fellow judge, among other infractions); *In re Mathesius*, 910 A.2d 594 (N.J. 2006) (judge improperly told law clerk of the author of an appellate opinion that reversed a criminal conviction arising from a trial over which defendant presided to deliver message to her judge that the judge was "inexperienced and not competent," and wrote a letter to that appellate judge stating that the judge was uninformed and impractical); *Disciplinary Counsel v. Ferreri*, 710 N.E.2d 1107 (Ohio 1999) (judge made derogatory comments about other courts and judges to television reporter shortly after one of his decisions was reversed; court stated this Code provision does not distinguish between comments on and "off the record," noting that "[w]e recognize that on occasion a judge may unwittingly make an inappropriate casual remark. However, respondent's remarks about the appellate court were not unwitting, inadvertent 'slips.'").

Lack of Judicial Temperament

When rude or hostile behavior becomes a pattern of conduct, judges have received differing sanctions reflecting the severity of the offenses. *Compare In re Elliston*, 789 S.W.2d 469 (Mo. 1990) (judge suspended for 15 days without pay for repeatedly discourteous, abrasive, and abusive conduct toward attorneys, litigants, witnesses, and colleagues), *and In re Bowers*, 721 So. 2d 875 (La. 1998) (judge censured for using foul language, being impatient, discourteous, and insensitive to attorneys, witnesses, and parties appearing before him) *with In re Flournoy*, 990 P.2d 642 (Ariz. 1999) (six month suspension of judge for outbursts of temper) *and In re Moore* 626 N.W.2d 374 (Mich. 2001) (six month suspension without pay for judge who exhibited pattern of interference in cases; discourteous and severe attitudes toward jurors, witnesses, counsel, and others present in courtroom; and use of controversial tone in addressing litigants, jurors, witnesses, and counsel).

In some jurisdictions, the severity of the sanction may also depend on whether the court concludes that the judge is willing to take steps to eliminate the pattern of behavior. *Compare In re Wood*, 720 So. 2d 506 (Fla. 1998) (public reprimand for a pattern and practice of rude, intemperate, and inappropriate comments given judge's candor, his voluntary submission to anger and stress management therapy, and his assurances that he will continue to undergo therapeutic treatment until no longer necessary) *with In re Sloop*, 946 So. 2d 1046 (Fla. 2006) (judge who was rude and abusive toward defendant and who failed to promptly release 11 citizens whom he improperly ordered arrested was removed from office after court found that judge had irreparably damaged public confidence in the judiciary and lacked the proper temperament and judgment to continue to serve as a judicial officer).

In particularly egregious situations, courts have found that removal of the judge is necessary to restore public confidence in the judiciary. *See, e.g., In re Shea*, 759 So. 2d 631 (Fla. 2000) (judge removed for pattern of hostile conduct toward attorneys, court personnel, and fellow judges); *Inquiry Concerning a Judge re Graziano*, 696 So. 2d 744 (Fla. 1997) (removal of judge for, among other misdeeds, the persistent practice of using inappropriately harsh, insulting, embarrassing, and threatening language toward numerous court employees in public and private); *In re Inquiry Concerning a Judge*, 566 S.E.2d 310 (Ga. 2002) (removal of magistrate for general pattern of unacceptable behavior and judicial incompetence); *In re Inquiry Concerning Holien*, 612 N.W.2d 789 (Iowa 2000) (removal of district court judge for repeated ethics violations, including her rude, hostile treatment of fellow judges, attorneys, defendants, court reporters, court clerk's office staff, peace officers, and other court personnel; the court, noting the frequent conflicts with almost everyone with whom the judge came into contact, stated "[t]he depth and breadth of her hostilities must have touched every aspect of her judicial services in Marshall County. She has been like the proverbial bull in a china shop."); *In re Esworthy*, 568 N.E.2d 1195 (N.Y. 1991) (family court judge removed for pattern of egregious conduct including abusing rights of litigants, flouting the law, conveying the impression of bias, being intemperate, and making racist statements).

Judging While Under the Influence or While Intoxicated

Judges who are impaired by alcohol or drugs while on the bench violate Rule 1.2. *See, e.g., In re Lodge*, 12-176 (Ariz. Comm. on Jud. Conduct 2012) (judge reprimanded for conducting court proceedings while under the influence of alcohol); *In re Krake*, 942 So. 2d 18 (La. 2006) (judge's public intoxication at judicial and bar conferences, and his appearance and demeanor on the bench and in chambers, either when he was severely hung over or appeared to be hung over violated Canon regarding observing high standards of personal conduct so that the integrity of the judiciary could be preserved and maintaining decorum in judicial proceedings); *In re Disciplinary Action Against Tessmann*, 638 N.W.2d 883 (N.D. 2002) (municipal court judge resigned where court ordered censure of judge who frequently smelled of alcoholic beverages); *In re Hey*, 457 S.E.2d 509 (W. Va. 1995) (judge admitted to appearing on bench in an intoxicated state; court noted, "it is widely recognized and perceived that intoxication impairs an individual's judgment, and we believe that the appearance of a judge on the bench in an intoxicated state would be a circumstance, which would create in reasonable minds the perception that the judge's ability to carry out his judicial responsibilities with integrity, impartiality, and competence was impaired."); *but see Idaho Jud. Council v. Becker*, 834 P.2d 290 (Idaho 1992) (judge found to have been under the influence of alcohol while working, whose behavior detracted from public confidence in the integrity of the judiciary, received only three-month suspension without salary, the court noting that alcoholism is a disease that can be treated and controlled).

In at least one jurisdiction, whether a judge is actually intoxicated while on the bench, as opposed to suffering from the effects of having been drunk prior to taking the bench, may determine the sanction imposed. *Compare In re Doggett*, 874 So. 2d 805 (La. 2004) (holding that judge's persistent public intoxication while performing judicial duties warrants removal from office) *with In re Krake*, 942 So. 2d 18 (La. 2006) (holding that judge who did not consume alcohol at the courthouse and was not "drunk on the bench" but instead suffered from being severely hung over and, therefore, did not perform his duties as a judge to the best of his abilities warranted suspension). Another factor with regard to the type of sanction imposed is whether the judge has shown an effort to change his or her behavior by seeking treatment for the problem. *Matter of Purple*, 1997 WL 633512 (N.Y. Comm'n on Jud. Conduct, Sept. 29, 1997) (judge drove his car into a tree and pleaded guilty to DWI; Commission decided judge should be censured rather than removed from office, noting that he sought treatment for alcoholism, had been a judge for more than 26 years, and his conduct had never been called into question). *See* Cynthia Gray, *The Worst-Kept Secret in the Courthouse*, 90 Judicature 30 (July–Aug. 2006) (discussing how the appropriate sanction in cases involving impairment requires conduct commissions and courts to weigh the importance of public confidence against the fact that the judge is suffering from a disease).

Exceeding Authority

A violation of Rule 1.2 can come from misjudging the scope of one's judicial role. At one extreme is the judge who exceeds judicial authority or jurisdiction in deciding cases or imposing orders. *See, e.g., In re Comparet-Cassani* (Cal. Comm'n on Jud. Performance 2011) (judge admonished for revoking defendant's pauper status without legal basis, after being disciplined for similar conduct on two other occasions); *In re Graham*, 620 So. 2d 1273 (Fla. 1993) (judge removed for repeatedly exceeding and abusing his powers by imposing improper sentences and orders, by acting in an undignified manner, and by closing and attempting to close public proceedings); *In re Harkin*, 958 N.E.2d 788 (Ind. 2011) (city-court traffic judge abused his authority when he allowed court staff to refer traffic infraction litigants to a city-operated traffic school and then dismissed their cases upon their completion of the program without dismissal request from prosecutor); *In re Young*, 943 N.E.2d 1276 (Ind. 2011) (judge violated Rule 1.2 when he imposed "increased penalties against traffic-infraction litigants for exercising their trial rights so as to penalize them for doing so and to discourage others from doing so"); *Miss. Comm'n on Jud. Performance v. Sanders*, 708 So. 2d 866 (Miss. 1998) (judge disciplined for suspending the sentences of inmates when judge knew or should have known that she did not have jurisdiction); *Miss. Comm'n of Jud. Performance v. Russell*, 691 So. 2d 929 (Miss. 1997) (judge exceeded his authority by allowing for the post-sentencing release of four inmates after the term of court during which they were sentenced); *Miss. Comm'n on Jud. Performance v. Dodds*, 680 So. 2d 180 (Miss. 1996) (judge's infractions included issuing a restraining order against the pastor of a church when he had no authority to do so, signing an execution of judgment without authority, improperly handling DUI cases, engaging in ticket fixing, and interfering with the rotation of cases); *In re Pizzi*, 617 A.2d 663 (N.J. 1993) (judge failed to inform a defendant that he was facing a charge of contempt of court, prejudged the merits of the defendant's case, sentenced the defendant without taking a plea or hearing evidence, and imposed a sentence beyond judge's authority); *In re Brown*, 527 S.E.2d 651 (N.C. 2000) (judge overstepped his authority by converting a clear DWI to a charge of careless/reckless driving); *Disc. Counsel v. Medley*, 819 N.E.2d 273 (Ohio 2004) (judge's disposal at arraignment, when neither prosecutor nor counsel for defense was present, of some criminal charges against defendant in exchange for a guilty plea to other charges violated judicial Canons requiring a judge to uphold the integrity and independence of the judiciary); *Disc. Counsel v. Runyan*, 840 N.E.2d 623 (Ohio 2006) (in attempting to broker a "settlement" of allegations of prosecutorial misconduct in felony prosecution, judge went well beyond his judicial authority and ethical constraints); *In re Holley*, B14-5938 (Tenn. Bd. of Jud. Conduct 2015) (judge who ordered defendants to perform public service work or contribute to judge-selected charity to secure appointed counsel, denied appointed counsel without conducting indigency hearing, and required waiver of counsel and jury trial to grant continuance, violated rule); *In re Hammermaster*, 985 P.2d 924 (Wash. 1999) (judge exceeded role and abused authority by threatening life imprisonment or indefinite jail sentences; court stated, "judicial independence does not equate to unbridled discretion to bully and threaten, to disregard the requirements of the law or to ignore the constitutional rights of defendants"). For additional discussion of actions in excess of judicial authority, see Rule 2.2 and accompanying text.

Misuse of Contempt Power

Another example of exceeding judicial authority is the misuse of contempt powers. *See, e.g., In re Batiste* (Ala. Ct. of the Judiciary 2013) (judge suspended for 90 days without pay and ordered to attend training for exhibiting "cavalier disregard for the due-process rights of litigants and witnesses" and pattern and practice of disregarding contempt laws); *In re Salcido*, 189 (Cal. Comm'n on Jud. Performance 2010) (judge held defendant for 30 minutes in courtroom for direct contempt but did not provide defendant due process, ultimately recusing self and transferring case to other courtroom); *Matter of Inquiry Concerning a Judge No. 94-70*, 454 S.E.2d 780 (Ga. 1995) (magistrate issued orders and used contempt power "to intimidate and coerce other elected officials"); *In re Jefferson*, 753 So. 2d 181 (La. 2000) (judge dismissed 41 criminal cases without legal grounds and abused contempt power, thus creating public perception that judge has "unbridled power to haul people into court and, if they fail to please him, to jail them."); *In re Judge Sassone*, 959 So. 2d 859 (La. 2007) (judge who abused her contempt power did not preserve the integrity of the judiciary); *In re Stone*, CJD 2012-014 (Maryland Comm'n on Jud. Disabilities 2012) (judge improperly held 24 people in contempt for having their cell phones turned on in the courtroom); *In re Wiley*, 844 N.W.2d 1 (Mich. 2014) (judge who held indirect contempt proceedings based on unsworn conversations with staff failed to conduct himself in way that would enhance the public's confidence in the integrity and impartiality of the judiciary); *Miss. Comm. on Jud. Performance v. Harris*, 131 So. 3d 1113 (Miss. 2013) (public reprimand issued for judge who prevented defendants from defending against contempt charge); *Miss. Comm. on Jud. Performance v. Skinner*, 119 So. 3d 294 (Miss. 2013) (after all county judges recused from a matter in which family of a court employee was a litigant, judge issued contempt of court violations and bench warrants against parties); *In re Toth*, 978 A.2d 914 (N.J. 2009) (judge abused contempt power where defendant created yelling match resulting in colloquy wherein judge increased contempt jail sentence auction-style, ending at 180 days); *In re Feeder*, 2012 WL 975671 (N.Y. Comm'n on Jud. Conduct, Jan. 31, 2012) (New York judge removed from office for abusing summary contempt power when holding litigants in contempt without providing due process); *In re Hart*, 849 N.E.2d 946 (N.Y. 2006) (judge abused his summary contempt power, warranting discipline, by holding litigant in summary contempt for his counsel's attempt to place on record incident in which litigant approached judge in parking lot following hearing); *Disc. Counsel v. Cox*, 862 N.E.2d 514 (Ohio 2007) (stating that abuse of the contempt power to intimidate and demean someone "not only throws doubts on respondent's impartiality, but also weakens the public's perception of the integrity of the judiciary." (citations omitted)); *Disc. Counsel v. Karto*, 760 N.E.2d 412 (Ohio 2002) (judge committed misconduct by abusing his contempt power, among other infractions); *In re Roemer*, 06-244 (N.C. Jud. Standards Comm'n 2007) (judge publicly reprimanded for holding defendants in civil contempt and ordering them to be held in county detention center because they could not pay $2,480 fine awarded by court); *In re Jackson*, 11-4599 (Tenn. Ct. of the Judiciary 2012) (judge reprimanded for holding two defendants in contempt of court without appointing counsel or conducting a hearing). A judge need not find a person in contempt to abuse contempt powers; *In re Shelton*, CJC No. 6284-F-148 (Wash. Comm'n on Jud. Conduct 2011) (judge reprimanded for summarily incarcerating domestic violence victim overnight as a contempt sanction, without authority and contrary to law). *See also* Dennis A. Rendleman, *The Case of the Dirty T-Shirt: A Proposed Amendment to the Model Code of Judicial Conduct on the Exercise of the Power of Contempt*, 15 No. 4 Prof. Law. 18 (2005).

Ticket-Fixing

Many instances of discipline for ticket-fixing illustrate that such abuse of the law is not tolerated pursuant to the language of Rule 1.2. *See, e.g., In re Stanford*, 53 Cal.4th CJP Supp. 1 (Jan. 2012) (criminal felony department judge removed from office for "a pattern" of transferring family and friends' traffic citations to his call and ordering "unusually lenient dispositions"); *Miss. Comm'n on Jud. Performance v. Chinn*, 611 So. 2d 849 (Miss. 1992) (judge had engaged in roughly 100 violations of ticket-fixing, had attempted to influence other judges, and repeatedly violated sentencing statutes); *In re Inquiry Concerning a Judge*, 570 S.E.2d 102 (N.C. 2002) (judge disciplined for dismissing two cases of DUI); *In re Kelly*, 757 A.2d 456 (Pa. Ct. Jud. Disc. 2000) (judge held ex parte communications with a fellow district court judge in an attempt to influence the outcome of a traffic court proceeding for the benefit of a close associate); *In re O'Kelley*, 603 S.E.2d 410 (S.C. 2004) (judge reduced parking tickets issued to his relatives, employees, and acquaintances to warnings outside of court); *In re Kittrell*, No. B13-5454 (Tenn. Bd. of Jud. Conduct 2013) (judge reprimanded for asking court employee to dismiss relative's traffic ticket); *cf. In re Harvin*, 638 S.E.2d 49 (S.C. 2006) (judge who admitted converting money he received to pay traffic tickets failed to uphold integrity of the judiciary). For additional discussion of ticket-fixing, see Rules 1.3 and 2.2 and accompanying text.

Abdicating Role of Judge

Equally injurious to public confidence is the judge who abdicates the sworn duties of office. Thus, judges have been disciplined for dereliction of their duties or neglecting their work. *See, e.g., In re Landry*, 157 P.3d 1049 (Alaska 2007) (judge's conduct in making pre-signed bail orders available for use by prosecutors for all out-of-custody arraignments violated provisions of Code of Judicial Conduct requiring upholding the integrity and independence of the judiciary); *In re Yoder*, No. 85-2011 (W. Va. Jud. Investigation Comm'n 2011) (judge admonished for pre-signing orders and then allowing law clerk to preside over hearings regarding petitioners' name changes in judge's absence); *In re Browning*, 452 S.E.2d 34 (W. Va. 1994) (magistrate reprimanded when, after a scheduling dispute with the chief magistrate, the magistrate refused to assist a battered spouse in receiving a protective order; the magistrate claimed that she did not feel well but then proceeded to do paperwork and to assist other petitioners; court found a "total disregard and dereliction" of the magistrate's duty to uphold the public's confidence and the integrity of the judiciary); *but see In re Verbage*, 490 S.E.2d 323 (W. Va. 1997) (magistrate who refused to appear for a domestic violence petition when he was on duty violated the Code of Judicial Conduct; however, complaint dismissed due to mitigating circumstances including the fact that the magistrate was ill, another magistrate was scheduled to take his place in a very brief period, and did take his place and attend to the petition promptly, and the person bringing the petition suffered no substantial harm); *In re Codispoti*, 414 S.E.2d 628 (W. Va. 1992) (judge failed to perform his judicial duties on one occasion, where police were unable to contact him on a night when he was on duty; magistrate was ill, took prescribed medicine, did not hear telephone or knocking on his door, and discovered later that his telephone was broken; charges against magistrate were dropped since magistrate had made reasonable efforts to fulfill his duties).

Causing Delay

Causing delay, or failing to attend to the business of the court in a timely fashion also diminishes public confidence in the judiciary. *See, e.g., In re Carpenter*, 17 P.3d 91 (Ariz. 2001) (judge committed various violations including being consistently tardy and sleeping during court proceedings; court did not find judge's narcolepsy a mitigating factor, particularly in light of his failure to use bailiff provided to him as an accommodation to help him stay awake); *In re Gibson*, 852 N.W.2d 891 (Mich. 2014) (judge who eroded public confidence in judiciary by consistently beginning proceedings two hours later than the time when the morning call was set was suspended without pay for 30 days, and publicly censured); *In re Jelsema*, 625 N.W.2d 751 (Mich. 2001) (unwarranted delay, inaction, and failure to act timely, including taking 11 months to render a decision after hearing a matter, created impropriety and appearance of judicial impropriety and constituted conduct that erodes public confidence in the judiciary); *In re Hathaway*, 630 N.W.2d 850 (Mich. 2001) (judge disciplined for pattern of adjournments of proceedings without good cause, unnecessary and unexcused absences from judicial responsibilities during normal court hours, overall lack of industry and proper management of her court docket, as well as an unwillingness to take corrective action or accept constructive suggestions or assistance to improve case management); *In re Smith*, 687 A.2d. 1229 (Pa. Ct. Jud. Disc. 1996) (judge failed to render timely decisions in 61 cases that were pending before him and ready to be decided); *In re Daghir*, 657 A.2d. 1032 (Pa. Ct. Jud. Disc. 1995) (judge disciplined for misconduct including engaging in pattern of unreasonable and unjustified delay in disposition and decision of six cases); *In re Stocker*, 608 S.E.2d 865 (S.C. 2005) (magistrate's alleged conduct in failing to respond to inquiries about the status of a case, failing to promptly set a case for trial, and in failing to promptly issue a ruling in a case under advisement, violated several Canons including the Canon requiring a judge to uphold the integrity of the judiciary); *In re McCormick*, 521 S.E.2d 792 (W. Va. 1999) (judge improperly delayed the filing of a domestic violence protective order by screening the facts through an inappropriate ex-parte communication and by deterring a couple from coming to the courthouse on a Saturday to file a petition); *cf. In re Kouros*, 816 N.E.2d 21 (Ind. 2004) (judge's failure to provide Supreme Court with full and accurate information regarding her measures to ensure prompt processing of orders violated provisions of Code requiring judges to uphold integrity of judiciary and to avoid impropriety and appearance of impropriety).

Allowing Others to Perform Judicial Duties

Some judges have been disciplined under the language of Rule 1.2 for improperly allowing others to perform duties, even minor ones, that judges alone should perform. *See, e.g., In re Lockwood*, 804 P.2d 738 (Ariz. 1990) (justice of the peace improperly instructed and permitted court clerks to sign guilty pleas in misdemeanor DUI cases); *In re Best*, 719 So. 2d 432 (La. 1998) (judge's misconduct included taking a straw poll of courtroom audience regarding defendant's guilt); *In re Brown*, 662 N.W.2d 733 (Mich. 2003) (judge used a coin flip to determine issue of where children would spend holiday in custody dispute); *Miss. Comm'n on Jud. Performance v. Hopkins*, 590 So. 2d 857 (Miss. 1991) (judge engaged in several acts of willful misconduct, including allowing clerks and other officials to dismiss traffic tickets without an adjudication and failing to sign the court docket); *In re Eskridge*, 559 S.E.2d 575 (S.C. 2002) (prior to hearing, judge received from a public official a list of defendants scheduled to appear before him with letters "NG" beside the names of some of the defendants on the list; judge understood the letters to mean "not guilty" and subsequently found each defendant whose name appeared next to the letters "NG" not guilty, even the defendants who failed to appear in court); *In re Smith*, 559 S.E.2d 584 (S.C. 2002) (judge failed to sign various court orders issued in his name and failed to specify any factual basis for issuance of several orders); *In re Wilder*, 516 S.E.2d 927 (S.C. 1999) (judge committed numerous violations of Code including signing blank arrest warrants for his staff to complete).

PROVOCATION NO EXCUSE

Provocation is not an excuse for judicial misconduct. Even when judges are overworked, criticized, cursed, or insulted, they must nonetheless exercise restraint and maintain judicial composure. *See, e.g., In re Shea*, 110 So. 3d 414 (Fla. 2013) (judge reprimanded for acting in a manner unbecoming of the judiciary "even if provoked by the unprofessional behavior of those appearing before the judge"); *In re Zack*, 570 So. 2d 938 (Fla. 1990) (judge violated Canon by using "very profane" language upon arriving at work and finding a very heavy docket due to a drug sting operation the previous night); *Miss. Comm'n on Jud. Performance v. Guest*, 717 So. 2d 325 (Miss. 1998) (judge disciplined for engaging in scuffle and swearing at defendant who had proved uncooperative at trial and cursed at the court while leaving; court noted that the judge's misconduct occurred in a crowded courtroom and thus strongly debased the integrity of the court in the public eye); *In re Toth*, 978 A.2d 914 (N.J. 2009) (in arraignment for multiple traffic offenses, defendant in custody appearing via video conference making offensive gestures, noises, and challenging responses no justification for judge's verbal aggression and intemperate use of contempt); *In re Mogil*, 673 N.E.2d 896 (N.Y. 1996) (in response to criticism from a criminal attorney, judge sent eight anonymous communications that were harassing, threatening, and offensive; at a bar association social event, the judge circulated a statement on his stationary that included disparaging and offensive remarks regarding the conduct of criminal defense lawyers); *In re Bissell*, 429 S.E.2d 731 (N.C. 1993) (judge responded with open hostility when an attorney initiated a preliminary investigation of the judge; judge informed attorney that he was a persona non grata in her courtroom and should not practice before her); *cf. In re Bell*, 894 S.W.2d 119 (Tex. Spec. Ct. Rev. 1995) (judge held in direct contempt of court, fined, and jailed for three days a man who approached her in the hallway on her late return from lunch and told her that he thought her tardiness was "irresponsible and disrespectful;" judge's mischaracterization of the place where the exchange occurred as being in "open court" was "a violation of the mandate that a judge shall comply with the law and act in a manner that promotes the public's confidence in the integrity and impartiality of the judiciary.").

AVOIDING IMPROPRIETY AND THE APPEARANCE OF IMPROPRIETY

The language in Rule 1.2 regarding impropriety and its appearance, though "extremely broad in scope," can be traced back to the directive of the old Canon 4, "Appearance of Impropriety," which directed judges both on and off the bench to avoid impropriety and the appearance of impropriety. *See* Nancy J. Moore, *Is the Appearance of Impropriety an Appropriate Standard for Disciplining Judges in the Twenty-First Century?*, 41 Loy. U. Chi. L.J. 285 (Winter 2010) *and* Lisa L. Milord, *The Development of the ABA Judicial Code* 13 (1992). The Commission added this language to Rule 1.2 at the urging of the judiciary and others, in order to make creating "an appearance of impropriety" an independent basis for discipline. Charles G. Geyh & W. William Hodes, *Reporters' Notes to the Model Code of Judicial Conduct* 17–18 (2009). For criticism of this addition to the black letter, *see* Raymond J. McKoski, *Judicial Discipline and the Appearance of Impropriety: What the Public Sees Is What the Judge Gets*, 94 Minn. L. Rev. 1914 (2010); Ronald D. Rotunda, *Judicial Ethics, The Appearance of Impropriety, and the Proposed New ABA Judicial Code*, 34 Hofstra L. Rev. 1337 (2006).

Rationale

The Commentary to Rule 1.2 notes the rationale for the standard: public confidence in the judiciary is eroded when judges engage in misconduct. Therefore, judges must be prepared to avoid both impropriety and the appearance of impropriety. Model Code of Judicial Conduct Rule 1.2 cmt. [1]. Courts have echoed this rationale. *See, e.g., In re Dean*, 717 A.2d 176, 185 (Conn. 1998) ("Avoiding the appearance of impropriety is as important to developing public confidence in the judiciary as avoiding impropriety itself."); *In Interest of McFall*, 617 A.2d 707 (Pa. 1992) ("[T]he appearance of bias or prejudice can be as damaging to public confidence in the administration of justice as would be the actual presence of either of these elements." (citation omitted)); *Earls v. Earls*, 2001 WL 504905 (Tenn. Ct. App 2001) ("It is of immense importance not only that justice be administered impartially but also that the public perceive that it is being administered impartially." (citation omitted)). *See generally* Cynthia Gray, *The 2007 ABA Model Code: Taking Judicial Ethics Standards to the Next Level*, 90 Judicature 284 (2007); Cynthia Gray, *Avoiding the Appearance of Impropriety: With Great Power Comes Great Responsibility*, 28 U. Ark. Little Rock L. Rev. 63 (2005); Kathleen Maher, *Keeping Up Appearances*, 16 No. 1 Prof. Law. 1 (2005).

Impropriety Defined

The prohibition against "impropriety and the appearance of impropriety" is cast in general terms. *See* Lisa L. Milord, *The Development of the ABA*

Judicial Code 12 (1992) (noting that the majority of commentators on the 1972 Code expressed belief that general language is necessary, although a significant minority criticized vagueness of the provisions). Difficulties have arisen, as might be expected, when this general language serves as a basis for disciplining a judge. It may be difficult to determine what is "impropriety" or the appearance of impropriety, without meaningful definitions of these terms. Thus, this language has been subject to criticism by both courts and commentators. Raymond J. McKoski, *Judicial Discipline and the Appearance of Impropriety: What the Public Sees Is What the Judge Gets*, 94 Minn. L. Rev. 1914 (2010); Ronald D. Rotunda, *Judicial Ethics, The Appearance of Impropriety, and the Proposed New ABA Judicial Code*, 34 Hofstra L. Rev. 1337 (2006); Leslie W. Abramson, *Canon 2 of the Code of Judicial Conduct*, 79 Marq. L. Rev. 949 (1996) (suggesting lack of specificity as to what conduct creates "appearance of impropriety" raises serious due process concerns; citing Justice Arthur Goldberg's comments to Congress that "appearance of impropriety" Canon was "unbelievably ambiguous," and that judges "can benefit greatly from having some ground rules against which to measure their conduct . . . particularly . . . in this area of avoiding even the appearance of impropriety." (*quoting Nonjudicial Activities of Supreme Court Justices: Hearing on S. 1097 and S. 2109 Before the Subcommittee on Separation of Powers of the Senate Comm. on the Judiciary*, 91st Cong. 1st Sess. (1969)); *see also In re Hey*, 452 S.E.2d 24 (W. Va. 1994) (court emphasized the "subjectivity and elasticity, or vagueness" of the language used in Rule 1.2, which is especially problematic when applied to judicial expression). *But see* Cynthia Gray, *Avoiding the Appearance of Impropriety: With Great Power Comes Great Responsibility*, 28 U. Ark. Little Rock L. Rev. 63 (2005) (asserting that the appearance of impropriety standard is not too vague and that "given their power and prestige, requiring judges to consider the implications of their conduct for public confidence in the judiciary is not too much to ask").

In 2007, because of the importance of the appearances created by judges, the Commission added a definition of impropriety to the Terminology section of the Code. According to that definition, impropriety "includes conduct that violates the law, court rules, or provisions of this Code, and conduct that undermines a judge's independence, integrity, or impartiality." ABA Model Code of Judicial Conduct, Terminology. The Commentary also fleshes out the prohibition somewhat by stating that "actual improprieties . . . include violations of law, court rules, or other specific provisions of this Code." Model Code of Judicial Conduct Rule 1.2 cmt. [5]. *See In re Eriksson*, 36 So. 3d 580 (Fla. 2010) (judge who retaliated against litigants by increasing bail when one defendant sought a motion to recuse, and discouraging multiple people seeking protection orders, violated this rule).

The Test for Appearance of Impropriety

When the analysis involves the "appearance of impropriety," as opposed to actual impropriety, the waters get murky. In an effort to provide some guidance, the Commentary to Rule 1.2 offers a test for the appearance of impropriety: "whether the conduct would create in reasonable minds a perception that the judge violated this Code or engaged in other conduct that reflects adversely on the judge's honesty, impartiality, temperament, or fitness to serve as a judge." Model Code of Judicial Conduct Rule 1.2 cmt. [5]. *But see* Raymond J. McKoski, *Judicial Discipline and the Appearance of Impropriety: What the Public Sees is What the Judge Gets*, 94 Minn. L. Rev. 1914 (2010) (concluding the "appearance-of-impropriety standard is no standard at all. It only appears to be a standard.").

Objective Standard

The appearance of impropriety standard, though elastic, is considered an objective standard. *See, e.g., Inquiry Concerning a Judge*, 822 P.2d. 1333 (Alaska 1991) (test is whether a judge fails "to use reasonable care to prevent objectively reasonable persons from believing an impropriety was afoot"; "[t]he objectively reasonable person is not a well trained lawyer or a highly sophisticated observer of public affairs. Neither is this person a cynic skeptical of the government and the courts. Moreover, an objectively reasonable person is not necessarily one who is informed of every conceivably relevant fact. He or she is the average person encountered in society."); *In re Flanagan*, 690 A.2d 865 (Conn. 1997) (judge censured for engaging in a three and one half years' consensual affair with married court reporter regularly assigned to his courtroom; court stated "[t]he duty to avoid creating an appearance of impropriety is one of taking 'reasonable precautions' to avoid having 'a negative effect on the confidence of the thinking public in the administration of justice.'" (citations omitted)); *Blaisdell v. City of Rochester*, 609 A.2d 388 (N.H. 1992) ("[w]hether an appearance of impropriety exists is determined under an objective standard, i.e., would a reasonable person, not the judge himself, question the impartiality of the court"); *In re Reddin and Keegan*, 111 A.3d 74 (N.J. 2015) (the test to determine whether a judge's personal behavior creates an appearance of impropriety is whether an individual who observes the judge's personal conduct has "a reasonable basis to doubt the judge's integrity and impartiality." Judges who socialized in public with defendant awaiting trial on criminal charges violated rule). *See also In re Chmiel*, 08-CC-1 (Ill. Cts. Comm'n 2010) (the focus of the inquiry is on "the perception of the general public to the conduct at issue").

In order to determine whether an appearance of impropriety under Rule 1.2 exists, some courts have looked to the "totality of the circumstances." *See, e.g., In re Johnstone*, 2 P.3d 1226 (Alaska 2000) (totality of circumstances regarding judge's hire of chief justice's personal friend as coroner for judicial district created "unmistakable appearance that something improper was afoot" under objectively reasonable person test for determining whether judge's actions have created the appearance of impropriety); *In re Herbert Ray* (N.Y. Comm'n on Jud. Conduct 1999) (judge appointed two attorneys as guardians in a disproportionate number of cases, circumventing the rotation system through which law guardians were usually assigned by the court clerk and failed to scrutinize the lawyers' bills, permitting them to grossly inflate their charges and collect thousands of unearned dollars in public funds; commission found that the combination of these factors created the appearance that lawyers were getting favored treatment from the judge).

Rule 1.2's "appearance of impropriety" language is akin to the "appearance of impartiality" language of Rule 2.11 wherein a judge's disqualification is mandated whenever a judge's impartiality "might reasonably be questioned." *See, e.g., State v. Ross*, 974 P.2d 11 (Haw. 1998) (test for disqualification due to the "appearance of impropriety" is an objective one, based on "the assessment of a reasonable impartial onlooker apprised of all the facts," which is consistent with the test for appearance of impropriety); *Gibilisco v. Gibilisco*, 637 N.W.2d 898 (Neb. 2002) (Nebraska Supreme Court clarified its test for judicial recusal as follows: "a trial judge should recuse himself or herself when a litigant demonstrates that a reasonable person, who knew the circumstances of the case, would question the judge's impartiality under an objective standard of reasonableness, even though no actual bias or prejudice is shown"). For further discussion of the appearance of impartiality standard for judicial disqualification, see Rule 2.11.

Irrelevance of Judge's Perception of Behavior

Because the standard for determining the appearance of impropriety is objective, a judge's own perception of motivation for behavior is irrelevant to the analysis. *See, e.g., In re Adams*, 932 So. 2d 1025 (Fla. 2006) (judges must do all that is reasonably necessary to minimize the appearance of impropriety, and they must remain cognizant of the fact that even in situations where they personally believe that their judgment would not be colored, public perception may differ); *In re Removal of a Chief Judge*, 592 So. 2d 671 (Fla. 1992) (judge removed for making racially insensitive remarks in a newspaper interview; court noted that even if remarks had been misinterpreted and did not reflect his personal beliefs, they were widely read in the community and "significantly eroded his ability to work effectively with all segments of the community in administering the courts"); *People for Ethical Treatment of Animals v. Bobby Berosini, Ltd.*, 894 P.2d 337 (Nev. 1995) *overruled in part on other grounds, Towbin Dodge, LLC v. Dist. Ct.*, 112 P.3d 1063 (2005) (court found that a judge who had served on the advisory board of a local animal shelter that had connections to one of the parties should have been disqualified because "reasonable person, knowing all the facts, would harbor reasonable doubts about [the judge's] impartiality"; the judge's subjective impartiality was irrelevant); *In re Case of Snow*, 674 A.2d 573 (N.H. 1996) (rejecting judge's claim that he did not intend to fix his brother's ticket, court noted, "There is no intent requirement in these Canons. In fact, it is practically impossible to impose a mens rea element on the 'appearance of impropriety' standard" (citations omitted)); *In re Blackman*, 591 A.2d 1339 (N.J. 1991) (judge's attendance at a highly publicized labor day picnic hosted by long-time friend, a local politician convicted on federal racketeering charges, created a perception of impropriety; court stated, "[t]he issue is not whether a reasonable person would probably conclude the judge had become vulnerable to political influence, but whether there is a fair possibility that some portion of the public might become concerned on that score. . . . It does not matter whether that interpretation was reasonable or whether it might have been at odds with respondent's true motives. As a judge, respondent had a duty to foresee that his actions might be open to criticism by the press or members of the public. Even if such criticism might be a misinterpretation of his motives, respondent, nonetheless, had an obligation to avoid any conduct that might lead to such criticism."); *In re Larsen*, 616 A.2d 529 (Pa. 1992) (ex parte communications with other judge relating to matter pending before judge "warrants disciplinary action despite the absence of an improper motive, because the conduct by itself raised an appearance of impropriety, which could undermine public confidence in our judiciary.").

Examples of Appearance of Impropriety

Courts have found that a great variety of judicial conduct creates the appearance of impropriety. *See, e.g., In re Judicial Misconduct (Cebull)*, 751 F.3d 611 (U.S. Jud. Conf. Comm. on Jud. Conduct and Disability 2014) (judge publicly reprimanded for sending "hundreds" of disrespectful emails lambasting politicians, racial minorities, religions, gays, and women); *In re Inquiry Concerning a Judge*, 788 P.2d 716 (Alaska 1990) (judge, a vice-president of a defunct airline, validated reduced fare tickets under questionable circumstances, where a reasonable lawyer would have consulted a trustee; action created the appearance of impropriety); *Huffman v. Ark. Jud. Disc. & Disability Comm'n* 42 S.W.3d 386 (Ark. 2001) (judge who owned 12,000 shares of Wal-Mart stock worth about $700,000 created an appearance of impropriety when he presided over proceeding in which Wal-Mart sought a temporary restraining order against a labor union; appearance of impropriety existed even though judge's action was unlikely to affect the value of his stock, which was "but a minuscule percent of the total stock" of Wal-Mart); *Ark. Jud. Disc. & Disability Comm'n v. Proctor*, 360 S.W.3d 61 (Ark. 2010) (judge failed to avoid the appearance of impropriety when he sent money to convicted robber who judge sentenced, allowed a defendant appearing before him to live in his house for one week, giving rides to at least eight defendants in his personal car, having lunch with other defendants); *In re Mills* (Cal. Comm'n on Jud. Performance 2013) (judge publicly admonished for creating appearance of impropriety when he discussed his son's case with courtroom clerk and pro tempore judge in nonpublic area of courthouse); *In re Barrett*, 593 A.2d 529 (Del. Jud. 1991) (judge created an appearance of impropriety by conducting gratuitous title searches for police officers who appeared before her); *In re Chmiel*, No. 08-CC-1 (Ill. Cts. Comm'n 2010) (judge who conducted emergency bond hearing, when not on call to do so, for brother of political supporter and friend created appearance of impropriety); *In re Hunter* (Ind. Comm'n on Jud. Qualifications 2011) (judge admonished for participation in television interview about a specific traffic case he adjudicated); *In re Hammond*, 559 N.E.2d 310 (Ind. 1990) (after taking the bench, judge maintained a fiduciary relationship with a non-family member as her attorney-in-fact under a power-of-attorney, thereby creating an appearance of impropriety); *In re Handy*, 867 P.2d 341 (Kan. 1994) (judge who was simultaneously employed as a municipal judge and a state district court judge demonstrated insensitivity to the appearance of impropriety in the purchase of property that was involved in a probate case assigned to him, among other infractions); *In re Granier*, 906 So. 2d 417 (La. 2005) (judge's hiring of a registered nurse with whom he was romantically involved to review and summarize medical records for cases in his court created an appearance of impropriety); *In re Ellender*, 889 So. 2d 225 (La. 2004) (judge's Halloween costume of blackface, afro wig, orange jumpsuit, and handcuffs with spouse as officer, worn in public, was an appearance of impropriety); *In re Mazur*, 871 N.W.2d 526 (Mich. 2015) (on behalf of former neighbor, judge spoke with judicial colleague about case pending before colleague asking that neighbor's child be released on a personal recognizance bond); *In re Logan*, 783 N.W.2d 705 (Mich. 2010) (judge authorized bond for county commissioner relying only on initial investigative report); *In re Baugh*, 334 P.3d 352 (Mont. 2014) (judge censured and suspended for 31 days for comments in open court disregarding law that a person under the age of 16 is legally incapable of consenting to sexual intercourse, issuing an unlawful sentence, providing an inappropriate rationale, and subsequently commenting publicly about the matter); *In re Lewis*, JC-13-042-C (N.H. Jud. Conduct Comm. 2014) (judge sanctioned for violating Rule 1.2 for disparaging comments about female attorneys that "may have been reasonably perceived as prejudiced or biased"); *In re Rivera-Soto*, 927 A.2d 112 (N.J. 2007) (judge created appearance of impropriety when he improperly interceded with police and the courts in a delinquency case against a youth accused of bullying his son by asking police chief to file charges, going to police station to sign a delinquency complaint, and calling county prosecutor and assignment judge to alert them to the case); *In re Van Woeart* (N.Y. Comm'n on Jud. Conduct 2012) (judge created appearance of impropriety by failing to keep complete and accurate records related to transfer of matters involving judge's family); *In re Gumo* (N.Y. Comm'n on Jud. Conduct 2014) (judge created appearance of impropriety for not disclosing to parties that daughter of court clerk was witness for plaintiff); *In re Hair*, 436 S.E.2d 128 (N.C. 1993) (judge, who was going through divorce proceedings and threatened attorneys representing his wife, as well as the judge presiding over the divorce, created the appearance of impropriety); *In re Disc. Action Against Hoffman*, 595 N.W.2d 592 (N.D. 1999) (judge harassed, stalked, and abused his former wife and her companion, showed disrespect for court that entered his judgment of divorce, and interjected himself in proceedings before him involving child custody and orders of protection by commenting on his own ongoing problems with his former wife); *Disc. Counsel v. Lisotto*, 761 N.E.2d 1037 (Ohio 2002) (judge accepted sporting event tickets from an attorney who appeared before him); *Disc. Counsel v. Medley*, 756 N.E.2d 104 (Ohio 2001) (judge talked to a newly arrested defendant on the telephone, and then picked up the defendant at the police station and drove her home; while the judge and defendant did not discuss the merits of the defendant's case, the judge's actions gave the impression of bias and made it appear that the defendant would receive special treatment); *In re Trkula*, 699 A.2d. 3 (Pa. Ct. Jud. Disc. 1997) (district justice who had made ex parte contact with administrator of appellate court and another judge violated the rule against creation of impropriety or appearance of impropriety by falsely informing FBI agents that no contact was made); *In re Lebedeff*, 2003 WL 22970547 (N.Y. Comm'n on Jud. Conduct 2003) (judge created an appearance of impropriety by failing to pay for income tax preparation services in the same four-year period that she awarded fiduciary appointments to her income tax accountant); *In re Newberry County Magistrate English*, 625 S.E.2d 919 (S.C. 2006) (magistrate created an appearance of impropriety during a DUI trial by ordering that arresting officer be located after arresting officer, defendant, and defense attorney failed to appear); Del. Jud. Ethics Adv. Comm. Op. 2006-2 (2006) (judge may not serve on board of directors of Police Athletic League of Delaware (PAL), which engages in juvenile crime prevention activities, because public identifies PAL with law enforcement and service on its Board would create an appearance of impropriety); *In re Evans*, 702 S.E.2d 557 (S.C. 2010) (judge removed from office in part for attending judicial conference and sharing hotel suite with 20-year-old defendant charged in the judge's jurisdiction with possession of drug paraphernalia); S.C. Adv. Comm. on Stands. of Jud. Conduct Op. 8-2007 (2007) (a magistrate serving in the same county in which the judge's spouse is employed by the sheriff and may appear before the magistrate would create an appearance of impropriety); S.C. Adv. Comm. on Stand. of Jud. Conduct Op. 08-2006 (2006) (part-time magistrate serving as a part-time municipal judge, who is paid on a per-ticket basis creates the appearance of impropriety); *In re Henry*, No. 5850-F-147 (Wash.

Comm'n on Jud. Conduct 2004) (judge who made inappropriate sexual remark to one lawyer and engaged in conduct, which was "reasonably perceived to be offensive and unwelcome" and did not avoid appearance of impropriety); *In re deVilla* CJC No. 4169-F-112 (Wash. Comm'n on Jud. Conduct 2004) (judge created appearance of impropriety by attending only one of five sessions at American Judges Association's Annual Education Conference in Hawaii, even though judge reimbursed city for expenses, because his conduct created appearance that he used conference as pretext for vacation at public expense). *See generally* Jeffrey Shaman, *The Illinois Code of Judicial Conduct and the Appearance of Impropriety*, 22 Loy. U. Chi. L.J. 581 (1991) (examination of core body of law interpreting provisions of Illinois Code of Judicial Conduct (a modified version of the 1990 ABA Model Code of Judicial Conduct) that concern the appearance of impropriety).

Employment Negotiations

A judge's negotiation of employment with a party's law firm creates an appearance of impropriety. *See, e.g., Denike v. Cupo*, 958 A.2d 446 (N.J. 2008) (trial judge's negotiation of and post-trial employment with plaintiff's counsel's law firm created an appearance of impropriety such that defendant was entitled to a new trial).

Not Every Questionable Act Creates an Appearance of Impropriety

An appearance of impropriety does not occur every time a judge engages in disagreeable or unpopular conduct. *See, e.g., In re Lemoine*, 686 So. 2d 837 (La. 1997) ("[A]ny number of minor failings on the part of a judge may . . . fall short of the high standards of conduct required of judges . . . or constitute acts, which do not promote public confidence in the integrity and impartiality of the judiciary . . . less serious failings may violate the Code of Conduct, yet not constitute sanctionable misconduct subject to punishment through the disciplinary process. Of course, an accumulation of minor ethical transgressions may together amount to sufficiently serious misconduct to qualify as sanctionable misconduct.").

Further, not all potentially suspect behavior is improper. *See, e.g., Inquiry Concerning a Judge*, 822 P.2d. 1333 (Alaska 1991) (judge's courthouse parking lot discussion of settlement stipulation with judge assigned to case did not violate judicial Canons where it was apparent at time of contact no further legal proceedings were contemplated); *Parks v. State*, 734 N.E.2d 694 (Ind. App. 2000) (police detective's incidental contact with jurors outside of courtroom did not warrant mistrial; however, appellate court warned that judges must manage a trial in such a way as to avoid even the appearance of impropriety, thus, "care should be taken by court personnel to avoid even such seemingly innocent and accidental contact between jurors and others involved in the trial"); *In re Hasay*,

686 A.2d 809 (Pa. 1996) (neither magistrate's possession of marijuana nor his conduct in keeping 14-year-old girl at his residence overnight warranted sanction where judge did not intentionally or knowingly possess the marijuana, the judge did nothing improper with the girl, and the situation arose out of the judge's concern for the girl's welfare after he found her walking on a rural highway in the middle of the night); *Eldridge v. Eldridge*, 137 S.W.3d 1 (Tenn. Ct. App. 2002) (in divorce case, wife contended that donations made by her husband's lawyer to the judge's election campaign created an appearance of impropriety; argument rejected on a number of grounds, notably that wife's counsel also donated to the judge's campaign); *Vt. Sup. Ct. Admin. Directive No. 17 v. Vt. Sup. Ct.*, 576 A.2d 127 (Vt. 1990) (in response to cuts in the judicial budget, the state Supreme Court issued a directive establishing a moratorium on civil jury trials; plaintiffs challenging directive unsuccessfully sought to have Supreme Court Justices disqualified on the grounds that the participation of justices created an appearance of impropriety because the justices themselves had promulgated the challenged directive; court noted, "[a] court or judicial officer is often called upon to render an opinion of law on a matter on which the court or officer has formally rendered an opinion. Prior knowledge of a legal issue is not grounds to disqualify a judge").

Disqualification

Judicial disqualification is generally governed by Rule 2.11, however sometimes, considerations of bias for purposes of judicial disqualification also involve analysis under the "appearance of impropriety" standard of Rule 1.2. *See, e.g., White v. Sun Trust Bank*, 538 S.E.2d 889 (Ga. App. 2000) (Code of Judicial Conduct provision requiring judges to avoid appearance of impropriety required probate court judge to voluntarily disqualify herself from hearing probate matter or, at minimum, to disclose her financial interest to parties, because executor was bank in which judge owned stock); *In re Gerard*, 631 N.W.2d 271 (Iowa 2001) (judge who had an intimate relationship with an assistant county attorney who regularly appeared before him in matters of litigation failed to recuse himself from these matters when he should have and failed to disclose the relationship to anyone violated Code; court noted, "[i]t is immaterial that the judge's association may not have had a detrimental impact on defendants appearing before him . . . once the public learned of the judge's relationship with the State's attorney who appeared before him daily, the appearance of bias was very real"); *In re Lafayette D. Young Jr.*, 974 N.E.2d 658 (N.Y. 2012) (judge who heard six cases involving family members of significant other did not preserve the integrity of the judiciary); *In re Braswell*, 600 S.E.2d 849 (N.C. 2004) (judge who failed to recuse himself from civil litigation brought by a plaintiff who had unrelated civil lawsuit pending against judge failed to act in a manner that promotes public confidence in the integrity and impartiality of the judiciary); *Sanjines v. Sanjines*, 1998 WL 761849 (Tenn. Ct. App. 1998) (trial judge announced denial of motion, prior to hearing, allegedly stating, "I'm going to deny your motion, but you can put on any proof you want to"; non-rebutted, although controverted claims of statement made by the trial judge created the appearance of impropriety necessitating judge's recusal); *In re K.E.M.*, 89 S.W.3d 814 (Tex. App. 2002) (juvenile court judge who presided over habeas corpus proceedings disqualified because judge had been county attorney when underlying juvenile case was prosecuted by that office, even though record was "entirely free of the slightest suggestion of prejudice or impropriety" on the part of the judge; the court explained, "[a]ll judges have the duty to sit and decide matters before them unless a basis exists for disqualification or recusal. Judges have as much of an obligation not to step down from a case when there is no reason to do so as they have to do so when there is a reason. However, a judge also must avoid the appearance of impropriety. In the context of judicial disqualification, 'avoiding the appearance of impropriety' means that the judge must comply with the law applicable to judicial disqualification and act 'in a manner that promotes public confidence in the integrity and impartiality of the judiciary.'" [citations omitted]).

However, not every perceived appearance of impropriety under Rule 1.2 mandates judicial disqualification. *See, e.g., Walls v. State*, 20 S.W.3d 322 (Ark. 2000) (trial judge's remarks to a local television reporter on the day the defendant's first appeal was issued, in which judge disagreed with the appellate court's conclusions, may have violated the Code of Judicial Conduct, however, the "apparent ethical lapses" were characterized by the court as disagreement with court's decision rather than bias requiring recusal at resentencing); *Town of Groton v. Lewis*, 754 A.2d 189 (Conn. App. Ct. 2000) (judge was not required to recuse where, prior to appointment, the trial court judge practiced at the same firm as one of plaintiff's attorneys but there was no evidence that their practices overlapped and nothing suggested impropriety); *Rosas v. State*, 76 S.W.3d 771 (Tex. App. 2002) (in an appeal from a conviction of sexual assault of a child, defendant contended that the trial judge should have recused herself from the case because of her membership in a children's assessment center judicial council; court rejected argument in spite of Texas Judicial Ethics Op. 270 (2001), stating that recusal should be necessary because a judge violates Canon 2 of the Texas Judicial Canon of Ethics (requiring judges to avoid impropriety and the appearance of impropriety) by serving on the judicial council of the Children's Assessment Center; appellate court held recusal was unnecessary because there was no showing of actual bias and noted "[e]thical violations alone are not grounds for a recusal"); *Sears v. Olivarez*, 28 S.W.3d 611 (Tex. App. 2000) (appellate court dismissed a challenge to the decision of numerous appellate court justices not to recuse themselves; plaintiff, an attorney and Republican running for judicial office, unsuccessfully argued that his clients would be unfairly prejudiced because all the judges on the court were Democrats). For a detailed discussion on judicial disqualification and recusal generally, see Rule 2.11.

Ex Parte Contacts

Even certain ex parte contacts do not create an appearance of impropriety when they involve merely administrative matters. Allowances for this type of contact facilitate the efficient handling of court business. *See, e.g., Mahrdt v. State*, 629 N.E.2d 244 (Ind. App. Ct. 1994) (judge's ex parte communications with sheriff regarding a breathalyzer machine was administrative in nature, therefore, the judge did not create an appearance of impropriety); *Doerman v. Doerman*, 2002 WL 1358792 (Ohio App. Ct. 2002) (court gives short shrift to argument that the trial court was biased in divorce case due to judge's numerous ex parte conversations with the juvenile court, court security, the guardian ad litem, and counselors; court stated, "[n]othing in the judicial code 'preclude[s] a judge from non-substantive ex parte communications on procedural matters affecting prompt disposal of the business of the court'"). Similarly, innocuous judicial conversation does not necessarily rise to the level of creating an appearance of impropriety. *See, e.g., Janson v. State*, 785 So. 2d 731 (Fla. App. Ct. 2001) (no violation when the judge invited jurors to tour his chambers and engaged the various jurors in conversation regarding a Ford hunting truck he owned and the fact that he had been part of the architectural committee when the courtrooms were designed); *Harman ex rel. Harman v. Borah*, 756 A.2d 1116 (Pa. 2000) (judge had a private conversation with an expert witness during deliberations in the sight, but not hearing, of jurors, and later gave the jury instructions and stated that her conversations with one side or the other should not be interpreted as her favoring one side or the other; court determined that the judge's statement cured any appearance of impropriety caused by the private conversation); *but cf. Salaiscooper v. Eighth Judicial Dist. Court ex rel. County of Clark*, 34 P.3d 509 (Nev. 2001) (judge may discuss legal issues in the context of hypothetical situations, but justice court exceeded its jurisdiction by collaborating with other justices to reach a "collective" or "en banc" decision). For a detailed discussion of ex parte contacts, see Rule 2.9.

Relationship with Parties

While courts have found an appearance of impropriety when a judge has a close and direct relationship with parties or matters coming before him or her, the finding is less likely when the relationship is more attenuated. *E.g., compare Matter of Tyler*, 553 N.E.2d 1316 (N.Y. 1990) (removal from office warranted where judge presided over arraignment hearing pertaining to a dishonored check given to the complainant, judge's husband, by defendant; court noted that the judge's handling of the matter was "particularly egregious" and the judge "clearly displayed favoritism to her husband") *with State v. Smith*, 50 P.3d 825 (Ariz. 2002) (recusal in death penalty case not required where defendant argued that the sentencing judge's casual relationship with the son and daughter-in-law of the victim amounted to an "appearance of impropriety"; the casual relationship only involved the pair working in the same building as the judge and crossing paths a few times over the course of several years).

Sometimes, in declining to find an appearance of impropriety, courts will look to pragmatic considerations regarding the function of the court. *See, e.g., Donnell v. Donnell*, 567 So. 2d 1143 (La. App. 1990) (court found no appearance of impropriety where judge was good friends with a man who was dating the wife in a divorce-related proceeding before the judge; court emphasized the small size of the community, and the fact that judges were regularly called upon to adjudicate disputes involving community members known to the judge; court suggested that there may have been an appearance of impropriety if evidence of a "close, direct relationship was established between either the party and the trial judge or the party and the trial judge's family").

VIOLATION OF OTHER PROVISIONS OF THE CODE

Because a violation of another specific provision of the Code might fail to "promote[ ] public confidence in the independence, integrity, and impartiality of the judiciary," and could create the "appearance of impropriety" a judge may be found to have violated Rule 1.2 in instances where other specific code violations are proved. Former Canon 2A, on which Rule 1.2 is based, has often served as a "catch-all" provision where other Code violations are found. Thus, when judges have engaged in multiple acts of misconduct, courts often catalogue the judge's infractions, list all sections of the Code that apply, and include former Canon 2A. *See, e.g., In re Meyerson*, 581 So. 2d 581 (Fla. 1991) (judge, in closing his private practice, failed to pay trust funds in a timely fashion, charged his clients excessive fees, failed to comply with financial disclosure laws, and failed to obtain consent of clients regarding legal fees violated several Code provisions and also lessened public confidence in the integrity of the judiciary); *Matter of Edwards*, 694 N.E.2d 701 (Ind. 1998) (full-time judge who continued to practice law and maintained simultaneous employment as part-time commissioner in another court violated several Code provisions, including the provision requiring judges to avoid impropriety and the appearance of impropriety, and to act at all times in a manner promoting public confidence in the integrity and impartiality of the judiciary); *In re Groneman*, 38 P.3d 735 (Kan. 2002) (judge who allowed assistant to accept second job that conflicted with court duties violated several Code provisions, including the provision requiring judges to act at all times in a manner that promotes public confidence in the integrity and impartiality of the judiciary); *Matter of King*, 568 N.E.2d 588 (Mass. 1991) (judge made derogatory and obscene references to members of the bench and bar in violation of former Canons 1, 2A, 5A; was intoxicated and urinated in public in violation of former Canons 1, 2A; set unusually high bail for African-American defendants in violation of former Canons 1, 2A, 2B; and used improper bail procedure in violation of former Canons 2A, 3A(1)); *In re Waterman*, 625 N.W.2d 748 (Mich. 1999) (judge, who leased office space to several attorneys, failed to recuse himself when these attorneys appeared before him, and frequently assigned indigent clients to these attorneys impermissibly engaged in a prohibited ex parte communication, allowed social or other relationships to influence his conduct or judgment and also created the appearance of impropriety and engaged in conduct that harms public confidence in the integrity and impartiality of the judiciary); *Miss. Comm'n on Jud. Performance v. Britton*, 936 So. 2d 898 (Miss. 2006) (judge's ex parte communications violated provision of Code prohibiting such communications and provisions requiring judge to uphold integrity and independence of judiciary, to avoid appearance of impropriety, and to perform duties impartially).

CONSTITUTIONAL CHALLENGES

Challenges to the constitutionality of the provisions contained in Rule 1.2 have had varying degrees of success. In some instances, courts have found that the First Amendment offers protection for judges against such charges. *See, e.g., Scott v. Flowers*, 910 F.2d 201 (5th Cir. 1990) (public reprimand of justice of the peace who wrote open letter to county officials regarding dismissal of charges and fines reduced on appeal of traffic offense convictions violated justice's First Amendment rights); *Miss. Comm'n on Jud. Performance v. Wilkerson*, 876 So. 2d 1006 (Miss. 2004) (holding that judge could not be sanctioned for statements in letter to newspaper and on radio network proclaiming that homosexuals were mentally ill; such speech constituted speech regarding matter of political/public importance and private religious speech, and could only be sanctioned if doing so would serve compelling state interest); *Matter of Hey*, 452 S.E.2d 24 (W. Va. 1994) (judge may not be disciplined for public comments in radio interview wherein he criticized a panel member hearing his own disciplinary hearing and stated his intention to take lawful measures against the panel member; the court emphasized that the "subjectivity and elasticity, or vagueness," of general prohibitions in the Code is especially problematic when the Canons are applied to judicial expression, stating, "[t]his is not to say that [those provisions] are facially unconstitutional; rather, it means that [they] cannot constitutionally be manipulated to apply to a judge's off-the-bench remarks about a subject of public concern that is neither presently pending before him nor likely to come before him and that does not violate some other more specific provision of the Code or the law."). In *Rangra v. Brown*, 566 F.3d 515 (5th Cir. 2009) the court reaffirmed its interpretation of *Republican Party of Minn. v. White*, 536 U.S. 765 (2002) that a strict scrutiny test is required to determine whether a state judiciary commission's order violated the First Amendment when it censured an elected judge's speech on the basis of its content. *See generally* Tobin A. Sparling, *Keeping Up Appearances: The Constitutionality of the Model Code of Judicial Conduct's Prohibition of Extrajudicial Speech Creating the Appearance of Bias*, 19 Geo. J. Legal Ethics 441 (2006).

In other cases, constitutional arguments have been unsuccessful. *See, e.g., In re Disc. Action Against McGuire*, 685 N.W.2d 748 (N.D. 2004) (North Dakota Code of Judicial Conduct was not unconstitutionally vague, for due process purposes, as to its provisions regarding upholding integrity of judiciary, avoiding impropriety and appearance of impropriety, and being patient, dignified, and courteous towards people subject to judge's direction and control); *In re Compl. Against Harper*, 673 N.E.2d 1253 (Ohio 1996) (judge authorized a campaign advertisement stating that her opponent had received large sums of money from plaintiff's lawyers and suggesting that such lawyers were dishonest; court concluded that the advertisement undermined public confidence in the judiciary and its impartiality; Code provision prohibiting conduct that diminishes confidence in integrity of judiciary and requiring judge to maintain dignity of judicial office did not unconstitutionally infringe upon First Amendment rights and was not void for vagueness or overbroad); *In re Conduct of Schenck*, 870 P.2d 185 (Or. 1994) (judge wrote newspaper "guest editorial" criticizing competence and maturity of the district attorney; First Amendment did not insulate judge because the prohibition on comments that undermine the public's confidence in the judge's impartiality are directly related to the furtherance of "profound" public interest in protecting both the fact and appearance of the impartiality and integrity of the judiciary; thus, the Code provision is not impermissibly overbroad on its face); *In re Lowery*, 999 S.W.2d 639 (Tex. Rev. Trib. 1998) (finding that Canons of judicial discipline were not unconstitutionally vague or overbroad in permitting discipline for certain willful or persistent conduct or incompetence, in requiring judges to act in manner promoting public confidence in judiciary); *cf. In re Inquiry of Broadbelt*, 683 A.2d 543 (N.J. 1996) (collecting and analyzing cases on whether placing restrictions on a judge's speech violates the First Amendment). *See generally* Erwin Chemerinsky, *Is It the Siren's Call?: Judges and Free Speech While Cases Are Pending*, 28 Loy. L.A. L. Rev. 831 (1995) (discussing Canons governing judicial speech; concluding judicial speech should be regarded as constitutionally protected "unless the government can prove that speech posed a substantial likelihood of materially prejudicing an adjudicatory proceeding, or at the very least, prove that the statement might reasonably be expected to affect its outcome or impair its fairness"). For a discussion of limits on judicial speech, see William G. Ross, *Extrajudicial Speech: Charting the*

Boundaries of Propriety, 2 Geo. J. Legal Ethics 589 (1989). For more discussion of the constitutionality of restrictions on judicial speech, see Rule 2.10 and Canon 4.

Judges' Political Activities

A number of recent cases have focused on First Amendment concerns related to judges' political activity. In *Spargo v. N.Y. State Comm'n on Jud. Conduct*, 244 F. Supp. 2d 72 (N.D.N.Y. 2003), *vacated on other grounds*, 351 F.3d 65 (2d Cir. 2003), for instance, a U.S. District Court in New York held that the New York's Code provision requiring judges to "respect and comply with the law and act at all times in a manner that promotes public confidence in the integrity and impartiality of the judiciary" is facially unconstitutional and void for vagueness because it does not give a person of ordinary intelligence a reasonable opportunity to know what is prohibited, does not have specific standards, and leads judges and judicial candidates to more severely limit their conduct in order to avoid a violation. The U.S. Supreme Court also addressed the issue in *Republican Party of Minn. v. White*, 536 U.S. 765 (2002), holding that Minnesota's "announce clause," which prohibited candidates for judicial election from announcing their views on disputed legal and political issues, was insufficiently tailored to serve compelling interest under strict scrutiny analysis. Applying *White* to a Wisconsin rule that prohibited elected judges and judicial candidates from stating a political party affiliation, the U.S. District Court utilized strict scrutiny analysis to determine that the rule was not narrowly tailored to further a compelling state interest using the least restrictive means. Therefore, the court held the rule unconstitutional. *Siefert v. Alexander*, 597 F. Supp. 2d 860 (W.D. Wis. 2009). *See generally* Wendy R. Weiser, *Regulating Judges' Political Activity After* White, 68 Alb. L. Rev. 651 (2005).

Judges' First Amendment arguments in this context do not always prevail, however. *See, e.g., In re Raab*, 793 N.E.2d 1287 (N.Y. 2003) (disciplining judge who "acted as a party volunteer" in making improper campaign contribution, actively campaigning for legislative candidate, and assisting in candidate screening meeting; court rejected judge's First Amendment challenge to restrictions on judicial political conduct, distinguished *Republican Party of Minn. v. White*, 536 U.S. 765 (2002), and asserted that restrictions survive constitutional challenge because they are narrowly constructed to address compelling state interests in preventing political bias or corruption or the appearance thereof in the judiciary). *See also In re Kinsey*, 842 So. 2d 77 (Fla. 2003) (Canon prohibiting a judicial candidate from making pledges or promises of conduct in office and from making statements that commit or appear to commit the candidate with respect to cases or issues likely to come before the court, does not violate candidate's First Amendment right of free speech; state has compelling interest in maintaining public's confidence in impartial judiciary, and Canon is narrowly tailored to protect those interests without improperly restricting a candidate from stating personal views); *In re Code of Jud. Conduct*, 603 So. 2d 494 (Fla. 1992) (Canons prohibiting judge from public endorsement of candidate for public office do not unconstitutionally infringe on judge's freedom of speech; under strict scrutiny analysis court found Canons meet the compelling state interest in "maintaining the impartiality, the independence from political influence, and the public image of the judiciary as impartial and independent" and are "drawn and interpreted narrowly enough to be constitutional"; collecting cases illustrating that judicial office demands higher standards than is expected of general citizenry); *In re Vincent*, 172 P.3d 605 (N.M. 2007) (holding that provision in New Mexico Code of Judicial Conduct prohibiting judges from publicly endorsing political candidates did not unconstitutionally infringe on judge's First Amendment right to support the political candidates of his choosing). For more on the constitutionality of restrictions of judicial political activity, see Canon 4. *See also* Nat Stern, *The Looming Collapse of Restrictions on Judicial Campaign Speech*, 38 Seaton Hall L. Rev. 63 (2008); Joe Cutler, *Oops! I Said It Again: Judicial Codes of Conduct, the First Amendment, and the Definition of Impartiality*, 17 Geo. J. Legal Ethics 733 (2004). For additional discussion, see Canon 4 and accompanying text.

RULE 1.3 AVOIDING ABUSE OF THE PRESTIGE OF JUDICIAL OFFICE

A judge shall not abuse the prestige of judicial office to advance the personal or economic interests* of the judge or others, or allow others to do so.

COMMENT

[1] It is improper for a judge to use or attempt to use his or her position in order to gain personal advantage or deferential treatment of any kind. For example, it would be improper for a judge to allude to his or her judicial status to gain favorable treatment in encounters with traffic officials. Similarly, a judge must not use judicial letterhead to gain an advantage in conducting his or her personal business.

[2] A judge may provide a reference or recommendation for an individual based on the judge's personal knowledge. The judge may use official letterhead if the judge indicates that the reference is personal and if there is no likelihood that the use of the letterhead would reasonably be perceived as an attempt to exert pressure by reason of the judicial office.

[3] Judges may participate in the process of judicial selection by cooperating with appointing authorities and screening committees, and by responding

to inquiries from such entities concerning the professional qualifications of a person being considered for judicial office.

[4] Special considerations arise when judges write or contribute to publications of for-profit entities, whether related or unrelated to the law. A judge should not permit anyone associated with the publication of such materials to exploit the judge's office in a manner that violates this Rule or other applicable law. In contracts for publication of a judge's writing, the judge should retain sufficient control over the advertising to avoid such exploitation.

1990 Code Comparison

The term "abuse" was substituted for "lend." The Commission decided that the term "lend" created unnecessary confusion. For example, a judge who wrote a letter of recommendation for a law clerk "lends" the prestige of the judge's office to the recommendation, and some judges told the Commission that they declined to write letters on their clerks' behalf as a consequence. In the Commission's view, however, this is not the problem that Rule 1.3 seeks to address. Thus, "abuse" more accurately characterizes the conduct to be proscribed. "Economic interests" was added because even though a judge's "personal interests" might commonly encompass "economic interests," the Commission wanted to circumvent the possibility of confusion. Thus, there is no question that a judge may not abuse the prestige of office to advance either. The Rule was also revised to prohibit judges from allowing others to abuse the prestige of the judge's office to advance the judge's or others' personal or economic interests. "Personal" replaced "private" for stylistic reasons only. Charles G. Geyh & W. William Hodes, *Reporters' Notes to the Model Code of Judicial Conduct* 22–23 (2009).

Annotation

Abusing the Prestige of Judicial Office

Rule 1.3 of the Code prohibits a judge from abusing the prestige of judicial office to advance his or her own personal or economic interests or the personal or economic interests of others. A judge must also not allow others to so abuse the prestige of office. The Commentary to Rule 1.3 explains that it is improper for a judge to use or attempt to use his or her position to gain any kind of personal advantage or deferential treatment. The Commentary also provides two concrete examples of a judge's improper use of the prestige of office: 1) alluding to his or her judicial status to gain favorable treatment in encounters with traffic officials and 2) using judicial letterhead to gain an advantage in conducting his or her business. Model Code of Judicial Conduct Rule 1.3 cmt. [1]. *See also* Cynthia Gray, *The 2007 ABA Model Code: Taking Judicial Ethics Standards to the Next Level*, 90 Judicature 284 (2007).

Improperly Advancing the Judge's Own Interests

The prohibition against abusing the prestige of office applies to the advancement of a judge's own personal or economic interests as well as the advancement of others' interests. Thus, judges have been disciplined when they use their position to gain a personal advantage. *See, e.g., In re Salcido*, 189 (Cal. Comm'n on Jud. Performance 2010) (judge censured for allowing filming in her courtroom, scheduling challenging cases on days in which filming was to occur, and made disparaging remarks to litigants, all to promote herself for television role); *In re Richardson*, 760 So. 2d 932 (Fla. 2000) (judge, arrested for attempting to solicit prostitution from an undercover police officer, repeatedly told police he was a judge, that he was "pro-police," and that his campaign had been run by the president of the local police association thereby abusing his status; court stated, "[u]sing the prestige of judicial office to advance one's own interest undermines the very prestige and respect that is being traded upon and, inevitably, erodes public confidence in the judiciary."); *In re Brown*, 626 N.W.2d 403 (Mich. 2001) (judge used the prestige of his office to gain a personal advantage in the aftermath of a car accident in which the judge was involved); *In re Muller*, No. 069351, N.J. Sup. Ct. (2011) (judge reprimanded for repeatedly noting her position as a judge to rebuke local law enforcement officers responding to judge's 9-1-1 call concerning a state law enforcement officer's service of subpoena on judge's husband on unrelated matter); *In re Brigantti-Hughes*, 2013 WL 6981506 (N.Y. Comm'n on Jud. Conduct 2013) (judge censured for asking court staff to pray with her, attend her church, and make financial donations to her church as well as repeatedly using court staff to babysit daughter and run personal errands); *In re Gallagher*, 951 P.2d 705 (Or. 1998) (judge used state-paid services, property, and equipment to further judge's campaign fund-raising efforts including "Hizzoner's Annual Classic" golf tournament); *In re Mendelsohn*, 621 S.E.2d 661 (S.C. 2005) (judge used his judicial office to evade the policies of the arresting jurisdiction in order to obtain a non-scheduled bond hearing and early release from jail); *In re Corbin*, No. 10-0292-JP (Tex. Comm'n on Jud. Conduct 2011) (judge admonished for misusing position forcing a driver the judge encountered on the way to the courthouse to appear before the judge so that the judge could lecture the driver about the driver's speeding); *cf. In re Stephenson*, 552 S.E.2d 137 (N.C. 2001) (General Court of Justice judge who solicited support and votes for his re-election from defendants and attorneys appearing before him; judge disciplined under other Code provisions).

Judges have been disciplined for advancing their own economic interests. *See, e.g., Miss. Comm. on Jud. Performance v. Fowlkes*, 121 So. 3d 904 (Miss. 2013) (judge publicly reprimanded, fined, and assessed costs for trying to convince probation officer not to check for arrest warrant for tenant of judge. Such conduct advanced the private financial interests of the judge); In *re Hill*, 8 S.W.3d

578 (Mo. 2000) (judge used judicial office for private gain by ordering blanket reduction in fines and release of prisoners in order to compel payment of his health insurance); *In re Calderon*, (N.Y. Comm'n on Jud. Conduct 2010) (judge censured for using title when asking prison officials to confiscate inmate's papers related to judge's civil suit against inmate); *In re Brown*, 512 S.E.2d 114 (S.C. 1999) (probate judge performed 220 marriages and kept a fee charged for each one); *In re Thoma*, 873 S.W.2d 477 (Tex. Rev. Trib. 1994) (judge's misconduct included entering into a conspiracy to extort money from party in judicial proceeding and giving favorable treatment to defendants in exchange for favors); *Matter of Phalen*, 475 S.E.2d 327 (W. Va. 1996) (judge requested home visit with couple appearing before him in order to solicit couple to sell Amway products; judge's failure to disclose to the husband and wife that a decision had been entered on their case was evidence that judge was using his office to intimidate them into becoming Amway recruits); *In re Jud. Disc. Proc. Against Laatsch*, 727 N.W.2d 488 (Wis. 2007) (by highlighting his municipal court judgeship in Yellow Pages advertisement for his private legal practice, judge sought to use the prestige of his judicial office to advance his private interests and exploited the judgeship in the hopes of obtaining financial gain).

Misuse of the judicial office for personal vengeance clearly violates Rule 1.3. *See, e.g., Matter of Lehman*, 812 P.2d 992 (Ariz. 1991) (judge's misconduct included ordering an officer to retrieve the prize for his racehorse's win and then ordering another officer to arrest the first officer when he refused to do so); *Miss. Comm'n on Jud. Performance v. Bishop*, 761 So. 2d 195 (Miss. 2000) (judge suspended for trying to intimidate 15-year-old female minor with whom judge was accused of having sex, and interrogating and intimidating a male high school student who made inappropriate sexual remarks to the minor female); *Miss. Comm'n on Jud. Performance v. Walker*, 565 So. 2d 1117 (Miss. 1990) (judge jailed an attorney for 24 hours without bond for personal attacks, including racial slur against the judge; because the statement was directed to the judge personally and not at the court as an institution, the judge's conduct was an inexcusable abuse of power); *In re Samay*, 764 A.2d 398 (N.J. 2001) (judge disciplined when, after confrontation between judge's son and son's gym teacher, judge had teacher arrested and arraigned before him); *Matter of Hancock*, 483 S.E.2d 756 (S.C. 1997) (judge asked arresting officer for "as much help as you can give me" regarding friend's charge of speeding, resisting arrest, and DUI; dissatisfied with response, the judge called South Carolina Law Enforcement on behalf of his friend and asked that officer be investigated for excessive use of force); *Matter of Edwards*, 459 S.E.2d 837 (S.C. 1995) (after being served with process, judge issued bench warrant directing process server be arrested for contempt of court); *but see In re Jimenez*, 841 S.W.2d 572 (Tex. Spec. Ct. Rev. 1992) (judge who wrote letter to police chief accusing officer of perjury and selective prosecution after officer criticized judge's ruling as "chicken shit" did not violate Code; although insult triggered judge's response, court was not convinced by a preponderance of the evidence that any personal motive "exceeded the public motive of disciplining a police officer reasonably suspected of major crimes and minor bad manners.").

Ticket-Fixing

Some judges have been disciplined for impermissibly taking advantage of their position to try to avoid traffic tickets. *See, e.g., In re Heiple*, 97-CC-1 (Ill. Cts. Comm'n 1997) (Illinois Supreme Court Chief Justice avoided speeding tickets by producing judicial identification credential instead of driver's license when stopped by police on several occasions and stating "Don't you know who I am?"); *In re Pierce* (Indiana Comm'n on Jud. Qualifications 2010) (judge admonished for informing officer of the judge's position when officer was ticketing judge's car, then calling the board of public works, the deputy mayor, and mayor of the community to complain about the ticket and inform office holders of his judicial position); *Matter of Collester*, 599 A.2d 1275 (N.J. 1992) (during arrest for repeat DUI offense, judge lied to police officer that he was on his way to the courthouse on an emergency and attempted to use "the prestige and weight of his judicial office to try to gain some personal advantage."); *In re Garza*, 161 P.3d 876 (N.M. 2007) (while a passenger when girlfriend was pulled over for speeding, judge asked police officer "Do you know who I am?"); *In re Longoria*, CJC 14-1037-AP (Tex. Comm'n on Jud. Conduct 2015) (judge admonished when she "repeatedly identified herself as a judge and offered to show her judicial badge to the officers without being asked for that information"); *In re Ryan*, CJC No. 7150-F-156 (Wash. Comm'n on Jud. Conduct 2013) (judge who resigned after identifying self as judge during traffic stop for suspicion of DUI issued written admonishment).

Judicial Letterhead

Comment [1] to Rule 1.3 states that "a judge must not use judicial letterhead to gain an advantage in conducting his or her personal business." This Comment elaborates the core objective of the Rule by making plain that a judge should not use his or her position to gain personal advantage in business or daily life. The last sentence of the comment was changed to limit the admonition to situations in which the use of the letterhead could "gain advantage." There are times when a judge might draft a personal note on stationery that includes the judge's title that could not conceivably enable the judge to "gain advantage," as, for example, when the judge corresponds with a longtime acquaintance who is well aware of the judge's position. Charles G. Geyh & W. William Hodes, *Reporters' Notes to the Model Code of Judicial Conduct* 23 (2009).

However, a judge may be disciplined when using the judicial stationery for personal business or by using the honorific title "judge" to gain an advantage. *See, e.g., Inquiry Concerning a Judge*, 822 P.2d 1333 (Alaska 1991) (state Supreme Court justice used chambers stationery to correspond with opposing counsel in private litigation); *In re Combs* (Ky. Jud. Conduct Comm. 2015) (judge suspended for 180 days in part for using official letterhead to complain to police about illegal parking in lot of the church that judge attended, using official letterhead to make an open records request for a matter unrelated to the judge's duties, and using letterhead to complain to a local television station about programming the judge labeled political, and threatening to sue the station in the same letter); *In re Murphy*, 897 N.E.2d 1220 (Mass. 2008) (judge improperly used official court stationery in letters to publisher of newspaper against which judge had filed libel lawsuit); *In re Mosley*, 102 P.3d 555 (Nev. 2005) (judge improperly used judicial letterhead for two letters sent to principals at his child's school asking that school prohibit child's mother, with whom judge was involved in a custody battle, from visiting child at school); *In re Isabella*, 85 A.3d 937 (N.J. 2014) (judge admonished for lending prestige of the office to girlfriend when judge used judicial letterhead to communicate with school of girlfriend's children); *In re Gallagher*, 951 P.2d 705 (Or. 1998) (95 percent of judge's personal business letters went out on judicial stationery; repeated use of title and "colorful and conspicuous" judicial letterhead in correspondence was designed to obtain personal advantages, including financial advantages, for himself and those close to him; judge knew stationery "was likely to play a prominent role in the recipient's response to each such letter."); *In re Samay*, 764 A.2d 398 (N.J. 2001) (municipal court judge's designation of himself as a judge in his signature on a non-judicial, personal letter involving a dispute over a financial obligation violated provisions of Code of Judicial Conduct requiring judges to refrain from lending the prestige of office to advance the private interests of others); *but see In re Thibodeaux*, 737 So. 2d 1284 (La. 1999) (judge's personal "thank you" letter on court stationery did not violate Canon). For further discussion, *see* Raymond J. McKoski, *Ethical Considerations in the Use of Judicial Stationery for Private Purposes*, 112 Penn. St. L. Rev. 471 (2007); Cynthia Gray, *The 2007 ABA Model Code: Taking Judicial Ethics Standards to the Next Level*, 90 Judicature 284 (2007).

Judges may also be prohibited from using the prestige of office after leaving office. ABA Formal Ethics Opinion 95-391 (1995) (after a judge leaves office, use of honorific title such as "Judge" or "Your Honor" is improper; cites supporting ethics opinions from various jurisdictions); *see also* Joanne Pelton Pitulla, *Trading on Titles*, 6 No. 4 Prof. Law. 14 (1995) (use of honorific titles by ex-judges in the practice of law causes professional and ethical problems; former judges must gracefully relinquish the prestige of judicial office when they return to practice); *but see* Alaska Bar Ass'n Ethics Op. 2006-4 (2006) (advising that an attorney who runs for public office may use information indicating prior judicial service where the campaign information (e.g., campaign flier or mailing) only lists the candidate as having been a "former" judicial officer, and identifies the specific position along with the length and location of such service).

Advancing Interests of Others

Rule 1.3 prohibits a judge from abusing the prestige of judicial office to advance the personal or economic interests of others. To do so, or to convey that anyone is in a special position of influence, is to prostitute the office. *See* E. Wayne Thode, *Reporter's Notes to Code of Judicial Conduct* 49 (1972). The case law is full of examples of judges improperly advancing the interests of others. *See, e.g., In re Gottsfield*, 12-263 (Ariz. Comm'n on Jud. Conduct 2012) (judge gave appearance of abusing prestige of the office when judge sent an email and initiated a telephone conversation with psychologist involved in custody dispute involving family member of judge); *In re Pollard*, 11-187 (Ariz. Comm'n on Jud. Conduct 2012) (judge censured for making "inquiries to two other judges about a case on behalf of family friends involved in that case. While the judge assured his friends that he had no authority to change the decision previously made, his inquiries may have led the complainant to believe he could, in fact, impact the outcome of the underlying case."); *In re Morales*, Arizona Comm'n on Jud. Conduct 07-040 (2007) (judge's actions in quashing a warrant based solely on a motion filed by his own attorney presented the appearance that the judge was granting attorney a special favor); *In re Maloney*, 916 So. 2d 786 (Fla. 2005) (judge improperly used prestige of judicial office when he contacted police department to request that friend of judge's son, who had been arrested for DUI, be released from custody); *In re Holloway*, 832 So. 2d 716 (Fla. 2002) (judge improperly used the prestige of office by requesting schedule favor for a family member from a fellow judge; however, single phone call to detective handling criminal investigation involving family friend did not amount to abuse of judicial office); *In re Inquiry Concerning Eads*, 362 N.W.2d 541 (Iowa 1985) (judge interjected himself in the merits of a lawyer/friend's dissolution case and becoming legal advisor and advocate for the friend; judge engaged in campaign of intimidation against lawyer who represented friend's spouse in the dissolution); *In re Funke*, 757 N.E.2d 1013 (Ind. 2001) (judge allowed signature to be stamped on protective order in action brought by father and granting emergency protective orders with regard to property interests of judge's parents, aunt, and first cousin); *In re Justice of the Peace Adams*, 959 So. 2d 474 (La. 2007) (judge improperly lent prestige of judicial office to advance the private interests of another by issuing warrants for the arrest of two individuals for a parade permit violation and issuing excessive bonds in retaliation for the individuals' political opposition to mayor); *In re Decuir*, 654 So. 2d 687 (La. 1995) (judge allowed his former law partner to use court's secretary/receptionist, telephone system, post office box, office supplies, and law library); *In re Shannon*, 637 N.W.2d 503 (Mich. 2002) (judge allowed police officer to sit next to podium in courtroom with a bag of tickets from the Detroit Fire and Police Field Day; judge dismissed tickets of defendants and advised them to purchase tickets from the police officer, telling some to "dig deeper" or go to an ATM); *Miss. Comm'n on Jud. Performance v. Thompson*, 169 So. 3d 857 (Miss. 2015) (judge removed from bench, in part, for using his position to advance interest of private bail bondsman); *Miss. Comm'n on Jud. Performance v. Brown*, 918 So. 2d 1247 (Miss. 2005) (judge attempted to use his position to obtain favorable treatment for, and obstruct prosecution of charges against, his son, who had been charged with assaulting his now ex-wife); *In re Rivera-Soto*, 927 A.2d 112 (N.J. 2007) (judge censured for improperly interceding with police and the courts in a delinquency case against a youth accused of bullying his son by asking police chief to file charges, going to police station to sign a delinquency complaint, and calling county prosecutor and assignment judge to alert them to the case); *Matter of Carton*, 658 A.2d 1211 (N.J. 1995) (judge gave legal advice to defendant in criminal matter and sending fax to judge before whom the matter was pending); *In re Schatz*, 845 N.W.2d 273 (Neb. 2014) (judge publicly reprimanded for intervening in felony drunk driving case on behalf of friend); *In re Naranjo*, 303 P.3d 849 (N.M. 2013) (judge publicly censured for calling another judge hearing child support enforcement matter of step-son to assure that step-son was not a flight risk and should be let of our jail or have his bond reduced); *In re Garza*, 161 P.3d 876 (N.M. 2007) (judge repeatedly tried to influence other magistrate court judges presiding over his girlfriend's DWI case); *In re Daniels* (N.Y. Comm'n on Jud. Conduct 2011) (judge censured for "personally delivering his co-worker's traffic ticket" to court, "showing a video of the accident to court staff, and asking the staff to tell the judge of his visit to the court"); *Disc. Counsel v. Allen*, 684 N.E.2d 31 (Ohio 1997) (judge appeared in a law firm television advertisement in which judge did not speak, but appeared on bench in her judicial robes with her name plate visible, and led viewers to believe that firm had special relationship with judge); *In re Darlington County Magistrate Thomas*, 642 S.E.2d 736 (S.C. 2007) (county magistrate who issued subpoena in favor of his son-in-law, who was involved in a child support proceeding violated Code, including provision prohibiting a judge from lending the prestige of judicial office to advance the private interests of others); *Matter of Ward*, 448 S.E.2d 546 (S.C. 1994) (judge's improper issuance of arrest warrants for fraudulent checks, at request of individual engaged in illegal loan operation, essentially allowed individual to use magistrate's office to collect on illegal loans); *In re Williams*, 987 S.W.2d 837 (Tenn. 1998) (judge's misconduct included the use of inmate from county jail to help build a house for judge's son); *In re Sharp*, 2013 WL 979361 (Tex. Spec. Ct. Rev. 2013) (judge called juvenile detention center, county commissioner, and district court judge, identified self as judge on court of appeals, and requested release of acquaintance's daughter from hold at juvenile detention); *In re De La Paz*, 11-0804-JP (Tex. Comm'n on Jud. Cond. 2012) (judge lent the prestige of his judicial office to advance the private interests of landlord friend by threatening to evict tenant with notice of hearing); *In re De La Paz*, 14-0823-JP (Tex. Comm'n on Jud. Cond. 2014) (judge who intervened in private dispute between building tradesmen used prestige of office to advance one person's private interest); *In re Heavey*, No. 5975-F-145 (Wash. Comm'n on Jud. Conduct 2010) (judge who wrote letters to Italian authorities and spoke on behalf of American held in Italy lent prestige of the office to another).

Ticket-Fixing

Ticket-fixing for others is the classic case of abuse of judicial power and is subject to discipline. *See, e.g., Inquiry Concerning Judge Sarmiento* (Cal. Comm'n on Jud. Perfomance 2012) (judge censured for asking another judge to waive a $300 civil assessment cost for failure to timely pay wife's traffic ticket); *In re Justin*, 809 N.W.2d 126 (Mich. 2012) (judge removed for summarily dismissing traffic tickets issued to self, spouse, and court personnel); *Miss. Comm'n on Jud. Performance v. McKenzie*, 63 So. 3d 1219 (Miss. 2011) (judge requested copies of the tickets of friends, "gave those copies to a deputy clerk, and instructed the clerk to pass them along to the citing officer so the officer could help the defendants dispose of the charges"); *Miss. Comm'n on Jud. Performance v. Warren*, 791 So. 2d 194 (Miss. 2001) (judge dismissed speeding tickets without notice to the ticketing officer and without a hearing); *Miss. Comm'n on Jud. Performance v. Dodds*, 680 So. 2d 180 (Miss. 1996) (judge engaged in ticket-fixing in 32 cases); *In re Case of Snow*, 674 A.2d 573 (N.H. 1996) (after judge called police officer who had issued speeding ticket to judge's brother to ask if officer was aware of relationship, the speeding ticket was revoked; court rejected judge's argument that he did not intend to fix his brother's ticket because judge was aware ticket would be "taken care of" as result of call); *In re Ramirez*, 135 P.3d 230 (N.M. 2006) (judge who confronted police officers issuing citations for violation of municipal ordinance to judge's son and his son's friends, identifying himself as a judge and asking one of the officers if she knew who he was, improperly lent the prestige of judicial office to advance the private interest of the judge or others); *In re Hunt*, (N.Y. Comm'n on Jud. Conduct 2011) (judge disciplined for interceding on behalf of friend who was issued two traffic tickets by speaking with issuing officer, noting the judge's friendship with the ticket recipient, and asking the officer to "do whatever you can do"); *In re Hayes*, (N.C. Jud. Standards Comm'n 2011) (judge reprimanded for contacting fellow judge about traffic citations issued to county official); *In re Woodham*, 689 S.E.2d 605 (S.C. 2010) (judge fixed tickets for municipalities); *Matter of Chiles*, 490 S.E.2d 259 (S.C. 1997) (municipal judge exercised undue influence in getting arresting officer to dismiss DUI charges against personal friend); *but see Miss. Comm'n on Jud. Performance v. A Justice Court Judge*, 580 So. 2d 1259 (Miss. 1991) (judge received private reprimand rather than recommended public reprimand for fixing tickets; infractions were based upon good intentions and showed no hint of dishonesty or political gain–when the judge had accepted fines, he turned money over to clerk and produced a receipt). For additional discussion of ticket-fixing, see Rule 2.2.

Letters of Recommendation

A judge may provide a reference or recommendation for an individual as long as the reference is based on the judge's personal knowledge. *See, e.g.*, Fla. Jud. Ethics Adv. Comm. Op. 2007-06 (2007) (judge may write letter of recommendation for former staff attorney who applied for a Harvard Law School fellowship; when an attorney's employment is as a staff attorney for a judge, the judge is uniquely qualified to comment on the staff attorney's work performance); Neb. Jud. Ethics Adv. Comm. Op. 07-04 (2007) (judge may send a letter of recommendation to a college on behalf of high school student whom the judge has known for most of the student's life); Nev. Stand. Comm. on Jud. Ethics and Election Prac. Op. JE10-014 (2010) (judge may write letter of recommendation for person seeking foster care license); Nev. Stand. Comm. on Jud. Ethics and Election Prac. Op. JE 04-004 (2004) (judge may write letter of recommendation on behalf of candidate for admission to law school based on personal knowledge of candidate, but may not write one on behalf of a doctor in a medical licensing hearing because that would be lending the prestige of judicial office to advance the private interests of others and improperly testifying as a character witness); N.M. Adv. Comm. on Code of Jud. Conduct Op. 12-6 (2012) (judge may write a letter of recommendation for lawyer who has appeared before judge in connection with lawyer's application for a contract position); N.C. Formal Adv. Op. 2007-03 (2007) (judge may, based on personal knowledge, complete the North Carolina Board of Law Examiner's Certificate of Moral Character on behalf of an applicant seeking admission to practice law in North Carolina); N.Y. Adv. Comm. on Jud. Ethics Op. 10-07 (2010) (judge may write a letter of reference for lawyer who appears before judge regularly).

According to one jurisdiction, a judge may also recommend a lawyer or a former employee on a social networking site like LinkedIn. Utah Jud. Ethics Adv. Comm. Informal Op. 12-01 (2012). However, a judge may not recommend "someone who regularly appears before the judge" because the recommendation "may be perceived as an endorsement of the person's skills and credibility." *Id.*

Additionally, a judge may need to recuse himself or herself if the recommended lawyer has a matter before the judge, and the judge recommended the lawyer "based on the judge's interactions with the attorney in court." *Id.*

The judge may use official letterhead if the judge indicates that the reference is personal and if there is no likelihood that the letterhead would reasonably be perceived as an attempt to exert pressure through the judicial office. Model Code of Judicial Conduct Rule 1.3 cmt. [2]. *See, e.g.*, Mass. Comm. on Jud. Ethics Adv. Op. 2005-1 (2005) (judge may use court stationery for letter of recommendation to Judicial Nomination Commission on behalf of candidate for judicial position); Nev. Stand. Comm. on Jud. Ethics and Election Prac. Op. JE12-010 (2012) (judge may use official court letterhead for reference letter praising work of construction project manager with whom judge worked during construction project); Va. Jud. Ethics Adv. Comm. Op. 06-1 (2006) (listing steps judge must take to avoid lending prestige of judicial office when writing letter of recommendation including limiting the substance of the letter to what the judge has personally observed about the individual); *but see* N.C. Formal Adv. Op. 2007-02 (2007) (advising that personal stationary rather than official letterhead should be used as the recommendation was not done in the course of official duties as a judge).

When a judge goes beyond this limited exception, however, the letter of recommendation may constitute abuse of the prestige of office. *See, e.g., In re Steiner* (Cal. Comm'n on Jud. Performance 2014) (judge who: sent a recommendation letter on behalf of lawyer with whom judge was involved in a sexual relationship; contacted the district attorney's office about the employment application; asked questions about the interview and hiring processes, and expressed irritation that the judge's recommendation had not resulted in lawyer's hiring, exceeded the scope of conduct permitted). This result is consistent with the cases decided before the rule's language change from lending the prestige of the office to abusing it. *See, e.g., In re Whitaker*, 948 So. 2d 1067 (La. 2007) (judge who sent a letter on official court stationery to Chief Disciplinary Counsel in support of disbarred lawyer who was applying for readmission to the practice of law improperly lent the prestige of judicial office to advance the private interest of another); *In re Hill*, 8 S.W.3d 578 (Mo. 2000) (municipal judge's open letter in local newspaper in support of city police chief, who was involved in political battle with city mayor, was not a private letter of recommendation, such that it would fall within exception to judicial conduct rule prohibiting judges from lending prestige of judicial office to advance private interests); *In re Smith*, 2013 WL 3322456 (N.Y. Comm'n on Jud. Conduct 2013) (judge admonished for writing letter of support to parole division in matter); *In re Beckham*, 620 S.E.2d 69 (S.C. 2005) (magistrate's meeting with public official for purpose of recommending a personal friend for promotion within police department improperly lent prestige of judicial office for purpose of benefiting another); *In re Ochoa*, No. 11-0105-JP

(Tex. Comm'n on Jud. Conduct 2011) (judge reprimanded for writing recommendation letter on court stationary in support of neighbor facing immigration matter); Ariz. Jud. Ethics Adv. Comm. Op. 10-05 (2010) (judge may send a letter on behalf of a family member to the judge sentencing that family member if case is pending out of state and the letter "makes no reference to the writer's status as a judicial officer"); Ark. Jud. Ethics Advisory Op. 2005-01 (2005) (judge may not write a letter to the judge who is sentencing a life-long friend of the judge at the request of the friend's attorney); Utah Jud. Ethics Adv. Comm. Informal Op. 12-01 (2012) (judge may not write restaurant review and use title because to do so would lend prestige of the office to a for-profit entity). *See generally* Raymond J. McKoski, *Ethical Considerations in the Use of Judicial Stationery for Private Purposes*, 112 Penn. St. L. Rev. 471 (2007); Cynthia Gray, *Recommendations by Judges: What Are the Limits?*, 79 Judicature 310 (1996) (discussing contours of the rule on judicial letters of recommendation); Marla Greenstein, *Judicial Ethics*, 41 Judges' J. 38 (2002) (starting with hypothetical of judge using court stationery to write recommendation letter for courtroom janitor seeking new employment, article examines guiding principles in what may be confusing judicial ethics analysis).

The prohibition on abusing the prestige of judicial office to advance the interests of another is intended to prevent inappropriate exploitation of judges' positions, but there is nothing inappropriate about judges identifying themselves as such when judicial experience is germane to the recommendation. Therefore, a judge may write letters on the basis of a judge's experience on the job (e.g., law clerks) or general expertise in the law (e.g., a neighbor applying for admission to law school). Comment [2] does not admonish judges to avoid writing letters of reference on behalf of someone with respect to whom the judge's status is irrelevant, but rather, advises judges to consider whether their position might be perceived as exerting pressure by reason of their office and to refrain if it would. Charles G. Geyh & W. William Hodes, *Reporters' Notes to the Model Code of Judicial Conduct* 23–24 (2009).

On a related issue, some state judicial ethics committees have issued opinions addressing whether a judge may rate lawyers for various ratings services. Kan. Jud. Ethics Op. JE-148 (2006) (judge may respond to request from Martindale-Hubbell for opinion as to lawyer's legal ability and general ethical standards where judge believes he has sufficient personal knowledge of lawyer's skill and general ethical conduct); N.Y. Adv. Comm. on Jud. Ethics Op. 11-40 (2011) (judge may provide Martindale-Hubbell with opinion); *but see* S.C. Adv. Comm. on Stand. of Jud. Conduct Op. 04-2004 (2004) (judge may not rate the lawyers in his or her circuit for Martindale-Hubbell because publicized ratings which indicate that a judge believes one lawyer to be superior, in one way or another, to another lawyer, could certainly create the appearance of partiality).

Referring Lawyers to Others

At least one jurisdiction has advised that a judge who refers potential clients to particular lawyers creates the perception that the judge is improperly using the prestige of office to advance the private interest of that lawyer. Colo. Jud. Ethics Adv. Bd. Op. 2006-01 (2006). However, that opinion advises that the judge may recommend a lawyer to a family member or friend, provided that the judge's relationship with the family member or friend is of such a nature so as to require the judge's disqualification in any matter in which the relative or friend is involved. *Id. Cf.* N.Y. Adv. Comm. on Jud. Ethics Op. 93-89 (1993) (a judge may recommend an attorney to a friend or acquaintance, as long as the judge does not sit on the case and the judge makes it clear that it is not an official recommendation); N.Y. Adv. Comm. on Jud. Ethics Op. 97-60 (1997) (when a judge is asked to recommend an attorney to any other individuals, the judge should consider referring the individual to the local bar's attorney referral service or should recommend not less than three attorneys for consideration).

Participation in Judicial Selection Process

Judges are often in the best position to comment upon the qualifications of a particular judicial candidate, however, such comments may raise the specter of political involvement that goes beyond the bounds of propriety for sitting judges. The Commentary to Rule 1.3 strikes a balance by allowing judges to participate in judicial selection, but only in certain situations. For example, judges may cooperate with appointing authorities and screening committees seeking names for consideration. Model Code of Judicial Conduct Rule 1.3 cmt. [3]. Additionally, a judge may respond to official inquiries concerning the professional qualifications of a person being considered for judicial office. *Id. See, e.g.*, Nev. Stand. Comm. on Jud. Ethics and Election Prac. JE07-009 (2007) (judges with knowledge of an applicant's professional abilities can respond to requests for recommendations for judicial appointments, so long as such requests come from or at the direction of agencies or groups officially tasked with selecting candidates for appointment); N.M. Jud. Adv. Op. 05-03 (2005) (judge may write a letter to a judicial nominating commission, based on his personal knowledge, supporting their nomination of a judge for appointment to the bench); Pa. Jud. Ethics Comm. Informal Op. 3/7a/05 (2005) (judge may ask other judges, who are familiar with the judge's qualifications and experience, to write letters of recommendation for the federal bench).

In affirming that a judge may write a letter of recommendation to a Judicial Nomination Commission on behalf of a candidate for judicial appointment, the Oklahoma Judicial Ethics Advisory Panel provided the following guidelines: (1) the judge should have personal knowledge of the applicant; (2) the judge's recommendation must be factual, discreet, and directed only to factors relevant to performance of the office; (3) the judge should avoid lending the judge's name to any publicity campaign for candidate; (4) the judge should avoid pleading for a candidate of judge's choosing over others being considered; and (5) the judge should not provide the letter of endorsement if the judge could reasonably expect the endorsement to be announced publicly. Okla. Jud. Ethics Op. 2002-1 (2002).

This limited permission, however, does not allow for a judge to otherwise use the influence of office to support another's candidacy. *See, e.g., In re Shea*, 815 So. 2d 813 (La. 2002) (judge made campaign contributions to his son's campaign for the New Orleans City Council and donated his excess campaign coffers to other candidates for public office); *In re Koon*, 580 S.E.2d 147 (S.C. 2003) (public reprimand of part-time municipal court judge was warranted, where judge participated in a taped telephone message that solicited support for a candidate for lieutenant governor, and judge stated in the message that he was a former magistrate for county); *but see In re Hecht*, 213 S.W.3d 547 (Tex. Spec. Ct. Rev. 2006) (Canon that prohibits judge from lending the prestige of judicial office to advance the private interests of others did not apply to Supreme Court justice's support for United States Supreme Court nominee; life tenure and the power and prestige of the office were public interests, rather than private interests).

Broadcast Media Appearances

A relatively recent development in the area of lending judicial prestige is the problem of judges appearing on commercial television programs. In the case of *In re Broadbelt*, 683 A.2d 543 (N.J. 1996), the leading case on this issue, a municipal court judge appeared as guest commentator more than 50 times on "Court TV" and other shows to discuss pending cases, including the O.J. Simpson case. The New Jersey Supreme Court held that in addition to violating the prohibition against making public comments regarding pending proceedings, which appears in Rule 2.10(A), the judge's television appearances violated the prohibition against lending the prestige of office to advance the private interests of others.

Facing a dearth of case law on the point, the court looked to several ethics opinions regarding media appearances by judges. *Id.* (citing ABA Comm. on Professional Ethics, Formal Op. 298 (1961)) (advised that judges may not appear on commercial television simulating judicial proceedings, but did not determine whether panel discussion or interview were improper); ABA Comm. on Professional Ethics, Informal Op. C-230(g) (1961) (appearance by judge on "Meet the Press" permissible as "distinctly … a public service type [of show]"); S.C. Adv. Comm. on Stand. of Jud. Conduct Op. No. 14-1991 (1991) (judge prohibited from answering questions on radio talk show on regular basis).

Acknowledging the difficulty of the question of whether a judge lends prestige of office to a television program merely by appearing on it, the court articulated several factors to be analyzed: "the frequency with which a judge appears on a program, the intended audience, the subject matter, and whether the program is commercial or non-commercial." In the *Broadbelt* case, the frequency of appearances led the court to find a violation, however, the court was careful to state "isolated" appearances might be permissible. *In re Broadbelt*, 683 A.2d 543, 550 (N.J. 1996). Additionally, some state ethics committees have advised that a judge may participate in a television program involving a case the judge worked on while he or she was a lawyer, as long as the judge avoids references to his or her judicial office. S.C. Adv. Op. 09-2008 (2008) (judge may participate in television program concerning case judge prosecuted as an assistant solicitor prior to election).

Following the *Broadbelt* decision, the New Jersey Supreme Court approved a new guideline that requires judges to exercise "exceptional caution and discretion" when participating in television and radio programs, particularly programs that potentially reach a large audience. N.J. Judicial Guideline III A. 6. Additionally, the Guideline limits commentary on pending cases to an explanation of legal issues involved and advises judges to avoid making appearances that convey the impression that a program sponsor or anyone else is in a special position to influence the judge. *Id.*

For further analysis of *Broadbelt, see generally* Christine Kormanik, *Survey of Recent Development in New Jersey Law*, 27 Seton Hall L. Rev. 872 (1997); Joseph Wharton, *Judge Must Forgo TV Commentary Gigs*, 83 ABA J. 37 (March 1997). For a discussion of First Amendment issues raised in *Broadbelt* and other cases involving judicial speech, *see* Honorable Howland W. Abrahamson and Gary Lee, *Judicial Ethics Advisory Committees Should Render Opinions Which Adhere to Binding United States Constitutional Precedents*, 41 Duq. L. Rev. 269 (2003) (analyzing state and federal cases on campaign and non-campaign speech); Cynthia Gray, *When Judge's Speak Up: The Code of Judicial Conduct and Public Education*, 38 Judges' J. 6 (Fall 1999) (outlining the contours of Code provisions that expressly permit judges to educate public); Ronald D. Rotunda, *Judicial Comments on Pending Cases: The Ethical Restrictions and the Sanctions—A Case Study of the Microsoft Litigation*, 2001 U. Ill. L. Rev. 611 (2001) (addressing the contours of the Public Comment Restrictions of the ABA Model Code of Judicial Conduct).

A related issue is whether judges can appear in print or televised advertisements. Some state ethics committees have advised that a judge should not do so because it would use the prestige of judicial office to advance the private interests of others and create the appearance of impropriety. *See* Md. Jud. Ethics Op. 2006-11 (2006) (judge who recently underwent surgery performed by a local physician may not appear in an infomercial in which the physician would explain the procedure and the judge's successful recovery and rehabilitation).

Online Social Networking

Judicial ethics opinions are split on whether judges may friend or connect on social networking sites with lawyers who appear before them. Florida has determined that a judge may not accept from or offer to a lawyer who appears before the judge a "friend" or connection request. To allow such would convey to others that the lawyer is in a special position to influence the judge. Fla. Jud. Ethics Adv. Comm. Op. 2009-20 (2009) (to violate Canon 2B, the judge must establish the social networking page, the judge must have discretion to accept or reject contacts or "friends," and "friends" or contacts selected by the judge must be communicated to others); Fla. Jud. Ethics Adv. Comm. Op. 2012-12 (2012) (judge may not connect through LinkedIn with lawyers who may appear before the judge). *See also* Mass. Comm. on Jud. Ethics Adv. Op. 2011-06 (2011) (Code does not permit judge to friend any lawyer who may appear before the judge); Okla. Jud. Ethics Op. 2011-3 (2011) (friending a lawyer who appears before the judge "would or could" convey the impression that the lawyer is in a special position to influence the judge). A disclaimer on the judge's page that explains that a "friend" is actually only an acquaintance is not effective. Fla. Jud. Ethics Adv. Comm. Op. 2010-06 (2010).

Although the California Judges Association, in Advisory Opinion 66 (2010), rejected a per se prohibition of social networking with lawyers who may appear before a judge, it looked to four factors to determine whether interacting on social media with a lawyer who creates an impression that the lawyer "is in a special position to influence the judge and cast doubt on the judge's ability to be impartial . . ." The factors included (1) the nature of the networking site, i.e., whether the site is a personal page or one "used to facilitate professional interactions"; (2) the number of friends on the page; (3) the judge's practice for accepting friends or links; and (4) how regularly the lawyer appears before the judge. Opinion 66 explained that if a judge hosts a personal site, the judge should not connect with lawyers who appear before or who have a pending matter before the judge. If a lawyer who is connected to the judge on the judge's personal social media page does, in fact, appear before the judge, the judge must disclose the connection, "unfriend" the lawyer, and "the judge should disqualify him or herself."

The Ethics Committee of the Kentucky Judiciary rejected the idea that a judge who has connected with a lawyer, or others who regularly appear before the judge on a social networking site, conveys the impression that the connection is in a special position to influence the judge. Ky. Jud. Ethics Op. JE 119 (2010). *See also* N.Y. Jud. Ethics Adv. Op. 08-176 (2008) (nothing inherently inappropriate about a judge joining and making use of a social network); Ohio Bd. of Comm. on Grievances and Discipline Op. 2010-7 (2010) (judge may friend lawyer who appears before judge); S.C. Adv. Comm. on Stands. of Jud. Conduct Op. 17-2009 (magistrate judge may friend law enforcement officers who appear before judge); Utah Jud. Ethics Adv. Comm. Informal Op. 12-01 (2012) (judge may be Facebook friend with lawyer who appears before the judge; opinion also addresses 20 other social media-related questions).

Judges may be members of a bar association's social networking site. Fla. Jud. Ethics Adv. Comm. Op. 2010-06 (2010) ("because the organization, as opposed to the judge, determines and controls who may have access and participate in that type of social networking site, it is ethically permissible for a judge to be a member of a voluntary bar association's Facebook page and the judge is not required to "de-friend" lawyers who are also members on that organization's Facebook page and who use Facebook to communicate among themselves about that organization and other non-legal matters.").

Retaining Control over Advertising on Judicial Writings

Although issues concerning a judge's writings are dealt with elsewhere in the Code (Rule 3.1 on extrajudicial activities), the Commentary to Rule 1.3 makes mention of the fact that a judge must retain control over the advertising of any publication of the judge's writing so as to ensure that the prestige of judicial office is not exploited. Model Code of Judicial Conduct Rule 1.3 cmt. [4].

Using Prestige of Judicial Office for Fund-Raising Solicitations

A judge may not use or permit the use of the prestige of the judicial office for fund-raising solicitations. Such impermissible conduct may occur on the bench or off. *See* Raymond J. McKoski, *Charitable Fund-Raising by Judges: The Give and Take of the 2007 ABA Model Code of Judicial Conduct*, 2008 Mich. St. L. Rev. 769. For instance, a judge may not use the judicial position to encourage criminal defendants to donate to charity in lieu of paying a fine or other sentence. *See In re Wagner*, 25 Cal. Rptr. 2d 201 (Cal. App. 4th Dis. 2005) (judge improperly required a probationer to pay a certain amount to a battered women's shelter as a condition of probation, as authorized by law); *In re Shannon*, 637 N.W.2d 503 (Mich. 2002) (judge censured and suspended for advising defendants found guilty of traffic citations to purchase tickets for Detroit Fire and Police Field Day from police officer sitting in the courtroom; judge's conduct, whether well-intentioned or not, gave the appearance of using power of his position to solicit money from defendants for charitable cause); *In re Davis*, 946 P.2d 1033 (Nev. 1997) (judge removed from office for misconduct including suggesting that criminal defendants contribute money to charities on a list prepared by judge in lieu of paying fines to the city); Mich. Comm. on Jud. Ethics Op. JI-48 (1992) (sentencing judge may not give offenders the option of performing community service work or making monetary contribution to charity designated by judge); N.M. Adv. Comm. on Code of Jud. Conduct Op. 12-04 (2012) (judge may not order defendant to make a contribution to local Crime Stoppers organization as condition of deferred sentence); *cf.* Fla. Jud. Ethics Adv. Comm. Op. 97-32 (1997) (judge may not advise jurors of option to donate jury service compensation to domestic violence shelter or organization specified by guardian ad litem program); Wash. Ethics Adv. Comm. Op. 95-18 (1995) (judge may not provide jurors with option of contributing their compensation to the city combined charities fund); *but see* Mich. Comm. on Jud. Ethics Op. JI-64 (1992) (judge may offer defendant, as an alternative to incarceration, the option of performing services or attending an organization's educational or rehabilitative program); Pa. Jud. Ethics Comm. Informal Op. 5/15/00 (2000) (judge may give proceeds of late fines to charity that provides free child care for parties who attend court because the sole purpose is to improve the administration of justice); *In re Carney*, 79 A.3d 490 (Pa. 2013) (judge did not advance private interest when lending his name to campaign to eliminate graffiti; private gain of business owners and religious institutions incidental); Wash. Ethics Adv. Comm. Op. 99-10 (1999) (judge may give a lawyer the option to pay a bona fide monetary fine to either a pro bono program or civic or charitable organization of the lawyer's choice). *See generally* Sylvia Shaz Shweder, Note, *Donating Debt to Society: Prosecutorial and Judicial Ethics of Plea Agreements and Sentences That Include Charitable Contributions*, 73 Fordham L. Rev. 377 (2004).

A judge also improperly uses judicial influence when he raises funds by selling items to people whom the judge associates and works with during work hours. *See, e.g., In re Arrigan*, 678 A.2d 446 (R.I. 1996) (judge solicited lawyers, law firms, and other judges to buy jewelry for a nonprofit organization, sold sweaters knit for benefit of another nonprofit organization from his chambers and sold raffle tickets to help sponsor memorial event); Fla. Jud. Ethics Adv. Comm. Op. 03-16 (2003) (judge's art work or crafts may not be sold or auctioned at bar association fund-raising event).

Off the bench, a judge may not permit an organization to use the judge's position or title in an effort to raise funds. *See* Ariz. Jud. Ethics Adv. Comm. Op. 94-4 (1994) (agreeing to have lunch with successful bidder at charity auction improperly used judicial prestige to advance private interest); Mich. Comm. on Jud. Ethics Op. JI-115 (1997) (judge's attendance at testimonial dinner sponsored by political party where admission price exceeds reasonable cost of attendance would be exploiting judicial office); Neb. Jud. Ethics Adv. Comm. Op. 02-03 (2002) (judge may not provide supportive quotes for legal service's fund-raising pamphlet where the organization's request amounts to "leveraging the judge's title and influence to solicit funds or pro bono legal services"); Okla. Jud. Ethics Op. 2006-1 (2006) (judge may not allow his or her name to be on the letterhead or stationery of a county leadership group who uses the stationery to solicit funds for worthwhile community projects); Pa. Jud. Ethics Comm. Informal Op. 4/11/05 (2005) (judge can attend charitable events, but must be sensitive as to whether he or she is being "showcased" as a means to encourage others to contribute or to advance the private interest of the host); S.C. Adv. Comm. on Stand. of Jud. Conduct, Op. 10-1995 (1995) (judge may not write letter of reference for organization in an effort to obtain funding).

While a judge does not shed all First Amendment associational rights upon taking office, the judge must exercise great care in interactions that can give the appearance of bias in favor of certain groups or organizations. *See generally* Cynthia Gray, *A Judicial Survival Guide to Balancing Social Commitments with the Code of Judicial Conduct*, 35 Judges' J. 18 (Fall 1996) (discussing guidance from advisory committees regarding judges' social and community commitments, limitations on accepting hospitality from attorneys, involvement in specialty bar associations, guidelines for charitable fund-raising activities, and judges' attendance at political events). For more on judicial membership in invidiously discriminating organizations, see Rule 3.6.

Using Judge's Name or Likeness in Image Campaigns

Some jurisdictions permit schools and other organizations to use a judge's name or image in promotions intended for purposes other than fund-raising, such as recruitment. *See, e.g.*, Fla. Jud. Ethics Adv. Comm. Op. 97-28 (1997) (judge may authorize his college alma mater to feature him in advertising campaign, which is not used to generate funding, but which profiles successful alumni in order to inspire others to consider higher education); Ill. Jud. Ethics Comm. Op. 99-3 (1999) (judge's name may be included on list of donors to fund-raiser honoring retired public defender where list is not used for fund-raising); N.Y. Adv. Comm. on Jud. Ethics Op. 02-21 (2002) (judge's photograph, name, and biographical information may be used by university in advertisements appearing in the subway, in college and high school newspapers, and on school website where purpose of advertisement is to "encourage and recruit students to [its] colleges and law school."); S.C. Adv. Comm. on Stand. of Jud. Conduct Op. 04-2002 (2002) (judge's image may appear on billboard as part of an image campaign on behalf of Girl Scouts); Wash. Ethics Adv. Comm. Op. 02-1 (2002) (judge may appear in county bar foundation's informational video discussing foundation's scholarship program that permitted judge to attend law school); *but see* Kan. Jud. Ethics Op. JE-159 (2007) (judge improperly lends prestige of judicial office to judge's alma mater by permitting his or her image, name, and title to appear in newspaper advertisements with comment "[m]y educational experience at [university] prepared me to keep focused on my goals and to keep a positive attitude toward life and my career."); Mass. Comm. on Judicial Ethics Adv. Op. 2000-6 (2000) (judge may not permit alma mater to use judge's photograph and a quotation from judge's commencement address praising university in newspaper and magazine advertising campaign); Pa. Jud. Ethics Comm.

Informal Op. 4/29/2005 (2005) (judge may not give an interview to a nonprofit organization that would feature the judge's interview, and other interviews, in a national promotion because doing so would lend the prestige of the judge's office to advance the private interests of another); Wis. Jud. Conduct Adv. Comm. Op. 05-1 (2005) (judge's name, image, and title may not be used on billboards promoting a university).

Allowing Others to Abuse the Prestige of the Judge's Office

Rule 1.3 provides that a judge may not allow others to abuse the prestige of judicial office to advance the personal or economic interests of the judge or of others. This provision is new to the Code. The Commission determined that judges should not be permitted to look the other way if friends or relatives seek to trade on the judge's position to benefit themselves or others. Charles G. Geyh & W. William Hodes, *Reporters' Notes to the Model Code of Judicial Conduct* 23 (2009).

Canon 2

A judge shall perform the duties of judicial office impartially, competently, and diligently.

1990 Code Comparison

Canon 2 addresses solely the judge's professional duties as a judge, which previously appeared in Canon 3 of the 1990 Code. The element of "competence" was added to the Canon in recognition of the importance that competence plays in a judge's discharge of his or her duties. Charles G. Geyh & W. William Hodes, *Reporters' Notes to the Model Code of Judicial Conduct* 25 (2009).

This Canon is at the heart of the Rules, that is, it governs core judicial functions. The judicial function has changed over time. Judicial activities or conduct are not limited to the adjudication of cases. As a result, this Canon includes rules governing judicial discipline, administration, and reporting. *Id.*

Rule 2.1 Giving Precedence to the Duties of Judicial Office

The duties of judicial office, as prescribed by law,* shall take precedence over all of a judge's personal and extrajudicial activities.

Comment

[1] In order to ensure that judges are available to fulfill their judicial duties, judges must conduct their personal and extrajudicial activities to minimize the risk of conflicts that would result in frequent disqualification. See Canon 3.

[2] Although it is not a duty of judicial office unless prescribed by law, judges are encouraged to participate in activities that promote public understanding of, and confidence in, the justice system.

1990 Code Comparison

This language of Rule 2.1 previously appeared in Canon 3A of the 1990 Code, with some changes. "[A]ll the judge's other activities" was replaced with "all of a judge's personal and extrajudicial activities." "Judicial duties" became "duties of judicial office" to emphasize that its application goes beyond adjudicative functions to reach the broader scope of responsibilities that accompany the judicial office. The Joint Commission to Evaluate the Model Code of Judicial Conduct added the word "shall" to make clear that this rule was doing more than making the descriptive point that judicial functions do take precedence; by inserting the term "shall," the Code clearly imposes an ethical duty on judges to give priority to the duties of judicial office. Charles G. Geyh & W. William Hodes, *Reporters' Notes to the Model Code of Judicial Conduct* 25–26 (2009).

Comment 1 was added to highlight the relationship between Canon 2 and Canon 3. Because judges must disqualify themselves from cases in which they have a conflict of interest, they must conduct their extrajudicial activities in ways that minimize their need to disqualify themselves. Comment 2 is also new and was added to underscore the value of judicial outreach. *Id.*

ANNOTATION

PRIORITY TO JUDICIAL DUTIES

Rule 2.1 instructs judges that the duties of judicial office, as prescribed by law, take precedence over all of their other activities. These include duties provided by statutes, constitutional provisions, and decisional law. Model Code of Judicial Conduct, Terminology. Rule 2.1 corresponds with Rule 3.1(A), which provides that a judge should conduct all of the judge's extrajudicial activities so that they do not interfere with the proper performance of judicial duties.

A judge does not violate Rule 2.1 simply by engaging in private, extrajudicial pursuits. "[W]e cannot say that a judge commits an ethical violation every time his or her secretary performs a task that someone might say is personal rather than judicial." Ariz. Sup. Ct. Jud. Ethics Adv. Comm. Op. 97-8 (1997). However, a judge may violate this Rule when extrajudicial pursuits detract from the performance of judicial duties. *In re Woodard*, 919 So. 2d 389 (Fla. 2006) (while running for re-election, judge left an arraignment to conduct a radio campaign interview); *In re Brown*, 512 S.E.2d 114 (S.C. 1999) (judge reprimanded for performing 901 marriages in one year and charging and retaining fees for personal use); Nev. Stand. Comm. on Jud. Ethics and Election Prac. Op. JE01-001 (2001) (full-time justice of the peace may not serve as a receiver in bankruptcy cases because such appointment would have a significant possibility of interfering with the ability of the judge to perform judicial duties in a diligent or proper manner); N.Y. Adv. Comm. on Jud. Ethics Op. 96-141 (1996) (judge may not maintain full time teaching position at local university, but may maintain a part-time position if it does not interfere with the proper performance of judicial duties); Tex. Advisory Op. on Jud. Ethics No. 221 (1998) (while judge may attempt two separate careers, when a judge is an independent agent selling products or services for a communications company, his selling duties could interfere with the proper performance of judicial duties). *See also In re Phalen*, 475 S.E.2d 327 (W. Va. 1996) (ruling that even though a judge's attempt to solicit litigants to become Amway sales representatives violated numerous Canons, the conduct did not violate this provision, because it did not involve any dereliction of judicial duties); Va. Jud. Ethics Adv. Comm. Op. 00-09 (2000) (judge may serve as an officer or director of homeowners' association if the position does not interfere with the judge's judicial duties).

While judges are expected to give precedence to the duties of judicial office, they may not use Rule 2.1 to justify delegating routine personal matters to their staff, such as picking up laundry or selling cookies for a child's scout troop. Ariz. Sup. Ct. Jud. Ethics Adv. Comm. Op. 97-8 (1997). A judge who repeatedly uses court personnel for personal errands, even in an effort to maximize productivity, creates a reasonable question about the judge's integrity, demeans employees, and detracts from the professionalism of the court in violation of Rule 2.1.

Presence in Court

Judges are required to be on the bench on time and as scheduled. Judges violate Rule 2.1 and may implicate other sections of the Code, including Rules 2.7 and 2.5(A) (regulating judges' adjudicative and administrative responsibilities), when they are late for court or not on the bench when they are supposed to be. *See, e.g., In re McVay*, 158 P.3d 198 (Ariz. 2007) (judge disciplined for misconduct, including being habitually late for court); *In re Braun*, 883 P.2d 996 (Ariz. 1994) (judge was habitually tardy in conducting court business), *In re Woodard*, 919 So. 2d 389 (Fla. 2006) (judge was frequently late in beginning scheduled hearings and once, while running for re-election, left an arraignment to conduct a radio campaign interview); *In re Peters*, 715 S.E.2d 56 (Ga. 2011) (judge who refused to work hours assigned by chief judge violated this provision); *In re Cahill*, 13-32, 13-41, 13-42 (Minn. Bd. on Jud. Standards 2014) (judge reprimanded in part for habitual tardiness); *In re Osburn*, 315 S.E.2d 640 (W. Va. 1984) (finding a violation when a magistrate tried to handle an arraignment from his home); *In re Harshbarger*, 314 S.E.2d 79 (W. Va. 1984) (judge censured for leaving night court three-and-a-half hours before the end of his shift); *In re Sheldon* (Cal. Comm'n on Jud. Performance 1998) (judge admonished for misconduct, including leaving courthouse with his pretrial calendar ongoing and not covered by another judge). *But see In re Verbage*, 490 S.E.2d 323 (W. Va. 1997) (finding mitigating circumstances and dismissing charges even though magistrate left night court half way through his shift after taking ill with the flu); *In re Codispoti*, 414 S.E.2d 628 (W. Va. 1992) (finding no violation when a magistrate on night duty took ill in the middle of his shift but obtained a replacement to cover his office duties and came in at 9:00 p.m., despite his illness, to handle an arraignment).

Judges may also violate Rule 2.1 by refusing to cooperate with other judges in scheduling time off from work. *See In re Browning*, 452 S.E.2d 34 (W. Va. 1994); *cf.* Fla. Jud. Ethics Adv. Comm. Op. 2004-38 (2004) ("[Rule 2.1] implies that judges must discharge their duties as constitutional officers before taking a vacation, and must schedule their vacation days in a manner consistent with the needs of the court.").

In some types of cases, such as workers' compensation cases, a judge may be permitted to appoint a clerk or a master to act as a special judge in the judge's absence. However, in such cases, the trial judge's absence from the courtroom must be necessary, meaning that the appointment of a special judge must be indispensable, rather than merely convenient. *Reece v. Findlay Indus., Inc.*, 83 S.W.3d 713 (Tenn. 2002); *Ferrell v. Cigna Property & Cas. Ins. Co.*, 33 S.W.3d 731 (Tenn. 2000) (a judge may not use mere convenience as basis for being absent from court).

RULE 2.2 IMPARTIALITY AND FAIRNESS

A judge shall uphold and apply the law,* and shall perform all duties of judicial office fairly and impartially.*

COMMENT

[1] To ensure impartiality and fairness to all parties, a judge must be objective and open-minded.

[2] Although each judge comes to the bench with a unique background and personal philosophy, a judge must interpret and apply the law without regard to whether the judge approves or disapproves of the law in question.

[3] When applying and interpreting the law, a judge sometimes may make good-faith errors of fact or law. Errors of this kind do not violate this Rule.

[4] It is not a violation of this Rule for a judge to make reasonable accommodations to ensure pro se litigants the opportunity to have their matters fairly heard.

1990 CODE COMPARISON

This Rule is taken from the first half of the first sentence of former Canon 3B(2), which spoke in terms of judges being "faithful" to the law. In its stead, the Joint Commission to Evaluate the Model Code of Judicial Conduct substituted the phrase "uphold and apply the law." In the Commission's view, "fidelity" lacked clear meaning; the essential point was, and remains, that judges should interpret and apply the law as they understand it to be written, and the Rule has been revised to make that point more clearly. Charles G. Geyh & W. William Hodes, *Reporters' Notes to the Model Code of Judicial Conduct* 27 (2009).

The Comments to Rule 2.2 are new to the Code. Comment [1] defines impartiality with reference to the two definitions accepted by the Supreme Court in *Republican Party of Minnesota v. White*, lack of bias toward a participant in the judicial process and open-mindedness. Comment [2] underscores the distinction between judges whose honest understanding of the law is influenced by upbringing, education, and life experience, which is neither avoidable nor improper, and judges who disregard the law. Comment [3] was added to emphasize that the rule is not aimed at good-faith errors of fact or law, but rather, at judges who deliberately or repeatedly disregard court orders or other clear requirements of law. Comment [4] was added to make clear that judges do not compromise their impartiality by making reasonable accommodations to pro se litigants, but rather, by leveling the playing field, judges ensure that pro se litigants receive a fair hearing. However, judges should resist unreasonable demands for assistance that might give an unrepresented party an unfair advantage. *Id.* at 27–28.

ANNOTATION

INTRODUCTION

Rule 2.2 requires judges to uphold and apply the law and perform all duties of judicial office fairly and impartially. "Judicial impartiality implies judicial objectivity and resides at the core of what Justice Kennedy . . . has called the 'promise' of 'neutrality.'" Donald L. Burnett, *A Cancer on the Republic: A Critical Appraisal of State Courts and the Challenge to Judicial Selection*, 34 Fordham Urb. L. J. 265 (2007).

Although there is some similarity between this Rule and Rule 1.1, their purposes are fundamentally different. While Rule 1.1 addresses the judge's duty to comply with the law in his or her daily life, this Rule directs the judge to follow the rule of law when deciding cases. The duty to follow the law is inextricably linked to a corresponding duty to be fair and impartial. Although the duty to decide cases with impartiality was implicit in numerous provisions in the former Code, it was not stated explicitly. This Rule corrects that oversight and does so by linking the judge's obligation to decide cases with impartiality to a corresponding duty to apply the law. *See, e.g., Matter of Inquiry Concerning a Judge*, 462 S.E.2d 728 (Ga. 1995) (judge's misconduct included refusing to set appeal bonds when obligated by law to do so, issuing bench warrants without probable cause, and forcing defendant to enter guilty plea in absence of counsel); *Matter of Boles*, 555 N.E.2d 1284 (Ind. 1990) (judge ordered a juvenile defendant's family to pay costs associated with the juvenile's defense by a public defender, even though the judge had not conducted a hearing to determine whether the juvenile's family was able to pay, in contravention to governing statute; judge refused to amend his order even when the illegality of the order was brought to his attention, stating on one of the related orders, "under no circumstances would the taxpayers of Hendricks County be required to pay the legal costs on the extraordinary bill submitted by" the public defender); *In re Aucoin*, 767 So. 2d 30 (La. 2000) (judge used "instanter" trial procedure immediately after defendants entered a not guilty plea at arraignment); *Matter of Markey*, 696 N.E.2d 523 (Mass. 1998) (judge's misconduct included a pattern of failing to engage in plea colloquies required under U.S. and state constitutional law); *Miss. Comm'n on Jud. Performance v. Brown*, 918 So. 2d 1247 (Miss. 2005) (judge's attempt to use his position to obtain favorable treatment for, and obstruct prosecution of charges against, his son, who had been charged with assaulting his now ex-wife, constituted conduct that was not faithful to the law, because judge promoted personal gain at expense of law enforcement and court personnel); *Miss. Comm'n on Jud. Performance v. Byers*, 757 So. 2d 961 (Miss. 2000) (judge's violations included improperly sentencing a defendant under the wrong statute and improperly extending a defendant's probationary period); *Disc. Counsel v. O'Neill*, 815 N.E.2d 286 (Ohio 2004) (judge used variety of coercive tactics, including threatening to revoke or revoking bond for no acceptable reasons, in order to expedite dispositions in criminal cases); *In re Dash*, 564 S.E.2d 672 (S.C. 2002) (judge entered directed verdict of guilty without giving defendant opportunity to present evidence).

Duty to Uphold and Apply the Law

Rule 2.2 requires judges to "uphold and apply the law." Some jurisdictions may not find a violation of the rule, unless the conduct of the judge occurred in an adjudicative capacity. *See, e.g., In re Trkula*, 699 A.2d 3 (Pa. Ct. Judicial Discipline 1997). Violations of this provision, therefore, typically involve rulings and orders in excess of a judge's authority, either through the denial of constitutional rights or through a failure to comply with the requirements set down by statutes, rules, or cases. *See, e.g., In re Stolz*, CJC No. 5456-F-138 (Wash. Comm'n on Jud. Conduct 2008) (judge failed to "be faithful to the law" when she required a defendant to remove head garment that he wore for religious reasons; judge abridged defendant's religious liberty protected by the First Amendment); Arizona 06-059 (2006) (judge reprimanded for applying Arizona Revised Statute §12-502 to dismiss a lawsuit against a minor defendant when the statute only applies to minor plaintiffs who are trying to file lawsuits).

Legal Error Distinguished

While it is easy to see that a judge's willful non-compliance with the law should be disciplined, courts have struggled with the issue of whether a judge's legal error rises to the level of sanctionable conduct under Rule 2.2 and other provisions of the Code. To discipline a judge for mere legal error would threaten judicial independence because judges might consciously or unconsciously render decisions based on how they think the disciplinary body would view the decision, instead of what they think would be the right decision in a particular case. Ben F. Overton, *Grounds for Judicial Discipline in the Context of Judicial Disciplinary Commissions*, 54 Chi.-Kent L. Rev. 59 (1977) ("To allow disciplinary proceedings to evaluate judicial decisions could force judges to walk an ill-defined and standardless line between propriety and impropriety. Clearly, such a sword over a judge's head would have a tendency to chill his independence."). *See also In re Quirk*, 705 So. 2d 172 (La. 1997) ("subjecting a judge to discipline because of an erroneous legal ruling has the potential to trammel the exercise of judicial discretion and stifle the independence of the judiciary."); *Miss. Comm'n on Jud. Performance v. Justice Court Judge T.T.*, 922 So. 2d 781 (Miss. 2006) (to maintain an independent judiciary, mere errors of law or simple abuses of judicial discretion should not amount to judicial misconduct); *In re Comm'n on Jud. Tenure and Disc.*, 916 A.2d 746 (R.I. 2007) ("To safeguard the independence of our judiciary, we take this opportunity to recognize that at times judges err."); Jeffrey M. Shaman, *Judicial Ethics*, 2 Geo. J. Legal Ethics 1 (1988) ("the disciplinary process should not be used as a substitute for appeal."). *See also* Cynthia Gray, *The Line Between Legal Error and Judicial Misconduct: Balancing Judicial Independence and Accountability*, 32 Hofstra L. Rev. 1245 (2004).

There can be disagreement on what are "errors of judgment or errors of law" versus judicial misconduct. *In re Tucker*, 501 S.E.2d 67 (N.C. 1998). *See Matter of Hart*, 577 A.2d 351 (Me. 1990) ("the Rules governing judicial misconduct confer upon the Committee the authority to prosecute only those instances of judicial misconduct that exceed in seriousness the mistakes and frailties of the ordinary judge"). For a critique of this case, *see* Harold T. Kelly, Jr., Note, *Hart Failure: The Supreme Judicial Court's Interpretation of Nonjudicial Demeanor*, 44 Me. L. Rev. 175 (1992) (discussing rules governing judicial demeanor and criticizing decision in *Hart*, that judge's 100-minute berating of attorney "may have resulted in discourtesy or unfairness" but did not rise to the level of seriousness warranting sanction). In *Jud. Inquiry & Review Comm'n v. Taylor*, 685 S.E.2d 51 (Va. 2009), a divided court determined that the judge engaged in misconduct by threatening a juvenile's right to appeal detention and denial of bail; the dissent believed that the judge's conduct was an unknowing mistake of law not appropriate for disciplinary censure. *See also Jud. Inquiry & Rev. Comm'n of Va. v. Peatross*, 611 S.E.2d 392 (Va. 2005) (judge's conduct involving courtroom interaction with attorneys and ex parte communications with judicial superiors was not violative of rules); *W. Va. Jud. Inquiry Comm'n v. Dostert*, 271 S.E.2d 427 (W. Va. 1980) (judge's error of judgment, absent proof of improper motive, is not basis for discipline).

Decisions that fall into the category of mere legal error include those made pursuant to a statute that was unclear or ambiguously worded, *People ex rel.*

Harrod v. Ill. Cts. Comm'n, 372 N.E.2d 53 (Ill. 1977); *In re Quirk*, 705 So. 2d 172 (La. 1997); *In re Benoit*, 487 A.2d 1158 (Me. 1985); Ariz. Sup. Ct. Jud. Ethics Adv. Comm. Op. No. 92-10 (1992) (advising that there is no misconduct in an honest difference of opinion over what constitutes "good cause," substantial compliance," or "excusable neglect"), and those involving a situation or issue of first impression. *See, e.g., In re Curda*, 49 P.3d 255 (Alaska 2002) (no misconduct where judge conducted ex parte contempt hearing and confined intoxicated witness in criminal trial without notice and a hearing because judge was motivated by good faith and was facing a unique situation for which there was no legal template); *Miss. Comm'n on Jud. Performance v. Martin*, 921 So. 2d 1258 (Miss. 2005) (justice court judge's error in denying bail in violation of state constitutional provision, under which only county judges and circuit judges had authority to deny bail, did not violate Code where judge identified several statutes, which led to her confusion and error; she honestly believed that she had authority to deny bond, and she testified that issue was not addressed in training or judicial seminars); but see *Miss. Comm'n on Jud. Performance v. Britton*, 936 So. 2d 898 (Miss. 2006) (disciplining judge who set aside default judgment in violation of statute; court stated that there is a difference between error made in complex legal analysis necessary to reconcile statutes as seen in *Martin* and a failure to learn even the basic requirements of the Code of Judicial Conduct and the court's rules).

Additionally, some cases fall into the category of legal error when the judge acts in good faith but exercises poor judgment. *See, e.g., In re Thomson*, 494 A.2d 1022 (N.J. 1985) (due to aberrational facts of the case, a judge did not commit misconduct when he failed to advise a defendant of his rights, to swear in the witnesses, and to inform the defendant of the reasons for his sentence).

In other instances, however, legal error can raise questions about a judge's fitness for office, particularly if the error is egregious (*see, e.g., In re Inquiry Concerning a Judge Renfer*, 493 S.E.2d 434 (N.C. 1997) (judge entered guilty pleas for two defendants who intended to plead not guilty)) or motivated by bad faith (*see, e.g., In re Duckman*, 699 N.E.2d 872 (N.Y. 1998) (judge removed from office for misconduct, including dismissing cases in willful disregard of the law, abusing power of office, and injudicious behavior)).

The line between "mere error" and judicial misconduct is also frequently crossed when isolated improper judicial decisions, any one of which could be corrected on appeal, begin to display a pattern of overreaching or abuse of power. *In re Keith*, 3 Ill. Cts. Comm'n 39 (1994) ("Where . . . the conduct of a judge in matters before him, whether they be contempt proceedings or other judicial matters, demonstrate that going beyond mere error, the judge is brazenly and outrageously demonstrating a pattern of violation of the canons of judicial conduct, a case has been presented, which demands the imposition of sanctions against the judge."). *In re Curda*, 49 P.3d 255 (Alaska 2002) (legal error in conducting ex parte contempt hearings and confining intoxicated witnesses did not constitute violation of Code of Judicial Conduct; court noted that legal errors were neither willful nor part of a pattern of misconduct, therefore did not constitute ethical misconduct); *In re Elloie*, 921 So. 2d 882 (La. 2006) (judge's legal error in failing to hold contradictory hearings prior to granting motions to expunge felony arrests and convictions rose to level of judicial misconduct; judge had a pattern or practice of legal error); *Miss. Comm'n on Jud. Performance v. Justice Ct. Judge T.T.*, 922 So. 2d 781 (Miss. 2006) (court found that mistake was latest in emerging pattern of legal errors); *In re Walsh*, 587 S.E.2d 356 (S.C. 2003) (judge's conduct, based on his history of intemperate behavior in the courtroom, his failure to modify his behavior after previous letters of caution, and his failure to abide by an administrative order of the Chief Justice to relieve certain defendants making demands for a jury trial from having to appear at the originally scheduled bench trial); *In re Michels*, 75 P.3d 950 (Wash. 2003) (commission found 12 cases in a two-and-half-year period in which judge deprived defendants of their constitutional rights by acting as both judge and defense counsel, and eight instances where he failed to use proper guilty plea forms); *In re Hammermaster*, 985 P.2d 924 (Wash. 1999) ("While we recognize that legal error is usually a matter for appeal and does not generally trigger judicial discipline, a repeated pattern of failing to protect a defendant's constitutional rights can constitute misconduct.").

In some instances, courts have found that a repeated pattern of legal error calls for a judge's removal from office. *See, e.g., In re Yengo*, 371 A.2d 41 (N.J. 1977) (judge removed for persistent misconduct in judicial performance); *In re Tripp*, (N.Y. Comm'n on Jud. Conduct, 2010) (judge removed from office for repeatedly denying litigants constitutional rights to be heard and to have appointed counsel). In other cases, a judge has been given a lesser penalty, such as censure or suspension, *see, e.g., In re Hammermaster*, 985 P.2d 924 (Wash. 1999) (judge censured and suspended for engaging in a pattern of threatening to impose sentences outside his lawful authority) and in some instances, has been ordered to participate in remedial programs. Charles Gardner Geyh, James J. Alfini, Steven Lubet, & Jeffrey M. Shaman, *Judicial Conduct and Ethics*, § 2.02 at 2–8 (5th ed. 2013).

Another factor to consider in distinguishing legal error from misconduct is the availability of appeal, with some courts holding that discipline is unnecessary when an error, particularly one that is not flagrant or part of a pattern, can be corrected on appeal. Charles Gardner Geyh, James J. Alfini, Steven Lubet, & Jeffrey M. Shaman, *Judicial Conduct and Ethics*, § 2.02 at 2–10 (5th ed. 2013). *See, e.g., In re Thomson*, 494 A.2d 1022 (N.J. 1985) (in finding that judge's failure to advise criminal defendant of his constitutional right to counsel, to swear in witnesses, and to inform defendant of reasons for his sentence do not constitute judicial misconduct, court noted that this was a single incident of misconduct in judge's long career and that defendant could appeal judge's rulings).

Some courts, however, have held that even if a judicial decision constitutes legal error subject to appeal, it may still be grounds for discipline under the Code of Judicial Conduct. *See, e.g., Oberholzer v. Comm'n on Judicial Performance*, 975 P.2d 663 (Cal. 1999) ("legal error does not preclude a finding of misconduct"); *People ex rel. Harrod v. Ill Cts. Comm'n*, 372 N.E.2d 53 (Ill. 1978) ("Although all misconduct arising during the course of a judicial proceeding may be the subject of an appeal, an individual defendant's vindication of personal rights does not necessarily protect the public from a judge who repeatedly and grossly abuses his judicial power."); *In re King*, 568 N.E.2d 588 (Mass. 1991) (judges are generally immune from sanctions based solely on appealable errors of law or abuse of discretion; however, sanctions are appropriate for judges who utterly disregard law and establish rules of practice in face of contrary orders); *In re Lowery*, 999 S.W.2d 639 (Tex. Rev. Trib. 1998) ("[L]egal error and judicial misconduct are not mutually exclusive; a judge is not immune from discipline merely because the judge's conduct also constitutes judicial error.").

Different Standards

Different standards have been used in evaluating whether erroneous decisions are simply appealable legal error or whether they cross over the line into ethical misconduct. The Maine Supreme Court uses an objective standard and asks whether a "reasonably prudent and competent judge would consider that conduct obviously and seriously wrong in all the circumstances." *In re Benoit*, 487 A.2d 1158, 1163 (Me. 1985); *see also In re DiLeo*, 83 A.3d 11 (N.J. 2014) (New Jersey adopting the Maine objective standard plus "the error must be 'made contrary to clear and determined law about which there is no confusion or question as to its interpretation,' and that the error must be 'egregious, made in bad faith, or made as part of a pattern or practice of legal error'"). Another standard draws on a set of criteria developed by Professor Jeffrey Shaman. Under this standard, a judge can be disciplined for legal error if that error is egregious, if it is motivated by bad faith or if it is part of a pattern of continuing error. Jeffrey M. Shaman, *Judicial Ethics*, 2 Geo. J. Legal Ethics 1, 8 (1988). *See also* Charles Gardner Geyh, James J. Alfini, Steven Lubet, & Jeffrey M. Shaman, *Judicial Conduct and Ethics*, § 2.02 at 2–7 (5th ed. 2013); *see, e.g., In re Jud. Comm'n on Tenure and Disc.*, 916 A.2d 746 (R.I. 2007) (legal error may amount to misconduct if it is repeated, motivated by bad faith, accompanied by intemperate or abusive conduct, or irremediable by appeal); *In re Blackman*, JDDC 09-345 and 10-361 (Ark. Jud. Disc. & Disability Comm'n 2014) (Arkansas adds the question of whether there is an appellate remedy). Louisiana has attempted to synthesize the Maine approach with Professor Shaman's factors, and has decided that a ruling can be misconduct if it is "made contrary to clear and determined law about which there is no confusion or question as to its interpretation and where this legal error was egregious, made in bad faith, or part of a pattern or practice of error." *In re Quirk*, 705 So. 2d 172, 181 (La. 1997). California looks to whether, in addition to legal error, the judge's conduct "reflected bad faith, bias, abuse of authority, disregard for fundamental rights, intentional disregard of the law, or any purpose other than the faithful discharge of judicial duty." *Oberholzer v. Comm'n on Jud. Performance*, 975 P.2d 663 (Cal. 1999).

Ignorance of the Law Not an Excuse

The fact that a judge makes a mistake out of ignorance does not necessarily insulate him or her from discipline if the error results in prejudice to the administration of justice. *In re Quirk*, 705 So. 2d 172 (La. 1997) (collecting cases from various jurisdictions on legal error as grounds for judicial misconduct; announcing standard that misconduct occurs when "a legal ruling [is] made contrary to clear and determined law about which there is no confusion or question as to its interpretation and where this legal error was egregious, made in bad faith, or made as part of a pattern or practice of legal error"); *Miss. Comm'n on Jud. Performance v. Boykin*, 763 So. 2d 872 (Miss. 2000) (judge publicly reprimanded for ticket-fixing and holding ex parte communications with defendants; court stated, "misconduct does not have to be imbedded in any form of bad behavior. Negligence, ignorance, and incompetence are sufficient for a judge to behave in a manner prejudicial to the administration of justice which brings the judicial office into disrepute"); *accord Miss. Comm'n on Jud. Performance v. Lewis*, 830 So. 2d 1138 (Miss. 2002) (judge who improperly ordered forfeit of handgun should have known that his actions were not legal); *Miss. Commn. on Jud. Performance v. Neal*, 774 So. 2d 414 (Miss. 2000) (judge issued fines and handed down sentences in excess of his statutory authority; court stated, "mere negligence or ignorance of the law can constitute behavior prejudicial to the administration of justice."); *but see Miss. Comm'n on Jud. Performance v. Martin*, 921 So. 2d 1258 (Miss. 2006) (justice court judge's error in denying bail in violation of state constitutional provision under which only county judges and circuit judges had authority to deny bail did not violate Code where judge identified several statutes, which led to her confusion and error; she honestly believed that she had authority to deny bond, and she testified that issue was not addressed in training or judicial seminars).

Denial of Constitutional Rights

Judges must know the limits that the Constitution places on their exercise of authority if they are to "uphold and apply the law." One of the most serious violations of Rule 2.2 occurs when judges deprive parties or lawyers before the court of one or more of their constitutional rights. *See, e.g., Miss. Comm'n on Jud. Performance v. Thompson*, 169 So. 3d 857, 869 (Miss. 2015) (judge deprived drug court participants of due process rights when he "signed orders of contempt without the person being properly notified" and held contempt hearings without giving participants adequate time to secure counsel and present evidence); *In re Littlejohn*, 62 So. 3d 968 (Miss. 2011) (judge violated lawyer's First Amendment right to free speech for finding lawyer in contempt because lawyer did not recite the Pledge of Allegiance); *In re Santoya* (Tex. Comm'n on Jud. Conduct 2006) (prior to commencement of trial, justice of the peace did not advise defendant of her constitutional rights, including her right to counsel, right to remain silent, and right to a jury trial).

Right to Notice and Hearing

A judge may violate Rule 2.2 by holding a hearing in a case without giving notice of the hearing to a party or the party's lawyer. *See, e.g., Inquiry Concerning Miller*, 644 So. 2d 75 (Fla. 1994) (finding a violation of several Code provision when a judge held a hearing in a child custody case and failed to give the mother notice of the hearing until after it began); *In re Newberry County Mag. English*, 625 S.E.2d 919 (S.C. 2006) (magistrate's misconduct included convicting defendant of DUI in his absence when defendant's attorney had not been notified of the hearing).

A judge may also violate Rule 2.2 by issuing an order that affects an individual's rights without holding a hearing. For instance, a judge was removed from office for ordering a warrantless search of a party's home without first holding an evidentiary hearing to determine if probable cause existed or if the defendant was an immediate threat to others. *In re Inquiry Concerning a Judge (Hammill)*, 566 S.E.2d 310 (Ga. 2002). *See also In re Colby*, 629 So. 2d 120 (Fla. 1993) (judge reprimanded for convicting defendants without a plea or trial when defendants failed to appear); *Miss. Comm'n on Jud. Performance v. Wells*, 794 So. 2d 1030 (Miss. 2001) (judge reprimanded for finding a defendant guilty of disturbing the peace and simple assault based solely on the affidavits, without affording the defendant the opportunity to defend herself); *In re Dash*, 564 S.E.2d 672 (S.C. 2002) (judge's conduct in entering directed verdict of guilty without giving defendant opportunity to present evidence warranted public reprimand); *In re Baliles*, B12-5030 (Tenn. Bd. of Jud. Conduct 2013) (judge reprimanded for altering child's custody without notice or hearing); *In re Saldana*, CJC no. 11-471-DI (Tex. Comm'n on Jud. Conduct 2013) (judge admonished for issuing writ of attachment on child without notice to parent).

Other possible violations of Rule 2.2 include imposing a penalty on a defendant who wants to exercise his or her right to a hearing. *In re Cox*, 680 N.E.2d 528

(Ind. 1997) (judge added penalty against defendant for exercising her right to jury trial and forced another defendant to choose between proceeding involuntarily without counsel and facing contempt charges); *Disc. Counsel v. O'Neill*, 815 N.E.2d 286 (Ohio 2004) (judge threatened to revoke, or actually revoked, defendants' bonds because they wanted to exercise their rights to refuse an offered plea and go to trial or ordered that a party be incarcerated without making any finding regarding guilt or innocence).

In one particularly egregious case, a judge ordered a juvenile defendant sent to a correctional facility pending his trial, which was six weeks away, even though the State had not requested his incarceration. The juvenile spent a week in the facility before he was released on a habeas corpus petition. *In re Benoit*, 487 A.2d 1158, 1167 (Me. 1985) ("[The judge's] order detaining a juvenile for a period of nearly six weeks, before the boy had the assistance of counsel and without the court's taking any evidence, ignored the most basic liberties and procedural requirements of law."). *See also Miss. Comm'n on Jud. Performance v. Fletcher*, 686 So. 2d 1075 (Miss. 1996) (sending defendant to jail for three months and 29 days without notice or a hearing); *In re Roeder* (Cal. Comm'n on Jud. Performance 2003) (judge maintained a practice of stating, for the record, that defendants had waived their rights to have a speedy preliminary examination without obtaining the defendants' personal waivers of these rights, as required by law). A judge may also violate Rule 2.2 by threatening to put a defendant in jail if the defendant refuses to waive his or her right to a jury trial. *See In re Hathaway*, 630 N.W.2d 850 (Mich. 2001).

Alternatively, a judge may violate Rule 2.2 by dismissing criminal charges without giving the prosecution or the arresting officer, as opposed to the defendant, notice and an opportunity to be heard. *See, e.g., In re Hathaway*, 630 N.W.2d 850 (Mich. 2001) (judge conducted arraignment in absence of prosecu tor); *In re Conduct of Ginsberg*, 690 N.W.2d 539 (Minn. 2004) (judge dismissed charges in three criminal cases without hearing from the prosecution); *In re* Hartsfield, 722 N.E.2d 496 (N.C. 2012) (judge suspended in part for dismissing traffic tickets for friends and acquaintances without hearings); *In re Hearn*, 515 So. 2d 1225 (Miss. 1987); *In re Duckman*, 699 N.E.2d 872 (N.Y. 1998) (judge removed from office for, among other things, disregarding statutory requirements in dismissing charges).

Deprivation of Liberty

A judge's decision to sentence a defendant to jail may be grounds for discipline under Rule 2.2 if the incarceration violates either a state or federal constitutional provision prohibiting "cruel and unusual punishment," *In re Markle*, 328 S.E.2d 157 (W. Va. 1984) (judge incarcerated an alcoholic for public intoxication in violation of state constitution and state statute), or the guarantee against deprivation of liberty without due process of law. *See, e.g., In re Inquiry Concerning a Judge (Vaughn)*, 462 S.E.2d 728 (Ga. 1995) (judge incarcerated misdemeanor defendants pending appeal instead of granting appeal bonds as required by state law); *In re Benoit*, 487 A.2d 1158 (Me. 1985) (judge incarcerated a defendant in a civil traffic offense case for 35 days without respecting safeguards provided by state and federal constitutions).

Guilty Pleas

The Constitution requires judges to ensure that defendants who enter into guilty pleas waive their rights knowingly, voluntarily, and intelligently. *Boykin v. Alabama*, 395 U.S. 238 (1969). A judge can deprive a defendant of his or her constitutional rights, in violation of Rule 2.2, by accepting a guilty plea without ensuring that the defendant knew either the nature of the charges pending against him or her or the maximum and minimum penalties that could be imposed. *See, e.g., In re Hammermaster*, 985 P.2d 924 (Wash. 1999); *In re Quezada*, 13-210 (Ariz. Comm'n on Jud. Conduct 2013) (judge reprimanded for pattern of accepting guilty pleas without securing proper waiver of rights); *In re Michels*, 2002 WL 1591852 (Wash. Comm'n on Jud. Conduct 2002) (judge violated provision by accepting guilty pleas using a plea statement form that did not advise defendants of their constitutional rights).

Denial of Right to Counsel

A judge may violate Rule 2.2 by infringing upon a defendant's constitutional right to counsel. Judges have violated this right by completely failing to inform defendants that they have a right to counsel (*see, e.g., In re Prince*, 2013 WL 6925099 (N.Y. Comm'n on Jud. Conduct 2013) (judge admonished for ignoring ethical obligation to advise domestic violence defendant that he has a right to counsel); *In re Bauer*, 818 N.E.2d 1113 (N.Y. 2004) (judge censured despite argument that advising defendants of rights in some cases "was unnecessary because from their prior experiences, defendants knew their rights" and in others, because they "were not alert enough to understand the advice."); *Off. of Disc. Counsel v. Karto*, 760 N.E.2d 412 (Ohio 2002); *In re Pauley*, 318 S.E.2d 418 (W. Va. 1984)); by trivializing the right to counsel in the process of informing defendants of it (*In re Bozarth*, 604 A.2d 100 (N.J. 1992) ("They make me do it. I know you don't want one [an attorney], you know you don't want one, but I have to go through this and waste your time anyhow.")); by demanding that a defendant enter a guilty plea without his or her lawyer being present (*In re Inquiry Concerning a Judge (Vaughn)*, 462 S.E.2d 728 (Ga. 1995)); and by failing to immediately respond to a request for counsel (*In re Colglazier*, 06-090 (Ariz. Comm'n on Jud. Conduct, 2006)).

Another way judges have infringed on the right to counsel is by threatening defendants with more severe sentences (*In re Damron*, 487 So. 2d 1 (Fla. 1986);

In re Comm'n on Jud. Tenure and Disc., 916 A.2d 746 (R.I. 2007)) or with contempt if they insist on their right to be represented by an attorney, and by following through on those threats and imposing higher sentences on defendants who were convicted after they insisted on having an attorney represent them (*In re Cox*, 680 N.E.2d 528 (Ind. 1997) (judge added penalty against defendant for exercising her right to jury trial and forced another defendant to choose between proceeding involuntarily without counsel and facing contempt charges)).

Rulings and Orders in Excess of Authority

In their adjudicative duties, judges must comply not only with the constitution, but also with a myriad of other statutes, rules, and regulations. Failure to comply with these provisions can also be a violation of Rule 2.2's requirement that judges "uphold and apply" the law.

Arrest Warrants

Judges wield considerable authority in their ability to issue arrest warrants. However, failing to follow proper procedures when issuing arrest warrants may result in a violation of Rule 2.2. *See, e.g., In re Van Hook*, 13-306 (Ark. Jud. Disc. & Disability Comm'n 2015) (judge censured for sua sponte issuing arrest warrants in four cases); *In re Sloop*, 946 So. 2d 1046 (Fla. 2006) (removal from office was appropriate sanction for county judge who engaged in judicial misconduct by callously failing to seek prompt release of 11 citizens whom he had ordered arrested after they were directed to the wrong courtroom for traffic citation proceedings); *In re Inquiry Concerning a Judge (Vaughn)*, 462 S.E.2d 728 (Ga. 1995) (judge issued arrest warrant for defendant's failure to appear even though defendant was in the courtroom the entire day); *In re Just. of the Peace Alfonso*, 957 So. 2d 121 (La. 2007) (justice of the peace suspended for issuing arrest warrant against neighbor without probable cause); *In re Fuselier*, 837 So. 2d 1257 (La. 2003) (judge signed arrest warrants in worthless check cases supported by probable cause affidavits that contained merchants' facsimile signatures applied by court personnel); *In re Bailey*, 541 So. 2d 1036 (Miss. 1989) (judge issued arrest warrant based on defendant's alleged contempt of court for failure to pay a civil fine); *In re Bozarth*, 604 A.2d 100 (N.J. 1992) (judge issued bench warrant for the arrest of a defendant who arrived in court 15 minutes late); *In re Sims*, 462 N.E.2d 370 (N.Y. 1984) (Canon mentioned in disciplining judge for issuing an arrest warrant when her son was the complainant); *In re Eplin*, 410 S.E.2d 273 (W. Va. 1991) (judge violated Canon by signing blank re-arrest warrants and jail commitment release forms, and using or allowing the use of pre-signed blank forms to secure the commitment, release, or re-arrest of defendants); *In re Crislip*, 391 S.E.2d 84 (W. Va. 1990) (judge violated Canon by asking sheriff's office to return arrest warrant without executing it). *See also*

Miss. Comm'n on Jud. Performance v. Vess, 692 So. 2d 80 (Miss. 1997) (judge followed proper procedures in issuing arrest warrant, but acted improperly by subsequently hearing the case for which he issued warrant).

Judges may also be held accountable under Rule 2.2 when they are required to issue arrest warrants but fail to do so because the defendant was either a police officer (*In re Hall*, 356 S.E.2d 21 (W. Va. 1987)), a former client, (*In re Feeney*, 1987 WL 383091 (N.Y. Comm'n on Jud. Conduct 1987)), or a personal acquaintance, (*In re Wilder*, 516 S.E.2d 927 (S.C. 1999)).

Issuing Subpoenas

A judge may be disciplined for issuing a subpoena without authority to do so. *See, e.g., In re Darlington County Mag. Thomas*, 642 S.E.2d 736 (S.C. 2007) (60-day suspension was appropriate sanction for county magistrate who issued subpoena in favor of his son-in-law, who was involved in a child support proceeding, when judge knew, or should have known, that party to whom he issued subpoena was not bound by it).

Opposing a Motion to Recuse

In *In re Mullin*, 15-0002 (Tex. Special Ct. of Rev. 2015), a retired judge was disciplined for filing a motion to reconsider an order removing the judge from a matter. The Special Court of Review found that Mullin's motion was "wholly improper and without authority" because under Texas law, when a party files a motion to recuse a judge, the judge "is not a party to the motion, and thus is not represented at the recusal hearing nor allowed an opportunity to appear and defend against the motion." *Id.* The Special Court of Review rejected Mullin's argument that she had a due process right to notice of the recusal motion and hearing.

Setting Bail

State laws governing the circumstances and requirements for setting bail vary greatly, and there are a number of different ways that judges can exceed their authority in setting bail. For instance, a judge was disciplined for imposing bail in a civil traffic offense. *In re Benoit*, 487 A.2d 1158 (Me. 1985) ("The clearly improper use of bail as a weapon of the State in a civil matter, rather than as a mechanism to secure a defendant's liberty, thus had the effect of directly imposing a 35-day jail sentence for a civil traffic violation. This was an outrageous result."). Judges have also been disciplined for setting bail in other matters where there were charges for which imprisonment was not a legally permitted penalty (*see In re Bauer*, 818 N.E.2d 1113 (N.Y. 2004) (judge removed for misconduct including setting excessive bail amounts for defendants charged with petty crimes or violations)) and for an amount that exceeds the amount permitted by statute (*see Miss. Comm'n on Jud. Performance v. Sanders*, 749 So. 2d 1062 (Miss. 1999)).

Judges have been disciplined for failing to set bail (*see In re La Belle*, 591 N.E.2d 1156 (N.Y. 1992) (imposing discipline on a judge who committed non-felony defendants to jail without setting bail in violation of a state statute requiring either release on recognizance or bail in offenses below "felony grade.")) and for setting bail without authority to do so (*see, e.g., In re Davis*, 645 S.E.2d 243 (S.C. 2007) (off-duty magistrate's decision to set bond for release of law enforcement officer's friend warranted six-month suspension; magistrate was not on call that evening, did not seek permission to conduct the special bond hearing at his home, failed to ascertain whether other inmates were awaiting bond hearings, did not conduct bond hearings for any other inmates, and failed to inform the Chief Magistrate of the special bond hearing); *Miss. Comm'n on Jud. Performance v. Martin*, 921 So. 2d 1258 (Miss. 2005) (justice court judge's error in denying bail in violation of state constitutional provision under which only county judges and circuit judges had authority to deny bail did not violate Code where judge identified several statutes, which led to her confusion and error; she honestly believed that she had authority to deny bond, and she testified that issue was not addressed in training or judicial seminars)).

However, it is not misconduct for a judge to refuse to permit a bail bondsman to sign a bond where the bail bondsman was not certified to act in that court and had not presented the documentation that would permit the judge to authorize him. *In re Eplin*, 411 S.E.2d 862 (W. Va. 1991) (judge was not responsible rejecting bail bondsman where judge had never received an updated list authorizing the bail bondsman's bonding company).

Judges may also violate Rule 2.2 by using the money that was deposited as bail to satisfy a legal obligation that the defendant owed, even one arising from another case that was not the case for which bail had been posted. *See In re King*, 568 N.E.2d 588 (Mass. 1991) ("The judge's policies were in violation of the intent of [Massachusetts statutes], which recognize a surety's right to post cash bail and require that it be returned in cases where the defendant does not default.").

Plea Bargains

A judge may violate Rule 2.2 by participating in, or attempting to participate in, the process of negotiating a plea in a criminal case. *See, e.g., In re Cox*, 553 A.2d 1255 (Me. 1989) (judicial participation "in the specifics of a plea negotiation . . . runs afoul of the fundamental values set forth in these Canons."); *People v. Ellis*, 658 N.W.2d 142 (Mich. 2003) ("A decision to drop or plea bargain charges is one that lies with one or both of the parties, not the court."); *Jud. Inquiry & Rev. Bd. v. Fink*, 532 A.2d 358 (Pa. 1987) (ruling that a judge acted improperly and in violation of a state criminal procedural rule in negotiating a plea without the knowledge of the district attorney). *See generally* Jenia Iontcheva Turner,

Judicial Participation in Plea Negotiations: A Comparative View, 54 Am. J. Comp. L. 199 (2006). A judge may also violate Rule 2.2 by dismissing charges or acquitting a criminal defendant on charges that are supported by the evidence presented by the prosecutor in exchange for the defendant's waiver of his right to a jury trial. *People v. Ellis*, 658 N.W.2d 142 (Mich. 2003).

Beyond direct participation in the plea negotiations, judges may also violate Rule 2.2 by directly or indirectly using the power of their office to coerce a defendant to enter a guilty plea. *In re Keith*, 3 Ill. Cts. Comm'n 39 (1994); *see, e.g., In re Campbell*, 2 Ill. Cts. Comm'n 113, 123 (1988) (judge impaneled jury when neither the defendant, defense counsel, nor prosecutor were in the courtroom; as a result, the panel included both a police officer and the defendant's former mother-in-law, and the defendant pleaded guilty).

A Rule 2.2 violation may also result when a judge conducts a criminal proceeding and accepts guilty pleas or dismisses charges when no prosecutor is present. *In re Fuselier*, 837 So. 2d 1257 (La. 2003) (judge conducted arraignments and accepted guilty pleas in criminal cases when no prosecutor was present); *In re Jefferson*, 753 So. 2d 181 (La. 2000) (judge banned city prosecutor from courtroom until prosecutor apologized for wrongs judge perceived were committed against him and judge dismissed 41 criminal cases due to lack of prosecutor).

Pursuant to the United States Constitution and most states' laws, judges cannot accept a plea bargain unless the defendant has been informed of his or her rights and has knowingly and voluntarily waived those rights. Failing to adhere to these requirements may constitute misconduct (*see, e.g., In re Markey*, 696 N.E.2d 523 (Mass. 1998) (judge violated Canon by failing to engage in plea colloquies with defendants who were pleading guilty or nolo contendere or admitting to sufficient facts to permit a finding of guilt)), even if the judge's decision to accept the plea is not reversed on appeal (*In re Hammermaster*, 985 P.2d 924 (Wash. 1999) (judge engaged in a pattern and practice of accepting guilty pleas in a manner that denied defendant's basic due process rights and judge's argument that he cannot be disciplined because his decisions have not been overturned or appealed is unpersuasive)).

Other infractions of this rule may occur when judges permit defendants to plead to reduced charges in spite of a state statute that forbids such pleas for the conduct charged (*Miss. Comm'n on Jud. Performance v. Dodds*, 680 So. 2d 180 (Miss. 1996) (judge let defendant with a blood alcohol content of .14 percent charged with DUI to plead to lesser charges of possession of beer and whiskey in spite of a state law that prohibited reducing charges for defendants whose blood alcohol level was higher than .10 percent)), or when judges impose additional requirements on defendants as a condition to accepting a guilty plea (*In re Vonderheide*, 532 N.E.2d 1252 (N.Y. 1988) (it was improper for a judge to condition acceptance of a guilty plea from a teenager on the teenager's signing a statement implicating a third person in an alleged crime)).

Contempt

The law on contempt has often been described as "murky," and states differ considerably in their interpretations of contumacious behavior. D.D. Wozniak and Cynthia L. Lehr, *Dealing with a Double-Edged Sword: A Practical Guide to Contempt Law in Minnesota*, 18 Wm. Mitchell. L. Rev. 7, 8 (1992). However, most jurisdictions agree that criminal contempt differs from civil contempt in that the former attempts to vindicate the authority of the court when someone has been disrespectful, while the latter deals only with refusal to obey a court's order. Further, most jurisdictions agree that direct contempt differs from indirect contempt in that the former can be imposed summarily without notice and a hearing, while the latter requires the contemnor to be given some basic due process protection.

Judges have the right to hold someone in contempt for an affront to the authority and dignity of the court, and typically, the use of the contempt power will not violate the Model Code of Judicial Conduct. *See, e.g., In re Buford*, 577 S.W.2d 809 (Mo. 1979). However, an abuse of the contempt power can cross over the line into judicial misconduct when judges treat an indirect contempt as a direct contempt and summarily impose contempt for conduct that was not committed in the immediate presence of the court. *In re Bell*, 894 S.W.2d 119 (Tex. Spec. Rev. Ct. 1995) (judge held person in contempt for statement made in the hallway to the judge when court was not in session).

Another way that judges commit an ethical violation in their use of the contempt power is by inappropriately labeling conduct as criminal contempt and using their contempt power to punish someone because they are displeased with that person rather than because that person threatened the authority of the court. *Miss. Comm'n on Judicial Performance v. Walker*, 565 So. 2d 1117 (Miss. 1990) (judge reprimanded for holding party in contempt for statements directed to the judge personally and not directed at the authority of the court or the judicial system); *In the Matter of Singer*, (N.Y. Comm'n on Jud. Conduct 2009) (judge admonished, in part, for holding domestic violence victim's attorney in contempt for declining judge's order to reveal location of shelter, contrary to law); *Jud. Inquiry & Rev. Bd. v. Fink*, 532 A.2d 358 (Pa. 1987) ("holding an attorney in criminal contempt of court because [a judge] is displeased with the attorney . . . 'created a gross appearance of impropriety, contravened his obligation to be faithful to the law, and has undermined public confidence in the judiciary.'"). *See generally* Annotation, *Abuse or Misuse of Contempt Power as Grounds for Removal or Discipline of Judge*, 76 A.L.R. 4th 76 (1990); *see also* Dennis A. Rendleman, *The Case of the Dirty T-Shirt: A Proposed Amendment to the*

Model Code of Judicial Conduct on the Exercise of the Power of Contempt, 15 No. 4 Prof. Law. 18 (2005).

In addition to imposing contempt for conduct that does not fit the definition of either direct contempt or criminal contempt, judges commit misconduct when they use the contempt power vindictively (*see, e.g.*, *In re Littlejohn*, 62 So. 3d 968 (Miss. 2011) (judge violated lawyer's First Amendment right to free speech for finding lawyer in contempt because lawyer did not recite the Pledge of Allegiance); *In re Keith*, 3 Ill. Cts. Comm'n 3 (1994) (involving several vindictive uses of the contempt power such as jailing a defendant for 96 days after she asked the judge out of turn how long it would take for her case to be called) or to enforce an order they had no authority to make (*see, e.g.*, *In re Stocker*, 608 S.E.2d 865 (S.C. 2005) (judge violated Canon by holding a defendant in contempt of court for failing to adhere to his order to "get a regular job" when he had no authority to make such an order); *Inquiry Concerning McBrien* (Cal. Comm'n on Jud. Performance 2010) (judge abused authority by threatening contempt without issuing order to be obeyed)).

Likewise, Rule 2.2 may be violated by misuse of the contempt power when judges fail to follow the requirements of a contempt statute or constitutional due process requirements. *See, e.g.*, *In re Bennington*, 24 N.E.3d 958 (Ind. 2015) (judge violated contempt statute by not sentencing defendant to a set time in jail for contempt, indicating when defendant would be released, reducing the contempt order to writing, appointing defendant a lawyer before jailing defendant, or informing defendant of his right to appeal the contempt finding); *In re Judge Sassone*, 959 So. 2d 859 (La. 2007) (judge violated statute by refusing to afford the defendant "an opportunity to be heard orally by way of defense or mitigation" before holding him in contempt); *In re Leavitt*, 67987 (Nev. 2015) (judge violated rule when the judge held person in contempt without allowing a timely opportunity to be heard). The rule is also violated when a judge misrepresents the facts on which a contempt order is based (*In re McAllister*, 646 So. 2d 173 (Fla. 1994) (judge removed for misconduct including holding contempt hearing against lawyer for misrepresenting his availability for trial when the judge had been told that he had not done so); *In re Ross*, 428 A.2d 858 (Me. 1981) (judge falsely stated that a contempt hearing had been held when there had been no hearing); or when they try to enforce a contempt order that had been stayed by a higher court. *Jud. Inquiry and Rev. Comm'n v. Lewis*, 568 S.E.2d 687 (Va. 2002) (judge found father in contempt for violating judge's order requiring father to surrender custody of two children to mother, even though judge knew that his order had been stayed)).

Sentencing

A judge may violate Rule 2.2 by imposing or threatening to impose a harsher sentence or fine against a defendant than is permitted by state law. *See, e.g.*, *Miss. Comm'n on Jud. Performance v. Emmanuel*, 688 So. 2d 222 (Miss. 1996) (judge assessed costs in excess of statutory maximum in six criminal cases); *Miss. Comm'n on Jud. Performance v. Fletcher*, 686 So. 2d 1075 (Miss. 1996) (judge sentenced defendant to more jail time than allowed by law); *In re Hammermaster*, 985 P.2d 924 (Wash. 1999) (judge threatened to impose life imprisonment, or indefinite jail sentences, against defendants who had failed to pay fines imposed as part of sentencing obligations, which were penalties outside his lawful authority); *see also In re Walters*, 13-40 (Minn. Bd. on Jud. Standards 2014) (judge reprimanded for violating state rule of criminal procedure requiring court to advise the parties in open court of rejection of plea agreement and then call upon the defendant to affirm or withdraw the plea when sentencing defendant to longer jail term than the agreement).

In other cases, judges have been disciplined for ordering a shorter sentence or lower fine than is permitted by law (*Jud. Inquiry & Rev. Bd. v. Fink*, 532 A.2d 358 (Pa. 1987) (judge imposed sentence of incarceration that was less than the minimum time provided for under the sentencing guidelines); *In re Thoma*, 873 S.W.2d 477 (Tex. Rev. Trib. 1994) (judge violated Canon by granting credit for jail time in excess of time actually served); *In re Crislip*, 391 S.E.2d 84 (W. Va. 1990) (judge imposed less than the minimum fine)); or even no sentence at all. *In re Ross*, 428 A.2d 858 (Me. 1981) (judge violated Canon by continuing sentence on a day-to-day basis for six months when there was no authority to do so).

Rule 2.2 may also be violated when a judge alters or modifies a sentence, regardless of whether the sentence had originally been imposed by that judge or another judge. *See, e.g., Miss. Comm'n on Jud. Performance v. Sanders*, 708 So. 2d 866 (Miss. 1998) (judge reprimanded for suspending sentence of former client and placing second inmate on probation after his conviction and sentence had been affirmed by Court of Appeals); *Miss. Comm'n on Jud. Performance v. Russell*, 691 So. 2d 929 (Miss. 1997) (judge suspended sentences of four defendants when he lacked authority and jurisdiction to do so).

Although judges have been disciplined for imposing harsher or lighter sentences than they were permitted to impose under state law, they have typically not been disciplined for imposing unconventional sentences. *See, e.g., People ex rel. Harrod v. Ill. Cts. Comm'n*, 372 N.E.2d 53 (Ill. 1978) (expunging discipline imposed on judge for sentencing male defendants to get their hair cut, sentencing defendants convicted of illegal transportation of alcohol to pick up discarded bottles and cans alongside the road, and ordering probationers to give their drivers' licenses to the court clerk in exchange for a card identifying them as probationers); *In re Quirk*, 705 So. 2d 172 (La. 1997) (judge's use of church attendance as condition of probation was not judicial misconduct); *In re Richter*, 409 N.Y.S.2d 1013 (N.Y. Ct. Jud. 1977) (ordering defendants to attend church as a condition of probation did not involve judicial impropriety, but judge may not order defendants to contribute to various charities); *but see In re Johnson*, 1 So. 3d 425 (La. 2009) (judge presiding in drug court not authorized to order defendants to pay fines to civic or charitable organizations where the organizations not themselves crime victims); *In re Felsted*, 1990 WL 678957 (Wash. Comm'n on Jud. Conduct 1990) (Canon violated when judge dismissed charges in some cases if defendants made voluntary contributions to law enforcement-related services).

Ticket-Fixing

The predominant, but by no means only, way that judges improperly reduce charges is by ticket-fixing. Since many citizens have their only contact with the courts when they receive a traffic ticket, the high proportion of ticket-fixing cases compared to other types of irregular dismissals is not surprising. It is surprising, however, that the vast majority of disciplinary cases for ticket-fixing cases come from Mississippi. This high concentration does not mean that ticket-fixing only occurs in Mississippi. Some ticket-fixing has probably occurred in every state at one point or another. However, in the realm of judicial discipline, some states charge ticket-fixing as a violation of the state's constitution rather than as a violation of the Code of Judicial Conduct. *See, e.g., In re Diener*, 304 A.2d 587 (Md. 1973) (finding that judges of traffic division violated state constitution by disposing of cases for reasons other than honest appraisal of facts). Moreover, even states that charge ticket-fixing as a Code violation do not necessarily charge it under Rule 2.2 (or prior Section 3B(2)), but rather as a violation of other provisions of the Code. *See, e.g., In re Haddad*, 627 P.2d 221 (Ariz. 1981); *Inquiry Concerning a Judge No. 1035 (Spear)*, 361 S.E.2d 157 (Ga. 1987); *In re Jenkins*, 465 N.W.2d 317 (Mich. 1991); *In re DelRio*, 256 N.W.2d 727 (Mich. 1977); *In re Hardt*, 369 A.2d 5 (N.J. 1977). New York, which has removed dozens of judges for ticket-fixing, has sometimes charged it under the Code of Judicial Conduct, *In re Edwards*, 492 N.E.2d 124 (N.Y. 1986), and sometimes simply concluded that ticket-fixing is serious misconduct, which should be disciplined by removal. *In re Conti*, 516 N.E.2d 1207 (N.Y. 1987).

Mississippi, however, has consistently viewed ticket-fixing as a violation of former Canon 3, as well as a violation of former Canons 1 and 2, and, since it did not adopt the 1990 Code until April 2002, in its ticket-fixing cases, it consistently charged violations of Section 3A(1) and related Canons of the 1972 Code. Judges have typically fixed tickets either by reducing the charges to lesser offenses (*Miss. Comm'n on Jud. Performance v. Jones*, 735 So. 2d 385 (Miss. 1999)) or by dismissing the tickets completely (*Miss. Comm'n on Jud. Performance v. Gordon*, 955 So. 2d 300 (Miss. 2007); *Miss. Comm'n on Jud. Performance v. Chinn*, 611 So. 2d 849 (Miss. 1992)). Ticket-fixing is a violation of the Canons, regardless of whether it is done by the judge (*Miss. Comm'n on Jud. Performance v. Gunn*, 614 So. 2d 387 (Miss. 1993)) or by the judge's clerk at the judge's direction (*Miss. Comm'n on Jud. Performance v. Hopkins*, 590 So. 2d 857 (Miss. 1991)).

It is also a violation regardless of whether the judge does it at someone else's request (*In re Seal*, 585 So. 2d 741 (Miss. 1991)) or because the judge thinks that the ends of justice can be accomplished by some alternate means, such as a lecture (*In re Ross*, 428 A.2d 858 (Me. 1981)).

Other Improper Dismissals

Although traffic cases constitute the vast majority of improper dismissals, one judge was disciplined under this Canon for improperly dismissing other types of lesser criminal and quasi-criminal charges. *In re Hague*, 315 N.W.2d 524 (Mich. 1982) (judge improperly dismissed prostitution cases and cases brought under a gun control ordinance) and another judge was disciplined for dismissing several drug possession charges, in addition to a charge of DUI. *Wilson v. Judicial Retirement and Removal Comm'n*, 673 S.W.2d 426 (Ky. 1984). *See also In re Brown*, 527 S.E.2d 651 (N.C. 2000) (judge removed for misconduct including disposing of DWI charges by convicting defendants of careless and reckless driving, with which they were not charged, and which was not lesser included offense).

Attempting to Obtain Favorable Treatment for Family Members or Friends

A judge may violate Rule 2.2 by trying to obtain favorable treatment for a family member, friend, or other acquaintance. *In re Petrucelli* (Cal. Comm'n on Jud. Performance 2015) (judge censured for calling jail and ordering the "own recognizance" release of friend arrested for spousal abuse); *Miss. Comm'n on Jud. Performance v. Brown*, 918 So. 2d 1247 (Miss. 2005) (judge's attempt to use his position to obtain favorable treatment for, and obstruct prosecution of charges against, his son, who had been charged with assaulting his now ex-wife, constituted conduct that was not faithful to the law, because judge promoted personal gain at expense of law enforcement and court personnel).

Nonfeasance

When judges actively do something wrong, such as entering an order that they do not have authority to enter, they are not upholding and applying the law as required by Rule 2.2. *In re Gormley*, 332 S.W.2d 717 (Ky. 2010) (judge publicly reprimanded for entering order that "no modifications of child support shall be considered until December 31, 2009 for employees of Toyota Motor Manufacturing" upon request of county attorney, based on rumor that Toyota would not be issuing semi-annual bonus). A judge's failure to do something that should be done may constitute nonfeasance in violation of Rule 2.2 because a judge has "an ethical as well as legal obligation to apply the law." Ariz. Sup. Ct. Jud. Ethics Adv. Comm. Op. 92-10 (1992) (judge who regularly and continually fails to enforce rules of procedure violates Code). For example, when judges fail to advise defendants of their constitutional rights (*see, e.g., In re Williams*, 987 S.W.2d 837 (Tenn. 1998) (failure to advise defendant of his right to counsel, right to indictment by a grand jury, or right to subpoena and cross-examine witnesses); *In re Pauley*, 318 S.E.2d 418 (W. Va. 1984) (failure to advise defendant of right to counsel, right to remain silent, or right to a preliminary hearing)), the conduct could be considered nonfeasance since it is a failure to do what is legally required, even though any actions taken in violation of those rights would probably be considered misfeasance.

Another type of nonfeasance occurs when a judge refuses to issue an order that the law dictates should be issued, such as protective orders in domestic abuse cases. *In re Romano*, 1998 WL 543813 (N.Y. Comm'n on Jud. Conduct 1998) (judge's refusal to issue protective orders unless the victim showed extraordinary proof, such as "a turban of bandages" was deemed "negligen[ce] in properly applying the law"); *In re Chase*, 1991 WL 733643 (N.Y. Comm'n on Jud. Conduct 1991) (judge forced complaining witness who was seeking a temporary order of protection to come before him in open court when the law contained no such requirement). Similarly, a judge's failure to execute an appropriate order may be grounds for discipline. *See, e.g., In re Newman*, 858 N.E.2d 632 (Ind. 2006) (judge's failure to execute an appropriate order for inmate's release upon appellate court's remand order and failure to provide proper supervision and instruction to his court reporter, which led inmate to unnecessarily spend over one year incarcerated and one year on supervised parole warranted public reprimand).

Judges may also violate Rule 2.2 when they disregard state laws governing court procedures, such as rules regarding the collecting and reporting of fines and fees received by the court. *See, e.g., Miss. Comm'n on Jud. Performance v. Smith*, 109 So. 3d 95 (2013); *Miss. Comm'n on Jud. Performance v. Coleman*, 553 So. 2d 513 (Miss. 1989); *In re Hearn*, 515 So. 2d 1225 (Miss. 1987); *In re Garner*, 466 So. 2d 884 (Miss. 1985); *In re Sanders*, 564 S.E.2d 670 (S.C. 2002).

Other types of nonfeasance include failing to have a proper record made of court proceedings (*In re Collins*, 524 So. 2d 553 (Miss. 1987); *In re Cieminski*, 270 N.W.2d 321 (N.D. 1978)), failing to conform a judgment to the jury verdict (*In re Hearn*, 515 So. 2d 1225 (Miss. 1987)), failing to require the presentation of appropriate documents before entering an order requested by an attorney who was a family friend (*In re Jacobi*, 715 N.E.2d 873 (Ind. 1999)), and failing to sign records to dispose of cases as required by law (*Miss. Comm'n on Jud. Performance v. Spencer*, 725 So. 2d 171 (Miss. 1998)).

PRO SE LITIGANTS

Comment [4] to Rule 2.2 provides that it is not a violation of the Rule for a judge "to make reasonable accommodations to ensure pro se litigants the opportunity to have their matters fairly heard." State ethics committees have attempted to impose limits on what a judge may do on behalf of a pro se litigant. For instance, a judge may not sua sponte raise the defense of statute of limitations on behalf of pro se defendants because that would bring the court's impartiality into question. Md. Jud. Ethics Op. 2006-01 (2006). However, special circumstances may require the judge to look to the timeliness of a case. Md. Jud. Ethics Op. 2006-05 (2006) (judge may query sua sponte whether a collection action is time barred under the Fair Debt Collection Practices Act because the Act is intended to prevent collection of stale debts from unsophisticated debtors and places on the debtor creditor the affirmative duty to document compliance with the statute of limitation). *See generally* Cynthia Gray, *Reaching Out or Overreaching: Judicial Ethics and Self-Represented Litigants*, 27 Nat'l Admin. L. Judiciary 97 (2007); Jona Goldschmidt, *Judicial Ethics and Assistance to Self-Represented Litigants*, 28 The Justice System Journal 324 (2007).

Rule 2.3 Bias, Prejudice, and Harassment

(A) A judge shall perform the duties of judicial office, including administrative duties, without bias or prejudice.

(B) A judge shall not, in the performance of judicial duties, by words or conduct manifest bias or prejudice, or engage in harassment, including but not limited to bias, prejudice, or harassment based upon race, sex, gender, religion, national origin, ethnicity, disability, age, sexual orientation, marital status, socioeconomic status, or political affiliation, and shall not permit court staff, court officials, or others subject to the judge's direction and control to do so.

(C) A judge shall require lawyers in proceedings before the court to refrain from manifesting bias or prejudice, or engaging in harassment, based upon attributes including but not limited to race, sex, gender, religion, national origin, ethnicity, disability, age, sexual orientation, marital status, socioeconomic status, or political affiliation, against parties, witnesses, lawyers, or others.

(D) The restrictions of paragraphs (B) and (C) do not preclude judges or lawyers from making legitimate reference to the listed factors, or similar factors, when they are relevant to an issue in a proceeding.

Comment

[1] A judge who manifests bias or prejudice in a proceeding impairs the fairness of the proceeding and brings the judiciary into disrepute.

[2] Examples of manifestations of bias or prejudice include, but are not limited to, epithets; slurs; demeaning nicknames; negative stereotyping; attempted humor based upon stereotypes; threatening, intimidating, or hostile acts; suggestions of connections between race, ethnicity, or nationality and crime; and irrelevant references to personal characteristics. Even facial expressions and body language can convey to parties and lawyers in the proceeding, jurors, the media, and others an appearance of bias or prejudice. A judge must avoid conduct that may reasonably be perceived as prejudiced or biased.

[3] Harassment, as referred to in paragraphs (B) and (C), is verbal or physical conduct that denigrates or shows hostility or aversion toward a person on bases such as race, sex, gender, religion, national origin, ethnicity, disability, age, sexual orientation, marital status, socioeconomic status, or political affiliation.

[4] Sexual harassment includes, but is not limited to, sexual advances, requests for sexual favors, and other verbal or physical conduct of a sexual nature that is unwelcome.

1990 CODE COMPARISON

Paragraphs (A) and (B) are taken from former Canon 3B(5) while paragraphs (C) and (D) were formerly in Canon 3B(6). Former Canon 3B(5) required judges to avoid bias and prejudice, but included nothing in the black letter about harassment, which it relegated to a discussion in the Commentary limited to sexual harassment. The Joint Commission to Evaluate the Model Code of Judicial Conduct agreed that harassment was a form of bias or prejudice that the Rules proscribed but wanted to expand it beyond sexual harassment to reach other forms of harassment as well. Therefore, the Commission deleted the term "sexual" from the Commentary in an early draft. Witnesses, however, argued that the proposed change could be construed as deleting sexual harassment from the range of behaviors barred by the Rules, or at least diminishing its significance. The Commission was persuaded both that sexual harassment deserved special mention, given the significance of the problem, and that harassment per se was sufficiently distinct from bias and prejudice to deserve separate mention in the black letter of the Rule. Charles G. Geyh & W. William Hodes, *Reporters' Notes to the Model Code of Judicial Conduct* 29 (2009).

Although the Rule prohibits bias, prejudice, or harassment on any basis, sections (B) and (C) include an illustrative list, to which four new items were added: gender ("sex" is a term of art employed in sex discrimination statutes, but may not capture bias, prejudice, or harassment against transgendered individuals); ethnicity (which the Commission regarded as distinct from national origin; for example, in the case of an Arab-Canadian, discrimination on the basis of Arab ancestry would relate to ethnicity, while discrimination based on Canadian derivation would relate to national origin); marital status (the Commission was made aware of instances in which judges had berated a party for cohabiting or having a child outside of wedlock); and political affiliation (as, for example, when a judge displays animus toward plaintiffs affiliated with a particular political party). To ensure consistency with Title VII case law, the last sentence of Comment [2] includes the term "reasonably" to distinguish the "merely vulgar" from "deeply offensive." *Id.* at 29–30.

When a case before the judge raises issues of bias or prejudice, the judge must be in a position to discuss such issues without fear of violating this rule, for which reason an exception has been created in Rule 2.3(D). *Id.* at 30.

Comments [1] and [2] are taken from the Commentary to former Canon 3B(5), while the first paragraph of Commentary to former Canon 3B(5) was deleted. Comment [3], which is new to the Code, defines harassment and underscores that the prohibition in the black letter includes, but is not limited to, sexual harassment. Comment [4] is also new and elaborates on the meaning of "sexual harassment." *Id.*

Annotation

Introduction

Former Canons 3B(5) and 3B(6), upon which Rule 2.3 is based, were added to the Code in 1990 in order to emphasize the requirements of impartial decision-making and the appearance of fairness in the courtroom. The language of Rule 2.3 requires judges to act without bias and to refrain from engaging in harassment based on race, sex, gender, religion, national origin, ethnicity, disability, age, sexual orientation, marital status, socioeconomic status, or political affiliation. A judge also must not permit court staff, officials, or others subject to the judge's direction and control to do so. This provision is aimed at prohibiting both overt and covert lack of impartiality by judges. Lisa L. Milord, *The Development of the ABA Judicial Code* 17–18 (1992). The Commentary states that a "judge who manifests bias or prejudice in a proceeding impairs the fairness of the proceeding and brings the judiciary into disrepute." Model Code of Judicial Conduct Rule 2.3 cmt. [1].

The Commentary also states that in addition to speech, facial expressions and body language can convey to parties and lawyers in the proceeding, jurors, the media, and others an appearance of bias and prejudice. Model Code of Judicial Conduct Rule 2.3 cmt. [2]. To date, however, judges have been disciplined only for speech and conduct that manifest bias or prejudice and not facial expressions or body language. Since Rule 2.3 is directed only to sitting judges, it cannot constitute an independent violation as to a judicial candidate who is not yet a judge. *See In re Kinsey*, 842 So. 2d 77 (Fla. 2003) (holding that Section 3B(5), on which Rule 2.3 is based, does not apply to judicial candidate's campaign literature asserting that he is committed to the prosecution in criminal cases); *but see*

In re McMillan, 797 So. 2d 560 (Fla. 2001) (holding that judge violated Section 3B(5) when he made explicit campaign promises to favor the state and police in court proceedings).

Judicial candidates might be subject to discipline for their prejudicial speech under Rule 4.1(A)(12), which prohibits a judicial candidate from making "any statement that would reasonably be expected to affect the outcome or impair the fairness of a matter pending or impending in any court." Additionally, Rule 4.1(A)(13) prohibits a judge, in connection with cases, controversies, or issues that are likely to come before the court, from making "pledges, promises or commitments that are inconsistent with the impartial performance of the adjudicative duties of judicial office." *In re Kinsey*, 842 So. 2d 77 (Fla. 2003) (judicial candidate's conduct in running campaign on a platform that stressed her allegiance to police officers, pledging to "help law enforcement by putting criminals where they belong—behind bars," and to "bend over backward" to protect victims, violated Canon prohibiting a candidate from making pledges or promises of conduct). For additional discussion on restrictions on campaign speech, see Canon 4 and accompanying text.

SPEECH THAT INDICATES BIAS

Statements during a court proceeding that indicate that the judge has a preference for or is biased toward or against a party may violate Rule 2.3(A). *See, e.g., In re Osterfeld*, 12-029 (Ariz. Comm'n on Jud. Conduct 2012) (when accepting defendant's plea, judge "suggested that he endorsed" the defendant punching the victim); *In re Giss* (Cal. Comm'n on Jud. Performance, 2011) (judge who, during plea negotiations between counsel, said that "the only thing that would make the defendants plead was for the judge to come out in a white sheet and a pointy white hat, admonished for biased statement); *In re Pollard* (Cal. Comm'n on Jud. Performance 2011) (judge admonished for ethnic stereotyping after uttering, "I'm concerned about the throwing of the rocks and the spitting. I've been doing domestic violence now for 14 years. Usually that is the kind of behavior I see in Middle Eastern clients, but almost—if I read a declaration where they say, 'He spit on me, he threw rocks at me,' almost always it's a Middle Eastern client. If the declaration says, 'He drags me around the house by the hair,' it's almost always a Hispanic client."); *In re Wood*, 720 So. 2d 506 (Fla. 1998) (judge stated, during a hearing, that he was "for the little guy, not for the government"); *In re O'Brien*, 650 A.2d 134 (R.I. 1994) (judge openly criticized the ability of pro se litigants during a trial in which a party was appearing pro se); *In re Henderson*, 343 P.3d 518, 525 (Kan. 2015) (judge "inappropriately mixed his personal views on socio-politcal issues with his role as a judge" when judge wrote email concerning contract adoption lawyer's advocacy for gay adoptions); *In re Fletcher* (Ky. Jud. Conduct Comm'n 2013) (judge reprimanded for biased comments made during sentencing of male teacher who pleaded guilty to 14 counts of sexual offenses perpetrated on 13- and 14-year-old female students, including that defendant "was not blind and only human"); *In re Citta*, 991 A.2d 213 (N.J. 2010) (judge's statements relating to defendant's nationality, inability to speak English, and judge's desire that defendant be returned to his country of origin indicated bias toward immigrant defendant); *In re Fuller*, 798 N.W.2d 408 (N.D. 2011) (judge involuntarily retired—stayed with conditions—for pattern of misconduct that continued throughout tenure on bench including calling city police force "a bunch of racists," referring to juveniles as "peckerheads" and commenting that the legal profession was "better off" before women were admitted to the bar); *In re Gaul*, 936 N.E.2d 28 (Ohio 2010) (judge exhibited prejudice against the defendant when he accused "defendant of unproven acts such as obstruction of justice, kidnapping, and smoking crack," said to prosecutor that he was on the "same team" with the prosecution, and explained his behavior by saying that "sometimes you got to check somebody else into the boards"); *In re Nelson*, 532 S.E.2d 609 (S.C. 2000) (judge made derogatory comments about police department to defendants in criminal cases demonstrating bias against arresting authority); *In re Schildknecht*, CJC 14-1080-DI & 15-0002-DI (Tex. Comm'n on Jud. Conduct 2015) (judge admonished for describing a district attorney as a New York Jew and telling another district attorney that his beard made him look like a Muslim whom she would not hire); *In re Ladenburg*, CJC 7599-F-163 (Wash. Comm'n on Jud. Conduct 2015) (judge reprimanded for requesting Jewish defendant provide court with memorandum and religious justification for wearing fedora in courtroom); *cf. Barrett v. City of Margate*, 743 So. 2d 1160 (Fla. App. 1999) (holding that judge may not assist pro se party to detriment of other party as judge's behavior would be perceived as prejudicial); *but see In re J.D.*, 619 S.E.2d 818 (Ga. App. 2005) (judge did not violate code of judicial conduct or exhibit bias in favor of state in questioning fingerprint witness in order to fully develop the truth of the case; judge's questions did not exhibit discriminatory behavior applicable to race, sex, religion, national origin, disability, age, sexual orientation, or socioeconomic status); *In re Corrigan*, 826 N.E.2d (Ohio 2004) (holding that judge's use of the word "jackasses" in referring to attorneys who behave foolishly or who resolve cases too slowly was unfortunate, and his reference to clothing and jewelry worn by some attorneys in the domestic relations field was unnecessary but do not reflect bias or prejudice in violation of the Code); *Brown v. State*, 2007 WL 2012902 (Tex. App. 2007) (judge's comments in front of the jury, although perhaps rudely made, were in reference to points of procedure and not with regard to the guilt or innocence of appellant and therefore did not violate Canon).

Comments outside of the courtroom can also violate Rule 2.3(A). *See, e.g., In re Goetteman*, 12-315 (Ariz. Comm'n on Jud. Conduct 2013) (judge who said during a staff meeting, "Some of the most profane, manipulative, and back-stabbing people I've worked with have been women. Men tend to get physical and just hit you," violated rule); *Dodds v. Comm'n on Jud. Performance*, 906 P.2d 1260 (Cal. 1996) (telling a joke outside of the courtroom and in front of the plaintiff's family about the occupation of one of the parties suggested bias and was "clearly unjudicial"); *but see Miss. Comm'n on Jud. Performance v. Wilkerson*, 876 So. 2d 1006 (Miss. 2004) (holding that judge could not be sanctioned under Code of Judicial Conduct for statements in letter to newspaper and on radio network proclaiming that homosexuals were mentally ill; such speech constituted speech regarding matter of political/public importance and private religious speech and could only be sanctioned if doing so would serve compelling state interest). *See also* Tobin A. Sparling, *Judicial Bias Claims of Homosexual Persons in the Wake of* Lawrence v. Texas, 46 S. Tex. L. Rev. 255 (2004); LaDonna Childress, *To Fulfill a Promise: Using Canons 3B(5) and 3B(6) of the Judicial Code of Conduct to Combat Sexual Orientation Bias Against Gay and Lesbian Criminal Defendants*, 34 Sw. U. L. Rev. 607 (2005).

A judge likely does not violate Rule 2.3(A) by making comments that do not reflect his personal interest in the outcome of the case, but rather, express that he was offended by the facts of the crime committed by the defendant. *Cameron v. Nevada*, 968 P.2d 1169 (Nev. 1999) (comments by judge, who sentenced defendant to statutory maximum term of ten years' imprisonment for lewdness with a minor, that "We should be concerned with punishment," did not reflect his personal interest in the outcome of the case or improper judicial bias).

CONDUCT THAT INDICATES BIAS

Judges may violate Rule 2.3(A) by engaging in conduct that indicates that they strongly favor one side of a dispute over the other. *See, e.g., In re Chiles*, 12-012 (Ariz. Comm'n on Jud. Conduct, 2012) (judge reprimanded for behavior that "facilitated an impression of bias in favor of the prosecutors" when judge allowed prosecutors into the building at 8:00 a.m., denied the same access to defendant and counsel, dismissed jury when defendant and counsel were not in courtroom at 8:00 a.m., denied defense an opportunity to explain, then disqualified self from matter, and managed reassignment of it); *In re Cresap*, 940 So. 2d 624 (La. 2006) (judge's numerous actions indicated a bias in favor of plaintiff over defendant including allowing plaintiffs' counsel to engage in untimely argument and speaking objections without limit, but frequently interrupting, shortening, or curtailing argument or objection by defense counsel; frequently following the suggestions made by plaintiffs' counsel for conducting the proceedings, even when the procedures they suggested required him to take things out of their normal order; granting every request for a break or recess made by the plaintiffs' counsel, but refusing to delay the proceedings even momentarily when the request was made by defense counsel; refusing to allow defense counsel to proffer evidence or testimony on at least seven occasions, and on at least one occasion stating that he did not want the defense to "taint" the record); *Inquiry Concerning McBrien* (Cal. Comm'n on Jud. Performance 2010) (judge ordered transcript of part of divorce hearing regarding respondent's failure to disclose certain information of state economic interest document, consulted with Agency attorney and provided transcript to Agency resulting in respondent's dismissal from employment); *In re Boyett*, CJC No. 11-0047-JP (Tex. Comm'n on Jud. Conduct 2011) (judge who set bond of $50,000 for defendant accused of stealing college ring from student who attended judge's alma mater when bond schedule threshold was $5,000 exhibited bias).

Judges may also violate the rule by allowing their own personal situation to influence their official conduct. For instance, a judge's conduct was "colored by his own situation" when the judge, whose harassment and stalking of his former wife resulted in a dual protection order, interjected himself in a proceeding before his court involving child custody and orders of protection. *In re Hoffman*, 595 N.W. 2d 592 (N.D. 1999) (in hearing on a husband's violation of protection order, judge told state's attorney's representative at hearing that he wanted to report a violation of the protection order by wife).

Judges allowing their personal beliefs to influence their conduct on the bench may also violate Rule 2.3(A). *See, e.g., In re Ballew*, M2013-02345-BJC-DIS-FC (Tenn. Bd. of Jud. Conduct 2014) (judge who changed baby's name from Messiah to Martin, explaining that Messiah is a title earned only by Jesus Christ, violated the anti-bias rule by inappropriately interjecting and applying judge's personal religious beliefs); *Cleveland Bar Ass'n v. Cleary*, 754 N.E.2d 235 (Ohio 2001) (judge's decision to impose prison sentence, rather than probation, on pregnant defendant in order to prevent an abortion violated the requirement to perform duties without bias or prejudice; judge allowed her personal feelings about abortion to influence her decision to deny probation to a pregnant defendant who was charged with a fifth degree felony, unless the defendant promised to carry her pregnancy to term).

The fact that a judge has a general opinion about a legal or social matter relating to a pending case, however, does not automatically render the judge biased or prejudiced within the meaning of the rule. Charles Gardner Geyh, James J. Alfini, Steven Lubet, & Jeffrey M. Shaman, *Judicial Conduct and Ethics* § 4.06 at 4–15 (5th ed. 2013). *See also Voss v. State*, 856 N.E.2d 1211 (Ind. 2006) (fact that a judge may have a personal opinion regarding an issue in a case does not, standing alone, create a rational inference that the judge's decision will be governed by bias and prejudice). While a judge is free to hold his or her own personal beliefs, those beliefs may not be translated into action or inaction that displays bias or partiality. *In re Inquiry Concerning a Judge J.Q.C. No. 77-16*, 357 So. 2d 172 (Fla. 1978).

Judges may also violate Rule 2.3(A) by allowing their actions to be influenced by a personal relationship with an individual. *See, e.g., In re Adams*, 932 So. 2d 1025 (Fla. 2006) (judge's conduct in entering into romantic relationship with lawyer who practiced before him and then continuing to preside over matters in which the lawyer appeared as counsel, with judge granting numerous continuances requested by the lawyer in five cases and dismissing the charges in four traffic cases in which the lawyer represented the defendant violated Canon); *In re Inquiry Concerning a Judge re Graziano*, 696 So. 2d 744 (Fla. 1997) (judge's misconduct, including using her position to obtain a job and substantial salary increase for a friend, warranted public reprimand); *In re Funke*, 757 N.E.2d 1013 (Ind. App. 2001) (judge took action that helped improve the property interests of family members); *In re Davis*, 645 S.E.2d 243 (S.C. 2007) (off-duty magistrate's decision to set bond for release of law enforcement officer's friend warranted a six-month suspension from judicial duties); *In re Gosnell*, 621 S.E. 2d 659 (S.C. 2005) (magistrate's efforts to show favoritism toward judge in order to secure release of judge on bond following arrest, and racial remark made toward a defendant appearing before the magistrate, violated standards set forth in judicial conduct rules regarding, inter alia, preservation of integrity and independence of the judiciary, and performance of duties with impartiality); *In re Wilder*, 516 S.E.2d 927 (S.C. 1999) (judge helped an acquaintance forge a request for dismissal of prosecution form); *In re Nickolds*, CJC No. 13-0496-JP (Tex. Comm'n on Jud. Conduct 2013) (judge reprimanded for moving case from another docket to the judge's docket and hearing DWI case involving close personal friend). A judge charged with violating Rule 2.3(A), due to the influence of personal relationships, is likely to also be charged with violating Rule 1.3 ("A judge shall not abuse the prestige of judicial office to advance the personal or economic interests of the judge or others or allow others to do so.").

Judges may also not give special treatment or favors to someone because they or their family members or friends are in a powerful position. *See In re Sessions*, 538 S.E.2d 1 (S.C. 2000) (judge reprimanded for dismissing defendant's traffic ticket because defendant was son of city council member and continuing case and altering sentence, without prosecution's knowledge, of defendant whose father called city council member to ask for assistance).

HARASSMENT

As noted previously, the proscription against harassment is new to the Code. Former Canon 3B(5), upon which Rule 2.3 is based, referred to "sexual harassment" in the Commentary, stating that judges must refrain from speech, gestures, or other conduct that could reasonably be perceived as sexual harassment, but made no mention of harassment generally. Rule 2.3(A) states in the black letter that judges must not "engage in harassment . . . based on race, sex, gender, religion, national origin, ethnicity, disability, age, sexual orientation, marital status, socioeconomic status, or political affiliation." The Commentary to Rule 2.3 states that harassment "is verbal or physical conduct that denigrates or shows hostility or aversion toward a person on bases such as race, sex, gender, religion, national origin, ethnicity, disability, age, sexual orientation, marital status, socioeconomic status, or political affiliation." Model Code of Judicial Conduct Rule 2.3 cmt. [3].

Sexual Harassment

The commentary to Rule 2.3 states that "[s]exual harassment includes but is not limited to sexual advances, requests for sexual favors, and other verbal or physical conduct of a sexual nature that is unwelcome." Model Code of Judicial Conduct Rule 2.3 cmt. [4]. *See, e.g, In re Henderson*, 343 P.3d 518, 524 (Kan. 2015) (judge's "pervasive comments of a sexual nature which were offensive and demeaning to female attorneys" violates the rule); *In re Corwin*, 843 N.W.2d 830 (N.D. 2014) (judge who persistently asked court reporter for dates and time alone for one year after court reporter told judge that she was not interested in a personal relationship with him violated the rule and was suspended for one month without pay; whether this conduct also violated federal or state law "was not relevant to the inquiry" because the North Dakota judicial code does not require "the establishment of sexual harassment under federal or state law to constitute a violation" of the code). Those cases finding a violation of Section 3B(5) usually involved a judge's inappropriate comments toward court employees. *See, e.g., In re Servaas*, 774 N.W.2d 46 (Mich. 2009) (judge publicly censured for inappropriate sexual drawings and comments directed toward female court employees); *In re Empson*, 562 N.W.2d 817 (Neb. 1997) (finding violation of Section 3B(5) when judge repeatedly made inquiries into the sexual lives of court employees); *In re Nelson*, 532 S.E.2d 609 (S.C. 2000) (judge violated Canon by making sexually oriented remarks to a female deputy).

REQUIRING LAWYERS TO REFRAIN FROM MANIFESTING BIAS OR PREJUDICE OR ENGAGING IN HARASSMENT

Rule 2.3(C), the corollary to Rule 2.3(A), places upon judges the responsibility to require lawyers in proceedings before them to "refrain from manifesting bias or engaging in harassment based on, but not limited to, race, sex, gender, religion, national origin, ethnicity, disability, age, sexual orientation, marital status, socioeconomic status, or political affiliation." Judges are likely to be found to have violated Rule 2.3(C) when they fail to reprimand or otherwise sanction a lawyer for making comments that suggest bias or prejudice. For instance, one court held that a suggestion by a husband's attorney, in a divorce proceeding, that physical violence would have been appropriate against his client's wife was reprehensible and unacceptable, and the district court judge's failure to censure the lawyer was a violation of former Section 3B(6), upon which Rule 2.3(C) is based. *Johnson v. Johnson*, 544 N.W.2d 519 (N.D. 1996). Similarly, a judge was found to have violated this provision when he failed to rebuke a defense attorney who made an inappropriate joke about domestic violence. *In re Romano*, 712 N.E.2d 1216 (N.Y. 1999). However, Rule 2.3(C) is not limited to proceedings within the courtroom. Judges must monitor the conduct of lawyers throughout the judicial process. For instance, a judge may take action to ensure that lawyers refrain from manifesting bias or prejudice during pretrial proceedings. *Mullaney v. Aude*, 730 A.2d 759 (Md. Ct. Spec. App. 1999) (appellate court upheld decision of trial court judge to sanction a lawyer for using sexist language toward opposing counsel during a discovery deposition).

EXCEPTION FOR ISSUES IN A PROCEEDING

Rule 2.3(D) allows lawyers to make "legitimate reference" to matters of "race, sex, gender, religion, national origin, ethnicity, disability, age, sexual orientation, marital status, socioeconomic status, or political affiliation" or "similar factors" when they are relevant to an issue in a proceeding. However, there must be a sufficient relationship between the use of such factors and the issues in the proceeding. For instance, in *State v. Roberts*, 1998 WL 748472 (Tenn. Crim. App. 1998), the appellate court concluded that a trial court judge could not allow a prosecutor to discredit a defendant's witness by questioning the witness's gender. The appellate court stated that allowing the prosecutor to use the witness's status as a hermaphrodite "as a ground for general impeachment" would unfairly prejudice the witness's testimony.

RULE 2.4 EXTERNAL INFLUENCES ON JUDICIAL CONDUCT

(A) A judge shall not be swayed by public clamor or fear of criticism.

(B) A judge shall not permit family, social, political, financial, or other interests or relationships to influence the judge's judicial conduct or judgment.

(C) A judge shall not convey or permit others to convey the impression that any person or organization is in a position to influence the judge.

COMMENT

[1] An independent judiciary requires that judges decide cases according to the law and facts, without regard to whether particular laws or litigants are

popular or unpopular with the public, the media, government officials, or the judge's friends or family. Confidence in the judiciary is eroded if judicial decision making is perceived to be subject to inappropriate outside influences.

1990 Code Comparison

Rule 2.4(A) is the second sentence of former Canon 3B(2), Rule 2.4(B) is the first sentence of former Canon 2B, and Rule 2.4(C) is the second half of the second sentence of former Canon 2B. "Financial" relationships were added to the list of influences that judges should avoid. Although the pre-existing rule referred to "other" relationships, the Joint Commission to Evaluate the Model Code of Judicial Conduct regarded financial relationships as important enough to warrant separate mention. Charles G. Geyh & W. William Hodes, *Reporters' Notes to the Model Code of Judicial Conduct* 31 (2009).

The scope of the Rule was expanded slightly in paragraph (C). As previously drafted, the Rule forbade a judge from permitting others to convey the impression that they, meaning the others, were in a position to influence the judge. As a technical matter, that prohibition did not reach the situation in which "others" conveyed the impression that a third person was in a position to influence the judge, and the change has been made to cover that scenario. *Id.*

The 1990 Code spoke in terms of those in a "special" position to influence the judge, presumably to distinguish those who influenced the judge through appropriate advocacy. The Commission determined that such a distinction went without saying and removed the term "special." *Id.*

Comment [1] is new to the Code and is intended to underscore the general purpose underlying paragraphs (A) and (B) by linking the duty not to be swayed by the public, friends, or family to the judge's primary obligation to follow the law and facts impartially. *Id.*

Annotation

Duty to Avoid Partisan Interests, Public Clamor, and Fear of Criticism

Rule 2.4(A) requires judges not to be "swayed by public clamor or fear of criticism." This section essentially directs judges to decide cases on their merits and not on the basis of an outcome that the judge or someone else would like to accomplish or avoid. *See, e.g., In re Kinsey*, 842 So. 2d 77 (Fla. 2003) (during election campaign, judge violated provision by stating in an interview that it was a judge's responsibility to be "absolutely a reflection of what the community wants"); *In re Eskridge*, 559 S.E.2d 575 (S.C. 2002) (finding that public reprimand was appropriate sanction for judge who received a list of defendants scheduled to appear before him with letters "NG" beside the names of some of the defendants and understood the letters to mean "not guilty," and subsequently found each defendant whose name appeared next to the letters "NG" not guilty, even the defendants who failed to appear in court); *In re Cox*, CJC 10-1018-JP (Tex. Comm'n on Jud. Conduct 2011) (judge admonished for unilaterally dismissing case because of fear of future potential lawsuits).

As discussed below, a judge may violate Rule 2.4(A) when his or her professional conduct is motivated by a desire to harass, humiliate, or retaliate against lawyers that the judge dislikes or to help their friends and acquaintances.

Carrying Out Personal Vendettas

Judges may not use the power and authority of their office to carry out vendettas against lawyers for either personal or political reasons. *See, e.g., In re McAllister*, 646 So. 2d 173 (Fla. 1994) (judge removed for misconduct including holding a contempt hearing against public defender for misrepresenting his availability for trial when the judge had been told that he had not done so; shortly thereafter, judge told another judge that she "couldn't stand" the public defender and that she "was going to get him"); *In re Damron*, 487 So. 2d 1 (Fla. 1986) (judge set aside a dismissal he had entered in litigant's case after finding out that litigant had supported his opponent in an election); *State ex. rel. Comm'n on Jud. Qualifications v. Rome*, 623 P.2d 1307 (Kan. 1981) (disciplining a judge for his discriminatory treatment of certain lawyers who had taken a public position in favor of a ballot item that he opposed); *Jud. Inquiry & Rev. Bd. v. Fink*, 532 A.2d 358 (Pa. 1987) (judge engaged in a pattern of conduct designed to undermine the career and reputation of the local District Attorney).

It may be a violation of Rule 2.4(A) for a judge to retaliate in the courtroom against someone who has done something that annoys or irritates the judge. *See, e.g., In re Keith*, 3 Ill. Ct. Comm'n 38 (1994) (it is misconduct for a judge to hold someone in contempt of court for being a few hours late for court, particularly if the judge fails to ask the party for a reason why he or she was late). Judges have also been disciplined for abusing the power of their office to retaliate against someone who criticized them (*In re Ross*, 428 A.2d 858 (Me. 1981) (judge increased sentence because of defendant's alleged derogatory remarks); *Miss. Comm'n on Jud. Performance v. Walker*, 565 So. 2d 1117 (Miss. 1990) (judge improperly jailed litigant for contempt based on a personal affront, which did not threaten the dignity of the court)) or who questioned their fairness (*In re Graham*, 620 So. 2d 1273 (Fla. 1993) (judge increased sentence after defendant questioned its fairness); *In re Boles*, 555 N.E.2d 1284 (Ind. 1990) (judge vacated attorney's fee award after lawyer questioned the method in which they were awarded)).

Lastly, judges have been disciplined for imposing harsher sentences on defendants who insisted on exercising their constitutional rights, such as a right to go to trial (*In re Cox*, 680 N.E.2d 528 (Ind. 1997) ("A critical distinction exists between the appropriate consideration of cooperation and remorse as mitigating circumstances in fashioning a sentence and the inappropriate imposition of an added penalty for the exercise of constitutional rights.")) or the right to have an attorney (*see, e.g., In re Damron*, 487 So. 2d 1 (Fla. 1986) (judge routinely threatened individuals who requested the services of an attorney with substantial periods of incarceration)).

Favoritism

Judges may violate Rule 2.4(A) when they cease being objective and decide cases based on their friendship or familial relationship with one of the parties. *See, e.g., In re Funke*, 757 N.E.2d 1013 (Ind. 2001) (judge should not have granted emergency protective orders in cases in which judge's parents, aunt, and first cousin had property interests); *Wilson v. Jud. Ret. & Removal Comm'n.*, 673 S.W.2d 426 (Ky. 1984) (judge misused power of his office to commit acts specifically designed to aid and benefit a close personal friend); *Miss. Comm'n on Jud. Performance v. Milling*, 651 So. 2d 531 (Miss. 1995) (judge issued a fugitive warrant so that a friend could be released from jail and then dismissed the warrant without notice or hearing); *In re Marcuzzo*, 770 N.W.2d 591 (Neb. 2009) (judge suspended without pay for 120 days for involving himself in nephew's criminal case, including ex parte contact with prosecuting attorney and another judge and leaving profane and threatening message for prosecutor); *In re Inquiry Concerning a Judge Ammons*, 473 S.E.2d 326 (N.C. 1996) (in criminal matter involving a worthless check where the prosecuting witness was a personal friend, judge refused to continue the case to enable defendant to obtain counsel; and tried defendant without counsel on the defendant's not guilty plea, cross-examined the defendant, and found the defendant guilty).

Judges may also violate Rule 2.4(A) by issuing rulings that favor one religious viewpoint over another (*Jud. Inquiry & Rev. Bd. v. Fink*, 532 A.2d 358 (Pa. 1987) (judge favored Christians over non-Christians in judicial rulings)) or that advance their own political interests (*In re Haddad*, 627 P.2d 221 (Ariz. 1981) (judge dismissed traffic citations issued just before the election to avoid political embarrassment); *In re Damron*, 487 So. 2d 1 (Fla. 1986) (judge terminated jail sentence of defendant when, just before the election, at the judge's request, the defendant wrote a letter to the paper thanking the judge for setting her straight); *In re Eplin*, 416 S.E.2d 248 (W. Va. 1992) (judge circumvented normal procedures on a traffic ticket issued to an employee of a state senator in order to "curry favor" with the senator)).

Not only is it misconduct for a judge to be influenced in his or her own decision making to advance the judge's private interests or the interests of friends or family members, but it is also improper and a violation of this Canon for a judge to attempt to influence others in the decision-making process to advance these relationships and interests. *See, e.g., In re Kiley*, 546 N.E.2d 916 (N.Y. 1989) (referring generally to Canon in ordering censure of judge for attempting to get District Attorney to reduce charges against friends).

ALLOWING RELATIONSHIPS TO INFLUENCE IMPROPERLY

The language of Rule 2.4(B), a general standard about the necessity of a judge maintaining independence from improper influence by those close to the judge, derives from the first sentence of Canon 2B in the 1990 Code, which reiterates this notion from the 1972 Code which, in turn, echoes Canons 4, 25, and 33 in the original *Canons of Judicial Ethics*. *See* E. Wayne Thode, *Reporter's Notes to Code of Judicial Conduct* 49 (1972); *In re Chmeil*, 88 CC-1 (Ill. Cts. Comm'n 2010) (judge reprimanded under Canon 2B when he agreed to conduct a bond hearing after he received a phone call from a longtime friend and former client whose brother was in the process of being arrested).

Perhaps because of the general language in Rule 2.4(B), it has often been included in "a kitchen sink" approach, where it is added to a litany of other violations. *See, e.g., Adams v. Comm'n on Jud. Performance*, 882 P.2d 358 (Cal. 1994) (judge violated several Code provisions by seeking and receiving favorable price on automobile from litigant in matter pending before him); *Miss. Comm'n on Jud. Performance v. Gunter*, 797 So. 2d 988 (Miss. 2001) (judge's misuse of judicial position, intemperate treatment of minor defendant, and abuse of contempt power violated former Canons 1, 2A, 2B, 3A(1), 3A(2), 3A(3), 3A(4), and 3A(6)) and Miss. Const. art. 6, § 177A, Miss. Code Ann. § 45-27-13, 18 U.S.C. §§ 641, 1030, 1343, 1351, 1952); *Miss. Comm'n on Jud. Performance v. Atkinson*, 645 So. 2d 1331 (Miss. 1994) (municipal judge setting accused person's bail and subsequently seeking to reduce bail while acting as practicing attorney representing the accused violated former Canons 1, 2A, 2B, 3A(1), and 5C(1)).

Family

Even though steering clear of improper relational influence is a well-established ethical norm, judges continue to be disciplined under the language of Rule 2.4(B) for allowing certain relationships to interfere with judicial duties. *See generally* Leslie W. Abramson, *Canon 2 of the Code of Judicial Conduct*, 79 Marq. L. Rev. 949 (1996).

For instance, judges have crossed the ethical line in permitting undue influence by family members. *See, e.g., In re Inquiry Concerning a Judge*, 832 So. 2d 716 (Fla. 2002) (judge requested a scheduling favor for her family member from a fellow judge); *In re Burgess*, 85 So. 3d 604 (La. 2012) (judge censured for intervening in niece's domestic relations case to secure protective order from another judge not assigned to matter); *In re Davis*, 865 So. 2d 693

(La. 2004) (judge appointed his father, who was a practicing attorney, to represent indigent criminal defendants); *In re Parro*, 847 So. 2d 1178 (La. 2003) (judge intervened with district attorney, presiding judge, and others on behalf of niece facing felony theft charges; though actions were not part of official duties, "prestige of office was brought to bear," thus undermining judicial process); *In re Johnson*, 763 S.E.2d 812 (S.C. 2014) (judge publicly reprimanded for telephoning magistrate judge to enter plea and pay fine on behalf of grandson); *In re Darlington County Mag. Thomas*, 642 S.E.2d 736 (S.C. 2007) (county magistrate's issuance of subpoena in favor of his son-in-law, who was involved in a child support proceeding, when judge knew or should have known that party to whom he issued subpoena was not bound by it); *In re Dillion County Mag. Davis*, 630 S.E.2d 281 (S.C. 2006) (magistrate's misconduct in conducting special bond proceeding for a relative who was arrested for DUI, although magistrate was not on call and did not seek permission to conduct proceeding or ascertain if other inmates were awaiting bond hearings, amounted to preferential treatment in violation of Code of Judicial Conduct); *In re McKinney*, 478 S.E.2d 51 (S.C. 1996) (judge assisted daughter in extortion efforts by issuing arrest warrants at daughter's request, accepting payment for dismissal of charges, and expressing willingness to mislead probation officer to advance daughter's interests); *In re Reese*, 495 S.E.2d 548 (W. Va. 1997) (magistrate's ex parte conversations with defendant and their mutual relatives created implication that they had struck a deal to reduce charge against defendant); *In re Rice*, 489 S.E.2d 783 (W. Va. 1997) (judge contacted arresting officer and prosecuting attorney concerning charges of public intoxication and possession of a controlled substance against his son in-law); *In re Boese*, 410 S.E.2d 282 (W. Va. 1991) (judge left telephone message on her ex-husband's answering machine in which she tried to use her official position to threaten ex husband with arrest); *cf. In re Van Rider*, 715 N.E.2d 402 (Ind. 1999) (judge whose son appeared before him as criminal defendant failed to recuse himself and used authority to order son's release from jail; court issued reprimand based on judge's failure to recuse himself rather than for a violation of Rule 2.4(B), noting that no such violation had been charged, "although such a charge may have been appropriate under the facts of this case"); *cf. In re JQC No. 97-61*, 499 S.E.2d 319 (Ga. 1998) (municipal court judge removed from office due to familial relationship with city's mayor, who was judge's mother; relationship gave rise to appearance of impropriety, though there was no evidence that judge had disregarded his duty of neutrality).

Nepotism is an obvious abuse of power in favor of a family member. *See* Ind. Comm'n on Jud. Qualifications Op. 2-98 (1998) (outlining factors against nepotism and favoritism, to be considered by judge hiring relative or friend). For more on nepotism, see Rule 2.13(A)(2).

Friends and Acquaintances

Judges are not expected to break off friendships and live in isolation when they ascend to the bench. A judge may not, however, give friends or acquaintances special judicial treatment or allow personal friendships to color professional judgment. *See, e.g., In re Petrucelli* (Cal. Comm'n on Jud. Performance 2015) (judge censured for calling jail and ordering the own recognizance release of friend arrested for spousal abuse); *In re Adams*, 932 So. 2d 1025 (Fla. 2006) (judge's conduct in entering into romantic relationship with lawyer who practiced before him and then continuing to preside over matters in which the lawyer appeared as counsel, with judge granting numerous continuances requested by the lawyer in five cases and dismissing the charges in four traffic cases in which the lawyer represented the defendant, violated Canons prohibiting a judge from allowing social or other relationships influence the judge's judicial conduct or judgment); *In re Trettis*, 577 So. 2d 1312 (Fla. 1991) (judge allowed personal relationships to influence his judicial conduct and used the prestige of his office to create an employment position in judicial system for others); *In re Simpson*, 11-CC-1 (Ill. Cts. Comm'n 2011) (judge censured for discussing with another judge acquaintance's pro se matter pending before that judge); *In re Cooks*, 694 So. 2d 892 (La. 1997) (judge's failure to recuse herself from case in which she had close personal relationship with litigant warranted public censure); *In re Markey*, 696 N.E.2d 523 (Mass. 1998) (on behalf of a former colleague and neighbor, judge made ex parte communication with family court judge that led to dismissal of prevention order); *In re Jenkins*, 465 N.W.2d 317 (Mich. 1991) (judge improperly released an individual whom he thought was a friend of a close friend but who was actually an undercover agent); *In re Hartzog*, 32 So. 3d 1188 (Miss. 2010) (judge disciplined for trying to negotiate sale of property from one litigant acquaintance to another litigant acquaintance instead of hearing evidence in the eviction matter); *In re George*, 22 N.Y.3d 323 (2013) (judge removed from office for, in part, sua sponte dismissing traffic ticket of family friend); *In re Going*, 761 N.E.2d 585 (N.Y. 2001) (judge reinstated friend's driver's license that had been suspended for failure to pay child support, even though judge knew friend was in arrears in child support payments); *In re Backal*, 660 N.E.2d 1104 (N.Y. 1995) (judge engaged in financial dealings with a close associate involved in money laundering and drug dealing); *In re Inquiry Concerning a Judge Ammons*, 473 S.E.2d 326 (N.C. 1996) (judge bent procedures in case where personal friend was a prosecuting witness); *In re Beckham*, 620 S.E.2d 69 (S.C. 2005) (judge's conduct in meeting with public official in order to recommend a personal friend for promotion within the police department and speaking with police officer about traffic ticket issued to family friend violated Code of Judicial Conduct); *In re Wilder*, 516 S.E.2d 927 (S.C. 1999) (judge issued a blank arrest warrant for a man after an acquaintance complained of abuses by that man; judge also ordered the release of a criminal defendant, a high school senior planning to leave for a trip to the Bahamas the day of his arrest, because the defendant's mother called the judge). *See generally* Vincent R. Johnson, *The Ethical Foundations of American Judicial Independence*, 29 Fordham Urb. L.J. 1007 (2002) (discussing various provisions in the judicial ethics code that deal with problematic relationships between judges and other individuals or entities).

Merely contacting those in a position of authority, however, is insufficient to establish that a judge has misused the judicial office. There must be "some affirmative expectation or utilization of position to accomplish that which otherwise would not have occurred." *In re Frank*, 753 So. 2d 1228 (Fla. 2000) (contacting bar grievance attorneys and expressing displeasure with handling of a grievance proceeding, but not demanding special treatment due to judicial position, was not abuse of office; court noted "Judge Frank did not forfeit the right to make proper inquiry concerning the pending matters simply because he held judicial office"); *accord In re Inquiry Concerning a Judge (Holloway)*, 832 So. 2d 716 (Fla. 2002) (telephone call to detective handling criminal investigation of sexual abuse situation involving family friend did not amount to abuse of judicial office absent any indication call was attempt to influence investigation or a demand for special treatment on account of judge's position). *See also In re Charge of Jud. Misconduct*, 91 F.3d 1416 (10th Cir. 1996) (magistrate's calling of district attorney for release of arrestee, who was related to magistrate's secretary, did not constitute judicial misconduct; magistrate identified himself as judicial officer merely to illustrate that he was not acting as attorney for arrestee).

Extramarital Affairs

Judges are held to a higher standard than the public at large, and thus, off-bench conduct is also subject to scrutiny. *In re Tamsen*, 789 N.E.2d 613 (N.Y. 2003), *citing Aldrich v. State Comm'n on Jud. Conduct*, 447 N.E.2d 1276 (N.Y. 1983) (it is imperative to also consider "the effect of the judge's conduct on and off the Bench upon public confidence in his [or her] character and judicial temperament").

Courts have taken various positions regarding whether extramarital affairs, for example, constitute a basis for discipline. *See generally* Jeffrey M. Shaman, *The Illinois Code of Judicial Conduct and the Appearance of Impropriety*, 22 Loy. U. Chi. L.J. 581 (1991) (discussing split in authority among various jurisdictions on this issue). When a judge's romantic involvements are seen to have a negative impact on the judge's impartiality, however, a judge is subject to discipline under Rule 2.4(B). *See, e.g., In re Miller*, 949 So. 2d 379 (La. 2007) (judge removed for misconduct including engaging in sexual relationship with secretary and wrote letter of recommendation, on court stationery, to secretary's eventual new employer); *In re Harris*, 713 So. 2d 1138 (La. 1998) (judge suspended for engaging in extramarital affair with paroled felon who was released from prison on parole pursuant to sentence judge imposed); *In re Chrzanowski*, 636 N.W.2d 758 (Mich. 2001) (judge appointed as counsel to 56 indigent defendants an attorney with whom she was having intimate relationship and judge gave misleading statements to police investigating the murder of her lover's wife); *Miss. Comm'n on Jud. Performance v. Milling*, 651 So. 2d 531 (Miss. 1995) (discipline of judge stemming from personal relationship and ultimate marriage to criminal defendant in her court; judge obtained a fugitive warrant on defendant's behalf and then dismissed it, allowed defendant to drive with a suspended license, openly lived with defendant, an accused felon, and actively participated in the defendant's criminal case in another state); *In re Brown*, 540 S.E.2d 452 (S.C. 2000) (judge blackmailed woman with whom he had an affair; judge used court funds to pay her, and therefore, let his personal relationship interfere with his official duties); *cf. In re Flanagan*, 690 A.2d 865 (Conn. 1997) (judge censured for engaging in three-and-a-half-year consensual affair with married court reporter in his courtroom; court stated, "[a]lthough it may be difficult to assess the degree to which the public at large now may condone or disapprove of one having a sexual affair with a married person, we are persuaded that, in general, such conduct is regarded as improper when it involves a subordinate in a professional, highly sensitive public context. . . . [P]ublic confidence in the integrity of the judiciary is compromised by extended sexual relationships between judges and married court reporters assigned to their courtrooms").

Colleagues and Former Clients

A judge must be careful not to allow loyalty to former clients, colleagues, or co-workers to improperly influence the judge's conduct. *See, e.g., In re Santini*, 597 A.2d 1388 (N.J. 1991) (municipal court judge lent the prestige of the office to advance private interests by contacting three public officials on behalf of former client); *In re Cornelius*, 436 S.E.2d 836 (N.C. 1993) (judge improperly intervened in dispute of friend, a former county employee, giving legal advice and threatening to convene a grand jury to investigate the circumstances of employee's termination; judge improperly conveyed impression that former employee had special influence with judge even though judge was not motivated by desire for personal gain); *In re Gosnell*, 621 S.E. 2d 659 (S.C. 2005) (magistrate's efforts to help judge to secure release on bond following arrest violated Canon); *In re Sullivan*, 68 Conn. L. J. 24 (Conn. Jud. Rev. Council 2006) (Chief Justice of Connecticut Supreme Court suspended for 15 days for delaying release of a controversial opinion in order to facilitate appointment process of another justice of the Supreme Court to position of Chief Justice; Council found that Chief Justice improperly allowed his social or other relationships to influence his judicial conduct and judgment); *In re Plunk*, CJC Nos. 03-1016-DI & 04-1119-DI

(Tex. Comm'n on Jud. Conduct 2006) (judge's close relationship with opposing counsel, the daughter of his longtime court coordinator, influenced his conduct and judgment in cases, causing litigants to form legitimate concerns that judge would not be fair, neutral, or impartial).

Political Relationships

Independence and judicial neutrality require judges to eschew political connections. *See generally* Charles W. Wolfram, *Modern Legal Ethics* § 17.5.4, at 986–87 (1986). For this reason, except for voting and activities involving improvement of the law, legal system, or administration of justice, a judge must refrain from partisan political activities that other citizens can enjoy. See *generally* Canon 4.

Although political activity by judges usually falls under the aegis of Canon 4, a judge may violate Rule 2.4(B) by allowing political interests or relationships to influence his or her judicial conduct or judgment. *See, e.g., In re Benge*, 24 So. 3d 822 (La. 2009) (judge removed from bench after ruling contrary to evidence in favor of plaintiff preferred by political-judicial mentor/campaign contributor); *In re Adams*, 959 So. 2d 474 (La. 2007) (justice of the peace improperly issued arrest warrants for two individuals for a parade permit violation and issued excessive bonds, admittedly in retaliation to the individuals' political opposition to mayor); *Disc. Counsel v. Medley*, 819 N.E.2d 273 (Ohio 2004) (judge's undue delay in disposition against defendant, who was chair of county political party of which judge was member, and judge's misrepresentation of facts regarding that case violated Canons prohibiting a judge from allowing family, social, political, or other relationships to influence judge's judicial conduct or judgment); *In re Sessions*, 538 S.E.2d 1 (S.C. 2000) (judge dismissed reckless driving charge against son of local city council member, even though son wanted to plead guilty); *In re Romo*, CJC No. 12-0787-MU (Tex. Comm'n on Jud. Conduct 2014) (judge who defended dismissing tickets without prosecutor motion because judge felt political pressure to do so violated rule); *In re Eplin*, 416 S.E.2d 248 (W. Va. 1992) (magistrate asked police officer investigating a hit-and-run accident to reduce charge as a favor to defendant's employer, a state senator).

A related issue arises when a judge gets involved in supporting a spouse's political interests. *See, e.g., Allen v. State*, 737 N.E.2d 741 (Ind. 2000) (judge's wife was president of an area domestic abuse support organization; judge spoke at a telethon raising money for wife's organization; no sustainable inference that judge's wife's activities, or his appearance and support of her organization, affected his ability to make proper decisions in cases regarding domestic violence). For more on the impact of political activities of a judge's spouse, *see generally* Andrew L. Kaufman, *Judicial Ethics: The Less-Often Asked Questions*, 64 Wash. L. Rev. 851 (1989) (discussing, among other topics, advisory opinions regarding political activities of judge's spouses; concluding "spouses may do what they wish," though their political activities may result in a judge's disqualification in some instances).

Financial Influences

As noted previously, in 2007, the Commission added "financial" relationships to the list of influences the judge should avoid. Past examples of this type of financial relationship can be found in *Adams v. Comm'n on Jud. Performance*, 882 P.2d 358 (Cal. 1994) (judge received substantial financial benefits in the form of discounts and favorable prices for the purchase of automobiles and repairs from person who was a litigant in favor of whom the judge had previously awarded a substantial monetary judgment. Readily inferable from these allegations is that the judge was attempting to receive favors for past deeds) and *In re Hartzog*, 32 So. 3d 1188 (Miss. 2010) (judge should have recused himself from dispute between landlord and tenant involving property for which judge's landscaping business provided services).

POSITION TO INFLUENCE JUDGE

Rule 2.4(C) makes clear that a judge has a responsibility to avoid conveying the impression that any person or organization is in a position to influence the judge. Whether the pressure comes from individuals or corporate interests, a judge must exercise judgment free of such influence. *See, e.g., White v. Jud. Inquiry & Rev. Bd. of Penn.*, 744 F. Supp. 658 (E.D. Pa. 1990) (judge accepted and failed to report $300 given to him by a court employee associated with the roofers union, and used the money to buy gift certificates for other court employees; receipt of money gave roofers union officials impression that they were in special position of influence; subsequent disposition of cash did not eradicate that impression); *In re Cresap*, 940 So. 2d 624 (La. 2006) (judge improperly conveyed impression that others are in a position to influence him by allowing plaintiff's counsel to persuade him to repeatedly ask counsel for the state for the name of the person who had approved the filing of a recusal motion and then holding counsel for state in contempt when he refused to answer); *Miss. Comm'n on Jud. Performance v. Lewis*, 913 So. 2d 266 (Miss. 2005) (judge, by discussing litigant's cases ex parte, conveyed the impression that the litigants were in a special position to influence the judge); *Miss. Comm'n on Jud. Performance v. Peyton*, 645 So. 2d 954 (Miss. 1994) (judicial misconduct in dismissing burglary charges pursuant to ex parte communications with defendant and defendant's aunt to effect that complainant desires to drop charges); *In re Davis*, 645 S.E.2d 243 (S.C. 2007) (off-duty magistrate improperly held bond hearing for law enforcement officer's friend; magistrate was not on call that evening, did not seek permission to conduct special bond hearing at his residence, failed to ascertain whether other inmates were awaiting bond hearings, did not conduct bond hearings for any other inmates, and failed to inform the Chief Magistrate of the special bond hearing); Nev. Standing Comm. on Jud. Ethics and Election Prac., Op. JE01-001 (2001) (justice of the peace may not own and operate a paralegal service because of risk of impression of improper influence); Okla. Jud. Ethics Op. 2005-1 (2005) (judge may accept social invitations from attorneys who are former partners or associates of the judge or from social friends who are regularly on judges docket, as long as it would not reasonably be construed, either in the legal community or the general community in which the judge lives and serves, as likely to carry the impression that such persons are in a special position to influence the judge).

Rule 2.4(C) also requires a judge to take action to stop others from conveying an impression of special influence. To allow influence peddling, or even the claim of special influence, is to discredit the individual judge and the entire judiciary. E. Wayne Thode, *Reporter's Notes to Code of Judicial Conduct* 49 (1972); *In re White Crane Trading Co., Inc.* 170 B.R. 694 (Bkrtcy. E.D. Cal. 1994) (bankruptcy judge intervened to stop a store from advertising "Court-authorized Bankruptcy Sale"; "[p]ermitting a merchant to trumpet court authorization amounts to entrusting the court's prestige to the care and custody of the merchant. It places that prestige at risk of being sullied by the actions of others. What if the merchandise is shoddy? Breaches of warranty? Dubious credit practices? 'Bait and switch' tactics? When a court recognizes that its name is being used in vain, it has an obligation to intervene sua sponte.").

RULE 2.5 COMPETENCE, DILIGENCE, AND COOPERATION

(A) A judge shall perform judicial and administrative duties, competently and diligently.

(B) A judge shall cooperate with other judges and court officials in the administration of court business.

COMMENT

[1] Competence in the performance of judicial duties requires the legal knowledge, skill, thoroughness, and preparation reasonably necessary to perform a judge's responsibilities of judicial office.

[2] A judge should seek the necessary docket time, court staff, expertise, and resources to discharge all adjudicative and administrative responsibilities.

[3] Prompt disposition of the court's business requires a judge to devote adequate time to judicial duties, to be punctual in attending court and expeditious in determining matters under submission, and to take reasonable measures to ensure that court officials, litigants, and their lawyers cooperate with the judge to that end.

[4] In disposing of matters promptly and efficiently, a judge must demonstrate due regard for the rights of parties to be heard and to have issues resolved without unnecessary cost or delay. A judge should monitor and supervise cases in ways that reduce or eliminate dilatory practices, avoidable delays, and unnecessary costs.

1990 CODE COMPARISON

Rule 2.5(A) governs competence, formerly governed by Canon 3B(2), and diligence, formerly governed by Canon 3C(1), and makes the requirements applicable to both adjudicative and administrative duties of a judge. Rule 2.5(B) regarding cooperation in the administration of court business was the second half of former Canon 3C(1). The duty of competence is analogous to a lawyer's professional duty of competence, while the duty to apply the law is discussed elsewhere (the term "fidelity" is no longer used). Charles G. Geyh & W. William Hodes, *Reporters' Notes to the Model Code of Judicial Conduct* 32 (2009).

The black letter rule was expanded slightly to extend the duty of diligence to all judicial duties and not just "judicial matters," which is generally understood to be limited to case adjudication. The obligation to cooperate with others in judicial administration was upgraded from hortatory to mandatory. Efficient and effective administration is a duty of the judicial office, the proper execution of which necessitates cooperation among the judges of the court. *Id.*

Comments [1] and [2] are new to the Code and Comments [3] and [4] were taken from the Commentary to former Canon 3B(8).

ANNOTATION

OBLIGATION TO PERFORM DUTIES COMPETENTLY AND DILIGENTLY

Competent Discharge of Duties

Rule 2.5(A) requires judges to perform judicial and administrative duties competently and diligently. Comment [1] states that "Competence in the performance of judicial duties requires the legal knowledge, skill, thoroughness, and preparation reasonably necessary to perform a judge's responsibilities of judicial office."

Thus a judge may violate Rule 2.5(A) by failing to obtain training and knowledge required for the position. *See, e.g., In re Fletcher*, 15-125 (Ariz. Comm'n on Jud. Conduct 2015) (judge reprimanded, in part, for simultaneous entry of judgment for the defendant and dismissing the case without prejudice reflecting a lack of knowledge of the law); *In re Burke* (N.Y. Comm'n on Jud. Conduct 2014) (judge who continued to issue $200 fines when statute only allowed $150 fines, and was warned by clerk of the error, did not maintain professional competence in the law); *In re Williams*, 987 S.W.2d 837 (Tenn. 1998) (nonlawyer judge who tried and convicted an individual for felony offense notwithstanding court's lack of jurisdiction lacked necessary knowledge and legal training and failed to take appropriate steps to correct these deficiencies).

A judge may also violate Rule 2.5(A) by failing to keep himself or herself apprised of changes in the law. *Disc. Counsel v. Karto*, 760 N.E.2d 412 (Ohio 2002) (judge who used an outdated statute book to impose sentence in juvenile justice proceeding violated Canon requiring judges to maintain professional competence); *In re Duncan* CJC No. 05-0254-MU (Tex. Comm'n on Jud. Conduct 2006) (judge publicly admonished for failing to fulfill his judicial education requirements); *but see Miss. Comm'n on Jud. Performance v. Martin*, 921 So. 2d 1258 (Miss. 2005) (judge who erred in denying bail on two separate occasions, in violation of state constitutional provision under which only county judges and circuit judges had authority to deny bail, did not violate Canon requiring judges to maintain professional competence in it; while the judge was not a lawyer, she had attended Judicial College and was required to complete 18 hours of continuing education each year, and denial of bail had not been addressed in any training or judicial seminars she had attended).

Diligent Discharge of Duties

In addition to performing their administrative and judicial duties competently, Rule 2.5(A) requires judges to do so diligently. *In re Keaton*, 11-201, 11-206, 11-265 (Ark. Jud. Disc. & Disability Comm'n 2012) (judge censured for delay of 17 months in issuing ruling); *In re Kirihara* (Cal. Comm'n on Jud. Performance 2012) (judge admonished for not issuing decisions in three matters for hundreds of days); *In re Allawas*, 906 So. 2d 1052 (Fla. 2005) (judge reprimanded for failing to issue rulings in dozens of cases, which adversely impacted the administration of justice); *In re Holmes*, Jud-11-1 (Me. Sup. Jud. Ct. 2011) (judge reprimanded for allowing five cases to languish); *Disc. Counsel v. Sargeant*, 889 N.E.2d 96 (Ohio 2008) (judge reprimanded for allowing six civil cases to languish); *In re Hudson*, 690 S.E.2d 72 (S.C. 2010) (judge suspended for failure to review clerk's documentation on remission of fines resulting in clerk's embezzlement of more than $5,000); *In re Rich* (Tenn. Ct. of the Judiciary 2009) (judge reprimanded for eight-month delay in deciding petition relating to custody of minor child); *In re Dobbs*, (Cal. Comm'n on Jud. Performance 2009) (retired commissioner of family court publicly censured and barred from further judicial office for lack of diligence by failing to resolve 15 cases for over 90 days and 14 cases between 60 and 90 days).

As Comment [3] to the Rule states, the "[p]rompt disposition of the court's business requires a judge to devote adequate time to judicial duties, to be punctual in attending court and expeditious in determining matters under submission, and to take reasonable measures to ensure that court officials, litigants, and their lawyers cooperate with the judge to that end." *See, e.g.*, *In re Merlo*, 58 A.3d 1 (Pa. 2012) (judge removed from bench in part for missing 30 percent of work days in a 26-month period and never arriving on time).

Rule 2.5(A) provides some guidance for judges on how to discharge their duties diligently. Comment [2], which was new to the Code in 2007, advises judges to "seek the necessary docket time, court staff, expertise, and resources to discharge all adjudicative and administrative responsibilities." This Comment was added to emphasize the need for judges to devote the necessary time and resources to perform all their duties diligently and competently. Charles G. Geyh & W. William Hodes, *Reporters' Notes to the Model Code of Judicial Conduct* 32 (2009). Comment [4] advises judges to "monitor and supervise cases in ways that will reduce or eliminate dilatory practices, avoidable delays, and unnecessary costs."

Violations of Rule 2.5(A) may involve a failure to adhere to court rules or other requirements regarding record keeping and handling financial funds. *See, e.g.*, *In re Braun*, 883 P.2d 996 (Ariz. 1994) (judge failed to administer competently, fairly, and diligently the day-to-day operations of the justice court to the detriment of court staff and litigants by constant lateness and irregular calendar); *In re Carstensen*, 316 N.W.2d 889 (Iowa 1982) (judge flagrantly and persistently disregarded local rule that required judges to compile and file accurate and complete records on pending matters); *In re Seitz*, 495 N.W.2d 559 (Mich. 1993) (judge who failed to file reports with state court administrator's office violated Canon); *In re Anderson*, 412 So. 2d 743 (Miss. 1982) (judge failed to keep accurate record of public money received and willfully and fraudulently made false entries in monthly reports); *In re Corning*, 741 N.E.2d 117 (N.Y. 2000) (judge removed for misconduct including failing to remit funds to state comptroller); *In re Sanders*, 564 S.E.2d 670 (S.C. 2002) (judge reprimanded for failing to properly report, prepare, and document deposits made to magisterial account, failing to comply with proper procedures for issuing checks, and failing to properly reconcile accounts); *In re Brown*, 540 S.E.2d 452 (S.C. 2000) (magistrate judge reprimanded for failing to follow rules regarding handling of judicial funds and financial record keeping, keeping records with false information, commingling personal funds with official funds); *In re Riley*, 380 S.E.2d 816 (S.C. 1989) (judge publicly reprimanded for mismanagement of office finances and court docket); *In re Rainville*, 13.001 (Vt. Jud. Conduct Board 2014) (judge made late, undated amendments to entry orders). *See generally* Annotation, *Removal or Discipline of State Judge for Neglect of, or Failure to Perform, Judicial Duties*, 87 A.L.R.4th 727 (1991).

However, a judge must not sacrifice fairness in an effort to be diligent. As Comment [4] to the rule states, "[i]n disposing of matters promptly and efficiently, a judge must demonstrate due regard for the rights of parties to be heard and to have issues resolved without unnecessary cost or delay." *See, e.g., Sierra Nevada Stagelines, Inc. v. Rossi*, 892 P.2d 592 (Nev. 1995) (judges have a duty to dispose of all judicial matters promptly, efficiently, and fairly, but a judge may not seek promptness and efficiency at the expense of fairness).

Pattern of Misconduct Generally Required

The majority of cases disciplining judges for failing to act diligently involve a pattern of repeated failure to perform judicial responsibilities in a timely manner. *See, e.g., In re Gerard*, 631 N.W.2d 271 (Iowa 2001) (judge suspended for 60 days for failing to make timely rulings and file monthly caseload report as required by court rule, where judge had earlier been admonished for failing to comply with rule); *In re Disc. Action Against Hagar*, 810 N.W.2d 338 (N.D. 2012) (judge disciplined for not issuing timely decisions in more than 10 cases); *Disc. Counsel v. Sargeant*, 889 N.E.2d 96 (Ohio 2008) (judge reprimanded for allowing six civil cases to languish); *but see In re Bell*, 344 S.W.2d 304 (Tenn. 2011) (requirement to act promptly does not require a pattern of delay).

A delay on only a few occasions, which is not reflective of a judge's usual performance, is not likely to result in discipline. *See, e.g., In re Alvino*, 494 A.2d 1014 (N.J. 1985) (inadvertent delay in disposing of matters before a judge that is not at all typical of judge's performance, warrants not judicial discipline but rather administrative correction). *See also In re Kilburn*, 599 A. 2d 1377 (Vt. 1991) (because a violation of this provision does not implicate a judge's honesty or integrity, it can be violated only "where there is a pattern of unreasonable delay or where a particular instance is so lacking in legitimate justification that it is willful"); *In re King*, 399 S.E.2d 888 (W. Va. 1990) (delay of a single decision for three and a half months not a violation of Canon). *See also* Charles Gardner Geyh, James J. Alfini, Steven Lubet & Jeffrey M. Shaman, *Judicial Conduct and Ethics* § 6.02[4] at 6–16 (5th ed. 2013) (stating that courts generally decline to sanction a judge when there are only one or two cases of delay); Annotation, *Removal or Discipline of State Judge for Neglect of, or Failure to Perform, Judicial Duties*, 87 A.L.R.4th 727 (1991).

Judges have been disciplined, however, for only a few instances of delay if the delays are particularly egregious. For instance, the Supreme Court of Louisiana found that a judge violated the Canon when he did not decide one case for 21 months after the trial, and another for over six years after the trial. *In re Tuck*, 683 So. 2d 1214 (La. 1996) (holding that the delays warranted discipline because the judge allowed attorneys to abuse the decision-making process by not holding them to briefing schedule, and because the judge did not continue to report these cases as being under advisement). *See also In re Kohn*, 568 S.W.2d 255 (Mo. 1978) (judge censured for taking four years to decide case taken under advisement and for taking 21 months to decide another case); *In re Edwards*, 12-075

(N.C. Jud. Standards Comm'n 2012) (judge reprimanded for delay of four years in issuing order on equitable distribution of marital property); *In re Frye*, 08-020 (N.C. Jud. Standards Comm'n. 2008) (judge reprimanded for failing to provide written judgment in a case nearly four years after case concluded). *But see Lloyd's of London v. Walker*, 716 S.W.2d 99 (Tex. App.-Dallas 1986) (holding that absent some proof of significant injury or of some other factor rendering delay unreasonable, six-year delay between trial and rendition of judgment was not unreasonable as matter of law).

Even if a delay is not especially long, courts may discipline a judge when the delay constitutes a blatant misuse of the judicial office. The Supreme Judicial Court of Maine, for example, publicly reprimanded a judge who permanently deferred issuing a decision in one case, and delayed deciding another for over a year after the trial of another, believing that his actions would serve to facilitate negotiations between the parties. *In re Barrett*, 512 A.2d 1030 (Me. 1986) ("The fault in Judge Barrett's course of purposeful conduct . . . does not lie alone in the months and years of delay that resulted; rather, the principal fault lies in the fact that he determinedly administered his own personal brand of justice."). *See also In re Kelly*, 407 N.W.2d 182 (Neb. 1987) (judge removed from office for single instance of delay when he prevented his son's case from being heard by hiding court files); *In re Crislip*, 391 S.E.2d 84 (W. Va. 1990) (judge violated Canon by retrieving unexecuted warrants from sheriff's office and placing them either in his desk or in court files to prevent them from being executed).

Preventable Delay Warrants Discipline

While courts will not typically discipline a judge for only a few cases of delay that were not motivated by an abuse of office, good faith is usually no defense if a judge has established a record of inability to fulfill responsibilities in a timely manner. The Supreme Court of California, for example, sanctioned a judge when he "repeatedly and unjustifiably delayed decisions" on cases before him. *In re Creede*, 729 P.2d 79 (Cal. 1987). Even though the court noted that the record revealed that the judge was "a diligent, hardworking and highly respected judge," the court found that "he could have taken steps to monitor his cases and to dispose more promptly of submitted matters." *Id. See also In re Weeks*, 658 P.2d 174 (Ariz. 1983) ("In the cases that have been decided regarding delay, the courts have unanimously held that unnecessary, unwarranted delay is a violation of the Canons of Judicial Conduct."); *In re Allawas*, 906 So. 2d 1052 (Fla. 2005) (judge publicly reprimanded for failing to expeditiously issue rulings in a dozen cases, which adversely impacted the administration of justice); *In re Long*, 772 P.2d 814 (Kan. 1989) (court censured judge for delaying decisions in nine cases for more than a year and stated that "we do not adopt the respondent's argument that inefficiency alone cannot be grounds for disciplining a judge"); *Miss.*

Comm'n on Jud. Performance v. U.U., 875 So. 2d 1083 (Miss. 2004) (judge reprimanded for pattern of delays when seven separate complaints were received over the approximate span of one year, each concerning lengthy delays between a hearing on a motion and entry of judgment on that motion); *In re Assini*, 720 N.E.2d 882 (N.Y. 1999) (judge's neglect of more than 100 cases over an eight-month period in spite of repeated reminders from court personnel, the town board, and state auditors, was willful violation of rule governing judicial conduct requiring judges to perform their duties impartially and diligently and warranted removal).

Some cases, however, have held that discipline is inappropriate, even when judges have a long record of delay, so long as the delays were not caused by a willful abuse of office. The Court of Appeals of New York, for example, found that a judge who had failed to decide nine cases within a reasonable amount of time had not committed judicial misconduct, because there were no allegations that he had shirked his work. Despite the fact that the judge's refusal to write a decision that did not meet his "high standards" burdened others, the court stated that discipline for decisional delay should be reserved for those judges who have "defied administrative directives or [have] attempted to subvert the system by, for instance, falsifying, concealing or persistently refusing to file records indicating delays." *In re Greenfield*, 557 N.E.2d 1177 (N.Y. 1990). *See also In re Bell*, 894 S.W.2d 119 (Tex. 1995) (holding that discipline is unwarranted unless judge acts with a "specific intent to use the powers of office to accomplish an end, which the judge knew or should have known was beyond the legitimate exercise of authority").

Heavy Caseload as Mitigating Factor

In some jurisdictions, a delay in carrying out administrative and judicial duties may be justified where the judge has an unusually heavy caseload. *See, e.g., In re Twyman*, 437 S.E.2d 764 (W. Va. 1993) (magistrate did not improperly delay hearing even though she granted several continuances and ultimately dismissed case because it was not heard in 120 days, where magistrate's office had unusually heavy caseload due to lengthy absence of another magistrate). *But see In re Reinholtzen* (Cal. Comm'n on Jud. Performance 2015) (judge admonished for delayed decision making; while the commission recognized "that a judge's workload may make prompt decision of all matters submitted to the judge impossible. . . . [a]s presiding judge, Judge Reinholtsen had the authority to '[a]pportion the business of the court, including assigning and reassigning cases to departments'"); *In re Long*, 772 P.2d 814 (Kan. 1989) (insufficient staff was not a defense to charges that judge failed to comply with statutory time period for setting hearings, delayed making decisions, and deliberately failed to comply with written report requirement of court rule).

Violations throughout the Adjudicatory Process

For the purpose of classifying Rule 2.5(A) violations, the adjudicatory process may generally be divided into three stages, each with an attendant possible violation. These violations are: failure or delay in holding hearings or trials, delay in routine trial rulings, and failure to make timely decisions on cases under submission. *See generally* Russell G. Donaldson, *Removal or Discipline of State Judge for Neglect of, or Failure to Perform, Judicial Duties*, 87 A.L.R.4th 727 (1991). However, at least one jurisdiction has also disciplined a judge for delaying pretrial and post-trial procedures. *See In re Emanuel*, 755 So. 2d 862 (La. 1999) (judge censured for refusal to issue scheduling orders or set status conferences and for failing to promptly respond to requests for such) and *In re Hunter*, 823 So. 2d 325 (La. 2002) (judge's repeated failures to produce transcripts timely, accurately, or frequently not at all, resulting in lengthening of appeal process, 11 appellate reversals of serious felony criminal convictions and sentences for violation of defendants' constitutional right to judicial review, and potential reversals and remands for new trials, and judge's continuous lack of cooperation with court of appeal in securing transcripts for appellate review, warranted removal from office).

Additionally, Comment [3] to Rule 2.5 states that "prompt disposition of the court's business requires a judge to . . . be punctual in attending court." A judge may violate Rule 2.5(A), and may implicate other sections of the Code including Rule 2.1, simply by being habitually tardy in commencing court sessions. *See, e.g., Doan v. Comm'n on Jud. Performance*, 902 P.2d 272 (Cal. 1995).

Failure or Delay in Holding Hearings or Trials

A judge may be disciplined for failing to hold timely hearings or trials. The acceptable amount of time between the filing of a petition and the holding of a hearing is sometimes governed by state statute. If a statute defines the acceptable amount of time between the filing of a petition and a hearing, a court's determination of whether particular delays constitute misconduct may hew closely to the statutory definition. *See In re Long*, 772 P.2d 814 (Kan. 1989) (judge failed to comply with Kansas statutory requirement that hearings be held no later than 30 days after petition is filed; "It was the responsibility of Judge Long to see that the mandatory provisions of the statute for setting the hearings were followed"). However, isolated violations of such statutes may not constitute judicial misconduct. *See In re King*, 399 S.E.2d 888 (W. Va. 1990) (while "the deliberate failure to follow mandatory criminal procedures constitutes a violation of the Judicial Code of Ethics," a single failure to follow civil procedures does not rise to the level of misconduct).

When a state statute does not specify the acceptable amount of time between the filing of a petition and a hearing, a court determining whether delays are unreasonable will examine whether the delays were unnecessary and avoidable. In one particularly egregious case of delay, a Michigan judge's persistent refusal to work with staff led to the delay of hearings in 21 cases for varying amounts of time. Even though the judge knew, or should have known, that most of the cases were ready for hearing, he refused to schedule them, which the court found to be "absolutely inexcusable." *In re Seitz*, 495 N.W.2d 559 (Mich. 1993). The court deemed discipline appropriate because "[a] great deal of time, personnel, and administrative effort was expended to bring about a routine disposition of a group of uneventful cases that could have been accomplished by engaging in the kind of routine communication that keeps courtrooms and court dockets functioning throughout the state." *Id.* at 621. *See also In re Johnson*, 903 So. 2d 408 (La. 2005) (juvenile court judge's failure to conduct hearings, as requested by other judge, who was appointed Supernumerary Judge pro tempore of Juvenile Court, after she was informed that juvenile drug court treatment center was closing was violation of Code of Judicial Conduct).

Delay in Routine Trial Holdings

A judge may also be disciplined for taking an unreasonable amount of time to issue determinations on routine motions arising during the course of trial. *See, e.g., In re Emanuel*, 755 So. 2d 862 (La. 1999) (judge violated Canon by failing to sign routine orders). However, compared to other types of violations for failing to discharge duties diligently, delays in issuing routine holdings have not frequently been grounds for discipline.

Failure to Make Timely Decisions

Decisional delay is the most common ground on which courts discipline judges, pursuant to the language of Rule 2.5(A). As one commentator has written, "decision-making delay is in fact a relatively complex phenomenon," resulting from a "myriad of causes." Charles Gardner Geyh, *Adverse Publicity as a Means of Reducing Judicial Decision-Making Delay: Periodic Disclosure of Pending Motions, Bench Trials and Cases Under the Civil Justice Reform Act*, 41 Clev. St. L. Rev. 511 (1993). Decisional delay, like other delays in the adjudicatory process, may be caused by an excessive caseload, a shortage of sitting judges, and other structural inefficiencies, or may be caused by the inefficiencies of individual judges, resulting from an inability to manage cases, indecisiveness, or simply sloth. *Id.* at 514–20. When a judge delays in rendering judgment in a case, the judge not only denies quick and certain justice to the litigants but also reinforces the negative images of the judicial system. James J. Alfini, Steven Lubet, Jeffrey M. Shaman, & Charles Gardner Geyh, *Judicial Conduct and Ethics* § 6.02[4] at 6–14 (5th ed. 2013).

A judge may be disciplined for failing to decide a matter within a statutorily prescribed time period (*see In re Anderson*, 252 N.W.2d 592 (Minn. 1977)), but the Rule can also be violated in the absence of a statutory time limit. *See In re Keaton*, 13-301 (Ark. Jud. Disc. & Disability Comm'n 2015) (judge reprimanded for issung decision 17 months after divorce hearing); *In re Avera*, 283 P.3d 923 (Ore. 2012) (judge censured for 16-month delay in issuing final divorce decree); *In re Merlo*, 58 A.3d 1 (Pa. 2012) (judge removed from office, in part, based on failure to timely issue truancy adjudications).

Some courts utilize six factors, as delineated in an opinion by West Virginia's Supreme Court, in deciding whether decisional delay constitutes misconduct. *See In re Sommerville*, 364 S.E.2d 20 (W. Va. 1987). Those factors are "the amount of delay from the date the case was ripe for decision, the complexity of the case, the administrative and judicial workload of the judge, the number of special assignments given to the judge, the amount of vacation time taken, and other complaints involving delayed decisions made against the judge." *Id.* at 23–24. The Supreme Court of Louisiana, for example, utilized these factors in deciding the case of a judge who had delayed decisions in only two cases, but had delayed one for over six years. *In re Tuck*, 683 So. 2d 1214 (La. 1996). While noting the judge's otherwise spotless record, the court stressed that this extreme delay, along with the fact that the judge had failed to report the cases as pending, presented an aggravating circumstance. *See also In re Lee*, 933 So. 2d 736 (La. 2006) (using factors in opinion sanctioning judge for failing to render timely judgments in 18 cases).

While *Sommerville* has not been universally adopted, courts generally approach decisional delay on a case-by-case basis, analyzing many of the same factors to determine whether delay constitutes misconduct. In *Jud. Qualifications Comm'n v. Cieminski*, 326 N.W.2d 883 (N.D. 1982), the Supreme Court of North Dakota noted that, while a judge's lengthy delay in issuing decisions appeared to be in part motivated by "a strong sense of morals and a gentle heart," a lack of organization had also contributed to his repeated failure to issue decisions in cases that should have been resolved expeditiously. *Id.* at 887–88. Additionally, his workload was not so large as to play a mitigating factor. Weighing the factors together, the court found a violation and elected to suspend the judge from office for a period of three months.

Another important factor in determining whether decisional delay constitutes misconduct is whether the judge has continued to report on the status of undecided cases. State court systems often require that judges periodically report to an administrative body cases that have been fully submitted and await only a decision. *See In re Alvino*, 494 A.2d 1014 (N.J. 1985) (describing a typical reporting system). Not only does a judge's failure to report cases constitute a willful violation of administrative rules, it makes administrative management of habitually slow judges more difficult. Courts then tend to view decisional delay in a harsher light when the offending judge has also failed to report delayed cases to the appropriate administrative body. *See In re Estelle*, 336 P.3d 692 (Alaska 2014) (judge suspended for 45 days without pay for filing 16 inaccurate reports regarding cases pending more than six months); *In re Guzman*, 14-398 (Ariz. Comm'n on Jud. Conduct 2015) (judge who delayed rulings in three DUI cases and then falsely reported his docket by not including said cases reprimanded for violating rule); *In re Long*, 772 P.2d 814 (Kan. 1989) (judge's failure to report cases was "clear and deliberate" non-compliance with written report requirement of court rule and warranted public censure); *In re Emanuel*, 755 So. 2d 862 (La. 1999) (judge's failure to report case as under advisement violated Canon); *In re Tuck*, 683 So. 2d 1214 (La. 1996) ("[W]e normally would not impose a sanction in such a case. However, respondent also failed to report accurately . . . cases as being under advisement."); *In re Perez*, 843 N.W.2d 562 (Minn. 2014) (judge did not issue decisions timely, falsely certified that docket did not contain delayed cases, and falsified dates on judicial orders); *but see In re Cappoadge* (Del. Ct. on the Judiciary 2013) (judge who delayed findings in eight family court matters and filed inaccurate reports on status of undecided cases only issued censure based, in part, on judge's acknowledgement of the error and misconduct, commitment to remedial steps to ensure future compliance, no history of disciplinary complaints, and support of the local chief judge).

DUTY TO COOPERATE WITH OTHER JUDGES AND COURT OFFICIALS IN THE ADMINISTRATION OF COURT BUSINESS

Pursuant to Rule 2.5(B), a judge may be disciplined for failing to cooperate with other judges and court officials in the administration of court business. *See, e.g., In re Woodward* (Cal. Comm'n on Jud. Performance 2014) (judge censured in part for misleading court administrators in four separate meetings about re-assignment of judge's courtroom clerk with whom judge was engaged in an intimate relationship); *In re Jefferson*, 753 So. 2d 181 (La. 2000) (judge removed from office for misconduct, including failing to obey order issued by state supreme court and failing to cooperate with supernumerary judge); *In re McDonough*, 296 N.W.2d 648 (Minn. 1979) (judge failed to get along with administrative superiors and instigated a number of confrontations that interfered with the performance of his judicial duties). Fighting with or criticizing other judges may be grounds for discipline under this provision. *See, e.g., In re Jones*, 800 So. 2d 828 (La. 2001) (judge failed to cooperate in the administration of court business when he engaged in a shoving match with another judge); *Disc. Counsel v. Ferreri*, 710 N.E.2d 1107 (Ohio 1999) (judge's statements to newspaper attributing problems at juvenile detention center to administrative judge of Juvenile Court and detention center director constituted failure to cooperate with other judges and court officials in administration of court's business).

RULE 2.6 ENSURING THE RIGHT TO BE HEARD

(A) A judge shall accord to every person who has a legal interest in a proceeding, or that person's lawyer, the right to be heard according to law.*

(B) A judge may encourage parties to a proceeding and their lawyers to settle matters in dispute but shall not act in a manner that coerces any party into settlement.

COMMENT

[1] The right to be heard is an essential component of a fair and impartial system of justice. Substantive rights of litigants can be protected only if procedures protecting the right to be heard are observed.

[2] The judge plays an important role in overseeing the settlement of disputes, but should be careful that efforts to further settlement do not undermine any party's right to be heard according to law. The judge should keep in mind the effect that the judge's participation in settlement discussions may have, not only on the judge's own views of the case, but also on the perceptions of the lawyers and the parties if the case remains with the judge after settlement efforts are unsuccessful. Among the factors that a judge should consider when deciding upon an appropriate settlement practice for a case are (1) whether the parties have requested or voluntarily consented to a certain level of participation by the judge in settlement discussions, (2) whether the parties and their counsel are relatively sophisticated in legal matters, (3) whether the case will be tried by the judge or a jury, (4) whether the parties participate with their counsel in settlement discussions, (5) whether any parties are unrepresented by counsel, and (6) whether the matter is civil or criminal.

[3] Judges must be mindful of the effect settlement discussions can have, not only on their objectivity and impartiality, but also on the appearance of their objectivity and impartiality. Despite a judge's best efforts, there may be instances when information obtained during settlement discussions could influence a judge's decision making during trial, and, in such instances, the judge should consider whether disqualification may be appropriate. See Rule 2.11(A)(1).

1990 CODE COMPARISON

Paragraph A of Rule 2.6 comes from the previous Canon 3B(7). Paragraph B of Rule 2.6 was formerly in the Commentary to Canon 3B(8). This new paragraph was added to the Rule in recognition of the fact that an out-of-court settlement is a commonly used method of case resolution. It is important for judges to remember that a litigant's right to be heard can inadvertently be impaired by a judge who is overzealous in encouraging an out-of-court resolution. Accordingly, the Rule draws a line between encouraging settlement, which is permitted, and coercing settlement, which is not. Some people urged the Joint Commission to Evaluate the Model Code of Judicial Conduct to adopt rules that would prohibit judges from presiding at trial over cases with respect to which they had previously conducted settlement negotiations that were ultimately unsuccessful. Several members of the Commission agreed that as a general matter, it was the better practice for judges not to try cases they had attempted to settle, given the risk that statements the judge made during settlement negotiations might later be construed as lack of impartiality, but the Commission declined to adopt such a rule. The Commission ultimately concluded that such an issue was better left for rules of practice and procedure than ethics. Charles G. Geyh & W. William Hodes, *Reporters' Notes to the Model Code of Judicial Conduct* 33–34 (2009).

The Comments to Rule 2.6 are new to the Code. Comment [1] emphasizes what is implicit in the Rule, that judges' duties include ensuring that those entitled have their day in court. The Comment underscores the relationship between substantive and procedural justice, that is, the protection of substantive rights depends in part on respecting procedural right to be heard. Comment [2] provides judges with guidance in conducting settlement talks and Comment [3] emphasizes that events transpiring during settlement talks may bias judges toward a party or create an appearance of bias necessitating disqualification. *Id.* at 34–35.

ANNOTATION

THE RIGHT TO BE HEARD

Rule 2.6(A) requires a judge to accord to every person who has a legal interest in a proceeding, or that person's lawyer, the right to be heard according to law. As noted in Comment [1], "[t]he right to be heard is an essential component of a fair and impartial system of justice. Substantive rights of litigants can be protected only if procedures protecting the right to be heard are observed."

Therefore, a judge may violate Rule 2.6(A) by entering a directed verdict of guilt without giving the defendant an opportunity to present evidence (*see, e.g., In re Dash*, 564 S.E.2d 672 (S.C. 2002) (judge publicly reprimanded)), by holding a party in contempt without issuing a summons or conducting a contempt hearing (*see, e.g., In re Dixon*, 559 S.E.2d 576 (S.C. 2002)), by not allowing a party to put on its case (*see, e.g., In re McBrien*, (Cal. Comm'n on Jud. Performance 2010); *In re Jones*, JC-10-069-C (N.H. Jud. Conduct Comm. 2011)), by dismissing a case sua sponte without notice or a hearing (*see, e.g., In re Lyons*, JD-2014-0001 (N.H. 2015)), or by adopting the State's proposed findings of fact and conclusions of law in a criminal case without giving the defendant the opportunity to be heard. (*Byford v. State*, 156 P.3d 691 (Nev. 2007)).

A judge may also violate Rule 2.6(A) by finding a defendant guilty when either the defendant or the prosecutor is not in the courtroom. *See, e.g., In re Edens*, 226 S.E.2d 5 (N.C. 1976) (judge accepted a defendant's guilty plea in the clerk's office rather than in the courtroom, outside of the presence of and without giving notice to the prosecutor); *In re Jordan*, 622 P.2d 297 (Or. 1980) (judge commenced trial of an absent defendant in a criminal case and entered a finding of guilty at the conclusion of the trial); *In re Eplin*, 416 S.E.2d 248 (W. Va. 1992) (judge suspended for authorizing a plea agreement on behalf of a defendant without input from the victim, complaining officer, or prosecutor); *but see In re Murphy*, 737 N.W.2d 355 (Minn. 2007) (judge's disposition of traffic ticket by ordering a continuance for dismissal, in chambers without prosecutorial input, did not constitute a violation of Canon requiring judge to afford all interested parties an opportunity to be heard because the disposition of the ticket was within the range of normal dispositions for similar traffic violations in county); *In re Tucker*, 501 S.E.2d 67 (N.C. 1998) (entering plea and judgment of not guilty in driving while impaired cases based on defense counsel's ex parte representations, without determining whether state consented or wanted to be heard, was permissible where judge acted pursuant to shorthand disposition practice acquiesced in by state and had no reason to suspect that defense counsel had not been authorized by state to proceed in that manner).

A judge also should not impose a sentence of imprisonment without a hearing (*see In re Ross*, 428 A.2d 858 (Me. 1981)), hold a hearing without giving notice to an interested party (*see In re Miller*, 644 So. 2d 75 (Fla. 1994) (finding a violation of several Canons when judge held a hearing in child custody case and failed to give the mother notice of the hearing until after it began)), or conduct a hearing or question a party whom the judge knows is represented by counsel in the absence of that counsel (*see In re Murphy*, 181 So. 3d 1169 (Fla. 2015) (judge removed from bench in part for calling "cases in which defendants were represented by the Public Defender's Office and were without the presence of their attorney, and inducing some of the defendants to waive speedy trial rights"); *In re Jorgensen*, CJC No. 4780-F-126 (Wash. Comm'n on Jud. Conduct 2006) (judge reprimanded for beginning custody hearing before scheduled hearing time when party's attorney was not yet in the courtroom even though judge knew party was represented by counsel)).

A judge may also violate this rule by conducting a proceeding with no interpreter when a litigant is unable to understand and communicate in English to the extent that the party cannot meaningfully participate in the court proceedings. *In re Merino* (N.Y. Comm'n on Jud. Conduct 2014) (court proceeding "is meaningless when, because of the party's limited proficiency in English, the proceeding is incomprehensible to him").

A judge has even been disciplined pursuant to this rule for entering the jury room unaccompanied by either counsel or a court reporter, to ask whether the jurors wished to continue deliberating or go home. *In re Mathesius*, 910 A.2d 594 (N.J. 2006) (judge disciplined for repeated intemperate and inappropriate remarks to jurors and attorneys and about other judges).

A judge's motives for denying a party the right to be heard are not relevant in determining whether Rule 2.6(A) was violated. *See, e.g., In re Dwyer*, 572 P.2d 898 (Kan. 1977) (judge told the defense lawyer not to bother to introduce any evidence because, the judge asserted, he wanted to prevent the young defendant from perjuring himself. The court held that regardless of how well-motivated the judge may have been, "he effectively foreclosed the defense from presenting its side of the dispute, thus giving the appearance of impropriety and denying to the defendant his full right to be heard"); *In re Branch*, 767 S.E.2d 47 (N.C. 2015) (despite judge's belief that court had discretion to proceed without appointing counsel for servicemember-defendant in domestic relations matter when servicemember was assigned overseas, court found judge violated this rule as a result of "insufficient inquiry" into Servicemember's Civil Relief Act of 2003); *In re Royster*, 648 S.E.2d 837 (N.C. 2007) (rejecting judge's argument that his ex parte disposition of a case was driven by a desire to see justice done stating that "a determination of disrepute 'depends not so much upon the judge's motives but more on the conduct itself, the results thereof, and the impact such conduct might reasonably have upon knowledgeable observers'"); *In re McBrien* (Cal. Comm'n on Jud. Performance 2010) (judge publicly censured, though he claimed that need to respond to brief emergency protection order telephone call and fact that attorney's estimated time for trial had expired justified judge's declaration that the trial had ended); *In re Pratt*, CJC 14-0102-DI (Tex. Comm'n on Jud. Conduct 2014) (judge's mistaken belief that dismissal of 600 cases for want of procesution was procedural mechanism for closing cases did not prohibit finding that judge violated rule).

ENCOURAGING BUT NOT COERCING PARTIES TO SETTLE

New Rule 2.6(B), which previously appeared in the Commentary to former Canon 3B(8), provides that a "judge may encourage parties to a proceeding and their lawyers to settle matters in dispute but shall not act in a manner that coerces any party into settlement." As noted in the Commentary, judges should be careful that efforts to further settlement do not undermine any party's right to be heard according to law.

The Commentary to Rule 2.6 acknowledges the important role that judges play in overseeing the settlement of disputes but cautions them against some potential problems, particularly when settlement negotiations are unsuccessful. Such negotiations may not only alter the judge's view of the case, but also create, in the minds of the lawyers and the parties, an appearance of coercing a settlement and thus undermining a party's right to be heard. Such negotiations also may create an appearance of impartiality if the case remains with the judge after unsuccessful attempts at settlement. Additionally, as noted in paragraph [3] of the Commentary, a judge may, despite his or her best effort, learn something during settlement discussions that could influence his or her decision making during the trial. In those instances, the judge should consider whether to recuse himself or herself from the trial.

The Commentary lists six factors, among others, that a judge should consider when deciding upon an appropriate settlement practice for a case: (1) whether the parties have requested or voluntarily consented to a certain level of participation by the judge in settlement discussions, (2) whether the parties and their counsel are relatively sophisticated in legal matters, (3) whether the case will be tried by the judge or a jury, (4) whether the parties participate with their counsel in settlement discussions, (5) whether any parties are unrepresented by counsel, and (6) whether the matter is civil or criminal.

RULE 2.7 RESPONSIBILITY TO DECIDE

A judge shall hear and decide matters assigned to the judge, except when disqualification is required by Rule 2.11 or other law.*

COMMENT

[1] Judges must be available to decide the matters that come before the court. Although there are times when disqualification is necessary to protect the rights of litigants and preserve public confidence in the independence, integrity, and impartiality of the judiciary, judges must be available to decide matters that come before the courts. Unwarranted disqualification may bring public disfavor to the court and to the judge personally. The dignity of the court, the judge's respect for fulfillment of judicial duties, and a proper concern for the burdens that may be imposed upon the judge's colleagues require that a judge not use disqualification to avoid cases that present difficult, controversial, or unpopular issues.

1990 CODE COMPARISON

The Rule is former Canon 3B(1), with a slight modification to cross-reference the disqualification rule explicitly and to acknowledge that in some instances disqualification may be required by other law. Charles G. Geyh & W. William Hodes, *Reporters' Notes to the Model Code of Judicial Conduct* 35 (2009). The Comment to the Rule, emphasizing the importance the importance of judges' availability to decide matters that come before the courts, is new to the Code.

ANNOTATION

DUTY TO SIT

Rule 2.7 mandates that judges hear and decide matters assigned to them, unless disqualification is required. This language was added to the Judicial Code in 1990 to emphasize the judicial "duty to sit" and to minimize potential abuse of the disqualification alternative. ABA Standing Committee on 1990 Code, Legislative Draft 15 (1990). Permitting judges to disqualify themselves for frivolous reasons or for no reason at all would contravene public policy by unduly delaying proceedings, increasing the workload of other judges, and fostering impermissible judge-shopping. Ronald D. Rotunda and John S. Dzienkowski, *Legal Ethics: The Lawyer's Deskbook on Professional Responsibility* 1480 (2016). However, although a judge has a duty to not sit where disqualified, a judge has an equally strong duty not to recuse himself when the circumstances do not require recusal. *Laird v. Tatum*, 409 U.S. 824 (1972). Nor should a judge exercise recusal for reasons that have nothing to do with a lack of impartiality. The New York State Commission on Judicial Conduct censured a judge who used recusal from cases, where an attorney involved was a state legislator, as a political tactic over the issue of judicial salaries. The judge encouraged other judges to engage in the same practice. *In re Himelein* (N.Y. Comm'n on Jud. Conduct 2009) For additional discussion of disqualification, see Rule 2.11 and accompanying text.

The relatively little case law that exists construing the language of Rule 2.7 suggests that it imposes an "affirmative duty not to avoid justiciable issues." *In re Respondent U.*, 1995 WL 405060 (Cal. Bar Ct., Review Dep't July 6, 1995); *see Parker v. Priest*, 932 S.W.2d 320 (Ark. 1996) (in denying motion to disqualify, judge asserted that because there is no conflict of interest, real or apparent, there is no basis for disqualification, and that the Code requires that I "shall hear and decide matters" assigned to me); *Peterson v. Borst*, 784 N.E.2d 934 (Ind. 2003) (judge asserted that if his appointment by mayor to Cultural Development Commission creates appearance of impartiality when mayor is litigant in judge's court, appropriate action is to resign from Commission rather than recuse himself); *Hi-Country Ests. Homeowner's Ass'n v. Bagley & Co*, 996 P.2d 534 (Utah 2000) ("unless a justification for reassignment exists, a judge has a duty to retain a case until it is completed."); N.Y. Adv. Comm. on Jud. Ethics Op. 92-75 (1992) (advising a village justice not to disqualify himself from cases where the village attorney appears as private counsel unless there is some other basis for the disqualification because the "duty to sit where not disqualified . . . is as strong as the duty not to sit where disqualified").

Relevant Federal Statute

Prior to a 1974 amendment, 28 U.S.C.A. Section 455 required a federal judge to sit in a case where there was no violation of the disqualification statute, though there may have been an appearance of impartiality. Ronald D. Rotunda and John S. Dzienkowski, *Legal Ethics: The Lawyer's Deskbook on Professional Responsibility* 1480–81 (2016). Amended Section 455 adopted an objective standard, mandating that a judge sit in a case unless there is a reasonable question as to the judge's impartiality. Therefore, while federal judges do not have a duty to sit where their impartiality might be reasonably questioned, they should not disqualify themselves simply to avoid sitting on difficult or controversial cases. *Id.*; *see, e.g., U.S. v. Glick*, 946 F.2d 335 (4th Cir. 1991) (when there is no reasonable basis to question judge's impartiality, it would be improper for judge to recuse); *Hinman v. Rogers*, 831 F.2d 937 (10th Cir. 1987) (there is as much obligation not to recuse when there is no occasion for him to do so as there is for him to do so when there is).

RULE 2.8 DECORUM, DEMEANOR, AND COMMUNICATION WITH JURORS

(A) A judge shall require order and decorum in proceedings before the court.

(B) A judge shall be patient, dignified, and courteous to litigants, jurors, witnesses, lawyers, court staff, court officials, and others with whom the judge deals in an official capacity, and shall require similar conduct of lawyers, court staff, court officials, and others subject to the judge's direction and control.

(C) A judge shall not commend or criticize jurors for their verdict other than in a court order or opinion in a proceeding.

COMMENT

[1] The duty to hear all proceedings with patience and courtesy is not inconsistent with the duty imposed in Rule 2.5 to dispose promptly of the business of the court. Judges can be efficient and businesslike while being patient and deliberate.

[2] Commending or criticizing jurors for their verdict may imply a judicial expectation in future cases and may impair a juror's ability to be fair and impartial in a subsequent case.

[3] A judge who is not otherwise prohibited by law from doing so may meet with jurors who choose to remain after trial but should be careful not to discuss the merits of the case.

1990 CODE COMPARISON

Paragraph (A) of Rule 2.8 is former Canon 3B(3). Paragraph (B) is former Canon 3B(4), modified to extend the duty of courtesy to court staff, where episodes of abusive behavior have occasionally arisen. "Court officials" was added to be consistent with the list used later in the same paragraph. Paragraph (C) is the first sentence of former Canon 3B(11). The Joint Commission to Evaluate the Model Code of Judicial Conduct moved discussion permitting judges to express appreciation to jurors from the black letter to the Comment on the grounds that it should not be considered subject matter for disciplinary enforcement. Charles G. Geyh & W. William Hodes, *Reporters' Notes to the Model Code of Judicial Conduct* 36 (2009).

Comment [1] is the Commentary to Canon 3B(4) and Comment [2] is the Commentary to Rule 3B(4). Comment [3] is new to the Code and was added to make clear that judges can commend jurors for their service and that providing an opportunity for judges to learn more about the jury's experience can be valuable, as long as the merits of the case are not discussed. *Id.* at 36–37.

ANNOTATION

ORDER AND DECORUM

Rule 2.8(A) requires that judges maintain order and decorum in their courtrooms. In carrying out this duty, a judge may admonish parties to keep their voices down in court or cease behavior that may be distracting or threatening. *See, e.g., State v. Lovelace*, 607 P.2d 49 (Kan. 1980) (judge acted properly in admonishing defendant to keep his voice down when he was conversing with his lawyer in a loud voice that could be heard by others in the courtroom; court rejected defendant's assertion on appeal that judge's admonishment prejudiced the jury); *State v. Lewis*, 781 So. 2d 650 (La. App. 2001) (finding that judge's admonishing murder defendant to cease his distracting and discourteous behavior of nodding his head and staring at jury was not an improper comment on the defendant's character). According to at least one state ethics opinion, a trial judge has the authority to control the dress code of people appearing before the court, if the dress is inappropriate and jeopardizes the dignity of the proceeding. Fla. Jud. Ethics Adv. Comm. Op. 83-12 (1983) (judge may prohibit inappropriate attire to maintain decorum and order in courtroom). *But see* Dennis A. Rendleman, *The Case of the Dirty T-Shirt: A Proposed Amendment to the Model Code of Judicial Conduct on the Exercise of the Power of Contempt*, 15 No. 4 Prof. Law. 18 (2005).

A judge may violate Rule 2.8(A) by failing to take control of a case and permitting lawyers to engage in unprofessional conduct without sanctioning them. *Jud. Inquiry & Rev. Bd. v. Snyder*, 523 A.2d 294 (Pa. 1987); *In re Cresap*, 940 So. 2d 624 (La. 2006) (judge admittedly lost control of hearing and was unable to find a way to rein in behavior of lawyers before him). A judge may be permitted to preserve or restore order in the courtroom by temporarily ejecting disruptive and disorderly persons, including lawyers. However, a judge may not use that power as an artifice or guise to eject counsel with whom the judge has a personal or professional disagreement. Ronald D. Rotunda and John S. Dzienkowski, *Legal Ethics: The Lawyer's Deskbook on Professional Responsibility* 1481–82 (2016); *see also In re Jefferson*, 753 So. 2d 181 (La. 2000) (judge removed for misconduct including banning city prosecutor from courtroom until judge received apology for wrongs that judge perceived were committed against him); *In re Hague*, 315 N.W.2d 524 (Mich. 1982) (misconduct, including improperly excluded attorneys from the courtroom, is misconduct warranting suspension from office).

Judges' Lack of Decorum

Cases construing the language of Rule 2.8(A) are likely to involve judges' lack of decorum in the courtroom, rather than their failure to regulate behavior of litigants or lawyers. For instance, judges may violate Rule 2.8(A) by being hung-over while on the bench (*In re Krake*, 942 So. 2d 18 (La. 2006)) or by yelling or making inappropriate remarks to litigants, lawyers, and others appearing before them (*see, e.g., In re Trettis*, 577 So. 2d 1312 (Fla. 1991) (judge reprimanded for directing verbal tirades at jurors, defendants and attorneys); *In re Inquiry Concerning a Judge (Hammill)*, 566 S.E.2d 310 (Ga. 2002) (judge made inappropriate comments to parties in three separate cases); *In re Ellender*, 16 So. 3d 351 (La. 2009) (judge suspended for failing to treat pro se applicant for domestic abuse protection seriously and for demeaning and condescending attitude); *In re Jefferson*, 753 So. 2d 181 (La. 2000) (judge removed for misconduct including using bench as a pulpit from which to chastise lawyers and court staff); *In re Bowers*, 721 So. 2d 875 (La. 1998) (judge used inappropriate language and was insensitive and impatient toward those appearing in courtroom); *In re Rice*, 515 N.W.2d 53 (Minn. 1994) (judge reprimanded for shouting at and intimidating court employees); *Miss. Comm'n on Jud. Performance v. Spencer*, 725 So. 2d 171 (Miss. 1998) (judge demonstrated outrageous, erratic conduct and hostile demeanor toward those exposed to him); *In re Albano*, 384 A.2d 144 (N.J. 1978) (judge censured for making sarcastic remarks to student attorneys from a law school legal clinic); *In re Romano*, 690 N.Y.S.2d 849 (N.Y. 1999) (judge removed for misconduct including making insensitive remarks about charges of domestic violence); *In re Griffin*, 357 S.E.2d 682 (N.C. 1987) (judge censured for injudicious response to comments by a spectator in court); *In re Barr*, 13 S.W.3d 525 (Tex. Rev. Trib. 1998) (judge made sexist comments and gestures to women in courtroom); *In re Hammermaster*, 985 P.2d 924 (Wash. 1999) (judge intimidated defendants with threats of life imprisonment or indefinite jail sentences)). *See generally* Annotation, *Disciplinary Action Against Judge on Ground of Abusive or Intemperate Language or Conduct Toward Attorneys, Court Personnel, or Parties to or Witnesses in Actions, and the Like*, 89 A.L.R.4th 278 (1991). In many of these cases, the judge's conduct also violates Rule 2.8(B), which requires judges to be "patient, dignified, and courteous."

Judges have been disciplined for unconventional conduct that compromises the order and decorum of the courtroom while sitting on the bench. *See, e.g., In re Anderson*, 814 P.2d 773 (Ariz. 1991) (judge made phone calls from the bench to obtain advice on cases from "friends of the court"); *In re Best*, 719 So. 2d 432 (La. 1998) (judge asked courtroom audience to vote on the guilt or innocence of a defendant); *In re Greene*, 403 S.E.2d 257 (N.C. 1991) (judge polled courtroom spectators in a domestic dispute to find out how many had "little spats" with their spouses).

Engaging in physical altercations with litigants also violates Rule 2.8(A). *See, e.g., In re Best*, 719 So. 2d 432 (La. 1998) (during juvenile court hearing, judge grabbed juvenile defendant by the shirt, pulled him so that their eyes met and their noses almost touched and then chastised him); *Miss. Comm'n on Jud. Performance v. Guest*, 717 So. 2d 325 (Miss. 1998) (judge left the bench in front of a crowded courtroom and initiated a physical confrontation with a handcuffed defendant).

Where the Conduct Takes Place

There is some debate over whether a judge can be charged under the language of Rule 2.8(A) for conduct that does not occur in the courtroom. Some courts assert that since the language of Rule 2.8(A) requires order and decorum in "proceedings" before the judge, the Canon can only be violated by "conduct, which takes place in open court, while the judge is on the bench, fulfilling an adjudicative function." *In re Barr*, 13 S.W.3d 525 (Tex. Rev. Trib. 1998). However, a judge was found to have violated the Canon requiring him to "maintain order and decorum in proceedings before him" by holding arraignments and initial appearances in criminal cases in his chambers and by being disrespectful to litigants during those in-chambers proceedings. *In re Dwyer*, 572 P.2d 898 (Kan. 1977). In another case, a judge was disciplined for off-the-bench conduct when he refused to schedule a magistrate to sit on the bench in retaliation for the magistrate's reporting an improper order issued by the judge. *In re Inquiry Concerning a Judge (Hammill)*, 566 S.E.2d 310 (Ga. 2002) (judges must maintain decorum and be patient, dignified, and courteous to everyone they deal with in their official capacity).

JUDICIAL TEMPERAMENT

Rule 2.8(B) deals with judicial demeanor. It requires "[a] judge to be patient, dignified, and courteous to litigants, jurors, witnesses, lawyers, court staff, court officials, and others with whom the judge deals in an official capacity." As noted in the Commentary, this duty is not inconsistent with the duty to promptly dispose of the court's business. Judges are expected to be efficient and businesslike while being patient and deliberate. Model Code of Judicial Conduct Rule 2.9 cmt. [1].

Rule 2.8(B) sets a high standard, one that is explained more fully by Standards 6-3.4 and 6-3.5 of the ABA Standards Relating to the Function of the Trial Judge, which say:

> Standard 6-3.4(a): The trial judge should be the exemplar of dignity and impartiality. The judge should exercise restraint over his or her conduct and utterances. The judge should remain neutral regarding the proceedings at all times, suppress personal predilections, control his or her temper and emotions, and be patient, respectful, and courteous to defendant, jurors, witnesses, victims, lawyers, and others with whom the judge deals in an official capacity. The judge should not permit any person in the courtroom to embroil him or her in conflict, and should otherwise avoid conduct which tends to demean the proceedings or to undermine his authority in the courtroom.
>
> Standard 6-3.5(b): When it becomes necessary during the trial for the judge to comment upon the conduct of witnesses, spectators, counsel, or others, or upon the testimony, the judge should do so outside the presence of the jury, if possible. Any such comment should be in a firm, dignified and restrained manner, avoiding repartee, limiting comments and rulings to what is reasonably required for the orderly progress of the trial, and refraining from unnecessary disparagement of persons or issues.

Judicial conduct inconsistent with the principles expressed in this standard will generally violate Rule 2.8(B). *See, e.g., In re Shea*, 759 So. 2d 631 (Fla. 2000) (judge removed for acting with hostility toward lawyers, court personnel, and other judges); *In re Inquiry Concerning Holien*, 612 N.W.2d 789 (Iowa 2000) (judge removed for rude, disrespectful, and hostile treatment of fellow judges, lawyers, defendants, court reporters, and other court personnel); *In re Krake*, 942 So. 2d 18 (La. 2006) (judge who appeared on bench hung-over, and sometimes disheveled, failed to maintain the dignity expected of a judge); *Disc. Counsel v. O'Neill*, 815 N.E.2d 286 (Ohio 2004) (judge who engaged in a pattern of rude, undignified, and unprofessional conduct that included abusive verbal outbursts, unjustified expulsions from the courtroom, and berating or humiliating persons in the presence of others violated professional rules that required a judge to be patient, dignified, and courteous to litigants, jurors, witnesses, lawyers, and others with whom the judge dealt with in an official capacity).

Rule 2.8(B) has several purposes, the most obvious of which is to require judges to act in a way that engenders respect for the judicial system. The people who come before the court, including lawyers, witnesses, jurors, spectators, and court staff cannot be expected to respect the judiciary when judges are rude, sarcastic, or impatient. As the court stated in *In re Jenkins*, 503 N.W.2d 425, 427 (Iowa 1993):

> The people who come to court, litigants, witnesses, jurors, even lawyers, cannot select the judge who is to preside over them. Although circumstances may on occasion demand sternness, a judge should strive to be kind. The authority exercised by a judge is so great as to easily break ordinary people who are rendered comparatively helpless in their relationship with a court. Such authority should not be entrusted to those who, either deliberately or through thoughtlessness, offend the ordinary sensibilities of citizens. This is true with regard to a judge's conduct throughout a trial, whether in the courtroom or in chambers. Nowhere is it more true than in the words chosen by a judge in a decision or decree that becomes a permanent record. Flamboyance in decorum and attempts at clever ridicule are not admired characteristics in a jurist.

A second purpose of Rule 2.8(B) is to ensure that judicial proceedings both are and appear to the public to be fair and impartial. *In re Brown*, 691 N.E.2d 573 (Mass. 1998) (it is not enough that judges know that they are fair and impartial, they must appear to be so as well, and "an impartial manner, courtesy and dignity are the outward sign of that fairness and impartiality"); *In re O'Dea*, 622 A.2d 507 (Vt. 1993) ("[J]udicial intemperance invariably conveys the message of a closed mind."). Berating an attorney or a witness may interfere with a lawyer's ability to represent a client effectively or with a witness's ability to testify calmly. Moreover, if a judge's abusive conduct is directed at one side only, the judge's attitude toward that side may prejudice the jury against it. Even if the judge is equally intemperate toward both sides, the conduct could compromise the fairness or the appearance of fairness of the proceeding, because a hostile or undignified atmosphere in the courtroom may not be conducive to impartial decision-making. *See generally* Leonard E. Gross, *Judicial Discipline and the First Amendment*, 36 Syracuse L. Rev. 1181 (1986).

Because judicial temperament is so important to the effectiveness of the judicial system, courts have construed Canon 3B(4), the predecessor to Rule 2.8(B), rather broadly. For instance, although the provision is within the section of the Model Code dealing with adjudicative behavior, and would seem to deal with conduct in the courtroom, courts have disciplined judges for intemperate conduct in chambers (*In re Cox*, 532 A.2d 1017 (Me. 1987)), in the hallways of the court building (*In re Greene*, 403 S.E.2d 257 (N.C. 1991)), in other offices of the courthouse (*In re Hair*, 436 S.E.2d 128 (N.C. 1993)), and even away from the court (*In re Lehman*, 812 P.2d 992 (Ariz. 1991) (judge publicly censured for various misconduct that occurred away from the court)). Courts have also applied the language of Rule 2.8(B) to appellate judges, as well as trial judges. *In re Brown*, 691 N.E.2d 573 (Mass. 1998) ("[T]he Canons do not distinguish between trial and appellate judging, . . . the appearance of impartiality and courtesy are as important in appellate judging as at trial.").

Additional Targets of the Conduct

In addition, although the Rule speaks of judges' conduct toward "litigants, jurors, witnesses, lawyers, court staff, court officials, and others with whom the judge deals in an official capacity," it can also apply to comments made about a person or an organization not before the court. *See In re Brown*, 691 N.E.2d 573 (Mass. 1998) ("[T]he spirit and purpose of [the Rule] would hardly be served by holding that a judge may act in an undignified manner while on the bench so long as he only chooses to berate persons not before him."); *but see In re Brown*, 879 S.W.2d 801 (Tenn. 1994) (holding that language of the Rule was not violated by a judge's comments that were directed at the structure and operation of the juvenile court and not at anyone with whom the judge had direct contact). The language of this provision has even been applied absent a showing that the judge's behavior raises sufficient doubts about the judge's impartiality. *In re Brown*, 691 N.E.2d 573 (Mass. 1998) ("Impatience, a lack of dignity, or discourtesy—the stuff of [Rule 2.8(B)]—may not suffice to demand recusal, but the bias and prejudice relevant in a recusal proceeding are not therefore necessary to find a violation of [Rule 2.8(B)].").

Requiring Similar Conduct of Others

Although Rule 2.8(B) instructs judges to "require similar conduct of lawyers, court staff, court officials, and others subject to the judge's direction and control," the case law under this Canon generally involves only displays of intemperate behavior by judges themselves and not their failure to control the intemperate behavior of others. *But see In re Kohn*, 568 S.W.2d 255 (Mo. 1978) (where judge was charged with failing to require staff to extend courteous treatment to litigants, lawyers, and others appearing before them, court found that judge could not be responsible for staff's conduct when it wasn't clear that he had been informed of incidents of rudeness); *In re Crow*, 151 P.3d 270 (Wyo. 2007) (judge's failure to supervise court staff, particularly his wife, who had been his chief clerk and the subject of numerous complaints involving her rude behavior to co-workers and members of the public, violated Canons requiring judge to be patient, dignified, and courteous to litigants and others with whom judge dealt in an official capacity, and to require similar conduct of staff and court officials).

Intemperate Speech to or About Lawyers, Litigants, and Court Employees

The "patience and dignity" standard of former Canon 3B(4) and current Rule 2.8(B) speaks in broad and ambiguous terms and is not susceptible to a precise definition. Ronald D. Rotunda and John S. Dzienkowski, *Legal Ethics: The Lawyer's Deskbook on Professional Responsibility* 1483 (2016).

Many of the cases construing the language of this provision involve intemperate speech by judges toward lawyers, litigants, court employees, and others appearing in their courtrooms. Sometimes, this speech is characterized by arrogance on the part of the judge that has been described as the judge "act[ing] like he was God" (*Miss. Comm'n on Jud. Performance v. Spencer*, 725 So. 2d 171 (Miss. 1998)) or treating people as if they "were stupid" (*Kloepfer v. Comm'n on Jud. Performance*, 782 P.2d 239 (Cal. 1989)). *See also In re Schwartz*, 755 So. 2d 110 (Fla. 2000) (during oral argument, appellate judge verbally abused law students who were making initial appearances before the court and made discourteous remarks about professor who was supervising students); *In re Mathesius*, 910 A.2d 594 (N.J. 2006) (judge's remarks to defense counsel who objected to judge's act of entering jury room without either counsel or a court reporter and asking whether jurors wished to continue deliberating or go home, which consisted of judge stating that "you can do that when you're a judge. I'll do it the way I do it when I am a judge," violated Canon requiring judges to be patient, dignified, and courteous to attorneys and others); *In re Houston*, 11-4749 (Tenn. Ct. of the Judiciary 2012) (judge reprimanded for stating he wished he could "pull a trap door" and send defendants accused of murder "straight to hell right now"); *cf. In re Disqualification of Corrigan*, 826 N.E.2d 302 (Ohio 2004) ("Judges are certainly entitled to express dissatisfaction with attorneys' dilatory tactics inside and outside the courtroom, but that dissatisfaction can and should be expressed in a way that promotes public confidence in the integrity, dignity, and impartiality of the judiciary."). *See generally* Annotation, *Disciplinary Action Against Judge on Ground of Intemperate or Abusive Language or Conduct Toward Attorneys, Court Personnel, or Parties to or Witnesses in Actions, and the Like*, 89 A.L.R.4th 279 (1991). Engaging in a pattern of misrepresentation in interactions with judges, litigants, attorneys, and court personnel may also violate this Code provision. *See, e.g., Disc. Counsel v. O'Neill*, 815 N.E.2d 286 (Ohio 2004).

Disparaging Lawyers and Their Staff

Violations of the language of Canon 3B(4), the predecessor to Rule 2.8(B) often entailed disparaging statements directed at lawyers. Judges have spoken contemptuously of lawyers' motives in filing cases or motions (*see, e.g., In re Wood*, 720 So. 2d 506 (Fla. 1998) (judge attacked good faith of lawyer who filed a motion requesting a continuance); *In re Eads*, 362 N.W.2d 541 (Iowa 1985) (accusing a lawyer of filing a lawsuit solely because of the fees)); of their professionalism (*see, e.g., In re Bowers*, 721 So. 2d 875 (La. 1998) (saying to a lawyer who was approving the wording of a judgment, "I wouldn't want you to go whining up to the Court of Appeal again.")); of their credibility (*see, e.g., In re Elliston*, 789 S.W.2d 469 (Mo. 1990) (telling a lawyer, "[i]f you think I'm going to make a commitment to you before I've heard all the evidence, you're sadly mistaken.")); and of their competence (*see, e.g., Kloepfer v. Comm'n on Jud. Performance*, 782 P.2d 239 (Cal. 1989) (disciplining a judge for, among other things, telling one lawyer that she was "an embarrassment to the People of the State" and another lawyer that he was appalled that the interests of the People of the State of California rested in her hands); *In re Eads*, 362 N.W.2d 541 (Iowa 1985) (claiming a lawyer had conducted a "shoddy" investigation); *In re Bennett*, 267 N.W.2d 914 (Mich. 1978) (judge gossiped about two lawyers, suggesting that one was an alcoholic and that another was incompetent); *In re McDonough*, 296 N.W.2d 648 (Minn. 1979) (calling an attorney's objections "childish and ridiculous and quite immature"); *Miss. Comm'n on Jud. Performance v. Spencer*, 725 So. 2d 171 (Miss. 1998) (telling a county prosecutor that she needed to resign); *In re Elliston*, 789 S.W.2d 469 (Mo. 1990) (calling a lawyer's work "sloppy"); *In re Chase*, 1991 WL 733643 (N.Y. Comm'n on Jud. Conduct, 1991) (accusing a lawyer of being a "lousy district attorney" and suggesting that his recent election loss was due to "poor lawyering skills"); *In re Hill*, 609 S.E.2d 221 (N.C. 2005) (judge's suggestion to defense attorney to use "big boy voice" when addressing jury violated Canon)).

Judges have also been disciplined for criticizing actions taken by a lawyer in a case. *See, e.g., Comm'n on Jud. Qualifications v. Rome*, 623 P.2d 1307 (Kan. 1981) (judge criticized county attorney's actions in reducing criminal charges against a particular defendant); *In re Bowers*, 721 So. 2d 875 (La. 1998) (judge criticized lawyers for seeking supervisory writs from the appellate court). And, judges have been disciplined for hostile questioning of lawyers' staff, including investigators. *See, e.g., In re Easterling* (Ky. Jud. Conduct Comm'n 2015) (judge reprimanded for confrontational tone and scolding of investigator for state Attorney General's office).

Disparaging Litigants and Witnesses

Judges have been disciplined for making disparaging comments to litigants, usually demeaning their character or their behavior. *See, e.g., In re Williams*, 15-085 (Ariz. Comm'n on Jud. Conduct 2015) (judge publicly reprimanded for mocking and demeaning debtor-litigant); *In re Holt*, 13-035 (Ariz. Comm'n on Jud. Conduct 2013) (judge publicly reprimanded for calling litigant's pleading "stupid and screwy" as well as telling litigant, "If you don't like it, move to

Mexico"); *In re Conn*, 13-178 (Ariz. Comm'n on Jud. Conduct 2013) (judge who called domestic violence victim "idiot" during sentencing hearing publicly reprimanded for violation of Rule 2.8); *In re Wood*, 720 So. 2d 506 (Fla. 1998) (ruling it was misconduct for a judge to criticize a defendant insurance company and the insurance industry as a whole); *In re Sloop*, 946 So. 2d 1046 (Fla. 2006) (judge who was condescending, rude, abrupt, and abusive toward criminal defendant, acting more like a prosecutor than a court judge, violated Canon of judicial conduct requiring that a judge be patient, dignified, and courteous to litigants, jurors, witnesses, lawyers, and others with whom the judge deals in an official capacity); *In re Inquiry Concerning Golden*, 645 So. 2d 970 (Fla. 1994) (judge told defendant to "quit having so many babies so you can afford to pay your fines"); *In re Best*, 719 So. 2d 432 (La. 1998) (judge told juvenile defendant, "you need to be taken behind a shed and whipped," and telling his mother, "you need to take him and stick him upside down in a trash can and haul him out to the yard"); *In re Complaint Against Lindner*, 710 N.W.2d 866 (Neb. 2006) (judge reprimanded for making racist remark in apparent reference to defendant or persons with him); *In re Yaccarino*, 502 A.2d 3 (N.J. 1985) (judge said to defendant in a case on falsification of tax refunds, "You are in this up to your hipboots with Uncle Sam. Forget about defending yourself. You are dead . . . "); *In re Horan*, 428 A.2d 911 (N.J. 1981) (commenting on an allegation that defendants did not maintain their property saying, "I don't think a neighborhood should have (to) live . . . while somebody's flaunting around Europe . . . and ivy growing up all over . . . and kids running around."); *In re McLeod*, (N.Y. Comm'n on Jud. Conduct 2012) (while Commission recognized that disrespectful defendant "baited" judge, it admonished judge for responding to defendant with similar language, convicted defendant who had yet to formally enter guilty plea); *In re Hannnigan*, 1997 WL 809945 (N.Y. Comm'n on Jud. Conduct, 1997) (judge told defendant that she was a "full-time nothing" and that she "elected to make her life into a garbage pit"); *In re Hill*, 609 S.E.2d 221 (N.C. 2005) (judge's question about witness' description of weapon by asking whether it was a "Bradley tank" violated Canon); *In re Weithman*, 34 N.E.3d 865 (Ohio 2015) (judge suspended for two years, disposition stayed, for "impatient, disrespectful, and discourteous treatment of the wife and her counsel, in contrast to his display of excessive familiarity toward the husband's counsel" including "ogling of a female litigant who sought redress for her former husband's alleged posting of her intimate photographs on multiple pornographic websites and his subsequent offer of a bounty to opposing counsel if he could make her cry during cross-examination—going so far as to remove a dollar bill from his wallet and place it on the bench—were also demeaning and degrading to that litigant and to all women"); *In re O'Brien*, 650 A.2d 134 (R.I. 1994) (judge intimidated pro se litigant by criticizing the ability of pro se litigants and stating disapproval of pro se representation); *In re*

Adams, no. 12-001, Tex. Special Court of Review (2012) (judge admonished, in part, for inappropriately referring to parts of a person's body and appearance in truancy proceedings); *In re Wulle*, no. 6707-F-154 (Wash. Comm'n on Jud. Conduct 2013) (judge reprimanded for four instances in which judge "demeaned and humiliated the litigants appearing before him"); *In re Hutchinson*, 1995 WL 902265 (Wash. Comm'n on Jud. Conduct 1995) (judge disparaged parties seeking name change after their sex change operations, suggesting that they would pose a risk to those who "send their daughters into the ladies' restroom" and that the procedure was immoral); *but see Miss. Comm'n on Jud. Performance v. Martin*, 921 So. 2d 1258 (Miss. 2005) (judge who referred to criminal defendant as a "public menace" when, in violation of state constitutional provision under which only county judges and circuit judges had authority to deny bail, she denied him bail, did not violate Canon requiring judges to be patient, dignified, and courteous; judge's bail decision was based on statements of arresting officers, information received from court clerks, frequency of defendant's alleged multiple offenses against his estranged wife, and judge's misunderstanding of applicable law regarding her authority to deny bail).

Judges have also been disciplined for making disparaging remarks to relatives of litigants (*see, e.g., Miss. Comm'n on Jud. Performance v. Spencer*, 725 So. 2d 171 (Miss. 1998) (judge said to someone who went to court to pay a fine for his brother-in-law, "what damn business is it of yours?"); *In re Complaint Against Staley*, 486 N.W.2d 886 (Neb. 1992) (judge told defendant's mother that she was being "manipulative" and "using her son")) and to witnesses (*see, e.g., In re Wood*, 720 So. 2d 506 (Fla. 1998) (finding a judge committed misconduct by making comments about the unreliability and credibility of a police officer who was a witness)).

Criticizing Court Employees and Other Judges

Judges have been disciplined pursuant to the language of Rule 2.8(B) for disparaging comments directed at court employees. *See, e.g., Kloepfer v. Comm'n on Judicial Performance*, 782 P.2d 239 (Cal. 1989) (judge berated court reporter in a courtroom and reduced her to tears when the reporter asked a witness to speak up); *In re Inquiry Concerning a Judge Graziano*, 696 So. 2d 744 (Fla. 1997) (disciplining a judge who reduced a court reporter to tears by approaching her in the midst of a trial in another judge's courtroom, demanding to know if her car was blocking the judge's assistant's car, and insisting that the court reporter move the car immediately); *In re Westra* (Cal. Comm'n on Jud. Performance 2007) (judge admonished for failing to be dignified, patient, and courteous with deputies from county sheriff's department); *In re Halverson*, 0801-1066 (Nev. Comm'n on Jud. Discipline 2008) (judge removed for misconduct including multiple instances of mistreatment of staff).

In most cases, the inappropriate speech involves critical comments about an employee's competence. *See, e.g., In re Flournoy*, 990 P.2d 642 (Ariz. 1999) (judge shouted and pointed his finger at the elected clerk and made derogatory comments, claiming that she did not know what she was doing and threatening to throw her in jail); *In re Inquiry Concerning a Judge Graziano*, 696 So. 2d 744 (Fla. 1997) (judge berated Clerk's office for not faxing a document correctly, calling the clerks "incompetent, morons, and idiots"); *In re Jefferson*, 753 So. 2d 181 (La. 2000) (judge reprimanded court clerk in loud and disparaging manner regarding tardiness of paychecks); *In re Rice*, 515 N.W.2d 53 (Minn. 1994) (judge suspended for displaying inappropriate anger and undignified conduct toward staff); *In re Elliston*, 789 S.W.2d 469 (Mo. 1990) (judge said about a court employee, "once again she's proven her incompetence"); *In re Lyons*, JD-2014-001 (N.H. 2015) (judge demeaned deputy sheriff for following a policy of sherrif's office that judge believed violated separation of powers).

Judges have also been disciplined for making critical statements about other judges. *See, e.g., Comm'n on Jud. Qualifications v. Rome*, 623 P.2d 1307 (Kan. 1981) (finding a violation of a predecessor to Rule 2.8(B) based on judge's criticism of another judge's work release order). *But see In re Brown*, 879 S.W.2d 801 (Tenn. 1994) (finding that predecessor to Rule 2.8(B) was not violated by a judge's criticism of a state law permitting a nonlawyer to serve as juvenile court judge, because the comments were directed at the structure and operations of the court and not at "litigants, witnesses, jurors and others with whom [the judge] deals in his official capacity"). *See generally* William G. Ross, *Civility Among Judges: Charting the Bounds of Proper Criticism By Judges of Other Judges*, 51 Fla. L. Rev. 957 (1999).

INTEMPERATE CONDUCT

Judges may violate Rule 2.8(B) by engaging in intemperate conduct toward lawyers, litigants, and others appearing before them. *See, e.g., In re Murphy*, 181 So. 3d (Fla. 2015) (judge removed for "threatening violence against an assistant public defender, leaving the bench to meet the assistant public defender in the hall to engage in a physical scuffle, returning to the bench to call cases in which defendants were represented by the Public Defender's Office and were without the presence of their attorney, and inducing some of the defendants to waive speedy trial rights"). This conduct may entail making derogatory gestures or sounds in the courtroom. *See, e.g., Spruance v. Comm'n on Judicial Qualifications*, 532 P.2d 1209 (Cal. 1975) (judge emitted a "raspberry" to indicate disbelief of a witness and gave a defendant "the finger" as a reprimand for coming to court late); *In re Schapiro*, 845 So. 2d 170 (Fla. 2003) (judge asked criminal defense attorney "Do you know what I think of your argument?" and pushed a button on a device that simulated the sound of a toilet flushing). Judges also belittle lawyers and others in the courtroom by issuing inappropriate orders. *See, e.g., In re Elliston*, 789 S.W.2d 469 (Mo. 1990) (judge refused to allow lawyer to have a glass of water when he was having trouble speaking while presenting his closing argument); *In re Millard*, 631 N.E.2d 224 (Ohio Comm'n of Judges 1994) (judge ordered lawyer to speak from the podium and not to make any more notes on the easel).

Ordering Arrest of Lawyer, Litigant, or Witness

Arguably, one of the most egregious actions taken by a judge that may violate Rule 2.8(B) is unnecessarily ordering a lawyer, litigant, or witness to be arrested and handcuffed in the presence of others, usually for failing to appear in court. *See, e.g., In re Inquiry Concerning a Judge Graziano*, 661 So. 2d 819 (Fla. 1995) (disciplining a judge who ordered officers to arrest and jail a witness, even though the witness had not been properly subpoenaed and even though at the time of the order the witness was attending a professional conference at which he was scheduled to speak, as a result of which he was arrested and led away in handcuffs in the presence of lawyers attending the conference); *In re Johnson*, 658 N.E.2d 589 (Ind. 1995) (disciplining a judge for ordering a lawyer arrested and brought into court in a jail uniform, where his client was present); *In re Elliston,* 789 S.W.2d 469 (Mo. 1990) (ordering a litigant who had not appeared in court to be arrested at work in the presence of her employer and fellow employees, even though the litigant's lawyer had notified the judge the previous day that he had a conflict and that he and the litigant would not be in court at the scheduled time).

Inappropriate Language in the Courtroom

Sometimes, judges violate Rule 2.8(B) by using particularly opprobrious language, either as a personal attack on someone in the courtroom or as an inappropriate expression of anger.

Racial and Ethnic Slurs

While some of the most egregious incidents involving racial and ethnic slurs by judges never refer to the predecessors of Rule 2.8(B), Canon 3B(4) of the 1990 Code or Canon 3(3) of the 1972 Code (*see, e.g., Gonzalez v. Comm'n on Jud. Performance*, 657 P.2d 372 (Cal. 1983) (judge disciplined for racially and ethnically offensive remarks); *In re Stevens*, 645 P.2d 99 (Cal. 1982) (judge disciplined for repeated racial and ethnic epithets and stereotype remarks); *In re Agresta*, 476 N.E.2d 285 (N.Y. 1985) (judge censured for use of racially offensive phrase); *In re Gorenstein*, 434 N.W.2d 603 (Wis. 1989)), there is no doubt that the use of "racially charged language" directed at someone before the court would be a violation of Rule 2.8(B). *See, e.g., In re Golden*, 645 So. 2d 970 (Fla. 1994) (judge made racist remark regarding Hispanic Americans by responding to a public defender's assertion that her client had gotten married and was doing well by saying, "He's Hispanic, get real"); *Miss. Comm'n on Jud. Performance v. Guest*, 717 So. 2d 325 (Miss. 1998) (judge called an African-American defendant a "black son of a bitch" and said to him "sit down, boy and shut up"); *In re Schiff*, 635 N.E.2d 286 (N.Y. 1994) (judge stated in the presence of a Hispanic Legal Aid attorney that he "recalled a time when it was safe for young women to walk the streets 'before the blacks and Puerto Ricans moved here'"); *In re Esworthy*, 568 N.E.2d 1195 (N.Y. 1991) (judge used racially charged language that was highly insulting to certain ethnic groups); *In re Fabrizio*, 480 N.E.2d 733 (N.Y. 1985) (judge used racial slurs); *In re Ain*, 1992 WL 752853 (N.Y. Comm'n on Jud. Conduct 1992) (judge extended his middle finger and said to a lawyer of Arab ancestry "you're our sworn enemies"); *Disc. Counsel v. Mestemaker*, 676 N.E.2d 870 (Ohio 1997) (judge said to Hispanic defendant "Why is America being punished? Did we do something to you folks? We have to pay for all your crimes . . . . Could we get foreign aid from your native land for you being here? Did they send you to get even with us for something? Montezuma's revenge").

Judges have been disciplined for using ethnic slurs to refer to someone who was not directly before the court. *See, e.g., In re Matter of Disc. Proc. Against Buchanan*, 669 P.2d 1248 (Wash. 1983) (judge instructed staff not to cooperate with a lawyer whom the judge referred to as a "little rich Jew kid" and a "rotten, spoiled Jew"), and when the judge was not on the bench. *See, e.g., In re Velie*, 1992 WL 778716 (Wash. Comm'n on Jud. Conduct 1992) (judge said "nuke the sand niggers" in reference to the Middle-East crisis in the presence of others in the clerk's office coffee room in the courthouse). In one case, a judge was disciplined, not for racially offensive language, but for ridiculing the inability of a defendant named "Baljit Hundal" to speak English. *In re Moroney*, 914 P.2d 570 (Kan. 1996).

Sexist Comments

Sexist comments by a judge may constitute sexual harassment in violation of Rule 2.3(B). However, a judge's sexist comments may also violate Rule 2.8(B) even if the allegations against the judge do not mention sexual harassment. Typically, the inappropriate conduct involves sexist remarks by male judges toward women appearing before them. *See, e.g., In re Marko*, 595 So. 2d 46 (Fla. 1992) (saying that there are all kinds of "bimbos" in single bars); *Compl. Concerning Kirby*, 354 N.W.2d 410 (Minn. 1984) (referring to female lawyers as "lawyerette" and "attorney generalette" and asking a female attorney why she was not wearing a necktie); *In re Greene*, 403 S.E.2d 257 (N.C. 1991) (referring to a battered women's support group, which had a representative in the courtroom to support an abused victim as "a one-sided, man-hating, bunch of females" and "a pack of she-dogs"); *In re Disc. Action Against McGuire*, 685 N.W.2d 748 (N.D. 2004) (judge engaged in a pattern of making inappropriate comments to and inappropriate physical contacts with female employees); *In re Barr*, 13 S.W.3d 525 (Tex. Spec. Rev. Ct. 1998) (judge referred to female district attorneys in his court as "babes," and made inappropriate sexual remarks to women required to appear in his court); *In re Jud. Disc. Proc. Against Michaelson*, 591 N.W.2d 843 (Wis. 1999) (judge called the daughter of a woman before the court a "slut"); *In re Rohleder*, 1997 WL 360850 (Kan. Comm'n on Jud. Qualifications 1997) (suggesting in open court that 13- and 14-year-old female victims in statutory rape cases had invited the defendants' sexual acts).

A judge may also violate Rule 2.8(B) by publicly referring to women's bodies or to sex in a demeaning way. *In re Inquiry Concerning a Judge, No. 1496 (Noland)*, 407 S.E.2d 743 (Ga. 1991) (judge said that a particular witness would be welcomed if she was as "sharp looking" as another witness had been); *In re Deming*, 736 P.2d 639 (Wash. 1987) (judge said to a prosecuting attorney, "I would really like to jump your bones"); *In re Matter of Disc. Proc. Against Buchanan*, 669 P.2d 1248 (Wash. 1983) (referring in a sexual manner to female employees' bodies and to the type of lingerie worn by an employee). Such inappropriate comments are not exclusively made by male judges. A female judge was removed from office for misconduct that included commenting on her judicial assistant's body and sex life. *In re McAllister*, 646 So. 2d 173 (Fla. 1994).

The use of sexual innuendoes may also violate Rule 2.8(B). *See, e.g., In re Tripp,* (N.Y. Comm'n on Jud. Conduct 2010) (judge's repeated, gratuitous sexual comments about litigant's t-shirt were ribald and violated Rule); *Disc. Counsel v. Campbell*, 623 N.E.2d 24 (Ohio 1993) (judge responded to a prosecutor who said she was "ready to go" with the day's docket by saying, "when a young woman tells me she's ready, I'm ready to go"); *In re Barr*, 13 S.W.3d 525 (Tex. Spec. Rev. Ct. 1998) (beckoning a female attorney with his index finger and saying to her, "I just wanted to see if I would make you come"); *In re Deming*, 736 P.2d 639 (Wash. 1987) (judge responded to a male attorney who indicated that a female attorney was in court on a matter that would be "very quick" by saying, "Oh, she's here for a quickie").

Sometimes, the sexist comments that have been the subject of discipline under Canon 3B(4), the predecessor to Rule 2.8(B), are not directed to any woman in particular, but rather, are crude or unseemly comments about women. *In re Lehman*, 812 P.2d 992 (Ariz. 1991) (in a case involving a person charged with sex-related crimes, judge said, "everyone knows that the girls in Duncan are easy"); *In re Romano*, 690 N.Y.S.2d 849 (N.Y. 1999) (judge said about charges that a man assaulted his wife, "What's wrong with that? You've got to keep them in line once in a while."); *In re Greene*, 403 S.E.2d 257, 260 (N.C. 1991) (judge said about a victim of sexual abuse, "How is a man supposed to react?").

Use of Profanity

Judges may be disciplined under Rule 2.8(B) for using profane language while acting in their official capacity. Typically, disciplinary cases that have found a violation of Canon 3B(4), the predecessor to Rule 2.8(B), involve the use of profane language along with other types of misconduct. *See, e.g., In re Jones*, 581 N.W.2d 876 (Neb. 1998) (judge repeatedly used profane words, sent death threats to another judge, set off fireworks in bathroom area of colleagues office, and engaged in other misconduct); *In re Romano*, 690 N.Y.S.2d 849 (N.Y. 1999) (judge made profane comments about a complaining witness, as well as insensitive comments to an assault victim and abused judicial authority). *See also In re Schapiro*, 845 So. 2d 170 (Fla. 2003) (judge reprimanded for pattern of belittling, embarrassing, and screaming at attorneys as part of longtime rude and intemperate behavior); *In re Golden*, 645 So. 2d 970 (Fla. 1994) (judge reprimanded for sexist, racial, profane, and otherwise inappropriate language); *In re Bowers*, 721 So. 2d 875 (La. 1998) (censure for inappropriate, insensitive, discourteous language); *In re Del Rio*, 256 N.W.2d 727 (Mich. 1977) (judge persistently and repeatedly referred to his sexual prowess and other profane language); *In re Bennett*, 267 N.W.2d 914 (Mich. 1978) (public use of obscene, profane, and abusive language a gross lack of judicial temperament); *Miss. Comm'n on Jud. Performance v. Spencer*, 725 So. 2d 171 (Miss. 1998) (judge used intemperate and sexual language); *In re Sadofski*, 487 A.2d 700 (N.J. 1985) (reprimand for intemperate and offensive language during proceedings); *In re Mulroy*, 731 N.E.2d 120 (N.Y. 2000) (judge removed for pattern of racial epithets and ethnic slurs).

Cases rarely involve a single incident with a single profane word, and those that do, have conflicting results. *Compare In re Hamrick*, 512 S.E.2d 870 (W. Va. 1998) (judge did not violate Code when he used the word "damn" once to express his exasperation to an evasive witness) *and In re Pauley*, 314 S.E.2d 391 (W. Va. 1983) (discipline not warranted for magistrate who stated, "When I am elected sheriff, this shit will stop," in reference to bailiff's failure to produce a prisoner as ordered; language in this context was not profanity, but vulgar slang for "nonsense") *with In re Frankel*, 323 N.W.2d 911 (Mich. 1982) (judge violated Code when he called a lawyer a "despicable son-of-a-bitch"). Thus, it is not clear whether certain words are offensive enough by themselves to violate the Rule, or whether a pattern of offensive words without other types of misconduct would violate the Rule.

Inappropriate Expressions of Anger

Physical Confrontations

Judges may violate 2.8(B) when they lose their tempers and inappropriately express their anger in the courtroom. One of the most obvious displays of anger occurs when a judge engages in a physical confrontation with someone in the courtroom. *See, e.g., In re Best*, 719 So. 2d 432 (La. 1998) (judge grabbed a juvenile defendant's shirt and pulled the juvenile toward him until their noses touched); *In re Barr*, 13 S.W.3d 525 (Tex. Spec. Rev. Trib. 1998) (judge disciplined for engaging in a tug-of-war with a deputy sheriff over a defendant, whereby the judge was pulling on the defendant's right arm while the deputy sheriff was pulling on the defendant's left arm); *In re Troisi*, 504 S.E.2d 625 (W. Va. 1998) (judge initiated physical confrontation with criminal defendant in the courtroom). However, in *In re Bullock*, 377 S.E.2d 743 (N.C. 1989), the North Carolina Supreme Court did not discipline a judge who grabbed a police officer and escorted him out of anteroom. That court said that "[n]ot every intemperate outburst of a judge, especially when it is an isolated, single event, occurring in the privacy of the judge's office and brought on by what the judge might reasonably have perceived to be some provocation, amounts to conduct deserving of discipline. To rule otherwise would be asking judges to be more than they can be; it would be asking them to be more than human."

Judges may also violate Rule 2.8(B) by expressing their anger in other ways, such as by slamming doors (*In re Rice*, 515 N.W.2d 53 (Minn. 1994) (slamming a door so hard that a clock fell off the wall); *In re Hair*, 436 S.E.2d 128 (N.C. 1993)), or by throwing objects such as pens and files (*In re Morales*, JC-98-0002 (Ariz. Comm'n on Jud. Conduct 1998)).

Yelling during Court Proceedings

Yelling during a court proceeding is neither dignified nor courteous. Thus, it is not unusual for judges who raise their voices in this way to be found to have violated Rule 2.8(B). However, because judicial discipline hearings are largely based on oral characterizations of something that occurred in the past, there is room for a difference of opinion on what is loud enough to be within the reach of this rule. *In re Pauley*, 314 S.E.2d 391 (W. Va. 1983) ("The characterization of . . . speech as 'loud' is conclusory. . . loudness of speech is in the ear of the hearer. What some may interpret as 'loud,' others may find 'forceful,' 'assertive,' or 'resolute.' 'Loud' as a characterization upon which to base a conclusion of abusiveness is overly broad."); *accord In re McGraw*, 359 S.E.2d 853 (W. Va. 1987). *See also In re Johnson*, 395 A.2d 1319 (Pa. 1978) (refusing to discipline a judge where testimony as to judge's tone of voice was conflicting and the judge's comments did not indicate that he had lost his self-restraint).

Judges are most likely to be disciplined for loud and abusive language where the evidence of their tone of voice can be verified, either through a tape recording of the proceeding (*see e.g., In re Inquiry Concerning Perry*, 641 So. 2d 366 (Fla. 1994)), or through someone asking the court reporter to put on the record that the judge was yelling or shouting (*see, e.g., Fletcher v. Comm'n on Jud. Performance*, 968 P.2d 958 (Cal. 1998)). Likewise, it is easier for courts to conclude that judges were loud enough to warrant discipline when they admit to raising their voices inappropriately (*see, e.g., In re Flournoy*, 990 P.2d 642 (Ariz. 1999); *Fletcher v. Comm'n on Jud. Performance*, 968 P.2d 958 (Cal. 1998) (among other conduct, judge repeatedly yelled at attorney during proceeding); *In re Rice*, 515 N.W.2d 53 (Minn. 1994) (shouting abuse among other conduct toward court staff violates Canons); *In re Andrus*, 20140240-SC (Utah 2014) or when there is corroborating testimony regarding their tone of voice (*see, e.g., In re Cox*, 532 A.2d 1017 (Me. 1987) (judge's loud berating of police captain in chambers could be heard by others and conversation was not private in the strict sense of the word); *Miss. Comm'n on Jud. Qualifications v. Spencer*, 725 So. 2d 171 (Miss. 1998) (testimony of court staff, law enforcement officers, the county prosecutor, the other sitting justice court judge in the county and litigants who had appeared before the judge); *In re Elliston*, 789 S.W.2d 469 (Mo. 1990) (16 local attorneys testifying to judge's abusive behavior); *In re Complaint Against Staley*, 486 N.W.2d 886 (Neb. 1992)).

Because loudness is a relative term, absent verifiable or strongly corroborated evidence, courts typically discipline a tone of voice that is described in stronger terms than simply "loud." *In re McGraw*, 359 S.E.2d 853 (W. Va. 1987). Thus, discipline will be imposed when the judge's treatment of people before the court is described as "berat[ing]" (*Kloepfer v. Comm'n on Jud. Performance*, 782 P.2d 239 (Cal. 1989) (rude, abusive, hostile behavior); *In re McAllister*, 646 So. 2d 173 (Fla. 1994) (abusive and hostile toward attorneys and sexual harassment toward judicial clerk); *In re Inquiry Concerning Perry*, 641 So. 2d 366 (Fla. 1994)), "yelling" (*Dodds v. Comm'n on Judicial Performance*, 906 P.2d 1260 (Cal. 1996) (discipline rejected for brusque judicial style); *In re Moroney*, 914 P.2d 570 (Kan. 1996) (angry and intemperate behavior in and out of court); *In re Elliston*, 789 S.W.2d 469 (Mo. 1990) (pattern of discourteous, abrasive, and abusive conduct); *In re Staley*, 486 N.W.2d 886 (Neb. 1992) (intemperate in court behavior)); speaking in a "raised voice" (*In re Eastmoore*, 504 So. 2d 756 (Fla. 1987); *Miss. Comm'n on Jud. Qualifications v. Spencer*, 725 So. 2d 171 (Miss. 1998) (offensive sexual comments); *In re Millard*, 631 N.E.2d 224 (Ohio Comm'n of Judges 1994)), "shouting" (*In re Rice*, 515 N.W.2d 53 (Minn. 1994); *In re McDonough*, 296 N.W.2d 648 (Minn. 1979)), or speaking "angrily" (*In re Hair*, 436 S.E.2d 128 (N.C. 1993) (angry and hostile treatment of attorneys and witnesses after personal dissolution case); *In re Yengo*, 371 A.2d 41 (N.J. 1977) (consistent disrespectful and discourteous treatment of litigants and witnesses warrant removal)).

Retaliatory Responses

Pursuant to Rule 2.8(A), judges are permitted to use their judicial authority to respond to unruly or improper courtroom behavior. *See, e.g., Hinton v. Jud.*

Ret. & Removal Comm'n, 854 S.W.2d 756 (Ky. 1993), *overruled on other grounds* (ruling that discipline was inappropriate when a judge jailed an attorney for contempt, after the attorney interrupted a trial in which neither of the parties was his client). However, a judge may violate Rule 2.8(B) by reacting angrily to a minor provocation or to a legitimate exercise of rights. For instance, it is not acceptable for a judge to hold, or threaten to hold, a lawyer in contempt, remove a lawyer from court, or take other onerous actions simply because a lawyer filed a complaint with a judicial discipline commission (*In re Bissell*, 429 S.E.2d 731 (N.C. 1993)), moved to disqualify a judge (*Fletcher v. Comm'n on Jud. Performance*, 968 P.2d 958 (Cal. 1998)), filed an appeal (*Spruance v. Comm'n on Jud. Qualifications*, 532 P.2d 1209 (Cal. 1975)), requested a continuance (*Kloepfer v. Comm'n on Jud. Performance*, 782 P.2d 239 (Cal. 1989)), or engaged in conduct that the judge perceived as a slight (*In re Jefferson*, 753 So. 2d 181 (La. 2000) (judge banned prosecutor from courtroom for perceived slights)). A judge also should not punish, or threaten to punish, a lawyer for being late for court without allowing the lawyer to explain (*In re Crowell*, 379 So. 2d 107 (Fla. 1979)), for a client's failure to appear (*In re Del Rio*, 256 N.W.2d 727 (Mich. 1977)), or for asking to approach the bench to state an objection on the record (*In re Weddel*, 414 N.W.2d 178 (Minn. 1987)).

Judges have also been disciplined for reacting vindictively toward parties, witnesses and others in the courtroom. *See, e.g., In re Hammermaster*, 985 P.2d 924 (Wash. 1999) (judge threatened defendants with life sentences when they failed to pay fines); *In re Keith*, 3 Ill. Cts. Comm'n 39 (1994) (judge may not detain a party or witness or threaten to raise a fine or penalty when someone accompanies a relative to court or asks how long he is expected to remain in the courtroom); *In re Keller* (Vt. Jud. Conduct Board 2011) (judge disciplined for discouraging grandparents from filing for guardianship of grandchild and, when they sought to move forward with the guardianship directing that they would have to pay a $10,000 retainer to the child's counsel, a position not supported by law).

It is equally inappropriate for judges to retaliate against court staff or public officials who have done something that annoys them. *See, e.g., In re Inquiry Concerning a Judge Graziano*, 696 So. 2d 744 (Fla. 1997) (finding a judge violated the Canon by threatening a court clerk with jail because the clerk circulated a memorandum explaining the status of efforts to install computer network for judiciary), *In re Jefferson*, 753 So. 2d 181 (La. 2000) (judge held clerk in contempt for late delivery of paychecks); *In re Staley*, 486 N.W.2d 886 (Neb. 1992) (judge ordered the delivery of juveniles to custody of county administrator in retaliation for parking space reassignment); *In re Meurer*, CJC Nos. 09-0413-RT, 09-0488-RT, 09-0489-RT, 09-0637-RT (Tex. Comm'n on Jud. Conduct 2010) (judge put three government employees, court volunteer, and mother of juvenile in secure holding area for recommending to judge that juvenile be detained until medical profile could be updated).

Inappropriate Humor

It may often be harmless or even beneficial for a judge to have a sense of humor. *See, e.g., U.S. v. Syufy Enter.*, 903 F.2d 659 (9th Cir. 1990) (judge incorporated over 200 movie titles into an opinion in an antitrust case involving the movie industry). However, some attempts at humor may be inappropriate and subject a judge to discipline pursuant to Rule 2.8(B), if they display bias (*see Dodds v. Comm'n on Jud. Performance*, 906 P.2d 1260 (Cal. 1996) (judge made a joke about chiropractors shortly after reducing a chiropractor's lien)), risk hurting someone (*see In re Jones*, 581 N.W.2d 876 (Neb. 1998) (finding that a judge's writing a threatening note to a fellow judge and setting off firecrackers in the fellow judge's office to be "juvenile, immature and clearly prejudicial to the administration of justice")), or insult someone's character or abilities (*see, e.g., In re Elliston*, 789 S.W.2d 469 (Mo. 1990) (finding a judge to be discourteous for making a remark that embarrassed a lawyer in front of his client)).

Judges may violate Rule 2.8(B) by making inappropriate jokes or by failing to admonish a lawyer for an inappropriate joke. *See In re Romano*, 690 N.Y.S.2d 849 (N.Y. 1999). Courts do consider the context in which the attempt at humor was made and are less likely to impose discipline when the person against whom the humor is directed understands it to be a joke than when it offends or harms that person. *Compare In re Empson*, 562 N.W.2d 817 (Neb. 1997) (judge's "will I love you more than I already do" statement to female attorney during telephone conversation was not an ethical violation where attorney stated that she eventually took telephone conversation as a joke) *with In re Jones*, 581 N.W.2d 876 (Neb. 1998) (finding a violation when a judge said he wanted to turn a court employee's head into "pink mist" and when a threatening note, which he intended as a prank, was taken seriously by its recipient).

Sarcasm toward Litigants and Others

Judges may violate Rule 2.8(B) by treating litigants, lawyers, and others appearing before them with sarcasm or ridicule. *See, e.g., In re Schwartz*, 755 So. 2d 110 (Fla. 2000) (judge made sarcastic remarks to law students appearing under the student practice rule, who were making initial appearances before the court and law professor who was supervising students); *In re Rome*, 542 P.2d 676 (Kan. 1975) (disciplining a judge for writing a memorandum decision about the defendant in a prostitution case in the form of a poem that "portrayed [her] in a ludicrous or comical situation—someone to be laughed at and her plight found amusing"); *In re Judge Sassone*, 959 So. 2d 859 (La. 2007) (judge violated code of judicial conduct by acting in a rude, impatient, and sarcastic manner toward an attorney); *In re Kellam*, 503 A.2d 1308 (Me. 1986) (judge said to husband who was afraid because of death threats from his wife, "You're here, aren't you? She didn't kill you yet" and told a party who wanted to read something in a small claims case, "No, we're not going to let you read it. If you don't know anything about this case, why don't you just say so in the beginning?"); *Miss. Comm'n on Jud. Performance v. Spencer*, 725 So. 2d 171 (Miss. 1998) (egregious erratic and outrageous demeanor); *In re Complaint Against Staley*, 486 N.W.2d 886 (Neb. 1992) (snide and disrespectful court language and demeanor warrants removal); *In re Yaccarino*, 502 A.2d 3 (N.J. 1985) (ridicule of attorneys and litigants warranted removal); *In re Yengo*, 371 A.2d 41 (N.J. 1977) (describing a judge's statement that "this looks like one of those habituals" as "undignified, discourteous and partial to the interests of the State"); *In re Hoffman*, 595 N.W.2d 592 (N.D. 1999) (judge responded to wife's complaint about her former husband making over 100 harassing phone calls by telling her that she had a duty to "facilitate the psychological relationship between her child and her former husband"). As one court stated, "An attempt at judicial sarcasm or humor directed at a litigant, witness, attorney or law student [appearing under the student practice rule] has no place in a courtroom. It is deeply resented and inevitably demeans the judge himself." *In re Albano*, 384 A.2d 144 (N.J. 1978).

Mockery of Judicial Process

Beyond ridiculing people who come before the court, judges may sometimes violate Rule 2.8(B) when their actions or words make a mockery of the entire judicial process. Judges have thus been disciplined for holding a mock auction on the amount of a fine (*In re Keith*, 3 Ill. Cts. Comm'n 39 (1994)) or the amount of bail (*In re Yengo*, 371 A.2d 41 (N.J. 1977)) and for loading a gun while sitting on the bench and displaying it while questioning an unruly defendant (*In re Fleet*, 610 So. 2d 1282 (Fla. 1992)). Judges have also been disciplined for calling the proceedings in front of them "garbage" and a "waste of time" (*In re O'Dea*, 622 A.2d 507 (Vt. 1993)) and for ridiculing the *Miranda* rights and comparing them to the Last Rites (*In re Yengo*, 371 A.2d 41 (N.J. 1977) (commenting on judge's conduct as "heavy-handed humor" and "sneering at and deriding the supreme law of the land")).

Rude Behavior

A judge's rude behavior shows a lack of judicial demeanor. Judges have been disciplined for insulting or disregarding the feelings of courtroom participants, interrupting or cutting off lawyers or witnesses, and ignoring people who come to see them on legitimate business. *See, e.g., In re Eiler*, 236 P.3d 873 (Wash. 2010) (judge suspended for five days without pay for repeatedly rude behavior, including interrupting pro se litigants, being condescending to them, and threatening to rule against pro se litigants who annoyed her).

Name Calling

When judges refer to others in insulting terms, they fall short of the demeanor expected of them. Referring to courtroom participants in derogatory terms is usually part of a larger pattern of disrespectful behavior that has resulted in discipline. *See, e.g., Fletcher v. Comm'n on Jud. Performance*, 968 P.2d 958 (Cal. 1998) (judge called criminal defendant a "punk"); *Kloepfer v. Comm'n on Jud. Performance*, 782 P.2d 239 (Cal. 1989) (telling a witness that he was "one of the Magnificent Seven bad guys"); *In re Jenkins*, 503 N.W.2d 425 (Iowa 1993) (judge called witness a "beer-bellied, full-bearded, unemployed, seedy, coverall-clad lout"); *Miss. Comm'n on Jud. Performance v. Spencer*, 725 So. 2d 171 (Miss. 1998) (calling a litigant a "God-damn liar"); *In re Sadofski*, 487 A.2d 700 (N.J. 1985) (telling a mother that her son, who was the defendant was "a punk, a no-good rotten punk"); *In re Greene*, 403 S.E.2d 257 (N.C. 1991) (calling a battered women's support group, members of which were in court, a "one-sided, man-hating bunch of females and a pack of she-dogs"). Judges have also been disciplined for name-calling that was directed at someone not present in the courtroom. *In re Bowers*, 721 So. 2d 875 (La. 1998) (calling a litigant's husband, who was in another state, a "pimp" and a "little two-bit hoodlum"); *In re O'Brien*, 650 A.2d 134 (R.I. 1994) (calling the boyfriend of the mother of two minors involved in litigation a "leech").

Interrupting People Who Appear in Courtroom

A judge who interrupts lawyers, witnesses, and others who appear in his or her courtroom may be disciplined for a lack of decorum. *See, e.g., Fletcher v. Comm'n on Jud. Performance*, 968 P.2d 958 (Cal. 1998) (judge interrupted and yelled loudly at litigant and her lawyer); *Kloepfer v. Comm'n on Jud. Performance*, 782 P.2d 239 (Cal. 1989) (judge interrupted a defense witness and told her to "keep her mouth shut"); *In re Inquiry Concerning a Judge, No. 1496 (Noland)*, 407 S.E.2d 743 (Ga. 1991) (during witness's testimony establishing her qualifications as an expert, judge interrupted her with wholly irrelevant remarks); *In re Kellam*, 503 A.2d 1308 (Me. 1986) (judge interrupted witnesses and litigants in small claims cases); *In re Moore*, 626 N.W.2d 374 (Mich. 2001) (judge frequently interrupted trials); *In re Sadofski*, 487 A.2d 700 (N.J. 1985) (judge repeatedly interrupted lawyer and party). As one court observed, "when a judge, clothed with the prestige and authority of his judicial office, repeatedly interrupts a litigant and yells angrily without adequate provocation, the judge exceeds his proper role and casts disrepute on the judicial office." *Dodds v. Comm'n on Jud. Performance*, 906 P.2d 1260 (Cal. 1995).

Discipline has also been imposed on judges who interrupt proceedings before another judge. *In re Inquiry Concerning a Judge Graziano*, 696 So. 2d 744 (Fla. 1997) (judge entered another judge's courtroom through the judge's private entrance when court was in session and demanded to know if the court reporter's car was blocking her assistant's car in the parking lot); *In re Matter of Disc. Proc. Against Buchanan*, 669 P.2d 1248 (Wash. 1983) (judge's misconduct included disrupting proceedings in another judge's court in order to continue an argument with a lawyer who was appearing in that court).

Restricting Testimony, Statements, and Court Availability

A judge may violate Rule 2.8(B) by cutting off or limiting the examination or cross-examination of witnesses. *See, e.g., In re Hocking*, 546 N.W.2d 234 (Mich. 1996) (before lawyer could argue the merits of a motion, judge told her it was not justified, denied the motion, and awarded costs and attorney's fees; when lawyer asked him to explain his rationale, he "instigated a confrontational exchange" with her in a "caustic abusive tone"); *In re Horan*, 428 A.2d 911 (N.J. 1981) (judge curtailed party's questioning of his witnesses and cross-examination of opposing party's witnesses); *In re O'Dea*, 622 A.2d 507 (Vt. 1993) (stressing that the court "cannot let the judiciary become an impersonal and authoritarian institution, relying for legitimacy solely on its power"); *In re Millard*, 631 N.E.2d 224 (Ohio Comm'n of Judges 1994) (finding misconduct when a judge questioned a prosecutor about the prosecutor's refusal to disclose the name of an informant and limited a prosecutor's responses to "yes" or "no"); *cf. Disc. Counsel v. O'Neill*, 815 N.E.2d 286 (Ohio 2004) (judge violated Canon by using a variety of coercive tactics to expedite dispositions in criminal cases, including threatening to revoke or actually revoking defendants' bonds because they wanted to exercise their rights to refuse an offered plea and go to trial).

A judge may also violate Rule 2.8 by limiting the hours in which the court will hear a matter. *See, e.g., In re Vega*, no. 1203-324 (Nev. Comm'n on Jud. Discipline 2013) (judge violated Rule 2.8 when he concluded daily court sessions early during murder trial so that he could attend daughter's soccer matches and then forced jurors in the same matter to work through evening hours to conclude case prior to holiday season).

Judges may also violate Rule 2.8(B) by refusing to allow lawyers or court staff an opportunity to explain the reasons for an error or oversight. *Kloepfer v. Comm'n on Jud. Performance*, 782 P.2d 239 (Cal. 1989) (disciplining judge for a pattern of misconduct that included his refusal to hear a clerk's explanation about why she had not been available in his courtroom as he had requested); *In re Crowell*, 379 So. 2d 107 (Fla. 1979) (disciplining judge for, among other things, refusing to allow a sheriff to respond to an accusation and refusing to allow a lawyer to explain why he was late to court).

Refusing to Speak to People

Judges may violate Rule 2.8(B) by refusing to see people who have come to speak with them on legitimate business. *See, e.g., In re Dwyer*, 572 P.2d 898

(Kan. 1977) (finding a judge engaged in misconduct when he refused to speak to the father of a young boy he had sentenced to jail regarding what he could do to get his son out of jail); *Miss. Comm'n on Jud. Performance v. Dodds*, 680 So. 2d 180 (Miss. 1996) (finding that a judge's refusal to speak with someone who wanted to press charges was part of a pattern of misconduct in violation of several Code provisions). A judge may also violate Rule 2.8(B) by refusing to acknowledge someone's presence (*In re Rice*, 515 N.W.2d 53 (Minn. 1994) (ruling that part of a judge's misconduct resulted from his ignoring the presence of staff members that had been asked to come into his chambers)) or acknowledge that a party has made a request (*In re Conduct of Gustafson*, 756 P.2d 21 (Or. 1988) (part of judge's pattern of misconduct consisted of his refusal to acknowledge a defendant's request to be represented by the same public defender who had represented him on a related matter, partly based on judge's personal bad feelings about public defender)). *Cf. Hinton v. Jud. Ret. & Removal Comm'n*, 854 S.W.2d 756 (Ky. 1993), *overruled on other grounds* (ruling that judge presiding over murder trial did not act in undignified, discourteous, or impatient manner to degree required to impose public censure when he refused to permit intervention by a lawyer who represented a witness, rather than a party, and who had failed to follow the local rules of procedure regarding participation of lawyers of non-parties).

Sexual Harassment

Rule 2.3(B) provides that a "judge shall not, in the performance of judicial duties . . . engage in harassment, including but not limited to, harassment based on sex." The Comment to that Rule explains that "[s]exual harassment includes but is not limited to sexual advances, requests for sexual favors, and other verbal or physical conduct of a sexual nature that is unwelcome." While it is likely that states that adopt this new rule will bring disciplinary cases involving sexual harassment under that Rule, many of the disciplinary cases addressing the issue of sexual harassment have arisen under Rule 2.8(B)'s mandate that judges be dignified and courteous.

Generally, few victims of sexual harassment file formal charges or complaints, making it difficult to get a sense of the prevalence of this problem among the judiciary. Better evidence of its magnitude can be found in reports from state supreme court task forces on gender bias in the courts. *See* Marina Angel, *Sexual Harassment by Judges*, 45 U. Miami L. Rev. 817 (1991) (detailing several states' reports and asserting that despite the seriousness of the problem, sanctions against judge have been minimal). Of the cases that do exist, most involve sexually harassing comments or conduct by male judges toward female victims, including lawyers, litigants, court employees, and jurors. *See, e.g., In re Disc. Action Against McGuire*, 685 N.W.2d 748 N.D. (2004) (judge suspended for inappropriate comments to, and inappropriate physical contacts with, female courthouse employees, where judge's acts were repeated over lengthy period of time and they offended, shocked, and intimidated employees under his supervision). To date, few female judges have been disciplined for sexual harassment. *But see In re McAllister*, 646 So. 2d 173 (Fla. 1994) (female judge making unwanted comments and giving unwanted invitations to female employee). *Cf. In re Miera*, 426 N.W.2d 850 (Minn. 1988) (charging a male judge's harassment of both male and female court employees as a violation of former Canons 1 and 2 of the 1990 Code).

When a judge sexually harasses a court employee, the employee often acquiesces for fear of losing her job. Female lawyers face a different dilemma. If they try to put an end to the harassment by speaking to the judge or reporting the conduct to the disciplinary authorities, they risk angering the judge, who may retaliate against their clients. On the other hand, if they ignore the conduct to protect their clients' interests, they risk allowing the conduct to go unchecked. *See* Marina Angel, *Sexual Harassment by Judges*, 45 U. Miami L. Rev. 817, 821 (1991). As the court in *In re Barr*, 13 S.W.3d 525, 534-35 (Tex. Rev. Trib. 1998), explained:

> Gender bias in general and sexual harassment in particular, is personally offensive, extraordinarily invasive, psychologically damaging, and deeply embarrassing to the intended victim. [citation omitted] It is insulting, belittling, and inappropriate in an exchange between a judge and attorney and is to be condemned for the simple reason that it is wrong. Sexual harassment in the administration of justice is harmful and offensive conduct, which clearly indicates a lack of respect for the judge's victim, and, by reasonable extension, a lack of respect for the citizens of the State of Texas at large.

According to the Equal Employment Opportunity Commission (EEOC), sexual harassment involves "[u]nwelcome sexual advances, requests for sexual favors, and other verbal or physical conduct of a sexual nature" when the conduct affects terms or conditions of employment, interferes with work performance, or creates a hostile environment. 29 C.F.R. § 1604.11 (1999). However, sexually harassing behavior can also involve an exploitation of judicial authority. As a result, judges may violate Rule 2.8(B) even when their conduct falls short of the legal requirements established by the EEOC. *Miss. Comm'n on Jud. Performance v. Just. Ct. Judge R.R.*, 732 So. 2d 224 (Miss. 1999) ("[W]hether [the judge's] behavior . . . meets the legal definition of sexual harassment is not germane . . . [t]he question to be decided is whether there is clear and convincing evidence that [the judge] violated the . . . cannons [sic]."); *In re Seaman*, 627 A.2d 106 (N.J. 1993) ("[T]he inquiry before the court is not whether [the judge's] behavior constituted sexual harassment as such. Although undoubtedly all forms of behavior that cross the legal threshold of sexual harassment would constitute judicial misconduct, many forms of offensive interpersonal behavior that would otherwise violate the Code of Judicial Conduct would not meet the legal definition of sexual harassment.").

Inappropriate Comments

Judges who are disciplined for sexually harassing comments have usually engaged in a pattern of misconduct. Judges will generally not be disciplined for a single inappropriate comment, particularly if there is no indication that the woman objected to it. *See, e.g., In re Brenner*, 687 A.2d 725 (N.J. 1997) (finding that a judge's observation that an employee was getting taller, which was intended as a comment about her short skirt, was "inappropriate, but relatively minor and neither a violation of the Code of Judicial Conduct nor an act of sexual harassment.").

Sexually harassing comments by judges usually include comments about a woman's physical appearance. *See, e.g., In re McAllister*, 646 So. 2d 173 (Fla. 1994); *In re Disc. Action Against McGuire*, 685 N.W.2d 748 (N.D. 2004); *In re Deming*, 736 P.2d 639 (Wash. 1987). Other inappropriate comments include comments about a woman's bodily functions (*Miss. Comm'n on Jud. Performance v. Spencer*, 725 So. 2d 171 (Miss. 1998); *In re Barr*, 13 S.W.3d 525 (Tex. Rev. Trib. 1998); *In re Buchanan*, 669 P.2d 1248 (Wash. 1983)) and her clothes or manner of dress (*see, e.g., In re Moore*, 626 N.W.2d 374 (Mich. 2001) (judge commented in criminal case that only reason prosecution wanted to cross-examine witness was because she was not wearing a bra); *Miss. Comm'n on Jud. Performance v. Spencer*, 725 So. 2d 171 (Miss. 1998) (judge commented that he wanted to buy a clerk a pair of red underwear and offered to wash a clerk's jeans if she took them off "right now"); *Disc. Counsel v. Campbell*, 623 N.E.2d 24 (Ohio 1993) (judge told female lawyer he wanted to "connect the dots" on her patterned stockings to "see where it lead to"); *In re Buchanan*, 669 P.2d 1248 (Wash. 1983) (deeming "undignified" a judge's speculation about his female employees' lingerie)); *but see In re Empson*, 562 N.W.2d 817 (Neb. 1997) (refusing to impose discipline where judge asked court reporter to stand up and turn around because he was concerned about inappropriateness of clerk's casual attire).

It is also improper for judges to make reference to a woman's marital status (*Disc. Counsel v. Campbell*, 623 N.E.2d 24 (Ohio 1993)) or to her sexual relationships (*In re Empson*, 562 N.W.2d 817 (Neb. 1997) (judge's misconduct included speculating about court employees' sexual relationships with their husbands)).

Judges may also violate Rule 2.8(B) when their comments deal with their own sexual desire (*Miss. Comm'n on Jud. Performance v. Spencer*, 725 So. 2d

171 (Miss. 1998) (finding impropriety in a judge's statement to a female judge about his strong sexual desire); *In re Nelson*, 532 S.E.2d 609 (S.C. 2000) (finding impropriety where judge told female deputy that after seeing her, he would need to go home and take a cold shower); *In re Deming*, 736 P.2d 639 (Wash. 1987) (finding impropriety in a judge's statement that he had "reached a heightened state of excitement" when seeing a deputy prosecutor on the witness stand)) or when they boast of their sexual prowess. *See also In re Seaman*, 627 A.2d 106 (N.J. 1993) (judge removed for verbal and physical sexual harassment of law clerk).

Physical Contact

Courts have disciplined judges for unwanted physical contact with female court clerks, attorneys, interns, and other women who work in the courthouse. The inappropriate contact includes rubbing (*Inquiry Relating to Alvord*, 847 P.2d 1310 (Kan. 1993) (rubbing back of neck and behind); *In re Jones*, 581 N.W.2d 876 (Neb. 1998) (judge rubbed up against female judge in elevator), touching (*Disc. Action Against McGuire*, 685 N.W.2d 748 (N.D. 2004) (judge flipped employee's hair, "framed" an employee's face, touched an employee's cheek and back); *In re Seaman*, 627 A.2d 106 (N.J. 1993) (lifting up skirt and touching legs); *In re Deming*, 736 P.2d 639 (Wash. 1987)), and kissing (*Disc. Counsel v. Campbell*, 623 N.E.2d 24 (Ohio 1993); *In re Hey*, 457 S.E.2d 509 (W. Va. 1995)); *cf. In re Brenner*, 687 A.2d 725 (N.J.) (1997) (court found that judge did not engage in sexual harassment but that hugging and kissing a subordinate employee warranted private reprimand)). However, physical contact is a basis for discipline only when it is without the woman's consent. In cases where the evidence showed consensual behavior, judges have not been disciplined, even if they were disciplined for other incidents of harassing behavior or other misconduct. *See, e.g., In re Empson*, 562 N.W.2d 817 (Neb. 1997) (handholding incident involving male judge and female court reporter was not ethical violation where judge and court reporter were eating dinner together after first day of trial, judge placed his hand on table prior to saying prayer, and court reporter placed her hand on judge's hand).

Gestures

Judges have been disciplined under the language of Rule 2.8(B) when they make unwanted sexual gestures. *In re Katic*, 595 N.E.2d 259 (Ind. 1992) (male judge pulling down pants in front of female employee of clerk's office); *In re Barr*, 13 S.W.3d 525 (Tex. Rev. Trib. 1998) (crooking an index finger and saying, "I wanted to see if I could make you come with one finger"); *In re Deming*, 736 P.2d 639 (Wash. 1987) (winking and kissing at a female attorney from the bench).

Pictures and Displays

In private litigation, employers have been held liable for sexual harassment when a male worker has displayed pictures of naked women or women in sexually suggestive poses in the workplace. Similarly, judges have been disciplined for displaying inappropriate pictures of nude women on their computer screens when a female employee entered the office (*In re Litson*, 1997 WL 360847 (Kan. Comm'n on Jud. Qualifications 1997)) and for accessing sexually explicit images on a county computer in chambers, which exposed other court employees to the images (*Harris v. Smartt*, 57 P.3d 58 (Mont. 2002)). The Michigan Supreme Court censured a judge, in part, for inappropriate sexual drawings on notes attached to court files. *In re Servaas*, 774 N.W.2d 46 (Mich. 2009).

Invitations and Favors

Extending unwanted invitations, by itself, would probably not be misconduct. However, persistently extending unwanted invitations while engaging in other sexually harassing behavior likely violates Rule 2.8(B). *See, e.g., In re McAllister*, 646 So. 2d 173 (Fla. 1994) (disciplining female judge who frequently invited her judicial assistant out for lunch or drinks and once invited her to a judicial conference, while also making sexually explicit remarks to assistant). Judges may also violate Rule 2.8(B) by explicitly requesting sexual favors. *See, e.g., In re Seaman*, 627 A.2d 106 (N.J. 1993) (judge asked legal intern to have sex with him); *Disc. Counsel v. Campbell*, 623 N.E.2d 24 (Ohio 1993) (judge told female prosecutor that the procedure to be followed in certain cases depended on "whether [she] wanted to be his lover or not"); *In re Deming*, 736 P.2d 639 (Wash. 1987) (ruling that judge violated the Canon in asking a female intern to come into his chambers, take her clothes off, and bend over); *In re Buchanan*, 669 P.2d 1248 (Wash. 1983) (finding a violation where judge asked female job applicants irrelevant questions about their spouses' jealousies and whether they would go on personal outings with the judge in his airplane or boat); *In re Hey*, 457 S.E.2d 509 (W. Va. 1995) (judge engaged in sexual harassment of female court employees including unwanted and unwelcome touching and kissing, making crude sexual comments, and asking for sexual favors).

Judges have also been disciplined for retaliating after their unwanted invitations or request for sexual favors were rebuffed. *See, e.g., Disc. Counsel v. Campbell*, 623 N.E.2d 24 (Ohio 1993) (after director of court's psycho-diagnosis clinic rebuffed judge and compared his behavior to the conduct described by Anita Hill in the Clarence Thomas confirmation hearings, the judge questioned her salary and sent a letter criticizing her office to her and to the court's executive officer; court found the conduct "particularly intolerable by an attorney and abhorrent for a member of the judiciary" and suspended him from the practice of law for a year).

COMMENDING OR CRITICIZING JURORS FOR THEIR VERDICT

Rule 2.8(C) requires judges to refrain from commenting upon a jury's verdict other than in a court order or opinion. Canon 3B(11) of the 1990 Code, on which Rule 2.8(C) is based, permitted judges to "express appreciation to jurors for their service to the judicial system and the community." The Joint Commission to Evaluate the Model Code of Judicial Conduct removed that provision from the Rule on the grounds that it was advice not needed in the black letter. Instead, the Commission added a new comment stating that a "judge who is not otherwise prohibited by law from doing so may meet with jurors who choose to remain after trial," but warns that the judge "should be careful not to discuss the merits of the case." Model Code of Judicial Conduct Rule 2.8 cmt. [3]. According to the Commission, the Comment was added in light of the growing recognition that judicial outreach is a valued part of the judicial role and includes outreach to jurors. The "Comment makes clear," the Reporters' notes explain, "that judges can commend jurors for their service and that the prohibition on judges commending or criticizing the jury for their verdict does not foreclose other communications between judges and jurors." *See, e.g.,* Ariz. Sup. Ct. Jud. Ethics Adv. Comm. Op. 01-01 (2001) (judge may issue certificates or letters of appreciation for jury service without reference to the outcome of a particular case). The Commission added this Comment because it "saw value in creating an opportunity for the judge to learn more about the jury's experience, as long as the merits of the case were not discussed." Charles G. Geyh & W. William Hodes, *Reporters' Notes to the Model Code of Judicial Conduct* 36–37 (2009). As noted in the Comment to the Rule, "[c]ommending or criticizing jurors for their verdict may imply a judicial expectation in future cases and may impair a juror's ability to be fair and impartial in a subsequent case." *See also ABA Standards for Criminal Justice: Discovery and Trial by Jury*, Standard 15-4.3(d) ("Under no circumstances should the court state or imply an opinion on the merits of the case, or make any other statements that might prejudice a juror in future jury service.").

The language of Rule 2.8(C) was first added to the Code in 1990 as former Canon 3B(11), and to date, there are only a few disciplinary cases construing it. *See, e.g., In re Goshgarian*, No. 98-CC-2 (Ill. Cts. Comm'n 1998) (judge suspended for three months for misconduct, including calling a jury in a criminal case "stupid" and "gutless" for its verdict of "not guilty" and stating that the verdict was the "worst" he had seen in years); *In re Salerno*, 28 N.E.3d 84 (Ohio 2015) (after the jury returned a not-guilty verdict in a criminal trial, judge told the jurors that they had reached the wrong verdict and disclosed that the defendant had additional criminal charges pending against him, although that information had not been admitted into evidence); *In re*

Private Admonition of a District Judge (2/10/00) (Tex. Comm'n on Jud. Conduct 2000) (judge's negative post-verdict comments to jurors about the integrity and professionalism of a litigant's lawyer, and comments indicating that the judge would not be fair and impartial concerning the litigant's case in the future violated provision); *In re Austin*, CJC No. 4880-F-129 (Wash. Comm'n on Jud. Conduct 2006) (judge admonished for telling jurors that he thought defendant was not guilty and that the jury reached an incorrect verdict in criminal trial). *See also In re Cunningham* 1994 WL 897477 (N.Y. Comm'n on Jud. Conduct 1994) (judge censured for praising jurors for their verdict in criminal trial); *Dougherty v. State*, 746 So. 2d 486 (Fla. App. 2d Dist. 1999) (judge's improper public criticism of a jury's acquittal in an unrelated criminal case involving a different defendant was a flagrant violation of Canon prohibiting judge from commending or criticizing jurors for their verdict; court held that in subsequent case, individual voir dire was justified so that prospective jurors would not learn of comments but judge's disqualification was not warranted). A judge's intent in making comments to jurors appears to be irrelevant in determining a violation of this section. *In re Dillon*, 2002 WL 275083 (N.Y. Comm'n on Jud. Conduct 2002) (judge's comments expressing his agreement with jury's verdict were improper and could not be justified by judge's intent to allay apparent emotionalism of jurors in highly charged murder trial).

In some cases, parties have sought to disqualify a judge for comments the judge made to jurors in a previous, unrelated case. In addition, parties have sought to overturn an adverse decision on appeal by arguing that a judge's comment to jurors shows that the judge was biased against the appellant. However, courts have generally been reluctant to grant such a disqualification motion or reverse a lower court decision based on judicial comments to a jury absent proof that those comments actually prejudiced jurors. *See, e.g., U.S. v. Quesada-Bonilla*, 952 F.2d 597 (1st Cir. 1991) (judge's comments at end of trial that he would have reached the same conclusion had he been trying the case without a jury did not bias two jurors who then sat at trial of defendant, which was presided over by the same judge and involved the same defense lawyer). *See also Walter v. Wal-Mart Stores, Inc.*, 748 A.2d 961 (Me. 2000) (trial judge's improper post-verdict comment telling jury that it had sent "a message about the duty and care of a pharmacist" and that it was a step "we took together" was not enough in and of itself to support discount store's contention that judge was, in fact, prejudiced or biased against store in pharmacist malpractice case). *But see Everitt v. U.S.*, 281 F.2d 429 (5th Cir. 1960) (judge's comments create reversible error when his praise for a speedy guilty verdict in codefendant's trial were likely to create prejudice in appellant's trial).

RULE 2.9 EX PARTE COMMUNICATIONS

(A) A judge shall not initiate, permit, or consider ex parte communications, or consider other communications made to the judge outside the presence of the parties or their lawyers, concerning a pending* or impending matter,* except as follows:

(1) When circumstances require it, ex parte communication for scheduling, administrative, or emergency purposes, which does not address substantive matters, is permitted, provided:

(a) the judge reasonably believes that no party will gain a procedural, substantive, or tactical advantage as a result of the ex parte communication; and

(b) the judge makes provision promptly to notify all other parties of the substance of the ex parte communication, and gives the parties an opportunity to respond.

(2) A judge may obtain the written advice of a disinterested expert on the law applicable to a proceeding before the judge, if the judge gives advance notice to the parties of the person to be consulted and the subject matter of the advice to be solicited, and affords the parties a reasonable opportunity to object and respond to the notice and to the advice received.

(3) A judge may consult with court staff and court officials whose functions are to aid the judge in carrying out the judge's adjudicative responsibilities, or with other judges, provided the judge makes reasonable efforts to avoid receiving factual information that is not part of the record, and does not abrogate the responsibility personally to decide the matter.

(4) A judge may, with the consent of the parties, confer separately with the parties and their lawyers in an effort to settle matters pending before the judge.

(5) A judge may initiate, permit, or consider any ex parte communication when expressly authorized by law* to do so.

(B) If a judge inadvertently receives an unauthorized ex parte communication bearing upon the substance of a matter, the judge shall make provision promptly to notify the parties of the substance of the communication and provide the parties with an opportunity to respond.

(C) A judge shall not investigate facts in a matter independently, and shall consider only the evidence presented and any facts that may properly be judicially noticed.

(D) A judge shall make reasonable efforts, including providing appropriate supervision, to ensure that this Rule is not violated by court staff, court officials, and others subject to the judge's direction and control.

COMMENT

[1] To the extent reasonably possible, all parties or their lawyers shall be included in communications with a judge.

[2] Whenever the presence of a party or notice to a party is required by this Rule, it is the party's lawyer, or if the party is unrepresented, the party, who is to be present or to whom notice is to be given.

[3] The proscription against communications concerning a proceeding includes communications with lawyers, law teachers, and other persons who are not participants in the proceeding, except to the limited extent permitted by this Rule.

[4] A judge may initiate, permit, or consider ex parte communications expressly authorized by law, such as when serving on therapeutic or problem-solving courts, mental health courts, or drug courts. In this capacity, judges may assume a more interactive role with parties, treatment providers, probation officers, social workers, and others.

[5] A judge may consult with other judges on pending matters, but must avoid ex parte discussions of a case with judges who have previously been disqualified from hearing the matter, and with judges who have appellate jurisdiction over the matter.

[6] The prohibition against a judge investigating the facts in a matter extends to information available in all mediums, including electronic.

[7] A judge may consult ethics advisory committees, outside counsel, or legal experts concerning the judge's compliance with this Code. Such consultations are not subject to the restrictions of paragraph (A)(2).

1990 CODE COMPARISON

Rule 2.9(A) derives from former Canon 3B(7) with some modifications. In paragraph (A)(1)(a), "substantive" was added in recognition of the fact that a scheduling, administrative, or emergency ex parte communication that is unrelated to substantive matters per se could nonetheless, in some instances, enable a party to gain an inappropriate substantive advantage. Charles G. Geyh & W. William Hodes, *Reporters' Notes to the Model Code of Judicial Conduct* 39 (2009).

Paragraph (A)(1)(b) of Rule 2.9 is former Canon 3B(7)(a)(ii), but reworded to clarify that the judge may delegate the task of notifying other parties of ex parte communications undertaken for administrative and scheduling purposes.

Paragraph (A)(2) is former Canon 3B(7)(b), but modified to add the requirement of advance notice. Under the 1990 Code, a judge could consult with an outside legal expert ex parte before notifying the parties. If such a consultation was problematic for reasons that had not occurred to the judge, post-consultation notification to the parties would come too late to prevent the problem from arising. As revised, the Rule calls upon the judge to notify the parties before the ex parte contact is made and to make any advice received available in writing. *Id.* at 39.

Paragraph (A)(3) is a modified version of Canon 3B(7)(c). The permissibility of a judge's consultation on a case with other court personnel was qualified to include the common sense limitations that the judge must not relinquish ultimate responsibility for deciding the case and, in the course of such consultation, should be careful not to acquire factual information to which he or she is not entitled. *Id.*

Paragraph (B) is new and addresses an issue not covered by the former Code. If a judge inadvertently receives an unauthorized ex parte communication, the new Rule directs the judge to notify all the other parties of the substance of the communication and give them an opportunity to respond. In an age when misdirected faxes and email are common, the Commission was impressed of the need for some provision to deal with inadvertent disclosures of ex parte information. *Id.* at 39–40.

Paragraph (C) is also new to the Code. In the Commission's view, the judge's duty to consider only the evidence presented is a defining feature of the judge's role in an adversarial system and warrants explicit mention in the black letter Rules. Commentary in the 1990 Code that prohibited a judge from undertaking independent factual investigations was largely unsupported by the black letter. Specific acknowledgement of the category of evidence or facts that are judicially noticed was considered a beneficial clarification, and was therefore added to this paragraph. *Id.* at 40.

Paragraph (D) was moved to the black letter from the Commentary to former Canon 3B(7). In the Commission's view, a judge's duty to take steps to avoid violating the Rule against ex parte communications through staff could not be inferred from the black letter of the former Rule. Comments [4] through [7] are new to the Code. Comment [4] notes that the exception for ex parte communications authorized by law enables jurisdictions to devise special rules for their problem-solving and therapeutic courts. Comment [5] was added to clarify that while a judge may consult with another judge about a case, the judge should not consult with other judges who have been disqualified from hearing the case.

Additionally, the Comment clarifies that judges should not consult with any judge who has appellate jurisdiction over the matter. Comment [6] emphasizes that judges must be vigilant in avoiding independent investigation of facts, particularly given the ease of access to information via electronic databases and the Internet. Comment [7] makes clear that judges may seek ex parte guidance concerning their compliance with the Code without violating Rule 2.9. *Id.* at 40–41.

ANNOTATION

INTRODUCTION

Pursuant to Rule 2.9, a judge must not "initiate, permit, or consider ex parte communications" or "consider other communications made to the judge outside the presence of the parties or their lawyers concerning a pending or impending matter." An ex parte communication is one that excludes any party who is legally entitled to be present or notified of the communication and given an opportunity to respond. *See* Leslie W. Abramson, *The Judicial Ethics of Ex Parte and Other Communications*, 37 Hous. L. Rev. 1343 (2000).

Ex parte communications are prohibited generally because they undermine the adversary system, threaten the fairness of a proceeding, and create an appearance of bias and impartiality. *In re Marek*, 609 N.E.2d 419 (Ind. 1993) ("Improper ex parte communications undermine our adversarial system, which relies so heavily on fair advocacy and an impartial judge. [Such communications] threaten not only the fairness of the resolution at hand, but the reputation of the judiciary and the bar, and the integrity of our system of justice."); Charles Gardner Geyh, James J. Alfini, Steven Lubet, & Jeffrey M. Shaman, *Judicial Conduct and Ethics* § 5.02 at 5–3 (5th ed. 2013) ("[a]t the very least, participation in ex parte communications will expose the judge to one-sided argumentation, which carries the attendant risk of an erroneous ruling on the law or the facts. At worst, ex parte communication is an invitation to improper influence if not outright corruption.") As one court noted, "[n]othing is more dangerous and destructive of the impartiality of the judiciary than a one-sided communication between a judge and a single litigant. Even the most vigilant and conscientious of judges may be subtly influenced by such contacts. No matter how pure the intent of the party who engages in such contacts, without the benefit of a reply, a judge is placed in the position of possibly receiving inaccurate information or being unduly swayed by unrebutted remarks about the other side's case. The other party should not have to bear the risk of factual oversights or inadvertent negative impressions that might easily be corrected by the chance to present counter arguments." *Rose v. State*, 601 So. 2d 1181 (Fla. 1992).

Therefore, as noted in the Commentary, "[t]o the extent reasonably possible, all parties or their lawyers shall be included in communications with a judge." Model Code of Judicial Conduct Rule 2.9 cmt. [1]. Whenever the presence of a party or notice to a party is required, the party's lawyer must be given notice or if the party is appearing pro se, then notice must be given to the party. Model Code of Judicial Conduct Rule 2.9 cmt. [2]. A judge should treat a pro se party as he or she would treat a party's lawyer and may not communicate ex parte with opposing counsel in the pro se party's absence. *See, e.g., Strothers v. Strothers*, 567 N.E.2d 222 (Mass. App. Ct. 1991) (judge committed reversible error in divorce case where wife appeared pro se and judge asked husband and wife to leave courtroom and discussed with husband's lawyer the amount husband could afford to pay in child support).

A judge may violate Rule 2.9 by permitting someone else to initiate an ex parte communication (*see Miss. Comm'n on Jud. Performance v. Chinn*, 611 So. 2d 849 (Miss. 1992) ("For a judge to merely listen to another person involved in a pending litigation is a violation."); *In re Complaint Against White*, 651 N.W.2d 551 (Neb. 2002) (while judge's communication with lawyer was "not initiated by the respondent, it was clearly permitted by her.")) or by considering information that he or she obtained ex parte (*see, e.g., Horton v. Ferrell*, 981 S.W.2d 88 (Ark. 1998) (trial court's acceptance of special master's report constituted error in action for an accounting following dissolution of partnership); *State ex rel. Bryan v. McDonald*, 662 S.W.2d 5 (Tex. Crim. App. 1983) (judge may not view presentence investigation reports prior to determination of guilt); Fla. Jud. Ethics Adv. Comm. Op. 99-19 (1999) (judge may not review unsworn comments of a law enforcement officer, attached to a traffic citation, when the comments are not disclosed to defendant)). A judge does not violate the "consider" provision of the rule if the information that was received ex parte was already known to the judge. *Foster v. United States*, 615 A.2d 213 (D.C. 1992) (judge did not violate "consider" provision of rule by speaking to member of parole board because information was already known to judge and on the record, and therefore, available to the defendant).

A judge who engages in ex parte communications may be subject to discipline (*see generally* Annotation, *Disciplinary Action Against Judge for Engaging in Ex Parte Communication With Attorney, Party or Witness*, 82 A.L.R. 4th 567 (1990)); *In re Foret*, 144 So. 3d 1028 (Louisiana 2014) (judge suspended for 60 days without pay, in part, for ex parte communication with parties); *In re Solomon*, 51 A.3d 836 (N.J. 2012) (judge censured and disqualified from holding future office for five years for ex parte communication). Judges also may be required to recuse themselves from proceedings under Rule 2.11's general provision mandating disqualification where a judge's "impartiality might reasonably be questioned." *See, e.g., In re Parker*, 11-259 (Ariz. Comm'n on Jud. Conduct 2012) (judge censured for continuing to discuss matter with petitioner over telephone after defendant disconnected from telephone hearing); *Miss. Comm'n on Jud. Performance v. Vess*, 10 So. 3d (Miss. 2009) (judge's ex parte communication with person charged with crime and proceeding with case violated Code); *In re Morton*, 770 N.E.2d 827 (Ind. 2002) (judge publicly reprimanded for engaging in ex parte communications with father's lawyer in child custody proceeding, failing to disclose ex parte communication, and refusing to disqualify himself); *Miss Comm'n on Jud. Performance v. Britton*, 936 So. 2d 898 (Miss. 2006) (judge publicly reprimanded and suspended without pay for engaging in ex parte communications with litigants in several cases and setting aside default judgment entered by another judge after ex parte communication); *but see Ex Parte Hunt*, 642 So. 2d 1060 (Ala. 1994) (judge not required to recuse where ex parte communication did not prejudice defendant). See also Rule 2.11 and accompanying text regarding Disqualification.

The permissibility of ex parte communications is likely to vary between jurisdictions and may depend on the level of formality required in a particular locality. For instance, a judge in a small rural community is likely to treat ex parte communications very differently than a federal district judge in a large city. Jack M. Weiss, *It Depends on the Meaning of "Ex Parte,"* 29 No. 2 Litig. 27 (2003). At the same time, new technology developments also raise questions about the meaning of ex parte: when is "blogging" improper ex parte communication? Rachel C. Lee, Student Author, *Ex Parte Blogging: The Legal Ethics of Supreme Court Advocacy in the Internet Era*, 61 Stan. L. Rev. 1535 (2009).

PENDING AND IMPENDING MATTERS

Rule 2.9 prohibits ex parte communications concerning a "pending" or "impending" matter. General legal discussions about the law between a judge and a party or lawyer outside the context of pending or impending litigation are not usually considered ex parte communications. *See* Charles Gardner Geyh, James J. Alfini, Steven Lubet, & Jeffrey M. Shaman, *Judicial Conduct and Ethics*, § 5.03[1] at 5–4 (5th ed. 2014). A case has generally been considered "pending" after the case begins and until the appellate process is complete. *See, e.g., Hovelson v. U.S. Swim & Fitness, Inc.*, 450 N.W.2d 137 (Minn. 1990) (judge did not violate Canon by hearing ex parte motion to amend default judgment to include defendant's other names because the motion was made following the judgment and no appeal was pending); *In re Complaint Against White*, 651 N.W.2d 551 (Neb. 2002) (judge violated Canon when, after district court vacated judge's sentence and remanded case for resentencing by another judge, judge had ex parte contacts with deputy county attorney to provide advice for appeal from district court's judgment); *In re Young*, 984 P.2d 997 (Utah 1999) (initiating ex parte phone conversation with attorney and commenting on pending attorney fees motion violated Canon, even though judge had issued bench order dismissing case and judge was technically no longer assigned to case because he had completed his rotation in county; case was still pending, even though it was not pending before that judge). Not every contact between a judge and a party or lawyer, even while a trial is pending, violates Rule 2.9, if the case is not discussed. Charles Gardner Geyh, James J. Alfini, Steven Lubet, & Jeffrey M. Shaman, *Judicial Conduct and Ethics*, § 5.03[1] at 5–4 (5th ed. 2013). *See, e.g., In re McGraw*, 359 S.E.2d 853 (W. Va. 1987) (ex parte telephone call between magistrate and mother of divorce litigant appearing in magistrate's court did not violate Canon where their discussion did not concern divorce case).

The prohibition on ex parte communications also applies to proceedings pending before other judges. As one court noted, "the language of [Rule 2.9] simply proscribes ex parte communications concerning a 'pending or impending' proceeding and does not limit that prohibition by reference to the docket of a particular judge." *In re Complaint Against White*, 651 N.W.2d 551 (Neb. 2002) (judge's contacts with deputy county attorney, after district court had vacated the judge's revocation of probation for violation of domestic protection order and had remanded the case for resentencing by another judge, constituted improper ex parte communications while case was pending). *See also In re Ramos*, 2014-094 (N.M. 2014) (judge publicly censured and ordered to participate in mentoring program for contacting another judge to personally vouch for a defendant in matter appearing before that judge); *In re Young*, 984 P.2d 997 (Utah 1999) (judge violated Canon prohibiting unauthorized ex parte communications with attorneys involved in any pending proceedings by initiating ex parte phone conversation with lawyer and commenting on pending attorney fees motion that was pending before another judge). *But see Miss. Comm'n on Jud. Performance v. Brown*, 918 So. 2d 1247 (Miss. 2005) (judge's communications with jailer, arresting officer, and prosecutor in an effort to obtain favorable treatment for his son who was charged with assaulting his ex-wife were improper but did not violate the Code provision prohibiting ex parte communications because that Canon addresses communications between judge and parties to a case over which judge is presiding); Ill. Jud. Ethics Comm. Op. 94-19 (1994) (an assistant state's attorney assigned to retry a case that was previously tried by a former state's attorney who is now a judge may have a detailed discussion about the case with the judge because the judge is not sitting on the case).

A case is generally deemed to be "impending" when it is anticipated but has not yet begun. Judges who engage in ex parte communications regarding impending proceedings create an appearance of impropriety and should recuse themselves from the subsequent litigation. *See, e.g., Scogin v. State*, 227 S.E.2d 780 (Ga. App. 1976) (judge was required to recuse himself where he gave advice to a person regarding her inability to collect child support from the father of her child and the abandonment case against the father subsequently came before judge's court); *Stivers v. Knox County Dept. of Public Welfare*, 482 N.E.2d 748 (Ind. App. 1985) (judge's participation in community child protection team meeting prior to presiding over proceedings instigated by child protection team, which included petition for termination of parental rights was impermissible and judge was required to recuse himself). The "impending proceeding" limitation was added to the 1972 Code to preclude forum shopping by a party or lawyer who tries, before a claim is filed, to obtain some idea about how the judge would rule on the particular fact situation. E. Wayne Thode, *Reporter's Notes to Code of Judicial Conduct* 54 (1973).

Judges may need to take affirmative steps to distance themselves from pending and impending cases by taking reasonable precautions to avoid extrajudicial contacts. For instance, a judge may have clerks screen telephone calls, mail, and e-mail to ensure that they do not pertain to matters presently pending before the court. *Miss. Comm'n on Jud. Performance v. Chinn*, 611 So. 2d 849 (Miss. 1992) ("For a judge to merely listen to another person involved in a pending litigation is a violation of [Rule 2.9]."). At least one jurisdiction, Florida, has addressed the issue of judges' participation in e-mail forums regarding legal issues. Florida's Judicial Ethics Advisory Committee has issued an opinion advising that judges may participate in such forums with lawyers, but must limit their participation to reading the postings and may not ask questions or respond to pending questions. Fla. Jud. Ethics Adv. Comm. Op. 2001-02 (2001).

Impermissible Ex Parte Communications

Ex Parte Communications with Lawyers

A judge may not communicate ex parte, either in person or in writing, with a lawyer who is representing a party in a proceeding in the absence of opposing counsel or the opposing party, if he or she is appearing pro se. *See, e.g., In re Free*, 158 So. 3d 771 (La. 2014) (judge who telephoned one party's counsel after counsel wrote to judge raising issue of recusal communicated ex parte with lawyer and violated rule); *In re Royster*, 648 S.E.2d 837 (N.C. 2007) (judge's conduct in mother's action to recover unpaid child support, in participating in ex parte conference with father's attorney, and as result, entering order striking earlier order by different district court judge that had found father in contempt warranted public censure, violated rule); *In re Mosley*, 102 P.3d 555 (Nev. 2004) (judge assigned to post-plea bargain sentencing violated Canon by meeting defendant's attorney in chambers without notifying district attorney and discussing procedural advantage to be gained by forcing judge's recusal based upon fact that defendant and his wife could provide evidence in judge's bitter child custody case against judge's former girlfriend now living with defendant); *Jud. Inquiry & Rev. Bd. v. Snyder*, 523 A.2d 294 (Pa. 1987) (judge held frequent ex parte conferences with plaintiff's counsel regarding evidentiary and other legal issues); *Matter of Disc. Proc. Against Aulik*, 429 N.W.2d 759 (Wis. 1988) (judge suspended for telling attorney for one litigant about law clerk's conclusions that attorney's firm might be involved in frivolous lawsuit and by mailing law clerk's summary of research on contested issue to attorney).

Lawyers are similarly prohibited from ex parte communications by Model Rule of Professional Conduct 3.5(b), which provides that a lawyer "shall not communicate ex parte with a [judge] during the proceeding unless authorized to do so by law or court order." Such communications, though they may be harmless, "often partake of all of the evils that the rule against ex parte communications was designed to prevent: bias, prejudice, coercion, and exploitation." Charles Gardner Geyh, James J. Alfini, Steven Lubet, & Jeffrey M. Shaman, *Judicial Conduct and Ethics*, § 5.03[2] at 5–6 (5th ed. 2013). *See also In re Conduct of Merkel*, 138 P.3d 847 (Or. 2006) (the purpose of the disciplinary rule prohibiting an attorney from engaging in ex parte communications with the court as to the merits of the case is to prevent a party from improperly influencing or inaccurately informing a judge).

A guardian ad litem in a child custody case, like any other lawyer in the case, is not permitted to have ex parte communications with the judge regarding issues before the court because such communications are a violation of the opposing party's due process rights. *Ex Parte R.D.N.*, 918 So. 2d 100 (Ala. 2005).

Ex Parte Communications with Prosecutors

The relationship between prosecutors and judges is often of a more cooperative nature than the relationship between the judge and a defendant's lawyer and may lead to frequent improper ex parte communications. *See* Roberta K. Flowers, *An Unholy Alliance: The Ex Parte Relationship Between the Judge and the Prosecutor*, 79 Neb. L. Rev. 251 (2000) (discussing why prosecutors and judges have a close relationship and how that can result in impermissible ex parte communications). *See also Haller v. Robbins*, 409 F.2d 857 (1st Cir. 1969) (noting that the relationship between prosecutor and judge may lead to ex parte communications).

A judge may violate Rule 2.9 by engaging in ex parte communications with a prosecutor about factual issues in a criminal case. *See, e.g., In re Cummings*, 211 P.3d 1136 (Alaska 2009) (judge suspended without pay for ex parte communication with prosecution by giving notes to state trooper witness referencing specific information in key document); *State v. Cash*, 867 S.W.2d 741 (Tenn. Crim. App. 1993) (judge required to recuse after he spoke with prosecutor in the absence of defense counsel about factual issues that were subject of remand); *but see Westbrook v. State*, 29 S.W.3d 103 (Tex. Crim. App. 2000) (even if judge violated Canon by meeting ex parte with prosecutor three days before murder trial started, such violation did not require disqualification of trial judge, where defendant failed to demonstrate any judicial bias resulting from trial judge's participation in such meetings).

A judge may also violate Rule 2.9 by offering legal or tactical advice to a prosecutor. *See, e.g., In re Cummings*, 292 P.2d 187 (Alaska 2013) (judge removed for ex parte communications with prosecutor directing prosecutor to relevant case law on issue at trial); *In re Irwin*, 14-400 (Ariz. Comm'n on Jud. Conduct 2015) (trial court judge reprimanded for sending an email to prosecutor demanding prosecutor notify supreme court of misstatement defense counsel made to supreme court when that court heard the appeal of matter initially heard by trial judge); *In re McClosky*, 50 A.3d 15 (N.J. 2012) (judge reprimanded for ex parte conversation with prosecutor in which judge told the prosecutor to ask "certain questions of State witnesses concerning issues relevant to the State's case and critical to the defense); *Disc. Counsel v. Plough*, 931 N.E.2d 575 (Ohio 2010) (judge disciplined for telephoning prosecutor to discuss judge's opposition to plea agreement); *Jones v. State*, 668 P.2d 1170 (Okla. Crim. App. 1983) (judge improperly initiated ex parte communications suggesting various procedures to prosecution); *In re Starcher*, 457 S.E.2d 147 (W. Va. 1995) (initiating ex parte telephone conversation to advise the assistant prosecutor on the style of the State's upcoming closing argument in ongoing criminal trial violated Canon); *In the Matter of Recant*, (N.Y. Comm'n on Jud. Conduct 2001) (judge censured for misconduct, including advising assistant district attorney that he was filing the wrong type of motion); *cf. People v. Garson*, 848 N.E.2d 1264 (N.Y. 2006) (judge improperly offered ex parte advice to attorney appearing in divorce case before the judge); *In re Kondo*, CJC No. 7772-F-166 (Wash. Comm'n on Jud. Conduct 2015) (judge improperly responded to prosecutor's email about location of defense counsel whom prosecutor was trying serve with a subpoena in pending case on another docket).

Judges have also been disciplined for ex parte communication with law enforcement officers and state investigators. *See In re Allen* (N.Y. Comm'n on Jud. Conduct 2011).

In addition, while the incidence is generally less frequent, judges have also been disciplined for providing ex parte legal assistance to a defense lawyer in a criminal case. *Public Admonishment of Judge Ronald Maciel* (Cal. Comm'n on Jud. Performance 1997) (judge called court-appointed defense lawyer to discuss with her the option of filing a peremptory challenge against the judge who was assigned to case).

Ex Parte Communications with Parties

Judges may not communicate ex parte with parties to a proceeding, even if the judge claims a seemingly positive motive for doing so. *See, e.g., Miss. Comm'n on Jud. Performance v. Carver*, 107 So. 3d 964 (Miss. 2013) (judge reprimanded and assessed costs for improper ex parte discussion with defendant and defendant's brother-in-law, whom the judge had known his entire life, about arraignment date, defendant's inability to appear on that date, and the automatic resetting for trial on a later date); *Miss. Comm'n on Jud. Performance v. Vess*, 10 So. 3d 486 (Miss. 2009) (judge received public reprimand, costs and fine after improperly communicating and convicting defendant even though judge was simply trying to help the defendant and believed that it was not improper to talk with parties in a case so long as they did not discuss the facts or the "meat of the case"); *Miss. Comm'n on Jud. Performance v. Dodds*, 680 So. 2d 180 (Miss. 1996) (judge's ex parte communications violated Canon even if judge did not possess any bad motives and engaged in the practice in order to accord fairness to the litigants); *In re Buchanan* (N.Y. Comm'n on Jud. Conduct 2012) (judge disciplined for improper contact with hospitalized juvenile who was subject of delinquency petition pending before judge); *In re Tarantino* (N.Y. Comm'n on Jud. Conduct 2011) (judge disciplined for taking defendant for a ride in his personal car over a lunch recess and speaking privately with him about personal issues, including the defendant's drug use and his mother's death); *Disc. Counsel v. Medley*, 819 N.E.2d 273 (Ohio 2004) (judge's disposal at arraignment of some criminal charges against defendant in exchange for a guilty plea to other charges, when defendant was present but prosecutor and defense counsel were not, violated Canon prohibiting ex parte communications, even though judge did not have malevolent intent and was likely simply trying to expedite the process); *In re Koetter*, no. CJC 12-0849-DI, (Tex. Comm'n on Jud. Conduct 2013) (judge admonished for ex parte remarks to party about considering mediation, followed by entering order in favor of that party without allowing opposing party to be heard); *In re Johnson*, no. 20130036-SC, (Utah Supreme Court, Mar. 26, 2013) (judge reprimanded for speaking, ex parte before issuing decision, with small claim defendant about paying the plaintiff, and for speaking with plaintiff about what the decision would be). *But see In re Yaccarino*, 502 A.2d 3 (N.J. 1985) (judge violated Canon by meeting individually with parties to discuss proposed settlement in order to conserve costs of litigation; judge was not disciplined because the parties and their lawyers consented to this procedure). *See also* Charles Gardner Geyh, James J. Alfini, Steven Lubet, & Jeffrey M. Shaman, *Judicial Conduct and Ethics*, § 5.03[3] at 5–11 (5th ed. 2013). ("Although some judges may believe in good faith that they can personalize or demystify the judicial system through direct contact with the parties, the more common result is some form of prejudgment or other unfair advantage." (citations omitted)). It is also irrelevant that the communication may be beneficial to the complaining party. *In re Kaufman*, 416 S.E.2d 480 (W. Va. 1992) (judge admonished for ex parte telephone conversation with party to the litigation; it is immaterial that the conversation may have been beneficial to the complaining party).

Communications with Criminal Defendants, Victims, or Their Families

A judge should generally not meet privately with criminal defendants, codefendants, or complaining witnesses in criminal or quasi-criminal cases. *See, e.g., In re Bravo*, JC-15-0001 (Ariz. 2015) (judge censured for exparte communications with petitioner seeking order of protection); *Ark. Jud. Disc. & Disability Comm'n v. Proctor*, 360 S.W.3d 61 (Ark. 2010) (judge removed from office, in part, for ex parte communications with multiple defendants); *Bell v. State*, 655 N.E.2d 129 (Ind. App. 1995) (judge abused his discretion in denying motion for new judge brought by defendant charged in drug conspiracy, where prior to trial judge had ex parte meeting with defendant's alleged co-conspirator); *In re Boothe*, 110 So. 3d 1002 (La. 2013) (judge suspended, in part, based on ex parte communication with pro se criminal defendant); *In re McCree*, 845 N.W.2d 458 (Mich. 2014) (judge suspended, in part, for ex parte communication with complaining witness in child support matter); *In re Burke* (N.Y. Comm'n on Jud. Conduct 2014) (judge rode in police car with defendant whom judge had just arraigned, provided legal advice to defendant, and recommended defendant hire judge's former partner); *In re Jordan*, 622 P.2d 297 (Or. 1980) (judge violated Canon by conversing privately with a complaining witness regarding a pending criminal case); *but see Walls v. State*, 20 S.W.3d 322 (Ark. 2000) (judge's public comments and ex parte meeting with victims' families did not amount to bias requiring recusal at resentencing).

A judge may also violate Rule 2.9 by communicating with family members of the defendant or the victim. *See, e.g., In re Peck*, 867 P.2d 853 (Ariz. 1994) (judge removed from office for meeting with the defendant's family and calling the police to tell them the defendant was a victim of mistaken identity); *In re Karren*, 11-236 and 11-239 (Ark. Jud. Disc. & Disability Comm'n 2012) (judge reprimanded for speaking ex parte with juvenile defendants parents, one of whom is employed by the judge); *State v. Scales*, 933 P.2d 737 (Kan. 1997) (proceeding was inherently unfair and homicide defendant was denied fair sentencing hearing due to judge's ex parte meeting with victim's family and ex parte consideration of petition requesting imposition of harsh punishment, as communications undermined any confidence in impartiality of proceeding); *In re Bass*, No. 2012-31 (Ga. Comm'n on Jud. Qualifications 2011) (judge publicly reprimanded for Facebook chat with DUI defendant's sister about matter).

Consent Given by Standard Practice in Jurisdiction

In some jurisdictions, ex parte communications may not violate Rule 2.9(A) if such communications are within normal procedures in that jurisdiction. For instance, in *In re Conduct of Stacey*, 737 N.W.2d 345 (Minn. 2007), the Minnesota Supreme Court held that a district court judge's disposition of a traffic ticket by ordering a continuance for dismissal, in chambers without prosecutorial input, did not violate the Canon that bars ex parte communications because there was undisputed testimony that prosecutors had given judges discretion to dispose of citations, both in open court and in chambers, without prosecutorial input. *See also Williams & Connolly, L.L.P. v. P.E.T.A.*, 643 S.E.2d 136 (Va. 2007) (attorneys' motion to recuse judge was not warranted by existing law or a good faith argument for the extension, modification, or reversal of existing law, and thus, sanctions were warranted against attorneys; attorneys had no reasonable basis for contending that judge violated his ethical duties in considering ex parte petition, and in issuing a rule to show cause given that a reasonable inquiry would have shown that the routine practice of the circuit court was to consider ex parte petitions for a rule to show cause and to issue rules to show cause upon the filing of a sufficient affidavit by the petitioning party).

Communications with Jurors

This issue of ex parte communications can arise when a judge addresses a jury in a criminal case prior to sentencing. In general, such communications are a violation of Rule 2.9 because the proceeding is still pending. However, such a violation may be deemed harmless if the jurors' disclosures in those communications did not form part of the judge's sentencing deliberations. For instance, in *Sloan v. U.S.*, 527 A.2d 1277 (D.C. 1986), during a post-verdict discussion, a juror told the judge's clerk that the jury acquitted the defendant of some of the charges because it misunderstood the court's jury instructions. The judge said that he did not consider the juror's communication when he subsequently sentenced defendant, and the court found that the judge's consideration of the information was "strictly limited to future application." Therefore, the court held that "the trial court's future utilization of the remarks is not consideration of an *ex parte* communication 'concerning a pending . . . proceeding.'" *See also Harris v. United States*, 738 A.2d 269 (D.C. 1999) (judge violated Canon by meeting with jurors after conviction and prior to sentencing to solicit their views in an effort to improve the judicial system; however, because jurors' disclosures did not form part of judge's sentencing deliberations, conviction was affirmed); *State v. Durant*, 892 A.2d 302 (Conn. App. 2006) (judge's ex parte communication with jury after jury acquitted defendant of assault did not require judge to recuse himself from presiding over defendant's subsequent probation revocation hearing as long as the judge fully disclosed to the parties his intention to speak with the jury and disclosed the subject matter to be discussed; error, if any, was harmless because judge stated that he had no reason to believe that conversation with jurors would influence his decision, and that he would not consider any information that was imparted during the ex parte discussion); *but cf. State v. Walkings*, 906 A.2d 504 (N.J. Super. 2006) (holding that trial judge violated defendant's right to be present when following entry of guilty verdict, he explored concern of one juror through ex parte, unrecorded discussions).

Some jurisdictions provide safeguards that judges should consider when speaking with a discharged jury following the return of a verdict. For instance, Arizona's Judicial Ethics Committee advises that before a judge meets with a jury: (1) counsel for all parties should be informed and given an opportunity to be present or to request that the meeting be on the record; (2) the judge must admonish the jurors before the meeting that he or she cannot answer questions regarding matters still pending and must prohibit any statements on such matters (it may be preferable to give this admonition in court on the record); and (3) the judge must also expressly and firmly prohibit any discussion of the jury deliberations. However, as the opinion notes, despite the judge's admonition and establishment of clear parameters, there remains the possibility that a juror may volunteer information a judge should be prohibited from hearing outside the presence of the parties, if at all. According to the Committee, such information should be treated like any other unsolicited communication to the judge, that is, it must be promptly disclosed to all parties on the record, and they must be given an opportunity to be heard on the matter. Ariz. Sup. Ct. Jud. Ethics Adv. Comm. Op. 01-01 (2001). The ABA Criminal Justice Standards similarly provide that a judge's post verdict discussions with jurors "should occur only on the record and in open court with counsel having the opportunity to be present." Standard 15-4.3(b) of the ABA Standards for Criminal Justice: Discovery and Trial by Jury.

JUDGE'S DISCLAIMER

A judge's disclaimer asserting that an ex parte communication had no effect on his or her decision in a case may be sufficient to avoid a Rule 2.9 violation. *See, e.g., Sloan v. U.S.*, 527 A.2d 1277 (D.C. 1986) (after jury's verdict, a juror told judge's clerk that the jury acquitted the defendant of some of the charges because it misunderstood some of the court's jury instructions; the judge said that he did not consider the juror's communication when he subsequently sentenced defendant and the judge's consideration of the information was "strictly limited to future application, not the present case" and, therefore, not a violation of Canon). Even if a reviewing court determines that the judge violated Rule 2.9, the judge's disclaimer may be sufficient to avoid recusal or reversal. *See, e.g., Cook v. State*, 36 P.3d 710 (Alaska App. 2001) (judge considering defendant's conditional no contest plea to first-degree stalking was not required to recuse himself due to fact that he heard victim's ex parte petition for temporary restraining order against defendant; judge declared that he had no contact with victim and obtained no information from her when he heard and granted her petition); *Harris v. U.S.*, 738 A.2d 269 (D.C. 1999) (judge violated Canon by meeting with jurors prior to sentencing to solicit their views on the jury system, however, the defendant was not substantially prejudiced and the communication was harmless because judge said that jurors' disclosures did not form part of his sentencing deliberations); *Belton v. U.S.*, 581 A.2d 1205 (D.C. 1990) (where judge engaged in ex parte communication and failed to offer assurances that he would not consider it when deliberating on a sentence, court could not be certain that he was aware of his obligation not to consider the ex parte conversation); *In re Marriage of Davison*, 48 P.3d 358 (Wash. App. 2002) (in the absence of at least an inference that a judge considered an improper communication, the judge's impartiality may not reasonably be questioned, and recusal is not required).

PERMISSIBLE EX PARTE COMMUNICATIONS

Rule 2.9(A) provides some exceptions to the general prohibition on ex parte communications. A judge may engage in ex parte communications for scheduling or administrative purposes, or for emergencies that do not deal with substantive matters. A judge may also obtain the written advice of a "disinterested expert" on the law applicable to a proceeding before the judge and consult with "court staff and court officials" who aid the judge in carrying out his or her adjudicative responsibilities or with other judges, if the judge makes "reasonable efforts" to avoid receiving factual information that is not part of the record and does not abrogate responsibility to decide the matter. A judge may confer separately with parties in order to settle a matter, with the consent of the parties, and a judge may initiate, permit, or consider ex parte communications when "expressly authorized by law to do so."

Ex Parte Communications for Scheduling, Administration, or Emergencies

Rule 2.9(A)(1) permits a judge to engage in ex parte communications, where circumstances require, for "scheduling, administrative, or emergency purposes, which does not address substantive matters." For instance, a telephone conversation in which the court informs a party's lawyer when certain forms have to be filed and when a hearing would take place is permissible. *See Hall v. Hall*, 482 A.2d 974 (Pa. Super. 1984); *see also Rodriguez v. State*, 919 So. 2d 1252 (Fla. 2005) (ex parte communication was purely administrative and permissible when the state attorney, on the public records request, informed the judge that the hearing was not a status hearing, but an evidentiary hearing); *Foundation Intern., Inc. v. E.T. Ige Const. Inc.*, 78 P.3d 23 (Haw. 2003) (judge's telephone call to defendant's attorney to discuss conclusion of law attorney had drafted and to clarify judge's reasons for his ruling and instruct attorney to delete sentence from proposed order was administrative or "housekeeping" and not grounds for recusal); *Mahrdt v.*

State, 629 N.E.2d 244 (Ind. App. 1st Dist. 1994) (judge's ex parte communication with sheriff's office concerned scheduling of the inspection of blood alcohol machine in sheriff's custody, the communication could be viewed reasonably only as administrative, and thus, it did not create the appearance of impropriety); *Baker v. Charlotte Motor Speedway, Inc.*, 636 S.E.2d 829 (N.C. App. 2006) (judge's ex parte communication with racetrack and company that constructed racetrack's pedestrian walkway, requesting that track and company create a proposed schedule of damages trials remaining, arising out of consolidated liability action after the walkway collapsed, was entirely administrative in nature, concerning only timing and order of the dozen or more consolidated cases still to be tried, and thus, did not provide a basis for recusal order). *But see In re Johnson*, 658 N.E.2d 589 (Ind. 1995) (hearing prosecutor's ex parte request to reset a hearing date after the defendant's lawyer had rescheduled the hearing is not permissible).

Most litigation under the emergency exception concerns ex parte communications regarding public safety concerns. Leslie W. Abramson, *The Judicial Ethics of Ex Parte Communications*, 37 Hous. L. Rev. 1343 (2000). For instance, an ex parte communication may be permitted to protect the safety of an incarcerated defendant (*see In re Varain*, 969 P.2d 305 (Nev. 1998) (due to defendant's unusual 3:00 a.m. arrest, judge's limited jailhouse communication to ensure defendant's personal safety not improper where judge knew defendant, victim, and victim's mother and disqualified himself from case)) or to protect the safety of third parties (*see, e.g., Mathew Zaheri Corp. v. New Motor Vehicle Bd.*, 64 Cal. Rptr. 2d 705 (Cal. Ct. App. 1997) (stating that a judge could receive an ex parte communication from counsel who believes that an opposing party was unlawfully carrying a concealed weapon)).

However, there are two limitations on ex parte communications for scheduling, administration, or emergencies. First, the judge must reasonably believe that no party will gain a procedural or tactical advantage. *See, e.g., Kail v. State*, 14 S.W.3d 878 (Ark. 2000) (judge's ex parte contact with victim's wife, through case coordinator regarding a visit to the crime scene was not grounds for recusal, as communication in no way gave any party a tactical advantage in the case); *Foundation Intern., Inc. v. E.T. Ige Const. Inc.*, 78 P.3d 23 (Haw. 2003) (judge did not abuse discretion in denying motion to recuse based on alleged improper ex parte communication, where judge had called defendant's attorney to discuss conclusion of law attorney had drafted, telephone call was administrative or "housekeeping" and entailed only the proposed order attorney had circulated, call was to clarify judge's reasons for his ruling and to instruct attorney to delete sentence from proposed order, and call did not provide any advantage to defendant or deprive plaintiff of the opportunity to argue its case); *Garage Doors of Indianapolis, Inc. v. Morton*, 682 N.E.2d 1296 (Ind. App. 1997) (court refused to infer that a party gained an advantage from an ex parte contact merely because he filed his answer and counterclaim immediately after the communication).

Second, the judge must promptly notify all other parties of the substance of the ex parte communication and allow an opportunity to respond. *See In re Anonymous*, 729 N.E.2d 566 (Ind. 2000) (a judge who fails to comply fully with these procedural safeguards, engages in impermissible ex parte communications). *See, e.g., Tessmann v. Tiger Lee Const. Co.*, 634 A.2d 870 (Conn. 1993) (in civil jury trial, answering jurors' questions in order to promote good public relations, and solicit feedback regarding performance of members of bar are within court's administrative functions and are permissible as long as judge fully discloses his intention to speak with jury and discloses subject matter to be discussed); *Cagle v. Davis*, 513 S.E.2d 16 (Ga. App. 1999) (no improper ex parte communications where judge's clerk notified counsel of communications); *James v. State*, 716 N.E.2d 935 (Ind. 1999) (recusal not required where judge relied upon prosecutor's good faith assertion that he would promptly inform defense counsel of ex parte conversation wherein prosecutor informed judge on eve of defendant's retrial of police officer's recollection of defendant's confession); *Timberlake v. State*, 753 N.E.2d 591 (Ind. 2001) (judge's ex parte communication with expert witness was ministerial and not grounds for recusal where judge reasonably believed that neither side gained a tactical advantage, and the parties were notified of the communication).

Substantive Matters

Rule 2.9(A) permits ex parte communications for scheduling, administrative, or emergency purposes that do not address "substantive matters." *See Aztec Minerals Corp. v. State*, 987 P.2d 895 (Colo. Ct. App. 1999) (trial judge's limited ex parte communication with defendants' counsel in which trial judge asked counsel to prepare draft of order awarding attorney fees to defendants but did not the involve a discussion of the substance of the case or the attorney fee request was permissible). Communications that touch upon issues of "critical significance to the judge's ruling in the case" are not permitted. *See Goebel v. Benton*, 830 P.2d 995 (Colo. 1992); *see also Rose v. State*, 601 So. 2d 1181 (Fla. 1992) (judge should not engage in ex parte communication about pending case, unless conversation concerns strictly administrative matters not dealing in any way with merits of case); *In re Conduct of Schenck*, 879 P.2d 863 (Or. 1994) (former judge reprimanded for sending letter to judge urging that case be resolved and that further delay was merely an effort to force a settlement; court rejected argument that letter was not "on the merits"); *State v. Cash*, 867 S.W.2d 741 (Tenn. Crim. App. 1993) (judge required to recuse after he spoke with prosecutor in the absence of defense counsel about factual issues that were subject of remand). A judge may also violate the rule when an ex parte communication indirectly concerns the substance of a pending proceeding. *See, e.g., In re Phalen*, 475 S.E.2d 327 (W. Va. 1996) (family law master violated Canon by engaging in ex parte discussion with litigants regarding selling home products to increase their incomes where income was the heart of the litigation).

Prompt Disclosure of Ex Parte Communication

Rules 2.9(A) instructs judges to "make provision promptly to notify the parties of the substance of the communication and provide the parties with an opportunity to respond." Va. Jud. Ethics Adv. Comm. Op. 00-04 (2000) (advising that to remedy an improper ex parte communication, a judge should disclose promptly to all parties all such oral and written communications on the record, offer the parties an opportunity to respond and direct the person who caused the ex parte communication to cease such communications). *But see In re Fine*, 13 P.3d 400 (Nev. 2000) (judge's ex parte communications with experts in order to decide disputed substantive issues, rather than to resolve administrative matters, were not validated under Code by judge's subsequent reports to the parties that such discussions had occurred).

"Courts have held that prompt disclosure of the ex parte communication to all affected parties may avoid the need for other corrective action." Charles Gardner Geyh, James J. Alfini, Steven Lubet, & Jeffrey M. Shaman, *Judicial Conduct and Ethics*, § 5.05 at 5–25 (5th ed. 2013). *See, e.g., Kamelgard v. Am. College of Surgeons*, 895 N.E.2d 997 (Ill. App. 1st Dist. 2008) (judge's clerk's communication to attorneys for defendants was ex parte and was substantive; therefore, it was improper; but notice was delivered by opposing counsel in accordance with state rules, negating this argument for recusal); *Bauer v. Memorial Hospital*, 879 N.E.2d 478 (Ill. App. 5th Dist. 2007) (ex parte communication during trial between judge and plaintiffs' counsel regarding possible testimony by defendant's lead attorney improper, but harmless error, in part because all the parties and their attorneys knew it was occurring); *A.H. v. P.B.*, 2 P.3d 627 (Alaska 2000) (trial court acted appropriately in forwarding ex parte communications received from child's mother in connection with visitation proceedings to child's incarcerated father who was appearing pro se); *Mallory v. Hartsfield Almand & Grisham, LLP*, 86 S.W.3d 863 (Ark. 2002) (judge's law clerk's ex parte telephone conversation with lawyer was impermissible but not grounds for judge's recusal where judge notified all of the parties and gave them an opportunity to respond); *Matheney v. State*, 688 N.E.2d 883 (Ind. 1997) (magistrate in post-conviction proceedings did not violate rule where magistrate was approached by prosecutor who inquired about subpoena she received from petitioner's counsel regarding her presence in magistrate's chambers when he allegedly made "injudicious" remarks about motion filed by petitioner; magistrate did not seek out contact with witness against petitioner, and he immediately made both parties aware of what prosecutor said to him); *see also* Alaska Comm'n on Jud. Cond. Adv. Op. 99-3 (1999) (when a judicial officer receives an ex parte communication by a court employee concerning facts affecting a pending case, the judge should make full disclosure; where the parties have inquired as to the identity of the person that initiated the communication, absent any legal basis for maintaining the anonymity of that individual, the name should be disclosed).

Obtaining Advice from Disinterested Expert

Rule 2.9(A)(2) permits a judge to "obtain the written advice of a disinterested expert on the law applicable to a proceeding before the judge." The judge must give advance notice to the parties of the person to be consulted, the subject matter of the advice to be solicited and give the parties reasonable opportunity to object and respond to the notice and the advice received. Under the 1990 Code, a judge could consult with an outside legal expert before giving notice to the parties. *See Time Warner Entertainment Co., L.P. v. Baker*, 647 So. 2d 1070 (Fla. Dist. Ct. App. 1994) (judge is not required to give notice prior to communicating with expert on subject matter of lawsuit). However, the 2007 Code requires the judge to notify the parties before the ex parte contact is made. The current Rule also requires that the advice obtained from the "disinterested expert" be in writing, whereas no such requirement was in the 1990 Code.

A judge's ex parte solicitation of information from consultants and experts concerning a technical issue, as opposed to a legal issue, in a case pending before the judge may not fall into this exception. *See In re Baker*, 813 So. 2d 36 (Fla. 2002) (while presiding over a breach of contract trial regarding computer software, judge violated Canon by soliciting information from unnamed computer consultants and experts concerning technical issues relating to the issue of damages in the case pending before him without the involvement of the litigants or their lawyers). *See generally* George D. Marlow, *From Black Robes to White Lab Coats: The Ethical Implications of a Judge's Sua Sponte, Ex Parte Acquisition of Social and Other Scientific Evidence During the Decision-Making Process*, 72 St. John's L. Rev. 291 (Spring 1998) (discussing whether judicial ethics standards should be adjusted to permit judges to engage in sua sponte, ex parte research while a case is pending or impending, and how they may do so while also protecting due process rights).

A judge may also decide to consult ethics advisory committees, outside counsel, or legal experts on judicial ethics to obtain advice about the judge's compliance with the judicial code. Such consultations are not subject to Rule 2.9(A)(2). Model Code of Judicial Conduct Rule 2.9 cmt. [7].

Judges must be aware of possible bias on the part of an expert. As one court noted: "[I]t cannot be assumed that legal and other experts will give only objective advice. They may have developed philosophical loyalties, which affect the advice that they give; as practicing attorneys they may have cases involving the same problems on which they are rendering advice; as consultants, they may owe allegiance to business or other interests that could benefit from acceptance by courts of their viewpoints. Unless the parties are given the opportunity to respond to the expert and the substance of his advice, his prejudices and preconceptions may go unchallenged." *In re Fuchsberg*, 426 N.Y.S. 2d 639, 648 (N.Y. Ct. Jud. 1978). Judges must also be aware of an appearance of bias that consultations with experts might create, which could result in disqualification. *See In re Kensington Intern. Ltd.*, 368 F.3d 289 (3d Cir. 2004) (judge required to recuse himself from asbestos litigation where two of the five "advisors" judge appointed to assist him simultaneously served as advocates in unrelated asbestos-related bankruptcy, representing future asbestos personal injury claimants).

Consulting with Court Personnel and Other Judges

Rule 2.9(A)(3) permits a judge to consult ex parte with "court staff and court officials whose functions are to aid the judge in carrying out the judge's adjudicative responsibilities, or with other judges." *See, e.g., Gaston v. Hunter*, 588 P.2d 326 (Ariz. Ct. App. 1978) (trial judge did not act improperly in consulting disinterested judges and attorneys on certain questions of law); *People v. Farmer*, 254 Cal. Rptr. 508 (Cal. 1989) ("[C]ollegial interchanges on abstract legal matters are not improper."); *Cannon v. State*, 866 N.E.2d 770 (Ind. 2007) ("Judges may certainly seek each other's counsel in the performance of their judicial duties."); *Miss. Comm'n on Jud. Performance v. Martin*, 921 So. 2d 1258 (Miss. 2005) (a judge's conversations with a court clerk are not considered ex parte communications prohibited by the Code of Judicial Conduct); *In re Ferrell*, 378 S.E.2d 662 (W. Va. 1989) (magistrate did not violate Canon when he was contacted by and consulted with another magistrate concerning a civil action in which the magistrate had issued a writ of execution to satisfy a default judgment); *but see In re Fine*, 13 P.3d 400 (Nev. 2000) (expert who was first approached, hired, and paid for by one of the parties in child custody matter was not "court personnel" with whom judge could conduct even limited ex parte communications pursuant to judicial Canon).

The 2007 Code places two new limitations on such consultations: a judge must make reasonable efforts to avoid receiving factual information that is not part of the record, and a judge must not relinquish ultimate responsibility for deciding the case. In *In re Segal*, the Arizona Commission on Judicial Conduct reprimanded a judge for receiving factual information about the defendant's courthouse behavior from court security and not disclosing the contents of the communication to defendant. *In re Segal*, 12-308 (Ariz. Comm'n on Jud. Conduct 2013). This second limitation is well supported by the case law and advisory opinions. *See, e.g., People v. Farmer*, 254 Cal. Rptr. 508 (Cal. 1989)

("[C]ollegial interchanges on abstract legal matters are not improper," but the "court must reach its own conclusions and shoulder responsibility for them"); *Andrews v. State*, 505 N.E.2d 815 (Ind. Ct. App. 1987) (found it a harmless error where judge stated that he had discussed the admissibility of evidence with other judges but that final decision on issue was his own); *Executive Mgmt., Ltd., v. Ticor Title Ins. Co.*, 963 P.3d 465 (Nev. 1998) (even if judge's ex parte consultation of judge in prior case was error, it was harmless where judge did not rely on conversation in deciding to dismiss on basis of res judicata); *McNair v. McNair*, 856 A.2d 5 (N.H. 2004) (even assuming that judge's ex parte communication with a Texas court constituted error, it was harmless as court identified independent grounds for its decision); Colo. Jud. Ethics Adv. Bd. Op. 2004-02 (2004) (a mentee judge may consult with his or her mentor judge as long as the final adjudicative responsibility for any decisions resides solely with the mentee judge).

Some jurisdictions have found that consultations between judges are permissible so long as the judges are from the same jurisdiction. Leslie W. Abramson, *The Judicial Ethics of Ex Parte Communications*, 37 Hous. L. Rev. 1343 (2000). *See, e.g., In re Ferrell*, 378 S.E.2d 662 (W. Va. 1989) (magistrate did not violate Canon when he was contacted by and consulted with another magistrate concerning a civil action in which the magistrate had issued a writ of execution to satisfy a default judgment). *See also* Oregon Code of Judicial Conduct, JR 2-102, which expressly provides that a judge may consult with another judge who is "at the same level." Other jurisdictions have held that a judge may not initiate an ex parte communication with another judge in order to influence that judge's decision. *See, e.g., In re Markey*, 696 N.E.2d 523 (Mass. 1998). An appellate court judge also may not write letters to a lower court judge assuring the judge that he will not overturn the sentences the trial judge imposed. *In re Cunningham*, 442 N.E.2d 434 (N.Y. 1982). A comment to the Rule added in 2007 provides that when consulting with other judges on pending matters, a judge must avoid ex parte discussions of a case with judges who have previously been disqualified from hearing the matter, and with judges who have appellate jurisdiction over the matter. Model Code of Judicial Conduct Rule 2.9 cmt. [5].

A number of cases have arisen regarding judges' ex parte communications with probation officers. Such officers have generally been deemed court employees, and therefore, a judge's ex parte communications with them are not improper. *See, e.g., State v. Mayer*, 834 P.2d 165 (Ariz. App. 1992) (because probation officer is an officer of the court, judge's private conference with probation officer concerning the officer's presentence report prepared for and at the direction of the trial court does not violate Canon); *People v. Smith*, 378 N.W.2d 384 (Mich. 1985) (ex parte communication between sentencing judge and probation officer concerning correction of technical error about statutorily permitted maximum sentence was not improper); *In re Chad S.*, 639 N.W.2d 84

(Neb. 2002) (juvenile probation officer was court personnel, and thus, communication in chambers between probation officer and judge regarding disposition of juvenile's case was not ex parte communication); Utah Jud. Ethics Adv. Op. 97-4 (1997) (juvenile court probation officers are employees of the judiciary and come under the exception permitting ex parte communications with court personnel). A comment added to the 2007 Code provides that when a judge is serving on a therapeutic or problem-solving court, mental health court or drug court, the judge "may assume a more interactive role with . . . probation officers." Model Code of Judicial Conduct Rule 2.9 cmt. [4]. Under Rule 2.9(A)(3), a judge is not required to give the parties notice of the communications with court personnel or fellow judges or an opportunity to respond. Ronald D. Rotunda and John S. Dzienkowski, *Legal Ethics: The Lawyer's Deskbook on Professional Responsibility* 1497–98 (2016).

Settling Pending Matters

Rule 2.9(A)(4) permits a judge, with the consent of the parties, to "confer separately with the parties and their lawyers in an effort to settle matters pending before the judge." *See, e.g., Bland v. Graves*, 650 N.E.2d 117 (Ohio App. 1994) (probate court's ex parte and in camera review of the settlement agreements did not violate Canon). While it may be preferable to have the parties' lawyers present during these settlement negotiations, a judge does not violate the Code provision by not doing so. *See Dutton v. Dutton*, 713 N.E.2d 14 (Ohio Ct. App. 1998) (judge did not engage in impermissible ex parte communication when he engaged in settlement negotiations with husband and wife in divorce case for three hours in chambers without their lawyers). A judge may violate Rule 2.9 by initiating ex parte communications with a party's representative if that individual's role is unclear. *In re Disqualification of Williams*, 657 N.E.2d 1352 (Ohio 1993) (judge violated Canon where there was no indication that judge had parties consent to engage in negotiations and role of the person judge spoke to was unclear). A judge does not violate Rule 2.9, however, by engaging in ex parte settlement discussions with a party the judge believed to be an authorized representative of the defendant. *In re Disqualification of Christiansen*, 723 N.E.2d 1100 (Ohio 1999) (the parties authorized judge to conduct ex parte settlement discussions with representatives of each party and the discussion at issue was between the judge and an individual who attended the trial as the corporate agent of the defendants).

Although Rule 2.9(A)(4) permits judges to confer with the parties and their lawyers in order to settle a matter, if a judge's participation in settlement negotiations becomes too extensive, the judge may be disqualified from the proceeding. *See, e.g., Collins v. Dixie Transport, Inc.*, 543 So. 2d 160 (Miss. 1989) (in proceeding for enforcement of oral settlement agreement, trial judge assumed role of a fact witness on critical credibility issues and had no alternative but to recuse himself).

Ex Parte Communications Expressly Authorized by Law

Rule 2.9(A)(5) permits ex parte communications that are "expressly authorized by law." "Law" includes "court rules as well as statutes, constitutional provisions, and decisional law." Model Code of Judicial Conduct, Terminology. *See, e.g., State v. Peeler*, 857 A.2d 808 (Conn. 2004) (ex parte communication between judge and attorney for key state witness did not violate Canon because it was expressly authorized by state statute). Some federal statutes permit certain ex parte and in camera communications to safeguard classified material. The permissibility of ex parte communications under these statutes has been the subject of commentary following 9/11 and the so-called War on Terror. *See generally* Kathleen Kerr, Note, *Ex Parte Communications in a Time of Terror*, 18 Geo J. Legal Ethics 551 (2005) (discussing the Classified Information Procedures Act (CIPA), which expressly permits limited forms of ex parte communication); Brian M. Tomney, *Contemplating the Use of Classified or State Secret Information Obtained Ex Parte on the Merits in Civil Litigation: Bl(a)ck Tea Society v. City of Boston*, 57 Me. L. Rev. 641 (2005).

Many states' domestic abuse statutes permit a judge to communicate ex parte with a petitioner seeking a protective order. *See, e.g., Cook v. State*, 36 P.3d 710 (Alaska App. 2001). See also Neb. Jud. Ethics Adv. Op. 98-1 (1998) (a judge may have ex parte communications with a petitioner requesting a protection order because the Nebraska Domestic Abuse statute permits such contact). And some states have held that an indigent defendant's ex parte request for expert assistance is "expressly authorized by law" because it is expressly authorized by the due process clauses of the state constitution and the United States constitution. *See, e.g., Ex Parte Moody*, 385 S.E.2d 81 (Ala. 1996) (holding criminal defendant entitled to *ex parte* hearing on whether expert assistance is necessary based on Fifth, Sixth, Fourteenth Amendments to Constitution); *Brooks v. State*, 385 S.E.2d 81 (Ga. 1985) (court upheld ex parte, in chambers application for funds by indigent defendant); *State v. Barnett*, 909 S.W.2d 423 (Tenn. 1995); *but see State v. Apelt*, 861 P.2d 634 (Ariz. 1993) (indigent defendant was not entitled to ex parte hearing on request for expert assistance); *Stevens v. State*, 770 N.E.2d 739 (Ind. 2002) (indigent defendant had no constitutional right to ex parte hearing). *See generally* Justin B. Shane, *Money Talks: An Indigent Defendant's Right to an Ex Parte Hearing for Expert Funding*, 17 Cap. Def. J. 347 (2005).

Some states' statutes permit a judge from one state to communicate ex parte with a judge from another state. *See, e.g., In re Simons*, 693 N.E.2d 1111 (Ohio App. 1997) (Ohio juvenile court judge's ex parte communications with Kentucky court concerning status of two pending child custody proceedings was authorized under Ohio's Uniform Child Custody Jurisdiction Act).

Ex parte communications may also be permitted under court rules. *See, e.g., Matter of Disc. Action Against Wilson*, 461 N.W.2d 105 (N.D. 1990) (ex parte communication between judge and party's lawyer and ex parte order clarifying judgment was permitted by court rule); Ariz. Sup. Ct. Jud. Ethics Adv. Comm. Op. 99-3 (1999) (judge may refer to police report at initial appearance or arraignment stage without prosecutor present for the limited purpose of supplementing the release questionnaire and for determining conditions of release, amount of bail, and appointment of counsel because use of such report is referred to in court rule).

If a litigant fails to point to express authority permitting ex parte communications, a judge does not err by refusing to permit them. *State v. Apelt*, 861 P.2d 654 (Ariz. 1993) *habeas corpus denied sub. nom. Aplet v. Schriro* 2007 WL 2288109 (D. Ariz. 2007) (since there is no statutory authority for granting indigent defendant an ex parte hearing regarding the need for expert assistance, permitting such a hearing would violate Canon); *State v. Goulet*, 593 N.W.2d 345 (N.D. 1999) (court did not err in disclosing defendant's ex parte application for funds to depose a witness where defendant's application did not invoke court rule governing ex parte applications for discovery, but instead cited deposition rule that specifically required notice to prosecutor and rule relating to information not subject to disclosure by the defendant). An ex parte communication that is expressly authorized by law need not be disclosed to all parties.

Requesting a Party to Submit Proposed Findings of Fact and Conclusions of Law

A judge may ask one party in a case to submit proposed findings of fact and conclusions of law so long as the other parties are apprised of the request and given an opportunity to respond. *See, e.g., Williams v. Farmers Ins. Group, Inc.*, 720 P.2d 598 (Colo. App. 1985) (it is proper to request order or submission of proposed findings of fact and conclusions of law so long as request is not ex parte between court and one party to case). Notifying only one party of the request creates an appearance of impropriety. *Rose v. State*, 601 So. 2d 1181 (Fla. 1992). *See also Perlow v. Berb-Perlow*, 875 So. 2d 383 (Fla. 2004) (judge's verbatim adoption of wife's proposed final divorce judgment, which created appearance that trial court did not independently make factual findings and legal conclusions amounting to appearance of impropriety, was reversible error; judgment was entered two hours after submission, husband was not given opportunity to submit his own proposed final judgment or to object to wife's proposal, and trial court made no indication on record of findings or conclusion that formed basis for judgment prior to its entry); *Hanson v. Hanson*, 678 So. 2d 522 (Fla. Dist.

Ct. App. 1996) (judge's ex parte meeting with counsel for husband after which judge directed counsel to draft final judgment in marital dissolution proceeding created appearance of impropriety and required reversal); Ind. Comm'n on Jud. Qualifications Adv. Op. 1-98 (1998) (advising that it is appropriate for a judge to inform one party of a decision the judge has made for the purpose of instructing that party to prepare an order for the judge's signature); Mich. Standing Comm. on Jud. Ethics, Op. RI-195 (1994) (lawyer may not draft an order upon an ex parte request from a judge without compliance with appropriate rules).

When requesting that a party draft findings of fact and conclusions of law, the judge may not touch upon the merits of the case. *Aztec Minerals Corp. v. State*, 987 P.2d 895 (Colo. Ct. App. 1999); *Jake C. Byers, Inc. v. J.B.C. Invs.*, 834 S.W.2d 806 (Mo. App. 1992) (judge did not act improperly in requesting suggested findings of fact and conclusions of law or requesting that party prepare order opposing other party's motion where there was no indication that judge and counsel discussed merits of motion). Nor may the communication suggest the form and content of the proposed order. See *Williams v. Farmers Ins. Group, Inc.*, 720 P.2d 598 (Colo. App. 1985) (ex parte communication was not limited to request to prepare order but also dealt with form and content of proposed order).

A judge's improper ex parte communication with a party regarding findings of fact and conclusions of law may be deemed harmless if there is no evidence that a party's right to a neutral, unbiased judge was compromised. *See, e.g., Ex parte Masonite Corp.*, 681 So. 2d 1068 (Ala. 1996) (judge's ex parte communication with party's counsel to facilitate drafting order was not impermissible where judge reached a firm decision before telephoning lawyer and gave opposing party full opportunity to argue its assertion of prejudice); *Aztec Minerals Corp. v. State*, 987 P.2d 895 (Colo. Ct. App. 1999) (judge's limited ex parte communication with defendants' counsel requesting a draft of order awarding attorney fees to defendants did not require that the order be vacated, as plaintiffs had not objected to the substance of the order and had not proposed modifications, and plaintiffs did not show trial judge's bias or prejudice to the plaintiffs' interests); *Randolph v. State*, 853 So. 2d 1051 (Fla. 2003) (judge's law clerk engaged in improper ex parte communication by preparing judgment in defendant's death penalty case, with the assistance of the state attorney, however, defendant's right to a neutral judge was not prejudiced because the judge independently weighed the aggravating and mitigating circumstances in the case); *Fuller v. Fuller*, 621 S.E.2d 419 (Ga. 2005) (judge's ex parte communication with counsel for husband in divorce action, for purpose of revising husband's drafts of proposed orders, did not implicate wife's right to due process, where judge played active and independent role by considering proposals of both parties, deciding to use primarily orders prepared on husband's behalf, and directing inclusion of provisions requested by wife, and wife had full opportunity to present her arguments in trial court and on appellate review); *but see State v. Reichmann*, 777 So. 2d 342 (Fla. 2000) (sentencing order prosecutor prepared in response to ex parte request by trial judge deprived defendant of an independent weighing of aggravating and mitigating circumstances).

REMEDYING AN EX PARTE COMMUNICATION

Inadvertently Receiving Unauthorized Ex Parte Communications

Rule 2.9(B), which was added to the Code in 2007, provides that if a judge inadvertently receives an unauthorized ex parte communication bearing upon the substance of a matter, the judge must promptly notify the parties of the substance of the communication and provide them an opportunity to respond. (See earlier discussion regarding Rule 2.9(A) and prompt disclosure of ex parte communication.) Even prior to the addition to the Code, some jurisdictions advised that an undisclosed inadvertent ex parte communication creates an appearance of bias in violation of the Code. *See, e.g.*, Alaska Comm'n on Jud. Cond. Formal Ethics Op. 016 (1993) (judge who had inadvertent informal contact with witness in former related proceeding and did not disclose contact to the parties at a hearing that immediately followed that contact, created an appearance of bias on the part of the court; at minimum, the judge would have stated that nature of the judge's communication with the witness on the record before making other comments. The fact that the judge did not hold the hearing as scheduled, but instead used the opportunity to make brief statements to one party concerning prior orders, contributed to the appearance of bias). Additionally, some jurisdictions advise judges to take precautions to avoid inadvertent ex parte communications. *See, e.g., Jocius v. Jocius*, 580 N.W.2d 708 (Wis. App. 1998) (recognizing that well-intentioned parties and friends might often attempt to communicate with judges in divorce cases in the hope of influencing the judge's decision, court advises judges to institute procedures so that these communiqués do not inadvertently violate the ex parte communication directive); *cf.* L.A. County Bar Assn. Formal Op. 514 (2005) (advising judges on steps to take to avoid inadvertent ex parte communications that can occur through list serve communications).

Recusal and Reversal

Ex parte communications can "cause legal as well as ethical problems." Va. Jud. Ethics Adv. Comm. Op. 00-4 (2000). In some instances, prompt disclosure is not sufficient and a judge may be required to recuse himself or herself from further participation in a proceeding where the ex parte communication creates an appearance of impartiality. *See, e.g., Disc. Counsel v. Karto*, 760 N.E.2d 412 (Ohio 2002) (judge should have immediately recused himself from juvenile delinquency proceedings after ex parte communication with prosecutor; instructing prosecutor to bring felony charges against juvenile indicated bias); *In re Elizabeth S.*, 698 N.W.2d 252 (Neb. App. 2005) (judge's solicitation and consideration of ex parte communication with child psychiatrist or child psychologist on subject of visitation amounted to plain error requiring recusal); Va. Jud. Ethics Adv. Comm. Op. 00-4 (2000) (if a judge becomes biased or prejudiced, recusal is mandated).

When an ex parte communication is discovered post-verdict, a party may seek reversal of the judgment on appeal because of the ex parte communication. Courts take different positions on whether a case should be reversed on appeal because the judge participated in an ex parte communication. For instance, the Wyoming Supreme Court has held that to justify the reversal of a judgment, there must not simply be the occurrence of an ex parte communication, there must also be a "manifest injustice." *Moore v. Moore*, 809 P.2d 261 (Wyo. 1991). The Hawaii Supreme Court has similarly held that an ex parte communication is not grounds for reversal if the excluded party's right to a fair trial was not unfairly prejudiced. *State v. Birano*, 126 P.3d 357 (Haw. 2006) (trial judge's participation in ex parte communication with prosecutor, prosecution witness, and witness' attorney, without the presence of defendant's attorney, in violation of judicial conduct Canons, did not unfairly prejudice defendant's right to a fair trial, based on judge's alleged impartiality, where nothing in the record indicated that judge made improper remarks or engaged in other improprieties during trial). *But cf. State v. Barker*, 420 N.W.2d 695 (Neb. 1988) (court held that if an ex parte communication is invited or initiated by the judge, no prejudice needs to be shown).

In a case where an ex parte communication was not invited or initiated by the judge, the South Dakota Supreme Court has held that reversible error occurs only if the adverse party is prejudiced by an inability to rebut the facts communicated and if improper influence appears with reasonable certainty. *O'Connor v. Leapley*, 488 N.W.2d 421 (S.D. 1992). *But see In re Marriage of Wheatley*, 697 N.E.2d 938 (Ill. Ct. App. 1998) (judgment vacated in custody case; judge created appearance of impropriety by failing to disclose receipt of a letter from a former Congressman that sought to influence judge to award custody of child to wife).

INDEPENDENT INVESTIGATIONS PROHIBITED

Pursuant to Rule 2.9(C), a judge must not independently investigate facts in a case and must consider only the evidence presented. This prohibition now extends to information available in all mediums, including electronic. Model Code of Judicial Conduct Rule 2.9 cmt. [6]; *In re Cahill*, 13-32, 13-41, 13-42 (Minn. Bd. on Jud. Standards 2014) (judge reprimanded in part for accessing electronic criminal file of party's fiancé during child custody trial); *but see* N.M. Adv. Comm. on Code of Jud. Conduct Op. 14-01 (2014) (judge may take judicial notice at arraignment phase of information in judiciary's case management system about defendant). The addition of this language in the Code reflects the ease with which factual investigation can be accomplished via electronic databases and the Internet and the need for judges to be vigilant to ensure that they and their staff members do not inadvertently violate the Rule. Charles G. Geyh & W. William Hodes, *Reporters' Notes to the Model Code of Judicial Conduct* 41 (2009). *See, e.g.*, S.C. Advisory Op. 1-2005 (2005) (advising magistrates that they may not use NCIC, a computerized index of criminal justice information, during guilt phase of a case, but may use it to assist during bail proceedings, sentencing phases and similar situations). For a discussion of judges' use of the Internet to investigate elements of a case, *see generally* David H. Tennant and Laurie M. Seal, *Judicial Ethics and the Internet: May Judges Search the Internet in Evaluating and Deciding a Case?*, 16 No. 2 Prof. Law 2 (2005).

Rule 2.9(C) does not prohibit a judge from conducting general research about topics that may arise in a matter before the judge. Cal. Judges Ass'n Jud. Ethics Comm. Adv. Op. 68 (2013) (judge may research basic principles of medicine or other disciplines prior to being assigned a matter, judge may not investigate relevant facts that are germane to the case). For a discussion of the difference between improper factual research and judicial notice, *see generally* Alaska Comm'n on Jud. Cond. Adv. Op. 2014-01 and N.M. Adv. Comm. on Code of Jud. Conduct Op. 14-01 (2014)

Independent investigations by a judge create an appearance of partiality and may provide a judge with personal knowledge of disputed facts, which is a specific ground for judicial disqualification. Leslie W. Abramson, *The Judicial Ethics of Ex Parte Communications*, 37 Hous. L. Rev. 1343 (2000). For instance, a judge in a criminal case may be disqualified from a proceeding for investigating the defendant's prior record. *See State v. Emanuel*, 768 P.2d 196 (Ariz. Ct. App. 1989) (judge who personally investigates defendant's background, ex parte, prior to sentencing, must recuse himself from sentencing); *State v. Cash*, 867 S.W.2d 741 (Tenn. Crim. App. 1993) (upon remand, judge independently investigated and conversed ex parte with assistant district attorney).

While the Code of Conduct for United States Judges does not include an equivalent to Model Rule 2.9(C), Federal Rule of Evidence 201(b) notes that a "court may judicially notice a fact that is not subject to reasonable dispute because it is generally known within the trial court's territorial jurisdiction; or can be accurately and readily determined from sources whose accuracy cannot reasonably be questioned." The question of what is generally known and what can be readily determined from accurate sources has been addressed by a number of federal courts. In *Rowe v. Gibson*, 798 F.3d 622 (7th Cir. 2015), the Seventh Circuit explained that, "We must acknowledge the need to distinguish between judicial web searches for mere background information that will help the judges and the readers of their opinions understand the case, web searches for facts or other information that judges can properly take judicial notice of . . . and web searches for facts normally determined by the factfinder after an adversary procedure that produces a district court or administrative record." In *Rowe*, an Indiana prisoner appealed the district court's granting of summary judgment on the question of whether prison administrators and medical services company working for the state were deliberately indifferent to his serious medical condiction when they did not provide the inmate with heartburn medication before he ate meals and not at all for 33 days in violation of 42 U.S.C. Section 1983. Relying on website research conducted independent of the parties to the matter, the Seventh Circuit Court of Appeals explained, "When medical information can be gleaned from the websites of highly reputable medical centers, it is not imperative that it instead be presented by a testifying witness. Such information tends to fall somewhere between facts that require adversary procedure to determine and facts of which a court can take judicial notice, but it is closer to the second in a case like this in which the evidence presented by the defendants in the district court was sparse and the appellate court need only determine whether there is a factual dispute sufficient to preclude summary judgment." *Rowe*, 798 F.3d at 628–629. *See also Gent v. CUNA Mutual Insurance Society*, 611 F.3d 79, 84 n.5 (1st Cir. 2010) (court takes judicial notice of definition of Lyme Disease provided by Centers for Disease Control and Prevention on its website); *Matthews v. NFL Management Council*, 688 F.3d 1107, 1113 (9th Cir. 2012) (NFL player filing workers' compensation claim in California court did not allege facts necessary to show California law applied; court took judicial notice that Matthews' teams played 13 games in California during Matthews' 19-year career, citing Matthew's team website); *United States v. Bari*, 599 F.3d 176, 17881 (2d Cir. 2010) (District Court's Internet search regarding variety of yellow rain hats available not reversible error because Court can take judicial notice of this fact during supervised release revocation hearing alleging appellant robbed a bank while wearing a yellow rain hat).

Similarly, a judge may not investigate records from an earlier proceeding involving the parties before the judge. *See, e.g., In re J.A.*, 601 A.2d 69 (D.C. 1991) (in child neglect proceeding, judge obtained and read court file of child's parents' divorce proceedings; because mother raised the issue for the first time on appeal, the court used the plain error standard and found no plain error). A judge also may not independently investigate the veracity of a witness's testimony. *State v. Dorsey*, 701 N.W.2d 238 (Minn. 2005) (trial judge's act of independently investigating correctness of witness's testimony concerning date of alleged firearm owner's death deprived defendant of his right to a fair trial and an impartial finder of fact, and thus, defendant was entitled to new trial). Nor may a judge visit a site that is the subject of litigation or obtain information from someone else who visited the site. *See Kennedy v. Great A. & P. Tea Co., Inc.*, 551 F.2d 593 (5th Cir. 1977) (judge reversed where in slip and fall case judge's law clerk visited defendant's store after a rainstorm to determine if it was wet in the area where plaintiff claimed that he fell and gave that information to judge); *but see Creative Soft Solutions, LLC v. Soaring Eagle Consulting, Ltd.*, 190 Fed. Appx. 348 (5th Cir. 2006) (district court's viewing of website of consultant's principal was harmless error in breach of contract action brought by consultant against staffing company; website was noted in passing in opinion footnote and was unrelated to core of district court's reasoning, and outcome of proceedings was not affected) (unpublished opinion); *Abington Ltd. P'ship v. Heublein*, 717 A.2d 1232 (Conn. 1998) (trial judge's visit to property that was the subject of a quiet title action was not an improper independent investigation warranting his disqualification from the case, absent evidence that judge drew on his independent knowledge in deciding the case). For an article arguing in favor of permitting judges to engage in independent library research when facing unfamiliar and complex admissibility issues, see Edward K. Cheng, *Independent Judicial Research in the Daubert Age*, 56 Duke L.J. 1263 (2007).

A judge also may not contact third parties to verify or obtain information. *See, e.g., Edgar v. K.L.*, 93 F.3d 256 (7th Cir. 1996) (judge's ex parte meeting with panel of experts appointed by judge to investigate Illinois mental health institutions and programs to receive preview of panel's conclusions and to persuade judge that their methodology was sound was grounds for disqualification of judge; allowing off the record briefing on issues and prohibiting opposing counsel from discovering what was said in meetings resulted in unauthorized private investigation by judge and examples of judge's comments to counsel raised concerns about judge's impartiality); *In re Anderson*, 814 P.2d 773 (Ariz. 1991) (judge called arresting officers and others to help in reaching a decision about matters before the court); *Wilson v. Armstrong*, 686 So. 2d 647 (Fla. Dist. Ct. App. 1996) (trial judge, in evaluating estate beneficiary's objections to accountings filed by estate trustees, engaged in prohibited ex parte communication when he visited estate's accountant, without beneficiary, to discuss substantive objections to accountings); *In re Guardianship of Garrard*, 624 N.E.2d 68 (Ind. App. 1993) (judge's initiation of ex parte communication with expert who had prepared report in connection with guardianship proceeding was improper and merited new trial); *State v. Romano*, 662 P.2d 406 (Wash. Ct. App. 1983) (judge's ex parte communication with two of his friends in the jewelry business to verify defendant's statements regarding seasonality of his income, for purpose of adjusting restitution plan, violated due process by creating an appearance of unfairness); *but see Cobell v. Norton*, 237 F. Supp. 2d 71 (D.D.C. 2003) (disqualification of judge not warranted where consultations between judge and special masters were appropriate exercises of judicial oversight function, and judge possessed no personal knowledge of disputed evidentiary facts concerning the proceedings, inasmuch as masters did not communicate to judge information regarding contested issues that might have been obtained during ex parte interviews).

A judge may not direct an employee of the court to conduct an independent investigation. *See, e.g., In re Crow*, 12-160 (Arkansas Judicial Disc. & Disability Comm'n 2013) (judge reprimanded for directing court assistant to investigate facts underlying defendant's prior DUI convictions); *Davis v. U.S.*, 567 A.2d 36 (D.C. 1989) (auto theft case reversed and remanded where law clerk discovered that defendant had a driver's license under an alias after the judge asked the clerk to investigate defendant's background); *In re Foret*, 144 So. 3d 1028 (La. 2014) (judge suspended for 60 days without pay, in part, for allowing court employee to improperly investigate matter by obtaining police report); *Sherman v. State*, 905 P.2d 355 (Wash. 1995) (judge violated Canon when he directed legal extern to contact physicians charged with monitoring physician's chemical dependency for information about monitoring process). Nor may a judge rely on information obtained through a court employee's independent investigation. *See, e.g., Horton v. Ferrell*, 981 S.W.2d 88 (Ark. 1998) (trial court's acceptance of special master's report, which relied upon master's independent investigation and ex parte communications with third parties constituted error in action for an accounting following dissolution of partnership).

Ex Parte Communications by Court Staff

Rule 2.9(D) requires a judge to make "reasonable efforts," including providing appropriate supervision, to ensure that court staff, officials, and others subject to the judge's control do not violate Rule 2.9. *See e.g., Reichmann v. State*, 966 So. 2d 298 (Fla. 2007) ("[T]rial judges should be careful to avoid ex parte contacts of any kind, even through the use of judicial assistants, that could be perceived to have been made without the knowledge of all parties."); Mich. Comm. on Jud. Ethics Op. JI-134 (2006) (in seeking not to permit ex parte communications through court personnel, a judge should instruct his or her staff regarding the requirements of the Canon prohibiting ex parte communications and the need to avoid improper *ex parte* communications). Staff members' ex parte communications with litigants or lawyers involved in a proceeding may be imputed to the judge. *See, e.g., In re Kern*, 774 N.E.2d 878 (Ind. 2002) (judge engaged in improper ex parte communication where court staff helped a litigant draft an ex parte custody order and judge signed order without informing other parent's lawyer). However, even if an ex parte communication between court staff and a lawyer is improper, it may be deemed harmless if it is determined that a party's right to a neutral judge was not prejudiced. *See, e.g., Randolph v. State*, 853 So. 2d 1051 (Fla. 2003) (holding that even though conversation between judge's law clerk and prosecutor concerning wording of sentence amounted to improper ex parte communication, defendant's right to a neutral judge was not prejudiced, because contact was ministerial in nature and did not deal in any way with judge's independent weighing of aggravating and mitigating circumstances and his determination to impose sentence of death.").

RULE 2.10 JUDICIAL STATEMENTS ON PENDING AND IMPENDING CASES

(A) A judge shall not make any public statement that might reasonably be expected to affect the outcome or impair the fairness of a matter pending* or impending* in any court, or make any nonpublic statement that might substantially interfere with a fair trial or hearing.

(B) A judge shall not, in connection with cases, controversies, or issues that are likely to come before the court, make pledges, promises, or commitments that are inconsistent with the impartial* performance of the adjudicative duties of judicial office.

(C) A judge shall require court staff, court officials, and others subject to the judge's direction and control to refrain from making statements that the judge would be prohibited from making by paragraphs (A) and (B).

(D) Notwithstanding the restrictions in paragraph (A), a judge may make public statements in the course of official duties, may explain court procedures, and may comment on any proceeding in which the judge is a litigant in a personal capacity.

(E) Subject to the requirements of paragraph (A), a judge may respond directly or through a third party to allegations in the media or elsewhere concerning the judge's conduct in a matter.

COMMENT

[1] This Rule's restrictions on judicial speech are essential to the maintenance of the independence, integrity, and impartiality of the judiciary.

[2] This Rule does not prohibit a judge from commenting on proceedings in which the judge is a litigant in a personal capacity, or represents a client as permitted by these Rules. In cases in which the judge is a litigant in an official capacity, such as a writ of mandamus, the judge must not comment publicly.

[3] Depending upon the circumstances, the judge should consider whether it may be preferable for a third party, rather than the judge, to respond or issue statements in connection with allegations concerning the judge's conduct in a matter.

1990 CODE COMPARISON

Paragraphs (A) and (C) of Rule 2.10 derive from former Canon 3B(9). Paragraph (A) is the first sentence of Canon 3B(9), which was reworded to improve clarity. Paragraph (C) is the second sentence of Canon 3B(9). The term "court personnel" was broadened to "court staff, court officials, and others" subject to the judge's direction and control. Paragraph (D) is also from former Canon 3B(9), while paragraph (B) is former Canon 3B(10).

Paragraph (E) is new to the Code. Judges are justifiably reluctant to speak about pending cases. However, the Commission wanted to make clear that when a judge's conduct is called into question by the media or elsewhere, the judge may respond as long as the response will not affect the fairness of the proceeding, as well as not involving an improper pledge or promise. Charles G. Geyh & W. William Hodes, *Reporters' Notes to the Model Code of Judicial Conduct* 42 (2009).

ANNOTATION

INTRODUCTION

Rule 2.10 governs what judges may and may not say to the public about cases that either are or could come before them or before other judges. Specifically, paragraph (A) prohibits judges, while a proceeding is pending or impending in any court, from making any public statement that might reasonably be expected to affect its outcome or impair its fairness. Additionally, a judge may not make any nonpublic comment that might substantially interfere with a fair trial or hearing. There are exceptions, however, to Rule 2.10(A)'s restrictions. Paragraph (D) states that notwithstanding the restrictions in paragraph (A), a judge may make public statements in the course of official duties, may explain court procedures, and may comment on any proceeding in which the judge is a litigant in a personal capacity. However, as one court noted, these exceptions are very narrow. *In re Hey*, 425 S.E.2d 221 (W. Va. 1992) (Neely, J., concurring) (these exceptions "create a narrow path that is similar to the Straits of Messina. If a judge's comments stray to a specific case, the snarling dogs of Scylla await; if a judge fails to maintain a public image, the whirlpool of Charybdis awaits"). A second exception, in paragraph (E), permits a judge, subject to the requirements of paragraph (A), to respond directly or through a third party to allegations in the media or elsewhere concerning the judge's conduct in a matter.

Paragraph (B) of the Rule prohibits a judge from making "pledges, promises, or commitments" in connection with cases, controversies, or issues that are likely to come before the court that are inconsistent with impartial performance of the judge's adjudicative duties. Paragraph (C) provides that judges must require court staff, court officials, and others subject to the judge's direction and control to refrain from making statements that the judge may not make under paragraphs (A) and (B).

COMMENTING ON PENDING OR IMPENDING CASES

The issues that arise under Rule 2.10(A) involve, first, the question of whether a proceeding is pending or impending such that judicial comments are prohibited and second, whether a judge's comments cross the dividing line between permissible explanations of court procedures or "statements in the course of official duties" and improper comments on a "matter . . . in any court." *See, e.g., In re Allred* (Ala. Ct. of the Judiciary 2013) (judge who posted to Facebook and emailed all state court judges comments about pending contempt proceedings against lawyer violated prohibition on public comment on pending matters); *In re Bearse*, 15-17 (Minn. Bd. on Jud. Standards 2015) (judge reprimanded for comments posted to Facebook about pending matters). The restrictions on judicial comments on pending and impending cases are intended to protect the public's confidence in the integrity and impartiality of the judiciary. *In re Benoit*, 523 A.2d 1381 (Me. 1987) ("This Canon prevents a judge from publicly prejudging or creating the appearance that he is prejudging any aspect of an issue that has not been finally decided. It thereby minimizes the risk that such comments will either unfairly prejudge individuals' rights or create a public impression that citizens are not being treated fairly because different judges may not agree as to how those citizens' rights should be decided under the law.").

A judge who violates Rule 2.10(A) by publicly commenting about a pending case may not be required to recuse himself or herself from that case. *See, e.g., Cmmw. v. Druce*, 848 A.2d 104 (Pa. 2004) (judge's violation of Canon directing that judge should abstain from making public comment about pending court proceeding does not per se require judge's recusal; such per se rule would remove any introspective discretion from jurist, defeat spirit of judicial processes, and undermine legitimacy of judges).

Pending Cases

Rule 2.10(A) prohibits judges from commenting on cases that are impending or pending. According to the Code Terminology section, a pending matter is a "matter that has commenced." The requirement that judges abstain from public comment regarding a pending proceeding continues through any appellate process and until final disposition. Ronald D. Rotunda and John S. Dzienkowski, *Legal Ethics: The Lawyer's Deskbook on Professional Responsibility*, 1507–08 (2016). *See, e.g., In re Roe*, 931 So. 2d 1076 (La. 2006) (judge censured for participating in a newspaper interview regarding a case that was pending on appeal); Kan. Jud. Ethics Op. JE 163 (2008) (judge may not submit letter to editor of a newspaper in response to editorial regarding individual who either faces criminal charges or has been convicted in five counties and faces additional charges and civil suits).

Comments are not permitted while a case is on appeal because they could create the appearance that the judge is trying to influence the appellate court (*Broadman v. Comm'n on Jud. Performance*, 959 P.2d 715 (Cal. 1998)) and because there is a chance that the case could be remanded back to that judge (*see In re Ballew*, M2013-02345-BJC-DIS-FC (Tenn. Bd. of Jud. Conduct 2014) (magistrate judge who changed baby's name from Messiah to Martin and explained her decision in television interview while matter pending before chancery judge charged with reviewing magistrate's decision violated Rule 2.10); *In re Benoit*, 523 A.2d 1381 (Me. 1987) ("egregious" violation of the Canon occurred when a judge, before conducting proceedings in a remanded case, commented on the opinion that had vacated his ruling and had sent the case back to him); Ariz. Sup. Ct. Jud. Ethics Adv. Comm. Op. 95-4 (1995) (justice of the peace may only write about cases if they are completely resolved, including appeals); N.J. Sup. Ct. Advisory Comm. on Extrajudicial Activities, No. 3-88, 1988 WL 356383 (1988) (participation by judge in bar association panel on case pending on appeal inapprorpriate)).

Similarly, a judge may not comment on a case if one of the parties in the proceeding has sought review in a higher court of an order issued by the judge. *See, e.g., Ryan v. Comm'n on Jud. Performance*, 754 P.2d 724 (Cal. 1988) (judge commented on case while the validity of his contempt order was pending before superior court); *In re Hey*, 425 S.E.2d 221 (W. Va. 1992) (judge made comments on television program pertaining to case over which he presided and which was before appellate court, pursuant to petition to prohibit enforcement of judge's order). Even if a judge is no longer presiding in a case or the case is not appealed, a judge must refrain from commenting on any outstanding issues in the case. *See, e.g., In re Young*, 984 P.2d 997 (Utah 1999) (judge improperly commented on attorney's fees issue in case; even though judge had completed rotation in county and was no longer assigned to case, he had presided over all prior proceedings and case could be and was later reassigned to judge); Fla. Jud. Ethics Adv. Comm. Op. 00-30 (2000) (judge may not respond to newspaper reporter's questions regarding emergency shelter hearing over which judge presided; though no appeal was filed, parents were seeking recovery of attorney's fees).

Once a case has reached its "final disposition" and is no longer pending, a judge may comment on the case without violating Rule 2.10(A). *See, e.g., Wenger v. Comm'n on Jud. Performance*, 630 P.2d 954 (Cal. 1981) (judge's statement to the press regarding superior court judge's ruling in a habeas proceeding did not violate Canon because litigation had "concluded"); *Goldman* v. *Nev. Comm'n on Jud. Qualifications*, 830 P.2d 107 (Nev. 1992) (judge was permitted to make comments about the disciplinary case because they were made "*after* the commission conducted its probable cause hearing and *after* the commission entered its order of formal complaint"); *In re Codispoti*, 438 S.E.2d 549 (W. Va. 1993) (magistrate did not violate Canon by running newspaper advertisements criticizing his wife's opponent's conduct in handling a murder case since the prosecutor had dropped the charges against the defendant in that case almost two years earlier).

Cases Pending "In Any Court"

Rule 2.10(A) prohibits judges from making public statements that might reasonably be expected to affect the outcome or impair the fairness of a matter that is "pending . . . in any court." This includes cases before other judges in the jurisdiction where the judge sits (*Comm'n on Jud. Qualifications v. Rome*, 623 P.2d 1307 (Kan. 1981); *In re McCully*, 942 P.2d 327 (Utah 1997)) and, according to some courts and ethics opinions, it also applies to cases before judges in other jurisdictions (*see, e.g., In re Broadbelt*, 683 A.2d 543 (N.J. 1996) (New Jersey judge violated Canon by appearing as guest commentator on Court TV and CNBC to discuss O.J. Simpson trial); Ark. Jud. Ethics Adv. Comm. Op. 2000-02 (2000) (supreme court justice may not comment on pending federal court case even to correct mistakes reported in public media); N.Y. Adv. Comm. on Jud. Ethics, No. 93-133 (1994) (full-time judge may not act as commentator for out of state trial broadcast on television)). *See also* Ronald D. Rotunda and John S. Dzienkowski, *Legal Ethics: The Lawyer's Deskbook on Professional Responsibility* 1508–10 (2016).

Impending Cases

In addition to prohibiting comments on pending proceedings, Rule 2.10(A) prohibits commentary on impending proceedings. The Code Terminology section defines an impending matter as one that is "imminent or expected to occur in the near future." Therefore, a judge must refrain from commenting on a case that is about to be brought in his or her court or in another judge's court. Additionally, many of the controversial national issues can be considered "impending." One author has clarified this to say that "impending matters are those that if they continue on their regular course will end up in a court." However, impending does not include "every possible social or community issue that could come before the court." Marla N. Greenstein, *Commenting on Pending or Impending Matters*, 46 No. 2 Judges' J. 41 (2007).

A controversial local issue may also be considered "impending" because there is a reasonable likelihood that litigation concerning the issue could be filed. *See, e.g.*, Mich. Standing Comm. on Professional and Jud. Ethics, No. JI-52 (1992) (precluding judge from signing resolution asking local government officials to take action regarding a plant closing because the issue was extremely controversial, and lawsuits arising from the closing could be filed). *But see Jud. Inquiry Comm'n of W. Va. v. McGraw*, 299 S.E.2d 872 (W. Va. 1983) (approving a decision not to discipline a judge who made public statements about the judiciary's independent budget-making power because "a considerable body of law . . . holds that a judge will not be disqualified to sit on a case merely by expressing his opinion on a question of law involved in a case in his court or which may later come before him"). Finally, even a remote chance that an issue or a class of litigant may come before a judge in a future could make an issue "impending" and might restrict a judge's right to engage in activities that could be viewed as "symbolic speech." *See, e.g.*, Mich. Comm. on Jud. Ethics Op. JI-109 (1996) (advising that a judge may not participate in a protest against a militia group that advocates discrimination because some of the people targeted by the protest "presumably . . . may appear before the judge on unrelated matters").

Prohibited Comments

Merits of a Case

Rule 2.10(A) clearly prohibits judges from commenting on the merits of a case pending in their court or in another court. *See, e.g., U.S. v. Microsoft Corp.*, 253 F.3d 34 (D.C. Cir. 2001) (judge violated Code by disclosing to reporters his opinions about the credibility of witnesses, the validity of legal theories, the culpability of the defendant, and the choice of remedy); *In re Conard*, 944 S.W.2d 191 (Mo. 1997) (judge suspended because his comments went to the merits when he publicly disagreed with the arrest and detention of a defendant and said that no meritorious charges could be brought against that defendant); Ill. Jud. Ethics Comm. Op. 96-5 (1996) (judge violated Canon by commenting about his decision to require defendant in child support proceeding to increase defendant's reporting requirements). *See also* Ronald D. Rotunda, *Judicial Comments on Pending Cases: The Ethical Restrictions and the Sanctions: A Case Study of the Microsoft Litigation*, 2001 U. Ill. L. Rev. 611 (2001); William G. Ross, *Extrajudicial Speech: Charting the Boundaries of Propriety*, 2 Geo. J. Legal Ethics 589 (1989).

Judges are not only prohibited from commenting on the merits of cases pending before them, they are likewise prohibited from commenting on the merits of cases in other courts, as well as other judges' decisions or court practices. *Comm'n on Jud. Qualifications v. Rome*, 623 P.2d 1307 (Kan. 1981) (criticism of a fellow judge for accepting a plea to a reduced charge violated predecessor to Rule 2.10(A)); *In re Complaint Against White*, 651 N.W.2d 551 (Neb. 2002) (judge violated Canon by bringing a motion for appointment of a special prosecutor to appeal another judge's resentencing in a criminal case after the district court vacated the judge's sentence; motion involved public comments on merits of a matter pending before the county court); *In re Inquiry of Broadbelt*, 683 A.2d 543 (N.J. 1996) (commentary on O.J. Simpson case violated predecessor to Rule 2.10(A)); *Disc. Counsel v. Ferreri*, 710 N.E.2d 1107 (Ohio 1999) (judge violated the Canon when he called a decision that reversed and remanded one of the judge's custody decisions "purely political" and said that it was "written by a law clerk"); *Jud. Inquiry & Rev. Bd. of Sup. Ct. of Pa. v. Fink*, 532 A.2d 358 (Pa. 1987) (judge's intemperate criticism of the Pennsylvania Supreme Court violated predecessor to Rule 2.10(A)). Under the predecessor to Rule 2.10(A), Canon 3B(9), judges were also prohibited from preparing an affidavit in support of a party in litigation that is intended to influence the judge before whom that litigation is pending. *In re McCully*, 942 P.2d 327 (Utah 1997) (juvenile court judge was publicly reprimanded for preparing an affidavit that contained not only facts regarding operation of juvenile courts but also the judge's opinion as to ultimate issue before court in which affidavit was submitted).

Decisions to Be Issued

A judge may violate Rule 2.10(A) by indicating what his or her decision will be prior to issuing a ruling in a case. *See, e.g., Ryan v. Comm'n on Jud. Performance*, 754 P.2d 724 (Cal. 1988) (judge violated predecessor of Rule 2.10(A) by providing a draft copy of an opinion to the press before providing it to the parties, and by publicly stating his intentions to vacate a contempt order before he actually did so); *In re Young*, 984 P.2d 997 (Utah 1999) (judge reprimanded for giving a party advance warning of his inclination on attorney's fee issue). Further, once a decision is issued, a judge may not try to explain or defend the decisions if the case is not final. *See, e.g., In re Boston Children's First*, 244 F.3d 164 (1st Cir. 2001) (judge defended her rulings in telephone interview with reporter); *Yoder v. Workman*, 224 F. Supp. 2d 1077 (S.D. W. Va. 2002) (judge may not publish press release on court's Internet website explaining why she was recusing herself from case); *Broadman v. Comm'n on Jud. Performance*, 959 P.2d 715 (Cal. 1998) (judge censured for making public comments to explain his decisions in cases that were pending in an appellate court); *In re Benoit*, 523 A.2d 1381 (Me. 1987) (judge disciplined for writing letters to newspapers defending his decision in criminal cases after appellate court vacated sentence judge imposed and remanded case to judge for resentencing); Ill. Jud. Ethics Comm. Op. 96-5 (1996) (judge may not comment on ruling in pending case to a report, except to explain administrative procedures of the court or restate matters in the written opinion or transcript); N.J. Sup. Ct. Adv. Comm. on Extrajudicial Activities, No. 3-88, 1988 WL 356383 (1988) ("The opinion should rest on its own footing without further elaboration."). *But see Metropolitan Opera Ass'n, Inc. v. Local 100*, 332 F. Supp. 2d 667 (S.D.N.Y. 2004) (recusal of judge was not required when, in CLE conference following judgment in favor of plaintiff on question of liability, entered as sanction for defense counsel's discovery abuses, judge allegedly previewed decision on motion for reconsideration by commenting on proliferation of counsel at meeting and reminding counsel that motion for reconsideration was not a "do over"); *Disc. Counsel v. Souers*, 611 N.E.2d 305 (Ohio 1993) (finding a judge's defense of a sentencing order was permissible as an explanation of court procedures).

Once a case is fully resolved and no longer pending, a judge is free to engage in any extrajudicial comments. *See, e.g., Goldman v. Nev. Comm'n on Jud. Disc.*, 830 P.2d 107 (1992); *In re Broadbelt*, 683 A.2d 543 (N.J. 1996) (court affirms opinion prohibiting judge from serving as television commentator during trial, but allows comment once case is no longer pending); Ariz. Sup. Ct. Jud. Ethics Adv. Comm. Op. 95-4 (1995) (newspaper column explaining judge's reasoning "could be interesting, educational, and informative," as long as judge does not violate another provision of the Code or include identifying information other than "situational" facts). *See also* Stephen J. Fortunato, Jr., *On a Judge's Duty to Speak Extrajudicially: Rethinking the Strategy of Silence*, 12 Geo. J. Legal Ethics 679 (Summer 1999) (suggesting that judges have an obligation to respond to baseless attacks on their integrity, such as an editorial asserting that a judge made a decision based on a party's race, ethnic background, or status).

Criticism of Party or Lawyer in a Case

A judge may violate Rule 2.10(A) by criticizing the parties in a pending or impending case. *See, e.g., Papa v. New Haven Fed'n of Teachers*, 444 A.2d 196 (Conn. 1982) (judge violated predecessor to Rule 2.10(A) by criticizing teachers who went on strike while a case to enjoin a teachers' strike was pending before him); *In re Hayes*, 541 So. 2d 105 (Fla. 1989) (judge disciplined for discussing with a journalist, the judge's opinions about the behavior of parties and attorneys, witnesses, and the jury); *In re Roe*, 931 So. 2d 1076 (La. 2006) (judge censured for participating in a newspaper interview regarding a case that was pending on appeal and publicly criticizing attorney); *Disc. Counsel v. Gaul*, 936 N.E.2d 28 (Ohio 2010) (judge disciplined for accusing the defendant of unproven misconduct and telling defendant that judge would ensure defendant's indictment, conviction, and sentencing for obstruction of justice); *Disc. Counsel v. Ferreri*, 710 N.E.2d 1107 (Ohio 1999) (ruling that a judge violated predecessor to Rule 2.10(A) by making an erroneous accusation to a TV reporter that a party had filed for bankruptcy and "stuck people—thousand dollars [sic] for court reporters fees"); *In re Hey*, 425 S.E.2d 221 (W. Va. 1992) (judge made negative comments on television program about parties involved in a custody dispute case that was pending in appellate court on petition to prohibit judge from enforcing his order in the case); *cf. Shapley v. Tex. Dept of Human Resources*, 581 S.W.2d 250 (Tex. Civ. App. 1979) (finding fault with a judge's discussing facts of a pending case with a reporter, but declining to reverse on this ground).

Nor may a judge criticize lawyers practicing in the judge's court. *See Comm'n on Jud. Qualifications v. Rome*, 623 P.2d 1307 (Kan. 1981) (judge violated predecessor to Rule 2.10(A) by criticizing county attorney's office); *In re Schenck*, 870 P.2d 185 (Or. 1994) (judge violated predecessor to Rule 2.10(A) by writing letter to editor of newspaper criticizing district attorney); *cf. In re Hocking*, 546 N.W.2d 234 (Mich. 1996) (request for investigation by Attorney Grievance Commission is a proper response to arguably defamatory statements made by attorneys about judges; direct response by the judge in the media is problematic because "[r]egardless of the merits of the dispute, a media war of words may erode public confidence in the judiciary").

Intent Not Required

In determining whether a judge's comments fall within the prohibitions of Rule 2.10(A), intent is likely irrelevant. Even if the judge does not intend for certain comments to influence the outcome or fairness of a case, the comments may still violate the rule. *See, e.g., U.S. v. Microsoft*, 253 F.3d 34 (D.C. Cir. 2001) (where judge disclosed his views on factual and legal matters at the heart of the case, "it is no excuse that the Judge may have intended to 'educate' the public about the case or to rebut 'public misperceptions' purportedly caused by the parties"); *U.S. v. Garwood*, 16 M.J. 863 (N.M.C.M.R. 1983) (ruling that judge's comment was inappropriate even though motivated by a desire to inform, but finding no reversible error was caused by the comment); *In re Schenck*, 870 P.2d 185 (Or. 1994). Moreover, even if the judge's comments include some permissible statements about court procedure, if some of the statements are impermissible, the permitted statements will not insulate the prohibited ones. *Id.*

Forum Not Relevant

If judges limit their public comments to general issues about courts and court procedures, they may appear on radio or television or in print. However, if a judge's comments fall within the prohibitions of Rule 2.10(A), virtually any public expression in any forum is subject to discipline. Judges have been disciplined for comments appearing in newspaper news stories (*see, e.g., In re Sheffield*, 465 So. 2d 350 (Ala. 1984) (judge suspended for two months for commenting to media about substance of pending case and failing to recuse when issue raised); *Ryan v. Comm'n on Jud. Performance*, 754 P.2d 724 (Cal. 1988) (among 18 different misconduct charges justifying removal, judge discussed pending cases, including decisions not yet issued, with media); *Disc. Counsel v. Ferreri*, 710 N.E.2d 1107 (Ohio 1999) (judge suspended for derogatory remarks to various media about court personnel)) and letters to the editor of local papers (*see, e.g., Ryan v. Comm'n on Jud. Performance*, 754 P.2d 724 (Cal. 1988) (judge improperly communicated with representatives of the media on four different occasions on pending matters); *In re Benoit*, 523 A.2d 1381 (Me. 1987) (judge's public comment on pending matter warranted discipline); *In re Conduct of*

Schenck, 870 P.2d 185 (Or. 1994) (judge's letters to the editor criticizing district attorney improper)). Judges have also been disciplined for comments made on national television news and talk shows (*see, e.g., U.S. v. Garwood*, 16 M.J. 863 (N.M.C.M.R. 1983) (trial judge erred in giving interviews about the case to CBS evening news, national TV correspondents, and Nightline); *In re Inquiry of Broadbelt*, 683 A.2d 543 (N.J. 1996) (judge appeared as a commentator on Court TV and CNBC both with and without approval of supervising judge); *In re Hey*, 425 S.E.2d 221 (W. Va. 1992) (judge discussed pending state supreme court case and criticized party in case where judge's conduct was also subject of case)) and local television news programs (*see, e.g., Comm'n on Jud. Qualifications v. Rome*, 623 P.2d 1307 (Kan. 1981) (judge intentionally sought to promote to the local news media his memorandum, which was critical of the county attorney and another judge regarding past and pending cases); *Disc. Counsel v. Ferreri*, 710 N.E.2d 1107 (Ohio 1999)). *See also* Gary A. Hengstler, *Pressing Engagements: Courting Better Relationships between Judges and Journalists*, 56 Syracuse L. Rev. 419 (2006). Judges have been disciplined for comments appearing in guest editorials, *In re Conduct of Schenck*, 870 P.2d 185 (Or. 1994); information provided to local radio stations, *Comm'n on Jud. Qualifications v. Rome*, 623 P.2d 1307 (Kan. 1981); and affidavits or motions filed in court, *In re Complaint Against White*, 651 N.W.2d 551 (Neb. 2002) (judge filed motion for special prosecutor and made public comments in support of his actions in case where his sentencing decision was reversed by other judge); *In re McCully*, 942 P.2d 327 (Utah 1997). Judges have also been disciplined for comments made on the Internet. *See, e.g., In re Maggio*, 440 S.W.3d 333 (Ark. 2014) (judge removed from office for comments posted on Internet forum about cases pending before judge). In addition, advisory ethics opinions have counseled judges against serving as an editor of a journal of public opinion (Mich. Comm. on Jud. Ethics Op. JI-99 (1995)) and participating in a bar association symposium about a case that was pending before the state supreme court (N.J. Adv. Comm. on Extrajudicial Activity, No. 3-88, 1988 WL 356383 (1988)). *See generally* Ronald D. Rotunda, *Judicial Comments on Pending Cases: The Ethical Restrictions and the Sanctions A Case Study of the Microsoft Litigation*, 2001 U. Ill. L. Rev. 611 (2001) (asserting that there should be an absolute prohibition on ex parte commentary about ongoing cases in print or electronic media).

Nonpublic Comments

In addition to restricting public comments, Rule 2.10(A) prohibits a judge from making nonpublic comments that might interfere with a fair trial or hearing. For instance, a judge was disciplined for commenting on an issue pending in a case during a telephone call with an attorney in a case (*In re Young*, 984 P.2d 997 (Utah 1999)) and for discussing the merits of a trial with other witnesses while subpoenaed as a potential witness in a case (*In re Horry County Mag. Johnson*, 579 S.E.2d 308 (S.C. 2003)). *See also Public Admonishment of Revak* (Cal. Comm'n on Jud. Performance 2000) (judge admonished for telling two friends who had a financial interest in a $100 million jury verdict that the verdict had been reversed on appeal; even if intended as a joke, judge's comments adversely impacted public confidence in integrity and impartiality of judiciary).

FIRST AMENDMENT CONSIDERATIONS

Legal Standard Applied

A number of judges have argued that disciplining them for making comments prohibited by Rule 2.10(A) violates their right to freedom of speech under the First Amendment. In order to resolve these challenges, courts have first had to choose from among several Supreme Court tests for evaluating the constitutionality of restrictions on speech. The test most commonly applied in cases involving Rule 2.10(A) is the one used in cases involving the discipline of public employees. The test is often called the "*Pickering-Connick* test," because it was first enunciated in *Pickering v. Bd. of Ed.*, 391 U.S. 563 (1968), and refined through a line of cases ending with *Connick v. Myers*, 461 U.S. 138 (1983). *Garcetti v. Celballos*, 547 U.S. 410 (2006) (applying *Pickering-Connick* test). *See generally* Leonard E. Gross, *Judicial Discipline and the First Amendment*, 36 Syracuse L. Rev. 1181 (1986). Under this test, a court must first ask whether the speech involves a matter of public concern. If it doesn't, there is no constitutional issue. *See, e.g., In re Davis*, 82 S.W.3d 140 (Tex. Spec. Ct. Rev. 2002) (judge's letter to newspaper reporter criticizing prosecutor and defending judge's actions did not address issue of legitimate public concern).

If, however, a judge's speech involves a matter of public concern, and it typically does in cases involving Rule 2.10, the court must determine whether the speech is constitutionally protected by balancing the interests of the state in ensuring public confidence in the judiciary against the judge's interest in the freedom to express his or her ideas without fear of reprisal. *See Broadman v. Comm'n on Jud. Qualifications*, 959 P.2d 715 (Cal. 1998) (applying test and ruling that judge's First Amendment rights were not violated, because "the burden that the . . . Canon imposes on the general interest of judges in making public comments is outweighed by the benefits it achieves in furthering the state's interest in the soundness of the judicial system"); *In re Schenck*, 870 P.2d 185 (Or. 1994) (applying test in holding that judge's First Amendment rights were not violated because the government's interest was "profound," the restriction was "directly related to the furtherance of that interest," and the "prohibition [was] closely drawn to achieve [the government's interest]"); *but see Scott v. Flowers*, 910 F.2d 201 (5th Cir. 1990) (applying test in ruling that the commission's public reprimand of a justice of the peace for writing open letter criticizing the administration of the county judicial system, under which the great majority of convicted traffic offenders who appealed to the county court at law had charges against them dismissed or their fines sharply reduced, violated the justice's First Amendment rights). *See generally* Annotation, *First Amendment Protection for Judges or Government Attorneys Subjected to Discharge, Transfer, or Discipline Because of Speech*, 108 A.L.R. Fed. 117 (1992).

A second test used in First Amendment cases generally is the strict scrutiny test, whereby the government can only restrict speech if it can show that the restriction meets a compelling state interest, and the restriction is narrowly drawn to serve this interest. *See* Erwin Chemerinsky, *Is It the Siren's Call?: Judges and Free Speech While Cases Are Pending*, 28 Loy. L.A. L. Rev. 831 (1995). This test has never been applied in its pure form to cases charging violations of the language of Rule 2.10, but it has been applied in tandem with the *Pickering-Connick* test. This hybrid test uses a two-prong inquiry: whether the state could accomplish its legitimate interest in restraining judge's speech through narrowly tailored limitations and whether the regulation exceeded that which is necessary to accomplish the state's interest. *See, e.g., In re Hey*, 452 S.E.2d 24 (W. Va. 1994) (applying hybrid test in determining that a judge's statements about his own disciplinary proceeding were entitled to First Amendment protection).

New Jersey has adopted a third approach so that it could analyze both lawyers' and judges' comments about pending cases under the same legal standard. Called the "*Gentile-Hinds* test" after the New Jersey and U.S. Supreme Court cases upholding its constitutionality, it is a "middle-tier scrutiny test." The *Gentile-Hinds* test permits a state to regulate an attorney's, and now under New Jersey law, a judge's speech, if the regulation furthers a substantial government interest unrelated to the suppression of expression, and is no more restrictive than necessary. *See In re Inquiry of Broadbelt*, 683 A.2d 543 (N.J. 1996) (finding that the predecessor to Rule 2.10 serves substantial government interests of preserving the independence and integrity of the judiciary and maintaining public confidence in the judiciary and does not place greater than necessary restrictions on a judge's speech).

Balancing of Interests

All of these constitutional tests require balancing the competing interests of the judge and the state in order to determine whether disciplining a judge for violating Rule 2.10 abridges that judge's First Amendment rights. Judges' interests worthy of protection are twofold. One interest is the protection of judicial independence. Judges must be allowed to decide cases freely and impartially without fear of reprisal for politically unpopular statements or decisions. As one commentator has observed, "If judges feared that they could be disciplined for reasons unrelated to the efficiency of the judicial system, but related instead to the content of their speech, their actions as well as their words might be affected. In short, they might fear discipline for making politically unpopular decisions, as well as for making politically unpopular statements." Leonard E. Gross, *Judicial Discipline and the First Amendment*, 36 Syracuse L. Rev. 1181, 1187 (1986). The right to judicial independence comes into play, in particular, when the public is aware of a disciplinary proceeding, either because of news leaks or because the proceeding has reached a public stage. The judge's defense of his professional reputation both in the disciplinary proceeding and to the public at large is entitled to considerable protection. *In re Hey*, 452 S.E.2d 24 (W. Va. 1994) (saying that it would be unconstitutional to charge a judge with misconduct for his comment about the fairness of a prior discipline proceeding against him and his intent to do something about it).

The second interest entitled to protection is a judge's right, as a citizen, to comment on matters of public concern, including the right to engage in a robust public debate. Judges often have access to information that is relevant to public decision-making, such as, for example, knowledge of "the administration of justice as it passes through" their courts. Members of the public, of course, need information about the functioning of government so that they can exercise the franchise responsibly. Thus, judges have a right to inform the public about matters of judicial administration so that the public can decide whether to vote for or against those responsible for certain decisions regarding the administration of the courts. *See Scott v. Flowers*, 910 F.2d 201 (5th Cir. 1990) (ruling that a judge's First Amendment rights were violated when he was reprimanded for publicly commenting on a local practice that gave more rights to those "in the know" than to less sophisticated individuals).

The state, however, has a countervailing interest in ensuring not only that judges are impartial in their decision-making, but also that the public believes them to be impartial. Judges who comment on pending or impending matters create two risks. One risk is that if the matter commented upon is pending in their own courts, the public will see the comment as an indication that the judge has either pre-judged the matter or that the judge has such a strong bias that he cannot render or provide an arena where the jury can render an impartial decision based solely on the evidence. The other risk is that if the matter commented on is pending before another judge, the public will see the comment either as an improper attempt to influence a fellow jurist to rule in the manner advocated by the judge, or as an inappropriate defense of a decision previously rendered. *Broadman v. Comm'n on Jud. Performance*, 959 P.2d 715 (Cal. 1998) (upholding the constitutionality of a public censure when a judge, among other things, gave interviews to the press about two pending cases).

PLEDGES, PROMISES, OR COMMITMENTS ABOUT CASES, CONTROVERSIES, OR ISSUES LIKELY TO COME BEFORE COURT

Rule 2.10(B) prohibits a judge from making pledges, promises, or commitments in connection with cases, controversies, or issues that are likely to come before the court that are inconsistent with the impartial performance of judicial duties. *See, e.g., In re Seitz*, CJC No. 7365-F-159 (Wash. Comm'n on Jud. Conduct 2014) (judge who encouraged and accepted guilty pleas in 12 criminal cases without a written plea and in exchange for a promised sentence violated Rule 2.10(B)); *but see In re Slaughter*, 15-001 (Tx. Special Ct. of Review 2015) (disciplinary commission failed to prove judge's statements posted to Facebook about pending cases would cause reasonable person to doubt judge's impartiality). The language of this Rule was first added to the Code in 2003 as Canon 3B(10). The language of Rule 2.10(B) mirrors the speech restriction for judicial candidates in Rule 4.1 but is applicable to all sitting judges during the administration of their regular and adjudicative responsibilities, therefore serving the prevailing goal of preserving judicial independence, integrity and impartiality. *American Bar Association Standing Committee on Judicial Independence and the Standing Committee on Ethics and Professional Responsibility Report 105B to the House of Delegates* (August 2003).

PERMITTED STATEMENTS

Statements Made in Course of Official Duties or to Explain Court Procedures

Rule 2.10(D) permits judges to make public comments "in the course of [their] official duties" or to explain "court procedures." In general, a judge's public statements shall be considered to be in an official capacity when they are part of an official duty, related to an official duty, or sought from or given by the judge because of his or her official position. *See In re Hey*, 425 S.E.2d 221 (W. Va. 1992). *Accord In re Complaint Against White*, 651 N.W.2d 551 (Neb. 2002); *In re Inquiry of Broadbelt*, 683 A.2d 543 (N.J. 1996). Permissible comments thus include written opinions issued by the court, statements made from the bench while the press is present in the courtroom (*Ryan v. Comm'n on Jud. Performance*, 754 P.2d 724 (Cal. 1988); Ill. Jud. Ethics Comm. Op. 96-5 (1996) (permitting judge to speak about the merits of a case if the comments are part of the public record)) as well as statements to the press (*Smith v. Mahoney*, 2007 WL 869624 (D. Mont. 2007) (judge's comments that appeared in newspaper article did not violate Canon because they pertained to procedural matters and did not touch on the merits of the case)) and restatements of what the judge previously said in open court (*U.S. v. Yonkers Bd. of Educ.*, 946 F.2d 180 (2d Cir. 1991)).

Rule 2.10(D) also does not restrict judges from explaining court procedures. *See In re Sheffield*, 465 So. 2d 350 (Ala. 1985) ("While judges may not comment on the merits of a pending case, a judge may and should explain legal terms, and concepts, procedures, and the issues involved in that case so as to permit the news representatives to cover the case more intelligently . . . . Often there is no one, other than the judge, who is in a position to give a detailed and impartial explanation of the case to the news media."), quoting National Conference of State Trial Judges, Judicial Guidelines for Dealing with News Media Inquiries and Criticism (5th Draft, June 5, 1984). *See generally* Cynthia Gray, *When Judges Speak Up: The Code of Judicial Conduct and Public Education*, 38 No. 4 Judges' J. 6 (Fall 1999). Generally, this exception permits judges to explain pending cases in "abstract" terms. *See In re Sheffield*, 465 So. 2d 350 (Ala. 1984) (disciplining a judge because an explanation of a contempt order was not a discussion in abstract terms but a direct comment on the merits of a pending case). *But see Disc. Counsel v. Souers*, 611 N.E.2d 305 (Ohio 1993) (determining that a judge's defense of a sentence he imposed was a permitted explanation of court procedures). It also permits judges to comment on or advocate general issues concerning the administration of the courts or the legal system itself. *See, e.g., Jud. Inquiry Comm'n of W. Va. v. McGraw*, 299 S.E.2d 872 (W. Va. 1983) (justice who had spoken publicly on the judiciary's independent budgetary authority was not required to disqualify himself from hearing a mandamus action seeking restoration of certain items that had been cut from the judicial budget); Ariz. Sup. Ct. Jud. Ethics Adv. Comm. Op. 89-2 (1989) (association of lower court judges could file an amicus brief on the issue of separation of powers). *Cf.* N.J. Sup. Ct. Adv. Comm. on Extrajudicial Activities, No. 3-88, 1988 WL 356383 (1988) (advising that judge could not participate in a state bar symposium regarding his decision in a case that was pending on appeal because to do so would be "tantamount to an amicus curiae brief in support of the judge's own opinion").

However, there is often a fine line between comments about court procedures, which are permitted under Rule 2.10(D), and comments about the merits of a case, which are not. *See In re Sheffield*, 465 So. 2d 350 (Ala. 1984) ("[O]n the one hand, a judge is strictly prohibited from public comment on the merits of a pending case . . . yet, on the other hand, a judge is encouraged to explain a pending case in abstract terms. Obviously, judges walk a fine line between the duties and prohibitions of [Rule 2.10(D)]."). *See also* Ill. Jud. Ethics Comm. Op. 96-5 (1996) (judge's comments to the media should be limited to administrative procedures and matters from transcript, written opinion, or court order); Mass. Comm. on Jud. Ethics Adv. Op. 2008-1 (2008) (judge may be interviewed by author for book about high profile criminal case and discuss administrative matters, such as "extra concerns" in managing high profile matter, including security and media concerns; however, judge may not discuss his "impressions" or thoughts about the case as the trial judge "in the context of those times," how he "approached" the case, or anything else that "stood out" for him about the case if it would reveal information about adjudicative process that is outside public record; topics such as special concerns for families involved lie on or near border of administrative and adjudicative matters and would need to be addressed cautiously to prevent the conversation from calling judges' impartiality into question).

Judge Is a Litigant in a Personal Capacity

Rule 2.10(D) also permits judges to comment on proceedings in which the judge is a litigant in a personal capacity. *See, e.g., In re Hey*, 452 S.E.2d 24 (W. Va. 1994) (judge's comments were permissible when they were intended to indicate publicly that he intended to subpoena and depose someone in a civil proceeding against him). However, where the judge is a litigant in his or her official capacity, such as in a writ of mandamus, the judge may not make public comments. Model Code of Judicial Conduct Rule 2.9 cmt. [3]. Additionally, at least one court has held that this exception does not apply if the judge's public comments were intended to influence the courts and the public by lending the prestige of his office to the advancement of his private interests. *In re Miller*, 949 So. 2d 379 (La. 2007) (judge violated predecessor to Rule 2.10(A) when, after former employee filed sexual harassment suit and employee's husband filed filiation suit against judge, he gave an interview to a reporter, which formed the basis of a newspaper article and issued two press releases discussing the facts of the cases; court found that judge's comments were intended to influence the courts and the public by lending the prestige of his office to the advancement of his private interests).

Responding to Public Attacks

Rule 2.10(E), added to the Code in 2007, permits a judge to "respond directly or through a third party to allegations in the media or elsewhere concerning the judge's conduct in a matter." Before the addition of this provision, some states had carved out an exception to the prohibition in Rule 2.10(A) that would permit judges who have been publicly attacked to publicly explain their position in "moderate, unmalicious, and unabusive language." *In re Miera*, 426 N.W.2d 850 (Minn. 1988) (quoting *In re Kelly*, 238 So. 2d 565 (Fla. 1970) (Ervin, C.J., dissenting)). This exception is referred to as a "qualified privilege." The privilege must be "limited to a moderate and dignified response to the attack made upon the judge and may not be of a nature in quantity or substance that creates more harm than benefit to the judicial system." *In re Conard*, 944 S.W.2d 191 (Mo. 1997) (after judge was attacked in the press by chief of police and defendant's wife for his decision in spousal abuse case, judge could properly respond to those charges in the press). *See generally* Stephen J. Fortunato, Jr., *On a Judge's Duty to Speak Extrajudicially: Rethinking the Strategy of Silence*, 12 Geo. J. Legal Ethics 679 (Summer 1999) (asserting that judges have an obligation to respond to baseless attacks on their integrity); Robert M. O'Neil, *Assaults on the Judiciary*, 34 Trial 54 (1998). *See also* Meghan K. Jacobson, Note, *Assault on the Judiciary: Judicial Response to Criticism Post-Schiavo*, 61 U. Miami L. Rev. 931 (2007). Despite the exception, a judge may need to pursue other avenues to respond to criticism. *See In re Hocking*, 546 N.W.2d 234 (Mich. 1996) (request for investigation by Attorney Grievance Commission is a proper response to arguably defamatory statements made by attorneys about judges; direct response by the judge in the media is problematic because "[r]egardless of the merits of the dispute, a media war of words may erode public confidence in the judiciary").

The ABA adopted a similar provision for judicial candidates. Comment [8] to Rule 4.1 provides that a judicial candidate may "make a factually accurate public response" to "false, misleading, or unfair allegations made by opposing candidates, third parties, or the media."

A comment to Rule 2.10 suggests that it may be appropriate in some instances for statements that explain or defend the role or action of a judge in a particular matter to be made by a third person, rather than by the judge. Model Code of Judicial Conduct Rule 2.10 cmt. [3]. This suggestion is meant to present a way to avoid the perception that the judge is less than impartial. Charles G. Geyh & W. William Hodes, *Reporters' Notes to the Model Code of Judicial Conduct* 42 (2009).

RULE 2.11 DISQUALIFICATION

(A) A judge shall disqualify himself or herself in any proceeding in which the judge's impartiality* might reasonably be questioned, including but not limited to the following circumstances:

(1) The judge has a personal bias or prejudice concerning a party or a party's lawyer, or personal knowledge* of facts that are in dispute in the proceeding.

(2) The judge knows* that the judge, the judge's spouse or domestic partner,* or a person within the third degree of relationship* to either of them, or the spouse or domestic partner of such a person is:

(a) a party to the proceeding, or an officer, director, general partner, managing member, or trustee of a party;

(b) acting as a lawyer in the proceeding;

(c) a person who has more than a de minimis* interest that could be substantially affected by the proceeding; or

(d) likely to be a material witness in the proceeding.

(3) The judge knows that he or she, individually or as a fiduciary,* or the judge's spouse, domestic partner, parent, or child, or any other member of the judge's family residing in the judge's household,* has an economic interest* in the subject matter in controversy or in a party to the proceeding.

(4) The judge knows or learns by means of a timely motion that a party, a party's lawyer, or the law firm of a party's lawyer has within the previous [insert number] year[s] made aggregate* contributions* to the judge's campaign in an amount that is greater than $[insert amount] for an individual or $[insert amount] for an entity [is reasonable and appropriate for an individual or an entity].

(5) The judge, while a judge or a judicial candidate,* has made a public statement, other than in a court proceeding, judicial decision, or opinion, that commits or appears to commit the judge to reach a particular result or rule in a particular way in the proceeding or controversy.

(6) The judge:

(a) served as a lawyer in the matter in controversy, or was associated with a lawyer who participated substantially as a lawyer in the matter during such association;

(b) served in governmental employment, and in such capacity participated personally and substantially as a lawyer or public official concerning the proceeding, or has publicly expressed in such capacity an opinion concerning the merits of the particular matter in controversy;

(c) was a material witness concerning the matter; or

(d) previously presided as a judge over the matter in another court.

(B) A judge shall keep informed about the judge's personal and fiduciary economic interests, and make a reasonable effort to keep informed about the personal economic interests of

the judge's spouse or domestic partner and minor children residing in the judge's household.

(C) A judge subject to disqualification under this Rule, other than for bias or prejudice under paragraph (A)(1), may disclose on the record the basis of the judge's disqualification and may ask the parties and their lawyers to consider, outside the presence of the judge and court personnel, whether to waive disqualification. If, following the disclosure, the parties and lawyers agree, without participation by the judge or court personnel, that the judge should not be disqualified, the judge may participate in the proceeding. The agreement shall be incorporated into the record of the proceeding.

COMMENT

[1] Under this Rule, a judge is disqualified whenever the judge's impartiality might reasonably be questioned, regardless of whether any of the specific provisions of paragraphs (A)(1) through (6) apply. In many jurisdictions, the term "recusal" is used interchangeably with the term "disqualification."

[2] A judge's obligation not to hear or decide matters in which disqualification is required applies regardless of whether a motion to disqualify is filed.

[3] The rule of necessity may override the rule of disqualification. For example, a judge might be required to participate in judicial review of a judicial salary statute, or might be the only judge available in a matter requiring immediate judicial action, such as a hearing on probable cause or a temporary restraining order. In matters that require immediate action, the judge must disclose on the record the basis for possible disqualification and make reasonable efforts to transfer the matter to another judge as soon as practicable.

[4] The fact that a lawyer in a proceeding is affiliated with a law firm with which a relative of the judge is affiliated does not itself disqualify the judge. If, however, the judge's impartiality might reasonably be questioned under paragraph (A), or the relative is known by the judge to have an interest in the law firm that could be substantially affected by the proceeding under paragraph (A)(2)(c), the judge's disqualification is required.

[5] A judge should disclose on the record information that the judge believes the parties or their lawyers might reasonably consider relevant to a possible motion for disqualification, even if the judge believes there is no basis for disqualification.

[6] "Economic interest," as set forth in the Terminology section, means ownership of more than a de minimis legal or equitable interest. Except for situations in which a judge participates in the management of such a legal or

equitable interest, or the interest could be substantially affected by the outcome of a proceeding before a judge, it does not include:

(1) an interest in the individual holdings within a mutual or common investment fund;

(2) an interest in securities held by an educational, religious, charitable, fraternal, or civic organization in which the judge or the judge's spouse, domestic partner, parent, or child serves as a director, officer, advisor, or other participant;

(3) a deposit in a financial institution or deposits or proprietary interests the judge may maintain as a member of a mutual savings association or credit union, or similar proprietary interests; or

(4) an interest in the issuer of government securities held by the judge.

1990 CODE COMPARISON

Rule 2.11(A) and (B) derive from former Canons 3E(1) and 3E(2). Rule 2.11(C) is former Canon 3F. Most changes to this Rule and its accompanying Comment are stylistic and structural rather than substantive. The substantive changes include the addition of "domestic partner" to paragraphs (A)(2), (A)(3), and (B). In paragraph (A)(2)(a), "general partner" and "managing member" were added to ensure completeness of the list. In Paragraph (A)(2)(d), "to the judge's knowledge," which was in former Canon 3E(1)(d)(iv), was deleted as unnecessary.

Rule 2.11(A)(6)(b) makes explicit in the black letter what former Canon 3E(1)(b) stated only in Commentary. Judges must not sit on cases concerning matters with which they were involved as government lawyers, for the same reason that they must not sit on cases concerning matters in which they were involved as lawyers, and the Rule has been revised to so state. Rule 2.11 (A)(6)(d), regarding recusal when a judge has presided over a matter in another court, is new to the Code. Comments [2] and [6] are also new. Charles G. Geyh & W. William Hodes, *Reporters' Notes to the Model Code of Judicial Conduct* 46–47 (2009).

ANNOTATION

INTRODUCTION

Judicial impartiality is a fundamental principle of the administration of justice. To that end, Rule 2.11(A) tries to ensure that no judge presides in a case in which he or she is not disinterested and impartial. Rule 2.11(A) not only mandates disqualification where a judge is biased or prejudiced, but also when there is an appearance of impropriety. *See Tennant v. Marion Health Care Found., Inc.*, 459 S.E.2d 374 (W. Va. 1995) (administration of justice should be beyond appearance of unfairness). This requirement protects the due process rights of litigants and helps to maintain public confidence in the integrity of the judicial system. When determining whether or not to recuse, a judge must be guided not only by his or her true state of impartiality, but also by the public's perception of the judge's fairness. *Stamper v. Commw.*, 324 S.E.2d 682 (Va. 1985); *Billips v. Commw.*, 630 S.E.2d 340 (Va. 2006) (judge's knowledge of jury's act insufficient to require judge to recuse from imposing sentence on juvenile). *Joyner v. Comm'r of Corrections*, 740 A.2d 424 (Conn. 1999) (where no showing of actual bias or showing that a reasonable person would perceive an appearance of bias, recusal was not required). A comment to the Rule explains that "[a] judge's obligation not to hear and decide matters in which disqualification is required applies regardless of whether a motion to disqualify has been filed." Model Code of Judicial Conduct Rule 2.11 cmt. [2].

Disqualification is perhaps the most litigated area related to standards of judicial conduct. The general disqualification standard set out in Rule 2.11(A) provides that a judge must disqualify himself or herself from a proceeding if his or her "impartiality might reasonably be questioned." This section of the Canon creates an objective standard, requiring recusal where there is an appearance of bias and prejudice sufficient to permit the average person reasonably to question the judge's impartiality. *Pride v. Harris*, 882 P.2d 381 (Alaska 1994) (court affirmed judge's decision not to recuse though litigant felt judge biased); *Abington Ltd. P'ship v. Heublein*, 717 A.2d 1232 (Conn. 1998) (appearance of impropriety existed from judge's visit to property in question even though no substantive information gained beyond what was within record); *Anderson v. U.S.*, 754 A.2d 920 (D.C. 2000) (prisoner's appeal from recusal motion in post trial proceedings against trial judge fails, in part, as the allegations of personal bias or prejudice were not beyond the actions within the courtroom); *State v. Mann*, 512 N.W.2d 528 (Iowa 1994) (court applies a "reasonable person" test analogizing when a judge should recuse to challenges for cause to potential jurors); *Rogers v. Bradley*, 909 S.W.2d 872 (Tex. 1995) (two justices express contrary views on recusal and obligation to sit based upon specific litigant's direct involvement of his case in political campaign); *Ball v. Melsur Corp.*, 633 A.2d 705 (Vt. 1993) (court declines to adopt a per se requirement of recusal whenever a judge has been the subject of a judicial conduct complaint by an attorney appearing before him). The subsections that follow Rule 2.11(A) illustrate specific circumstances where a judge must be disqualified. However, they do not exhaust the field, and disqualification will be required in any other case where the judge's impartiality might reasonably be questioned. *Buchanan v. Buchanan*, 587 So. 2d 892 (Miss. 1991) (appellant entitled to evidentiary hearing on post-trial motion to disqualify judge on basis that judge's son-in-law was student at professional school where appellee and many witnesses taught, though no evidence presented on appeal that any "legal" interest existed in the outcome of the case).

"Impartial," "impartiality," and "impartially" are defined in the Terminology section of the Model Code to mean "absence of bias or prejudice in favor of, or against, particular parties or classes of parties, as well as maintenance of an open mind in considering issues that may come before a judge." Model Code of Judicial Conduct, Terminology. In *Republican Party of Minnesota v. White*, 536 U.S. 765 (2002), Justice Scalia's majority opinion suggests that impartiality might also mean "a lack of preconceived notion in favor of or against a particular *legal view*." 536 U.S. at 777. *See also* Joe Cutler, Student Author, *Oops! I Said It Again: Judicial Codes of Conduct, the First Amendment, and the Definition of Impartiality*, 17 Geo. J. Legal Ethics 733 (Summer 2004).

Related Federal Statutes

Although there are some differences, Rule 2.11 corresponds closely to 28 U.S.C.A. § 455, which governs the disqualification of federal judges. Therefore, federal case law interpreting that statute can be instructive to an understanding of the Canon. *See, e.g., Marshall v. Marshall*, 403 B.R. 668 (2009) (although appellant cited eight bases to show appearance of bias or prejudice or lack of neutrality, even taken in toto, there is no reasonable inference of bias or prejudice warranting recusal); *In re Evergreen Security, Ltd.*, 570 F.3d 1257 (2009) (contentious conduct by attorney, including improper filings implying misbehavior by judge, insufficient to create grounds for recusal of said judge). Two other federal statutes, 28 U.S.C.A. § 47 and 28 U.S.C.A. § 144, also govern disqualification in federal court. Pursuant to 28 U.S.C.A. § 47, a judge is prohibited from hearing an appeal in any case over which the judge presided as a trial judge. And, 28 U.S.C.A. § 144 disqualifies district court judges for actual bias or prejudice as alleged in a party's affidavit. *See generally* Debra Lyn Bassett, *Judicial Disqualification in the Federal Courts*, 87 Iowa L. Rev. 1213 (2002); Matthew E. Kaplan, Comment, *Judicial Process at Risk: Scales of Justice Unequal Under Present Federal Judicial Disqualification Statutes*, 8 U. Miami Bus. L. Rev. 273 (2000); Susan B. Hoekema, Comment, *Questioning the Impartiality of Judges: Disqualifying Federal District Court Judges Under 28 U.S.C. § 455(a)*, 60 Temp. L.Q. 697 (1987); Notes, *Disqualification of Judges and Justices in the Federal Courts*, 86 Harv. L. Rev. 736 (1973). Rule 2.11 is also substantially similar to Canon 3C of the Code of Conduct for United States Judges.

"Recusal" or "Disqualification"

Traditionally, "recusal" has referred to a judge's voluntary, discretionary decision to step down in a case, while "disqualification" refers to a motion for the statutorily or constitutionally mandated removal of a judge from a case. Richard E. Flamm, *Judicial Disqualification: Recusal and Disqualification of Judges* § 1.1 at 4–5 (1986). However, "in many jurisdictions, the term 'disqualification' has been defined in such a way as to include both removal by a judge on his own motion and removal at the request of a party. In fact, in modern practice the terms 'disqualification' and 'recusal' are frequently viewed as synonymous and are often used interchangeably." *Id.* This is reflected in the comment to the rule, which states that "[i]n many jurisdictions, the term 'recusal' is used interchangeably with the term 'disqualification'." Model Code of Judicial Conduct Rule 2.11 cmt. [1].

Timeliness of Motion

Comment [2] to Rule 2.11, which was added in 2007, states that "[a] judge's obligation not to hear and decide matters in which disqualification is required applies regardless of whether a motion to disqualify has been filed." However, when a motion is filed seeking a judge's disqualification, it must be done in a timely manner. Most state and federal courts have stringent timeliness standards and require that the motion be filed at the first opportunity after the lawyer learns of the disqualifying facts. *Travelers Ins. Co. v. Liljeberg Enters., Inc.*, 38 F.3d 1404 (5th Cir. 1994) (post-judgment motion relating to three cases to disqualify trial judge on basis of membership in a social club of which some attorneys from opposing law firms were also members rejected as untimely); *U.S. v. Studley*, 783 F.2d 934 (9th Cir. 1986) (motion for recusal filed weeks after trial ended untimely); *Wakefield v. Stevens*, 290 S.E.2d 58 (Ga. 1982) (litigant's motion for recusal not timely as facts known when judge first assigned to case, but motion not filed until after judge heard motions and arguments and insufficient time to assign substitute judge without delaying trial); *Madsen v. Prudential Sav. & Loan Assoc.*, 767 P.2d 538 (Utah 1988) (litigants failed to file motion to disqualify at earliest possible moment); *cf. Towbin Dodge, Inc., v. Eighth Jud. Dist. Court of State ex rel. County of Clark*, 112 P.3d 1063 (Nev. 2005) (if new grounds for a judge's disqualification are discovered after time limits have passed for filing a statutory affidavit of bias and prejudice, a party may file a motion to disqualify based on the Nevada Code of Judicial Conduct alleging the judge's impartiality might reasonably be questioned, as soon as possible after becoming aware of the new information). *Aetna Cas. & Sur. Co. v. Berry*, 669 So. 2d 56 (Miss. 1996) (failure of defendant to seek recusal until after adverse decision did not preclude determination that judge should have recused himself when opposing counsel representation of judge in divorce and heavy involvement in judge's re-election campaign not knowledge chargeable to defendant). Some courts have held that failure to timely file the motion results in a waiver of the right to question the judge's impartiality. *See Reno v. Glen R. Gale, Corner of State and William P'ship*, 418 N.W.2d 434 (Mich. App. 1987) (defendants waived the issue of disqualification by failing to assert in a timely manner); *State v. Lucero*, 725 P.2d 266 (N.M. App. 1986) (while defendant failed to timely file motion for disqualification and therefore may have waived constitutional right to disqualify judge, fact decision being reversed for rehearing, court directs case be reheard by different judge); *Reilly by Reilly v. S.W. Pa. Transp. Auth.*, 489 A.2d 1291 (Pa. 1985) (eight-month delay in bringing motion for disqualification waived the issue where party seeking disqualification had actual knowledge of the facts forming the basis of the motion); *Kinard v. Kinard*, 986 S.W.2d 220 (Tenn. App. 1998) (a party may lose right to challenge judge's partiality by engaging in strategic conduct); *Fielding v. State*, 719 S.W.2d 361 (Tex. App. 1986) (appellant's failure to raise issue of trial judge's impartiality until appeal waived issue).

One reason for imposing strict timeliness standards is to ensure that a party who has a reasonable basis for moving to disqualify a judge does not delay in the hope of obtaining a favorable ruling and then file the motion only if the result is unfavorable. *Madsen v. Prudential S. & Loan Assoc.*, 767 P.2d 538 (Utah 1988); *Disc. Counsel v. Au*, 113 P.3d 203 (Haw. 2005) (litigants cannot take the heads-I-win-tails-you-lose position of waiting to see whether they win and if they lose moving to disqualify a judge who voted against them); *Carpenter v. State*, 575 P.2d 26 (Kan. 1978) ("a party may not test the water before deciding whether to request a change of a judge"); *In re Michael M.*, 761 A.2d 865 (Me. 2000) (litigant's recusal motion filed after judgment largely based upon facts known throughout proceedings); *Reilly by Reilly v. Southeastern Pennsylvania Transp. Auth.*, 489 A.2d 1291 (Pa. 1985) (once verdict is entered, party is deemed to have waived right to have a judge disqualified and cannot thereafter be heard to complain following an unfavorable result). Courts frown upon such manipulation of the impartiality issue. *Kinard v. Kinard*, 986 S.W.2d 220 (Tenn. App. 1998). Delay imposes unnecessary disruption on the judicial system and litigants and may evidence a belief that the judge is not in fact biased. Therefore, "a party must move with dispatch once a basis for disqualification is discovered." *Madsen*, 767 P.2d at 542. However, if a party neither knew, nor should have known of the disqualifying factor, the recusal issue is not waived. *Aetna Cas. and Sur. Co. v. Berry*, 669 So. 2d 56 (Miss. 1996).

A Duty to Sit

Judges should not recuse themselves merely because an unfounded claim of bias or prejudice has been lodged against them. Nor should they recuse them selves in order to avoid difficult or controversial cases. H.R. Rep. No. 1453, 93d Cong. 2d 5 (1974). Recusing for these reasons or for no reason at all would contravene public policy by unduly delaying proceedings, increasing the workload of other judges, and fostering impermissible judge-shopping. Although a judge has a duty to recuse when required by Rule 2.11(A), a judge has an equally strong duty not to recuse when the circumstances do not require recusal. *Laird v. Tatum*, 409 U.S. 824 (1972) (a judge "has a duty to sit where not disqualified, which is equally as strong as the duty to not sit where disqualified"); *U.S. v. Glick*, 946 F.2d 335 (4th Cir. 1991) (when there is no reasonable basis to question judge's impartiality, it would be improper for judge to recuse); *U.S. v. Holland*, 501 F.3d 1120 (9th Cir. 2007) (absent a legitimate reason to recuse himself, a judge has a duty to sit in judgment in all cases coming before him); *Carton v. Mo. P. R.R. Co.*, 865 S.W.2d 635 (Ark. 1993) (judge has a duty to sit in a case unless there is some valid reason to disqualify); *State v. Fleming*, 267 S.E.2d 207 (Ga. 1980) (it is as much the duty of a judge not to grant motion to recuse when the motion is legally insufficient as it is to recuse when the motion is meritorious); *Adair v. State Dept. of Educ.* 709 N.W.2d 567 (Mich. 2006) (pursuant to federal courts' "duty to sit" doctrine, there is an obligation to remain on any case absent grounds for recusal). The "duty to sit" is affirmed by Rule 2.7, which requires judges to hear and decide matters, "except when disqualification is required." This provision was added to the 1990 Code "to emphasize the judicial duty to sit and to minimize potential abuse of the disqualification process." ABA Standing Committee on 1990 Code, Legislative Draft 15 (1990).

However, at least one court suggests that in deciding whether to recuse, a judge should consider "whether cases may be unfairly prejudiced or unduly delayed, or discontent may be created through unfounded charges of prejudice or unfairness made against the judge in the trial of a cause." *Tennant v. Marion Health Care Found., Inc.*, 459 S.E.2d 374 (W. Va. 1995); *but cf. Cmmw. v. King*, 839 A.2d 237 (Pa. 2003) (judge who had presided over petitioner's capital murder trial did not abuse his discretion by recusing himself from petitioner's post-conviction relief proceeding alleging ineffective assistance of appointed trial counsel; judge believed recusal would expedite disposition of the petition, and judge's decision to recuse himself on such grounds exhibited a bias in favor of petitioner). *See also* Leslie W. Abramson, *Appearance of Impropriety: Deciding When a Judge's Impartiality "Might Reasonably Be Questioned,"* 14 Geo. J. Legal Ethics 55, 62 n.37 (2000) (asserting that the Code of Judicial Conduct's rules for disqualification suggest that the appearance of partiality outweighs the duty of a judge to sit and decide a particular case). Some courts have held that on close questions, "the balance tips in favor of recusal." *See In re Boston's Children First*, 244 F.3d 164 (1st Cir. 2001) (although judge did not necessarily demonstrate partiality, recusal required nevertheless due to unique idiosyncratic facts); *Nichols v. Alley*, 71 F.3d 347 (10th Cir. 1995) ("rumor, speculation, beliefs, conclusions, innuendo, suspicion, opinion, and similar non-factual matters" are not ordinarily sufficient to require recusal). Another court has held that when a judge and counsel for a party have a relationship that would warrant attorney disqualification or judicial recusal, the client's right to counsel of choice generally prevails over the judge's duty to sit, unless the lawyer was retained in order to disqualify the judge. *Millen v. Eighth Jud. Dist. ex rel. County of Clark*, 148 P.3d 694 (Nev. 2006).

The Rule of Necessity

The rule of necessity permits a judge who is otherwise disqualified from handling a case to preside if there is no provision allowing another judge to hear the matter. The rule ensures that no person seeking redress in the courts will be denied a forum. *U.S. v. Will*, 449 U.S. 200 (1980). The rule has been used by courts for years and was codified in the comment to Rule 2.11 that provides that the rule of necessity may override the rule of disqualification. The Code commentary acknowledges that although a judge's impartiality might reasonably be questioned, situations may arise that require the judge to sit in a case, such as the review of a judicial salary statute or a matter requiring immediate judicial action. In the latter situation, the judge must reveal the basis for disqualification and "transfer the matter to another judge as soon as practicable."

The rule of necessity has most often been applied in cases involving judicial salaries, pension benefits affecting state employees, and cases affecting all state citizens, including judges, as taxpayers or customers of a utility. *See, e.g., U.S. v. Will*, 449 U.S. 200 (1980) (in cases before Supreme Court challenging statutes enacted to stop or reduce previously authorized cost-of-living increases in compensation of high-level federal officials, including federal judges, since all federal judges had interest in the outcome, it was impossible to assign a substitute district judge or remit the appeal to division of Court of Appeals, and thus, common-law rule of necessity prevailed over statute governing disqualification of federal judges); *Jorgensen v. Blagojevich*, 811 N.E.2d 652 (Ill. 2004) (rule of necessity requires state supreme court to hear case by state court judges against state governor and comptroller regarding cost of living adjustment even though the benefit would accrue to supreme court justices along with all other judges); *D & M Healthcare, Inc. v. Kernan*, 800 N.E.2d 898 (Ind. 2003) (members of Indiana Supreme Court had personal financial interests about issue in case which would normally preclude participation in this case, but court decided that it must address claim because there is no one else to do it); *Chairman of Bd. of Trustees of Emp. Ret. Sys. v. Waldron*, 401 A.2d 172 (Md. 1979) (judge's interest in litigation challenging constitutionality of statute precluding retired judges who accept pension from subsequently practicing law for compensation did not disqualify members of court from participating in decision on the merits where case could not otherwise be heard); *Weinstock v. Holden*, 995 S.W.2d 408 (Mo. 1999) (where case involves validity of senate resolution relating to judicial pay, all judges of the state have potential stake in the outcome and unless rule of necessity is applied, parties can have no judicial resolution of their rights); *Hughes v. State*, 838 P.2d 1018 (Or. 1992) (all justices of state supreme court had financial interest in case involving taxation of public employees' retirement benefits, however, since court is only one authorized to hear case, rule of necessity permits justices to adjudicate claims); Ill. Jud. Ethics Comm. Op. 03-05 (2003) (assuming, without deciding, that a judge is disqualified from hearing cases in which a party is represented by a lawyer who concurrently represents all Illinois judges in a class action suit seeking a declaration that salary adjustments are being unconstitutionally withheld from members of the plaintiff class, the judge may nonetheless, under the "rule of necessity," preside over matters in which the attorney appears).

The rule of necessity has also been used when a party names all of the judges in a jurisdiction as defendants in a case that challenges a court's decision or the court's rule-making authority. *See, e.g., Scheehle v. Justices of the Sup. Ct. of the St. of Ariz.*, 120 P.3d 1092 (Ariz. 2005) (under rule of necessity, members of supreme court were not disqualified from proceeding to answer certified question from United States District Court whether supreme court could promulgate court rules mandating experienced attorneys to serve as arbitrators, even though supreme court justices were named defendants in their official capacity in attorney's underlying federal court action; supreme court was only body authorized to interpret scope of its powers to regulate practice of law in state). The rule of necessity may not be used as a vehicle to force removal of judges by naming them as parties when challenging the administrative actions of the court. *N.Y. St. Ass'n of Crim. Def. Laws. v. Kaye*, 744 N.E.2d 123 (N.Y. 2000) (rule of necessity requires participation by appellate judges who are named as parties in their administrative capacity in case challenging validity of court's administrative order).

Since the rule of necessity is an exception to the general rule precluding a disqualified judge from hearing a matter, it is strictly construed and applied only where there is no other person having jurisdiction to handle the matter who can be brought in to hear it. The rule of necessity should be used only sparingly to circumvent disqualification. *State ex rel. Brown v. Dietrick*, 444 S.E.2d 47 (W. Va. 1994). *See, e.g., Lorenz v. N.H. Admin. Off. of Cts.*, 858 A.2d 546 (N.H. 2004) (recusal was warranted in case challenging supreme court's administrative order terminating court stenographers' employment on the condition that substitute judges were available). Thomas McKevitt, Note, *The Rule of Necessity: Is Judicial Non-Disqualification Really Necessary?*, 24 Hofstra L. Rev. 817 (1996) (arguing that alternatives should be explored before a judge invokes the rule of necessity to justify acting where a conflict of interest occurs or where impartiality is questioned); Annotation, *Construction and Application of Rule of Necessity in Judicial Actions, Providing that a Judge Is Not Disqualified to Try a Case Because of Personal Interest If Case Cannot Be Heard Otherwise*, 27 A.L.R. 6th 403 (2007). The rule of necessity may not be invoked simply because another judge was not immediately available and the parties would have to wait until another judge could be found. *Huffman v. Ark. Jud. Disc. & Disability Comm'n*, 42 S.W.3d 386 (Ark. 2001).

Presumption of Impartiality

There is a general presumption that a judge is impartial, and the party seeking disqualification bears the burden of proving otherwise. *Turner v. State*, 926 S.W.2d 843 (Ark. 1996); *Garland v. State*, 788 N.E.2d 425 (Ind. 2003) (the law presumes that judge is unbiased and unprejudiced); *State v. Mann*, 512 N.W.2d 528 (Iowa 1994) (burden of showing grounds for recusal is on the party seeking it); *Hathcock v. Southern Farm Bureau Cas. Ins. Co.*, 912 So. 2d 844 (Miss. 2005) (supreme court presumes that a judge, sworn to administer impartial justice, is qualified and unbiased); *In re Disqualification of Kilpatrick*, 546 N.E.2d 929 (Ohio 1989) (judge is presumed to be fair and impartial); *Commw. v. Council*, 421 A.2d 623 (Pa. 1980) (burden to show bias and prejudice is always on the party seeking recusal of a judge); *Luce v. Cushing*, 868 A.2d 672 (Vt. 2004) (for the purpose of a motion to recuse a trial judge, the judge is accorded a presumption of honesty and integrity, with the burden on the moving party to show otherwise). To overcome the presumption of impartiality, the moving party must establish that the trial judge has or appears to have a personal prejudice for or against a party. *See Lasley v. State*, 510 N.E.2d 1340 (Ind. 1987). The evidence presented must produce a reasonable doubt about the validity of the presumption. *Turner v. State*, 573 So. 2d 657 (Miss. 1990). A party may overcome the presumption by illustrating that one of the disqualifying circumstances listed in the subsections to Rule 2.11(A) exists, or by showing that for some other reason, the judge's impartiality might reasonably be questioned.

Standard of Review on Motion to Disqualify: Abuse of Discretion

Depending on the jurisdiction, when a motion for disqualification is filed, the judge may personally decide the motion, pass only on the legal sufficiency of the motion, or assign the motion to another judge. In the majority of states, the decision to recuse is within the judge's discretion and will be reversed only in case of manifest abuse of discretion. *See, e.g., Long v. Long*, 816 P.2d 145 (Alaska 1991) (judge's decision not to disqualify himself based on the appearance of impartiality will not be reversed unless the appellate court finds that he abused his discretion); *Turner v. State*, 926 S.W.2d 843 (Ark. 1996) (trial judge did not abuse his discretion in not recusing himself even though he had previously prosecuted the defendant for a separate crime); *Los v. Los*, 595 A.2d 381 (Del. 1991) (no abuse of discretion in refusing to recuse himself when father named trial judge as defendant in federal suit challenging child support formula). An abuse of discretion, with respect to trial court's decision not to recuse, can be proved by showing evidence of bias or prejudice on the part of the trial court. *Owens v. State*, 128 S.W.3d 445 (Ark. 2003);

Nemeth v. Nemeth, 451 A.2d 1384 (Pa. Super. 1982) (the record must clearly show prejudice, bias, capricious disbelief, or prejudgment).

Some jurisdictions provide that if a judge is presented with a motion to disqualify, supported by an affidavit, the judge should not pass upon the truth or falsity of the facts alleged in the affidavit, but only upon the legal sufficiency and timeliness of a motion. If the motion is timely, the affidavit sufficient, and recusal would be warranted if some or all of the facts set forth in the affidavit are true, another judge must be assigned to hear the motion. *See State v. Fleming*, 267 S.E.2d 207 (Ga. 1980). In order to be legally sufficient, the documents must "'state facts from which it may reasonably be inferred that the judge has a bias or prejudice that will prevent him from dealing fairly. . . .' Facts are required; conclusory statements, conjecture, and innuendo do not suffice." *Zoline v. Telluride Lodge Ass'n*, 732 P.2d 635 (Colo. 1987) (trial judge abused his discretion when he failed to disqualify himself even though petitioner's motion and affidavit assert that the judge had an interest in a bank in which the respondent was a substantial customer); *Livingston v. State*, 441 So. 2d 1083 (Fla. 1983) (facts alleged in motion to disqualify a judge need only show that party making it has a well-grounded fear that he or she will not receive a fair trial at hands of judge).

Lastly, in some jurisdictions, by court rule or statute, upon receipt of a motion to recuse, the judge may not pass on the legal sufficiency or timeliness of the motion, but must either recuse or assign the motion to another judge to decide. *See* Alaska Stat. § 22.20.020 (c); Kan Stat. Ann. § 20-311d(b) (1999); S.D. Codified Law Ann. § 15-12-32 (1984); Tex. Rule Civ. Pro. 18a(d); Vt. Rule of Criminal Proc. Rule 50 (d) (the judge whose disqualification is sought shall either disqualify himself or herself or, without ruling on the motion, refer the motion to the Administrative Judge for Trial Courts or a designee).

DISQUALIFICATION WHEN JUDGE'S "IMPARTIALITY MIGHT REASONABLY BE QUESTIONED"

Rule 2.11(A) is a catchall provision mandating disqualification whenever a judge's impartiality "might reasonably be questioned." A party may seek a judge's disqualification under this general provision when the circumstances do not altogether fit into one of Rule 2.11(A)'s specifically delineated subsections or when the situation clearly falls outside one of those specified scenarios. Leslie W. Abramson, *Appearance of Impropriety: Deciding When a Judge's Impartiality "Might Reasonably Be Questioned,"* 14 Geo. J. Legal Ethics 55 (2000). The language of Rule 2.11(A) does not require that the judge must have engaged in any biased or prejudicial conduct, and disqualification is required "regardless of the source or circumstances giving rise to the question of impartiality and even though the source and circumstances may be beyond the judge's volition or control." *Id.*, *citing Rogers v. Bradley*, 909 S.W.2d 872 (Tex. 1995). *Smith v. Pepsico, Inc.*, 434 F. Supp. 524 (S.D. Fla. 1977) (disqualification not required where plaintiff's lawyer had served as judge's clerk two years earlier; not reasonable to question judge's impartiality absent any other evidence).

Objective or Subjective Test

The language of Rule 2.11(A) creates an objective test for the appearance of impartiality: whether the facts create reasonable doubt concerning the judge's impartiality, not in the mind of the judge, or even, necessarily, in the mind of the litigant filing the motion, but rather in the mind of a reasonable person with knowledge of all the circumstances. *State v. Logan*, 689 P.2d 778 (Kan. 1984) *citing U.S. v. Martorano*, 620 F. 2d 912 (1st Cir. 1980). *See also United Farm Workers of America, AFL-CIO v. Superior Court*, 170 Cal. App. 3d 97 (1985) (judge "ought to consider how his participation in a given case looks to the average person on the street"); *Papa v. New Haven Fed'n of Teachers*, 444 A2d 196 (Conn. 1982) (in evaluating motion for recusal, standard to be employed is objective one, not judge's subjective view as to whether he or she can be fair and impartial in hearing the case); *Tyson v. State*, 622 N.E.2d 457 (Ind. 1993) (question is not whether the judge's impartiality is impaired in fact, but whether there exists a reasonable basis for questioning a judge's impartiality); *State v. Mann*, 512 N.W.2d 528 (Iowa 1994) (test is not whether the judge self-questions his own impartiality, but whether a reasonable person would question it); *Farm Credit Bank of St. Paul v. Brakke*, 512 N.W.2d 718 (N.D. 1994) (appearance-of-partiality test is one of reasonableness, and judges should err on the side of caution by disqualifying themselves in cases raising close questions); Ariz. Sup. Ct. Jud. Ethics Adv. Comm. Op. 98-2 (1998) (would an objective, disinterested observer, fully informed of the facts underlying the grounds on which disqualification was contemplated, entertain a significant doubt that justice would be done in the case?). Courts have employed numerous definitions of the "reasonable person" including "a person of ordinary prudence" *Matter of Sheffield*, 465 So. 2d 350 (Ala. 1984); the "average man," *State ex rel. Brown v. Dietrick*, 444 S.E.2d 47 (W. Va. 1994); "objective onlooker" and "disinterested bystander" *Robin Farms, Inc. v. Bartholome*, 989 S.W.2d 238 (Mo. App. 1999); a "reasonable person with knowledge of all the circumstances" *State v. Logan*, 689 P.2d 778 (Kan. 1984); and a "reasonable, disinterested observer" *In re Illuzzi*, 670 A.2d 1264 (Vt. 1995).

Federal law also requires a judge to be disqualified if there is a *reasonable* question as to the judge's impartiality. 28 U.S.C.A. 455(a); *see, e.g., Yagman v. Republic Ins.*, 987 F.2d 622 (9th Cir. 1993) (recusal is appropriate where "a reasonable person with knowledge of all the facts would conclude that the judge's impartiality might reasonably be questioned"); *Pepsico, Inc. v. McMillen*, 764

F.2d 458 (7th Cir. 1985) (statute requires recusal whenever there is "a reasonable basis" for a finding of an "appearance of partiality under the facts and circumstances" of the case). *See also Liteky v. U.S.*, 510 U.S. 540 (1994) (Kennedy, J., concurring, joined by Blackmun, Stevens, and Souter, JJ.) (statute "is triggered by an attitude or state of mind so resistant to fair and dispassionate inquiry as to cause a party, the public, or a reviewing court to have reasonable grounds to question the neutral and objective character of a judge's rulings or findings").

Despite the objective standard of Rule 2.11(A), a few courts have applied a subjective test and do not require disqualification unless there is evidence that the trial judge's impartiality was compromised. Leslie W. Abramson, *Appearance of Impropriety: Deciding When a Judge's Impartiality "Might Reasonably Be Questioned,"* 14 Geo. J. Legal Ethics 55 (2000), *citing Lawson v. State*, 664 N.E.2d 773 (Ind. App. 1996) (whether a judge's impartiality might reasonably be questioned because of an ex parte communication is a subjective determination; the question was not whether the content of the conversation was prejudicial, "but whether it had an impact on the judge's impartiality, which is a question only the trial judge can answer"); *State v. Jones*, 979 S.W.2d 171 (Mo. 1998) ("judge . . . is in the best position to decide whether recusal is necessary").

Still, other jurisdictions utilize a two-part analysis when ruling on a motion to disqualify for impartiality. First, the judge must be satisfied as a matter of subjective belief that he or she can proceed to hear the cause free of bias or prejudice concerning that party. Second, even if the judge believes that he or she has no actual bias, the judge must recuse if there is the appearance of bias sufficient to cast doubt as to the judge's impartiality. *Los v. Los*, 595 A.2d 381 (Del. 1991); *Goodheart v. Casey*, 565 A.2d 757 (Pa. 1989) (applying a "two-tiered" assessment to issue of judge's impartiality); *Mitchell v. Class*, 524 N.W.2d 860 (S.D. 1994) (judge should initially determine whether a fair trial dictates recusal; the Code also provides an objective standard upon which to determine whether a judge should disqualify himself or herself); Ill. Jud. Ethics Comm. Op. 96-22 (1996) (first, the judge must determine, objectively, whether the judge's impartiality might be questioned; then, the judge must subjectively review whether he or she holds any personal or extreme hostility toward a lawyer). *But see* Leslie W. Abramson, *Appearance of Impropriety: Deciding When a Judge's Impartiality "Might Reasonably Be Questioned,"* 14 Geo. J. Legal Ethics 55 (2000) (arguing that a subjective analysis is appropriate in determining whether a judge has a personal bias or prejudice, but not whether a judge's impartiality might reasonably be questioned).

If a judge seeks his or her own recusal from a case, appellate courts presume that a reasonable person would have doubts about the judge's impartiality, regardless of whether the reviewing court itself would have recused on the same facts. Leslie W. Abramson, *Appearance of Impropriety: Deciding When a Judge's Impartiality "Might Reasonably Be Questioned,"* 14 Geo. J. Legal Ethics 55 (2000), *citing Tennant v. Marion Health Care Found., Inc.*, 459 S.E.2d 374 (W. Va. 1995) and *Jacobs v. Commw.*, 947 S.W.2d 416, (Ky. App. 1997).

THE APPEARANCE OF PARTIALITY

Rule 2.11(A) mandates a judge's disqualification "in any proceeding in which the judge's impartiality might reasonably be questioned, including but not limited to" those circumstances described in the rule's six subsections. Further, as expressed by the "not limited to" language, there may be additional circumstances that do not squarely fit into one of the subsections of Rule 2.11(A), but which raise an appearance of impartiality requiring disqualification. The question in each case is not necessarily whether the judge is impartial or not, but rather, whether another person might reasonably question the judge's impartiality under the circumstances. *Abington Ltd. P'ship v. Heublein*, 717 A.2d 1232 (Conn. 1998). That determination is necessarily fact bound, and requires an examination of the nature of the judge's business, personal, social, or political associations at issue, and his or her exercise of judgment regarding how close, extensive, and recent those associations have been. *Sears v. State*, 426 S.E.2d 553 (Ga. 1993).

Negotiating for Employment

Like the Commentary to Rule 2.11, the Commentary to Section 3E(1) of the 1990 Code provides that a judge is disqualified whenever the judge's impartiality might reasonably be questioned, regardless of whether any of the specific provisions under the rule apply. The Commentary to Section 3E(1) states as an example that a judge who is in the process of negotiating for employment with a law firm would be disqualified from any matters in which that law firm appeared, unless the parties waived the disqualification after disclosure by the judge. This language does not appear in the Commentary to the 2007 Code, but the case law holds that employment negotiations with a firm would likely be grounds for disqualification. *See, e.g., DeNike v. Cupo*, 958 A.2d 446 (N.J. 2008) (finding an appearance of impropriety and ordering a new trial where judge and lawyer talked about job offer with lawyer's firm while winding up a commercial dispute before judge; litigation took two-and-a-half years to complete, judge had already made his substantive decisions in the litigation, and only thing that remained to be done was the ministerial act of formalizing the substantive decisions); *Voeltz v. John Morrell & Co.*, 564 N.W.2d 315 (S.D. 1997) (administrative law judge should have recused herself from hearing workers' compensation dispute involving claimant and employer, where judge had applied, and was negotiating with employer, for future employment opportunity and took job with claimant's employer four days after issuing opinion adverse to claimant); U.S. Jud. Conf. Comm. on Codes of Conduct Adv. Op. 84 (1998) (after judge initiates post-judicial employment discussions with law firm, no matter how preliminary or tentative the exploration may be, judge should recuse on any matter in which firm appears before judge); Ill. Jud. Ethics Comm. Op. 07-01 (2007) (judge is disqualified from proceedings in which a law firm appears when the judge is negotiating future employment with firm). A similar provision appears in Rule 1.12 of the Model Rules of Professional Conduct, which provides that "a lawyer shall not negotiate for employment with any person who is involved as a party or as lawyer for a party in a matter in which the lawyer is participating personally and substantially as a judge or other adjudicative officer . . . ." *See generally* Leslie W. Abramson, *Appearance of Impropriety: Deciding When a Judge's Impartiality "Might Reasonably Be Questioned,"* 14 Geo. J. Legal Ethics 55 (2000) (asserting that "If the ABA believes that disqualification is necessary in that context without regard to additional facts, it is curious that the ABA did not simply include this factual context in the list of specific instances requiring disqualification, especially because the judge is subject to lawyer discipline for that same activity under the ABA's Rules of Professional Conduct for attorneys").

Judges have been disqualified for engaging in employment negotiations with prospective employers in the private and public sector. *See Scott v. United States*, 559 A.2d 745 (D.C. App. 1989) (judge violated Canon 3 when he presided at the prosecution of a defendant by the U.S. Department of Justice through the U.S. Attorney's Office while actively negotiating for employment with the Department's Executive Office for U.S. Attorneys). *See generally* Ronald D. Rotunda, *The Propriety of a Judge's Failure to Recuse When Being Considered for Another Position*, 19 Geo J. Legal Ethics 1187 (2006).

Disqualification may also be required if a person working on the judge's behalf mistakenly contacts a law firm regarding the judge's post-judicial employment. *See In Pepsico, Inc. v. McMillen*, 764 F.2d 458 (7th Cir. 1985). A person working on a judge's behalf mistakenly contacted law firms representing opposing parties in an antitrust action that was pending before the judge, concerning possible employment of the judge after his retirement from the bench. Even though no actual impropriety may be involved, recusal is required because "[t]he dignity and independence of the judiciary are diminished when the judge comes before the lawyers in the case in the role of a suppliant for employment." "A fully informed and objective observer might wonder whether the judge could decide the case with the requisite aloofness and disinterest when he had just solicited (if unintentionally) employment by the law firms in the case. This conclusion requires recusal." *Id.* at 461.

A judge's recusal is not warranted simply because the judge's name has been mentioned as a potential candidate for a job, when there is no evidence that the judge sought, applied for, or negotiated with anyone for the position. The speculations of unknown individuals about a judge's future prospects for a position would not *reasonably* call into question the judge's impartiality. *Anderson v. United States*, 754 A.2d 920 (D.C. App. 2000) (an account in a newspaper that unnamed persons frequently mentioned judge's name as a *potential* candidate is not a sufficient reason to require the judge to recuse for actual impartiality or the appearance of impartiality).

Some courts and ethics committees have provided guidance to judges regarding post-judicial employment negotiations. In *DeNike v. Cupo*, 958 A.2d 446 (N.J. 2008), the New Jersey Supreme Court stated that the safest course would be for a judge to wait until retirement before starting a job search. However, noting that this is not necessary and can be impractical, the court advised: (1) that judge should not have a discussion if the firm has a matter in which the judge is participating personally and substantially; (2) if the subject is raised, the judge should halt the conversation, rebuff any offer, and disclose what occurred on the record; and (3) judge should delay starting any discussions until shortly before their planned retirement, and keep such discussions to the fewest possible number of prospective employers. In federal court, judges are advised to wait for "the passage of a reasonable interval" of time before discussing jobs with firms that have appeared before them. U.S. Jud. Conf. Comm. on Codes of Conduct Adv. Op. 84 (1998).

Law Clerk Employment Negotiations

Disqualification may also be an issue when a judge's law clerk is seeking post-clerkship employment prior to the termination of the clerkship. Model Rule of Professional Conduct 1.12(b) permits lawyers serving as judicial clerks to negotiate for employment even with persons involved in a matter in which the clerks are participating personally and substantially, as long as they notify their judges. However, a law clerk's continuing participation in a case, in which a future employer is counsel, may mandate the judge's disqualification, even if there is no suggestion of any actual impropriety by the clerk, the judge, or any other party. *Hull v. Small Bus. Administration*, 695 F.2d 175 (5th Cir. 1983) (law clerk's continuing participation with magistrate in case in which her future employers were counsel gave rise to appearance of partiality which required magistrate's disqualification); *Miller Inds., Inc. v. Caterpillar Tractor Co.*, 516 F. Supp. 84 (S.D. Ala. 1980) (disqualification of judge required where clerk continued to work on case involving future employer). *See generally* Linda H. Green, *The Spotless Reputation and the Federal Law Clerk Employment Negotiations*, 25 U. Mem L. Rev. 127 (1994); Kevin D. Swan, Comment, *Protecting the Appearance of Judicial Impartiality in the Face of Law Clerk Employment Negotiations*, 62 Wash. L. Rev. 813 (1987).

Disqualification can be avoided if the law clerk is properly screened from cases involving a future employer. *See Hunt v. American Bank & Trust Co.*, 783 F.2d 1011 (11th Cir. 1986) (judge need not have recused himself on ground that two of his law clerks accepted offers of employment from law firm representing several defendants while case was pending before the court, where neither clerk worked on case or even talked with judge about it to any significant extent); *Hall v. Small Bus. Administration*, 695 F.2d 175 (5th Cir. 1983) (disqualification required unless judge isolates law clerk from all knowledge of and participation in case immediately after employment interviews begin); *In re Nazi Era Cases Against German Defendants Litigation*, 153 Fed Appx. 819 (2005) (district court did not abuse its discretion by refusing motion to recuse based on court's employment of law clerks who had former and future employment ties to defendants' two law firms where clerks were walled off from case) (unpublished opinion); U.S. Jud. Conf. Comm. on Codes of Conduct Adv. Op. 74 (1998) (advising that when a law clerk might accept employment with a lawyer or law firm in a pending case disqualification of judge is not mandated but the law clerk should have no involvement whatsoever in pending matters handled by the prospective employer). In addition, neither the clerk nor the judge would likely be required to recuse from a case when the clerk has merely applied for a job with one of the party's firms or offices. *See, e.g., U.S. v. Persico*, 2006 WL 2792761 (E.D.N.Y. 2006) (no appearance of impropriety when a law clerk works on a case where he or she has done nothing more than submit an application for employment to a firm or attorney that serves as counsel-of-record; the court should remain cognizant of the status of the clerk's application and revisit the issue if an offer of employment is extended and accepted).

Judge's Professional Association with Lawyer in Case

A judge must disqualify from a case if the judge or a lawyer with whom the judge previously practiced law served as a lawyer in the case during that association. *See* Rule 2.11(A)(6)(a). However, even if the judge's former associate began the representation after the association with the judge ended, the judge may still be required to disqualify if his prior association with the lawyer reasonably creates an appearance of impartiality under Rule 2.11(A).

Generally, the fact that a judge was once professionally associated with a lawyer for one of the parties in a case is not, without more, grounds for disqualification. *See In re Affidavit of Bias*, 947 P.2d 1152 (Utah 1997); ABA Comm. on Ethics and Professional Responsibility, Informal Op. 87-1524 (1987); *see generally* Annotation, *Judge's Previous Legal Association with Attorney Connected to Current Case as Warranting Disqualification*, 85 A.L.R. 4th 700

(1991). In the absence of other disqualifying circumstances, courts have consistently concluded that a judge is not disqualified when the lawyer for one of the parties is the judge's former law partner (*Alvarado Morales v. Digital Equipment Corp.*, 699 F. Supp. 16 (D. Puerto Rico 1988); *Bumpus v. Uniroyal Tire Co.*, 385 F. Supp. 711 (E.D. Pa. 1974)), a former associate (*National City Bank v. Shortridge*, 691 N.E.2d 1210 (Ind. 1998)), or a former co-counsel (*Bonelli v. Bonelli*, 570 A.2d 189 (Conn. 1990) (requiring disqualification for minimal prior co-counsel association that does not include a present financial interest or business or social relationship would place an unjustified burden on the judicial system)). A judge is also usually not disqualified solely because he or she may at one time have had an office sharing arrangement with a lawyer for one of the parties. *See Savani v. Savani*, 403 S.E.2d 900 (N.C. App. 1991); *Kinard v. Kinard*, 986 S.W.2d 220 (Tenn. Ct. App. 1998).

A judge may be disqualified, however, where the judge's former firm appears as counsel and the judge is still receiving payments from a former law firm of accounts receivable for legal services before assuming judicial office (*see* Ohio Adv. Op. 2007-2 (2007) (advising that an appearance of impropriety will always be implicated when a judge is receiving payments from a former firm)) or where there the judge is involved in litigation with her former partner, who is appearing before her (*see Chandok v. Chandok*, 968 A.2d 1196 (N.J. 2009) (trial judge should have recused self where wife's attorney was judge's former partner against whom judge had brought embezzlement and assault allegations).

When addressing a motion to disqualify based on a judge's former association with a lawyer, some state courts and judicial ethics committees utilize a "totality of the circumstances" test to determine whether a reasonable person would question a judge's impartiality. The factors courts generally look at are: (1) the nature and extent of the prior association, (2) the length of time since the association was terminated, (3) the possibility that the judge might continue to benefit from the relationship, and (4) the existence of personal or social relationships springing from the professional relationship. Leslie W. Abramson, *Appearance of Impropriety: Deciding When a Judge's Impartiality "Might Reasonably Be Questioned,"* 14 Geo. J. Legal Ethics 55 (2000), *citing Bonelli v. Bonelli*, 570 A.2d 189 (Conn. 1990) (disqualification from dissolution action not required by formal co-counsel relationship between judge and husband's lawyer in unrelated action that ended 14 months earlier). Other factors may include the size of the firm, any financial arrangement that the judge may have with the firm and the size of the judicial district. N.M. Jud. Adv. Op. 07-05 (2007). *See e.g., Kinard v. Kinard*, 986 S.W.2d 220 (Tenn. Ct. App. 1998) (judge's two-year office sharing arrangement with husband's lawyer, which ended eight years before husband sought divorce, did not require recusal, absent any indication of a social or personal relationship that would prevent the trial judge from being impartial); *In re*

Affidavit of Bias, 947 P.2d 1152 (Utah 1997) (disqualification not required where judge no longer had financial interest in former firm, had not maintained close personal relationships with members of the firm, did not represent the party and had left firm 13 years earlier); S.C. Adv. Comm. on Stand. of Jud. Conduct Op. 30-2001 (2001) (judge can hear cases of former law partner where judge has not been member of firm for four years and has divested himself of all business interests with firm); *but see James v. James*, 656 N.E.2d 399 (Ohio Ct. App. 1995) (in divorce action, husband was entitled to new trial based on fact that referee previously practiced law with wife's lawyer only seven months before case).

The Code does not provide guidance as to how long after the end of a relationship with a lawyer appearing in a case before him a judge must disqualify himself or give notice of the prior association. Some states apply a "reasonableness test," asking whether a person of ordinary prudence in the judge's position, knowing all that the judge knows, would find a reasonable basis for questioning the judge's impartiality. *See* Ariz. Sup. Ct. Jud. Ethics Adv. Comm. Op. 95-11 (1995).

The Advisory Committee on Judicial Activities, on the other hand, has recommended that a subjective standard be utilized. According to the Committee, no specific number of months must elapse before a judge begins to handle matters in which his or her former firm represents a party. Rather the key factor is the individual judge's feeling as to his or her disqualification. U.S. Jud. Conf. Comm. on Codes of Conduct Adv. Op. No 62 (1979). Other states have included specific time limits in their rules. For instance, in Illinois, a judge must disqualify from a case if within the last three years, the judge was in private practice with any law firm or lawyer representing a party (excluding cases when no monetary interest was retained). If the judge had represented the party while in private practice, the disqualification period extends to seven years. Disqualification is required even if the judge's representation of the client did not involve the matter currently before the court. Ill. Sup. Ct. R. 63C(1)(c).

Judge's Former Law Clerk Appears in Case

Judicial law clerks hold a unique position with the judges for whom they work. Beyond performing clerical and administrative tasks, law clerks may research; aid in drafting memoranda, orders, and opinions; and serve as a judge's sounding board. As a result, a clerk is likely to have insight into the judge's thoughts and viewpoints that others do not. *Fredonia Broadcasting Corp., Inc. v. RCA Corp.*, 569 F.2d 251 (5th Cir. 1978). *See generally* Nadine J. Wichern, Comment, *A Court of Clerks, Not of Men: Serving Justice in the Media Age*, 49 DePaul L. Rev. 621 (1999) (examining the relationship between law clerks and judges). Despite this seeming advantage over an opponent, judges are generally not required to disqualify themselves merely because a former law clerk appears in a case. *See Smith v. Pepsico, Inc.*, 434 F. Supp. 524 (S.D. Fla. 1977) (disqualification not required where plaintiff's lawyer had served as judge's clerk two years earlier; not reasonable to question judge's impartiality absent any other evidence); *Bonelli v. Bonelli*, 570 A.2d 189 (Conn. 1990) (disqualification not necessarily required when judge's former law clerk appears before trial judge); *Pope v. State*, 354 S.E.2d 429 (Ga. 1987) (law clerk's participation in case that was pending before the judge during the law clerk's term of service is improper, but standing alone hardly calls for a post-trial recusal of the trial judge); *Reilly by Reilly v. S.E. Pa. Transp. Auth.*, 479 A.2d 973 (Pa. 1984) (recusal not required when plaintiff's lawyer was judge's former law clerk absent any indication that lawyer was in any way involved in the case while serving as the judge's clerk).

Following a clerkship, many former clerks practice law in the same city or geographical area in which they clerked. Mandatory disqualification for every case before their former employer would unfairly penalize former law clerks. Additionally, potential clerks might be reluctant to accept a clerkship that would lessen the chances of finding employment when the clerkship ends, and the number of recruits available to judges would be limited. Ronald D. Rotunda and John S. Dzienkowski, *Legal Ethics: The Lawyer's Deskbook on Professional Responsibility* 1572 (2016); *Comparato v. Schait*, 848 A.2d 770 (N.J. 2004) (recusal of trial judge not warranted by fact that former law clerk's firm was representing wife in divorce action before judge; nothing suggests former clerk's subsequent representation of wife caused judge to be predisposed to rule against husband); *Marxe v. Marxe*, 570 A.2d 44 (N.J. Super. 1989) ("chilling effect upon present judicial system would be significant"). However, a judge may be required to recuse himself if the former law clerk was "actively involved as counsel for a party in a case in which the law clerk participated during his clerkship." *Fredonia Broadcasting Corp v. RCA Corp.*, 569 F.2d 251 (5th Cir. 1978) (judge should have recused himself when former law clerk had been on judge's staff during first trial and was subsequently employed by law firm representing plaintiff and participated in proceedings when case was before judge on remand).

Some courts have specific rules prohibiting former law clerks from practicing before a court or judge for a period after the clerkship ends. *See, e.g.*, U.S. Supreme Court Rule 7 (law clerk to U.S. Supreme Court Justice may not practice before Court for two years from date of separation); First Circuit Local Rule 46(e) (staff attorney or law clerk may not practice as an attorney in connection with any case pending in the court during the term of service, or appear at the counsel table or on brief in connection with any case heard during a period of one year following separation from service with the court); Minn. R U.S. Br. Ct. Rule 9010-3 (for a period of one year after clerkship ends, former law clerk cannot appear before judge, nor can clerk's name appear on any pleading or memorandum filed in connection with any case or adversary proceeding assigned to that judge or on any petition filed with the court unless the lawyer is a sole practitioner); Mo. Rule of Civil. Pro. 82.05 (a person who has been employed as a lawyer, law clerk, research attorney, or legal assistant by the state supreme court or by a district of the court of appeals may not appear at counsel table or sign any filing in any case before that court or district for six months after leaving employment).

In other jurisdictions, case law has determined that after a certain amount of time has elapsed following a clerkship, a judge's impartiality may not reasonably be questioned when the former clerk appears in a case. *U.S. v. Hollister*, 746 F.2d 420 (8th Cir. 1984) (judge's refusal to recuse himself when prosecutor served as judge's clerk three months earlier was not reversible error; however, a one-year recusal period is recommended); *Smith v. Pepsico, Inc.*, 434 F. Supp. 524 (S.D. Fla. 1977) (suggesting that as with former associates, recusal period of one year would be sufficient); *Ghee v. Artuz*, 285 F. Supp. 2d 328 (E.D.N.Y. 2003) (adopting rule that disqualified law clerks from appearing before the court in which they had served as a law clerk for a period of one year after the conclusion of the clerkship); *Schwartz v. Hosp. of Univ. of Pa.*, 1992 WL 102864 (E.D. Pa. 1992) (judge need not recuse himself in case litigated by former law clerk when former law clerk entered his appearance more than three years after leaving judge's employ and judge did not receive case until after clerkship expired). And some jurisdictions follow an informal policy with regard to the time between the end of a clerkship and when the former clerk may appear before the judge. *See. e.g.*, *Marxe v. Marxe*, 570 A.2d 44 (N.J. Super. 1989) ("The generally accepted policy for the Superior Court in Bergen County is to observe a one year hiatus before law clerks may appear before the judge under whom they served.").

Lawyer Currently Represents Judge

Rule 2.11(A)(1) requires a judge to disqualify himself or herself where the judge "has a personal bias or prejudice concerning a party or a party's lawyer." This provision may preclude a judge from sitting in a case in which a party is represented by a lawyer who is currently representing the judge in a separate matter, if the judge is biased for against his or her lawyer. *See, e.g.*, *In re Appleby*, 074945 (N.J. Sup. Ct. 2014) (judge suspended for one month for creating and concealing conflict with lawyer appearing before judge in two matters when judge asked lawyer to represent judge in post divorce matter); ABA Standing Comm. on Ethics and Prof'l Responsibility Formal Op. 07-449 (2007) (where lawyer is representing judge and a client who appears before that judge, judge must disqualify herself from the proceeding over which she is presiding if she maintains a bias or prejudice in favor of or against her lawyer). Absent such a bias, the judge may continue to participate in the proceeding if disqualification is waived pursuant to the requirements of Rule 2.11(C).

The participation of the judge's lawyer, however, might also create an appearance of partiality mandating disqualification. ABA Standing Comm. on Ethics and Prof'l Responsibility Informal Op. 1477 (1981); *see also Potashnick v. Port City Construction Co.*, 609 F.2d 1101 (5th Cir. 1980) (where trial judge and lawyer for a party had engaged in business dealings and where, while action was pending, lawyer represented judge in several unrelated matters, failure of judge to disqualify himself constituted an abuse of sound judicial discretion); *Texaco, Inc. v. Chandler*, 354 F.2d 655 (10th Cir. 1965) (judge disqualified because same lawyer represented judge in civil damage action and plaintiff in suit against oil company that was before judge's court); *Sargent County Bank v. Wentworth*, 500 N.W.2d 862 (N.D. 1993) (reversal of judgment required where judge trying foreclosure action had been represented by lender's law firm in unrelated action, even though record showed that judge fairly tried case and judge's findings were supported by evidence); Ariz. Comm'n on Jud. Conduct, Compl. 07-040 (2007) (judge should have recused himself rather than quash warrant based solely on a motion filed by his own attorney); Colo. Jud. Ethics Adv. Bd. Op. 2006-05 (2006) (advising that judge should disqualify himself or herself if an attorney or firm currently representing the judge, or representing the judge's adversary in a current matter, appears before the judge because the judge's impartiality might reasonably questioned and in order to avoid an appearance of impropriety); Ill. Jud. Ethics Comm. Op. 07-03 (2007) (judge who, in the midst of a dissolution of marriage discovers that the attorney who represents his spouse will be appearing before him on a regular basis, is disqualified, but, absent any personal bias or prejudice, should remit the disqualification to the parties and counsel).

Recusal is required whether the lawyer is representing the judge in a personal matter or in a matter pertaining to the judge's official position or conduct. ABA Comm. on Ethics and Prof'l Responsibility Informal Op. 1477 (1981). *See, e.g., In re Disqualification of Badger*, 546 N.E.2d 929 (Ohio 1989) (judge disqualified where lawyer representing defendant was representing judge in the judge's official position); Ariz. Comm'n on Jud. Conduct, Compl. 07-040 (Sept. 28, 2007) (judge should have disqualified himself when attorney who was representing judge before judicial conduct commission filed a motion in judge's courtroom to quash an arrest warrant on behalf of a client); Ethics Comm. of the Ky. Jud. Ethics Op. JE-96 (2002) (when judge is sued as executive head of an administrative body, judge is disqualified from cases brought by judge's lawyer or judge's lawyer's law firm); Utah Jud. Ethics Adv. Op. 00-4 (2000) (disqualification required in any proceeding involving a lawyer currently representing the judge before the Judicial Conduct Commission while the proceeding is pending and for six months after). However, disqualification will not be required where a lawyer appearing before a judge had previously represented the judge in a class action suit seeking increased compensation for all of the commonwealth's judges. The "rule of necessity" trumps the disqualification motion; otherwise, the lawyer would have to forego trial practice in the state and only those judges coming to the bench after the decision in that case would be permitted to sit in cases involving that lawyer. *Reilly by Reilly v. S.E. Pa. Transp. Auth.*, 489 A.2d 1291 (Pa. 1985).

Recusal is required regardless of whether the lawyer representing the judge charged a fee. *See* Wash. Ethics Adv. Comm., Op. 97-6 (1997) (judge must disqualify himself regardless of whether the judge receives legal services in a personal capacity from a lawyer sponsored by an organization like the ACLU, provided through an insurance company, or retained by the judge personally). However, if the lawyer's participation in the case before the judge is limited, the judge's disqualification may not be required. *See Ainsworth v. Combined Ins. Co. of America*, 774 P.2d 1003 (Nev. 1989) (lawyer's signature on an amicus brief did not constitute representation of a litigant before the judge when the lawyer also represented judge on unrelated matter and, therefore, there was no disqualifying appearance of impropriety); *In re Disqualification of Morgan*, 657 N.E.2d 1335 (Ohio 1990) (preparation of a stipulation for judge's signature does not constitute legal representation of judge).

In jurisdictions not mandating disqualification, the judge must disclose to all of the parties in a case that the judge's lawyer represents one of the parties, so that they may decide whether to move for the judge's disqualification. *See In re Frank*, 753 So. 2d 1228 (Fla. 2000) (judge publicly reprimanded for failing to disclose that his daughter's divorce lawyer was appearing in case); *Berry v. Berry*, 765 So. 2d 855 (Fla. App. 2000) (judge had affirmative duty to disqualify himself in dissolution proceeding or, at very least, to disclose his own client-lawyer relationship with the husband's lawyer); *In re Cooks*, 694 So. 2d 892 (La. 1997) (judge must disclose representation to all parties in matter pending before him and failure to make disclosure when client-lawyer relationship exists could subject judge to discipline).

Disqualification may also be mandated when a litigant is represented by one of the partners or associates of the lawyer who is representing the judge. ABA Comm. on Ethics and Prof'l Responsibility Informal Op. 1477 (1981); *Atkinson Dredging Co. v. Henning*, 631 So. 2d 1129 (Fla. App. 4th Dist. 1994) (judge should have recused herself where law firm representing one of the parties was same law firm representing trial judge in a separate, unrelated action); Ark. Jud. Ethics Adv. Comm. Op. No. 92-03 (1992) (judge must recuse himself from all cases in which the judge's lawyer's law partners appear while the litigation is pending and for a reasonable time thereafter). *But see Ex parte City of Dothan Personnel Board*, 831 So. 2d 1 (Ala. 2002) (judge not required to recuse himself where lawyer representing judge in divorce action withdrew from representing party before judge and lawyer's partner assumed responsibility for that case);

Nev. Stand. Comm. on Jud. Ethics and Election Pract. JE07-001 (2007) (judges are not disqualified from presiding over cases simply because the attorney for a party is associated with the law firm representing an association of which the judges are members before the legislature in support of legislation to increase the number of judges in the district in which the judges sit).

Some jurisdictions do not mandate automatic disqualification, but require the judge to disclose the existence of his or her relationship with the law firm and, if the party objects, the judge should recuse. Ariz. Sup. Ct. Jud. Ethics Adv. Comm. Op. 92-11 (1992) (judge could receive no benefit from partiality where same firm appearing in medical malpractice suit is also selected by judge's insurance company to defend judge in auto collision, but judge should disclose situation to all parties); Mich. Comm. on Jud. Ethics Op. J-5 (1992) (whether judges sued in official capacity and represented by private law firm required to recuse a question of law, but ethics does require disclosure to parties); Utah Jud. Ethics Adv. Op. 99-9 (1999) (judge can preside where prosecutor is in same firm as judge's private attorney so long as judge discloses same and parties do not object); Wash. Ethics Adv. Comm. Op. 93-14 (1993) (appellate judge, who retains a private attorney, should disclose same whenever any member of the attorney's firm appears before judge and disqualify self if there is an objection). *But see* Fla. Jud. Ethics Adv. Comm. Op. 99-13 (1999) (disclosure alone is insufficient; judge who is currently represented by a lawyer must recuse himself or herself whenever members of the lawyer's firm appear before the judge on contested or uncontested matters, even if the parties do not request recusal).

Lawyer Formerly Represented Judge

Courts and judicial ethics commissions offer disparate opinions on whether and for how long a judge must disqualify himself or herself from cases in which the judge's lawyer appears after the representation has concluded. Some courts have determined that disqualification is not required after the representation has ended (*see In re Snowshoe Co.*, 137 B.R. 619 (N.D. W. Va. 1991) (recusal not required where law firm represented judge prior to, and perhaps during, bankruptcy proceeding, where judge was unaware of continuing nature of representation)), while others have held that disqualification is required for a period of time following the representation (*see, e.g., Smith v. Sikorsky Aircraft*, 420 F. Supp. 661 (D.C. Cal. 1976) (judge concluded that his impartiality "might reasonably be questioned" where the firm representing the plaintiff associated a lawyer who had represented the judge in a personal matter ten years earlier and in mandamus action five years earlier); *but see Young v. Young*, 971 S.W.2d 386 (Tenn. Ct. App. 1997) (disqualification not required where lawyer's representation of judge in divorce action ended ten years earlier)). Still other courts mandate a judge's disqualification from cases in which the judge's former lawyer appears, without reference to how much time has passed since the lawyer represented the judge. *See City of Fort Lauderdale v. Palazzo Las Olas Group, LLC*, 882 So. 2d 1102 (Fla. App. 4th Dist. 2004) (disqualification of judge is required if counsel for one of the parties is representing or has recently represented the judge); *cf. Bole v. Nationwide Ins. Co.*, 379 A.2d 1346 (Pa. 1977) (when a contract calls for "disinterested" arbitrators, prior representation of one of the parties by a designated arbitrator will disqualify that arbitrator upon objection of the opposing party).

Some courts and ethics committees distinguish between a lawyer's past representation of a judge on a personal matter and representation of the judge in his or her official capacity. The former relationship may be viewed as a closer one and, therefore, more likely to warrant disqualification for a certain period of time. *See, e.g., Reilly by Reilly v. Southeastern Pa. Transp. Auth.*, 489 A.2d 1291 (Pa. Super. 1985) (judge not disqualified where lawyer had represented all commonwealth judges in class action seeking an increase in compensation); Colo. Jud. Ethics Adv. Bd. Op. 2006-05 (2006) (disqualification is not necessary after representation ends where judge was represented in an official capacity, but where judge was represented in a personal matter, the judge should continue to disqualify himself or herself for one year, unless the facts and circumstances make continued disqualification appropriate; judge should continue to disclose prior representation until the passage of time, the limited consequences of the prior matter and the nature of the judge's relationship with the lawyer have made the prior representation irrelevant); Utah Jud. Ethics Adv. Op. 00-4 (2000) (disqualification required for six months after lawyer's representation of judge before judicial conduct commission); *see generally* Leslie W. Abramson, *Judicial Disqualification under Canon 3 of the Code of Judicial Conduct* (American Judicature Society, 2d ed. 1992). Similarly, where the former representation is combined with a continuing social or professional relationship, disqualification is more likely to be mandated. *See Aetna Cas. and Sur. Co. v. Berry*, 669 So. 2d 56 (Miss. 1996) (judge should have recused himself when litigant was represented by lawyer who represented judge in divorce action and was heavily involved in judge's re-election); *cf.* Fla. Jud. Ethics Adv. Comm. Op. 93-17 (1993) (if there is a strong social relationship or the prior representation was in a "high profile" case or one of great monetary significance to judge or lawyer disclosure would be necessary).

Other courts and state ethics committees look at a series of factors to determine if a judge should disqualify himself or herself from a case involving a lawyer who previously represented the judge. The Minnesota Supreme Court held that a reviewing court should look at four factors in determining whether disqualification is required when a judge has had an attorney-client relationship with an attorney appearing before the judge. First, a court should consider the extent of the attorney-client relationship. "If the relationship consisted of a single, short episode, or even a series of sporadic contacts, disqualification of the judge is less likely than if it consisted of a long-term, continuous course of representation." Similarly, representation that had been concluded prior to the instant case is less likely to lead to disqualification than representation that is concurrent with the case. Second, the nature of the relationship should be considered. "A direct relationship, where the judge is represented personally, is more indicative of a reasonable question regarding the judge's impartiality than a relationship that only involves the judge in some institutional or technical role." Additionally, the more serious the matter for the judge, the greater the impact of the representation on the judge's impartiality. Third, the court should consider the frequency, volume, and quality of the contacts between the judge and the attorney or firm. The more frequent and substantial the contacts between the judge and the attorney or firm, the more likely the relationship is to create a reasonable question as to impartiality. Fourth, the court should consider any special circumstances that might enhance or limit the importance of disqualification, particularly in the eyes of the public. *Powell v. Anderson*, 660 N.W.2d 107 (Minn. 2003) (holding that appellate judge should have disqualified himself from hearing appeal in which law firm representing one of the parties also represented trust of which judge was trustee). *See also Washington Mut. Fin. Group LLC v. Blackmon*, 925 So. 2d 780 (Miss. 2004) (applying four *Powell* factors in holding that law firm's limited involvement with Supreme Court justices in judicial performance proceedings against fellow presiding justice did not disqualify the justices, even though the firm had filed an amicus curiae brief and represented a corporation with an interest in the outcome of the appeal) and *Aetna Cas. & Sur. Co. v. Berry*, 669 So. 2d 56 (Miss. 1996) (judge should have recused self where party's counsel had represented judge in divorce case and had been heavily involved in judge's re-election campaign).

Similarly, Illinois's judicial ethics advisory committee has advised that the following five factors should be considered when determining whether a judge's impartiality might reasonably be questioned after termination of an attorney-client relationship: (1) the number of legal matters in which the lawyer represented the judge or a member of the judge's family, (2) the complexity of the legal matters, (3) the length of time that the legal matter or matters were pending (4) the degree to which the legal matters were contested or adversarial in nature, and (5) the length of time that has elapsed since the legal representation concluded. Ill. Jud. Ethics Comm. Op. 05-01 (2005) (judge not disqualified from cases in which a lawyer appears where the lawyer was retained by the judge six years before the judge's appointment to the bench to assist the judge in responding to a letter from the Attorney Registration and Disciplinary Commission). *See also* N.Y. State Bar Ass'n Op. 574 (1986) (whether judge's impartiality might reasonably be questioned when lawyer representing a party previously represented judge depends on facts of prior representation and time that has elapsed since the representation, but recusal not automatically required when lawyer's partner or associate appears before the judge and recusal may be waived by the parties after disclosure of reasons for recusal).

Judge Appointed Lawyer to Fiduciary Position

A judge's impartiality might be called into question when sitting in a case involving a lawyer who was put into a position of trust by the court. Leslie W. Abramson, *Appearance of Impropriety: Deciding When a Judge's Impartiality "Might Reasonably Be Questioned,"* 14 Geo. J. Legal Ethics 55, 85 (2000). In two Alabama cases, lawyers who were active members of the bar, and were appointed by circuit judges to serve as guardians of conservatorships and estates, were entitled to recusal of judges in their circuits when charged with embezzlement and theft from those conservatorships and estates. The court concluded that a reasonable person would question the impartiality of the judges, whose trust the defendants were charged with breaching. *Id., citing Ex parte Price*, 715 So. 2d 856 (Ala. 1997); *Ex parte Bryant*, 682 So. 2d 39 (Ala. 1996).

Court Employee or Court Employee's Relative Is a Party or Lawyer in Case

A judge's impartiality might reasonably be questioned when a court employee is a party to a case before the judge. *See, e.g., Cook v. Struble*, 2007 WL 2947636 (N.J. Super. Ct. App. Div. 2007) (municipal judge's impartiality may be reasonably questioned when he signed a temporary restraining order for his court administrator after she discussed the matter with him).

Generally, a judge's disqualification is not mandated merely because a relative of a court employee is appearing as a lawyer or litigant in a case. *State v. Scott*, 578 N.E.2d 841 (Ohio App. 1989) (mere fact that the defense counsel was married to judge's bailiff did not result in appearance of impropriety so as to require recusal of judge); *Taylor v. Carr*, 572 N.E.2d 805 (Ohio App. 1989) (simple fact that judge's bailiff, and not judge himself, was related to one of parties to action did not require disqualification of judge; judge could have excused himself or used substitute bailiff if he felt there was appearance of impropriety, but was not required to do so); Ark. Jud. Ethics Adv. Comm. Op. 96-07 (1996) (disqualification is not required in each instance in which the spouse of the court reporter is the attorney of record); Wash. Ethics Adv. Comm. Op. 84-3 (1984) (mere fact that a fellow judge's spouse appears as a lawyer before the judge does not require the judge's disqualification). At least one jurisdiction has advised that under such circumstances, the employee, and not the judge, is disqualified. Ind. Comm'n on Jud. Qualifications Adv. Op. 4-93 (1993) (judge should issue an order stating that the intent of the court's action was to eliminate appearance of impropriety, that the employee was not to act in any capacity on cases involving the relative, and that neither was to discuss the pending court cases with the other).

The judge's disqualification may be required, however, if the relative's appearance in a case is accompanied by other factors, such as the employee's close working relationship with the judge. Utah Jud. Ethics Adv. Op. 98-14 (1998) (judge must immediately disqualify himself when case involves a member of a court employee's family or household when that employee has a close working relationship with the judge, such as the judge's clerk, bailiff, and reporter, the clerk of the court, and the trial court executive). A number of ethics committees have advised that a judge should disclose, on the record, the relationship between the court employee and the lawyer so that the opposing party may make any motions deemed necessary. *See* Ark. Jud. Ethics Adv. Comm. Op. 96-07 (1996) (disqualification is not required in each instance in which the spouse of the court reporter is the attorney of record); Utah Jud. Ethics Adv. Op. 98-14 (1998) (in cases involving a member of a court employee's family or household when employee does not have close relationship with judge, the judge should disclose the relationship and any relevant facts and circumstances and allow the parties to take whatever action they deem necessary); Wash. Ethics Adv. Comm. Op. 84-3 (1984) (when fellow judge's spouse appears as a lawyer, judge need not disqualify herself but should notify all the parties to the proceeding of the relationship and should seriously consider any party's request for recusal); Wis. Jud. Conduct. Adv. Comm. Op. 01-02 (2002) (judge must exercise discretion on a case-by-case basis in determining whether to disclose a marriage between the court reporter and the assistant district attorney).

Campaign Endorsement or Participation

As in the case of campaign contributions, the fact that a lawyer has endorsed a judge's candidacy or has agreed to be listed on a judicial candidate's campaign committee, without more, constitutes only an "insignificant interest" that does not raise a "reasonable question as to a judge's impartiality." A judge's disqualification may be required, however, if a lawyer is more actively involved in the campaign, such as serving as campaign chairperson or raising money on the candidate's behalf. *See Caleffe v. Vitale*, 488 So. 2d 627 (Fla. Dist. Ct. App. 1990) (grounds for disqualification exist when a lawyer serves as a chair of a judge's currently active campaign while litigation is in progress); *Aetna Cas. & Sur. Co. v. Berry*, 669 So. 2d 56 (Miss. 1996) (judge disqualified where a lawyer for one of the parties had formerly represented the judge and was heavily involved in judge's re-election efforts during the litigation), *overruled on other grounds by Owens v. Miss. Farm Bureau Cas. Ins.* Co., 910 So. 2d 1065 (Miss. 2005); *Doyle v. State Comm'n on Judicial Conduct*, 17 N.E.3d 1127 (N.Y. 2014) (appearance of impropriety where judge heard matters in which lawyer who exercised a leadership role and was heavily involved in judge's election campaign represented parties); *Pierce v. Pierce*, 39 P.3d 791 (Okla. 2001) (trial judge should have disqualified himself from divorce case where husband's lawyer and lawyer's father each gave $5,000 to judge's campaign and lawyer solicited contributions on judge's behalf while case was pending); Wis. Jud. Conduct Adv. Comm. Op. 03-1 (2004) (judge must, for a reasonable period of time after the cessation of the relationship, recuse himself or herself in all contested matters involving a former campaign manager but recusal is not necessarily required in matters involving former opponents or supporters who endorsed or opposed judge's election). *But see Massongill v. County of Scott*, 991 S.W.2d 105 (Ark. 1999) (judge not required to recuse himself when litigant's lawyer had served as judge's campaign treasurer, absent proof of bias or prejudice); *Nathanson v. Korvick*, 577 So. 2d 943 (Fla. 1991) (disqualification not required where party was represented by lawyer who made campaign contribution to judge's political campaign and served on campaign committee); *Reems v. St. Joseph's Hosp. and Health Center*, 536 N.W.2d 666 (N.D. 1995) (refusing to reverse jury verdict in favor of defendant hospital in medical malpractice action where defendant's lead attorney was finance co-chair of judge's re-election committee); *State v. Stockert*, 684 N.W.2d 605 (N.D. 2004) (fact that uncle of defendant's ex-wife had been trial judge's campaign manager in recently completed judicial campaign did not warrant judge's disqualification); *State v. Carlson*, 833 P.2d 463 (Wash. App. 1992) (disqualification not required where prosecutor was honorary co-chair of judge's re-election campaign, but case before judge was tried by deputy prosecutor); Okla. Jud. Ethics Op. 2007-3, 162 P.3d 986 (2007) (appearance before judge by attorney who had placed yard signs for judge during judicial campaign and had made a modest donation of $50 to judge's campaign did not require judge to recuse himself; such minimal campaign assistance would not cause a knowledgeable observer to suspect bias or undue influence).

Some jurisdictions enumerate factors that should be used in deciding whether a judge should be disqualified when a campaign participant or contributor appears in the judge's court. *See, e.g., State v. Stockert*, 684 N.W.2d 605 (N.D. 2004) (factors to consider include (1) significance of person's campaign involvement, (2) whether campaign is underway or how recently it ended, (3) whether there is ongoing relationship between person and judge, (4) significance of person's involvement in current case, including closeness or remoteness of involved individual to case, (5) whether issue was promptly raised, and (6) evidence of judicial bias); *State v. Carlson*, 833 P.2d 463 (Wash. App. 1992) (in deciding not to disqualify prosecutor who was honorary co-chair of judge's re-election campaign court looked at three factors: (1) prosecutor's specific role in the instant case, (2) size of the prosecutor's jurisdiction, and (3) unusual circumstances like the publicity surrounding the case or controversy about the prosecutor's handling of certain cases). *See also* Leslie W. Abramson, *Judicial Disclosure and Disqualification: The Need for More Guidance*, 28 Just. Sys. J. 302 (2007) (suggesting the Code should enumerate variables for state courts to use to determine if there is appearance of impartiality in cases involving campaign contributors or participants).

If a lawyer's involvement in a judge's campaign occurred several years in the past, a court may be more likely to find that the judge need not recuse from the case. For instance, in *Gluth Bros. Constr. Co. v. Union Nat. Bank*, 548 N.E.2d 1364 (Ill. App. Ct. 1989), the court found that disqualification was not required when the lawyer representing a party had served as the judge's campaign manager six years earlier. *See also Ainsworth v. Combined Ins. Co. of America*, 774 P.2d 1003 (Nev. 1989) (allegation that plaintiff's counsel acted as county campaign cochairmen in former chief justice's campaign years earlier does not constitute legally competent grounds for recusal). Courts have also declined to mandate disqualification on the basis that a party or lawyer previously worked on behalf of a judge's opponent in an election. *In re Disqualification of Celebrezze*, 657 N.E.2d 1341 (Ohio 1991) (disqualification from domestic relations matter sought by fellow judge from same general division based upon prior political campaign opposition denied).

Campaign Opponent Appears in Case

A party in a proceeding may move to disqualify a judge by asserting that he or she cannot receive a fair trial because his or her lawyer opposed the judge in an election campaign. These motions, however, are usually not successful. *See, e.g., Jones v. Kassouf & Co. P.C.*, 949 So. 2d 136 (Ala. 2006) (state supreme court justice's statement of nonrecusal where attorney for appellant and justice were electoral opponents two years earlier), citing *Reach v. Reach*, 378 So. 2d 1115 (Ala. Civ. App. 1979) (in child support proceeding, judge's recusal was not required where husband's lawyer was judge's opponent in re-election campaign and husband was lawyer's campaign manager); Nev. Stand. Comm. on Jud. Ethics and Election Practices Op. JE06-005 (2006) (judge is not disqualified from presiding over case in which party I represented by an attorney who is opponent of judge in upcoming election nor does judge need to disclose this information); *but see Tower Group, Inc. v. Doral Enterprises Joint Ventures*, 760 So. 2d 256 (Fla. Dist. Ct. App. 2000) (recusal of trial court judge was warranted where defendant's attorney had been an opponent of judge's in acrimonious judicial campaign); Ariz. Sup. Ct. Jud. Ethics Adv. Comm. Op. 04-02 (2004) (incumbent judges are required to disqualify themselves in cases filed by their announced opponents in judicial elections unless remittal occurs).

Acquaintance with Party or Witness in Case

Although a judge's longstanding, ongoing relationship with a party or witness in a case will likely require recusal (*see, e.g., In re Badeaux*, 65 So. 3d 1273 (La. 2011) (judge censured for failing to recuse from hearing divorce and custody matter involving close personal friend); Nev. Stand. Comm. on Jud. Ethics and Election Prac. JE04-002 (2004) (justice of the peace is disqualified from hearing civil eviction cases brought by owner of apartment complexes with whom judge discusses eviction matters and has a longstanding social relationship); *In re Perskie*, 24 A.3d 277 (N.J. 2011) (judge with 35-year business and social relationship with witness should have recused self from matter), a judge's casual or social acquaintance with a party or witness appearing in a case does not automatically create an appearance of impartiality requiring disqualification. Ronald D. Rotunda and John S. Dzienkowski, *Legal Ethics: The Lawyer's Deskbook on Professional Responsibility* 1558 (2016); *see, e.g., Cheney v. U.S. Dist. Ct.*, 541 U.S. 913 (2004) (Scalia, J., Mem.) (Justice Scalia denied respondent's motion to recuse from action involving Vice President Cheney; motion asserted that Justice Scalia should recuse because he was a friend of the Vice President and went with him on a hunting trip); *Cottrell v. N.C.A.A.*, 975 So. 2d 306 (Ala. 2007) (state supreme court justice's statement of nonrecusal rejecting assertion that he must recuse because he and former defendant in case were fellow law professors and friends ten years earlier); *State v. Clark*, 2007 WL 2083640 (Del. Super. 2007) (in rape case, fact that sentencing judge's spouse was an occasional patient of the victim's mother was not grounds for recusal; a reasonable person would not question the court's impartiality due to its minimal and remote connection to victim's mother); *Hill v. State*, 919 So. 2d 142 (Miss. App. 2005) (judge was under no obligation to recuse himself from capital murder case after stating on the record that he knew victim's daughter); *Commonwealth v. Perry*, 364 A.2d 312 (Pa. 1976) (fact that trial judge was acquainted with murder victim and attended his funeral did not require judge's recusal from trial of defendant); Va. Jud. Ethics Adv. Comm. Op. 01-08 (2001) (judge is not required to recuse himself or herself, and should not do so, merely because he or she is an acquaintance of a party, lawyer or witness involved in the proceeding before the judge). Mandating disqualification would be particularly egregious in smaller communities, where judges are familiar with many of the people appearing in their courts. *See Kalapp v. State*, 729 So. 2d 987 (Fla. Dist. Ct. App. 1999) (trial judge's comment that he knew everyone in his small town, including the families of the defendant and the victim, did not reasonably call the trial judge's impartiality into question); *In re Conduct of Jordan*, 624 P.2d 1074 (Or. 1981) ("judges cannot be expected to disqualify themselves in all cases in which they may be casually acquainted with parties or witnesses, particularly in smaller communities served by a single judge").

However, the existence of factors in addition to the judge's personal acquaintance may give rise to an appearance of impartiality, mandating disqualification. Ronald D. Rotunda and John S. Dzienkowski, *Legal Ethics: The Lawyer's Deskbook on Professional Responsibility* 1569 (2016). For instance, if a judge asserts that based on his acquaintance with the defendant he cannot believe she committed the crimes charged, a reasonable person might think the judge would be inclined to believe the testimony offered on the defendant's behalf. *In re Conduct of Jordan*, 624 P.2d 1074 (Or. 1981). *See also In re Hill*, 8 S.W.3d 578 (Mo. 2000) (judge required to recuse himself in case involving mayor's daughter where judge had public dispute with mayor and had spoken to mayor's daughter on many occasions); *Leombruno v. Leombruno*, 540 N.Y.S.2d 925 (N.Y. App. Div. 1989) (supreme court justice should have disqualified himself in divorce action where husband and judge lived near each other and had disagreements resulting in police intervention).

Judges also should recuse themselves if they have more than a casual social relationship with a party. *See, e.g., In re Edwards*, 694 N.E.2d 701 (Ind. 1998) (judge should have recused himself from child support proceeding when he had current and ongoing sexual relationship with mother and was contributing financially to her support); *Miss. Comm'n on Jud. Performance v. Milling*, 651 So. 2d 531 (Miss. 1995) (judge should have recused herself from criminal case after becoming personally involved with defendant); Ariz. Sup. Ct. Jud. Ethics Adv. Comm. Op. 05-01 (2005) (judge should disqualify himself or herself in any contested proceedings involving a business co-owned by a friend of the judge and the chairman of the judge's campaign committee). Additionally, a judge may be required to recuse where he or she discloses a personal relationship with a witness in a pending matter and suggests that if a motion for disqualification is filed it will be granted. *Stevens v. Americana Healthcare Corp. of Naples*, 919 So. 2d 713 (Fla. Dist. Ct. App. 2006) (where judge voluntarily disclosed a personal or social relationship with a witness in a pending matter, invited the parties to make a motion for disqualification, and suggests that the motion will be granted, the judge could not thereafter properly deny a timely motion for disqualification).

Social Relationship with Lawyer in Case

A judge's impartiality will also generally not be called into question merely because the judge has a social relationship with a lawyer appearing in a case. *See, e.g., U.S. v. Bobo*, 395 F. Supp. 1116 (N.D. Ala. 2004) (a judge's non-business relationship with counsel for a party and possible witnesses does not destroy his or her impartiality); *Matthews v. Rodgers*, 651 S.W.2d 453 (Ark. 1983) (fact that prevailing plaintiff's lawyer served as pallbearer for judge's father did not show prejudice on the part of the judge); *Schupper v. People*, 157 P.3d 516 (Colo. 2007) (judge was not disqualified from presiding over defendant's trial for theft based on judge's personal friendship with a member of prosecution team; friendship was not so close that a question of partiality might have reasonably been raised, given that judge had little present social involvement with friend, and friend appeared in theft case on only a single occasion more than five years before trial); *Demoulas v. Demoulas Super Markets, Inc.*, 703 N.E.2d 1141 (Mass. 1998) (although even limited social contact between a judge and lawyer appearing in the judge's court is discouraged, not "every chance meeting or a public social discussion between judge and lawyer" create an appearance of impartiality mandating disqualification); *State v. Dann*, 702 A.2d 105 (Vt. 1997) (allegation that judge is a "good friend" of the prosecutor is not sufficient to require recusal).

As with a judge's social acquaintances with parties or witnesses, however, factors in addition to the judge's social relationship with a lawyer may lead to an appearance of impropriety requiring disqualification. Leslie W. Abramson, *Appearance of Impropriety: Deciding When a Judge's Impartiality "Might Reasonably Be Questioned,"* 14 Geo. J. Legal Ethics 55 (2000) (*citing, Washington v. Montana Min. Properties, Inc.*, 795 P.2d 460 (Mont. 1990)) (social relationship between judge and members of law firm representing respondent did not require disqualification; however, newspaper article describing judge's social meeting with lawyers at football game "snowballed" to create an appearance of impropriety); *In re Oldfield*, 16 N.E.3d 581 (Ohio 2014) (judge publicly reprimanded for not recusing self in matters involving lawyer whom judge was allowing to stay at judge's home and whom judge was driving to work after lawyer arrested for DWI, a matter in which judge was potential witness). *See also* Ariz. Sup. Ct. Jud. Ethics Adv. Comm. Op. 05-01 (2005) (judge may not hear case involving a business co-owned by a friend of the judge who is also the chairman of the judge's campaign committee); Annotation, *Membership in Fraternal or Social Club or Order Affected by a Case as Ground for Disqualification of Judge*, 75 A.L.R.3d 1021 (1977).

Judge's Familial Connection to Case

Rule 2.11 includes provisions expressly mandating a judge's disqualification when a member of the judge's family has a connection to a proceeding. In particular, disqualification is mandatory if the judge knows that his or her spouse or domestic partner, parent or child, or another family member residing in the judge's household, has an economic interest in the subject matter in controversy or is a party to the proceeding. *See* Rule 2.11(A)(3). Disqualification is also required if the judge, the judge's spouse, or domestic partner, a person within a third degree of relationship to either of them, or that person's spouse or domestic partner is (1) a party to the proceeding or an officer, director or trustee of a party; (2) acting as a lawyer in the proceeding; (3) a person who has more than a de minimis interest that could be substantially affected by the proceeding; or (4) likely to be a material witness in the proceeding. *See* Rule 2.11(A)(2).

However, even if a judge is not disqualified under Rules 2.11(A)(2) or (A)(3), a party may seek a judge's disqualification due to the appearance of impartiality created where a relative of the judge has a connection to the case. For instance, a party may assert that the judge's impartiality might reasonably be questioned where a relative's law firm is counsel of record, even though the relative is not working on the case. *See generally* Leslie W. Abramson, *The Judge's Relative Is Affiliated with Counsel of Record: The Ethical Dilemma*, 32 Hofstra L. Rev. 1181 (2004). This argument may be successful when the lawyer in question is an equity partner with a financial interest in the case, but less likely to prevail when the relative is a non-equity associate in the firm. Since a judge's decision could have only a minimal impact on the amount of money flowing to the associate, several jurisdictions have concluded that the associate's lack of interest in the outcome of the proceeding creates neither an appearance of impartiality nor a need for disqualification. *See Keene Corp. v. Rogers*, 863 S.W.2d 168 (Tex. App. 1993) (judge's son-in-law was salaried associate at firm representing defendant and, as such, owned no interest in the firm and had no direct financial interest in the outcome). *See also U.S. ex rel. Weinberger v. Equifax, Inc.*, 557 F.2d 456 (5th Cir. 1977) (applying federal equivalent of Rule 2.11(A)); Utah Jud. Ethics Adv. Op. No. 90-3 (1990) (opines that appellate judge must be disqualified when lawyer-relative is partner in law firm of record but not if an associate with no special interest in the case); *U.S. v. Bobo*, 395 F. Supp. 2d 1116 (N.D. Ala. 2004) (if judge's relative is associate in law firm, and relative's compensation is in no manner dependent upon result of particular case before judge, recusal is not required); *cf.* S.C. Adv. Comm. on Stand. of Jud. Conduct Op. 06-2004 (2004) (Master-In-Equity need not automatically disqualify himself from a proceeding where a party is represented by a firm for which Master's son works as law clerk or practicing attorney, however, Master should disclose son's relationship with firm, allow parties to consider question out of the presence of Master, and act upon the parties' request). *But see Stephens v. Stephens*, 292 S.E.2d 689 (Ga. 1982) (judge disqualified from case in which employer of his lawyer son represented a party, since judge's impartiality might reasonably be questioned, even though there was no evidence of any wrongdoing or impropriety on part of judge, his son, or his son's employer and no direct monetary or other advantage would accrue to son as result of favorable ruling to son's employer's client); *Holloway v. Hopper*, 852 P.2d 711 (Okla. 1993) (judge required to disqualify himself where party had sought and received legal counsel from judge's wife, even though neither judge's wife nor her law firm entered appearance in case, and judge's wife never discussed case with judge); S.C. Adv. Comm. on Stand. of

Jud. Conduct Op. 15-2005 (2005) (family court judge may not hear matters in which judge's spouse's business attorney appears as counsel of record, but may hear matters in which other members of the attorney's firm appear).

A similar conclusion has been reached where the judge's relative is a government employee who has no financial interest in a case. *Trimble v. State*, 871 S.W.2d 562 (Ark. 1994) (employment of trial judge's 20-year-old son as errand boy in prosecutor's office did not require recusal of judge, even after allegations of prosecutorial misconduct were brought); *State v. Logan*, 689 P.2d 778 (Kan. 1984) (judge not disqualified from criminal case where judge's son was employed by the district attorney's office prosecuting case, but in which son was not involved); *State v. Loera*, 530 So. 2d 1271 (La. App. 1988) (judge not required to recuse himself because his daughter was an assistant district attorney). Disqualification might be required, however, where the judge's spouse, rather than a son or daughter is the government employee in question. *See, e.g., Smith v. Beckman*, 683 P.2d 1214 (Colo. App. 1984) (due to the close nature of the marriage relationship, judge was required to disqualify himself where wife was deputy district attorney, but was not involved in case); S.C. Adv. Comm. on Stand. of Jud. Conduct Op. 12-2005 (2005) (a magistrate cannot serve in same county in which spouse, who is captain of detective unit in county or spouse's employees will regularly appear before magistrate); *but see Sensley v. Albritton*, 385 F.3d 591 (5th Cir. 2004) (disqualification not required where judge's wife was employed as a state assistant district attorney in the office that was representing the defendants); *York v. U.S.*, 785 A.2d 651 (D.C. 2001) (recusal not required in assault case in which a complainant and witnesses were police officers, notwithstanding that the judge was married to a police detective and that her brother had previously been Chief of Police; judge's family relationships with police officers did not, in and of themselves, create an appearance of judicial bias warranting recusal, and there was no significant connections between the judge's relatives and the facts, parties, or witnesses involved in the assault case); *Adair v. State of Michigan*, 709 N.W.2d 567 (Mich. 2006) (employment of spouses of state supreme court justices in non-supervisory capacities by office of state Attorney General did not give rise to "appearance of impropriety" requiring recusal); *In re Disqualification of Carr*, 826 N.E.2d 294 (Ohio 2004) (denying motion for disqualification of judge whose spouse worked as a prosecutor in the same office that was prosecuting the case where the judge's spouse "neither entered an appearance in the case nor participated in the preparation or presentation of the case"); *State ex rel. Brown v. Dietrick*, 444 S.E.2d 47 (1994) (magistrate, married to police chief of small force, not automatically disqualified from issuing warrant sought by other police officers). *See generally* Leslie W. Abramson, *The Judge's Relative Is Affiliated with Counsel of Record: The Ethical Dilemma*, 32 Hofstra L. Rev. 1181, 1199–1201 (2004).

A judge's impartiality might reasonably be questioned when a relative of the judge is associated with a party to a proceeding. *See Buchanan v. Buchanan*, 587 So. 2d 892 (Miss. 1991) (party was entitled to evidentiary hearing on his post-trial motion for judicial recusal, based on his discovery that judge's son-in-law was student at medical school where other party to case was faculty member); *but see United Farm Workers of America, AFL-CIO v. Superior Court*, 170 Cal. App. 3d 97 (1985) (fact that judge's wife had worked for employer for two days during strike did not warrant disqualification of judge from action brought by employer against union arising from strike, where judge had forgotten about his wife's work until nearly two months into trial, and where judge's conduct during trial did not support inference of partiality); *cf. In re Application of Graves for Admission to Bar of State*, 677 N.W.2d 215 (N.D. 2004) (failure of State Board of Law Examiners chairperson to disclose husband's and brother-in-law's acrimonious business dealings with applicant's stepfather created possible appearance of impropriety necessitating disqualification from proceedings on applicant's petition for admission to bar; failure to make disclosure was particularly troublesome because Board's inquiry focused on applicant's involvement in stepfather's business). The judge's impartiality might also be called into question where a judge's relative works with someone who is a witness in a proceeding before the judge. *See State v. Lincoln*, 680 A.2d 110 (Vt. 1996) (judge's disqualification was warranted in drug prosecution where judge's husband was police officer who was supervised by a key state witness); *but see State v. Putnam*, 675 A.2d 422 (Vt. 1996) (disqualification not warranted, where officer who was potential witness worked in different division of barracks than judge's spouse).

Judge's Personal or Family Circumstances

Unless there is an overt display of partiality, a judge's personal and family circumstances are generally not appropriate considerations on which to presume bias or partiality for purposes of determining whether judge should be disqualified. For instance, a judge's status as an adoptive parent does not create an appearance of partiality in case seeking disclosure of information about adoption. *See In re Margaret Susan P.*, 733 A.2d 38 (Vt. 1999); *see also U.S. v. State of Alabama*, 828 F.2d 1532 (11th Cir. 1987) (minority judges not disqualified from civil rights litigation that could potentially affect their children, solely because of their minority status); Fla. Sup. Ct. Comm. on Stand. of Jud. Conduct Op. 2002-05 (2002) (judge in family division need not recuse himself or herself in litigation concerning children when the judge may potentially be involved in litigation concerning his or her children); *but see In re Woolbright*, JC-11-0004 (Ariz. Sup. Ct. 2012) (judge removed from office, in part, for hearing petitions for orders of protection without disclosing he was subject of an order of protection or disqualifying himself on that basis); *People v. Barton*, 121 P.3d 224 (Colo. App. 2004) (in case charging defendant with arson in setting wildfire in national forest judge should have granted defendant's motion to recuse where during the sentencing hearing, the judge acknowledged the impact of the fire on him and his neighbors); *Miss. Comm'n on Jud. Performance v. Bowen*, 123 So. 3d 381 (Miss. 2013) (judge hearing asbestos-related case who, after two weeks of trial, "mentioned to the attorneys in chambers that his father might have been tested for asbestosis" and then failed to provide defendant with father's name or information that both his father and mother received asbestos-related settlement monies from defendant should have recused self).

Judge or Family Member Has Been Victim of a Crime

A criminal defendant may seek to disqualify a judge from a criminal trial when the judge or a member of the judge's family has been the victim of a crime. If the judge exhibits no hostile feelings or ill will toward the defendant, the judge will likely be allowed to sit in the case. Courts may look at whether the judge has given assurances of objectivity, the judge's understanding of the concepts of the presumption of innocence and reasonable doubt, and the judge's recognition that the present defendant was not the one involved in the prior event. Additionally, the length of time since the victimization, the similarity of the incidents, and the lack of acquaintance with the present victim are to be considered. *See, e.g., State v. Mann*, 512 N.W.2d 528 (Iowa 1994) (fact that judge was sexually abused by a relative when he was a teenager is not grounds for disqualification from kidnapping and attempted murder prosecution involving sexual abuse of seven-year-old victim; judge's experience was so attenuated in time and so dissimilar in nature that no reasonable person could question judge's impartiality); *see also State v. Shabazz*, 719 A.2d 440 (Conn. 1998) (judge not disqualified from murder trial involving African-American defendant on basis that judge's father was killed in robbery by African-American; defendant's assertion of bias was "raw speculation."); *State v. Kolbet*, 638 N.W.2d 653 (Iowa 2001) (a trial judge was not required to recuse herself from the jury trial in prosecution for homicide by vehicle caused by drunk driving even though judge's father had been killed, 14 years earlier, in collision with intoxicated driver); *State v. Alderson*, 922 P.2d 435 (Kan. 1996) (judge was not required to recuse himself from a felony murder case in which the vehicle, which the defendant allegedly drove at the time of the shootings, belonged to judge's brother and was stolen from judge's father's house); Leslie W. Abramson, *Appearance of Impropriety: Deciding When a Judge's Impartiality "Might Reasonably Be Questioned,"* 14 Geo. J. Legal Ethics 55, 87 (2000).

Judge's Membership in Organization

Judges may take part in law-related and other extrajudicial organizations that help further public understanding of and respect for courts and the judicial system, as long as such participation does not appear to a reasonable person to undermine the judge's independence, integrity, or impartiality. Model Code of Judicial Conduct Rule 3.1. In general, courts have found that a judge does not have an affirmative duty to withdraw from cases that merely tangentially relate to the judge's participation in an organization or committee, unless the agenda is inconsistent with the judge's duty to judge impartially. *See State v. Knowlton*, 854 P.2d 259 (Idaho 1993) (trial judge's membership in governor's task force on child abuse did not impose affirmative duty on judge to recuse himself from probation revocation hearing involving conviction for statutory rape; nothing in makeup of task force or in its enumerated responsibilities cast doubt on judge's capacity to conduct hearing impartially); *see also Yates v. State*, 704 So. 2d 1159 (Fla. Dist. Ct. App. 1998) (Harris J., concurring) (judge not required to recuse from domestic violence case because of her participation in domestic violence task force; if the task force advocated stiffer penalties for domestic abusers, movant may have had basis for fear that judge would not be even-handed); *State v. Haskins*, 573 N.W.2d 39 (Iowa App. 1997) (judge's activities on domestic abuse coalition entailed improving the general framework of the system, not victim advocacy; therefore, it did not support claim for recusal from case involving spousal abuse); *but see In re Disqualification of Murphy*, 850 N.E.2d 712 (Ohio 2005) (judge required to disqualify from case where he was a board member of a private agency that provides residential community corrections programs and provides funding for or does business with defendant in case).

Judge's Religious Affiliation

Judges do not have an affirmative duty to withdraw from cases that merely tangentially relate to the judge's involvement with a religious organization. *Idaho v. Freeman*, 507 F. Supp. 706 (D. Idaho 1981). *State v. Wood*, 967 P.2d 702 (Idaho 1998) (common church affiliation of judge and witnesses and attorneys does not alone require recusal); *In re Disqualification of Fuerst*, 674 N.E. 2d 361 (Ohio 1996) (fact that Catholic judge presiding over a case in which Catholic Diocese of Cleveland and Catholic priest were parties was insufficient grounds to warrant disqualification under either actual bias or appearance of impropriety standards); *Treff v. Hinckley*, 26 P.3d 212 (Utah 2001) (allegation of bias based on judge's religious affiliation alone is not sufficient for recusal). *See generally* Rebekah L. Osborn, *Beliefs on the Bench: Recusal for Religious Reasons and the Model Code of Judicial Conduct*, 19 Geo J. Legal Ethics 895 (2006); Richard B. Saphire, *Religion and Recusal*, 81 Marq. L. Rev. 351 (1998).

Business Relationships and Financial Interests

Judges are not expected to abandon financial and business interests upon assuming the bench. Pursuant to Rule 3.11(A), "[a] judge may hold and manage investments of the judge and members of the judge's family." However, a judge's business relationship or financial ties with a lawyer or law firm that is counsel to a proceeding or with a party to the proceeding may create an appearance of impropriety requiring disqualification. *See U.S. v. Bobo*, 395 F. Supp. 2d 1116 (N.D. Ala. 2004) (where judge has business relationship with counsel for party to proceeding, judge's impartiality is reasonably questionable; however a judge's non-business relationship with counsel for a party and possible witnesses does not destroy his or her impartiality); *In re Drury*, 602 N.E.2d 1000 (Ind. 1992) (judge committed willful misconduct by soliciting, accepting, and failing to report a $2,000 loan from a lawyer practicing in his court; after accepting loan, the judge should have disqualified himself from all cases involving lawyer's law firm); Fla. Sup. Ct. Jud. Ethics Adv. Comm. Op. 00-34 (2000) (disqualification is required when a judge is receiving payments from a former law firm pursuant to the terms of a promissory note); *U.S. v. Gordon*, 354 F. Supp. 2d 524 (D. Del. 2005) (alleged business interactions between defendants and another judge of the district court, which might be relevant to the case, resulted in an appearance of partiality on the part of the trial judge, requiring recusal; allegations were specific enough to require inquiry, and reasonable people could question the trial judge's impartiality in matters involving a colleague's reputation and privacy). *See generally* Randall T. Shepard, *Judicial Professionalism and the Relations Between Judges and Lawyers*, 14 Notre Dame J.L. Ethics & Pub. Pol'y 223 (2000) (discussing disqualification when judge is involved in a business relationship with lawyer in case); Annotation, *Disqualification of Judge Under Section 455(b)(4) Providing for Disqualification Where Judge Has Financial or Other Interest in Proceeding*, 163 A.L.R. Fed. 575 (2000).

Two types of financial interests are often raised on motions for disqualification: ownership of real estate and stock.

Ownership of Real Estate, Including Judge as Landlord

A judge's co-ownership of property with a law firm or lawyer who appears in the judge's court generally "reflects adversely on the judge's impartiality and ability to fairly administer justice" and requires recusal, without a showing of actual bias or prejudice. *See, e.g., In re Fiftieth Dist. Court Judge*, 483 N.W.2d 676 (Mich. App. 1992) (when judge owned property on which the law firm's building was located, firm paid property taxes, and paid and discharged a mortgage for which the judge was jointly liable, automatic disqualification was required); Annotation, *Disqualification of Judge Based on Property-Ownership*

Interest in Litigation Which Consists of More Than Mere Ownership of Stock-State Cases, 56 A.L.R. 5th 783 (1998).

A landlord-tenant relationship between a judge and a lawyer may also require disqualification. There is disagreement among the state judicial ethics advisory committees as to whether judges ought to recuse themselves from cases in which one of the parties is represented by a lawyer who leases property owned by the judge. *See generally* Cynthia Gray, *The Judge as Landlord*, 23 Vt. B.J. & L. Dig. 19 (1997) (discussing division among judicial ethics advisory opinions when a lawyer rents office space in a building owned by the judge). Some states have advised that a judge may lease real property to a lawyer without having to be disqualified in cases where that lawyer appears as counsel. *See, e.g.*, Ky. Jud. Ethics Op. JE-007 (1980) ("there would seem to be no need for disqualification of the judge solely because of the existence of the landlord-tenant relationship"); Md. Jud. Ethics Adv. Op. 1979-03 (1980) (judge can hear cases involving a lawyer who leases a building from the judge); Wash. Ethics Adv. Comm. Op. 93-8 (1993) ("The relationship of landlord/tenant alone does not reflect adversely on their impartiality, interfere with the performance of judicial duties, exploit their position as judges or involve them in frequent transactions with those coming before them."). The Washington Committee also advised that the mere fact that a party or witness is either renting property or has rented property, which is managed by the judge's spouse, would not in itself require the judge's disqualification. However, the judge should disclose that his or her spouse owns the property management company if the judge's impartiality or the appearance of impartiality might reasonably be questioned because of the spouse's interest. Wash. Ethics Adv. Comm. Op. 00-5 (2000).

Other state ethics committees have suggested that judges should recuse themselves when they have a landlord-tenant relationship with a lawyer appearing in a case. *See, e.g.*, Wis. Jud. Conduct Adv. Comm. Op. 07-2 (2007) (judge may not hold shares in, or be an officer or director of a closely held corporation, which owns property that it leases as office space to law firm whose members are likely to appear before court on which judge serves). Alternatively, the judge can disclose the relationship on the record, and the parties can decide whether or not to waive disqualification. Ark. Jud. Ethics Comm. Op. 97-03 (1997). Okla. Jud. Ethics Op. 2000-1, 10 P.3d 893 (2000) (if judge's tenant appears as lawyer in contested matter, the judge must fully disclose to adverse counsel all of the circumstances of the landlord-tenant relationship, and should advise adverse counsel that the judge will recuse himself unless disqualification is waived).

Some ethics opinions assert that if the judge has leased the building to a former law partner and the law partner has subleased to another lawyer, the judge may hear cases in which the sublessee appears. However, the judge may need to disclose that the lawyer is a sublessee in a building in which the judge has an ownership interest. *See* Va. Jud. Ethics Adv. Comm. Op. 01-07 (2001) ("[a] judge is not disqualified where an attorney appears who subleases his office space from the judge's lessee unless the judge knows that his financial interests could be substantially affected by the outcome of the proceeding, or there are additional circumstances causing the judge's impartiality to be reasonably questioned.").

Ownership of Stock in a Party

While stock ownership in a party may be an "economic interest" and grounds for recusal under Rule 2.11(A)(3) if it is more than "de minimis," such ownership, regardless of whether it is de minimis, may also create in reasonable minds a perception that the judge's ability to carry out judicial responsibilities with integrity, impartiality, and competence is impaired. *See Huffman v. Ark. Jud. Disc. & Disability Comm'n*, 42 S.W.3d 386 (Ark. 2001) (judge who owned 12,000 shares of Wal-Mart stock worth about $700,000 created an appearance of impropriety in ruling on Wal-Mart's motion for a temporary restraining order against a union; recusal was required, even if ownership interest was de minimis and could not be substantially affected by judge's decision); *White v. SunTrust Bank*, 538 S.E.2d 889 (Ga. App. 2000) (judge must voluntarily disqualify herself from hearing probate matter or at least disclose her financial interest to parties where executor was bank in which judge owned stock); Tex. Comm. on Jud. Ethics Op. No. 35 (1978) (judge should recuse himself or herself from participating in litigation involving corporations in which the judge owns stock, regardless of the number of shares owned). *But see In re Disqualification of Lavrich*, 657 N.E.2d 1330 (Ohio 1990) (limited stock ownership in a bank that is a party to the action does not raise an appearance of impropriety).

A number of federal courts have addressed the question of whether a judge is disqualified from a case involving a bank that has been the victim of a crime if the judge owns stock in that bank. It would seem that the issue would come under 28 U.S.C.A. § 455(b)(4), which mandates recusal if a judge or his or her family has a financial interest in the subject matter or a party to the proceeding. However, when addressing the issue, courts have applied the general disqualification provision of Section 455(a). *See U.S. v. Nobel*, 696 F.2d 231 (3d Cir. 1982) (finding that a judge's financial interest as a stockholder in corporate victim of crime was not a "financial interest in subject matter" in controversy under Section 455(b)(4), and therefore, Section 455(a) applies). The case law on this issue has failed to produce a bright line rule, and instead courts have decided whether disqualification is required on a case-by-case basis. *See* Andrew L. Wright, Comment, *Invested in the Outcome: When the Judge Owns Stock in the Victim of a Crime*, 1998 U. Chi. Legal. F. 481 (1998) (arguing for automatic disqualification when judge owns stock in victim banks regardless of the amount of stock owned).

Three circuits, the Second, Fourth, and Ninth, have permitted a judge who owns stock in a victim bank to preside over the criminal trial. *U.S. v. Rogers*, 119 F.3d 1377 (9th Cir. 1997) (judge held a "limited financial interest" in the bank that did not appear to raise a reasonable question of impartiality); *U.S. v. Sellers*, 566 F.2d 884 (4th Cir. 1977) (stock ownership interest in the victim of a crime was an interest "so remote as to be for all practical purposes non-existent"); *U.S. v. Ravich*, 421 F.2d 1196 (2d Cir. 1970) (court focused on the size of the judge's interest and found that since it was relatively small interest, disqualification was not warranted); *U.S. v. Laurensen*, 348 F.3d 329 (2d Cir. 2005) (judge's ownership of .00009 percent of victim insurer's stock would not cause an objective observer to question judge's impartiality, and thus, did not require judge's recusal in prosecution for health care fraud). The Third Circuit, however, has held that a judge who owns a "substantial interest" in the victim of a crime must disqualify himself or herself under Section 455(a). *U.S. v. Nobel*, 696 F.2d 231 (1982). That court did not, however, define "substantial interest."

Judicial Comments

Comments by a judge during a court proceeding are usually not indicative of a disqualifying bias or prejudice as long as the judge remains open-minded and does not decide the case until all of the evidence has been heard. *Madsen v. Prudential Fed. Sav. & Loan Ass'n*, 767 P.2d 538 (Utah 1988). The standard for recusal of a federal judge based on remarks made in court is a fairly demanding one. The Supreme Court held in *Liteky v. U.S.*, 510 U.S. 540 (1994) that "[j]udicial remarks during the course of a trial that are critical or disapproving of, or even hostile to, counsel, the parties, or their cases, ordinarily do not support a bias or partiality challenge. [T]hey *will* do so if they reveal such a high degree of favoritism or antagonism as to make fair judgment impossible." *See, e.g., U.S. v. Wecht*, 484 F.3d 194 (3d Cir. 2007) (disqualification not justified by judge's allegedly hostile remarks to or about defense counsel; requisite high degree of favoritism or antagonism was not shown); *U.S. v. Nickl*, 427 F.3d 1286 (10th Cir. 2005) (judge's alleged statements during voir dire analogizing homosexuality to illegal drug use and characterizing male defendant's partner as his "wife" were arguably insensitive and inappropriate but did not suggest "such a high degree of favoritism or antagonism as to make fair judgment impossible"); *but see Sentis Group, Inc. v. Shell Oil Co.*, 559 F.3d 888 (8th Cir. 2009) (judicial comments made during court proceedings and court's statements and rulings revealed that the judge's impartiality might reasonably be questioned; while not usual standard for reassignment to different federal district judge on remand, these facts reflect a sufficiently high degree of antagonism to require reassignment).

State courts have similarly held that as long as the judge keeps an open mind about a case, the judge will be deemed to be sufficiently impartial despite certain comments. *See, e.g., City of New Haven v. Tuchman*, 890 A.2d 664 (Conn. App. 2006) (judge's statement, made during a recess, that party's demeanor might "work against him" was indicative of exasperation with party whom the judge believed was sleeping during the presentation of evidence, and fell far short of a reasonable cause for disqualification for bias or prejudice); *Banks v. Dept. of Human Resources*, 233 S.E.2d 449 (Ga. App. 1977) (judge did not err in refusing to disqualify himself in "deprived child" case when judge expressed disapproval of mother's conduct but stated that his mind was not closed and that he would hear the rest of the evidence); *Grissom v. Grissom*, 886 S.W.2d 47 (Mo. App. 1994) (judge may express his or her personal displeasure as long as it does not affect the judge's decisions); *State v. Gary*, 501 S.E.2d 57 (N.C. 1998) (judge did not manifest appearance of partiality by stating that "[i]t is readily apparent to anyone with an IQ level above room temperature that the differences between counsel and the defendant relate to trial strategy and tactics," as statement did not directly implicate either defendant or merits of case; thus, judge was not required to recuse himself); *but see Cmmw. v. Darush*, 459 A.2d 727 (Pa. 1983) (where trial judge could not affirmatively deny making derogatory remarks concerning appellant, resentencing by another judge was ordered because the comments allegedly made by the first judge could raise a reasonable question concerning his impartiality).

Some comments by a judge are clearly impermissible. For instance, racial or religious epithets and references by a trial judge to a lawyer's age, gender, or competence are improper and constitute reversible error upon showing of prejudice to defendant. *State v. Pace*, 447 S.E.2d 186 (S.C. 1994). *Mejia v. United States*, 916 A.2d 900 (D.C. 2007) (judge's comments during bench trial in which judge found defendant guilty of misdemeanor sexual abuse, to effect that there might be issues she was unclear about and immigration implications adverse to defendant and his family, indicated that appearance of bias and warranted reversal of conviction). For a discussion of the difficulty of using recusal as a tool to identify and control racial bias, see Frank M. McClellan, *Judicial Impartiality and Recusal: Reflections in the Vexing Issue of Racial Bias*, 78 Temp. L. Rev. 351 (2005) (asserting that despite the prevalence of racial bias by judges, the author could find only one published decision, *Marshall v. Georgia Pac. Corp.*, 484 F. Supp. 629 (E.D. Ark. 1980), where a judge recused herself based on racial bias).

Comments suggesting that the judge has taken a position favorable or unfavorable to a party may also require disqualification. *Alley v. State*, 882 S.W.2d 810 (Tenn. Crim. App. 1994) *aff'd by Alley v. Bell*, 307 F.3d 380 (6th Cir. Tenn. 2002) (judge's comments suggested that judge had predetermined factual issues against petitioner and judge repeatedly made references to need for swifter capital punishment); *McPherson v. U.S. Physicians Mut. Risk Retention Group*,

99 S.W.3d 42 (Mo. App. 2003) (holding that conduct or speech of a trial judge indicative of a belief as to the accused's guilt is the antithesis of impartiality); *Miller Dollarhide, P.C. v. Tal*, 163 P.3d 548 (Okla. 2007) (trial judge abused his discretion in refusing to disqualify himself where there was elevated tension between the judge and defendant and judge questioned defendant's veracity from the bench); *Jud. Inquiry & Rev. Bd. of Sup. Ct. of Pa. v. Fink*, 532 A.2d 358 (Pa. 1987) (judge's tongue-in-cheek remarks that he will favor one party over another are grossly improper, and require the judge's recusal); *In re Anderson*, 82 P.3d 1134 (Utah 2004) (juvenile court judge removed from office for ongoing situation where his impartiality might reasonably be questioned due to his intemperate remarks to government lawyers who regularly appear in his courtroom).

A judge's hostile reaction to a motion to disqualify may give rise to an appearance of impartiality. *See, e.g., Williams v. Reed*, 6 S.W.3d 916 (Mo. Ct. App. 1999) (when party's lawyer moved for disqualification of judge in child custody and support case because the judge was about to become involved in a dissolution proceeding with similar facts, judge questioned the lawyer on the source and factual basis for the allegation, called the lawyer's client to the stand, denied her request to consult with her lawyer and threatened to hold her in contempt if she failed do what he told her to do, told the lawyer that he was personally insulted and chastised the lawyer for filing a baseless motion).

To be disqualifying, the comments usually must indicate a personal bias or prejudice about a party. *See Green v. State*, 631 So. 2d 167 (Miss. 1994) (judge not disqualified from murder trial in which handgun was alleged murder weapon, even though judge stated at sentencing that he advocated strict handgun control; while judge's comment was clearly a statement reflecting judge's personal bias, it was not "personal bias or prejudice concerning a party," as contemplated by Code of Judicial Conduct provision governing disqualification).

Comments indicating a judge's personal moral conviction or which "reflect prevailing societal attitudes" are insufficient alone to mandate disqualification." *U.S. v. Norton*, 700 F.2d 1072 (6th Cir. 1983) (judge's general statements with respect to prevailing societal attitudes toward American Nazi Party and Ku Klux Klan did not evidence prejudicial attitudes that would require judge to recuse himself). However, when a judge's remarks indicate to a reasonable person that the judge's decision has been predetermined or adversely affected by personal experiences, a reviewing court will often find a disqualifying appearance of bias, even if the judge is not in fact biased. *See, e.g., Gibson v. U.S.*, 792 A.2d 1059 (D.C. 2002) (judge's comments, prior to imposing maximum possible sentence for armed voluntary manslaughter, regarding pain that his grandfather's murder caused his mother and the fact that nobody had been punished because the "life of a black man was thought to be not worth anything" created an appearance of bias sufficient to require recusal at sentencing). Similarly, comments indicating that the judge has an opinion about a litigant's trial strategy are not permissible. *Cmmw. v. Berrigan*, 472 A.2d 1099 (Pa. Super. 1984) (trial judge should not have commented on what he perceived to be defendants' trial strategy, as comments indicated to public way in which he viewed their position).

A judge's opinion or comments based on information the judge acquired during a current or prior proceeding do not stem from an extrajudicial source, and are generally not grounds for disqualification. Leslie W. Abramson, *Appearance of Impropriety: Deciding When a Judge's Impartiality "Might Reasonably Be Questioned,"* 14 Geo. J. Legal Ethics 55 (2000), *citing Ex parte Duncan*, 638 So. 2d 1332 (Ala. 1994) (judge's statements, in capital murder prosecution, that he was "tempted" to say that additional statutory aggravating circumstance of offense being especially heinous, atrocious, or cruel compared to other capital offenses had been proven, and that there was no excuse or justification for the "vile, conscienceless, pitiless murder," did not show bias, hostility, or prejudice against defendant arising from personal source so as to require recusal). *See also Barca v. Barca*, 546 A.2d 887 (Conn. App. 1988) (judge's comment in divorce action that husband lied on a financial statement did not demonstrate prejudice; comments did not stem from "extrajudicial source" since they were made after judge heard most of the evidence and statements related to the defendant's credibility and, therefore, were directed to the merits of the case rather than to the parties); *but see Jefferson-El v. State*, 622 A.2d 737 (Md. 1993) (judge's statement that jury's verdict was an "abomination" warranted recusal; source of bias, whether personal or extrajudicial, is not dispositive when issue is whether, having made statements evidencing bias against defendant and/or his or her cause, trial judge thereby created situation in which it would appear that judge could not, with impartiality, preside at subsequent trial). In a jury trial, statements made before the jury is impaneled and in no way communicated to the jury cannot constitute bias or prejudice. *Irvin v. State*, 49 S.W.3d 635 (Ark. 2001) (judge's statement to defendant that judge would tape defendant's mouth closed if he did not stop talking was not made in the presence of the jury and, therefore, did not constitute bias or prejudice).

Statements to the Press or Public

A judge's comments to the press may give rise to a disqualification motion if the comments indicate that the judge prejudged the case and is not able to approach the case from a detached and impartial perspective. *Roatch v. Puera*, 534 N.W.2d 560 (Minn. App. 1995); *see also U.S. v. Microsoft*, 253 F.3d 34 (D.C. Cir. 2001) (judge's interviews with reporters, which were highly critical of defendant and their defenses, created appearance of impartiality; members of public could reasonably question whether judge's desire for press coverage influenced his judgments). However, it does not necessarily follow that any interview or public comments by a judge about a pending case mandate disqualification. Whether the judge is disqualified by his or her public comments depends on the content of the comments and whether they indicate that the judge can be fair and open-minded. *Compare Papa v. New Haven Fed'n of Teachers*, 444 A.2d 196 (Conn. 1982) (judge's interview with newspaper concerning pending proceeding involving teachers' strike was a violation of Code of Judicial Conduct; since interview and judge's finding in response to it raised reasonable question about his ability to remain fair and impartial, trial judge erred in denying motion for recusal) *with Roatch v. Puera*, 534 N.W.2d 560 (Minn. App. 1995) (judge's statement in a newspaper that a pending case "might set a precedent" did not indicate that the judge prejudged the merits of the case of that the judge's impartiality could reasonably be questioned).

Statements to the press may also implicate Rule 2.10(A) of the Model Code, which provides that while a proceeding is pending or impending, a judge shall not "make any public statement that might reasonably be expected to affect the outcome or impair its fairness. . . ." Model Code of Judicial Conduct Rule 2.10(A).

Constitutional Challenges

As noted in Canons 1 and 4, the constitutionality of Code provisions that require judges to disqualify themselves if they have made a public statement that "commits or appears to commit" themselves has been challenged with varying degrees of success. However, most cases that have addressed the issue have held that the disqualification provisions that burden speech to the extent that judges may be hesitant to express their views on issues for fear that they may later have to recuse themselves survive strict scrutiny. *Indiana Right to Life, Inc. v. Shepard*, 463 F. Supp. 2d 879 (N.D. Ind. 2006) *rev'd in part on other grounds*, 507 F.3d 545 (7th Cir. 2007) (holding that recusal clause did not violate First Amendment); *Family Trust Found. of Ky. v. Wolnitzek*, 345 F. Supp. 2d 672 (E.D. Ky. 2004) (judicial Canon regarding recusal did not violate First Amendment due to vagueness); *N.D. Family Alliance v. Bader*, 361 F. Supp. 2d 1021 (D.N.D. 2005) (Canon requiring judges to recuse themselves from those proceedings in which their impartiality might reasonably be questioned was narrowly tailored to serve compelling state interest in maintaining judicial impartiality). For criticism of the amendment to the Rule, see Matthew J. Medina, *The Constitutionality of the 2003 Revisions to Canon 3(E) of the Model Code of Judicial Conduct*, 104 Colum. L. Rev. 1072 (2004) (examining the constitutionality of the ABA's revised disqualification rule in light of *White*, concluding that the rule is unlikely to survive strict scrutiny) and James Bopp, Jr. and Anita Y. Woudenberg, *An Announce Clause by Any Other Name: The Unconstitutionality of Disciplining Judges Who Fail to Disqualify Themselves for Exercising Their Freedom to*

Speak, 55 Drake L. Rev. 723 (2007) (asserting that "[o]ne cannot avoid the constitutional prohibition on disciplining judges for exercising their First Amendment right simply by labeling that discipline as a recusal").

Improper Comments or Actions of Judge's Law Clerk

Improper actions by the judge's law clerk can also lead to a reasonable appearance of impartiality and bias on the part of the judge. "Because of the close working relationship between judges and their law clerks, there comes a point where a law clerk's bias for or against a particular party or attorney, or a law clerk's potential interest in the outcome of particular litigation, rises to an intolerable level—a level where the judicial decision-making process comes under reasonable suspicion." *Vaska v. State*, 955 P.2d 943 (Alaska App. 1998) (case remanded to determine whether law clerk's revealing confidential memo to prosecutor created an appearance of partiality), *rev'd on other grounds*, 135 P.3d 1011 (Alaska 2006). *But see In re Corrugated Container Antitrust Litigation*, 614 F.2d 958 (5th Cir. 1980) (judge cannot be disqualified because of the actions and statements attributed to his law clerk). *See also* Code of Conduct for Law Clerks (1981); John Paul Jones, *Some Ethical Considerations for Judicial Clerks*, 4 Geo. J. Legal Ethics 771 (1991).

Judge Participated in Prior Case Involving Party

The fact that a judge sat on a prior case involving a party or a particular issue or ruled on prior matters in the case before the judge is legally insufficient as grounds for recusal. *See, e.g., In re Heather L.*, 874 A.2d 796 (Conn. 2005) (judge's participation in previous petition to terminate father's parental rights, by itself, did not warrant judge's disqualification from presiding over subsequent petitions to terminate parental rights involving other children, absent any showing that judge was biased against father); *Petition of Wittrock*, 649 A.2d 1053 (Del. 1994) (judge who presided over defendant's criminal trial is not required to recuse himself from hearing defendant's post-conviction motion); *Alexander v. State*, 623 S.E.2d 160 (Ga. Ct. App. 2005) (evidence judge who signed defendant's arrest warrant was same judge who presided over defendant's trial for aggravated sodomy, aggravated assault with intent to rape and burglary, without more, was legally insufficient to warrant recusal); *Poorman v. Commonwealth*, 782 S.W.2d 603 (Ky. 1989) (judge who made rulings at defendant's probable cause and bond hearings was not required to recuse herself when, as an appellate judge, she considered the same case on appeal; court agreed that a judge should not sit in review of a case she decided, but since appellate court did not review any previous decisions made at the trial court level, recusal was not necessary); *Farmer v. State*, 770 So. 2d 953 (Miss. 2000) (trial judge who heard guilty plea that was later overturned is qualified to sit for subsequent trial absent some showing of actual prejudice or bias); *Barlett By and Through Barlett v. Kansas City Southern Ry. Co.*, 854 S.W.2d 396 (Mo. 1993) (judge who presided over probate proceedings to have motorist injured in train accident declared incompetent was not required to recuse himself or herself from acting as judge in jury trial brought by representatives of motorist against railroad); *but see Perotti v. State*, 806 P.2d 325 (Alaska App. 1991) (judge's participation in sentencing hearing, after having participated in juvenile waiver hearing and exposed himself to improperly compelled psychiatric evidence, created appearance of partiality).

The judge's disqualification is not mandated even if the judge made an adverse ruling against the party in the first proceeding. *See Pride v. Harris*, 882 P.2d 381 (Alaska 1994) (disqualification not warranted in personal injury even though in previous child custody proceeding, judge reached negative conclusions regarding plaintiff's fitness as a parent and did not award him custody); *Tracey v. Tracey*, 903 A.2d 679 (Conn. App. 2006) (adverse rulings by the judge do not amount to evidence of bias sufficient to support a claim of judicial disqualification); *Weber v. State*, 547 A.2d 948 (Del. 1988) (judge is not disqualified per se because of adverse decision in former case involving entirely different and unrelated criminal charges against same party; judge stated that he barely remembered earlier case, which occurred several years earlier and that he had no bias for or against defendant); *Luce v. Cushing*, 868 A.2d 672 (Vt. 2004) (to establish prejudice "it is not enough merely to show the existence of adverse rulings, no matter how erroneous or numerous, or that the judge expressed a comment or opinion, uttered in the course of judicial duty, based upon evidence in the case"); *but see Watson v. State*, 934 A.2d 901 (Del. 2007) (appearance of bias was sufficient to cause doubt as to impartiality of Family Court judge who presided over juvenile's rape trial ten minutes after she found juvenile delinquent on unrelated assault and robbery charges, warranting judge's recusal from rape trial where both cases turned on juvenile's credibility). *See generally* Annotation, *Disqualification of Judge for Having Decided Case Against Litigant-State Cases*, 85 A.L.R. 5th 547 (2001).

Judge Participated in Prior Case Involving Criminal Codefendant

In criminal cases, there is no per se disqualification when a judge who has presided over the trial and sentencing of a codefendant presides over the trial of the defendant, even if the judge has heard unfavorable remarks about the defendant in the prior proceedings. *State v. Ellison*, 140 P.3d 899 (Ariz. 2006); *Manning v. Engelkes*, 281 N.W.2d 7 (Iowa 1979) (on motion by prosecution to dismiss pending criminal charge, trial judge was not under obligation to recuse himself merely because he had previously presided over separate trial of codefendant); *Boyd v. State*, 581 A.2d 1 (Md. 1990) (trial judge was not actually biased or prejudiced when he decided case of defendant charged with first-degree murder of her husband, notwithstanding that judge had previously decided case against codefendant); *State v. Page*, 709 N.W.2d 739 (S.D. 2006) (judge not required to recuse from sentencing criminal defendant even though he had sentenced co-defendant to death).

Judge Previously Served as Prosecutor in Criminal Case against Party

When a former prosecutor assumes the bench as a judge, he or she may confront defendants that he or she prosecuted in the past. Generally, a judge is not automatically disqualified from a criminal case where he or she prosecuted the defendant in an earlier, unrelated case. Leslie W. Abramson, *Appearance of Impropriety: Deciding When a Judge's Impartiality "Might Reasonably Be Questioned,"* 14 Geo. J. Legal Ethics 55, 81–82 (2000); *see, e.g., Irvin v. State*, 49 S.W.3d 635 (Ark. 2001) (fact that trial judge had formerly prosecuted defendant on other charges while serving as elected prosecuting attorney did not require recusal, absent any actual showing of bias or prejudice); *State v. Bunker*, 874 A.2d 301 (Conn. App. 2005) (judge's participation in defendant's probation modification proceeding that was unrelated to instant information did not warrant recusal) appeal dismissed, 909 A.2d 521 (Conn. 2006); *People v. Harris*, 498 N.Y.S.2d 893 (N.Y. App. Div. 1986) (judge's failure to recuse himself from robbery case, though he prosecuted defendant for grand larceny five years earlier, did not require reversal of defendant's robbery conviction); *Cmmw. v. Darush*, 459 A.2d 727 (Pa. 1983) (refusing to adopt a per se rule that a judge who had participated in the prosecution of a defendant may never preside as judge in future unrelated cases involving that defendant). *But see State v. Kettles*, 785 A.2d 925 (N.J. Super. Ct. App. 2001) (where judge, as assistant prosecutor, had presented evidence to a grand jury against the defendant in another case recusal was required and could not be waived by defendant); *State v. Murchison*, 687 N.W.2d 725 (N.D. 2004) (possibility that trial judge may have prosecuted defendant years ago on a prior offense did not warrant recusal of judge in prosecution for assault on a correctional institution employee). *See generally* Annotation, *Prior Representation or Activity as Prosecuting Attorney as Disqualifying Judge from Sitting or Acting in Criminal Case*, 85 A.L.R. 5th 471 (2001). Paul M. Friedman, Comment, *Don't I Know You From Somewhere?: Why Due Process Should Bar Judges From Presiding Over Cases When They Have Personally Prosecuted the Defendant*, 88 J. Crim. L. & Criminology 683 (1998).

In determining whether disqualification is required, factors to be considered include (1) whether there is a relationship between the two criminal proceedings, (2) the amount of time between the two proceedings, and (3) whether the past prosecution is relevant to the current case. Leslie W. Abramson, *Appearance of Impropriety: Deciding When a Judge's Impartiality "Might Reasonably Be*

Questioned," 14 Geo. J. Legal Ethics 55, 81–82 (2000). *Compare State v. Neeley*, 748 P.2d 1091 (Utah 1988) (trial judge was not required to recuse himself from case where judge determined he had no actual bias against defendant by reason of his involvement in defendant's prosecution 20 years earlier); *State v. Pellerin*, 670 A.2d 255 (Vt. 1995) (recusal not required where judge, while serving as state's attorney, signed information charging defendant with prior offense 22 years earlier, despite defendant's claim that judge's imposition of more severe sentence upon remand established presumption of vindictiveness) *with W.I. v. State*, 696 So. 2d 457 (Fla. App. 1997) (where presiding judge had prosecuted petitioner as a juvenile two years earlier, petitioner had a well-founded fear that he would not receive a fair trial before that judge).

If the prior conviction prosecuted by the judge could be used in sentencing, disqualification may be more necessary. *Compare Goines v. State*, 708 So. 2d 656 (Fla. Dist. Ct. App. 1998) (disqualification from drug case required where judge, when employed by the State Attorney's Office, had prosecuted defendant on drug charges six years earlier, and facts and circumstances of prior conviction would be used in sentencing) *with Cooper v. State*, 879 S.W.2d 405 (Ark. 1994) (trial judge need not recuse himself or herself where judge had previously prosecuted the defendant for two separate crimes that were to be used for sentence enhancement purposes).

Disqualification is more likely to be required where the judge was previously involved as a prosecutor in the criminal case *currently* pending before the judge. *See, e.g., Duerst v. Goldstein*, 654 So. 2d 1004 (Fla. App. Ct. 1995) (judge must disqualify himself from resentencing following reversal of death sentence when judge, while a former assistant state attorney, delivered document to trial lawyer during defendant's original trial and was supervising state attorney of division in which defendant was tried at time of defendant's conviction); *In re Detention of Hargett*, 786 N.E.2d 557 (Ill. App. 3d Dist. 2003) (judge who appeared on behalf of state in defendant's prior prosecution erred by not recusing himself from proceeding); *Jenkins v. State*, 570 So. 2d 1191 (Miss. 1990) (defendant was denied fair and impartial trial when judge, who was prosecuting attorney when defendant's indictment was returned, refused defendant's request for judge to disqualify himself; reasonable person who knew judge acted as prosecutor during indictment would question's judge's impartiality); *but see People v. Thomas*, 556 N.E.2d 1246 (Ill. App. 1990) (judge not required to recuse himself in DUI prosecution where judge had previously been chief of the criminal division of state's attorney's office and had supervisory authority over the defendant's case for approximately six months but did not act as counsel in case). Disqualification may also be required if the judge sitting in a civil case served as a prosecutor in a criminal case arising out of the same "matter in controversy." *Rushing v. City of Georgiana*, 361 So. 2d 11 (Ala. 1978).

Most jurisdictions hold that if the judge was merely employed in the prosecutor's office, but did not work on the defendant's case, disqualification is not required. Richard E. Flamm, *Judicial Disqualification: Recusal and Disqualification of Judges*, 328–29 (Aspen Publ'g Inc., 1996); *see, e.g., People v. Julien*, 47 P.3d 1194 (Colo. 2002) (mere fact that trial judge had been employed by district attorney's office five weeks before his assignment to defendant's case was not sufficient basis for disqualifying judge based on an appearance of bias where judge did not participate in investigation, preparation, or presentation of case against defendant and did not have any other involvement with case, such as being a supervising attorney of the attorneys conducting the prosecution, or gaining personal knowledge of disputed evidentiary facts of the case in his former employment); *State v. Connolly*, 930 So. 2d 951 (La. 2006) (trial judge sitting in post-conviction proceedings is ordinarily not disqualified solely by virtue of his or her prior employment as an assistant district attorney in the office responsible for prosecuting the petitioner); *State v. Whittey*, 821 A.2d 1086 (N.H. 2003) (trial judge was not required to recuse herself from murder prosecution, even though defendant claimed judge was employed with attorney general's office during period of time defendant's case was being investigated; judge did not serve as a lawyer in the matter in question, and nothing in the record indicated that judge had any direct involvement in the defendant's case by participating in the investigation or preparation of the case, or that she acquired any personal knowledge about the evidence in the case).

However, courts are split over whether a judge, who previously served as the head of an office, such as district attorney or attorney general or served in another supervisory capacity in such an office, is disqualified from presiding over a case pending in that office while he served in that position. *See, e.g., Ex parte Sanders*, 659 So. 2d 1036 (Ala. Crim. App. 1995) (judge who was district attorney when case files were first delivered to the office for investigation was required to recuse himself from the case, even though cases were nolle prossed and defendant was re-indicted, as he had been lawyer of record for case against defendant); *State ex. rel Corbin v. Superior Court*, 748 P. 2d 1184 (Ariz. 1987) (judge who was supervisory member of staff of prosecuting attorneys' office while defendant's murder case was tried, original sentence imposed, and direct appeal decided, was required to recuse himself from defendant's resentencing proceedings later assigned to him); *King v. State*, 271 S.E.2d 630 (Ga. 1980) (district attorney is "of counsel" in all criminal "cases" or matters pending in his circuit and would be disqualified from serving as judge in such cases); *Frierson v. State*, 606 So. 2d 604 (Miss. 1992) (judge should have recused himself on his own motion where judge served as district attorney at time defendant was initially indicted); Del. Jud. Ethics Adv. Comm. Op. 2007-03 (2007) (judge may not preside over criminal proceedings on charges filed when that judge was Attorney General). *But see Payne v. State*, 265 So. 2d 185 (Ala. Crim. App. 1972) (judge, who while serving as assistant attorney general was not assigned to criminal work, was not required to recuse himself in prosecution for crime committed on while serving in that position); *Rodriguez v. State*, 489 S.W.2d 121 (Tex. Crim. App. 1972) (where it was not shown that judge who had served as first assistant to criminal district attorney had actually investigated, advised, or participated in case in any way, judge was not disqualified from sitting). Annotation, *Prior Representation or Activity as Prosecuting Attorney as Disqualifying Judge from Sitting or Acting in Criminal Case*, 85 A.L.R.5th 471 (2001) (discussing judicial split). A criminal defendant may waive his or her objection to a trial judge, who was district attorney at time defendant was indicted, hearing his or her case by entering a voluntary plea of guilty and by specifically stating that he or she does not object to judge sitting in his or her case. *Banana v. State*, 635 So. 2d 851 (Miss. 1994) (although judge was district attorney when defendant was indicted for forgery, disqualification was not required because defendant was given an opportunity to object to judge sitting in case but conferred with lawyer and specifically waived objection).

The U.S. Supreme Court ruled in *Williams v. Pennsylvania*, 579 U.S. ___ (June 9, 2016), that the chief justice of the Pennsylvania Supreme Court should have granted a motion to disqualify himself in a case where he had been the district attorney who approved seeking the death penalty when defendant's case was initially prosecuted. Twenty-eight years after the case was decided, a post-conviction petition was granted by the lower court, criticizing the original conviction for, among other issues, *Brady* violations within the district attorney's office. On the state's appeal to the Pennsylvania Supreme Court, defendant filed a motion seeking the chief justice's recusal/disqualification or referral of that motion to the entire court. The chief justice denied the motions, heard the appeal, voted with the unanimous court to reverse the lower court, and wrote an opinion castigating the lower court.

In a 5–3 decision written by Justice Anthony Kennedy, the U.S. Supreme Court determined that the participation by the Pennsylvania chief justice in hearing the defendant's case—the failure to recuse—violated due process. The Court concluded, "The due process guarantee that 'no man can be a judge in his own case' would have little substance if it did not disqualify a former prosecutor from sitting in judgment of a prosecution in which he or she had made a critical decision." The Court rejected the argument of the Pennsylvania chief justice that his approval, as district attorney, to seek the death penalty for Williams was not a "significant, personal involvement in a critical trial decision." As such, the Pennsylvania chief justice's participation in the appeal "gave rise to an unacceptable risk of actual bias" that "so endangered the appearance of neutrality" that participation in the appeal must be forbidden to preserve due process.

The Court further noted that the due process rule represented the "outer boundaries of judicial disqualifications" because the ABA Model Code of Judicial Conduct and rules adopted by the various states are more stringent and require disqualification under circumstances such as this fact situation. The court implied that, under the Pennsylvania Code of Judicial Conduct applicable at the time, recusal/disqualification would have been required.

Judge Represented Party in Unrelated Case

Prior representation of a party with regard to matters wholly unrelated to the case presently before a judge, or only tangentially related to such matters, does not automatically mandate judicial qualification. Richard E. Flamm, *Judicial Disqualification: Recusal and Disqualification of Judges*, 310–20 (Aspen Publ'g Inc., 1996); *Beckum v. State*, 917 So. 2d 808 (Miss. App. 2005) (defendant in robbery trial did not overcome presumption of judge's impartiality by showing that judge formerly represented defendant as defense counsel on prior unrelated charge).

Some jurisdictions have delineated factors a court should look at to determine whether there exists a reasonable basis for doubting the judge's impartiality when a judge has previously represented a party in an unrelated matter including (1) the nature of the prior representation, (2) the duration of the client-lawyer relationship, (3) the extent to which the prior representation might in some limited way be related to the current case, and (4) the lapse of time between the prior representation and the appearance of the former client before the judge. *In re Edwards*, 694 N.E.2d 701 (Ind. 1998) (judge not obligated to disqualify himself from child visitation and support disputes because of his prior representation of mother in unrelated criminal proceeding that occurred one year and five years prior to visitation and support hearings); *State v. Pearson*, 698 N.W.2d 338 (Iowa Ct. App. 2005) (judge need not recuse herself where she previously represented defendant in probation revocation hearing); *State v. Ellis*, 889 A.2d 1 (N.H. 2005) (judge's prior representation in civil matter of defendant's non-lawyer representative, by itself, did not warrant judge's disqualification from presiding over trial for criminal trespass); *but see Ex Parte Atchley*, 951 So. 2d 764 (Ala. Crim. App. 2006) (evidence established appearance of impropriety sufficient to warrant recusal of judge where defendant stated in his affidavit that when judge represented him in previous criminal case, the two had heated confrontation because, he says, judge tried to coerce him into pleading guilty and refused to follow his wishes concerning resolution charge, and judge did not dispute defendant's account of confrontation or fact of his representation); *State v. McCann*, 919 A.2d 136 (N.J. Super. Ct. App. Div. 2007) (municipal court judge was required to recuse himself from presiding over proceeding in which application for search warrant for defendant's residence was sought, where judge had a long-term client-lawyer relationship with defendant). Other factors that might be considered are the amount of compensation paid and whether the judge voluntarily disclosed the representation to all of the parties. *See Robin Farms, Inc. v. Bartholome*, 989 S.W.2d 238 (Mo. App. 1999) (judge's prior representation of party in her capacity as personal representative of estate did not create appearance of impropriety in subsequent lawsuit, where suits were unrelated and dissimilar, they came several years apart, and fee was paid by estate).

Judge Currently Represents Party Appearing Before Him

A judge may not sit in a case in which one of the parties is being represented by the judge in a separate case. *Ohio State Bar Assn. v. Vukelic*, 811 N.E.2d 1127 (Ohio 2007) (part-time magistrate publicly reprimanded for failure of part-time magistrate to immediately transfer to a different jurisdiction for resolution cause in which his client in pending domestic relations case appeared before him in mayor's court on two charges for commission of criminal misdemeanors and allowing case against his client to be discussed in his presence).

Judge Participated in Same Case Involving Party

A judge may be required to recuse himself or herself where the judge presided over the same case involving the same party. *See, e.g., State v. Moore*, 988 So. 2d 597 (Ala. Crim. App. 2007) (state sufficiently demonstrated an appearance of impropriety in having judge who presided over defendant's trial for capital murder, and who subsequently granted defendant's motion for new trial and dismissal of indictment, preside over defendant's retrial, thus warranting judge's recusal; great deal of animosity existed between judge and the prosecutor, as judge was frustrated with prosecutor's failure to comply with its orders, and in dismissing the indictment, judge made factual findings concerning the credibility of some of the state's evidence, the strength of the state's case against defendant, and the credibility of a statement that defendant made to police).

Usually this issue arises when the judge participated in an earlier stage of the case, such as by issuing a search or arrest warrant. *See, e.g., Brent v. State*, 929 So. 2d 952 (Miss. Ct. App. 2005) (judge's failure to recuse himself was manifest error where prior to selection as circuit court judge, judge served as county court judge, and in that capacity, issued search warrant that led to defendant's arrest and indictment that brought defendant before judge in his capacity as circuit court judge, attack on validity of warrant signed by judge was major element of defense, so judge was essentially asked to review his former ruling on his issuance of search warrant, and judge formerly prosecuted defendant on charge of aggravated assault which was used to charge defendant as habitual offender); *State v. McCann*, 919 A.2d 136 (N.J. Super. Ct. App. Div. 2007) (municipal court judge was required to recuse himself from presiding over proceeding in which application for search warrant for defendant's residence was sought, where judge had a long-term client-lawyer relationship with defendant); *but see Hirning v. Dooley*, 679 N.W.2d 771 (S.D. 2004) (though it is the better practice to allow a different judge than the one who issued a search warrant to rule upon the validity of the warrant, it is not required); *State v. Chamberlin*, 162 P.3d 389 (Wash. 2007) (judge did not need to recuse from hearing on motion to suppress evidence seized pursuant to a search warrant issued by judge). A judge would also likely be required to disqualify himself or herself in the unusual circumstances in which the judge participated in a defendant's arrest. *See, e.g., Disc. Counsel v. Parker*, 876 N.E.2d 556 (Ohio 2007) ("By participating in this defendant's arrest, respondent impermissibly crossed the line between law enforcement and the judiciary, establishing strong evidence of an actual bias. He then exacerbated an already irreparably tainted situation by failing to disqualify himself from proceedings involving the defendant.").

Disciplinary Complaints

Party or Lawyer Filed against Judge

A judge is not automatically disqualified merely because a party or a lawyer appearing in a case has filed a judicial conduct complaint against the judge. *See Keene v. State*, 938 S.W.2d 859 (Ark. App. 1997) (recusal from criminal trial not required where defendant has filed complaint against judge with judicial disciplinary commission); *5-H Corp. v. Padovano*, 708 So. 2d 244 (Fla. 1997) (neither a previously filed complaint against the judge with the Judicial Qualifications Commission, nor the expressed intent to file a complaint constitute legally sufficient grounds for recusal); *Cherradi v. Andrews*, 669 So. 2d 326 (Fla. App. 1996) (party's expressed intent to file complaint against judge alone legally insufficient to require recusal); *State v. Millsap*, 704 N.W.2d 426 (Iowa 2005) (defendant's filing of complaint and letter writing campaign against judge did not require recusal); *Demoulas v. Demoulas*, 732 N.E.2d 875 (Mass. 2000) (party's filing of complaint judge with Judicial Conduct Commission did not require judge's recusal, absent showing that the complaint caused the judge to be biased or prejudiced against the party); *In re Antonio*, 612 A.2d 650 (R.I. 1992) (mere filing of complaint against judge not ground for recusal on appearance of impropriety basis); *Ball v. Melsur Corp.*, 633 A.2d 705 (Vt. 1993) (disqualification not required where plaintiffs' lawyer had filed ethical complaint against judge six or eight years earlier). Ariz. Sup. Ct. Jud. Ethics Adv. Comm. Op. 98-2 (1998) (automatic recusal not required when litigant has filed disciplinary complaint against judge); Ill. Jud. Ethics Comm. Op. 95-5 (1995) (judge not required to disqualify himself when lawsuit or disciplinary complaint filed against him); Neb. Jud. Ethics Adv. Comm. Op. 05-2 (2005) (judge need not recuse himself in a case during the pendency of which a pro se litigant in the action informs the judge that he has filed a complaint against the judge); Tenn. Jud. Ethics Comm. Op. 99-3 (1999) (complaint filed with Court of the Judiciary does not require judge's disqualification); Utah Jud. Ethics Adv. Op. 05-3 (2005) (disqualification is not required simply because a disciplinary complaint has been filed); Wash. Ethics Adv. Comm. Op. 98-4 (1998) (judge not required to be disqualified despite actual notice of complaint filed); *but cf. Siegel v. State*, 861 So. 2d 90 (Fla. App. 4th Dist. 2003) (trial judge should have disqualified herself from case where defendant's attorney had not only filed bar complaint alleging unprofessionalism against judge while she was state prosecutor but also attempted to prevent her appointment to the bench by accusing her of being unfit).

Mandating disqualification under such circumstances would permit manipulation of the court and judge-shopping by allowing litigants to eliminate judges they find unsatisfactory merely by filing a complaint against them. *In re Illuzzi*, 670 A.2d 1264 (Vt. 1995). *See also In re Ronwin*, 680 P.2d 107 (Ariz. 1983) ("[t]o honor such a technique would be to put the weapon of disqualification in the hands of the most unscrupulous"). Alternatively, a lawyer may withhold a legitimate complaint against a judge that would bar subsequent appearances before that judge. Either outcome "could undermine the integrity and goals of the judicial conduct review process." *Ball v. Melsur Corp.*, 633 A.2d 705 (Vt. 1993). However, a judge's recusal may be required if in response to the lawyer's judicial conduct complaint, the judge has harsh words with the lawyer in private and makes an affirmative effort to publicize the dispute. *See In re Conduct of Schenck*, 870 P.2d 185 (Or. 1994) (cumulative effect created a reasonable basis for questioning the judge's impartiality); *In re Stigler*, 607 N.W.2d 699 (Iowa 2000) (judge should have recused himself from ruling on temporary attorney-fee application where one party was represented by lawyer who had filed complaint against judge with Commission on Judicial Qualifications, and judge expressed a bias against that lawyer because of that complaint); *In re Bissell*, 429 S.E.2d 731 (N.C. 1993) (judge censured for barring lawyer from courtroom due to judge's angry feelings toward lawyer for initiating investigation of judge; when interest or prejudice may compromise the objectivity of a judge, the proper course of action is the judge's own recusal).

Judge Filed against Lawyer

A judge is also not automatically disqualified merely for reporting perceived lawyer misconduct to the state bar or disciplinary authorities. *U.S. v. Mendoza*, 468 F.3d 1256 (10th Cir. 2006) (judges do not demonstrate possible bias or prejudice, for purposes of subsequent recusal motion, when they discharge obligation to alert disciplinary authorities to possible unethical conduct by attorneys); *Joyner v. Comm'r of Correction*, 740 A.2d 424 (Conn. App. 1999) (habeas judge who asked the state grievance committee and the state's attorney to investigate lawyer's actions and who called state's attorney for status of investigation did not indicate bias or the appearance of a bias that would call into question his ability to decide the case impartially); *5-H Corp. v. Padovano*, 708 So. 2d 244 (Fla. 1997) (judge's report of perceived lawyer unprofessionalism to the Florida Bar is, in and of itself, legally insufficient to support that judge's disqualification); *cf. Conklin v. Warrington Twp.*, 476 F. Supp. 2d 458 (M.D. Pa. 2007) (court's decision to sanction landowner's counsel for unprofessional conduct in action brought against township, alleging unlawful application of local zoning ordinances, did not require judge's recusal); *State ex rel Metsch v. Traeger*, 834 So. 2d 877 (Fla. App. 2d Dist. 2002) (petitioners were not entitled to disqualification of trial court judge based on judge's appointment to serve as referee in pending disciplinary action against opposing counsel); Utah Jud. Ethics Adv. Op. 05-02 (2005) (judge is not automatically disqualified from a proceeding in which the judge has (1) previously held one of the lawyers in contempt; (2) sanctioned one of the attorneys; or (3) referred one of the lawyers to the Office of Professional Conduct). *But see Ex Parte Rollins*, 495 So. 2d 636 (Ala. 1986) (evidence that judge had filed complaint against lawyer with bar association alleging perjury, political vindictiveness and unfitness to practice law, and had asserted that lawyer was in some way responsible for letter criticizing judge that was published in local newspaper was sufficient to support contention that judge was biased against lawyer requiring recusal). *See also* Rule 2.15 regarding judges' disciplinary responsibilities.

WAIVER OF AN APPEARANCE OF IMPARTIALITY

If a judge is disqualified from a proceeding under Rule 2.11(A), the parties may waive disqualification unless the basis for disqualification is personal bias or prejudice against a party. Model Code of Judicial Conduct Rule 2.11(C). However, there is disparity between state and federal courts, as well as disagreement among the states, as to whether a party may waive disqualification when the judge's impartiality "might reasonably be questioned."

Federal Courts

Under federal statutes, a party may waive disqualification of a federal judge *only* if the ground for disqualification is that the "judge's impartiality might reasonably be questioned." If the ground for disqualification is one of those specifically enumerated in the subsections following the general provision, the parties may not waive disqualification. 28 U.S.C. § 455(e) (1994). In order to waive disqualification under the federal statute, the waiver must be preceded by a full disclosure on the record of the basis for disqualification. 28 U.S.C. § 455(e) (1994). The statute does not require that the waiver be in writing. However, in 1980, the Judicial Conference of the United States adopted a rule requiring that the parties and the lawyers, independently of the judge's participation, all agree in writing that the judge's disqualification should be waived. 101 F.R.D. 373, 392–93 (1980).

State Courts

Rule 2.11(C) of the Model Code of Judicial Conduct permits parties to waive disqualification unless it is grounded in a judge's personal bias or prejudice under Rule 2.11(A). After the judge discloses on the record the basis for the judge's disqualification, he or she may ask the parties to consider, outside the presence of the judge and court personnel, whether to waive disqualification. If the lawyers and parties, without the participation of the judge or court personnel, all agree that the judge should not be disqualified, the judge may participate in the proceeding. The agreement must be incorporated into the record of the proceeding. *See* Model Code of Judicial Conduct Rule 2.11(C). *See also City of Prattville v. Joyner*, 698 So. 2d 122, 124, n.1 (Ala. 1997) (since all parties had not filed a remittal of disqualification, judge transferred case to another judge); *Woods v. Durkin*, 539 N.E.2d 920 (Ill. App. Ct. 1989) (oral waiver by lawyers of judge's disqualification is insufficient); Ill. Jud. Ethics Comm. Op. 95-2 (1995) (judge is disqualified when lawyer who represents him in matrimonial matter appears before him; disqualification may be waived); *but see F.D.I.C. v. O'Malley*, 618 N.E.2d 818 (Ill. 1994) (although judge who has disclosed his disqualification must obtain written remittal before continuing with trial, parties must exercise due diligence and cannot use lack of written remittal as basis for new trial, in absence of actual prejudice, where they do not pursue matter until unfavorable judgment has been entered against them).

JUDGE HAS PERSONAL BIAS OR PREJUDICE OR KNOWLEDGE OF FACTS IN DISPUTE

Personal Bias or Prejudice

Rule 2.11(A)(1) states that a judge should disqualify himself or herself if the judge has a "personal bias or prejudice concerning a party or a party's lawyer, or personal knowledge of facts that are in dispute in the proceeding." An identical provision applies in federal court. *See* 28 U.S.C.A. § 455(b)(1); *see generally* Leslie W. Abramson, *Specifying Grounds for Disqualification in Federal Court*, 72 Neb. L. Rev. 1046 (1993). However, Louisiana has not adopted a comparable provision in their judicial conduct code and several states do not require disqualification if a judge has bias toward a party's lawyer.

To be disqualifying, a bias or prejudice must be personal rather than judicial (*Alley v. State*, 882 S.W.2d 810 (Tenn. Crim. App. 1994)) and generally must concern a party, not an issue (*see, e.g., Scheehle v. Justs. of the Sup. Ct. of the State of Ariz.*, 120 P.3d 1092 (Ariz. 2005) (under judicial Canon requiring disqualification for bias and prejudice, "bias and prejudice" means a hostile feeling or spirit of ill-will toward one of the litigants); *Papa v. New Haven Fed'n of Teachers*, 444 A.2d 196 (Conn. 1982) (judge presiding over attempt to enjoin teachers' strike is not disqualified because prior to the case he gave a speech criticizing teachers' strikes generally; extrajudicial statements concerning legal issues do not disqualify judges); *State v. Smith*, 242 N.W.2d 320 (Iowa 1976) ("only personal bias or prejudice, as distinguished from judicial predilection, constitutes a disqualifying factor"); *State v. Walker*, 153 P.3d 1257 (Kan. 2007) (bias and prejudice exist if a judge harbors a "hostile feeling or spirit of ill will against one of the litigants, or undue friendship or favoritism toward one"); *In re Barrows*, 917 A.2d 490 (Vt. 2007) (fact that judge who presided over post-conviction relief proceeding also participated in the underlying criminal case, did not preclude the judge from deciding post-conviction relief petition; any knowledge acquired by judge during pretrial proceedings was not "personal" but was information acquired by judicial proceedings which judges are routinely expected to set aside in presiding over subsequent cases of an accused)).

When a lawyer is simultaneously representing a judge and a litigant who is appearing before the judge in a separate matter, the judge must disqualify himself or herself if he or she maintains a bias or prejudice either in favor of or against the lawyer. ABA Standing Comm. on Ethics and Prof'l Responsibility Formal Op. 07-449 (2007). This disqualification obligation also applies when another lawyer in the lawyer's firm is representing a litigant before the judge. *Id.*

A judge's personal convictions or attitudes alone are usually insufficient to require disqualification. *Scheehle v. Justs. of the Sup. Ct. of the State of Ariz.*, 120 P.3d 1092 (Ariz. 2005) (that judge may have opinion as to merits of the cause, or a strong feeling about the type of litigation involved, does not make the judge biased or prejudiced and therefore subject to disqualification); *State v. Page*, 709 N.W.2d 739 (S.D. 2006) ("opinions formed by the judge on the basis of facts introduced or events occurring in the course of the current proceedings, or of prior proceedings, do not constitute a basis for a bias or partiality motion unless they display a deep-seated favoritism or antagonism that would make fair judgment impossible"); *Alley v. State*, 882 S.W.2d 810 (Tenn. Crim. App. 1994); *but see In re Boothe*, 110 So. 3d 1002 (La. 2013) (recusal is required not only when judge is biased or prejudiced against a party but also when judge is "personally interested in the cause to such an extent that he would be unable to conduct a fair and impartial trial"); *Voss v. State*, 856 N.E.2d 1211 (Ind. 2006) (judge's bias or prejudice with respect to a substantial issue in a case, even if not directly related to a party or a party's lawyer, can equally impair impartiality and should mandate disqualification); *State v. Dorris*, 2006 WL 925728 (Wash. Ct. App. 2006) (sex offender was denied due process in proceedings for revocation of his Special Sex Offender Sentencing Alternative (SSOSA) suspended sentence, where revocation was based on allegations involving sex and pornography, and judge repeatedly and specifically admitted his bias on those issues, including his "real problems" with SSOSA and allowing convicted sex offenders to have treatment and remain in community).

Litigants are entitled to a judge who will hear both sides and decide an issue on the merits of the law and the evidence presented. However, they are not entitled to a judge whose mind is a clean slate. Every judge "brings to the bench the experiences of life, both personal and professional. A lifetime of experiences that have generated a number of general attitudes cannot be left in chambers when a judge takes the bench." *Madsen v. Prudential Fed. Sav. & Loan Ass'n* 767 P.2d 538 (Utah 1988). *Dept of Revenue v. Golder*, 322 So. 2d 1 (Fla. 1975) ("It would appear from this commentary that the ABA's drafting committee specifically rejected the notion that judges should disqualify themselves for previously developed or expressed legal expertise."). Similarly, at least one jurisdiction has held that the fact that a judge may have or develop during the trial an opinion, or a bias or prejudice, does not make the trial judge so biased and prejudiced as to require his or her disqualification. *Irvin v. State*, 49 S.W.3d 635 (Ark. 2001); *Noland v. Noland*, 932 S.W.2d 341 (Ark. 1996). *See generally* Jeffrey M. Shaman, *The Impartial Judge: Detachment or Passion?*, 45 DePaul L. Rev. 605 (1996).

A party seeking judicial disqualification must clearly and affirmatively show bias or prejudice. *Cliche v. Fair*, 487 A.2d 145 (Vt. 1984). Prior adverse rulings against a party alone do not create the appearance of impropriety. *Liteky v. U.S.*, 510 U.S. 540 (1994) (judicial rulings alone almost never constitute a valid per se basis for a bias or partiality motion"); *see also In re I.B.M. Corp.*, 618 F.2d 923 (2d Cir. 1980) (rulings and conduct of trial judge legally insufficient for recusal under federal statute or Fifth Amendment due process); *Irvin v. State*, 49 S.W.3d 635 (Ark. 2001) (absent objective showing of bias or prejudice, recusal not required by appellate reversal and remand for new trial); *Weber v. State*, 547 A.2d 948 (Del. 1988) (trial judge not required to disqualify himself after having presided over prior unrelated trial of defendant); *Rivera v. State*, 717 So. 2d 477 (Fla. 1998) (trial judge's written opposition to consideration of executive clemency in response to parole commission inquiry does not warrant disqualification); *Reems v. St. Joseph's Hosp. and Health Center*, 536 N.W.2d 666 (N.D. 1995) (trial judge's rulings did not indicate a lack of impartiality despite fact lead attorney for defendant was co chair of judge's campaign finance committee); *but see Watson v. State*, 934 A.2d 901 (Del. 2007) (family court judge should have recused herself from juvenile's rape trial after having found juvenile delinquent on unrelated assaulted and robbery charges ten minutes earlier; court distinguished *Weber* noting that in that case judge's adverse ruling against defendant occurred several years earlier and judge barely remembered earlier case). A trial judge must be free to make rulings on the merits without the apprehension that if he makes a disproportionate number in favor of one litigant, he may have created the impression of bias. *In re I.B.M. Corp.*, 618 F.2d 923 (2d Cir. 1980). In addition, a judge's mere expression of opinion, "uttered in what [the judge] conceived to be the discharge of his judicial duty, based upon evidence produced before him" is not sufficient proof of bias or prejudice. *Pettengill v. New Hampshire Ins. Co.*, 270 A.2d 883 (Vt. 1970) *quoting Leonard v. Willcox*, 142 A. 762 (Vt. 1928). As with the appearance of impartiality, instances of actual bias or prejudice are usually fact-bound and therefore, must be examined on a case-by-case basis. Ronald D. Rotunda and John S. Dzienkowski, *Legal Ethics: The Lawyer's Deskbook on Professional Responsibility* 1579 (2016).

Extrajudicial Source Doctrine

In order for a judge's alleged bias to be disqualifying, it "must stem from an extra-judicial source and result in an opinion on the merits on some basis other than what the judge learned from his [or her] participation in the case." *Carter v. State*, 271 S.E.2d 475, 477, (Ga. 1980) *quoting U.S. v. Grinnell Corp.*, 384 U.S. 563 (1966). The moving party must show that the alleged bias, hostility, or prejudice is "personal" not "judicial." *Ex parte Duncan*, 638 So. 2d 1332 (Ala. 1994). "[O]pinions formed by the judge on the basis of facts introduced or events occurring in the course of the current proceedings . . . do not constitute a basis for a bias or partiality motion unless they display a deep-seated favoritism or antagonism that would make fair judgment impossible." *Liteky v. United States*, 510 U.S. 540, 555 (1994). *See also State v. Greenway*, 823 P.2d 22 (Ariz. 1991) (state law has held judge can separate admissible evidence from inadmissible and no error for judge to preside over codefendant's separate trials; therefore no recusal required absent showing of bias or prejudice); *Carter v. State*, 271 S.E.2d 475 (Ga. 1980) (bias must stem from an extrajudicial source and result in findings based upon something other than what the judge learned from participating in the case); Utah Jud. Ethics Adv. Comm. Op. 98-12 (1998) (bias or prejudice is illustrated by words or conduct that is undeserved, excessive, or results from an extrajudicial source). *Cf. State v. Eric M.*, 858 A.2d 767 (Conn. 2004) (sentencing judge's consideration of newspaper article, in which defendant stated that he and assault victim practiced consensual bondage before and during their marriage, did not reflect judicial bias requiring recusal where defendant did not establish that statements in article were materially false or unreliable or did dispute that he made them).

Knowledge gained in a prior proceeding is also generally not a sufficient ground to disqualify a judge in a subsequent matter. *See Ex parte Duncan*, 638 So. 2d 1332 (Ala. 1994) (judge's opinion based on information heard during a current or even an earlier proceeding does not stem from an extrajudicial source and is usually not considered to be grounds for disqualification); *State v. Rameau*, 685 A.2d 761 (Me. 1996) (knowledge judge acquired during criminal trial and fact that he referred to notes from that trial is insufficient to warrant recusal from subsequent probation proceeding); *State v. Stokcert*, 684 N.W.2d 605 (N.D. 2004) (when personal knowledge about a matter has been obtained by a judge within another legal proceeding, disqualification is not called for); *State v. Lohnes*, 432 N.W.2d 77 (S.D. 1988) (judge not disqualified even though he sat on two prior proceedings involving same matter). Definite views on the law or judicial predilection do not stem from an extrajudicial source and are also not disqualifying. *Dept. of Rev. v. Golder*, 322 So. 2d 1 (Fla. 1975) (the Code commentary indicates that the ABA's drafting committee specifically rejected the notion that judges should disqualify themselves for previously developed or expressed legal expertise).

The extrajudicial source doctrine applies when disqualification is sought for actual bias as well as for an appearance of impartiality. *Liteky v. U.S.*, 510 U.S. 540 (1994). *See generally* Jeremy S. Brumbelow, Note, *Liteky v. United States: The Extrajudicial Source Doctrine and Its Implications for Judicial Disqualification*, 48 Ark L. Rev. 1059 (1995); Adam J. Safer, Note, *The Illegitimacy of the Extrajudicial Source Requirement for Judicial Disqualification under 28 U.S.C. § 455(A)*, 15 Cardozo L. Rev. 787 (1993).

No Waiver of Personal Bias or Prejudice

When a judge has a personal bias or prejudice concerning a party, disqualification may not be waived. Rule 2.11(C) provides, in part, that "[a] judge subject to disqualification under this Rule, *other than for bias or prejudice* under paragraph (A)(1), may disclose on the record the basis of the judge's disqualification and may ask the parties and their lawyers to consider, outside the presence of the judge and court personnel, whether to waive disqualification." [emphasis added] Some jurisdictions have held that this waiver exclusion also applies if a judge has a bias or prejudice for or against a lawyer or law firm. *See State v. Davis*, 284 S.E.2d 51 (Ga. App. 1981) (judicial prejudice against counsel would vicariously result in judicial prejudice against a represented party and judge is required to recuse himself); *In re Platt*, 8 P.3d 686 (Kan. 2000) (judge publicly censured for refusing to automatically disqualify himself from proceedings involving lawyers against whom he harbored personal bias; distinction between bias against party or party's lawyer is dubious); ABA Standing Committee on Ethics and Professionalism Formal Op. 07-449 (2007) (a judge's bias or prejudice for or against a lawyer makes disqualification mandatory, with no possibility of waiver); Ohio Adv. Op. 2007-2 (2007) (remittal of disqualification, in most circumstances, will not be appropriate when a judge is receiving money from a former firm).

Actions of Party or Lawyer Intended to Create Bias

Courts frown upon manipulation of the impartiality issue in order to gain procedural advantage, and generally adhere to the notion that "[s]chemes to drive a judge out of a case . . . should not be allowed to succeed." *State v. Ahearn*, 403 A.2d 696 (Vt. 1979) *quoting* A.B.A. Standards Relating to the Judge's Role in Dealing With Trial Disruptions, § F.5, at 21 (1971). Therefore, a lawyer or party who acts deliberately and with the intent to cause the judge to become biased and prejudiced against him or her is not entitled to have the judge disqualified. *See, e.g., State v. Jeffers*, 661 P. 2d 1105 (Ariz. 1983) (defendant was not entitled to have trial judge disqualified from resentencing him where defendant admitted sending judge unsolicited goods from mail-order firms); *People v. Page*, 702 N.Y.S.2d 552 (Co. Ct. 2000) (judge's viewing of defendant's post-verdict disturbance in courtroom did not warrant judge's disqualification from sentencing); *City of Las Vegas Downtown Redevelopment Agency v. Hecht*, 940 P. 2d 134 (Nev. 1997) (lawyer supported judge's opponent in election and subsequently argued that judge had an express or implied bias against her; motion for disqualification denied).

For instance, when a party hires a particular lawyer or law firm in order to obtain the judge's recusal, it is the lawyer or firm, rather than the judge, that may be disqualified. *See, e.g., In re BellSouth, Corp.*, 334 F.3d 941 (11th Cir. 2003) (law firm rather than judge is disqualified where party contrived to obtain judge's recusal by hiring firm in which judge's nephew is a partner); *McCuin v. Texas Power & Light, Co.*, 714 F.2d 1255 (5th Cir. 1983) (counsel may not be chosen by parties to litigation solely or primarily for purpose of disqualifying the judge, and district court threatened with such maneuvers need not confine itself to grievance proceedings against errant counsel); *Grievance Adm'r. v. Fried*, 570 N.W.2d 262 (Mich. 1997) (lawyer's appearance as co-counsel filed principally to obtain judge's recusal is ground for lawyer discipline); Utah State Bar Ass'n Ethics Adv. Op. Comm. Op. 01-03 (2001) (discussing ethical considerations where lawyer seeks to disqualify judge from case by associating a lawyer from the judge's prior law firm).

A party also may not try to obtain a judge's disqualification by physically attacking the judge and then claiming that the judge is biased against him or her. *See Bigby v. Drekte*, 402 F.3d 551 (5th Cir. 2005) (defendant is not entitled to automatic recusal of trial judge based only on defendant's physical attack on judge; such per se rule would lead to deliberate manipulation of judicial system); *Wilks v. Israel*, 627 F.2d 32 (7th Cir. 1980) (defendant's deliberate attack on trial judge calculated to disrupt the proceedings will not force the judge out of the case); *State v. Ahearn*, 403 A.2d 696 (Vt. 1979); *State v. Bilal*, 893 P.2d 674 (Wash. App. 1995) (recusal from sentencing not required where defendant assaulted judge immediately after verdict). *See also State v. Brown*, 825 P. 2d 482

(Idaho 1992) (disqualification not required when a party had made death threats against the judge); Utah Jud. Ethics Adv. Op. 98-12 (1998) (disqualification is not required because judge orders extra security measures in response to a risk posed by a particular party; such action does not constitute bias or prejudice); Annotation, *Disqualification of Judge Because of Assault or Threat Against Him By Party or Person Associated With Party*, 25 A.L.R.4th 923 (1983).

Ex Parte Communications

Ex parte communications may indicate partiality since, by definition, they involve one party to the exclusion of another. However, courts have declined to adopt a categorical rule that whenever a judge engages in an ex parte communication, the judge is deemed to be partial, biased, or prejudiced such that disqualification is mandated. Generally, to support a reasonable inference of a judge's prejudice or appearance of prejudice against a party or lawyer, the communication must stem from or be motivated by actual or apparent bias for or against a party or lawyer. *In re Young*, 984 P.2d 997 (Utah 1999). *See also S.S. v. Wakefield*, 764 P.2d 70 (Colo. 1988) (motion for disqualification denied because judge's ex parte communication with party regarding effectiveness of lawyer was not sufficient evidence of bias); *Disc. Counsel v. Karto*, 760 N.E.2d 412 (Ohio 2002) (judge should have immediately recused himself from juvenile delinquency proceedings after ex parte communication with prosecutor; instructing prosecutor to bring felony charges against juvenile indicated bias); *but see In re Moses W.*, 842 N.E.2d 783 (Ill. App. Ct. 2006) (judge's ex parte communication with juvenile about factual matter at issue in connection with state's petition to revoke juvenile's probation required judge's recusal even though judge's affidavit, indicated that he maintained "an open mind and objective perspective on what disposition may be most appropriate"). *See generally* Leslie W. Abramson, *The Judicial Ethics of Ex Parte and Other Communications*, 37 Hous. L. Rev. 1343 (2000). *See also* Rule 2.9 and accompanying text regarding Ex Parte Communications.

Even if an ex parte communication does not indicate actual bias or prejudice, it may warrant disqualification under the general standard of Rule 2.11(A) by creating an appearance of impartiality. *See In re Morton*, 770 N.E.2d 827 (Ind. 2002) (judge publicly reprimanded, in part, for engaging in and failing to disclose ex parte communication with father's lawyer in child custody proceeding; the combination of all of the facts indicate that a reasonable person would have doubted Respondent's impartiality); *In re K.L.W.*, 131 S.W.3d 400 (Mo. Ct. App. 2004) (ex parte communications between child's former foster parent and family court commissioner and hand-written notes on former foster parent's letters, if placed there by commissioner, would cause reasonable layman to question propriety of communications and commissioner's actions and to conclude that there was at least an appearance of impropriety); *Disc. Counsel v. Medley*, 756 N.E.2d

104 (Ohio 2001) (judge violated Code when he talked to a newly arrested defendant on the telephone, and then picked her up at the police station and drove her home, even though judge and defendant did not discuss the facts or merits of her case; actions gave impression of bias on judge's part when it came time to hear the case).

Animosity toward Counsel

Under Rule 2.11(A)(1), a judge's antipathy toward a lawyer in a proceeding may raise an issue as to the judge's ability to render impartial justice to that lawyer's client. *See, e.g., In re Platt*, 8 P.3d 686 (Kan. 2000) (judge should have automatically disqualified himself from hearing cases involving lawyer whom judge accused of lying in connection with prior matter and against whom judge admitted harboring personal bias); *Davis v. Neshoba County General Hosp.*, 611 So. 2d 904 (Miss. 1992) (recusal required where personal tension between plaintiff's counsel and judge would lead reasonable-minded person to question whether the judge would have personal bias or prejudice concerning plaintiff); *Wilson v. Com.*, 630 S.E.2d 326 (Va. 2006) (judge's failure to recuse himself was an abuse of discretion where the judge's actions reflected a personal bias and prejudice against defendant's counsel and raised concerns about the judge's impartiality and about the public's perception of his fairness in the case). *See generally* Annotation, *Disqualification of Judge for Bias Against Counsel for Litigant*, 54 A.L.R. 5th 575 (1998). A judge's friendliness or favorable treatment of a lawyer may also be raised as an issue, but is far less common.

To mandate disqualification, a judge's antipathy toward a lawyer generally must be extreme, *United States v. Ahmed*, 788 F. Supp. 196 (S.D.N.Y. 1992); *City of Las Vegas Downtown Redev. Agency v. Hecht*, 940 P.2d 127 (Nev. 1997) (judge's campaign comments about attorney's contributions to opponent did not show egregious facts to demonstrate bias); *In re Duckman*, 898 A.2d 734 (Vt. 2006) (judge not disqualified from presiding over summary criminal contempt proceedings despite previous hostile disputes with attorney). *See also* Richard E. Flamm, *Judicial Disqualification: Recusal and Disqualification of Judges*, 121–24 (Aspen Publ'g. Inc., 1996) ("to warrant judicial disqualification . . . the judge's bias toward the attorney ordinarily must be extreme. Situations in which judges have manifested such extreme bias toward an attorney are exceedingly rare") or accompanied by other prejudicial circumstances. *Ohio State Bar Ass'n v. Evans*, 999 N.E.2d 674 (2013) (judge who retaliated against contract public defender by removing lawyer from all cases assigned to judge's courtroom violated rule requiring a judge to disqualify self when judge's impartiality might reasonably be questioned); *Wash. Mut. Fin. Group LLC v. Blackmon*, 925 So. 2d 780 (Miss. 2004) (judge's conduct warranted recusal where he said he did not want defendant's attorney appearing in the court building as court-appointed attorney, he believed that defendant's changing his request from bench trial, to jury trial, then back to bench trial stemmed from attorney's "shenanigans" to avoid being tried by trial judge; he suggested to chief judge that he be assigned the case because a defendant shouldn't be allowed "to avoid a particular courtroom solely by asking for a jury trial," and he rejected plea agreement agreed to by Commonwealth and defendant).

Some courts have held that where hostility toward the lawyer is not also accompanied by evidence of bias against the party, recusal will not be required. *See, e.g., Henderson v. Dept. of Pub. Safety & Corrections*, 901 F.2d 1288 (5th Cir. 1990) (bias for or against attorney, who is not party, is not enough to require disqualification of judge unless it can also be shown that such controversy would demonstrate bias for or against the party itself); *A.J. by L.B. v. Kierst*, 56 F.3d 849 (8th Cir. 1995) (controversy between judge and lawyer does not require disqualification of judge in absence of proof of bias or judicial prejudice to parties); *U.S. v. Carignan*, 600 F.2d 762 (9th Cir. 1979) (judge's 4-year-old squabble with defendant's attorney in previous case statutorily insufficient and no violation of due process); *Draper v. Reynolds*, 369 F.3d 1270 (11th Cir. 2004) ("bias against a lawyer, even if found to exist, without more is not bias against his client") *quoting In re Drexel Burnham Lambert, Inc.*, 861 F.2d 1307, 1314 (2d Cir. 1988); *Ainsworth v. Combined Ins. Co. of America*, 774 P. 2d 1003 (Nev. 1989) (allegation of judge's bias in favor of or against counsel for litigant states insufficient ground for disqualification because it is not indicative of extrajudicial bias against a party); *Reilly by Reilly v. S.E. Pa. Transp. Auth.*, 489 A.2d 1291 (Pa. 1985) (animosity between a lawyer and a judge, standing alone, is irrelevant in the absence of allegation of bias toward the party); *cf. State v. Cherichel*, 2006 WL 2529561 (Minn. App. 2006) (judge who called defendant's expert witness's testimony "junk science" need not recuse himself because he did not express personal bias or prejudice concerning defendant or defendant's lawyer; "[b]ecause the Canon does not prohibit a judge from hearing a case when the judge has an unfavorable opinion of a party's witness, the trial judge's statements do not demonstrate [a violation]"); *but see Wilson v. Com.*, 630 S.E.2d 326 (Va. 2006) (finding that judge whose comments exhibited personal prejudice against defendant's counsel should have recused himself because an apparent bias against a litigant's attorney gives rise to a perception that by the litigant and the public that the judge may not be fair and impartial in the conduct of the proceeding). Other courts have found that prejudice against a lawyer is sufficient grounds for disqualification, but have denied the motion because the movant failed to provide sufficient evidence of bias. *See S.S. v. Wakefield*, 764 P.2d 70 (Colo. 1988) (motion denied because judge's ex parte communication with party regarding effectiveness of lawyer was not sufficient evidence of bias); *In re Young*, 984 P.2d 997 (Utah 1999) (improper ex parte conversation about pending fee request to lawyer did not require disqualification of judge for partiality, absent evidence that judge was motivated by any personal or extrajudicial bias or prejudice concerning parties or their lawyers).

Separate Action against Judge

A judge is not disqualified simply because a litigant sues or threatens to sue the judge. *U.S. v. Grismore*, 564 F.2d 929 (10th Cir. 1977). *Los v. Los*, 595 A.2d 381 (Del. 1991) (party's naming of trial judge as defendant in federal suit challenging child support formula did not require recusal of trial judge in state court child support proceeding); *Rice v. Cannon*, 641 S.E.2d 562 (Ga. App. 2007) (frivolous law suits against sitting judges cannot be used by litigants to delay the administration of justice and to judge shop); *Cmmw. v. Leventhal*, 307 N.E.2d 839 (Mass. 1974) (lawsuit pending between judge and party may be good cause for recusal but party cannot disqualify judge from sitting on case by bringing an action against the judge after the principal suit has been commenced); Charles Gardner Geyh, James J. Alfini, Steven Lubet & Jeffrey M. Shaman, *Judicial Conduct and Ethics* § 4.09 at 4–41 (5th ed. 2013) ("a judge is not ordinarily disqualified from presiding over a case where one of the attorneys has filed a disciplinary complaint against the judge"); Nev. Stand. Comm. on Jud. Ethics and Election Prac. JE 00-001 (2000) (judge not required to disqualify under Section 3E(1)(a) because a lawyer for one of the parties filed a lawsuit against the judge on behalf of a different client). Nor is there a per se requirement for the judge to recuse herself from cases involving a defendant who is threatening the judge. *State v. Riordan*, 209 P.3d 773 (N.M. 2009) (supreme court held that judge did not abuse discretion in denying to recuse herself in three pending cases involving criminal defendant who was subsequently charged with conspiracy to commit assault with a deadly weapon on the judge).

A judge may be required to recuse from a case filed by a person who already has a case pending against the judge. *See In re Braswell*, 600 S.E.2d 849 (N.C. 2004) (judge censured for failing to recuse himself from civil litigation brought by a plaintiff who had unrelated civil lawsuit pending against judge); *Eastside Baptist Church v. Vicinanza*, 603 S.E.2d 681 (Ga. App. 2004) (judge was required to recuse himself from case against church by parents whose child was allegedly molested by martial arts instructor employed by the church, where lead counsel in that case had previously filed another suit against a university of which the judge was a trustee).

Bias against Class of Litigants

Recusal has been mandated where the record indicates that a judge has a bias or prejudice against a certain class of litigants. For instance, a judge was required to recuse himself where he expressed his disagreement with sentencing guidelines and said that the maximum penalty should be imposed in all drug cases. The reviewing court found that the judge's statements indicated a predetermined policy in regard to sentencing drug offenders and a personal bias against a particular class of litigants, which required recusal from the drug case over which he was presiding. *Cmmw. v. Lemanski*, 529 A.2d 1085 (Pa. Super. 1987); *U.S. v. Thompson*, 483 F.2d 527 (3d Cir. 1973) (judge required to disqualify himself from prosecution for violation of Selective Service Act where judge stated that it was his policy to sentence selective service violators to 30 months in prison if they were good people).

KNOWLEDGE OF FACTS IN DISPUTE IN PROCEEDING

A judge is disqualified under Rule 2.11(A)(1) if the judge has personal knowledge of facts that are in dispute in the proceeding. A similar provision can be found in the federal statute. 28 U.S.C.A. § 455(b)(1). To be disqualifying, the knowledge must be obtained extrajudicially rather than in the judge's official capacity during the course of a proceeding. *Los v. Los*, 595 A.2d 381 (Del. 1991); *Poorman v. Commonwealth*, 782 S.W.2d 603 (Ky. 1989) (fact that judge had made probable cause and bond rulings did not require per se disqualification of judge from appellate review where those matters were not at issue); *In re T.L.S.*, 481 A.2d 1037 (Vt. 1984) (disqualification not required in remanded case where judge, three years earlier in the original proceeding, had heard evidence subsequently ruled inadmissible). For instance, disqualification was required where a judge contacted the presiding judge in a contempt hearing and told him that the defendant was guilty. *In re Bell*, 373 A.2d 232 (D.C. 1977). However, Rule 2.11(A)(1) is not intended to preclude participation of a judge who has obtained knowledge of a case through previous judicial participation in it. *See Roe v. Dietrich*, 835 S.W.2d 289 (Ark. 1992) (judge not disqualified from partnership dissolution proceeding where he presided over the previous litigation involving the dissolution of the partnership); *Boyd v. State*, 581 A.2d 1 (Md. 1990) (information obtained in an earlier proceeding involving a codefendant is "judicial" not "personal"). In addition, evidentiary facts may not be considered "disputed" if they are readily conceded by the party who made them. *See State v. Ortiz*, 848 A.2d 1246 (Conn. App. 2004) (judge was not required to recuse himself from assault case even though judge heard defendant admit his guilt prior to trial in hopes of receiving a lighter sentence; admissions did not involve "disputed" evidentiary facts since they were consistent with admissions defendant to police when arrested and with admissions made while testifying at trial).

Minnesota has held that the requirement that a judge must disqualify herself if she has "personal knowledge of disputed evidentiary facts" is a narrow prohibition and pertains to knowledge that arises out of a judge's private, individual connection to particular facts, and does not conclude the vast realm of general knowledge that a judge acquires in his or her day-to-day life as a judge and citizen. *State v. Dorsey*, 701 N.W.2d 238 (Minn. 2005) (judge not required to disqualify herself where her knowledge of and individual's date of death, which was a disputed evidentiary fact in the case, apparently arose in the course of her general judicial capacity or as a result of her day-to-day life as a citizen taking an interest in local news and not out of a private, individual connection to decedent).

A judge may be disqualified if he or she inspects property that is the subject matter of litigation (*In re Yengo*, 371 A.2d 41 (N.J. 1977)) or directs an employee to do so (*Price Bros. Co. v. Philadelphia Gear Corp.*, 629 F.2d 444 (6th Cir. 1980)); *but cf. Hass v. State, Dept. of Transp.*, 843 N.E.2d 994 (Ind. App. 2006) (fact that judge has general knowledge of property that is the subject of eminent domain action because he lives in the area and drives past property twice a day is not the sort of "personal knowledge" requiring recusal under the Code of Judicial Conduct). A judge may not make an investigation of a case, even an inadvertent one, off the record, and base a holding on the information obtained. *See Vaughn v. Shelby Williams of Tenn., Inc.*, 813 S.W.2d 132 (Tenn. 1991) (reversible error for trial judge in a workers' compensation case to base his decision on his inadvertent observations of employee outside of court). Similarly, disqualification was required where the judge conducted an unrecorded interview with a child during a child custody proceeding, *In re Marriage of Donley*, 819 S.W.2d 98 (Mo. App. 1991), and where a judge interviewed a child in chambers without the presence of counsel and without a record. *Plunkett v. Plunkett*, 757 S.W.2d 286 (Mo. App. 1988). *See also In re Moses W.*, 842 N.E.2d 783 (Ill. App. Ct. 2006) (judge's ex parte communication with juvenile about factual matter at issue in connection with state's petition to revoke juvenile's probation required judge's recusal). *See generally* George D. Marlow, *From Black Robes To White Lab Coats: The Ethical Implications of a Judge's Sua Sponte, Ex Parte Acquisition of Social and Other Scientific Evidence During The Decision-Making Process*, 72 St. John's L. Rev. 291 (1998) (discussing whether judicial ethics standards should be adjusted to permit judges to engage in sua sponte, ex parte research in pending or impending cases). *See also* Rule 2.9(C).

JUDGE'S OR FAMILY MEMBER'S CONNECTION TO PROCEEDING

Rule 2.11(A)(2) mandates a judge's disqualification where the judge, the judge's spouse, domestic partner, or a person within "the third degree of relationship" to either of them or that person's spouse or domestic partner is a party to the proceeding, or an officer, director, general partner, managing member, or trustee of a party, is acting as a lawyer in the proceeding, a person who has more than a de minimis interest that could be substantially affected by the proceeding, or is likely to be a material witness in the proceeding. Beginning in 2007, the rules regarding disqualification due to a family relationship include a "domestic partner," which is defined as "a person with whom another person maintains a household and an intimate relationship, other than a person to whom he or she is legally married." Model Code of Judicial Conduct, Terminology.

As for extended family, a person within the third degree of relationship includes great-grandparents, grandparents, parents, uncles, aunts, brothers, sisters, children, grandchildren, great-grandchildren, nephews, and nieces. Model Code of Judicial Conduct, Terminology. This disqualification provision is expansive because the drafters thought "that to maintain the appearance of impartiality the disqualification standard should encompass all persons within the third degree of relationship to a judge or his spouse even though the relationship arises only through marriage." E. Wayne Thode, *Reporter Notes to 1972 Judicial Code* 67–68 (1973). Even if a person is not within the third degree of relationship to the judge or his or her spouse, disqualification may still be required if, under Rule 2.11(A), the judge's impartiality might reasonable by questioned. Ronald D. Rotunda and John S. Dzienkowski, *Legal Ethics: The Lawyer's Deskbook on Professional Responsibility* 1584 (2016).

PARTY TO THE PROCEEDING

Pursuant to Rule 2.11(A)(2)(a), disqualification is required where the judge is a party to the proceeding or an officer, director, general partner, managing member, or trustee of a party. A nearly identical provision can be found at 28 U.S.C.A. Section 455(b)(5)(i). Although the language of Rule 2.11(A)(2)(a) implies automatic disqualification, most courts have not construed it in this manner. For instance, a judge will not be disqualified merely because a plaintiff names the judge as a defendant in order to obtain a disqualification. *See, e.g., Andersen v. Roszkowski*, 681 F. Supp. 1284 (N.D. Ill. 1988) (judge named as defendant in plaintiff's amended complaint; disqualification not required because plaintiff had no legitimate basis for adding judge as defendant). N.M. Jud. Adv. Op. 08-03 (2008) (judge need not recuse from case where it can be reasonably inferred that lawsuit filed against judge by one of the parties is a sham designed to impede him in the performance of his judicial responsibilities; the mere filing of a complaint does not mandate judge's disqualification without consideration of the circumstances). Similarly, a judge cannot be disqualified merely because a litigant sues or threatens to sue the judge. *See In re Ronwin*, 680 P.2d 107 (Ariz. 1983) (bar applicant who filed numerous actions against eleven judges did not establish basis for recusal); *Lorenz v. N.H. Admin. Off. of Cts.*, 858 A.2d 546 (N.H. 2004) (recusal not required where court was named party in case regarding labor issue with court stenographers). Disqualification may also not be required where a party names a judge or judges as defendants when challenging administrative actions of the court. *See, e.g., N.Y. State Assn. of Crim. Def. Laws. v. Kaye*, 721 N.Y.S.2d 588 (N.Y. 2000) (where judges were named as respondents only in their administrative capacity and had no pecuniary or personal interest, designation of substitute judges was not appropriate); *Vt. Sup. Ct. Admin. Directive No. 17 v. Vt. Sup. Ct.*, 576 A.2d 127 (Vt. 1990) (where justices were nominal parties in case challenging constitutionality of Administrative Directive, recusal not required; principle of necessity applied).

Courts have not mandated automatic disqualification under Rule 2.11(A)(2)(a), in part to prevent manipulation of the court and judge shopping. *State v. Rome*, 685 P.2d 290 (Kan. 1984). A party could name a judge as a defendant merely to obtain a newly assigned and possibly more favorable judge. *Andersen v. Roszkowski*, 681 F. Supp 1284 (N.D. Ill 1988); *Vt. Sup. Ct. Admin. Directive No. 17 v. Vt. Sup. Ct.*, 576 A.2d 127 (Vt. 1990) ("[w]e cannot encourage such an easy method of disqualification"). Therefore, when ruling on the disqualification issue where the judge is also a party, the court may look at the nature of the conflict posed by acting as both judge and party in the particular case, and the efficacy of replacing the judge. *N.Y. State Assn. of Crim. Def. Laws. v. Kaye*, 721 N.Y.S.2d 588 (N.Y. 2000). Additionally, the rule of necessity may require that a judge or group of judges sit in a case despite being named as a party. *Id.* For additional discussion, see "The Rule of Necessity" section.

Rule 2.11(A)(2)(a) also provides for disqualification whenever the judge's spouse or domestic partner or other relative of the judge covered under the provision is a party to the proceeding or an officer, director, general partner, managing member, or trustee of a party. *See, e.g., Ex Parte Jackson*, 508 So. 2d 235 (Ala. 1987) (recusal is mandated where judge's brother is director of bank, which is party to litigation); *In re Van Rider*, 715 N.E.2d 402 (Ind. 1999) (judge publicly reprimanded for failing to recuse himself from criminal proceeding against his son); *Cuyahoga County Bd. of Mental Retardation v. Assn. of Cuyahoga County Teacher's of Trainable Retarded*, 351 N.E.2d 777 (Ohio App. 1975) (judge had a mandatory duty to disqualify himself when the judge's brother was an officer on the board of one of the parties); *In re Johnson*, 532 S.E.2d 883 (S.C. 2000) (judge publicly reprimanded, in part, for failing to recuse herself from case involving her grandson); S.C. Adv. Comm. on Stand. of Jud. Conduct, Op. 2-2003 (2003) (associate municipal judge may not preside over municipal court where judge's daughter is the clerk and judge's son-in-law is the chief of police). However, some courts have held that disqualification is not automatic, and a judge may be able to sit in the case if the judge has not been influenced by the relative's role in the proceeding. *See, e.g., Johnson v. Cullman Medical Center*, 615 So. 2d 621 (Ala. Civ. App. 1992) (recusal not required, even though judge's son was member of defendant hospital's board of directors, because record showed that judge was not influenced by son's position); *but see Morton v. Benton Pub. Co. Inc.*, 727 S.W.2d 824 (Ark. 1987) (when relationship between judge and party in case is within proscribed limits, neither frequency of conduct nor closeness of individuals bears on whether judge should recuse himself).

Class Actions

If a judge is a member of a class that has been certified, and the class is a party to litigation in which the judge is considering participating as a judge, the judge would be disqualified pursuant to Rule 2.11(A)(2)(a). *New Orleans Public Service, Inc. v. United Gas Pipe Line Co.*, 719 F.2d 733 (5th Cir. 1983); *Gordon v. Reliant Energy, Inc.*, 141 F. Supp. 2d 1041 (S.D. Cal. 2001) (in class action brought by individual purchasers of electricity against generators and traders of wholesale electricity, recusal of federal district court judge who was a customer of a defendant was warranted); U.S. Jud. Conf. Comm. on Codes of Conduct Adv. Op. No. 90 (1999) ("The Committee adheres to its previous position that Rule 23 (b)(3) class members are 'parties' for purposes of [Rule 2.11(A)(2)(a)]."); *id.* (ch. V) at 26 ("All members of the class are parties whether named or unnamed so long as they have not opted out."). However, if the judge is a potential member of class, he or she is not a party to the action. Therefore, a judge is not disqualified if either the judge or a person within third degree of relationship to the judge or judge's spouse or domestic partner is merely a putative class member. *See New Orleans Public Service, Inc. v. United Gas Pipe Line Co.*, 719 F.2d 733 (5th Cir. 1983) (in suit by public utility, where class of ratepayers has been claimed but not certified, judges who are ratepayers and, therefore, potential parties, are not disqualified); *Tramonte v. Chrysler Corp.*, 136 F.3d 1025 (5th Cir. 1998) (fact that members of judge's family owned vehicles that may be subject of class action may require disqualification depending on distance of relationship and current status of ownership); *In re Initial Pub. Offering Secs. Litig.*, 174 F. Supp. 2d 70 (S.D.N.Y. 2001) (disqualification not warranted on basis that judge, in consolidated securities actions involving initial public offerings was once a putative class member since judge waived status as potential class member); *LeRoy v. City of Houston*, 592 F. Supp. 415 (S.D. Tex. 1984) (judge to whom election practices cases were assigned for resolution of attorney fee issue was not a "party" since action challenging at-large elections was not certified as a class action). For an examination of problems class actions raise in the area of disqualification in federal court see Ziona Hochbaum, Note, *Taking Stock: The Need to Amend 28 U.S.C. § 455 to Achieve Clarity and Sensibility in Disqualification Rules for Judges' Financial Holdings*, 71 Fordham L. Rev. 1669 (2003).

ACTING AS A LAWYER IN THE PROCEEDING

Absent waiver, Rule 2.11(A)(2)(b) requires recusal where the judge knows that a person covered by this section is acting as a lawyer in the proceeding. *See, e.g., In re Broome*, 264 S.E.2d 656 (Ga. 1980) (judge suspended from office where he presided over several cases in which his son-in-law represented one of the parties); *Abell v. Oliver*, 117 S.W.3d 661 (Ky. App. 2003) (judge was required to recuse herself in medical malpractice proceeding in which judge's spouse was associate of law firm representing patient); *State v. Vidales*, 571 N.W.2d 117 (Neb. App. 1997) (there is absolute disqualification of judge under code of judicial conduct when case brought by lawyer spouse is before judge spouse, as no one could reasonably suggest that judge's impartiality could not reasonably be questioned); *Disc. Counsel v. Kolmacic*, 541 N.E.2d 608 (Ohio 1989) (judge reprimanded for failing to recuse himself from three matters in which his son appeared as counsel); *Velardo v. Ovitt*, 933 A.2d 227 (Vt. 2007) (undisclosed sibling relationship between assistant judge and guardian ad litem in custody dispute required recusal of assistant judge); S.C. Adv. Comm. on Stand. of Jud. Conduct Op. 1-1995 (1995) (magistrate should disqualify himself from any proceeding where his son is acting as a lawyer); Wash. Ethics Adv. Comm. Op. 05-08 (2005) (judge may not preside over cases in which his or her spouse is acting as the prosecuting attorney or over any cases in which the spouse of the judicial officer is the supervisor of the deputy prosecuting attorney in the case); *see generally* Leslie W. Abramson, *The Judge's Relative Is Affiliated with Counsel of Record: The Ethical Dilemma*, 32 Hofstra L. Rev. 1181 (2004). This provision seeks to deter clients from believing that they can obtain special favor and consideration by retaining a lawyer who is a relative of a judge. Utah Jud. Ethics Adv. Op. No. 90-3 (1990).

Some courts have held that the judge must disclose to the parties the judge's relationship to a lawyer in the proceeding even if his or her impartiality is not questioned. *In re Broome*, 264 S.E.2d 656 (Ga. 1980) (there is an affirmative duty on a judge to disclose to the parties his relationship to an attorney within prohibited third degree, even without challenge); *Reilly by Reilly v. S.E. Pa. Transp. Auth.*, 479 A.2d 973 (Pa. Super. 1984) (if ground for recusal exists, it is burden of the judge either to recuse himself sua sponte or to disclose the ground and then preside only if no party objects. Other courts have held that waiver of a motion to disqualify a judge is implied if a party knows that the judge has a disqualifying relationship with a lawyer in a proceeding and fails to object); *Citizen's First Nat'l Bank v. Hoyt*, 297 N.W.2d 329 (Iowa 1980) (in action on promissory note, maker, whose lawyers were judge's uncle and first cousin impliedly waived judicial disqualification by failing to seek judge's disqualification until after judge ruled against maker).

The federal statute's counterpart to this provision can be found at 28 U.S.C.A. Section 455(b)(5)(ii). *In re Aetna Cas. & Sur. Co.*, 919 F.2d 1136 (6th Cir. 1990) (judge required to recuse from case where his daughter participated as a lawyer in depositions: "The statute contemplates a bright line test–if a person within the third degree of relationship to the judge or the judge's spouse is acting as a lawyer in the proceeding, the judge is disqualified"); *In re BellSouth, Corp.*, 334 F.3d 941 (11th Cir. 2003) (participation of district judge's nephew as counsel for a defendant called for recusal but district judge retained authority to refer plaintiffs' motion to disqualify counsel to the clerk of the court for reassignment to another judge). Federal courts have explained that the phrase "acting as a lawyer in the proceeding" focuses on the participation of the lawyer in the proceeding before the judge. *See Potashnick v. Port City Const. Co.*, 609 F.2d 1101 (5th Cir. 1980) ("actual participation is required"); *State ex rel. Weinberger v. Equifax, Inc.*, 557 F.2d 456 (5th Cir. 1997) (recusal of the judge was not necessary under federal statute because judge's son did not participate in the proceeding, although the son's firm did participate); *McCuin v. Tex. Power & Light Co.*, 714 F.2d 1255 (5th Cir. 1983) (disqualification required where judge's brother-in-law participated in discovery proceedings in cases pending before judge); *S.J. Groves & Sons v. Int'l Bhd. of Teamsters*, 581 F.2d 1241 (7th Cir. 1978) (judge's brother, prior to the withdrawal of his law firm as counsel for plaintiffs, was not "acting as a lawyer," by virtue of his relationship with the firm, where there was no actual participation by him in the case).

The Commentary to Rule 2.11(A)(2)(b) provides that a judge is not automatically disqualified merely because a lawyer in a proceeding is a member of a law firm with which a relative of the judge is affiliated. This provision has also been applied when the lawyer-relative is employed in the public sector rather than by a law firm. *See, e.g., Adair v. State of Mich.*, 709 N.W.2d 567 (Mich. 2006) (employment of spouses of state supreme court justices in non-supervisory capacities by office of state Attorney General did not require recusal); *In re Disqualification of Carr*, 826 N.E.2d 294 (Ohio 2004) (denying motion for disqualification of judge whose spouse worked as a prosecutor in the same office that was prosecuting the case where the judge's spouse "neither entered an appearance in the case nor participated in the preparation or presentation of the case"); *State v. Harrell*, 546 N.W.2d 115 (Wis. 1996) (disqualification not required when judge's spouse works in prosecutor's office but did not participate in or help prepare instant case); *but see* Ill. Jud. Ethics Comm. Op. 05-02 (2005) (advising that judge is disqualified from criminal cases in which the judge's son-in-law, in his capacity as an assistant state's attorney, signs the charging instrument or otherwise acts as a lawyer in the proceedings); N.M. Jud. Adv. Op. 07-04 (2005) (judge should disqualify himself in every criminal case when spouse is chief deputy district attorney). However, the judge can still be disqualified if the judge's impartiality might reasonably be questioned under Rule 2.11(A), or if the relative is known by the judge to have an interest in the law firm that could be substantially affected by the outcome of the proceeding under Rule 2.11(A)(2)(c). *See, e.g., Potashnick v. Port City Const. Co.*, 609 F.2d 1101 (5th Cir. 1980) (judge not disqualified under Rule 2.11(A)(2)(b) where judge's father was senior partner in law firm representing plaintiff, but is disqualified under Section 455(b)(5)(iii) because judge's father was "known by the judge to have an interest that could be substantially affected by the outcome"); *Jenkins v.*

Forrest County General Hosp. 542 So. 2d 1180 (Miss. 1988) (judge's impartiality "might reasonably be questioned" where judge's brother was senior partner in law firm representing a defendant).

INTEREST THAT COULD BE SUBSTANTIALLY AFFECTED BY THE PROCEEDING

Rule 2.11(A)(2)(c) requires recusal when the judge, the judge's spouse, or domestic partner, or a person within the third degree of relationship to either of them or the spouse or domestic partner of that person "is known by the judge to have a more than de minimis interest that could be substantially affected by the proceeding." *See, e.g., In re Lyons*, JC-12-031-C, N.H. Jud. Conduct Comm. (2013) (judge reprimanded for presiding over bail hearing for defendants accused of battery when victim was brother-in-law of judge's spouse); Section 455 (b)(5)(iii) is similar to Rule 2.11(A)(2)(c), however, the federal statute requires disqualification regardless of whether or not the interest is more than de minimis.

Judge's Relative Is Member of Law Firm

Rule 2.11(A)(2)(c) is frequently raised as grounds for disqualification when a judge's relative is a member of a law firm that is representing a party in a case before the judge. In determining what constitutes "an interest that could be substantially affected" by a case before the judge, the primary factor is the financial remuneration that the judge's relative might receive. *Regional Sales Agency, Inc. v. Reichert*, 830 P.2d 252 (Utah 1992); ABA Comm. on Jud. Activities Formal Op. 58 (1978); ABA Comm. on Jud. Activities Formal Op. 77 (1985). Some courts have held that when a judge is related within the third degree to a partner in a law firm representing a party-in-interest before that judge, that partner will always be "known by the judge to have an interest that could be substantially affected by the outcome of the proceeding." *Potashnick v. Port City Constr. Co.*, 609 F.2d 1101 (5th Cir. 1980) (disqualification required where judge's father was senior partner in law firm representing one of the parties and received one percent of firm's income); *Blaisdell v. City of Rochester*, 609 A.2d 388 (N.H. 1992) (where judge was nephew of senior partner in law firm representing defendant, judge disqualified, and his orders in case vacated even though there was no ongoing personal relationship between judge and uncle); *Regl. Sales Agency, Inc. v. Reichert*, 830 P.2d 252 (Utah 1992) (appellate judge must sua sponte disqualify self where brother-in-law and father-in-law are equity participants in the firm representing a party).

Other courts, however, have rejected such a per se rule of recusal and make the determination on a case-by-case basis. *Pashaian v. Eccelston Props., Inc.*, 88 F.3d 77 (2d Cir. 1996) ("[i]t would simply be unrealistic to assume . . . that partners in today's law firms invariably 'have an interest that could be substantially affected by the outcome of' any case in which any other partner is involved"); *SCA Services, Inc. v. Morgan*, 557 F.2d 110 (7th Cir. 1977) (judge disqualified where brother is senior partner of firm representing a party; although record did not include direct evidence as to degree of financial benefit to firm, it was undisputed that at least 35 days had been spent in pre-trial discovery and that, though case was not taken by firm on a contingency basis, a favorable outcome would obviously justify a higher fee). Some courts have listed factors that should be examined in deciding whether a law firm partner who is related to a judge has an interest that could be to be "substantially affected" when other lawyers in his or her firm represent a party before that judge, so as to required judicial disqualification. *See, e.g., In re Inquiry Concerning a Judge*, 81 P.3d 758 (Utah 2003) (factors include size of firm, status of judge's relative within firm, type of proceeding, amount in controversy, and fee arrangement between firm and client); Colo. Jud. Ethics Adv. Bd. Op. 2005-02 (2005) (factors to be considered include the status of the judge's relative as a partner or associate, the prominence of the judge's relative's name in the firm name, the size of the court, the size of the community, the size of the firm, and the frequency of the firm's appearance in the judge's court; opinion advised that judge should disqualify himself where a partner or associate in brother-in-law's firm is acting as counsel given that brother-in-law is senior member of firm that has fewer than five attorneys and practices within jurisdiction); Ill. Jud. Ethics Comm. Op. 94-18 (1994) (suggesting that in determining whether a relative has more than a de minimis interest that could be substantially affected by the proceeding a judge should consider (1) the nature of the case, in its financial or other impact on the relative's law firm; (2) the relative's position in the firm as a partner, shareholder, associate, or of counsel; and (3) the size of the firm); N.Y. State Bar Assn. Comm. on Prof. Ethics Formal Op. 703 (1998) (the nature of the attorney (public vs. private attorney), the nature of the fee (contingent vs. hourly fee), the size of the law firm, and the size of the community are all factors that the judge should take into account in deciding whether his or her impartiality may reasonably be questioned, and no one factor is determinative); Tenn. Adv. Op. 04-01 (2004) (considerations as to whether the judge's child has "a more than de minimis interest that could be substantially affected by the proceeding" include the size of the firm in question, the number and geographic spread of its offices, the nature of the matter, the potential impact on the child's firm of its client being awarded a large sum or substantial relief, or having such an award against it, as well as the child's involvement, if any, in the matter).

If the judge's relative is an associate in the firm or a salary, rather than an equity partner in the firm, recusal will generally not be required. *See U.S. ex rel. Weinberger v. Equifax, Inc.*, 557 F.2d 456 (5th Cir. 1997) (since judge's son was an associate of law firm representing defendant, he did not have a "financial interest" requiring judge's recusal); *U.S. v. Bobo*, 395 F. Supp. 2d 1116 (N.D. Ala. 2004) (if judge's relative is associate in law firm, and relative's compensation is in no manner dependent upon result of particular case before judge, recusal is not mandated); *Nobelpharma Ab v. Implant Innovations, Inc.*, 930 F. Supp. 1241 (N.D. Ill. 1996) (recusal not required where judge's daughter is a salary, not an equity, partner at defendant's law firm, performed no work on this case and did not represent defendant in any legal matter). *Miller Indus., Inc. v. Caterpillar Tractor Co.*, 516 F. Supp. 84 (S.D. Ala. 1980) (where judge's father was paid a fixed compensation as "of counsel" to a firm representing a party before the judge, father had no financial interest at stake or any discernible non-financial interest).

A second factor is the non-pecuniary benefits to the relative's law firm, such as enhanced reputation and increased good will that indirectly benefit the relative. *Reilly by Reilly v. S.E. Pa. Transp. Auth.*, 479 A.2d 973 (Pa. Super. 1984); *In re Kan. Pub. Employees Ret. Sys.*, 85 F.3d 1353 (8th Cir. 1996) (under 28 U.S.C.A. § 455 (b)(5)(iii), "interest" includes non-economic as well as economic interests); Nev. Stand. Comm. on Jud. Ethics and Election Prac. JE07-004 (2007) (in evaluating the interest of the judge's relative, the focus should not be exclusively on the potential monetary benefit to the relative's firm; the judge must look at the totality of the circumstances, including the possibility that future litigants may be drawn to the firm if they believe the judge would sit on cases involving his/her child's place of employment). To create sufficient benefit to judge's relative from enhanced reputation and good will to the relative's law firm so that disqualification may be appropriate, the case before the judge must be one that will greatly affect the reputation of the relative's firm. *Regional Sales Agency, Inc. v. Reichert*, 830 P.2d 252 (Utah 1992). This factor may affect both partners and non-partners, but one court noted that "[b]ecause non-pecuniary interests that might enhance a firm's goodwill will result in benefits only over time, an associate's lack of secure tenure with a firm, whether because of the probationary nature of an associate's status or because of significant inter-firm movement of young lawyers, reduces the likelihood of long-term benefit such that disqualification is not necessary." *Id.* at 258.

Judge or Judge's Relative Is Employed by a Party

A judge will likely not be disqualified merely because a party to a case has filed a civil action against the government entity that employs the judge. *See, e.g.*, S.C. Adv. Comm. on Stand. of Jud. Conduct Op. 11-2006 (2006) (municipal court may judge presiding over criminal matter in which defendant has a civil action pending against the city that employs judge; judge's interest is not more than a de minimis interest in that the judge will not be affected financially or otherwise). However, a judge may be disqualified if his or her spouse or relative is employed by a party appearing in a case before the judge. *See, e.g.*, Utah Jud. Ethics Adv. Op. 06-2 (2006) (judge is disqualified from a case involving a company which employs his wife part-time).

Ownership of Stock

A judge may be disqualified if the judge, the judge's spouse or domestic partner, or a person within the third degree of relationship to either or them or the spouse of that person owes a more than de minimis interest in stock of a company that is party to litigation before the judge. De minimis is defined in the Code as "an insignificant interest that could not raise reasonable question as to a judge's impartiality. "Model Code of Judicial Conduct, Terminology. *See also* Va. Jud. Ethics Adv. Comm. Op. 00-5 (2000) (ownership of 1 percent or less of the outstanding stock in a publicly held corporation is usually a de minimis interest and does not require disqualification of a judge in a case involving that corporation). Even if the stock interest does not meet the definition of de minimis, recusal may still be required if the judge's interest raises an appearance of impartiality under Rule 2.11(A). *See Huffman v. Ark. Jud. Disc. & Disability Comm'n*, 42 S.W.3d 386 (Ark. 2001) (although judge owned only a miniscule percent of the total stock of a corporate party, recusal was required because the judge's conduct would create in reasonable minds the perception that his ability to carry out judicial responsibilities with integrity, impartiality, and competence was impaired). *See generally* Annotation, *Disqualification of Judge Because of His or Another's Holding or Owning Stock in Corporation Involved in Litigation*, 25 A.L.R.3d 1331.

A judge's ownership of stock in a company that is not a party to a proceeding but is in the same industry as a party to the proceeding will not require the judge's recusal absent a showing that the judge's interest will be substantially affected by the decision in the case. *In re Placid Oil*, 802 F.2d 783 (5th Cir. 1986). *See, e.g., In re Kan. Pub. Employees Ret. Sys.*, 85 F.3d 1353, 1362 (8th Cir. 1996) ("we are reluctant to fashion a rule requiring judges to recuse themselves from all cases that might remotely affect nonparty companies in which they own stock"); *Gas Utils. Co. of Ala., Inc. v. Southern Natural Gas Co.*, 996 F.2d 282 (11th Cir. 1993) (judge whose wife and father-in-law held interests in land leased to gas producers was not required to recuse from antitrust action between gas suppliers who did not hold leases from judge's relatives); *cf. Wash. Mut. Fin. Group LLC v. Blackmon*, 925 So. 2d 780 (Miss. 2004) (judge's ownership of certificates of deposit in a bank did not require judge's recusal from case involving issues of loan practices and credit insurance).

LIKELY TO BE A MATERIAL WITNESS

Rule 2.11(A)(2)(d) and 28 U.S.C.A. Section 455(b)(5)(iv) require judges to disqualify themselves if they know that they are likely to be a material witness in a proceeding. *See, e.g., In re Crane*, 324 S.E.2d 443 (Ga. 1985) (judge should have disqualified himself in contempt trial of person who made telephone calls to judge's secretary and deputy clerk of court, using vulgar and insulting language because judge was a material witness); *Baier v. Hampton*, 440 N.W.2d 712 (N.D. 1989) (judge should have recused himself from criminal contempt trial based on conduct occurring before him in child support hearing); *Disc. Counsel v. Karto*, 760 N.E.2d 412 (Ohio 2002) (judge's actions in contempt proceedings, of disrobing and testifying, making a closing statement, and issuing the ruling violated judicial Canon); *In re Randolph*, 12-4849 (Tenn. Ct. of the Judiciary 2012) (judge reprimanded for presiding over hearing of defendant accused of burglarizing judge's office).

The rationale behind this provision is that a judge cannot be deemed capable of impartially deciding on the admissibility of his or her own testimony, or of weighing it against that of another. *Collins v. State*, 232 S.E.2d 635 (Ga. App. 1977). A judge is not a material witness where there are other witnesses to testify to the matter. *Callahan v. State*, 557 So. 2d 1292 (Ala. Crim. App. 1989) (judge's recusal not required on theory that he was a material witness, even though he entered room where defendant was being questioned by police officers to inform them lawyer hired by defendant's father wanted to speak with defendant, where assistant district attorney was present and able to testify to those facts); *In re Disqualification of Schweikert*, 850 N.E.2d 714 (Ohio 2005) (where judge was not sole observer of circumstances defendant hopes to explore at the post-conviction hearing, judge's disqualification is therefore not warranted on the grounds that judge is "likely to be a material witness"). In addition, grounds for disqualification may be limited to those situations in which a magistrate would be a material witness to the proceeding being heard *before* him or her, rather than a separate criminal proceeding that *may result* from incidents that happen to occur within the courtroom. *See In re Memic*, 2006 WL 3478421 (Ohio Ct. App. 2006) (judge not disqualified from child custody proceeding on grounds that he could be a witness in a potential criminal case that could be filed against mother after she physically attacked social worker who was involved in custody case).

Disqualification is also required if the judge's spouse or domestic partner, a relative within the prescribed degree or the relative's spouse or domestic partner is, to the judge's knowledge, likely to be a material witness in a proceeding. *See, e.g., Harris v. Champion*, 15 F.3d 1538 (10th Cir. 1994) (recusal required where judge would have to review rulings of state appellate court on which his uncle was judge and also named as party in habeas suit); *In re Sims*, 462 N.E.2d 370 (N.Y. 1984) (judge violated Code by signing arrest warrant for person involved in car accident with her son, since son was complaining witness); *Williams v. Reed*, 6 S.W.3d 916 (Mo. App. 1999) (trial judge's knowledge that his spouse was likely to be material witness in proceeding on motion for change of judge required recusal; motion was based on alleged similarity of judge's marital situation to that of parties, judge discussed veracity of allegation in motion with his wife prior to hearing, and judge relied on her testimony in ruling on motion); Wis. Jud. Conduct Adv. Comm. Op. 06-02 (2006) (judge may not handle cases where the judge's son, who is a police officer, was either in charge of or part of any investigation leading to citations or charges pending before the court). The Code does not define "material witness," but "the standard is probably analogous to that of Model Rule 3.7, of the Model Rules of Professional Conduct (the advocate-witness rule)." Ronald D. Rotunda and John S. Dzienkowski, *Legal Ethics: The Lawyer's Deskbook on Professional Responsibility* 1598 (2016).

Economic Interest in a Party or Subject of Proceeding

Pursuant to Rule 2.11(A)(3), a judge must disqualify himself or herself if the judge knows that he or she, individually or as a fiduciary, has an economic interest in the subject matter in controversy or in a party to the proceeding. The judge must also disqualify himself or herself if the judge knows that his or her spouse, domestic partner, parent or child, regardless of residence, or any other member of the judge's family residing in the judge's household has such an interest. Federal courts have a similar, though not identical provision, which states that a judge is disqualified if the judge knows that "he, individually or as a fiduciary, or his spouse or minor child residing in his household, has a financial interest in the subject matter in controversy or in a party to the proceeding . . . ." 28 U.S.C.A. § 455 (b)(4). *See generally* Annotation, *Disqualification of Judge under 28 U.S.C.A. § 455 (b), Providing for Disqualification Where Judge Has Financial or Other Interest in Proceeding*, 163 A.L.R. Fed. 575 (2000).

Economic Interest

The Code defines an "economic interest" as ownership of more than a de minimis legal or equitable interest. *See* Model Code of Judicial Conduct, Terminology. For instance, a justice of the peace who received court costs as fees had a direct interest in whether or not a party paid court costs, and therefore, was disqualified from deciding the issue of the truthfulness of pauper's affidavit. *Taylor v. Pub. Convalescent Serv.*, 267 S.E.2d 242 (Ga. 1980). A remote, contingent or speculative benefit or interest is not a economic interest in the subject matter in controversy or in a party to the proceeding. For example, a judge's interest in a refund as a utility customer or as a taxpayer is generally not considered a legal or equitable economic interest, though it could be disqualifying if it is "any other more than de minimis interest that could be substantially affected by the proceeding." *In re N.M. Natural Gas Antitrust Lit.*, 620 F.2d 794 (10th Cir. 1980) (remote, contingent benefit, such as possible beneficial effect on future utility bills, is not a "financial interest" within meaning of federal disqualification statute, but is an "other interest" requiring disqualification of judge under "substantially affected" test).

Exceptions

The Judicial Code expressly excludes a number of interests from the definition of "economic interest," ownership of which would not require disqualification. Model Code of Judicial Conduct, Terminology.

Mutual or Common Investment Fund

A judge is not disqualified because of a more than de minimis interest in a mutual or common investment fund unless the judge participates in the management of the fund, or the outcome of a proceeding before the judge could substantially affect the fund. Model Code of Judicial Conduct Rule 2.11 cmt. [6]. *See, e.g., N.Y. Hous. Dev. Corp. v. Hart*, 796 F.2d 976 (7th Cir. 1986) (interpreting similar federal provision, 28 U.S.C.A. § 455 (d)(4)(i), which states that the ownership of a mutual or common investment fund is "not a 'financial interest'" in the fund's securities, unless the judge participates in the management of the fund, court held that judge was not required to recuse himself from suit seeking injunction against redemption of certain municipal bonds on ground that his decision could affect value of bond trusts and funds in which judge had interest because; effects of such sort were both ubiquitous and too indirect to require disqualification). The second clause of the exception was added to the Code in 1990 "to cover situations such as an investment club where the outcome of a proceeding involving the club might affect the value of the judge's interest." ABA Standing Committee Report on 1990 Code, Legislative Draft 5 (1990).

Interest in Securities Held by Civic Organizations

An interest in securities held by an educational, religious, charitable, fraternal, or civic organization in which the judge or the judge's spouse, domestic partner, parent, or child serve as a director, an officer, an advisor, or other participant is not an "economic interest for purposes of determining whether a judge should disqualify himself from a proceeding unless the judge participates in the management of the interest or the interest could be substantially affected by the outcome of proceeding before the judge. Model Code of Judicial Conduct Rule 2.11 cmt. [6].

Financial Institution or Mutual Insurance Company

A deposit in a financial institution or deposits or proprietary interests the judge may maintain as a member of a mutual savings association or credit union or similar proprietary interest is an economic interest *only* if the judge manages the interest or the interest could be substantially affected by the outcome of a proceeding before the judge. Model Code of Judicial Conduct Rule 2.11 cmt. [6]. *See, e.g., Christiansen v. Nat. Sav. & Trust Co.*, 683 F.2d 520 (D.C. 1982) (federal judges need not disqualify themselves because of the interest they might have as subscribers to a government-wide health insurance plan); *Ex parte Dooley*, 741 So. 2d 404 (Ala. 1999) (judge's status as a policyholder of mutual insurance company did not entitle insured to judge's recusal or disqualification in suit to recover $70,000 in underinsured motorist benefits from company; the case would not substantially affect the value of the policy); *Wash. Mut. Fin. Group, LLC v. Blackmon*, 925 So. 2d 780 (Miss. 2004) (supreme court justice's ownership of certificates of deposit in bank that sold credit insurance and other products central to case before the supreme sourt did not require recusal; no showing was made that he would be substantially affected by the decision of the case).

Government Securities

Ownership of government securities is not an economic interest unless the proceeding pending or impending before the judge could substantially affect the value of those securities. Model Code of Judicial Conduct Rule 2.11 cmt. [6]. *See, e.g., In re Fuchsberg*, 426 N.Y.S.2d 639 (N.Y. Ct. Jud. 1978) (judge disciplined for failing to recuse himself or notify parties that he owned New York City bonds, the value of which could be substantially affected by outcome of proceeding).

Other Exceptions

In addition to the exceptions listed in the Code's terminology, courts have also concluded that certain other interests are not "economic interests" under the Code or "financial interests" under federal statute. For instance, a judge did not have a "financial interest" in a case simply because as a former borrower from a bank he was a "potential" member of the plaintiff class. *Madsen v. Prudential Fed. Sav. & Loan Assn.*, 767 P.2d 538 (Utah 1988). A judge's interest as stockholder also may not be a disqualifying "financial interest." *U.S. v. Nobel*, 696 F.2d 231 (3d Cir. 1982) (judge's financial interest as a stockholder in corporate victim of crime was not a "financial interest in subject matter" in controversy for purposes of statute providing that judge was to disqualify himself if he had financial interest in subject matter in controversy).

De Minimis Interest

The 1972 Code defined "financial interest" in the context of this Code provisions as ownership of a legal or equitable interest, "however small." ABA Code of Judicial Conduct Canon 3C(3)(b) (1972). The 1990 and 2007 Codes replaced "financial interest" with "economic interest" and "however small" with "de minimis" language and defined de minimis to mean "an insignificant interest that could not raise reasonable question as to a judge's impartiality." Model Code of Judicial Conduct, Terminology. *See, e.g., Huffman v. Ark. Jud. Disc. & Disability Comm'n*, 42 S.W.3d 386 (Ark. 2001) (fact that a judge and his wife owned approximately 12,000 shares of Wal-Mart stock worth about $700,000 created an appearance of impropriety in ruling on Wal-Mart's motion for a temporary restraining order against a union, and therefore, recusal was required, even if the judge's ownership interest could not be substantially affected by his decision). This language dispelled the notion that a judge is disqualified if he or she owns even one share of stock in a party to the litigation, regardless of how small its value, but does not provide a bright-line test to determine whether an interest is de minimis. The Code of Conduct for United States Judges, however, has maintained the "however small" language, and therefore, ownership of stock in any party, automatically requires a federal judge's disqualification. U.S. Jud. Conf. Comm. on Codes of Cond. Adv. Op. 101 (2001).

Knowledge of Economic Interests

Rule 2.11(A)(3) and 28 U.S.C.A. Section 455(b)(4) mandate disqualification only if the judge "knows" that he or she has a disqualifying economic interest. According to the Code's terminology, "knows" means that the judge has "actual knowledge" of the disqualifying interest, though a person's knowledge can be inferred from circumstances. Model Code of Judicial Conduct, Terminology.

Rule 2.11(B) requires judges to keep informed about their economic interests and make a "reasonable effort" to keep informed about the economic interests of their spouses or domestic partners and any minor children residing in their household. However, even if a judge does not have "actual knowledge" of such an interest, recusal may be required if the judge's participation in the case creates an appearance of impropriety. *See, e.g., Liljeberg v. Health Servs. Acq. Corp.*, 486 U.S. 847 (1988) (judge who was trustee of university, should have recused himself from proceedings in which university had interest; despite his lack of actual knowledge of university's interest in dispute during trial, judge's participation in case created strong appearance of impropriety).

Subject Matter in Controversy

To be disqualifying an economic interest must be "in the subject matter in controversy." The Code does not define the phrase "subject matter in controversy." One federal court relied on the dictionary to construe "subject matter in controversy" to mean "the matter acted upon," "the matter presented for consideration," or "the topic of dispute in a legal matter." *U.S. v. Nobel*, 696 F.2d 231 (3d Cir. 1982). Other courts have looked at how direct an effect the litigation will have on the judge's interest. These courts have held that "the effect of a favorable ruling must be direct, rather than indirect, speculative, or slight," to establish grounds for recusal. *McCann v. Commun. Design Corp.*, 775 F. Supp. 1535 (D. Conn. 1991) (citing *In re Placid Oil Co.*, 802 F.2d 783 (5th Cir. 1986)) (judge sitting on case involving 23 state banks had "financial interest" because of his large stock interest in non-party state bank, but financial interest was not in the "subject matter in controversy" because it was "remote, contingent, and speculative"). *See also In re Va. Elec. & Power Co.*, 539 F.2d 357 (4th Cir. 1976) (judge's remote and speculative interest in refund from utility company was not such ownership of a legal or equitable interest as to constitute a disqualifying financial interest in the litigation); *Allum v. Valley Bank of Nev.*, 915 P.2d 895 (Nev. 1996) (justice's personal indebtedness to respondent bank was too attenuated to require justice's disqualification from hearing appeal involving bank).

ECONOMIC INTERESTS OF JUDGE'S FAMILY

Rule 2.11(A)(3) mandates a judge's disqualification where a member of the judge's family owns a disqualifying interest. If the judge's spouse, domestic partner, parent, or child, regardless of where they are residing, or any other "member of the judge's family residing in the judge's household" has an economic interest or other interest that would be disqualifying if it were the judge's interest, the judge must disqualify himself or herself. *See, e.g., Corie v. City of Riviera Beach*, 954 So. 2d 68 (Fla. Dist. Ct. App. 2007) (judge whose father owned property in area that was subject of eminent domain proceedings as part of a redevelopment scheme should have disqualified herself from considering lawsuit brought by other property owners challenging redevelopment scheme, even if father's property was not scheduled to be taken by city; value of father's property could be affected by outcome of litigation, such that judge's impartiality could reasonably be questioned). Beginning in 2007, the rules regarding disqualification due to an economic interest include a "domestic partner," which is defined as "a person with whom another person maintains a household and an intimate relationship, other than a person to whom he or she is legally married." Model Code of Judicial Conduct, Terminology.

A family member's economic interest can be imputed to the judge only if the judge knows about the interest. Rule 2.11 requires that judges inform themselves about their own financial interests. However, a judge only needs to make a "reasonable effort" to learn of the personal economic interests of his or her spouse, domestic partner, and minor children residing in the judge's household. Rule 2.11(B). Factors that help determine if a reasonable effort has been made may include the following: "Did the interest of the spouse, [domestic partner], or child come from the judge or from another source? Does the spouse, [domestic partner] or child know the nature of the interest, or is he or she the beneficiary of a blind trust? Has the spouse's, [domestic partner's] or child's financial interest been supervised by the judge in the past, or has the judge not been involved in the handling of the interest?" E. Wayne Thode, *Reporter's Notes to 1972 Judicial Code* 68 (1973).

CAMPAIGN CONTRIBUTIONS FROM PARTIES OR LAWYERS

Legal campaign contributions from litigants or lawyers appearing before a judge, without more, generally do not raise a question as to the judge's impartiality. *See Dean v. Bondurant*, 193 S.W.3d 744 (Ky. 2006) (contributions to judicial campaigns by an attorney representing a party before the judge is not improper and is an insufficient basis to demand a judge's recusal); *Adair v. State of Mich.*, 709 N.W.2d 567 (Mich. 2006) (judge's receipt of a campaign contribution from a party, an attorney for a party, a law firm employing an attorney for a party, or a group having common interests with a party or an attorney, cannot reasonably require his or her disqualification); *City of Las Vegas Downtown Redevelopment Agency v. Eighth Jud. Dist. Ct. ex rel. County of Clark*, 5 P.3d 1059 (Nev. 2000) (campaign contributions to judge by casinos that stood to benefit from outcome of eminent domain action did not constitute proper grounds for judge's disqualification; contributions were not extraordinary in amount, and without more, constituted only an insignificant interest that did not raise reasonable question as to judge's impartiality); *In re Disqualification of Burnside*, 863 N.E.2d 617 (Ohio 2006) (judge not required to recuse from case where she received $8,300 in campaign contributions over a 13 year period from a law firm that was a defendant in the case until voluntarily dismissed by plaintiff); *but see In re Jayne*, No. 13-150 (Ariz. Comm'n on Jud. Conduct 2013) (judge reprimanded for failing to disqualify self from matter involving campaign contributor who personally contributed to judge's campaign, whose business paid judge's campaign debt, and whom judge appointed representative for granddaughter despite contributor's nonlawyer status).

With regard to contributions from lawyers, if a judge could not sit on a case in which a contributing lawyer is involved as counsel, elected judges in some jurisdictions would likely have to recuse themselves in a majority of cases filed in their courts. Leslie W. Abramson, *Appearance of Impropriety: Deciding When a Judge's Impartiality "Might Reasonably Be Questioned,"* 14 Geo. J. Legal Ethics 55, 85 (2000) *citing Rocha v. Ahmad* 662 S.W.2d 77, 78 (Tex. Ct. App. 1983).

However, Rule 2.11(A)(4), a provision that was first added to the Code in 1999, imposes a duty to disqualify themselves upon judges who have received campaign contributions in amounts exceeding certain limits from parties or their lawyers. The rule does not suggest specific dollar amounts. Instead, it leaves that issue up to individual jurisdictions, recognizing that jurisdictions vary with respect to the cost of judicial campaigns, the size of the electorate, the availability of alternative sources of funding, as well as other factors.

In order for there to be grounds for disqualification under Rule 2.11(A)(4), the judge must "know[ ] or learn[ ] by means of a timely motion that a party, a party's lawyer or a law firm of a party's lawyer" has made aggregate contributions to the judge's campaign exceeding a specified amount with a specified time period. According to the Code, "aggregate" in relation to campaign contributions means not only contributions in cash or in kind made directly to the candidate's campaign committee, but also all contributions made indirectly with the understanding that they will be used to support the candidate's election of oppose the election of the candidate's opponent. Model Code of Judicial Conduct, Terminology. A "contribution" includes "both financial and in-kind contributions, such as goods, professional or volunteer services, advertising, and other types of assistance, which if obtained by the recipient otherwise, would require a financial expenditure." Model Code of Judicial Conduct, Terminology.

The U.S. Supreme Court decision in *Caperton v. A.T. Massey Coal Co., Inc.*, 129 S. Ct. 2252 (2009) gave the discussion a new variable by holding that "[o]n these extreme facts the probability of actual bias rises to an unconstitutional level." *Id.* at 2265. *Caperton* ratifies the earlier belief of those commentators who had asserted that some contributions by lawyers and litigants do create an appearance of impropriety and had suggested that the system of selecting judges should be changed (*see, e.g.*, John D. Fabian, *The Paradox of Elected Judges: Tension in the American Judicial System*, 15 Geo. J. Legal Ethics 155 (2001) (asserting that a system of elected judges produces outcomes necessarily at odds with the goal of the ABA Model Code of Judicial Conduct and evaluating systems that would better balance the interests of independence and accountability)) or that limits or restrictions on contributions should be imposed (*see, e.g.*, Gerald F. Uelmen, *Disqualification of Judges for Campaign Support or Opposition*, 3 Geo. J. Legal Ethics 419 (1991) (suggesting automatic disqualification where a lawyer or litigant was a "'substantial contributor,'' that is, contributed more than $500, to a judge's campaign); Stuart Banner, *Disqualifying Elected Judges from Cases Involving Campaign Contributors*, 40 Stan. L. Rev. 449 (1988) (suggesting that a judge should be disqualified upon motion whenever a litigant has contributed anything, or a lawyer has contributed more than an amount such as $1,000, to the judge's most recent campaign)). *See also* Margaret S. Williams and Corey A. Ditslear, *Bidding for Justice: The Influence of Attorneys' Contributions on*

State Supreme Courts, 28 Just. Sys. J. 135 (2007) (examining the influence of attorneys' campaign contributions on the behavior of the judges of the Wisconsin Supreme Court); Stephen J. Ware, *Money, Politics and Judicial Decisions: A Case Study of Arbitration Law in Alabama*, 30 Cap. U. L. Rev. 583, 601–629 (2002) (finding a strong correlation between Alabama Supreme Court justices' voted in arbitration cases and the sources of their campaign funding).

However, the *Caperton* Court did not provide the guidance sought by such commentators. Rather than directly addressing the election of judges or contributions or standards for recusal or disqualification in the face of a party's campaign contributions, the court avoided establishing an overriding due process principle and focused on state judicial codes of conduct: "Because the codes of judicial conduct provide more protection than due process requires, most disputes over disqualification will be resolved without resort to the Constitution." 129 S. Ct. at 2267. *Caperton* has prompted critique from commentators. It has been said that: it was a mistake to "constitutionalize" state recusal practice. Terri R. Day, *Buying Justice: Caperton v. A.T. Massey: Campaign Dollars, Mandatory Recusal and Due Process*, 28 Miss. C. L. Rev. 359 (2009); it was a mistake to constitute new constitutional jurisprudence to address the state supreme court justice's bad behavior. Lawrence Lessig, Comment, *What Everybody Knows and What Too Few Accept*, 123 Harv. L. Rev. 104 (2009). Others have noted that the Court's highlighting of the large amount of the original verdict and the 3–2 vote to overturn it raised doubt about whether a constitutional violation would have been found if the result of the original appeal had not rested on the vote of the justice who did not recuse himself. Pamela S. Karlan, *Electing Judges, Judging Elections, and the Lessons of Caperton*, 123 Harv. L. Rev. 80 (2009).

Even before *Caperton*, some courts and state ethics committees had encouraged judges to disclose to all parties when they are aware that a party or party's lawyer has contributed to their campaigns, particularly if the contribution is extraordinary in amount. *See* Nev. Stand. Comm. on Jud. Ethics and Election Prac. Op. JE02-001 (2002) (when contribution is extraordinary in amount, disclosure should be made and judge should determine if recusal is required). *But see Ex parte Kenneth D. McLeod, Sr., Family Ltd. P'ship XV*, 725 So. 2d 271 (Ala. 1998) (disclosure not required where party's campaign contribution was on public record, and judge did not attempt to conceal information).

In *Citizens United v. FEC*, 558 U.S. 310 (2010), the Supreme Court did not exclude the judicial branch from the decision's reach and "is likely to make this type of conflict of interest [presented in *Caperton*] more common, and to increase pressures on judges who seek to remain independent and impartial." Adam Skaggs, *Buying Justice: The Impact of Citizens United on Judicial Elections*, Brennan Center for Justice at New York University School of Law, p. 1 (2015). The U.S. Supreme Court's decision in *Citizens United* explained that the First Amendment did not allow for the suppression of political speech on the basis of the speaker's corporate identity, and that the Bipartisan Campaign Reform Act of 2002 section that prohibited corporations and unions from advocating for the election or defeat of a candidate violated the First Amendment. The Brennan Center recently noted, "The prospect of increased corporate spending in judicial elections in the 21 states where *Citizens United* invalidated corporate spending bans is of particular concern because many of these states have already experienced some of the highest spending and nastiest races to date." Adam Skaggs, *Buying Justice: The Impact of Citizens United on Judicial Elections*, Brennan Center for Justice at New York University School of Law, p.8 (2015).

Public Statements That Commit or Appear to Commit Judge to Reach Particular Result

Rule 2.11(A)(5) requires disqualification if the judge or judicial candidate "has made a public statement, other than in a court proceeding, judicial decision, or opinion, that commits, or appears to commit, the judge to reach a particular result or rule in a particular way in the proceeding or controversy." The Rule derives from former Canon 3E(1)(f), which was first adopted by the ABA in August 2003 and was the product of the ABA's Working Group on the First Amendment and Judicial Campaigns that was formed to review provisions of the Model Code of Judicial Conduct in light of First Amendment challenges to restrictions on judicial campaign speech. The Working Group suspended its efforts in March 2002, after the Supreme Court heard oral arguments in *Republican Party of Minn. v. White*, 122 S. Ct. 2528 (2002). That case challenged a provision of the Minnesota Code of Judicial Conduct restricting a candidate's ability to "announce his or her views on disputed legal or political issues" and the Court found the "announce clause" unconstitutional on First Amendment grounds.

The members of the Working Group, in light of the Court's opinion, determined that it was important to include a provision within the disqualification provisions of the Code that related directly to judicial campaign speech. For criticism of the amendment to the Rule, see Matthew J. Medina, *The Constitutionality of the 2003 Revisions to Canon 3(E) of the Model Code of Judicial Conduct*, 104 Colum. L. Rev. 1072 (2004) (examining the constitutionality of the ABA's revised disqualification rule in light of *White*, concluding that the rule is unlikely to survive strict scrutiny) and James Bopp, Jr. and Anita Y. Woudenberg, *An Announce Clause by Any Other Name: The Unconstitutionality of Disciplining Judges Who Fail to Disqualify Themselves for Exercising Their Freedom to Speak*, 55 Drake L. Rev. 723 (2007) (asserting that "One cannot avoid the constitutional prohibition on disciplining judges for exercising their First Amendment right simply by labeling that discipline as a recusal").

Rule 2.11(A)(5) is designed to make the disqualification ramifications of prohibited speech violations explicit. A few states, in reviewing their codes of judicial conduct in light of the majority opinion in *Republican Party of Minnesota v. White*, have provided for disqualification as a remedy for preserving judicial impartiality. *See American Bar Association Standing Committee on Judicial Independence and the Standing Committee on Ethics and Professional Responsibility Report 105B to the House of Delegates* (August 2003). For a discussion of the use of disqualification and recusal rules as a means of balancing judicial candidates' free speech rights with litigants' due process rights to an impartial forum, see Thomas R. Phillips and Karlene Dunn Poll, *Free Speech for Judges and Fair Appeals for Litigants: Judicial Recusal in a Post-White World*, 55 Drake L. Rev. 691 (2007).

JUDGE SERVED AS LAWYER OR WAS ASSOCIATED WITH LAWYER WHO PARTICIPATED IN THE MATTER

Pursuant to Rule 2.11(A)(6)(a), a judge is disqualified from sitting in a case in which he or she previously served as a lawyer. *See, e.g., Ajadi v. Comm'r of Correction*, 911 A.2d 712 (Conn. 2006) (failure of trial judge, who had represented defendant when defendant pled guilty to credit card fraud, to remove himself from presiding over defendant's petition for habeas corpus alleging ineffective assistance of counsel in the credit card fraud case, constituted plain error); *Jud. Qualifications Comm'n v. Shirado*, 364 N.W.2d 50 (N.D. 1985) (judge censured for failing to disqualify himself from hearing case in which he previously represented one litigant and failing to inform parties in another case that he had represented one litigant's son on traffic charges arising out of accident at issue); *Disc. Counsel v. Runyan*, 840 N.E.2d 623 (Ohio 2006) (judge violated Canon by ruling on former client's motion to terminate his prison sentence). In general, "served as a lawyer" has been interpreted to mean that the judge's prior contact with a case has been more than simply administrative or "pro forma." *Muench v. Israel*, 524 F. Supp. 1115 (E.D. Wis. 1981); *Turner v. State*, 573 So. 2d 657 (Miss. 1990) (fact that supreme court justice had been attorney general when defendant was extradited from another state insufficient to overcome presumption justice qualified and unbiased, so as to require disqualification).

Recusal is also mandated when the judge's former law partner or associate served as a lawyer in the matter while the judge was practicing with the lawyer. Ronald D. Rotunda and John S. Dzienkowski, *Legal Ethics: The Lawyer's Deskbook on Professional Responsibility* 1626 (2016). On the other hand, a judge is not disqualified every time a lawyer with whom the judge previously practiced appears before him or her. *In re Affidavit of Bias*, 947 P.2d 1152 (Utah 1997) (inclusion of "at the time of their association" illustrates that Section 3E(1)(b) was narrowly drafted to avoid disqualifying a judge merely because the judge practiced with a lawyer then appearing before judge). However, depending on the circumstances, the judge may still have to recuse himself or herself under the catchall provision of Rule 2.11(A) if there is a reasonable question as to the judge's impartiality.

Some jurisdictions have strict rules requiring disqualification for a certain period following the judge's association with a law firm. For instance, in Illinois, a judge is disqualified if the judge was, within the last three years, associated in the private practice of law with any law firm or lawyer currently representing any party in the controversy (excluding cases when no monetary interest was retained). Ill. Sup. Ct. R. 63. Supreme Court Rule 63C(1)(c) also requires disqualification for a period of seven years following the last date on which the judge represented any party to the controversy while the judge was a lawyer engaged in the private practice of law. Disqualification is required even if the judge's representation of the client did not involve the matter currently before the court.

Former Government Lawyers

Rule 2.11(A)(6)(b), which was added to the Code in 2007, provides that a judge is disqualified if the judge "served in governmental employment, and in such capacity participated personally and substantially as a lawyer or public official concerning the proceeding, or has publicly expressed in such capacity an opinion concerning the merits of the particular matter in controversy." Provisions regarding former government lawyers previously appeared only in the Commentary to former Canon 3E(1)(b). A provision identical to Rule 2.11(A)(6)(a) applies to federal court judges and can be found at 28 U.S.C.A. Section 455(b)(3). That provision is "intended to cover the situations which can occur during the first two or three years of judicial service of a lawyer who is appointed to the bench form service as a government lawyer." H.R. Rep. No. 1453, 93d Cong., 2d Sess. 6 (1974). In practice, disqualification has only been required if the judge who had previously been in a government agency had "served as a lawyer" in the same or similar proceeding. *Hearing on S. 1064 Before the Subcommittee on Improvements in Judicial Machinery of the Committee on the Judiciary*, 93d Cong., 1st Sess. 100 (1971–73). *See, e.g.*, Nev. Stand. Comm. on Jud. Ethics and Election Prac. JE04-001 (2004) (noting that circumstances under which a judge may be required to disqualify in Nevada are extremely limited, Commission advised that a justice of the peace is not necessarily disqualified because he or she used to be an attorney for a public housing agency, which is now pursuing eviction cases in the judge's court); S.C. Adv. Comm. on Stand. of Jud. Conduct, Op. 13-1995 (1995) (newly elected administrative judge, who, as attorney general formerly represented Department of Revenue, need not automatically recuse himself from a proceeding involving Department of Revenue unless judge had served as lawyer in the matter in controversy).

Prior to taking the bench, some judges may have served as prosecutors or public defenders. A criminal defendant who was charged at the time that the judge served in that previous capacity may assert that the judge should be disqualified under this provision because he or she was "a lawyer in the matter in controversy." *Penoyer v. State*, 945 So. 2d 586 (Fla. Dist. Ct. App. 2006) (defendant's allegation that trial judge also served as prosecutor for the underlying conviction entitled him to have post-conviction motions reheard by another judge); *Holmes v. State*, 966 So. 2d 858 (Miss. App. 2007) (judge was required to recuse himself from ruling on defendant's motion for post-conviction relief, even though defendant waived conflict of interest where judge had actively participated in defendant's prosecution while serving as assistant district attorney, having sworn out arrest warrants against defendant); Ariz. Sup. Ct. Jud. Ethics Adv. Comm. Op. 06-01 (2006) (former city prosecutor now sitting as judge must disqualify himself or herself in cases that were issued or charged while judge was prosecutor).

Disqualification will likely not be required if the court determines that the subsequent case before the judge does not involve the "same matter," *Cmmw. v. Jackson*, 590 S.E.2d 518 (Va. 2004) (judge's service as commonwealth's attorney for city at time defendant was convicted of underlying offenses did not require judge to recuse himself from hearing probation revocation proceeding; revocation hearing, while criminal in nature, was not same proceeding as original trial), the judge's previous involvement in the case did not constitute "service as a lawyer" in the matter, *see People v. Del Vecchio*, 544 N.E.2d 312 (Ill. 1989) (defendant was not prejudiced by fact that judge had some involvement in conviction of defendant on murder charges 14 years earlier; in previous proceeding, judge worked in state's attorney's office and was only involved insofar as he received report on defendant's confession, was in courtroom during guilty plea and sentencing; and agreed to expedite indictment so that defendant could be tried as juvenile, but did not have direct, personal interest in seeing defendant punished); Ill. Jud. Ethics Comm. Op. 03-02 (2003) (new judge, who formerly served as public defender and assistant state's attorney, is not disqualified from cases involving defendants the judge previously prosecuted or defended, unless the judge personally participated in the case currently before the court), or if there is no evidence that the judge was biased. *State v. Conway*, 77 S.W.3d 213 (Tenn. Crim. App. 2001) (judge remembered prosecuting defendant for same offense ten years earlier, but felt he was fair and impartial and defendant presented no evidence of lack of impartiality).

Judge Has Been Material Witness Concerning Proceeding

Pursuant to Rule 2.11(A)(6)(c), a judge may not sit in a case in which he or she has been a material witness. *See, e.g., Lewis v. State*, 565 S.E.2d 437 (Ga. 2002) (after testifying as a material witness with regard to an issue in a case, judge could not consider and rule on defendant's motion for a new trial); *In re Dostert*, 324 S.E.2d 402 (W. Va. 1984) (judge recused himself from the disciplinary proceeding of another judge because he had been a material witness in judge's criminal contempt trial and could be called as a witness in the discipline proceeding). A judge will not be considered a "material witness" if there are other people who can testify as to the fact in issue. *Johnson v. State*, 2007 WL 2812234 (Ala. Crim. App. 2007). *In re Disqualification of Warren*, 863 N.E.2d 638 (Ohio 2007) (disqualification not warranted where not likely that judge will be required as material witness on basis of being shareholder in non-party bank that allegedly has interest in outcome of case). In addition, some courts have held that disqualification is not required if the judge's testimony did not affect the merits of the cause. *Rodriguez v. State*, 919 So. 2d 1252 (Fla. 2005) (judge who testified at defendant's public records hearing during post-conviction proceedings was not "material witness" where judge's testimony was limited to physical description of prosecutor's missing documents, his recollection of how he handled them, and his efforts to locate them after being notified they were missing, and he did not testify about nature of documents or why he ruled they were not public records).

Judge Previously Presided as a Judge over the Matter in Another Court

Rule 2.11(A)(6)(d), which was added to the Code in 2007, mandates judicial disqualification where the judge previously presided over the matter in another court. Trial judges sometimes sit by designation on courts of appeal, and vice versa. Such judges should not hear cases over which they presided in a different court, and this Rule makes that clear. This Rule, however, leaves unaffected the propriety of a judge who decided a case on a panel of an appellate court participating in the rehearing of the case en banc with that same court. Charles G. Geyh & W. William Hodes, *Reporters' Notes to the Model Code of Judicial Conduct* 46 (2009).

Keeping Informed About Economic Interests

Pursuant to Rule 2.11(B), a judge must keep informed about his or her own personal and fiduciary economic interests. However, a judge only has a duty to make a "reasonable effort" to keep informed about the personal economic interests of his or her spouse or domestic partner and minor children residing in the household. *See, e.g., Robertson v. State*, 484 S.E.2d 18 (Ga. App. 1997) (unreasonable to require a judge to know all of her lawyer-husband's clients; therefore, judge was not required to recuse herself, even though her husband was representing victim in connection with potential civil suit against defendant). Factors used in determining whether or not a judge has made that reasonable effort include: "Did the interest of the spouse[, domestic partner,] or child come from the judge or from another source? Does the spouse[, domestic partner,] or child know the nature of the interest, or is he or she the beneficiary of a blind trust? Has the spouse's[, domestic partner's,] or child's financial interest been supervised by the judge in the past, or has the judge not been involved in handling the interest?" E. Wayne Thode, *Reporter's Notes to 1972 Judicial Code* 68 (1973).

The Code does not require that a judge keep informed about other interests that may lead to disqualification, including some of those listed in Rule 2.11(A). *See* Leslie W. Abramson, *Appearance of Impropriety: Deciding When a Judge's Impartiality "Might Reasonably Be Questioned,"* 14 Geo. J. Legal Ethics 55 (2000) (arguing that the Code should be modified to impose a mandatory duty on judges to stay informed at least about any of the specific disqualifying circumstances listed in Rule 2.11(A)).

DISCLOSURE OF BASIS FOR, AND WAIVER OF, DISQUALIFICATION

If a judge is disqualified under Rule 2.11 for any reason other than personal bias or prejudice, Rule 2.11(C) permits the parties to waive disqualification if the proper steps are taken. The judge may disclose on the record the basis for the judge's disqualification, and ask the parties and their lawyers to consider, out of the judge's presence, whether to waive disqualification.

Although disclosure under the model rule is discretionary, some states require judges to disclose any information that may be grounds for disqualification. *See Berry v. Berry*, 765 So. 2d 855 (Fla. Dist. Ct. App. 2000) (judge had affirmative duty to disqualify himself or at the very least, to disclose his client-lawyer relationship with party's lawyer); *White v. Suntrust Bank*, 538 S.E.2d 889 (Ga. Ct. App. 2000) (judge was required to inform the parties of her financial interest and ask them whether they wanted to waive the disqualification; she was not authorized to keep such information private and proceed to try the case); *Forsmark v. State*, 349 N.W.2d 763 (Iowa 1984) (judge in medical malpractice action, who knew at commencement of trial that his brother's estate had a pending malpractice action against plaintiffs' chief expert witness, had a duty to disclose that fact to plaintiffs); *Blaisdell v. City of Rochester*, 609 A.2d 388 (N.H. 1992) (it is the judge's responsibility to disclose, sua sponte, all information of any potential conflict between himself and the parties or their lawyers when his impartiality might reasonably be questioned); *Velardo v. Ovitt*, 933 A.2d 227 (Vt. 2007) (when judge fails to disqualify himself, a reviewing court must consider (1) the risk of injustice to the parties, (2) risk that the denial of relief will produce injustice in other cases, (3) risk of undermining public's confidence in judicial process); *Reilly by Reilly v. S.W. Pa. Transp. Auth.*, 479 A.2d 973 (Pa. Super. 1984); no party has a burden, either of exercising due diligence or otherwise, to search out and discover whether there may exist some fact, known to the judge but unknown to the party, that requires recusal; rather, if ground for recusal exists, the judge has a duty to either recuse himself sua sponte or disclose the ground and then preside, only if no party objects thereto). *See also* Leslie W. Abramson, *Appearance of Impropriety: Deciding When a Judge's Impartiality "Might Reasonably Be Questioned,"* 14 Geo. J. Legal Ethics 55 (2000) (asserting that the ABA Code should be amended to impose a mandatory duty to disclose any information that may be grounds for recusal).

A failure to disclose grounds for disqualification cannot be corrected by subsequent disclosure. *Huffman v. Ark. Jud. Disc. & Disability Comm'n*, 42 S.W.3d 386 (Ark. 2001) (judge's violation of predecessor to Rule 2.11(A) by entering an ex parte temporary restraining order in favor of corporation in which judge owed stock could not be corrected by a subsequent hearing in which the judge disclosed his interest for the purpose of waiver of disqualification pursuant to predecessor to Rule 2.11(C)). In addition, failure to disclose may result in disqualification. *See Blaisdell v. City of Rochester*, 609 A.2d 388 (N.H. 1992).

Some courts have held that the duty to disclose is a "separate obligation" and may be required even where disqualification is not. *Matter of Edwards*, 694 N.E.2d 701 (Ind. 1998) (duty to disclose is "broader than the duty to disqualify"); *In re Frank*, 753 So. 2d 1228 (Fla. 2000) ("[r]eading the text of [Rule 2.11] . . . together with the Commentary, . . . it appears that the standard for disclosure is lower. In other words, a judge should disclose information in circumstances even where disqualification may not be required"). At least one court has held that a judge's failure to disclose can be a violation of the language the predecessor to Rule 2.11(A) and grounds for discipline. *In re Cox*, 680 N.E.2d 528 (Ind. 1997) (judge suspended for 30 days for failing to disqualify himself or to disclose that he had submitted written materials highly critical of the defendant).

While the parameters of the duty to disclose information relevant to disqualification are not completely clear, disclosure is generally seen as the better practice, even by states not adopting the Code commentary. *See, e.g.*, Ill. Jud. Ethics Comm. Op. 96-18 (1996) ("Disclosure avoids any suggestion that the judge concealed important information regarding disqualification and allows the parties to preserve the disqualification issue for appellate review."). *See also* Leslie W. Abramson, *Judicial Disclosure and Disqualification: The Need for More Guidance*, 28 Just. Sys. J. 302 (2007) (suggesting that the ABA Model Code of Judicial Conduct needs broader disclosure provisions).

Disclosure of information relevant to disqualification does not mandate a judge's disqualification, but rather, it gives the parties an opportunity to file a motion to recuse or to waive the issue. If the judge discloses relevant information and the parties do not file a motion to recuse, the issue is likely waived. *See Banana v. State*, 635 So. 2d 851 (Miss. 1994) (judge informed defendant he was the district attorney when case was presented to the grand jury and that defendant could object to his being judge; since defendant did not object, issue was waived). If, however, the judge withholds the relevant information, and the party has no knowledge or reason to know of the information, a failure to file a motion will likely not waive the issue. *See, e.g., Bride v. Heckart*, 556 N.W.2d 449 (Iowa 1996) (case reversed and remanded where judge's failure to disclose his prior representation by defense counsel's law firm deprived plaintiff the opportunity to make a timely request for disqualification); *Aetna Cas. and Sur. Co. v. Berry*, 669 So. 2d 56 (Miss. 1996) (judge should have given the parties an opportunity to object to his sitting in case by disclosing that opposing counsel represented judge in his divorce case and was heavily involved in judge's re-election campaign).

On appeal, a judge's failure to disclose information relevant to the issue of disqualification may be seen as harmless error (*see Tennant v. Marion Health Care Foundation, Inc.*, 459 S.E.2d 374 (W. Va. 1995) (the "appearance of impropriety" or a "sense of unfairness," without more, does not necessitate a new trial)) or grounds for a reversal or vacation of the judge's orders (*see Blaisdell v. City of Rochester*, 609 A.2d 388 (N.H. 1992) (since the disqualified justice's rulings were an integral part of rulings in two subsequent related cases, those rulings also had to be vacated); *Velardo v. Ovitt*, 933 A.2d 227 (Vt. 2007) (when judge fails to disqualify himself, a reviewing court must consider (1) the risk of injustice to the parties, (2) risk that the denial of relief will produce injustice in other cases, (3) risk of undermining public's confidence in judicial process)).

In *Hood v. Texas*, the U.S. Supreme Court denied a writ of certiorari in the highly publicized case of Charles Hood, who was convicted of capital murder and sentenced to death in Texas. Subsequent to the conviction, it was discovered that the trial judge and the trial prosecutor were engaged in an ongoing sexual relationship during the trial. The Court of Criminal Appeals of Texas rejected, on a six to three vote, Hood's argument that the secret affair denied him a fair trial. *Ex Parte Hood*, 2009 WL 2963854 (Tex. Crim. App.), *cert. denied*, 130 S. Ct. 2097 (2010).

If the parties and lawyers agree, without participation by the judge or court personnel, that the judge should not be disqualified, the judge may participate in the proceeding. *See, e.g., Pannell v. State*, 71 S.W.3d 720 (Tenn. Crim. App. 2001) (judge could preside over defendant's criminal trial even though judge was disqualified by virtue of his former step-father relationship with victim, which reasonably called his impartiality into question, where during pretrial motions judge disclosed basis for his disqualification, and defendant chose to waive disqualification); ABA Standing Comm. on Ethics and Prof'l Responsibility, Formal Op. 07-449 (2007) (where judge is represented by lawyer who is also representing litigant appearing before judge in separate matter, absent personal bias or prejudice for against lawyer, judge may continue to participate in proceeding if judge discloses on the record that she is being represented in the other matter by one of the lawyers, and the parties and their lawyers all consider such disclosure, out of the presence of the judge and court personnel, and unanimously agree to waive the judge's disqualification). To be valid, the agreement must be "incorporated into the record of the proceeding." *In re Johnson*, 532 S.E.2d 883 (S.C. 2000) (disclosing that defendant was judge's grandson is not sufficient to waive disqualification; the parties must also agree that the judge not be disqualified).

Although the Code permits a judge to disclose a reason for disqualification and seek a waiver, a judge is not required to do so. *Spring Creek Rancher's Assn., Inc. v. McNichols*, 165 P.3d 244 (Colo. 2007). In addition, even if the parties agree to validly waive the judge's disqualification, the judge should recuse himself or herself if the judge believes that he or she cannot be impartial. In deciding whether to accept a remittal, at least one jurisdiction has advised that a judge may take into account the fact that he or she sits in a multi-judge court and that recusal would not result in a significant delay. N.Y. State Bar Ass'n Ethics Op. 703 (1998). But, the opinion also advised, that factor alone does not preclude acceptance of a remittal.

Any method for obtaining a waiver of disqualification that deviates from the requirements of Rule 2.11(C) is not valid. *See, e.g., In re Platt*, 8 P.3d 686 (Kan. 2000) (judge's informed consent procedure was inappropriate; judge refused to acknowledge his disqualification and litigants who did not wish to waive the disqualification were required to either fire their lawyer or seek disqualification was inappropriate); *In re Johnson*, 532 S.E.2d 883 (S.C. 2000) (while judge disclosed that defendant was her grandson to grandson's girlfriend and police officer involved, she did not follow the procedure required by Canon); Ariz. Sup. Ct. Jud. Ethics Adv. Comm. Op. 97-2 (1997) ("The remittal procedure of [Rule 2.11(C)] must be strictly followed."). Additionally, a waiver by a party's lawyer, as opposed to a waiver by the party may not be sufficient. *See, e.g., Thomas G. Abbell M.D. v. Oliver*, 117 S.W.3d 661 (Ky App. 2003) (the defendant did not waive the conflict created by the fact that the judge's husband was a lawyer in the firm representing the plaintiff simply because the defendant's lawyer knew about the conflict). *But see Southwood v. Carlson*, 704 N.E.2d 163 (Ind. App. 1999) (plaintiff waived claim that trial judge erroneously failed to recuse himself, based on his alleged relationship with defendant physician, by failing to request disqualification until after trial court granted summary judgment for defendants, where plaintiff's lawyer had reason to know of judge's relationship with physician prior to entry of judgment against plaintiff).

Not every state has adopted Rule 2.11(C), or its predecessor Canon 3F of the 1990 Model Code. *See Tyson v. State*, 622 N.E.2d 457 (Ind. 1993) (noting that Indiana has omitted remittal provisions from its Code believing that parties should not be permitted to waive grounds for recusal that the public might find warranted). Several other states permit remittal under the standard of the 1972 Code, that is, where the judge's financial interest in a proceeding was insubstantial or the judge's relationship to the proceeding under former Canon 3C(1)(d) was immaterial. *See* Leslie W. Abramson, *Appearance of Impropriety: Deciding When a Judge's Impartiality "Might Reasonably Be Questioned,"* 14 Geo. J. Legal Ethics 55 (2000).

Remittal of Disqualification in Federal Court

Remittal of disqualification is generally more limited in federal court than in state courts. The federal statute, 28 U.S.C. § 455(e), permits waiver of disqualification only when the judge is disqualified because "his impartiality might reasonably be questioned." The statute provides that "[n]o . . . judge . . . shall accept from the parties to the proceeding a waiver of any ground for disqualification enumerated in [28 U.S.C. § 455(b)]." 28 U.S.C. § 455(e). The statute only requires that the basis for disqualification be disclosed on the record. *Id. See, e.g., Fletcher v. Conoco Pipe Line Co.*, 323 F.3d 661 (8th Cir. 2003) (plaintiffs did not explicitly waive their right to raise a recusal claim on the basis of trial judge's alleged social relationship with plaintiff's attorney nor judge's alleged client relationship with attorneys' law firm, since there was no disclosure on the record of the basis for disqualification). The Code of Conduct for United States Judges provides that the parties and their lawyers must "all agree in writing or on the record that the judge should not be disqualified." Code of Conduct for United States Judges, Canon 3D.

RULE 2.12 SUPERVISORY DUTIES

(A) A judge shall require court staff, court officials, and others subject to the judge's direction and control to act in a manner consistent with the judge's obligations under this Code.

(B) A judge with supervisory authority for the performance of other judges shall take reasonable measures to ensure that those judges properly discharge their judicial responsibilities, including the prompt disposition of matters before them.

COMMENT

[1] A judge is responsible for his or her own conduct and for the conduct of others, such as staff, when those persons are acting at the judge's direction or control. A judge may not direct court personnel to engage in conduct on the judge's behalf or as the judge's representative when such conduct would violate the Code if undertaken by the judge.

[2] Public confidence in the judicial system depends upon timely justice. To promote the efficient administration of justice, a judge with supervisory authority must take the steps needed to ensure that judges under his or her supervision administer their workloads promptly.

1990 CODE COMPARISON

Rule 2.12 is former Canons 3C(2) and (3), which were combined under a general rubric, "Supervisory Duties." Paragraph (A) was reworded to reflect a more comprehensive understanding of the standards of conduct required of court personnel. Judges must insist that court staff and officials act in a manner consistent with all of a judge's obligations under the Code and not simply those previously enumerated in Canon 3C(2) relating to diligence, fidelity, and lack of bias or prejudice. The Comments are new to the Code. Charles G. Geyh & W. William Hodes, *Reporters' Notes to the Model Code of Judicial Conduct* 47–48 (2009).

ANNOTATION

STAFF, COURT OFFICIALS, AND OTHERS SUBJECT TO JUDGE'S DIRECTION AND CONTROL

Pursuant to Rule 2.12(A), a judge must require court staff, court officials, and others subject to their control to act in a manner consistent with the judge's obligations under the Code. The Code does not define "staff," but the term has been extended to all those who are employed by the judiciary, including court clerks, law clerks, bailiffs, secretaries, as well as staff attorneys and appellate court mediators. Utah Jud. Ethics Adv. Op. 97-6 (1997) (appellate court staff attorney is a court employee).

The Joint Commission to Evaluate the Model Code of Judicial Conduct added a new Comment to Rule 2.12(A), stating that a judge "may not direct court personnel to engage in conduct on the judge's behalf or as the judge's representative when such conduct would violate the Code if undertaken by the judge." This Comment was added to emphasize the "critical position judicial staff occupy in the justice system—not only in terms of their relevance to the administration of justice but also in terms of their role in preserving public confidence in the system as a whole." A judge must never direct staff within his or her control to engage in conduct that would violate the Code if undertaken by the judge. Charles G. Geyh & W. William Hodes, *Reporters' Notes to the Model Code of Judicial Conduct* 47–48 (2009).

A judge violates this provision by encouraging or permitting a staff member to do something that would violate the Code. *See, e.g., In re Walters*, 13–40 (Minn. Bd. on Jud. Standards 2014) (judge reprimanded for signing clerk's inaccurate time records, which if filed by judge would have violated Rules 1.1 and 1.2); *Miss. Comm'n on Jud. Performance v. Brown*, 918 So. 2d 1247 (Miss. 2005) (judge's attempt to use his position to obtain favorable treatment for, and obstruct prosecution of charges against, his son by telling court clerk to abandon normal procedure and hold son's file on her desk rather than place it on other judge's desk violated judicial Canon governing judge's administrative responsibilities constituted encouraging, if not demanding, that others violate their own respective codes of conduct); *In re Judicial Ethics Op. 2006-4*, 136 P.3d 1085 (Okla. 2006) (judge may not allow court reporter whom judge supervises to campaign for election of court reporter's spouse to judiciary since it would be improper for judge to campaign for judicial candidate).

Judges may also violate Rule 2.12(A) by permitting court employees to perform judicial functions. *See, e.g., In re Seal*, 585 So. 2d 741 (Miss. 1991) (judge was reprimanded for allowing clerical personnel to adjudicate criminal cases and highway patrol officers and clerks to adjudicate traffic tickets); *In re Perea*, 711 P.2d 894 (N.M. 1986) (judge violated Canon by delegating the duty to perform marriages to a municipal court clerk). Judges have also been disciplined under this provision when they failed to adequately supervise court employees. *See, e.g., In re Briggs*, 595 S.W.2d 270 (Mo. 1980) (judge who was rarely in his office more than one day a week failed to adequately supervise his clerk, who illegally granted a limited driving license to her brother-in-law and repeatedly reduced traffic tickets without authority); *In re Rose*, 144 S.W.3d 661 (Tex. Rev. Trib. 2004) (holding that judge could be removed from office for failing to supervise his staff), and when they knew or should have known that employees were acting improperly. *See In re Lockwood*, 804 P.2d 738 (Ariz. 1990) (justice of the peace violated predecessor to Rule 2.12(A) by failing to prevent clerks from improperly signing guilty pleas in misdemeanor DUI cases).

Judges have also been disciplined pursuant to the predecessor to Rule 2.12(A) for misusing court staff by having them perform non-court related activities during court hours. *See, e.g., In re Troy*, 306 N.E.2d 203 (Mass. 1974) (judge was disciplined for using services of a court officer as a bulldozer operator during regular court hours). Similarly, a judge has been disciplined under this rule for permitting a court employee to work at a second job at the same time that the employee was scheduled to be at work for the court. *In re Groneman*, 38 P.3d 735 (Kan. 2002).

Application of the predecessor to Rule 2.12(A) has not been uniform among jurisdictions. For instance, the Texas Committee on Judicial Ethics advised that the rule requires court employees to adhere to all provisions of the Code of Judicial Conduct. Tex. Comm'n on Jud. Ethics Op. 106 (1987). Ariz. Sup. Ct. Jud. Ethics Adv. Comm. Op. 00-03 (2000) (advising that since it would be a violation of the Code for a judge to accept payment of bar dues by an employer law firm, the judge for whom the law clerk works must direct the law clerk not to accept payment of bar dues by the law firm). The Utah Judicial Advisory Committee has chosen not to extend all provisions of the Code of Judicial Conduct to court employees, but does not believe the rule should be limited to the administrative responsibilities of employees. Utah Jud. Ethics Adv. Op. 88-1 (1988) (advising that although this Canon is in the Administrative Responsibility section of the Code, a plain reading indicates that court employees must, at a minimum, observe all code provisions that require diligence and fidelity). *See also Okla. Jud. Ethics Op. 2001-6*, 73 P.3d 727 (Okla. 2001) (advising that the Code does not apply to judge's staff, but judges have managerial duties and must require the staff to comply with certain ethical standards; for instance, judges should prohibit staff from soliciting goods for charitable purposes because attorneys and litigants may be intimidated or may expect advantages in future litigation by acts of generosity to staff members).

JUDGES WITH SUPERVISORY POWER OVER OTHER JUDGES

Rule 2.12(B) governs judges who hold supervisory positions over other judges. Supervising judges must take "reasonable measures" to ensure that the judges they are supervising properly discharge their judicial responsibilities, including prompt disposition of matters before them. The 1992 Code drafting committee believed that adequate supervision by supervisory judges including, where appropriate, providing caseload management advice on subordinate administrative matters, as well as requiring adherence to ethical mandates, was a key element in the administration of justice. Lisa L. Milord, *The Development of the ABA Judicial Code* 23 (1992). The Commission added a Comment to the Rule requiring supervising judges to take the steps needed to ensure that judges under their supervision administer their workloads properly. This Comment underscores the importance of timely justice in maintaining public confidence in the judicial system. Charles G. Geyh & W. William Hodes, *Reporters' Notes to the Model Code of Judicial Conduct* 48 (2009).

RULE 2.13 ADMINISTRATIVE APPOINTMENTS

(A) In making administrative appointments, a judge:

(1) shall exercise the power of appointment impartially* and on the basis of merit; and

(2) shall avoid nepotism, favoritism, and unnecessary appointments.

(B) A judge shall not appoint a lawyer to a position if the judge either knows* that the lawyer, or the lawyer's spouse or domestic partner,* has contributed more than $[insert amount] within the prior [insert number] year[s] to the judge's election campaign, or learns of such a contribution* by means of a timely motion by a party or other person properly interested in the matter, unless:

(1) the position is substantially uncompensated;

(2) the lawyer has been selected in rotation from a list of qualified and available lawyers compiled without regard to their having made political contributions; or

(3) the judge or another presiding or administrative judge affirmatively finds that no other lawyer is willing, competent, and able to accept the position.

(C) A judge shall not approve compensation of appointees beyond the fair value of services rendered.

COMMENT

[1] Appointees of a judge include assigned counsel; officials such as referees, commissioners, special masters, receivers, and guardians; and personnel such as clerks, secretaries, and bailiffs. Consent by the parties to an appointment or an award of compensation does not relieve the judge of the obligation prescribed by paragraph (A).

[2] Unless otherwise defined by law, nepotism is the appointment or hiring of any relative within the third degree of relationship of either the judge or the judge's spouse or domestic partner, or the spouse or domestic partner of such relative.

[3] The rule against making administrative appointments of lawyers who have contributed in excess of a specified dollar amount to a judge's election campaign includes an exception for positions that are substantially uncompensated, such as those for which the lawyer's compensation is limited to reimbursement for out-of-pocket expenses.

1990 CODE COMPARISON

Paragraph (A) of the Rule is taken from Canon 3C(4), paragraph (B) is taken from Canon 3C(5), and paragraph (C) is the last sentence of former Canon 3C(4). The proscription in (B) against the appointment of a lawyer who has contributed a defined amount to the judge's election campaign is extended to the spouse or domestic partner of the lawyer. Comment [2], which clarifies the meaning of "nepotism" and Comment [3], which clarifies the meaning of "substantially compensated" are new to the Code. Charles G. Geyh & W. William Hodes, *Reporters' Notes to the Model Code of Judicial Conduct* 49 (2009).

ANNOTATION

NEPOTISM AND FAVORITISM IN JUDICIAL APPOINTMENTS

Pursuant to Rule 2.13(A), a judge may not make "unnecessary appointments" and must exercise the power of appointment impartially and on the basis of merit, avoiding nepotism and favoritism. *See, e.g., In re Granier*, 906 So. 2d 417 (La. 2005) (judge censured for hiring registered nurse with whom he was romantically involved to review and summarize medical records for cases in his court); Ala. Jud. Inquiry Comm'n Adv. Op. 90-394 (1990) (judge may not hire his daughter as bailiff); *In re Dumas* (Tenn. Ct. of the Judiciary 2010) (judge reprimanded for hiring daughter as court officer); Wash. Ethics Adv. Comm. Op 92-11 (1992) (judge should not appoint his or her child to serve as pro tem judge).

As noted in the Commentary, appointees include assigned counsel; officials such as referees, commissioners, special masters, receivers, and guardians; and personnel such as clerks, secretaries, and bailiffs. *See, e.g.*, Nev. Stand. Comm. on Jud. Ethics and Election Prac. Op. JE05-002 (2005) (judge may not hire a relative within the third degree as the judge's law clerk); *but see* S.C. Adv. Comm. on Stand. of Jud. Conduct Op. 03-2008 (2008) (judge may hire his or her nephew as law clerk since nephew is not within the prohibited degree of relationship).

A Comment to the Rule defines nepotism as "the appointment or hiring of any relative within the third degree of relationship of either the judge or the judge's spouse or domestic partner, or the spouse or domestic partner of such relative." Model Code of Judicial Conduct Rule 2.13 cmt. [2]. A judiciary free of nepotism and favoritism is critical to the public's trust in the fairness and integrity of the judicial system. Ind. Comm'n on Jud. Qualifications Op. 2-98 (1998). In addition to violating Rule 2.13(A), a judge who makes appointment decisions based on nepotism or favoritism, may also violate Rule 2.4(B), which provides that a judge should not allow family, social, political, financial, or other interests or relationships to influence his or her judicial conduct or judgment. *See, e.g.*,

In re Davis, 865 So. 2d 693 (La. 2004) (judge appointed his father, who was a practicing attorney, to represent indigent criminal defendants).

Rule 2.13(A) does not prohibit a judge from ever employing a relative, friend, or political ally. However, to avoid a violation, the prospective employee's merit and a concern for the proper administration of justice must be the overriding factors in that decision. *Caudill v. Jud. Ethics Committee*, 986 S.W.2d 435 (Ky. 1999) (a judge may employ his or her spouse as a secretary so long as the spouse possesses skills and competence requisite to performing job duties; appointment of relative, if based on merit and ability, does not, without exception, equate to nepotism); *In re Dalessandro*, 397 A.2d 743 (Pa. 1979) (no evidence that judge's appointment of someone not within the department to position of chief cashier in domestic relations probation office was not based on merit); Del. Jud. Ethics Adv. Comm. Op. 2004-4 (2004) (judge may hire brother's niece-in-law as judicial law clerk given the degree of familial separation between judge and clerk and objectively strong qualifications that clerk brings to the job); Fla. Jud. Ethics Adv. Comm. Op. 98-4 (1998) (judge did not violate predecessor to Rule 2.13(A) by hiring his niece-in-law as a judicial assistant as long as the niece-in-law's employment was based on her abilities and merit and not on favoritism or her relationship with the judge); Ill. Jud. Ethics Comm. Op. 97-18 (1997) (judge's hiring of fellow judge's child as a secretary does not violate rule where the judge interviewed several applicants and found the judge's child to be qualified); Ind. Comm'n on Jud. Qualifications Op. 2-98 (1998) (interpreting rule).

Indiana's Commission on Judicial Qualifications advises that judges consider the following factors when hiring a relative or friend: (1) the degree, extent, or depth of the relationship of the prospective employee to the judge; (2) whether or not the position for the prospective employee is relatively lucrative; (3) whether the position is permanent or temporary, full-time, or part-time; (4) the degree of the day-to-day supervision and contact the judge would have with the prospective employee; (5) the position for which the judge is considering hiring a friend or relative must be announced or advertised to the public in the same manner other vacancies within the court are announced or advertised, and other qualified applicants must be considered. Ind. Comm'n on Jud. Qualifications Op. 2-98 (1998). The opinion emphasizes that only if the friend or relative is objectively qualified for the position, and only after the judge has weighed every relevant factor, may the judge hire or appoint a friend or relative. The opinion also urges judges to seek the Commission's approval before hiring or appointing a relative or close friend to any position.

In addition to preferential hiring decisions, a judge may violate Rule 2.13(A) by appointing friends or relatives to represent parties in a case or serve as a mediator, guardian, or in another similar capacity. *See, e.g., Spruance v.*

Comm'n on Jud. Qualifications, 532 P.2d 1209 (Cal. 1975) (judge violated rule by appointing two lawyers who were friends and political supporters to represent indigent defendants in criminal cases without first determining that defendants are indigent and that public defender is unable to represent them); *In re Davis*, 865 So. 2d 693 (La. 2004) (judge violated Canon by appointing his father, who was a practicing attorney, to represent indigent criminal defendants); *In re Ford*, 535 N.E.2d 225 (Mass. 1989) (judge who was a member of an animal rights group violated rule by appointing lawyers who were also members of the group to probate cases that resulted in substantial attorney's fees); *In re Fine*, 13 P.3d 400 (Nev. 2000) (judge violated rule by appointing her first cousin as mediator in child custody case, even though cousin was the only mediator in the state known to the judge). *See also* Ariz. Sup. Ct. Jud. Ethics Adv. Comm. Op. 92-01 (1992) (judge may not order supervised visitation in a child custody case through a social services agency administered by a member of the judge's immediate family because an objective observer might conclude that referrals by the judge were improperly ordered or were ordered to generate agency business). A judge may not skirt Rule 2.13(A) "by 'laundering' judicial appointments." Ronald D. Rotunda and John S. Dzienkowski, *Legal Ethics: The Lawyer's Deskbook on Professional Responsibility* 1651 (2016). For instance, a judge may not appoint other judges' sons to represent defendants at the same time that those judges are appointing his son. *Spector v. State Comm'n on Jud. Conduct*, 392 N.E.2d 552 (N.Y. 1979).

Appointing Campaign Contributors

Rule 2.13(B) provides that a judge may not appoint a lawyer to a position if the judge knows or learns that the lawyer has contributed more than a specified amount of money within a specified number of years. The local jurisdiction sets the amount of money and the relevant time period. There are exceptions to this rule, where there is little likelihood that an appointment would create an appearance of impropriety. The prohibition does not apply where (1) the appointee is given a position that is substantially uncompensated; (2) the appointee is selected in rotation from a list of qualified and available lawyers compiled without regard to political contributions; or 3) the judge or another presiding judge affirmatively finds that no other lawyer is willing, competent, and able to accept the position. "Uncompensated positions" include those for which the lawyer's compensation is limited to reimbursement for out-of-pocket expenses. Model Code of Judicial Conduct Rule 2.13 cmt. [3].

Rule 2.13(B) corresponds with Model Rule of Professional Conduct 7.6, which prohibits a lawyer from accepting government legal engagements or appointments by a judge if the lawyer has made or solicited a political contribution in order to obtain or be considered for the appointment. Both Rule 2.13(B) and Rule 7.6, which was adopted in 2000, reflect the concern about the appearance of impropriety if lawyers make a political contribution to the judge and the judge then rewards or appears to reward those lawyers by appointing them to a government legal position. Ronald D. Rotunda, *Judicial Elections, Campaign Financing, and Free Speech*, 2 Election L.J. 79 (2003).

COMPENSATION FOR APPOINTEES

Rule 2.13(C) provides that a judge shall not approve compensation for employees beyond the fair value of the services rendered. Consent by the parties to an award of compensation is no defense. Model Code of Judicial Conduct Rule 2.13 cmt. [1].

RULE 2.14 DISABILITY AND IMPAIRMENT

A judge having a reasonable belief that the performance of a lawyer or another judge is impaired by drugs or alcohol, or by a mental, emotional, or physical condition, shall take appropriate action, which may include a confidential referral to a lawyer or judicial assistance program.

COMMENT

[1] "Appropriate action" means action intended and reasonably likely to help the judge or lawyer in question address the problem and prevent harm to the justice system. Depending upon the circumstances, appropriate action may include, but is not limited to speaking directly to the impaired person, notifying an individual with supervisory responsibility over the impaired person, or making a referral to an assistance program.

[2] Taking or initiating corrective action by way of referral to an assistance program may satisfy a judge's responsibility under this Rule. Assistance programs have many approaches for offering help to impaired judges and lawyers, such as intervention, counseling, or referral to appropriate health care professionals. Depending upon the gravity of the conduct that has come to the judge's attention, however, the judge may be required to take other action, such as reporting the impaired judge or lawyer to the appropriate authority, agency, or body. See Rule 2.15.

1990 CODE COMPARISON

Rule 2.14 is new. It governs a difficult and extremely important issue. Impairment can undermine judicial competence, diligence, and demeanor specifically, and public confidence in the courts generally. The Rule imposes a mandatory obligation to take appropriate action when a judge learns of a colleague's impairment. The objective of this provision is to guide and encourage judges to address impairment problems when they arise. Charles G. Geyh & W. William Hodes, *Reporters' Notes to the Model Code of Judicial Conduct* 50 (2009).

Annotation

The substance of Rule 2.14 was new to the Model Code in 2007, though at least one jurisdiction, West Virginia, had previously imposed upon judges an obligation to report another judge who is or may be incapacitated or impaired. West Virginia's former Canon 3D(3) provided that "A judge who has knowledge that another judge is incapacitated or impaired, raising a substantial question as to the judge's fitness for office, shall inform the Committee on Assistance and Intervention of the judiciary."

Rule 2.15 Responding to Judicial and Lawyer Misconduct

(A) A judge having knowledge* that another judge has committed a violation of this Code that raises a substantial question regarding the judge's honesty, trustworthiness, or fitness as a judge in other respects shall inform the appropriate authority.*

(B) A judge having knowledge that a lawyer has committed a violation of the Rules of Professional Conduct that raises a substantial question regarding the lawyer's honesty, trustworthiness, or fitness as a lawyer in other respects shall inform the appropriate authority.

(C) A judge who receives information indicating a substantial likelihood that another judge has committed a violation of this Code shall take appropriate action.

(D) A judge who receives information indicating a substantial likelihood that a lawyer has committed a violation of the Rules of Professional Conduct shall take appropriate action.

Comment

[1] Taking action to address known misconduct is a judge's obligation. Paragraphs (A) and (B) impose an obligation on the judge to report to the appropriate disciplinary authority the known misconduct of another judge or a lawyer that raises a substantial question regarding the honesty, trustworthiness, or fitness of that judge or lawyer. Ignoring or denying known misconduct among one's judicial colleagues or members of the legal profession undermines a judge's

responsibility to participate in efforts to ensure public respect for the justice system. This Rule limits the reporting obligation to those offenses that an independent judiciary must vigorously endeavor to prevent.

[2] A judge who does not have actual knowledge that another judge or a lawyer may have committed misconduct, but receives information indicating a substantial likelihood of such misconduct, is required to take appropriate action under paragraphs (C) and (D). Appropriate action may include, but is not limited to, communicating directly with the judge who may have violated this Code, communicating with a supervising judge, or reporting the suspected violation to the appropriate authority or other agency or body. Similarly, actions to be taken in response to information indicating that a lawyer has committed a violation of the Rules of Professional Conduct may include but are not limited to communicating directly with the lawyer who may have committed the violation, or reporting the suspected violation to the appropriate authority or other agency or body.

1990 CODE COMPARISON

This Rule derives from former Canon 3D. Paragraphs (A), (B), and (D) of the Rule were reworded to parallel the lawyer reporting obligations in Rule 8.3 of the Model Rules of Professional Conduct to require reporting to the "appropriate authority" whenever the judge has knowledge of another judge's violation of the Code or a lawyer's violation of the Rules of Professional Conduct that raises a substantial question as to the judge's or lawyer's "honesty, trustworthiness, or fitness" as a judge or lawyer in other respects. Charles G. Geyh & W. William Hodes, *Reporters' Notes to the Model Code of Judicial Conduct* 52 (2009).

Paragraph (C), which appeared in the first sentence of Canon 3D(1), was revised to state that when a judge receives information indicating a substantial likelihood that another judge has violated the Rules, the judge receiving such information "shall"—no longer "should"—take appropriate action. In the Joint Commission to Evaluate the Model Code of Judicial Conduct's view, in situations where the judge does not "know" but receives information making it substantially likely that another judge has violated the Rules, the judge receiving such information shall take action. The appropriate action would vary with the circumstances. In some instances, it could involve talking to the judge in question or in other instances, taking steps to verify the information received and report it to the appropriate authorities. *Id.*

Former Canon 3D(3), which declared that the acts of a judge in the discharge of disciplinary responsibilities were absolutely privileged, was deleted. Although there was no opposition to the concept that judges should be immune from suit in such situations, the Commission concluded that such a provision was inappropriate for the Model Code of Judicial Conduct. Neither the ABA nor an adopting court is in a position to grant or deny judicial immunity in the context of judicial conduct standards. Accordingly, Canon 3D(3) was viewed as a generalized statement of support for judicial immunity, which, in the Commission's view, was not appropriate for the Code. *Id.*

Comment [1] is new to the Code and was added to underscore the relationship between reporting serious misconduct of judges and lawyers and the judge's responsibility to preserve public confidence in the courts. *Id.*

ANNOTATION

REPORTING JUDICIAL MISCONDUCT

Subsections (A) and (C) of Rule 2.15(A) set forth the circumstances in which judges are to take disciplinary action with regard to the misconduct of other judges and lawyers. The Rule distinguishes between circumstances in which the judge "knows" that another judge has committed a violation of the Code of Judicial Conduct and those in which the judge receives information indicating "a substantial likelihood" that such a violation has occurred. A judge must inform the "appropriate authority" if he or she has "knowledge" that a violation of the Code of Judicial Conduct has been committed raising a substantial question about the judge's honesty, trustworthiness, or fitness as a judge. "Knowledge" means "actual knowledge of the fact in question" and can be "inferred from circumstances." Model Code of Judicial Conduct, Terminology. *See generally* Leslie W. Abramson, *The Judge's Ethical Duty to Report Misconduct by Other Judges and Lawyers and Its Effect on Judicial Independence*, 25 Hofstra L. Rev. 751 (1997) (comparing the judicial duty to disclose with a lawyer's ethical duty to disclose). If a judge does not have sufficient knowledge of another judge's violation of the Code of Conduct, the duty to report is not triggered. *See, e.g.,* Mass. Comm. on Jud. Ethics Adv. Op. 07-08 (2007) (judge did not have sufficient knowledge that judge may have violated Code of Judicial Conduct by failing to report attorney's misconduct and therefore duty to report judge was not triggered). Ill. Jud. Ethics Comm. Op. 95-01 (1995) (judge whose information that another judge may have violated the Code of Judicial Conduct comes from a litigant's filing of a Motion for Substitution of Judge does not have the actual knowledge contemplated to require judge to initiate disciplinary measures).

If a judge receives information indicating a "substantial likelihood" that a judge has committed a violation of the Code, the judge must take "appropriate action." The Canon does not require the judge to hold a hearing and make a definitive decision that a violation has occurred before the reporting requirement is triggered and at least one state's judicial ethics committee has advised that the reporting requirement is triggered when the judge has "sufficient information" to conclude that a "substantial issue" has been raised that a violation has occurred. *See* Mass. Comm. on Jud. Ethics Adv. Op. 2002-04 (2002).

According to the rule's commentary, "appropriate action" may include, but is not limited to, communicating directly with the judge who may have violated the Code, communicating with a supervising judge, or reporting the suspected violation to the appropriate authority or other agency or body. "Appropriate authority" is the authority with responsibility for initiation of disciplinary proceedings with respect to the violation reported. Some jurisdictions' rules specify to whom a judge must report misconduct. For instance, Massachusetts Rule 2.15(A) provides that if a judge becomes aware of another judge's unprofessional conduct he must report his knowledge to "the Chief Justice of the Supreme Judicial Court, the Chief Justice of the court on which the judge sits, and if the judge is a Trial Court judge, the Chief Justice of the Trial Court."

REPORTING LAWYER MISCONDUCT

Subsections (B) and (D) of Rule 2.15 address a judge's duty to report lawyer misconduct, and as with the duty to report judicial misconduct, these subsections distinguish between circumstances in which the judge "knows" that a lawyer has committed a violation of the Rule of Professional Conduct and those in which the judge receives information indicating "a substantial likelihood" that such a violation has occurred. In the latter situation, the Rule requires that the judge take "appropriate action," which may include, but is not limited to, communicating directly with the lawyer who may have committed the violation, or reporting the suspected violation to the appropriate authority or other agency or body. Model Code of Judicial Conduct Rule 2.15 cmt. [2]. A judge will likely need to make an independent assessment as to what corrective action is appropriate on a case-by-case basis. *See, e.g.*, Wash. Ethics Adv. Comm. Op. 02-15 (2002) (advising that where lawyer has been charged with DUI, it might be appropriate for the judge to speak to the lawyer or his or her supervisor, suggest the lawyer contact an assessment or treatment program such as the Bar's LAP or the judge may make a disciplinary complaint to the Washington State Bar Association).

In some states, "appropriate action" may mean reporting some types of lawyer misconduct to the disciplinary authority. *See e.g., Fravel v. Haughey*, 727 So. 2d 1033 (Fla. App. Ct. 1999) (although the code does not specify what the term "appropriate action" entails, at least in the case of lawyers who do not heed less severe judicial efforts to correct such conduct, referrals should be made to the Florida Bar); Fla. Jud. Ethics Adv. Comm. Op. 2001-06 (2001) (a judge must disclose to the Florida Bar potential unauthorized practice of law by a suspended lawyer in the judge's court. The judge should first investigate to determine if it is unauthorized practice. If so, the judge must report. If not, no report is required. If the judge is unable to satisfactorily complete an investigation, the judge may immediately report the matter to the bar); *AIG Hawaii Ins. Co. v. Bateman*, 923 P.2d 395 (Haw. 1996) (possibility that attorneys for automobile liability insurer and accident victim may have violated Rules of Professional Conduct by failing to disclose settlement, while appealing trial court's determination that driver was permissive user, warranted reference of record of case to office of disciplinary counsel for appropriate action); *In re Holzman*, (N.Y. Comm'n on Jud. Conduct 2012) (judge with information indicating substantial likelihood that lawyer who was court-appointed public administrator "committed act that strongly pointed to larcenous conduct" and overcharged estates censured for failing to fire and report lawyer to disciplinary and law enforcement authorities); *Johnson v. Johnson*, 948 S.W.2d 835 (Tex. Ct. App. 1997) (stating that court is bound by Canon to inform state bar of attorney misconduct); *Gum v. Dudley*, 505 S.E.2d 391 (W. Va. 1997) (when the Supreme Court of Appeals believes a case before it presents the appearance of conduct that does not comport with the Rules of Professional Conduct, the Court refers the matter to the Office of Disciplinary Counsel for its review).

In other states, reporting to the disciplinary authority may not be required unless a certain threshold is met. Ill. Jud. Ethics Comm. Op. 99-06 (1999) (advising that a judge must take appropriate disciplinary action against a lawyer whom the judge knows to have committed an ethical violation, and must report misconduct to disciplinary authority where the lawyer's conduct would constitute a crime); Ill. Jud. Ethics Comm. Op. 95-10 (1995) (lawyer's testimony about using cocaine confers on the presiding judge knowledge requiring the judge to report the attorney to the lawyer disciplinary authority).

Where a judge has "knowledge" that a lawyer has committed a violation of the Rules of Professional Conduct that raises a substantial question as to the lawyer's honesty, trustworthiness, or fitness as a lawyer in other respects, Rule 2.15(B) requires that the judge inform the "appropriate authority." *See, e.g.*, Mass. Comm. on Jud. Ethics Adv. Op. 07-08 (2007) (judge had knowledge of facts indicating a substantial likelihood that an attorney committed a violation of the Massachusetts Rules of Professional Conduct that raises a significant question as to his honesty, integrity, trustworthiness, or fitness for the practice of law and therefore must report the matter to bar counsel). Some jurisdictions, such as Arkansas, expressly provide that the judge must report the misconduct to the state's lawyer disciplinary authority. Other jurisdictions, however, such as Texas, provide that the judge must report such misconduct to the state's lawyer disciplinary authority *or take other appropriate action. In re J.B.K.*, 931 S.W.2d 581 (Tex. Ct. App. 1996) (when a judge receives information that raises substantial question as to lawyer's honesty, trustworthiness or fitness as lawyer in other respects, the judge is mandated to either inform the disciplinary authority or take other appropriate action). Judith A. McMorrow, Jackie A. Gardina, & Salvatore Ricciardone, *Judicial Attitudes Toward Confronting*

Attorney Misconduct: A View from the Reported Decisions, 32 Hofstra L. Rev. 1425 (2004).

The Code of Conduct for United States Judges, which applies to federal court judges, provides that "[a] judge should take appropriate action upon learning of reliable evidence indicating the likelihood that a judge's conduct contravened this Code or a lawyer violated applicable rules of professional conduct." Code of Conduct for United States Judges, Canon 3B(5). This language is similar to the language used in the 1972 version of the ABA Model Code of Judicial Conduct, which suggested but did not require that a judge take action when he or she becomes aware of unprofessional conduct. *See, e.g., Cobell v. Norton*, 212 F.R.D. 24 (D.D.C. 2002) (noting that "because not every violation for the ethics rules deserves punishment, there remains the question as to whether this matter warrants referral to the Disciplinary Panel for further proceedings") However, a federal court judge is likely to take such action where the lawyer's conduct affected the integrity of the proceeding. *See, e.g., U.S. ex rel. Crist v. Lane*, 577 F. Supp. 504 (N.D. Ill. 1983) (referring case to Illinois lawyer disciplinary authority where prosecutor's outrageous and inflammatory conduct denied petitioner a fair trial).

At least one jurisdiction had advised that when a judge reports attorney misconduct in a case that judge must disqualify from that case. Colo. Jud. Ethics Adv. Bd. Op. 2004-01 (2004) (judge's report of an attorney's misconduct in a case pending before the judge requires the judge to disqualify himself or herself).

REPORTING CRIMINAL CONDUCT DISCLOSED DURING PROCEEDINGS

On a related note, the Model Code of Judicial Conduct does not impose a duty to report misconduct by those who are not judges or lawyers. And most state ethics committees have advised that a judge does not have an affirmative ethical obligation to report criminal activity divulged during civil litigation. *See, e.g.*, Alaska Comm'n on Jud. Cond. Formal Ethics Op. 017 (1993) (judge who becomes aware of witness's illegal drug trafficking does not have an ethical duty to report it); Ga. Adv. Op. 166 (1992) (a "judge should not assume a prosecutorial role, nor chill public access to the courts by assuming the role of a policeman"); Wash. Ethics Adv. Comm. Op. 93-11 (1993) (no obligation to report tax violation). However, although a judge may not be required to report illegal activity, the judge is not prohibited from doing so. Most ethics committees have advised that it is within the judge's discretion to do "as judgment and conscience dictate." Ariz. Sup. Ct. Jud. Ethics Adv. Comm. Op. 92-15 (1992) (opining that a judge must weigh the severity of the criminal activity and stating that "a judge has no duty to report each and every witness who has admitted to having once smoked marijuana. On the other hand, a judge is under an obvious imperative to notify the police of a witness who, in court, admitted committing recent, unsolved serial murders. Between these two extremes lies the twilight zone of discretion. It is the nature of discretion that it can be abused both by action and inaction"). Some ethics committees have advised that a judge should expose obvious and egregious illegal activity where failure to do so could undermine confidence in the integrity of the judiciary. Cynthia Gray, *A Judge's Obligation to Report Criminal Activity*, 18 No. 3 Judges' Journal 3 (Fall 1996) *citing* Pa. Adv. Op. 95-1 (1995); U.S. Compendium of Selected Opinions § 1.1(c) (1995). If a judge decides to report the criminal activity, the appropriate authorities should be informed "at a time and in a manner that will not affect any ongoing litigation before the judge." Cynthia Gray, *A Judge's Obligation to Report Criminal Activity*, 18 No. 3 Judges' Journal 3 (Fall 1996) *citing* Alaska Comm'n on Jud. Cond. Formal Ethics Op. 017 (1993).

RULE 2.16 COOPERATION WITH DISCIPLINARY AUTHORITIES

(A) A judge shall cooperate and be candid and honest with judicial and lawyer disciplinary agencies.

(B) A judge shall not retaliate, directly or indirectly, against a person known* or suspected to have assisted or cooperated with an investigation of a judge or a lawyer.

COMMENT

[1] Cooperation with investigations and proceedings of judicial and lawyer discipline agencies, as required in paragraph (A), instills confidence in judges' commitment to the integrity of the judicial system and the protection of the public.

1990 CODE COMPARISON

The Rule and its Comment are new. In the Joint Commission to Evaluate the Model Code of Judicial Conduct's view, the need for a judge's cooperation in the disciplinary process is paramount. Moreover, for a judge to retaliate against a person for cooperating in disciplinary proceedings against him or her would be patently unethical. This Rule thus serves to address an important omission in the former Code. Charles G. Geyh & W. William Hodes, *Reporters' Notes to the Model Code of Judicial Conduct* 53 (2009).

ANNOTATION

Rule 2.16(A) requires judges to cooperate with and be candid and honest with judicial and disciplinary agencies. *See, e.g., In re Maggio*, 440 S.W.3d 333 (Ark. 2014) (judge removed from office, in part, for attempting to remove comments posted on Internet forum about cases pending before judge); *In re Adams*,

833 N.W.2d 897 (Mich. 2013) (judge committed perjury in personal divorce case and then lied to investigators from disciplinary agency about the same incidents); *In re James*, 821 N.W.2d 144 (Mich. 2012) (judge lied to disciplinary investigators about facts of matter investigated); *In re Leavitt*, 67987 (Nev. 2015) (judge was not honest in response to disciplinary agency questions regarding contempt proceedings); *In re Graham*, 1202-1083 (Nev. Comm'n on Jud. Discipline 2013) (judge lied about source of funds judge used to purchase property from third party who was restricted from dissipating property by pending divorce matter of which the judge had knowledge); *In re McAndrews*, (N.Y. Comm'n on Jud. Conduct 2013) (judge failed to respond to "numerous inquiries" from Commission investigating judge's failure to file 2010 financial disclosure statement). It requires a judge to "refrain from being dishonest and making deliberately false statements" to disciplinary agencies and includes a "duty not to make material omissions during a disciplinary investigations." *See In re Karasov*, 805 N.W.2d 255, 268 (Minn. 2011).

Rule 2.16(B) prohibits a judge from directly or indirectly retaliating against a person the judge knows or suspects has assisted or cooperated with an investigation of a judge or lawyer. *See, e.g.*, *In re Crow*, nos. 12-160 (Arkansas Jud. Disc. & Disability Comm'n 2013) (judge censured for investigating and filing disciplinary complaint against public defender in retaliation for lawyer's previous filling ethics complaint against judge).

Canon 3

A judge shall conduct the judge's personal and extrajudicial activities to minimize the risk of conflict with the obligations of judicial office.

1990 Code Comparison

New Canon 3 is largely drawn from Canon 4 of the 1990 Code, but "covers more ground." Some material involving the personal activities of a judge has been moved from Canon 2 of the 1990 Code to this Canon. Some activities governed by Canon 3 are closely related to a judge's professional life, but those activities are "extrajudicial" because they are not part of a judge's official duties. Yet, they are less formal and less public than participating in a seminar or accepting an award, such as membership in private clubs, accepting gifts, contributing to charities, etc. Accordingly, the word "personal" was added to the Canon title to make it more accurate and complete. Additionally, the phrase "conflict with judicial obligations" was replaced with "conflict with the obligations of judicial office" simply as a reminder that judges have a variety of duties, including administrative duties, that go with the judicial office. Charles G. Geyh & W. William Hodes, *Reporters' Notes to the Model Code of Judicial Conduct* 54–55 (2009).

Rule 3.1 Extrajudicial Activities in General

A judge may engage in extrajudicial activities, except as prohibited by law* or this Code. However, when engaging in extrajudicial activities, a judge shall not:

(A) participate in activities that will interfere with the proper performance of the judge's judicial duties;

(B) participate in activities that will lead to frequent disqualification of the judge;

(C) participate in activities that would appear to a reasonable person to undermine the judge's independence,* integrity,* or impartiality;*

(D) engage in conduct that would appear to a reasonable person to be coercive; or

(E) make use of court premises, staff, stationery, equipment, or other resources, except for incidental use for activities that concern the law, the legal system, or the administration of justice, or unless such additional use is permitted by law.

COMMENT

[1] To the extent that time permits, and judicial independence and impartiality are not compromised, judges are encouraged to engage in appropriate extrajudicial activities. Judges are uniquely qualified to engage in extrajudicial activities that concern the law, the legal system, and the administration of justice, such as by speaking, writing, teaching, or participating in scholarly research projects. In addition, judges are permitted and encouraged to engage in educational, religious, charitable, fraternal, or civic extrajudicial activities not conducted for profit, even when the activities do not involve the law. See Rule 3.7.

[2] Participation in both law-related and other extrajudicial activities helps integrate judges into their communities, and furthers public understanding of and respect for courts and the judicial system.

[3] Discriminatory actions and expressions of bias or prejudice by a judge, even outside the judge's official or judicial actions, are likely to appear to a reasonable person to call into question the judge's integrity and impartiality. Examples include jokes or other remarks that demean individuals based upon their race, sex, gender, religion, national origin, ethnicity, disability, age, sexual orientation, or socioeconomic status. For the same reason, a judge's extrajudicial activities must not be conducted in connection or affiliation with an organization that practices invidious discrimination. See Rule 3.6.

[4] While engaged in permitted extrajudicial activities, judges must not coerce others or take action that would reasonably be perceived as coercive. For example, depending upon the circumstances, a judge's solicitation of contributions or memberships for an organization, even as permitted by Rule 3.7(A), might create the risk that the person solicited would feel obligated to respond favorably, or would do so to curry favor with the judge.

1990 CODE COMPARISON

To the extent that Rule 3.1 serves as a general list of restrictions upon a judge's participation in extrajudicial activities, it is chiefly derived from Canon 4A of the 1990 Code. However, the new set of restrictions is somewhat different as it focuses attention more sharply on interference with the independence, integrity, and impartiality of judges. Rule 3.1(A) is essentially the same as Canon 4A(3) with the addition of the word "judge's" before "judicial duties." Rule 3.1(B) also derives from Canon 4A(3) but is a newly added specific instance of the prohibition contained in Rule 3.1(A).

Rule 3.1(C) is based on Canon 4A(1) but with expanded coverage and revised language. The Commission substituted the phrase "would appear to a reasonable person to undermine" for "cast reasonable doubt on," and broadened coverage from "act impartially" to "the judge's independence, integrity, or impartiality." The Commission decided that the words "cast reasonable doubt on" were too closely associated with criminal law and did not accurately express the proper level of certainty required. The new standard turns on the thought processes of a "reasonable person," which is a familiar standard in law, generally, and also suggestive of the "might reasonably be questioned" language of 28 U.S.C. § 455. Charles G. Geyh & W. William Hodes, *Reporters' Notes to the Model Code of Judicial Conduct* 56–57 (2009).

Rule 3.1(D) is a new provision that guards against overt or subtle efforts by a judge to coerce others into participating in extrajudicial activities favored by the judge. The Commission heard testimony suggesting that coercion of this kind can be a significant problem in small communities with only one judge or a small number of judges, and a small number of lawyers, who need to maintain good relations with the judiciary. *Id.*

Rule 3.1(E) is also new, but has some overlap with aspects of former Canon 2B ("lend the prestige of judicial office to advance the private interests of the judge or others"). The Rule adds a new prohibition against using court facilities and other resources for a judge's extrajudicial activities, but with an exception for incidental use in connection with a law-related event. The rationale for the general restriction is that favoring a particular charity or other extrajudicial event by providing access to facilities that are closed to others is an abuse of the prestige of judicial office. See Rule 1.3. The rationale for the exception, however, is that certain activities, such as opening a real courtroom for use in a moot court competition or using a court's conference room for a meeting of a bar association task force that includes the judge, are not abuses of judicial office. *Id.*

Comments [1] through [3] are derived from the Commentary to Canons 4A and 4B, while Comment [4], which is new to the Code, fleshes out the intention of Rule 3.1(D), which is also new.

Annotation

Introduction

"Rule 3.1 establishes the fundamental principle that none of a judge's personal, financial, or extrajudicial activities can be allowed to negatively affect the performance of the judge's judicial duties, including by generating frequent disqualification." Charles G. Geyh & W. William Hodes, *Reporters' Notes to the Model Code of Judicial Conduct* 56 (2009). The justifications for limiting a judge's off-bench activities generally fall into one of three categories: (1) the need to avoid the appearance of partiality, favoritism, or other collateral misuse of public office; (2) the need to maintain public confidence in the members of the judiciary; and (3) the need to ensure that judges will not be distracted by nonjudicial activities. Charles Gardner Geyh, James J. Alfini, Steven Lubet, & Jeffrey M. Shaman, *Judicial Conduct and Ethics* § 10.03 10–3 (5th ed. 2013). To that end, Rule 3.1 requires a judge to refrain from participating in activities that would interfere with the proper performance of the judge's judicial duties, lead to frequent disqualification, appear to undermine the judge's independence, integrity, or impartiality, or appear to be coercive. This rule also prohibits judges from using court premises, staff, stationery, equipment, or other resources for extrajudicial activities, except for incidental use for activities that concern the law, the legal system, or the administration of justice, or unless permitted by law. Some extrajudicial activities may need to be completely avoided upon assuming the bench while others may only need to be curtailed in order to ensure compliance with Rule 3.1. *See, e.g.*, Fla. Jud. Ethics Adv. Comm. Op. 2001-02 (2001) (upon taking the bench, judge may remain a member of an e-mail forum for real estate lawyers, but may only read the messages and may not ask or respond to questions). In a similar vein, Florida has opined that a judge may have his own social networking page, but may neither "friend" lawyers who appear before him nor allow the lawyers to "friend" him. Fla. Jud. Ethics Adv. Comm. Op. 2009-20 (2009).

The high standard of conduct imposed by Rule 3.1 is not intended to proscribe a judge's extrajudicial activities so as to isolate the judge from society. As noted in the Commentary, "[j]udges are uniquely qualified to engage in extrajudicial activities that concern the law, the legal system, and the administration of justice." Model Code of Judicial Conduct Rule 3.1 cmt. [1]. Judges are also permitted and encouraged to take part in extrajudicial activities that are not law-related, such as educational, religious, fraternal, or civic activities, so long as they are in connection with not-for-profit organizations. (For further discussion, see discussion following Rule 3.7.) Such participation helps to integrate judges into their communities, and furthers public understanding of and respect for courts and the judicial system. Model Code of Judicial Conduct Rule 3.1 cmt. [2]. Judges are expected to be active members of society and express or support their opinions and ideas. Ariz. Jud. Ethics Adv. Comm. Op. 98-4 (1998) (judge's writing and signing publicity pamphlets supporting legislative salary increases does not violate rule); *see generally* McKay, *The Judiciary and Non-judicial Activities*, 35 Law & Contemp. Probs. 9 (1970) (asserting that a "judge is likely to be a better dispenser of justice if he is aware of the currents and passions of the time, the developments of technology and the sweep of events"). However, judges' extrajudicial activities reflect not only on their judicial office but also on the entire judiciary. Judges must remember that although the judicial robes remain in the courthouse, the judicial aura remains with the judge. *See In re Koch*, 890 P.2d 1137 (Ariz. 1995) (judge's off-the-bench behavior required discipline because "although [a judge's] problems may be temporary, the harm to the public's faith in legal institutions is not").

Activities That Interfere with Proper Performance of Judge's Judicial Duties

Rule 3.1(A) requires a judge to regulate his or her extrajudicial activities to ensure that they do not hinder the performance of the judge's judicial duties. Judges must avoid the appearance that they are devoting a significant amount of time to matters unrelated to their judicial responsibilities. For instance, a judge's regular appearances on television news broadcasts could lead to a public perception that the judge has priorities other than proper performance of judicial duties. Fla. Jud. Ethics Adv. Comm. Op. 96-25 (1996) (television appearances may also demean the judicial office since they are largely commercial endeavors and not conducive to full and fair explanation of legal proceedings). Taking care of personal matters, such as exercising or running errands, when the judge should be on the bench, may also violate this rule. *See In re Sheldon* (Cal. Comm'n on Jud. Performance 1998) (judge admonished for misconduct including jogging on the stairs during afternoon pretrial calendar). Additionally, a judge's volunteer and civic activities, though commendable, may need to be curtailed if they interfere with his or her work as a judge. *See* Utah Jud. Ethics Adv. Comm. Informal Op. 89-11 (1989) (judge may not serve as volunteer for Special Olympics if service would require judge to be absent from court once a week).

Activities That Will Lead to Frequent Disqualification of the Judge

Rule 3.1(B) requires that judges refrain from participating in extrajudicial activities that will lead to frequent disqualification of the judge. The provision was added to the Code in 2007 as a specific instance of the type of extrajudicial activity that is prohibited. One way to interfere with the proper performance of judicial duties is to become involved in extrajudicial activities that will lead to frequent disqualification.

Activities That Would Appear to Undermine Judge's Independence, Integrity, or Impartiality

Pursuant to Rule 3.1(C), judges are required to ensure that their extrajudicial activities will not appear to a reasonable person to undermine the judge's independence, integrity, or impartiality. Therefore, judges must be upright and law-abiding. They should avoid membership in groups that advocate special interests and, similar to the prohibition in Rule 2.3(B) for adjudicative actions, they should not make jokes or other remarks that demean individuals based upon their race, sex, gender, religion, national origin, ethnicity, disability, age, sexual orientation, or socioeconomic status.

Violations of the Law

Judges must be impartial in their rulings, and convey the appearance of impartiality to the public. When a judge's extrajudicial conduct is criminal in nature, that conduct calls into question the judge's respect for the law and his or her ability to decide cases impartially according to the law. *See In re Koch*, 890 P.2d 1137 (Ariz. 1995) (judge who had been convicted of solicitation of prostitution violated rule and cast reasonable doubt cast on his impartiality when presiding over criminal cases); *see also* Annotation, *Sexual Misconduct as Grounds for Disciplining Attorney or Judge*, 435 A.L.R. 4th 1062 (1986). A judge's criminal conduct may also violate Rules 1.1 and 1.2, which require judges to "comply with the law" and "act at all times in a manner that promotes public confidence in the integrity and impartiality of the judiciary."

Membership or Participation in Groups That Advocate Special Interests

A judge's extrajudicial activities should not include membership in groups or organizations whose advocacy activities or public positions would cause a reasonable person to question the judge's impartiality. Ala. Jud. Inquiry Comm'n Adv. Op. 78-35 (1978) (being dues paying honorary member of Fraternal Order of Police would reflect adversely upon judge's impartiality because law enforcement officers frequently appear as witnesses); Ariz. Jud. Ethics Adv. Comm. Op. 96-4 (1996) (judge cannot be a member of the National Lawyer's Guild (NLG) since the opinions expressed by the NLG may cause the judge's impartiality to be questioned); Del. Jud. Ethics Adv. Comm. Op. 2006-6 (2006) (advising that judge should not accept an appointment to the Nominating Committee for the National Rifle Association); Fla. Jud. Ethics Adv. Comm. Op. 98-8 (1998) (judge's membership in domestic violence victims' rights council would cast a reasonable doubt on the judge's capacity to act impartially); Fla. Comm. on Stands. of Conduct Governing Judges Op. 82-18 (1982) (judge may not be a member of Mothers Against Drunk Drivers (MADD) because trial of DWI cases is the major stock and trade of the criminal division of the county court in which the judge sits); Fla. Comm. on Stands. of Cond. Governing Judges Op. 75-26 (1975) (judge may be member of Anti-Defamation League, but not chairman); Ill. Jud. Ethics Comm. Op. 01-03 (2001) (judge may not be guest of honor at non-fund-raising event held by nonprofit group whose employees regularly testify in adversary proceedings before judge); Mass. Comm. on Jud. Ethics Adv. Op. 95-8 (1995) (judge may not be member of Gay and Lesbian Advocates and Defenders that regularly engages in adversary proceedings, but may participate in its activities so long as appearance of impartiality is observed); N.Y. Adv. Comm. on Jud. Conduct Op. 13-134 (2013) (judge may not be a member of Fraternal Order of Police); S.C. Adv. Comm. on Stands. of Jud. Conduct Op. 01-2013 (2013) (magistrate judge who is graduate of FBI National Academy may not join FBI National Academy Associates, Inc., an organization of other graduates that meets monthly for social events, because membership would create an appearance of partiality); Tex. Adv. Comm. on Jud. Ethics Op. 240 (1999) (judge may not serve as a member of a board of directors of nonprofit corporation that trains volunteers and employs professional staff to be appointed by the judge to serve as guardian of incapacitated or minor persons); Wash. Ethics Adv. Comm. Op. 95-14 (1996) (judge may not be member of League of Women Voters because judge cannot be distinguished from position that League takes in matters unrelated to law); Wash. Ethics Adv. Comm. Op. 95-03 (1995) (judge may not be member of group of citizens who are joining together to encourage passage of school levy because code of judicial conduct prohibits judge from supporting ballot measure that is unrelated to law, legal system and administration of justice). *But see Miss. Comm'n on Jud. Performance v. Osborne*, 11 So. 3d 107 (Miss. 2009) (judge did not violate code of judicial conduct by being a member of Voters League and speaking at event on his behalf while running for re-election); *cf.* Fla. Sup. Ct. Jud. Ethics Adv. Comm. Op. 2009-13 (2009) (judge may join local gun club that requires proof of membership in National Rifle Association as condition precedent to membership).

Judges should also use discretion when accepting invitations to serve on committees or to speak at functions sponsored by special interest groups. *See* N.J. Sup. Ct. Adv. Comm. on Extrajudicial Activities Op. 1-93, 1994 WL 47152 (1994) (judge should not speak at function sponsored by a group that provides financial assistance to families of law enforcement officials since such activity may call into question the judge's ability to act impartially); S.C. Adv. Comm. on Stands. of Jud. Conduct Op. 6-2001 (2001) (judge's service on committee to determine qualification of prospective investigators for sheriff's department may help the legal system and the administration of justice, but could also create in reasonable minds a question of the judge's impartiality toward the sheriff's department); S.C. Adv. Comm. on Stands. of Jud. Conduct Op. 2-2001 (2001) (judge may not serve on committee to select winners of award for excellence in law enforcement because it may cast doubt on the judge's impartiality); Wash. Ethics Adv. Comm. Op. 95-08 (1995) (judge should not be speaker at annual dinner sponsored by MADD to honor police officers who issued the most DUI citations, since it would reflect adversely on the judge's impartiality in DUI cases and would interfere with the performance of judicial duties); *cf.* Ariz. Jud. Ethics Adv. Comm. Op. 06-03 (2006) (judge may not accept award for "Excellence in Adjudication" from MADD).

Mere attendance at an event sponsored by a special interest group, however, would generally not cast doubt on a judge's impartiality. *See* Ariz. Jud. Ethics Adv. Comm. Op. 95-13 (1995) (judge's attendance at reception hosted by attorneys' organization that represents specific classes of litigants would not cause "a reasonable and objective observer" to believe the organization would be favored by the judge); *but see* N.Y. Adv. Comm. on Jud. Ethics Op. 05-62 (2005) (judge should not attend functions sponsored by a domestic violence advocacy organization that focuses on providing court-related services solely on behalf of domestic violence victims).

Extrajudicial Conduct or Remarks Indicating Bias

Judges are not expected to come to the bench without personal opinions and beliefs. *See Laird v. Tatum*, 409 U.S. 824 (1972) ("Proof that a justice's mind at the time he joined the Court was a complete *tabula rasa* in the area of constitutional adjudication would be evidence of a lack of qualification, not lack of bias.").

However, expressions of bias by a judge outside of the courtroom may cast doubt on the judge's ability to act impartially inside the courtroom. The types of comments that may raise such a doubt include jokes or other remarks demeaning individuals on the basis of race, sex, religion, national origin, ethnicity, disability, age, sexual orientation, or socioeconomic status. Model Code of Judicial Conduct Rule 3.1 cmt. [3]. *See, e.g., In re Seiler*, CJC 12-0737-DI (Tex. Comm'n on Jud. Conduct 2015) (judge who hears challenges to civil commitment by persons adjudicated sexually violent predators reprimanded for statements made at a political action committee meeting, including calling such persons "nuclear radiation" and discussing details of cases adjudicated); *In re Davis*, 82 S.W.3d 140 (Tex. Spec. Ct. Rev. 2002) (judge reprimanded after he forwarded a letter to the media in which he characterized a prosecutor as "sneaky and surreptitious," alleged that she was guilty of "gross misconduct" and wrote several letters rebuking those who criticized him); *In re Tabor*, CJC No. 7251-F-158 (Wash. Comm'n on Jud. Conduct 2013) (judge admonished for expressing discriminatory intent when volunteering to perform marriages of opposite sex couples but stating in administrative meeting that judge was "uncomfortable" with performing same-sex marriages because of judge's "religious views").

Intemperate conduct outside the courtroom can also cast reasonable doubt on a judge's ability to act impartially, as well as demean the judicial office. *See, e.g., In re Disc. Action Against Hoffman*, 595 N.W.2d 592 (N.D. 1999) (judge's conduct in harassing, stalking, and abusing former wife violated Canon).

Other Extrajudicial Conduct That May Cast Doubt on Impartiality

A judge may be precluded from engaging in extrajudicial conduct, which though laudatory, casts doubt on the judge's impartiality. For instance, a judge was prohibited from appearing in his robe in a photograph in a newspaper advertisement intended to raise public awareness of the consequences of drinking and driving. Pa. Jud. Ethics Comm. Informal Op. 1/21/00 (2000); *see also* Ariz. Jud. Ethics Adv. Comm., Op. 03-02 (2003) (although justice of the peace's proposed "judge for a day" program, designed to educate high school students and adults about the courts, was laudable, permitting participants to wear robes and sit on bench with judge would place appearance of independent judiciary in jeopardy); Fla. Jud. Ethics Adv. Comm. Op. 98-7 (1998) (judges' signing and circulating petition to have victims of unresolved murder honored on postage stamp could impact the prosecution of any future defendant or defendants in their courts and cast reasonable doubt on the judge's capacity to act impartially as a judge); N.Y. Adv. Comm. on Jud. Ethics Op. 13-34 (2013) (criminal court judge prohibited from speaking at anti-violence program conducted at youth detention facility that held persons who could come before judge for sentenceing because judge's impartiality would be called into question); Wis. Jud. Conduct Adv. Comm. Op. 02-01 (2003) (judge who handles juvenile matters on a rotating basis may not serve as mentor to juvenile who has been diverted out of court system into alternative program; judge could be perceived as biased in favor of program or participants and may affect ability of mentoring judge's colleagues to be impartial if they were to consider impact of mentor judge on juvenile).

PERMISSIBLE EXTRAJUDICIAL CONDUCT

Speaking, Writing, and Teaching

Former Canon 4B provided that a judge may "speak, write, lecture, teach and participate in other extrajudicial activities concerning the law, the legal system, the administration of justice and non-legal subjects as long as they do not violate the Code." The provision was not addressed in a rule in the 2007 Code, but Comment [1] to Rule 3.1 notes that judges "are uniquely qualified to engage in extrajudicial activities that concern the law, the legal system, and the administration of justice, such as by speaking, writing, teaching, or participating in scholarly research projects."

Pursuant to former Canon 4B, and under the language of Comment [1] to Rule 3.1, "to the extent that time permits," judges are permitted to teach law courses, write legal articles and books, and lecture about the law so long as these activities do not interfere with judicial duties, lead to frequent disqualification of the judge, or undermine the judge's independence, integrity, or impartiality. *See* Ala. Jud. Inquiry Comm'n Adv. Op. 96-610 (1996) (judge may teach continuing legal education (CLE) as long as it will not interfere with judicial duties or cast doubt on impartiality); Colo. Jud. Ethics Adv. Bd. Op. 2008-3 (2008) (judge may speak at CLE which is, in effect, limited to only one component of the bar, provided that the judge is amenable to training advocates adverse to the position of the conference host, he refrains from giving legal advice, showing bias, or making comment on pending or impending cases, and avoids presenting on a topic such as trial strategy, which could raise questions regarding his impartiality); Conn. Comm. on Jud. Ethics Formal Adv. Op. JE 2010-21 (2010) (judge may speak to Connecticut Department of Health employees responsible for licencing and investigating daycare centers about children as witnesses in courtroom proceedings); Del. Jud. Ethics Adv. Comm. Op. 2006-3 (2006) (judge may serve as Special Editorial Advisor for the State Defense Force Publication Center (SDFPC), the purpose of which is to permit publication of material of interest and concern to the state defense force, State Guard community, and other interested organizations and individuals); Fla. Jud. Ethics Adv. Comm. Op. 2007-09 (2007) (judge may participate in panel discussion as part of a CLE seminar sponsored by a private organization so long as judge's participation is educational in nature and does not endorse products or materials offered by that organization); Kan. Jud. Ethics Op. JE-74 (1997) (judge may serve as a panelist and lecturer at in house law firm CLE programs); Md. Jud. Ethics Op. 2013-26 (2013) (judge may write introduction to criminal and civil procedure practice book); Md. Jud. Ethics Op. 2008-18 (2008) (judge may lecture attorneys at seminar regarding legal ethics and malpractice); Mass. Comm. on Jud. Ethics Adv. Op. 2011-1 (2011) (judge may moderate panel presentation at bar association conference for which the association has gathered "sufficiently diverse" sponsors "to negate any appearance of impropriety" and for which the judge will not use prestige of the office to raise funds for conference scholarships); N.M. Adv. Comm. on Code of Jud. Conduct Op. 12-01 (2012) (judge with extensive experience with bail and bondsmen may speak at national conference of bail bondsmen); N.M. Adv. Comm. on Code of Jud. Conduct Op. 05-05 (2005) (judge may teach evidence law for legal assistants program); Nev. Stand. Comm. on Jud. Ethics and Election Practices Op. JE10-016 (2010) (judge may serve as instructor at state university, but not as instructor at for-profit university or college); N.Y. Adv. Comm. on Jud. Ethics Op. 13-89 (2013) (judge may wear robe for author-picture that will appear on judge's book about the law); N.Y. Adv. Comm. on Jud. Ethics Op. 13-06 (2013) (judge may write and edit updates to for-profit legal publication; N.Y. Adv. Comm. on Jud. Ethics Op. 12-74 (2013) (judge may speak on panel about legal consequences of underage drinking hosted by treatment center and when co-panelists include two law enforcement officers); N.Y. Adv. Comm. on Jud. Ethics Op. 12-49 (2012) (judge may participate in mock trial to demonstrate new technology for video arrangement because it will educate the public and improve the legal system and administration of justice); Okla.

Jud. Ethics Op. 2004-1 (2004) (judge may serve as part-time adjunct faculty member at private university and be compensated for teaching classes pertaining to the law); S. C. Adv. Comm. on Standards of Jud. Conduct Op. 2-2011 (2011) (judge may speak at neighborhhod watch meeting on court's "function and role in criminal proceedings as well as the bond procedure"); S.C. Adv. Comm. on Stands. of Jud. Conduct Op. 22-2006 (2006) (municipal court judge may teach class to police officers on DUI, driving with unlawful alcohol concentration, and criminal domestic violence); Tenn. Jud. Ethics Comm. Adv. Op. 10-01 (2010) (judge may speak and write on Tennessee Constitution, the power of the Tennessee General Assembly, and judicial selection methods); Utah Jud. Ethics Adv. Comm. Informal Op. 06-4 (2006) (judge may participate on panel to train foster parents so long as panel consists of representation from the entities involved in juvenile court cases); *but see* Neb. Jud. Ethics Adv. Comm. Op. 06-04 (2006) (judge may not participate in seminar about defense of DUI cases because the totality of the factual circumstances bring a number of other Code provisions into consideration and raise significant concerns about judicial impartiality and prestige of the judicial office); N.M. Adv. Comm. on Code of Jud. Conduct Op. 12-13 (2012) (judge may not assist with mock trial organized by prosecutor and law enforncement agency to train officers how to testify in court because public may perceive judges is "promoting the interest of the state" and could lead to frequent disqualification).

Judges may also be permitted to host law-related radio programs (Wash. Ethics Adv. Comm. Op. 98-12 (1998)) and create a speakers' bureau and inform the public of judges' availability to speak on legal issues (Ill. Jud. Ethics Comm. Op. 94-17 (1994)). A judge may not, however, intimate in an article, lecture, or speech how he or she would rule on pending matters or matters that may come before the judge. Fla. Jud. Ethics Adv. Comm. Op. 99-14 (1999). Wash. Ethics Adv. Comm. Op. 87-11 (1987) (part-time judge may not write newspaper column expressing his opinion on recent legislation and court cases); *see generally* J. Clark Kelso, *Time, Place, and Manner Restrictions on Extra-Judicial Speech by Judges*, 28 Loy. L.A. L. Rev. 851 (1995).

Judges may create and write for blogs and websites. Fla. Sup. Ct. Judicial Ethics Adv. Comm. Op. 2012-07 (2012) (judge may create and write for blog on Florida Supreme Court and District Court of Appeal cases, where the writing is "neutral, non-judgmental, brief summaries of the facts and holdings, with a link to the full opinion of each case . . . The Code makes no distinctions among the activities of speaking, writing, lecturing, or teaching, or the technology used to engage in those activities"); *but see* N.Y. Adv. Comm. on Jud. Ethics Op. 10-172 (2010) (judge may not host a personal judicial website separate from the one hosted by the municipality to post court hours, court calendar, forms, and other information that could be "construed as legal advice" because judge's personal judicial website "could mislead members of the public" and would cause judge's impartiality to be questioned).

Pursuant to Comment [1], judges may also speak, write, lecture, and teach on nonlegal subjects. For instance, a judge may write a television screenplay and have his or her name appear in the screen credits (Ill. Jud. Ethics Comm. Op. 98-13 (1998)), give a speech at a company's private conference on a subject unrelated to the law (Mich. Comm. on Jud. Ethics Op. JI-80 (1994)); serve as a part-time college football referee (Fla. Sup. Ct. Judicial Ethics Adv. Comm. Op. 2013-07 (2013)), write a book of poems (N.M. Adv. Comm. on Code of Jud. Conduct Op. 09-05 (2009)), or write and host a website for high schoolers on college or trade school, "as long as the judge's website complies with all provisions of the Code" (Fla. Sup. Ct., Judicial Ethics Op. 2011-01 (2011)).

However, a judge's extrajudicial activities are subject to other provisions of the Code and may need to be avoided or curtailed if they run afoul of other Code requirements. *See, e.g., In re Broadbent*, 683 A.2d 543 (N.J. 1996) (judge's television appearances violated Section 3B(9), the predecessor to current Rule 2.10, prohibiting judge from making public comment on pending or impending proceeding in any court and Canon 2B, the predecessor to Rule 1.3, forbidding judge from lending prestige of office to advance private interests); Ala. Jud. Inquiry Comm'n Adv. Op. 00-750 (2000) (judge may not give speech at "Take Back the Night" rally as it would reflect adversely on the judge's impartiality in sexual assault cases); Mich. Comm. on Jud. Ethics Op. JI-137 (2012) (judge may not host television program, which is a public forum on topical issues because such actions may "detract from the dignity of the office or reflect adversely upon the judge's impartiality"); Nev. Stand. Comm. on Jud. Ethics Op. JE12-007 (2012) (judge may not host weekly current affairs television show on commercial, for-profit station because it could raise issues of the judge's impartiality and creates the "danger that a judge will lend the prestige of the office to a third party"); Va. Jud. Ethics Adv. Comm. Op. 01-04 (2001) (judge may lecture at police training academy regarding officers' courtroom appearances so long as the judge does not violate provisions of the Code requiring judges to uphold the integrity and independence of the judiciary and requiring judges to avoid impropriety and the appearance of impropriety). Stephanie Cotilla and Amanda Suzanne Veal, Comment, *Judicial Balancing Act: The Appearance of Impartiality and the First Amendment*, 15 Geo. J. Legal Ethics 741 (2002), James R. Noseda, *Limiting Off-Bench Expression: Striking a Balance between Accountability and Independence*, 36 DePaul L. Rev. 519 (1987).

Expressing Personal Opinions

Judges may express their personal views about legal and nonlegal subjects provided that they do so in a manner that promotes confidence in the integrity and impartiality of the judge. *See In re Miller*, 644 So. 2d 75 (Fla. 1994) (judge reprimanded for writing letters to newspaper criticizing judicial system; though judges are allowed to write about "activities concerning the law, the legal system, and the administration of justice," judges must "uphold the integrity and independence of the judiciary, avoid impropriety or its appearance, and perform the duties of office impartially and diligently"); *Miss. Comm'n on Jud. Performance v. Wilkerson*, 876 So. 2d 1006 (Miss. 2004) (judge could not be sanctioned for extra-judicial anti-gay statements contained in letter judge sent to newspaper; court held that remarks were political and could only be restricted if state demonstrated that Code provision at issue was narrowly tailored to serve a compelling state interest); *In re Hill*, 8 S.W. 3d 578 (Mo. 2000) (judge's "open letter" imploring citizens to support police chief in struggle with mayor did not promote public confidence in judiciary); *In re Schenck*, 870 P.2d 185 (Or. 1994) (judge's letters to newspaper criticizing district attorney are not permissible because they cast doubt on the judge's impartiality).

Judges may also express their disagreement and criticism about the present state of the law as long as they do not appear to substitute their concept of what the law ought to be for what the law actually is. *In re Gridley*, 417 So. 2d 950 (Fla. 1982) (judge's conduct in writing two letters to the editor of a newspaper and an article for a church newsletter opposing the death penalty did not violate Code since judge made it clear that he was duty bound to follow the law and would do so). *Owens v. American Cyanamid*, 2010 WL 597394 (E.D. Wis. 2010) (judge denied party's motion to disqualify based upon judge's co-authorship of law review article that briefly touched on general subject matter of pending case). *See generally* Nancy Gertner, *To Speak or Not to Speak: Musings on Judicial Silence*, 32 Hofstra L. Rev. 1147 (2004) (asserting that judges must not remain silent in debates on public policy).

Social Media Activities

Generally, judges may participate in social media if the judge's activities do not otherwise violate the Code. *See* ABA Formal Ethics Op. 462 (2013) (judge may participate in social media network); Cal. Judges Ass'n Jud. Ethics Comm. Adv. Op. 66 (2010) ("The same rules that govern a judge's ability to socialize and communicate in person, or on paper and over the telephone apply to the Internet."); Mass. Comm. on Jud. Ethics Adv. Op. 2011-6 (2011) (judge may be a member of social networking site, but may not identify self as judge); Ohio Bd. of Commissioners on Grievances and Disc. Op. 2010-7 (2010); Okla. Jud. Ethics Op. 2011-3 (2011); Tenn. Jud. Ethics Comm. Adv. Op. 12-01 (2012); Utah Jud. Ethics Adv. Comm. Informal Op. 12-01 (2012) (judge may be a member of social networking site, and may identify self as judge).

A judge's participation in a social media network does not per se "cast reasonable doubt on the judge's ability to act impartially, demean the judicial office, or interfere with the proper performance of the judge's judicial duties anymore than any other type of social activity." Cal. Judges Ass'n Jud. Ethics Comm. Adv. Op. 66 (2010). *See also* Fla. Sup. Ct. Jud. Ethics Adv. Comm. Op. 2009-20 (2009); (judge may post on social media); Ky. Jud. Ethics Op. JE-119 (2010) (judge may participate in Internet-based social networking site); S.C. Adv. Comm. on Stands. of Jud. Conduct Op. 17-2009 (2009) (magistrate judge may be a member of Facebook).

However, a judge "should exercise an appropriate degree of discretion in how he/she uses the social network and should stay abreast of the features of any such service he/she uses as new developments may impact his/her duties under the Rules." N.Y. Adv. Comm. on Jud. Ethics Op. 08-176 (2008). *See* Canon 2, generally, for a discussion of Internet social network connections and ex parte communications and recusal.

Legislative Activities

In addition to writing, speaking, and lecturing about the law, the legal system, and the administration of justice, judges have been permitted to engage in legislative activities, including submitting proposed legislation to the legislature, sitting as a member of an independent law revision commission, or testifying before a state legislative committee. *See* Fla. Jud. Ethics Adv. Comm. Op. 98-13 (1998) (judge assigned to domestic violence division may submit proposed legislation that increases the maximum periods of incarceration and probation for guilty defendants in domestic violence cases); Pa. Jud. Ethics Comm. Informal Op. 8/6/99 (1999) (judge may testify at a public hearing regarding the reach and extent of regulation of a certain subject).

As a general rule, judges have been permitted to participate in legislative activities as long as those activities do no cast doubt on the judge's ability to act impartially or exploit the judge's position. Ark. Jud. Ethics Adv. Comm. Op. 94-01 (1994) (judge may take public stand in favor of, opposed to, or indifferent to a proposed sales tax); Tex. Adv. Comm. on Jud. Ethics Op. 254 (1999) (judge may publicly support new legislation creating a judicial compensation commission); Utah Jud. Ethics Adv. Comm. Informal Op. 01-1 (2001) (judge may support or oppose a bill that is pending before the Utah legislature); Wash. Ethics Adv. Comm. Op. 92-05 (1992) (judge may actively promote passage of bond issue for a regional justice center); *but see* Ariz. Jud. Ethics Adv. Comm. Op. 96-9 (1996) (while judge may write and speak in neutral forums regarding a ballot proposition, the judge's appearance in television commercial endorsing the proposition would cause judge's impartiality to be questioned); N.Y. Adv. Comm. on Jud. Ethics Op. 06-120 (2006) (judge who presides over felony matters should not serve on local committee that will ask New York State legislature to mandate drug testing for middle and high school students as it would cast doubt on judge's independence and capacity to serve impartially).

The plain language of the Code does not prevent a judge from acting on his or her own initiative with regard to legislative issues. *See, e.g.*, Fla. Jud. Ethics Adv. Comm. Op. 98-13 (1998) (judge may submit proposed legislation to members of the legislature in an effort to improve the law); Wash. Ethics Adv. Comm. Op. 92-05 (1992) (the "[Canons] permit a judicial officer to actively promote the passage of a bond issue or levy for a regional justice center"). However, judges should be careful not to become too active in these matters. A judge who spends significant amounts of time speaking out on legislative issues during the legislative session could be perceived as allowing those activities to interfere with the judge's judicial duties and could be seen as attempting to exploit the judge's position. Utah Jud. Ethics Adv. Comm. Informal Op. 01-1 (2001); *see also* Cal. Judges Ass'n Judicial Ethics Comm. Adv. Op. 46 (1997) (judge's participation in a group that engages in advocacy towards the adoption, repeal, or modification of particular substantive laws or towards the courts' use and application of existing laws in a particular manner creates danger that judge's ability to act impartially may be cast in doubt). Joshua M. Dickey, Comment, *Judges as Legislators?: The Propriety of Judges Drafting Legislation*, 29 McGeorge L. Rev. 111 (1997) (asserting that when judges become too closely associated with a particular piece of legislation, they compromise the judiciary's role as a neutral arbitrator of our country's laws); J. Clark Kelso, *Time, Place, and Manner Restrictions on Extra-Judicial Speech by Judges*, 28 Loy. L.A. L. Rev. 851 (1995) ("Simply put, legislative drafting and lobbying is the wrong place for judges to exercise their rights of expression in an effort to improve the law. . . . A judge who wishes to contribute to legal development has to choose the proper forum, such as a law review article or a speech before a bar group.").

Participation in Law-Related Groups

Courts and judicial ethics committees have generally held that a judge may take part in activities of bar associations and other groups dedicated to the improvement of the legal system. *See, e.g.*, *Petition of Wiley*, 671 A.2d 308 (R.I. 1996) (holding that judge may attend meetings of professional associations as guest of organization or at his or her own expense, court stated that "avoiding intellectual exchange among lawyers and academics may lead [a] judge to a form of mental asphyxiation that will diminish his or her effectiveness. A judge should not be isolated from the current ideas abroad in his or her profession"); U.S. Committee on Codes of Conduct, Advisory Op. No. 85 (1991, Revised 1998) (judge may be member of and participate in ABA panel devoted to the improvement of the administration of justice); Wash. Ethics Adv. Comm.

Op. 86-03 (1986) (judge may remain a member of bar association after assuming the bench).

However, a judge's participation in a law-related organization is subject to other provisions of the Code, including the proscription in Rule 3.1(C) against extrajudicial activities that would appear to a reasonable person to undermine the judge's independence, integrity, or impartiality. *See, e.g.*, Wash. Ethics Adv. Comm. Op. 92-02 (1992) (judge may be regular or honorary member of county bar association and belong to particular section of association even though they take public positions and may be involved in legislative efforts, as long as judge does not take public positions on matters that do not involve the law, the legal system, and the administration of justice).

Jurisdictions have grappled with the question of whether the Code prohibits a sitting judge from seeking election to and serving as a bar association leader. For example, the Florida Supreme Court Judicial Ethics Advisory Committee opined that when a judge runs for a bar association leadership position, the "question will inevitably be raised whether the judge is exerting pressures on lawyers who must litigate before him. This gives the appearance of impropriety" and, as a result, violates the Code. Fla. Jud. Ethics Adv. Comm. Op. 2004-34 (2004); *but see* Fla. Jud. Ethics Adv. Comm. Op. 2010-03 (2010) (judge may serve as appointed president or vice president of American Board of Trial Advocacy). Other jurisdictions focus on the judge's role as a board member who could be asked to take positions on controversial issues to find that such service would violate Rule 3.1's demand that extrajudicial activities not appear to a reasonable person to undermine the judge's impartiality. *See* Mass. Comm. on Jud. Ethics Adv. Op. 2003-12 (2003); Nev. Stand. Comm. on Jud. Ethics and Election Practices Op. JE11-005 (2011).

Some jurisdictions have determined that a judge's service on the board of a bar association is appropriate. Ariz. Jud. Ethics Adv. Comm. Op. 91-02 (1991) (judge may serve as bar association president); Ill. Jud. Ethics Comm. Op. 93-8 (1993) (judges are frequently candidates for bar association offices); N.Y. Adv. Comm. on Jud. Ethics Op. 03-63 (2003) (judge may serve as president of women's bar association but may not participate in fund-raising activities and may not be involved in partisan political activity). Judges should not, however, recommend or endorse lawyer candidates for bar association office or sign a nominating petition for a candidate because to do so would lend the prestige of the office. *See* Ohio Bd. of Commissioners on Grievances and Disc. Op. 2011-3 (2011); S.C. Adv. Comm. on Stands. of Jud. Conduct Op. 3-2012 (2012).

There is no bright line between organizations concerned with the law and legal institutions, which judges are encouraged to participate in as members or officers, and those advocacy organizations that judges are forbidden from joining because of concerns about the appearance of partiality. Cal. Judges Ass'n Jud.

Ethics Comm. Adv. Op. 46 (1997). However, some states' ethics committees have delineated factors that a judge should consider before deciding to join or continue in a law-related organization. For instance, the California Judge's Association advised that judges consider (1) the extent to which the group engages in political or advocacy activities, (2) the extent to which the group is perceived by the public as engaging in political or advocacy activities, (3) the size and public prominence of the organization, (4) whether the issues that concern the group are likely to come before the court, (5) whether the group is concerned with procedural or substantive changes in the law or the application of the law, (6) whether the judge is participating in a policy making position, and (7) the fund-raising activities of the group. Cal. Judges Ass'n Jud. Ethics Comm. Adv. Op. 46 (1997). *See also* Ala. Jud. Inquiry Comm'n Adv. Op. 99-732 (1999) and Wash. Ethics Adv. Comm. Op. 93-19 (1993) (listing additional factors including: whether participation may create an appearance of partiality to a particular cause; whether participation may erode public confidence in the members of the judiciary; whether the organization files amicus briefs on disputed issues; whether the organization endorses nonjudicial political candidates; and whether the organization subscribes to a particular legal philosophy). According to the California opinion, "[n]o single one or combination of these factors is determinative. The ultimate test for judicial participation in such bodies is whether the judge's association with the group and the necessarily resulting public perception that the judge supports the group, is likely to lead to a public perception that the judge's impartiality in administering the law may be questioned." Cal. Judges Ass'n Jud. Ethics Comm. Adv. Op. 46 (1997).

Specialty Bar Associations

While judges are encouraged to take part in bar association activities, participation in specialty bar associations created for lawyers practicing in specific areas of the law may be more problematic. The drafters of the 1972 Code concluded that the "'impartiality' standard would . . . prevent a judge from participating as a member or officer of a partisan legal organization that champions one special interest in litigation that may be heard in the court on which he sits. Such a relationship would almost certainly cast doubt on a judge's capacity to decide impartially the issues in that type of litigation." E. Wayne Thode, *Reporter's Notes to Code of Judicial Conduct* 76–77 (1973). Therefore, judges may be advised not to become a member of or continue a membership in a specialty bar group. *See, e.g.*, Ill. Jud. Ethics Comm. Op. 01-08 (2001) (judge may not accept complimentary membership as judicial fellow in specialized bar association if membership gives appearance of favoritism toward a particular class or category of litigants); S.C. Adv. Comm. on Stands. of Jud. Conduct Op. 5-2001 (2001). *See generally* Cynthia Gray, *Judges' Participation in Bar Association*

Activities, 20 Vol. Nos. 2–3 Judicial Conduct Reporter 12 (Summer–Fall 1998) (summarizing state ethics opinions on judge's participation in bar associations and specialty bar associations).

For instance, several state ethics opinions advise that judges may not be members of the American Trial Lawyers Association (ATLA)* or similar plaintiffs' bar associations. Alaska Comm'n on Jud. Cond. Adv. Op. 99-4 (1994) (judge may not be a member of ATLA); Ark. Jud. Ethics Adv. Comm. Op. 99-04 (1999) (judge may not be a member of the ATLA or any other organization that outwardly favors one side or consistently takes one side in legal issues); Ethics Comm. of the Jud. Op. JE-91 (1998) (judge may not be a member of ATLA); Nev. Stand. Comm. on Jud. Ethics and Election Prac. Op. JE05-004 (2005) (judge may not accept a solicitation from ATLA to become a member as a "Judicial Fellow"); S.C. Adv. Comm. on Stands. of Jud. Conduct Op. 27-1998 (1998) (judge may not accept complimentary membership in the South Carolina Trial Lawyers Association); *but see* Pa. Jud. Ethics Comm. Informal Op. 4/7b/00 (2000) (judge may join ATLA as a fellow).

Attending Legal Education Programs

Judges may attend educational programs concerning the law and the legal system designed to educate judges on a particular topic. *See, e.g.*, Wash. Ethics Adv. Comm. Op. 00-18 (2000) (judge may attend domestic violence summit and other educational venues covering this topic). Similarly, a judge may attend an educational program designed for and attended by lawyers since it may improve the administration of justice in the area of law that is addressed. Fla. Jud. Ethics Adv. Comm. Op. 98-5 (1998) (judge may attend CLE program designed for and conducted by criminal defense lawyers); Wash. Ethics Adv. Comm. Op. 96-05 (1996) (judge may attend seminar on community-based policing); Wash. Ethics Adv. Comm. Op. 92-10 (1992) (judge may take part in seminar sponsored by state toxicologist providing information on breath and alcohol testing).

However, judges may be advised not to attend educational seminars or conferences that could raise questions about the judge's independence and impartiality, such as those presented by law enforcement agencies. *See, e.g.*, Ariz. Jud. Ethics Adv. Op. 03-08 (2003) (judges should not attend seminars or training programs sponsored by or presented at a law enforcement agency in which officers might discuss new devices, technologies, or police procedures because it would impair, if not directly contravene, the fundamental principles of judicial independence, integrity, and impartiality); Kan. Jud. Ethics Op. JE-126 (2005) (judge may not attend conferences sponsored by Kansas Department of Transportation

---

*American Trial Lawyers Association (ATLA) is now known as American Association for Justice.

and Kansas Highway Patrol designed to present law enforcement perspective on drunk and drugged drivers cases); N.Y. Adv. Comm. on Jud. Ethics Op. 94-31 (1994) ("It is unethical for judges to attend 'training sessions' sponsored by a law enforcement agency if the purpose is 'to maximize enforcement.").

Privately Funded Educational Programs

A number of private institutions, with sponsorship from corporations, law firms, and other private organizations, offer educational seminars for judges, addressing topics such as the environment, law, and economics. Frequently, judges are invited to attend such seminars at no charge, and the sponsoring institutions often provide food and lodging and reimburse all, or some, of the judges' travel expenses. Some questions have been raised as to whether a judge's attendance at privately funded seminars, such as ones sponsored by corporations, special interest groups, and other non-governmental entities, whose interests may come before the judge, create an appearance of impropriety. *See, e.g.*, Douglas T. Kendall & Jason C. Rylander, *Tainted Justice: How Private Judicial Trips Undermine Public Confidence in the Judiciary*, 18 Geo J. Legal Ethics 65 (2004) (asserting that privately funded seminars can result in at least the appearance of impropriety and "[l]eft unaddressed . . . seriously threaten public confidence in the American judicial system"). However, to date, it appears that no judicial body has found that judges are prohibited from attending such seminars. *See* Bruce A. Green, *May Judges Attend Privately Funded Educational Programs? Should Judicial Education be Privatized? Questions of Judicial Ethics and Policy*, 29 Fordham Urb. L.J. 941 (2002). *See, e.g., In re Aguinda*, 241 F.3d 194 (2d Cir. 2001) (judge's attendance at expense-paid environmental law seminar sponsored by organization that received general funding from oil company was not grounds to reasonably question judge's impartiality).

The United States Judicial Conference Committee on Codes of Conduct addressed the issue of judges' attendance at educational seminars in an opinion issued in 1980 and reissued in 1998 and 2004. The opinion states that "payment of tuition and expenses involved in attendance at an independent seminar constitutes a gift" permitted by the Canons. (See Rule 3.13 regarding gifts). According to the Committee, "the education of judges in various academic and law-related disciplines serves the public interest. That a lecture or seminar may emphasize a particular viewpoint or school of thought does not necessarily preclude a judge from attending." The opinion notes, however, that a variety of factors may affect the propriety of a judge's attendance at an independent seminar. The Committee lists the following as factors for judges to consider: (1) the identity of the seminar sponsor, noting that sponsorship by a corporation, law firm, or attorney should be carefully examined while sponsorship by a bar association or accredited institution of higher learning usually raises fewer concerns; (2) the nature and source of the funding, for instance, whether there are several contributors or one entity contributing a substantial portion of the cost; (3) whether a sponsor or a source of substantial funding of the seminar is currently involved as a party or attorney in litigation before the judge or is likely to be so involved; (4) the subject matter of the seminar, including whether the topics covered are likely to be in some manner related to the subject matter of litigation before the judge in which the sponsor is involved as a party or attorney; (5) the nature of expenses paid or reimbursed, that is, whether the expenses are reasonable and whether the seminar is primarily educational and not recreational; and (6) whether the seminar provider makes public disclosure about the sources of seminar funding and curriculum, noting that public disclosure obviate the need for further inquiry. The opinion acknowledges that other factors may be relevant in particular cases and advises that a judge consider the totality of the circumstances.

The opinion states that "if, in light of all the relevant factors, the judge concludes that there is a reasonable question concerning the propriety of attendance, the judge should not attend the seminar." If there is insufficient information to make a decision, the judge should decline the invitation or take reasonable steps to obtain additional information. If such information is not available, the opinion advises the judge not to attend the seminar. The opinion also advises that if the information obtained by the judge does not resolve the question of the propriety of attending the seminar, the judge should not do so. In addition to all of these factors, the opinion advises judges to keep in mind other provisions on the Code of Conduct, in particular Canon 2A, advising judge to "act at all times in a manner that promotes public confidence in the integrity and impartiality of the judiciary," and Canon 3C(1) advising judges to recuse from proceedings in which their impartiality might be questioned. United States Judicial Conference Committee on Codes of Conduct Adv. Op. 67 (1980 and reissued in 1998 and 2004).

Of the states that have addressed the issue, most advise that "there is no general ethical impropriety in attending expenses paid educational programs sponsored by non-governmental organizations." *See* Ariz. Jud. Ethics Adv. Comm. Op. 00-02 (2000); Kan. Jud. Ethics Op. JE-127 (2005) (judge may attend conference sponsored by National Foundation for Judicial Excellence who would pay for judge's transportation, meals, and lodging); N.Y. Adv. Comm. on Jud. Ethics Op. 96-106 (1996) (judges may attend a land use judicial education seminar conducted and sponsored by National Judicial College and funded by home builder trade association).

Some jurisdictions, however, have placed restrictions on judges' attendance at these seminars. Ariz. Jud. Ethics Adv. Comm. Op. 00-02 (2000) advised that (1) corporate, foundation, or business sponsorship of seminars must be indirect to an entity that independently determines course content; (2) the sponsoring organization may not be in or likely to be litigation before the judge; (3) compensation for expense reimbursement may not exceed actual costs; and (4) the judge must report the compensation as a gift. South Carolina's Advisory Committee on Standards of Judicial Conduct advised that a magistrate may attend a three-day conference hosted and financed by a local housing authority, but must pay his or her own expenses and not accept any gift or remuneration. S.C. Adv. Comm. on Stands. of Jud. Conduct Op. 9-1998 (1998). That Committee also addressed the issue of judges' attendance at a "lunch and learn" session sponsored by a children's center to inform judges about the center's mission and current issues in children's law. The Committee advised that since the center has a specific purpose that comes before the judiciary, the contents of the presentation must be reviewed to ensure that the contents did not unduly influence the judiciary to a particular point of view. S.C. Adv. Comm. on Stands. of Jud. Conduct Op. 22-1998 (1998) (judges "must be cautious not to attend functions where only one side of legal issues are or may be presented, by an interested group, so as to avoid the appearance of impropriety"). *See also* Alaska Comm'n on Jud. Conduct Adv. Op. 99-5 (1999) (advising that judges should not accept offer of free travel to judicial conference sponsored by the Roscoe Pound Foundation, which is a trust set up for educational purposes by the ATLA; since ATLA is a plaintiff's bar association, a gift of travel would give the appearance of a gift by the plaintiffs' bar to judges). For a discussion of reimbursement and reporting requirements for expenses related to privately-funded educational seminars, *see* Rules 3.14 and 3.15 and accompanying text.

ENGAGING IN COERCIVE CONDUCT

Rule 3.1(D), which is new to the Code, prohibits judges from engaging in overt or subtle efforts to coerce others to participate in extrajudicial activities favored by the judge. As an example, the Commentary states that "depending upon the circumstances, a judge's solicitation of contributions or memberships for an organization, even as permitted by Rule 3.7(A), might create the risk that he person solicited would feel obligated to respond favorably, or would do so to curry favor with the judge." Model Rule of Judicial Conduct Rule 3.1 cmt. [4].

In Ethics Opinion 13-05, the New Mexico Advisory Committee on the Code of Judicial Conduct opined that a judge could not participate in a school district's truancy court in which the judge would preside over a hearing-like proceeding in which the truant student, the student's parents, and school personnel would report on the truancy. The committee explained that judge had no jurisdiction to conduct the quasi-hearing and the extrajudicial activity was coercive. N.M. Adv. Comm. on the Code of Jud. Conduct Op. 13-05 (2013).

USING COURT RESOURCES FOR EXTRAJUDICIAL ACTIVITIES

Rule 3.1(E) provides that when engaging in extrajudicial activities, judges shall not "make use of court premises, staff, stationery, equipment, or other resources, except for incidental use for activities that concern the law, the legal system or the administration of justice, or unless such additional use is permitted by law." *See* N.M. Adv. Comm. on the Code of Jud. Conduct Op. 13-05 (2013) (school district truancy court does not concern the law, the legal system, or the administration of justice); Wash. Ethics Adv. Comm. Op. 12-04 (state capitol building furnishings preservation committee is not related to the law, the legal system, or the administration of justice and use of the Temple of Justice building where state supreme court sits for fund-raiser is more than incidental use).

Although Rule 3.1(E) was new to the Code in 2007, some courts had previously issued opinions prohibiting judges from engaging in extrajudicial activities during working hours, using court resources or involving court employees in personal activities or using their judicial privileges to personal advantage. *See, e.g., In re Cooley*, 563 N.W.2d 645 (Mich. 1997) (judge violated rule by using court's office equipment and court employees during court hours for work-related to personal business activity); *In re Davis*, 946 P.2d 1033 (Nev. 1997) (judge violated rule when he employed court employees during business hours for personal business, told employees to run personal errands, and was driven to work by a court employee).

RULE 3.2 APPEARANCES BEFORE GOVERNMENTAL BODIES AND CONSULTATION WITH GOVERNMENTAL OFFICIALS

A judge shall not appear voluntarily at a public hearing before, or otherwise consult with, an executive or a legislative body or official, except:

(A) in connection with matters concerning the law, the legal system, or the administration of justice;

(B) in connection with matters about which the judge acquired knowledge or expertise in the course of the judge's judicial duties; or

(C) when the judge is acting pro se in a matter involving the judge's legal or economic interests, or when the judge is acting in a fiduciary* capacity.

COMMENT

[1] Judges possess special expertise in matters of law, the legal system, and the administration of justice, and may properly share that expertise with governmental bodies and executive or legislative branch officials.

[2] In appearing before governmental bodies or consulting with government officials, judges must be mindful that they remain subject to other provisions of

this Code, such as Rule 1.3, prohibiting judges from using the prestige of office to advance their own or others' interests, Rule 2.10, governing public comment on pending and impending matters, and Rule 3.1(C), prohibiting judges from engaging in extrajudicial activities that would appear to a reasonable person to undermine the judge's independence, integrity, or impartiality.

[3] In general, it would be an unnecessary and unfair burden to prohibit judges from appearing before governmental bodies or consulting with government officials on matters that are likely to affect them as private citizens, such as zoning proposals affecting their real property. In engaging in such activities, however, judges must not refer to their judicial positions, and must otherwise exercise caution to avoid using the prestige of judicial office.

1990 CODE COMPARISON

Rule 3.2 is derived from Canon 4C(1) with some minor modifications. The word "voluntarily" was added to make clear that judges who are formally summoned to appear before various governmental bodies may not refuse to appear on the ground that it would be unethical to do so. Rule 3.2(A) is essentially the same as the middle clause of former Canon 4C(1), while Rule 3.2(C) modified the language of Canon 4C(1) by substituting "the judge's legal or economic interests" for "the judge's interests," and by extending the exception to situations in which a judge is "acting in a fiduciary capacity." Rule 3.2(B) is a newly added provision. Charles G. Geyh & W. William Hodes, *Reporters' Notes to the Model Code of Judicial Conduct* 59–60 (2009).

All of the Comments to Rule 3.2 are new to the Code. Comment [1] was added to explain the rationale of Rule 3.2(A) and, implicitly, of Rule 3.2(B). Comment [2] notes that though a judge may consult with appropriate governmental branch personal under Rules 3.2(A) or 3.2(B), the judge remains subject to other restrictions of the Code. Comment [3] describes the types of interests judges may address in their appearances before or consultations with government bodies.

ANNOTATION

INTRODUCTION

Pursuant to Rule 3.2(A), a judge generally may appear at a public hearing or otherwise consult with an executive or legislative body or official on matters concerning the law, the legal system, or the administration of justice. *See, e.g.*, Pa. Jud. Ethics Comm. Informal Op. 8/6/99 (1999) (judge may testify at a public hearing before a state legislative committee regarding the reach and extent of regulation of a certain subject). As noted in the Commentary to the Rule, "[j]udges possess special expertise in matters of law, the legal system, and the administration of justice, and may properly share that expertise with governmental bodies and executive or legislative branch officials." Model Code of Judicial Conduct, Rule 3.2, cmt. [1].

Also, as noted in the Commentary, when appearing before a governmental body or consulting with government officials, judges must be mindful of other provisions of the Code, including Rules 1.3, 2.10, and 3.1(C). Model Code of Judicial Conduct Rule 3.2 cmt. [2]. For instance, a judge may need to limit involvement in legislative issues to avoid the perception that those activities are interfering with judicial duties or exploiting the judge's position. Judges must also ensure that their communications do not compromise their independence, integrity, or impartiality and must not take positions on issues that may come before the judiciary. Utah Jud. Ethics Adv. Comm. Informal Op. 01-1 (2001); Ala. Jud. Inquiry Comm'n Adv. Op. 99-732 (1999) (judge may not participate as member of citizens' group that lobbies for legislation mandating seat belts on school buses because related issues are likely to come before judge).

"THE LAW, THE LEGAL SYSTEM, OR THE ADMINISTRATION OF JUSTICE"

To constitute a matter concerning "the law, the legal system, or the administration of justice" with regard to legislative activities, the issues usually must have a connection to the regular judicial or administrative activities of the judge. Utah Jud. Ethics Adv. Comm. Informal Op. 01-1 (2001). Issues concerning judges' compensation and the compensation and terms of employment of court personnel fall into this category. *See, e.g.*, Ala. Jud. Inquiry Comm'n Adv. Op. 91-436 (1991) (active retired judge may communicate with a member of the legislature regarding the compensation of judges and court personnel); Pa. Jud. Ethics Comm. Informal Op. 5/4/00 (2000) (judge may offer testimony about a proposed new county code that will include terms of employment for court employees and may subject them to an ethics code). However, increased funding for judge's alma mater, *see* Kan. Jud. Ethics Adv. Comm. Op. JE 35 (1990), and resolutions regarding business closings and loss of jobs for union workers are not matters concerning "the law, the legal system, or the administration of justice." *See* Mich. Comm. on Jud. Ethics Op. JI-52 (1992). *See also In re Chaisson*, 549 So. 2d 259 (La. 1989) (judge's involvement with legislative and executive branch officials concerning legislation necessary to effectuate settlement of action over which judge did not preside is not conduct concerning the administration of justice); Colo. Jud. Ethics Adv. Bd. Op. 2006-08 (2006) (judge should not accept appointment to a blue ribbon panel of public and private leaders charged with making recommendations to executive and legislative branches for "reducing the state's contribution and vulnerability to a changed climate" because climate control issues are unconnected with the law, the legal system, the administration of justice, or the role of the judiciary); Nev. Stand. Comm. on Jud. Ethics and Election Prac., JE07-002 (2007) (judge may not serve on a committee to develop and recommend a mandatory, but random, drug testing program for a high school's student athletes); *but see* Ill. Jud. Ethics Comm. Op. 07-05 (2007) (judge may appear at public hearing before mayor and city council to recommend a reduction in hours of liquor sales where reduction of public harm from alcohol consumption is part of administration of justice to the extent it decreases alcohol related offenses, civil litigation, and other court matters). If legislation applies to both judicial and nonjudicial officers, a judge may be permitted to support those aspects of the legislation addressing the concerns of members of the judiciary but not the applicability of the legislation to all elected officials or individuals. Wash. Ethics Adv. Comm. Op. 00-16 (2000).

According to the United States Committee on Codes of Conduct, judges may appear before a legislative or executive body or official, at a public hearing or in private consultation, with respect to matters concerning the administration of justice. Examples of such issues include matters relating to court personnel, budget, equipment, housing, and procedures, which are all necessary to the smooth operation of the dispensation of justice generally. United States Committee on Codes of Conduct, Advisory Op. 50 (1977, revised 1998). Less clear, according to the Committee, is the propriety of judges appearing on behalf of or against, particular proposed legislation that relates to a subject matter other than the administration of justice. Although Canon 4(B) of the Code of Conduct for United States Judges (the counterpart to Rule 3.2 of the Model Code) speaks of "matters concerning the law," which could be broadly construed, the U.S. Committee on Codes of Conduct concluded that the reach of the Canon was intended to be comparatively narrow. Therefore, the Committee advised, with the exception of matters involving the judge or the judge's interest, a judge may appear before a legislative or executive body on matters not concerning judicial administration only if (1) the hearing is public and (2) the subject matter reasonably may be considered to merit the attention and comment of a judge as a judge, and not merely as an individual. United States Committee on Codes of Conduct, Advisory Op. 50 (1977, revised 1998).

MATTERS ABOUT WHICH JUDGE ACQUIRED KNOWLEDGE OR EXPERTISE

Rule 3.2(B) permits judges to appear voluntarily before a governmental body or consulting with government officials in connection with matters about which the judge acquired knowledge or expertise in the course of the his or her judicial duties. This provision was added in 2007 to reflect the growing recognition that in the course of carrying out their judicial duties, judges often gain expertise and special insight into legal and social problems and matters of public policy and should be permitted to share that information with other governmental bodies and officials. Charles G. Geyh & W. William Hodes, *Reporters' Notes to the Model Code of Judicial Conduct* 59 (2009).

PRO SE APPEARANCES

Rule 3.2(C) permits judges to appear at public hearings when acting pro se in a matter concerning the judge's legal or economic interest, or when the judge is acting in a fiduciary capacity, which includes serving as an executor, administrator, trustee, or guardian. Model Code of Judicial Conduct Terminology. A comment to the rule states that "it would be an unnecessary and unfair burden to prohibit judges from appearing before governmental bodies or consulting with government officials on matters that are likely to affect them as private citizens," but added that when engaging in such activities, "judges must not refer to their judicial positions, and must otherwise exercise caution to avoid using the prestige of judicial office." Model Code of Judicial Conduct Rule 3.2 cmt. [3].

Pursuant to former Canon 4C(1), upon which Rule 3.2(C) is based, a judge could appear at public hearings when acting pro se "in a matter involving the judge or the judge's interest." *See, e.g.*, Kan. Jud. Ethics Op. JE-125 (2005) (judge can appear and speak at zoning board hearing where developer is requesting zoning change from single family zoning to a much less restrictive high density zoning approximately one block from judge's home); *but see* Nev. Stand. Comm. on Jud. Ethics and Election Prac. Op. JE04-004 (2004) (judge may not appear publicly on behalf of his neighborhood association to advocate for or against rezoning matters because he would not be acting pro se). Under Canon 4C(1) some states' judicial conduct codes, provided that "[t]he word 'interests' should be interpreted broadly" and that judges should be permitted to "speak on matters concerning the judge's social interests as well as matters affecting the judge's economic interests." Alaska Code of Judicial Conduct, Canon 4C(1), Commentary. However, the Arkansas Supreme Court found that the "judge's interests" exception violated the First Amendment because it is neither sufficiently defined nor narrowly tailored so as not to restrict legitimate free speech. *Griffen v. Ark. Jud. Disc. & Disability Comm'n*, 130 S.W.3d 524 (Ark. 2003) (majority of court granted writ of certiorari quashing admonishment of judge for comments he made while speaking before a meeting of the Arkansas Legislative Black Caucus).

The revised Code tried to address the problem raised by *Griffen* by retaining the exception but limiting it to matters involving the judge's "legal or economic interests or when the judge is acting in a fiduciary capacity." Charles Gardner Geyh, James J. Alfini, Steven Lubet, & Jeffrey M. Shaman, *Judicial Conduct and Ethics* § 9.03[3] at 9–13 (5th ed. 2013).

A Comment to Rule 3.2 states that the types of interests judges may address in their appearances before government bodies include "zoning proposals affecting their real property." Model Code of Judicial Conduct Rule 3.2 cmt. [3]. This is in accord with an advisory opinion of The United States Committee on Code of Conduct, which stated that judges may appear at a hearing regarding zoning or rezoning of the judge's property or for the imposition of assessments for improvements. United States Committee on Codes of Conduct, Advisory Op. 50 (1977, revised 1998).

RULE 3.3 TESTIFYING AS A CHARACTER WITNESS

A judge shall not testify as a character witness in a judicial, administrative, or other adjudicatory proceeding or otherwise vouch for the character of a person in a legal proceeding, except when duly summoned.

COMMENT

[1] A judge who, without being subpoenaed, testifies as a character witness abuses the prestige of judicial office to advance the interests of another. See Rule 1.3. Except in unusual circumstances where the demands of justice require, a judge should discourage a party from requiring the judge to testify as a character witness.

1990 CODE COMPARISON

Rule 3.3 originates from the last sentence of Canon 2B and the Comment is the last sentence of the Commentary to Canon 2B. Rule 3.3 substituted the phrase "except when duly summoned" for "testify voluntarily," and added the phrase "otherwise vouch for the character of a person in a legal proceeding." New language, specifying that the Rule applies in all forms of "adjudicatory proceedings," was also added as a reminder that Rule 3.3 is not limited to civil or criminal trials in courts, but applies whenever testimony is taken on a formal record. Charles G. Geyh & W. William Hodes, *Reporters' Notes to the Model Code of Judicial Conduct* 60–61 (2009).

ANNOTATION

Rule 3.3 is clear in prohibiting a judge from testifying as a character witness, unless duly summoned. The commentary explains the rationale behind this prohibition. A judge who testifies as a character witness without being subpoenaed abuses the prestige of office to advance the interests of another in violation of Rule 1.3. A judge must actively discourage a party from requiring the judge to testify as a character witness, except in the unusual circumstances when the demands of justice require such testimony. Rule 3.3 also provides that a judge shall not "vouch for the character of a person in a legal proceeding." This language was added to the Code in 2007 in recognition of the fact that under oath is not the only mode in which judges might abuse the prestige of office when the character of a person is at issue in a legal proceeding. Charles G. Geyh & W. William Hodes, *Reporters' Notes to the Model Code of Judicial Conduct* 60–61 (2009).

The 1972 Code drafters learned of numerous instances where judges were called upon to exploit the dignity and prestige of their office when asked to testify as character witnesses. In fact, some judges sought protection from the demands of being asked to testify as character witnesses. E. Wayne Thode, *Reporter's Notes to Code of Judicial Conduct* 49 (1972). As a result, the 1972 Code imposed a ban against judges voluntarily testifying as character witnesses. The Commentary to the 1972 Code, however, stated that the Canon "does not afford [the judge] a privilege against testifying in response to an official summons." 1972 Code of Judicial Conduct, Canon 2, Commentary, Paragraph 2.

Unfortunately, by the time of the 1990 Code review, it was clear that the "official summons" exception could be misused to circumvent the rule. The comment language discouraging a judge from testifying as a character witness "except in unusual circumstances" was added in response to the problem of avoiding the ban through the "friendly subpoena." Lisa Milord, *The Development of the ABA Judicial Code* 14 (1992). Although it has always been understood that judges should not encourage a party to issue a sham subpoena for what is in fact voluntary testimony, the comment to Rule 3.3 suggests that judges should actively discourage parties from seeking their testimony as character witnesses. Charles G. Geyh & W. William Hodes, *Reporters' Notes to the Model Code of Judicial Conduct* 61 (2009).

The case law and state judicial ethics opinions have followed the approach that it is improper for a judge to testify as a character witness unless necessitated by the demands of justice. *See, e.g., In re Abel*, 632 So. 2d 600 (Fla. 1994) (improper for judge to testify as character witness in any proceeding, except in response to official witness subpoena); *In re Fogan*, 646 So. 2d 191 (Fla. 1994) (rejecting argument that judge's letter to sentencing judge was not "testifying" because it was not under oath or affirmation; court noted that Canon prohibiting judge from being a character witness was broad enough to include written statements voluntarily submitted with the understanding that such statements may be used by a court); *Hatcher v. McBride*, 650 S.E.2d 104 (W. Va. 2006) (a judge who is requested to testify as a witness shall discourage the party from requiring him or her to testify; however, the judge may testify when properly summoned upon approval of the trial court and with such limitations as may be imposed by the trial court); Ky. Jud. Ethics Op. JE-104 (2004) (in the absence of a formal request from the Governor, a judge may not communicate with the Governor's office regarding a pardon, and in the absence of a formal request from the parole board, may not communicate with the board regarding a parole proceeding);

Mass. Comm. Jud. Ethics Adv. Op. 04-4 (2004) (judge may not send unsolicited letter to the Chief Justice for Administration and Management opposing termination for disciplinary reasons of court employee with whom judge worked; however, judge may furnish character information to a decision-maker who requests it or testify if properly summoned to do so); N.Y. Adv. Comm. on Jud. Ethics Op. 11-16 (2011) (judge may not write letter on behalf of court officer for use in the court officer's disciplinary proceeding because "voluntarily writing such a letter in a professional disciplinary matter would be tantamount to testifying as a character witness"); *cf. Kaufman v. Zakaib*, 535 S.E.2d 727 (W. Va. 2000) (denying demand for judge's deposition, noting "the temptation that some litigants may feel to engage in a form of 'judicial sabotage' by calling judge as witness"; collecting cases on exclusion of testimony of judges and dangers in forcing judges to testify); *Muniz v. Johnson*, 132 F.3d 214 (5th Cir. 1998) (appropriate for a judge to advise witness, a court official subject to the trial judge's control, that she could not testify voluntarily for defendant because prohibition on voluntary testimony extends to judge's staff; testimony may have signaled to the jury that the court disfavored a death penalty in the case or may have created public perception of unfair favor toward one litigant over another; requirement of issuing a subpoena for testimony does not violate Eighth or Fourteenth Amendment when applied to capital sentencing because "it is designed to protect the institutional impartiality of the courts").

When a judge is subpoenaed to testify, however, the judge is obligated to appear and testify like any other citizen. *See, e, g*, Nev. Stand. Comm. on Jud. Ethics and Election Prac. Op. JE06-007 (2006) (judge obligated to answer a subpoena commanding him or her to appear for a hearing or trial and may take steps to avoid providing character evidence). *See generally* Alan B. Rabkin, *Can Judges Be Witnesses*, 9 Nev. Law. 28 (2001) (analysis of voluntary judicial testimony; concluding character testimony should be obtained from other sources); Alan B. Rabkin, *Who Is a Judge Under the Code of Judicial Conduct?* 9 Nev. Law. 32 (2001) (discussing gray areas where rules for pro tem judges differ, such as, a pro tem may act as a character witness except when dealing with a case); Leslie W. Abramson, *Canon 2 of the Code of Judicial Conduct*, 79 Marq. L. Rev. 949 (1996) (analyzing prohibition again judges testifying as character witnesses and analyzing pertinent case law).

Testifying in Attorney Malpractice and Discipline Cases

The reasoning behind the prohibition, namely the implication of judicial partiality, applies equally to attorney malpractice or disciplinary cases in which a judge may be called to testify regarding a lawyer's conduct in proceedings before the judge. Such testimony may be allowed in exceptional circumstances. *See e.g., People v. Morley*, 725 P.2d 510 (Colo. 1986) (finding meritless respondent's claim that his due process rights were violated by refusal to allow retired judge to testify as character witness on his behalf, court noted "in passing" that there might be "exceptional circumstances" that render it appropriate to permit a judge's testimony, such as where judge is only available character witness).

Generally, however, character testimony by judges is discouraged. *See, e.g., In re Reardon*, 759 A.2d 568 (Del. 2000) (court explains that "unless a judge's testimony is relevant to the underlying facts of the disciplinary charges, the judge should not willingly agree to be subpoenaed to testify as a witness. Given that members of the Board include lawyers who may have to appear in other proceedings before the judge-witness, the testimony of the judge-witness may be accorded undue deference simply because of the witness' position as a judge"; compare Delaware Judges' Code of Judicial Conduct language, "a judge should not testify voluntarily as a character witness" with New Jersey and Virginia codes, both which omit the word "voluntarily" from the rule so that a judge cannot testify as a character witness under any circumstances); *accord, In re Howard*, 765 A.2d 39 (Del. 2000). *See also Battle v. Thornton*, 646 A.2d 315 (D.C. 1994) (because of position and authority of judges, there is considerable risk that jury will accord judge's testimony in legal malpractice case substantially greater weight than it deserves); *Cornett v. Johnson*, 571 N.E.2d 572 (Ind. App. 5th Dist. 1991) (judge's testimony at summary judgment hearing in attorney malpractice suit was improper because judge's statements gave impression that he was backing one litigant with weight of his authority and position); *Marrs v. Kelly*, 95 S.W.3d 856 (Ky. 2003) (administrative law judge (ALJ) should not have been permitted to testify in legal malpractice claim against attorney alleging that attorney failed to introduce expert witness testimony in a workers' compensation case heard by ALJ); *In the Matter of Thomason*, 304 S.E.2d 821 (S.C. 1983) (improper for judge to testify as character witness, either in person or by deposition or affidavit, in disciplinary hearing, noting risk of "official testimonial," injecting prestige of office into proceedings is "especially true in disciplinary proceedings where the Hearing Panel is comprised of lawyers"); *Joachim v. Chambers*, 815 S.W.2d 234 (Tex. 1991) (retired district judge who continues to serve as a judicial officer by assignment may not testify as expert witness in legal malpractice action; court stated that "[a]lthough [Rule 3.3] specifically restricts judges only from testifying as character witnesses, the underlying principles may apply to other judicial testimony, especially expert testimony. A judge who testifies as an expert witness for a private litigant provides more than evidence; the judge also confers the prestige and credibility of judicial office to that litigant's position, just as a judge who testifies to the litigant's character"; court uses case at bar to illustrate problems of allowing a judge to testify as expert witness); Nev. Stand. Comm. on Jud. Ethics and Election Prac. Op. JE06-001 (2006) (judge may not testify as an expert in a legal malpractice action for which the judge was engaged prior to taking the bench); *cf. In re Wilkinson*, 678 A.2d 1257 (Vt. 1996) (in petition for post-conviction relief, alleging ineffective assistance of counsel, permitting judge who presided over criminal trial to give expert testimony concerning effect of defense counsel's unprofessional conduct was error); Ill. Jud. Ethics Comm. Op. 04-03 (2004) (judge may not write letter to Illinois Courts Commission in support of a judge against whom disciplinary proceedings are pending, pursuant to the rule that provides that "[a] judge should not testify voluntarily as a character witness"); *but see Sansone v. Garvey, Schubert & Barer*, 71 P.3d 124 (Or. App. 2003) (holding that public policy does not warrant creation of rule categorically prohibiting judge from testifying in legal malpractice action regarding her personal observations of events from prior trial over which judge presided).

RULE 3.4 APPOINTMENTS TO GOVERNMENTAL POSITIONS

A judge shall not accept appointment to a governmental committee, board, commission, or other governmental position, unless it is one that concerns the law*, the legal system, or the administration of justice.

COMMENT

[1] Rule 3.4 implicitly acknowledges the value of judges accepting appointments to entities that concern the law, the legal system, or the administration of justice. Even in such instances, however, a judge should assess the appropriateness of accepting an appointment, paying particular attention to the subject matter of the appointment and the availability and allocation of judicial resources, including the judge's time commitments, and giving due regard to the requirements of the independence and impartiality of the judiciary.

[2] A judge may represent his or her country, state, or locality on ceremonial occasions or in connection with historical, educational, or cultural activities. Such representation does not constitute acceptance of a government position.

1990 CODE COMPARISON

Rule 3.4 is derived from the first sentence of Canon 4C(2). The word "board" was added to the list of governmental entities for completeness and, as has been done throughout the revised Code, "improvement in the law," has been changed to "concerns the law," because what constitutes an "improvement" is almost always debatable. Charles G. Geyh & W. William Hodes, *Reporters' Notes to the Model Code of Judicial Conduct* 61–62 (2009).

Comment [1] draws on the Commentary to Canon 4C(2) but was reworded to more clearly reflect the point that service on governmental bodies should not be allowed to distract judges from their judicial duties or otherwise compromise their independence, impartiality, or integrity. Comment [2] was moved to the Comments from the black letter text of Canon 4C(2) of the 1990 Code. Charles G. Geyh & W. William Hodes, *Reporters' Notes to the Model Code of Judicial Conduct* 62 (2009).

ANNOTATION

INTRODUCTION

The 1972 Code drafting committee adopted the view that the time and prestige of the judicial office should not be expended on the resolution of nonjudicial issues. E. Wayne Thode, *Reporter's Notes to Code of Judicial Conduct* 91 (1973).

This view was carried forward into the 1990 Code and subsequently into the 2007 Code, which provides, subject to listed exceptions, that a judge may not accept appointment to a governmental committee, board, commission, or other governmental position. *See, e.g.*, Ariz. Jud. Ethics Adv. Comm. Op. 94-09 (1994) (judge may not serve as member of Advisory Council on Spinal and Head Injuries because it does not fall into narrow confines of "improvement of the law, the legal system, or the administration of justice"); Del. Jud. Ethics Adv. Comm. Op. 2006-7 (2006) (advising that judge may not accept appointment as Chair of Governor's Consortium on Hispanic Affairs because the position does not appear to be directly concerned with improvement of the law, the legal system or administration of justice); Del. Jud. Ethics Adv. Comm. Op. 2012-3 (judge may not serve on Child Placement Review Board that monitors child placements to ensure children in state custody are receiving adequate care because it is not directly concerned with the improvement of the law; the Review Board's broad mandate "extends beyond what is permissible"); Fla. Jud. Ethics Adv. Comm. Op. 2002-14 (2002) (judge may not participate in independent, state-registered, and regulated political action committee since it does not focus on improvement of law, legal system, or administration of justice); Kan. Jud. Ethics Op. JE-176 (2012) (judge may not serve as volunteer fire chief or on fire board, but may serve as volunteer medical technician); Kan. Jud. Ethics Op. JE-149 (2006) (judge may not serve as Commissioner of Kansas Wildlife and Parks Commission because commission is concerned with issues of policy other than the improvement of the law, the legal system, and the administration of justice); Ky. Jud. Ethics Op. JE-126 (2014) (judge may not become a member or serve on the board of group seeking to establish and fund long-term residential substance abuse treatment housing); N.Y. Adv. Comm. on Jud. Ethics Op. 06-173 (2007) (judge may not serve as inspector for New York State Athletic Commission, which has jurisdiction over boxing matches in the state, because such activity does not concern improvement of the law, the legal system, or the administration of justice); Okla. Jud. Ethics Op. 2010-6 (2010) (judge may not serve on rural water district without approval of the state Supreme Court); S.C. Adv. Comm. on Stands. of Jud. Conduct Op. 08-2013 (judge may not serve on city's employee grievance committee); S.C. Adv. Comm. on Stands. of Jud. Conduct Op. 03-2013 (2013) (judge may not serve on local school advisory board); S.C. Adv. Comm. on Stands. of Jud. Conduct Op. 33-2006 (2006) (full-time magistrate may not serve on the State Board of Education); Wash. Ethics Adv. Comm. Op. 90-16 (1990) (judge may not chair an ethics committee established by the mayor).

The exceptions apply to appointments that concern the "law, the legal system, or the administration of justice." *See., e.g.*, Ariz. Jud. Ethics Adv. Comm. Op. 90-11 (1990) (judge may serve on governor's task force on the seriously mentally ill and on the governor's select commission on juvenile corrections); Ark. Jud. Ethics Adv. Comm. Op. 2007-01 (2007) (judge may serve on the board of visitors for the University of Arkansas); Ark. Jud. Ethics Adv. Comm. Op. 2001-01 (2001) (judge may serve on Board of Advisers for Legal Assistants at a community college); Colo. Jud. Ethics Adv. Bd. Op. 2012-05 (judge may serve on child welfare executive leadership council because the council "has some relationship to the law, legal system, or administration of justice); Fla. Jud. Ethics Adv. Comm. Op. 2004-05 (2004) (county court judge may accept an appointment from a local legislative body to its advisory Commission on the Status of Woman if the Commission is concerned with the improvement of the law, the legal system, or the administration of justice, and the group is not an advocacy group); Maryland Jud. Ethics Comm. Op. 2011-24 (2011) (judge may serve on Public Defender Regional Advisory Board but may only advise on issues concerning the law, the legal system, or the administration of justice; judge may not advise on executive functions like office management, funding, or budget issues); N.M. Adv. Comm. on Code of Jud. Conduct Op. 10-01 (2010) (probate judge may serve on U.S./Mexico Border Health Commission); N.Y. Adv. Comm. on Jud. Ethics Op. 10-91 (2010) (judge may serve on state-sponsored advisory group developing policy on the law and judge may vote on requests for funds).

Some jurisdictions utilize a "direct nexus" test, requiring that there be a direct link between the government commission's work and how courts go about the business of meeting their statutory or constitutional duties. If the nexus is indirect, incidental, or tangential, or if the permitted subjects are just one aspect of a broader mission or focus, service by a judge is not permitted. Additionally, even if there is a close nexus, participation on a particular commission is appropriate only where it would not cast reasonable doubt on a judge's capacity to act. *Compare* Conn. Comm. on Judical Ethics Formal Adv. Op. JE 2011-21 (2011) (applying nexus test determines that sentencing commission concerns the law) *with* Mass. Comm. on Jud. Ethics Adv. Op. 2003-13 (2003) (applying nexus test to advise that judges may not serve on subcommittees of Governor's

Commission on Criminal Justice because the focus of the subcommittees is too broad and does not address directly how courts go about their business); Nev. Stand. Comm. on Jud. Ethics and Election Practices Op. JE11-007 (2011) (judge may not serve on team charged with review of death of domestic violence victim because a "critical purpose and function of the team is to make policy and other recommendations to prevent domestic violence crimes . . .") *and* Utah Jud. Ethics Adv. Comm. Informal Op. 98-11 (1998) (applying test, advises that if Utah Antidiscrimination Advisory Council is primarily concerned with issues like ensuring compliance with requirements of Antidiscrimination Act, improving methods for fair resolution of complaints, and improving access to victims of discrimination to courts, service would be permitted but if council is more frequently concerned with policy initiatives, employer education, sensitivity education in the workplace, etc., service would not be permitted).

The exemption for governmental committees or positions concerning the law, the legal system, or the administration of justice is acknowledgement of the value of permitting judges, who have experience in administering the judicial system, to take part in state and national efforts to upgrade the system of justice. However, as noted in the Commentary to Rule 3.4, before accepting such an assignment, a judge must assess the appropriateness of accepting the appointment, particularly focusing on "the subject matter of the appointment and the availability and allocation of judicial resources, including the judge's time commitments, and giving due regard to the requirements of the independence and impartiality of the judiciary." *See, e.g.*, Ariz. Jud. Ethics Adv. Comm. Op. 97-6 (1997) (judge's membership on a domestic violence commission may "give the appearance of favoritism and raise a question as to the judge's ability to preside fairly over certain cases"); Ark. Jud. Ethics Adv. Comm. Op. 2004-04 (2004) (judge may not serve on sex offenders assessment committee that will promulgate guidelines and procedures for disclosure of relevant information, develop evaluation protocol for preparing reports to assist courts in making determinations against offenders, and set qualifications for examiners because doing so may cast doubt on judge's ability to act impartially and may interfere with proper performance of judicial duties); Ark. Jud. Ethics Adv. Comm. Op. 96-10 (1996) (judge may not accept appointment to state commission that sets policy and budget for operations of state parks and tourism); Del. Jud. Ethics Adv. Comm. Op. JPC 1991-1 (1991) (judge cannot serve as chairman of committee to revise the mental health laws); Fla. Jud. Ethics Adv. Comm. Op. 2013-03 (2013) (judge may not serve on county elections task force); Fla. Jud. Ethics Adv. Comm. Op. 2001-16 (2001) (judge may not serve as appointed member of commission charged with fiscal oversight of government funds); Mich. Comm. on Jud. Ethics Op. JI-65 (1993) (judge may not serve on legislative affairs and political action committee whose mission is to support pro-business interests); Ohio Bd.

of Commissioners on Grievances and Disc. Op. 2003-9 (2003) (common pleas court judges should not serve on judicial corrections boards for community-based correctional facilities and programs); Wash. Ethics Adv. Comm. Op. 96-02 (1996) (judge may not join domestic violence task force that has specific goals regarding judicial policy); *cf.* Conn. Comm. on Judical Ethics Formal Adv. Op. JE 2011-21 (2011) (judge may serve on sentencing commission, noting membership "is diverse and represents more than one point of view" and commission is "unlikely to be viewed by the public as a political or advocacy group").

For criticism asserting that exemption for governmental committees or positions concerning the law, the legal system or the administration of justice is too broad to provide useful guidance to judges, *see* Charles Gardner Geyh, James A. Alfini, Steven Lubet, & Jeffrey M. Shaman, *Judicial Conduct and Ethics* § 9.03[2] at 9–5 (5th ed. 2013).

EXCEPTIONS

There are a few exceptions to the limitations imposed by Rule 3.4. A judge may represent his or her country, state, or locality on ceremonial occasions or in connection with historical, educational, or cultural activities. Model Code of Judicial Conduct Rule 3.4 cmt. [2]. *See, e.g.*, Ariz. Jud. Ethics Adv. Comm. Op. 96-10 (1996) (judge may accept position on board of directors of Arizona Historical Society, which is nonprofit and created specifically for historical, educational, and cultural purposes). In addition, Rule 3.4 does not govern a judge's service in non-governmental positions. Rule 3.7 allows a judge to participate in activities sponsored by organizations or governmental entities concerned with the law, the legal system, or the administration of justice and those sponsored by or on behalf of nonprofit educational, religious, charitable, fraternal, or civic organizations.

MAINTAINING APPEARANCE OF IMPARTIALITY

In addition to the limitations listed in Rule 3.4, Rule 3.1 provides that judges must not participate in extrajudicial activities that would "appear to a reasonable person to undermine the judge's independence, integrity, or impartiality." Therefore, whether a judge may sit on any board or committee, turns not only on whether that board or committee concerns the law, the legal system, or the administration of justice, but also on whether participation by a judge would lead to an appearance of partiality in cases coming before that judge. Alaska Comm'n on Jud. Conduct Adv. Op. 2000-1 (2000) (advising that before accepting appointment to particular commission judge should consider (1) whether commission members represent only one point of view or whether membership is balanced; (2) whether group will discuss controversial legal issues likely to come before courts, or merely administrative or procedural issues; (3) whether group will be viewed by public as a political or an advocacy group or merely as an administrative group; (4) whether group will take public policy positions that are more appropriate to the other two branches of government than to the courts, or whether the policy positions could be viewed as clearly central to the administration of justice; opinion, however, also provided that regardless of these factors, judges may provide information on matters concerning the law or the administration of justice to groups in which their membership would be precluded by the Code). *See generally* Cynthia Gray, *Ethics and Judges' Evolving Roles Off the Bench: Service on Governmental Commissions*, 24 No. 1 Judicial Conduct Reporter 1 (Spring 2002) (summarizing state advisory opinion guidelines for determining whether judicial participation on a particular commission is acceptable under the Code). *See also* Colo. Jud. Ethics Adv. Bd. Op. 2010-02 (2010) (judge must resign from interagency advisory board because newly adopted memorandum of understanding on fund distribution creates situation in which judge's impartiality of juvenile placement decisions could be questioned).

CONTROVERSIAL COMMITTEES

A judge may be precluded from serving on a government committee due to the controversial nature of the committee's work. *See, e.g.*, Del. Jud. Ethics Adv. Comm. Op. 1991-1 (1999) (judge may not serve on committee reviewing ethics policies and procedures of school district facing allegations of unauthorized spending and purchases that have been source of public discussion). A judge working extrajudicially with such a committee "must assess the nature and extent of the controversy, but need not resign as long as that extrajudicial service does not tend[ ] to erode the appearance of impartiality, which is essential to judging itself." Steven Lubet, *Beyond Reproach: Ethical Restrictions on the Extrajudicial Activities of State and Federal Judges* 28 (1984).

RULE 3.5 USE OF NONPUBLIC INFORMATION

A judge shall not intentionally disclose or use nonpublic information* acquired in a judicial capacity for any purpose unrelated to the judge's judicial duties.

COMMENT

[1] In the course of performing judicial duties, a judge may acquire information of commercial or other value that is unavailable to the public. The judge must not reveal or use such information for personal gain or for any purpose unrelated to his or her judicial duties.

[2] This rule is not intended, however, to affect a judge's ability to act on information as necessary to protect the health or safety of the judge or a member of a judge's family, court personnel, or other judicial officers, if consistent with other provisions of this Code.

1990 CODE COMPARISON

Rule 3.5 is based on former Canon 3B(12), with minor revisions. The word "intentionally" was added because it would be unfair to impose discipline for an unintentional disclosure. In the 1990 Code, this provision was found in the Canon on the performance of *judicial* duties. It was repositioned to Canon 3, which addresses personal and extrajudicial activity, because it is a form of misuse of judicial office for personal gain or advantage. The two comments to the Rule are new to the Code. Charles G. Geyh & W. William Hodes, *Reporters' Notes to the Model Code of Judicial Conduct* 62–63 (2009).

ANNOTATION

INTRODUCTION

Rule 3.5 prohibits judges from using or disclosing information acquired in a judicial capacity in order to further nonjudicial purposes. *See* Fla. Jud. Ethics Adv. Comm. Op. 2013-13 (2013) (judge may not use former law office in building where former law firm continues to practice in part because "using a law firm's computer and other equipment for research, e-mailing, and composing judicially related work, allows nonjudicial personnel potential access to confidential nonpublic judicial work information"). The 1990 Code clarified that this restriction applies only to "nonpublic" information, that is, information that, by law, is not available to the public. Such information may include, according to the Code's Terminology section, information that is sealed by statute or court order or impounded or communicated in camera, and information offered in grand jury proceedings, presentencing reports, dependency cases, or psychiatric reports. This section was added to the Code in 1990, primarily to prohibit judges from abusing the public trust for their private gain. For instance, a judge would be subject to discipline for investing in stock based on a tip the judge had learned of through information sealed by court. Lisa L. Milord, *The Development of the ABA Judicial Code* 22 (1992). However, Comment [2] points out that the rule is not intended to prevent the judge from acting on information as necessary to protect the health or safety of the judge or a member of the judge's family, court personnel, or other judicial officers, if consistent with other provisions of the Code. Model Code of Judicial Conduct Rule 3.5 cmt. [2]. This comment was added to the Code in 2007 in recognition of the increased prevalence of physical violence in and around courts. If a judge learns of nonpublic information that constitutes a credible threat of violence against court personnel or family members, the judge may take protective measures on the basis of that information. Charles G. Geyh & W. William Hodes, *Reporters' Notes to the Model Code of Judicial Conduct* 63 (2009).

USE OF NONPUBLIC INFORMATION FOR FINANCIAL GAIN

Canon 3B(12), the predecessor to Rule 3.5, has most often been cited in proceedings against judges who have used nonpublic information acquired in their judicial capacity to enhance their personal financial position. For instance, a judge was removed from office for misconduct, including using inside information he obtained during judicial proceedings to develop an interest in property that was subject of litigation in his court. *In re Yaccarino*, 502 A.2d 3 (N.J. 1985). Even if a judge is not actually using inside information for personal gain, a judge may be disciplined for activities that create the appearance of an unfair advantage. *See, e.g., In re Fuchsberg*, 426 N.Y.S.2d 639 (N.Y. 1978) (judge censured for transactions in New York City bonds while cases affecting the value of the bonds were before New York courts; even though there was no evidence that judge traded on inside information, court concluded that "these purchases could reasonably create the impression, despite the absence of a factual basis for such impression, that respondent was purchasing securities on the basis of some information or advantage not generally available to the public"). *But see* Colo. Jud. Ethics Adv. Op. 2012-04 (2010) (judge may purchase "property that had previously been the subject of a foreclosure proceeding in the judge's judicial district so long as (1) the purchase does not result or appear to result from exploitation of the judicial office or the use of information acquired by the judge in his or her judicial capacity; (2) the judge does not receive preferential treatment in the sale or otherwise have an advantage over other potential purchasers based on his or her position as a judge or affiliation with any person or entity involved in the foreclosure proceedings or sale; and (3) the purchase does not undermine the judge's impartiality or give rise to the appearance of impropriety").

Use of nonpublic information does not have to be so egregious to draw censure under Rule 3.5, however. A judge who approached a divorced couple with a proposal that they become Amway distributors, after learning of their financial problems in a confidential child support proceeding, was found to have violated the predecessor to Rule 3.5. *In re Phalen*, 475 S.E.2d 327 (W. Va. 1996).

OTHER NONJUDICIAL PURPOSES

Although the predecessor to Rule 3.5 has most often been invoked when a judge has used nonpublic information for financial gain, the provision is violated whenever a judge uses nonpublic information for any nonjudicial purpose. For instance, a judge seeking re-election who, in a campaign statement, criticizes the majority decision in a case in which he or she dissented, may be violating Rule 3.5. *See* Vincent R. Johnson, *Ethical Campaigning for the Judiciary*, 29 Tex. Tech L. Rev. 811 (1998). And, a judge revealing nonpublic information about a private adoption on an Internet forum violated Rule 3.5. *In re Maggio*, 440 S.W.3d 333 (Ark. 2014). On the other hand, using nonpublic information in order to avoid acting in a way that might create the impression of judicial impropriety likely does not violate Rule 3.5. *See, e.g.,*

In re Swift, Ca. Comm. on Jud. Performance (Feb. 11, 1997) (judge avoided potential discredit to the judiciary by transferring a search warrant request to another judge after learning that the house that was the subject of the search was co-owned by the judge and occupied by the judge's stepson; judge's use of nonpublic information helped to uphold the reputation of the judiciary as a whole). In addition, a judge likely does not violate Rule 3.5 by disclosing nonpublic information that is within the purview of the judge's judicial duties. For instance, a judge was advised that reporting a physician for over-prescribing drugs based on information learned in the course of a child custody proceeding was not a violation of the predecessor to Rule 3.5. Va. Jud. Ethics Adv. Comm. Op. 2001-01 (2001).

INTENT REQUIRED

Unlike some other provisions of the Model Code of Judicial Conduct, Rule 3.5 and its predecessor may not be violated through carelessness–a judge must intentionally use nonpublic information to run afoul of this Section. *See, e.g., In re Handy*, 867 P.2d 341 (Kan. 1994) (judge who purchased a condominium three weeks after hearing a probate case that involved the condominium did not violate the Canon because it appeared that the judge had learned of the condominium's availability through a real estate agent and did not recall signing orders regarding the property).

RULE 3.6 AFFILIATION WITH DISCRIMINATORY ORGANIZATIONS

(A) A judge shall not hold membership in any organization that practices invidious discrimination on the basis of race, sex, gender, religion, national origin, ethnicity, or sexual orientation.

(B) A judge shall not use the benefits or facilities of an organization if the judge knows* or should know that the organization practices invidious discrimination on one or more of the bases identified in paragraph (A). A judge's attendance at an event in a facility of an organization that the judge is not permitted to join is not a violation of this Rule when the judge's attendance is an isolated event that could not reasonably be perceived as an endorsement of the organization's practices.

COMMENT

[1] A judge's public manifestation of approval of invidious discrimination on any basis gives rise to the appearance of impropriety and diminishes public

confidence in the integrity and impartiality of the judiciary. A judge's membership in an organization that practices invidious discrimination creates the perception that the judge's impartiality is impaired.

[2] An organization is generally said to discriminate invidiously if it arbitrarily excludes from membership on the basis of race, sex, gender, religion, national origin, ethnicity, or sexual orientation persons who would otherwise be eligible for admission. Whether an organization practices invidious discrimination is a complex question to which judges should be attentive. The answer cannot be determined from a mere examination of an organization's current membership rolls, but rather, depends upon how the organization selects members, as well as other relevant factors, such as whether the organization is dedicated to the preservation of religious, ethnic, or cultural values of legitimate common interest to its members, or whether it is an intimate, purely private organization whose membership limitations could not constitutionally be prohibited.

[3] When a judge learns that an organization to which the judge belongs engages in invidious discrimination, the judge must resign immediately from the organization.

[4] A judge's membership in a religious organization as a lawful exercise of the freedom of religion is not a violation of this Rule.

[5] This Rule does not apply to national or state military service.

1990 CODE COMPARISON

Rule 3.6(A) is very similar to Canon 2C of the 1990 Code, but expands the list of prohibited bases of invidious discrimination by adding gender, ethnicity, and sexual orientation. Rule 3.6(B) derives chiefly from the last paragraph of the Commentary to Canon 2C of the 1990 Code, which, in effect, provided a one-year grace period for a judge to maintain membership in an organization that practiced invidious discrimination if the judge made efforts to have the organization discontinue its discriminatory practices. This commentary was revised to change its focus, and moved to the black letter text because of its practical importance. Because Rule 3.6(B) does not allow any active engagement with an organization that practices invidious discrimination, the one-year "grace period" to try to effect change has been eliminated. The Commission concluded that any active involvement would constitute too much of an endorsement of the organization; even good-faith behind-the-scene activities would not sufficiently negate the public's perception of bias. New Comment [3] confirms that a judge must resign immediately upon learning of the organization's practices. Charles G. Geyh & W. William Hodes, *Reporters' Notes to the Model Code of Judicial Conduct* 64–66 (2009).

Comments [1] and [2] are based on the Commentary to Canon 2C of the 1990 Code. As noted previously, Comment [3] is new to the Code, as are Comments [4] and [5].

ANNOTATION

MEMBERSHIP IN ORGANIZATION THAT PRACTICES INVIDIOUS DISCRIMINATION

Rule 3.6(A) is predicated upon the concern that the public perception of judicial integrity and impartiality can be compromised when a judge holds membership in an organization that discriminates invidiously in its membership policies. As noted in Comment [1], a "judge's membership in an organization that practices invidious discrimination creates the perception that the judge's impartiality is impaired." *See also In re Complaint of Judicial Misconduct*, No. C.C.D. 11-01, U.S. Jud. Conference Comm. on Judicial Conduct and Disability (2011) ("We are not concerned here only with the sort of discriminiation prohibited by the Civil Rights Act, Title VII, of the Constitution . . . Quite simply, judges may not be members of organizations that would reasonably appear to the public to discriminiate in their membership practices on any of the grounds listed.").

Whether the judge shares the views of the organization or not, the fact of the judge's membership in a discriminatory organization can lead to the public perception of the judge's support of the discriminatory policies. *See generally* Charles Gardner Geyh, James J. Alfini, Steven Lubet, & Jeffrey M. Shaman, *Judicial Conduct and Ethics* § 10.05[1] at 10–23 (5th ed. 2013) (even in jurisdictions that have not adopted the Model Code, all judges should refrain from membership in invidiously discriminatory organizations because of perception of bias); Cynthia Gray, *Organizations that Practice Invidious Discrimination* (American Judicature Society 1996, rev. 1999). For a criticism of the wording of Canon 2C, the predecessor to Rule 3.6, and a consideration of five alternatives, including the elimination of the rule, see Andrew L. Kaufman, *Judicial Correctness Meets Constitutional Correctness: Section 2C of the Code of Judicial Conduct*, 32 Hofstra L. Rev. 1293 (2004) ("the choice of Canon 2C and its Commentary to focus on 'invidious' discrimination left considerably more 'muddle' than is either necessary or wise").

A Balancing of Interests

The issue of judicial membership in restrictive organizations presents the problem of balancing a judge's associational rights against public confidence in an impartial judiciary. In Rule 3.6, the balance is struck in favor of the public's interest in judicial impartiality. *See generally* Robert J. Aalberts & Kenneth C. Fonte, *Is Section 2C of the Model Code of Judicial Conduct Justified? An*

Empirical Study of the Impropriety of Judges Belonging to Exclusive Clubs, 8 Geo. J. Legal Ethics 597 (1995) (canvassing commentators' arguments allowing judges to be members in discriminatory clubs—a judge's freedom to associate, the desirability of a social outlet for judges and their families, and the undesirability of isolating judges from the public—and concluding with support for the prohibition in Canon 2C, the predecessor to Rule 3.6); Randall T. Shepard, *Campaign Speech: Restraint and Liberty in Judicial Ethics*, 9 Geo. J. Legal Ethics 1059 (1996) (discussing the problem of weighing a judge's associational rights against litigants' due process interests in the context of a judge's membership in advocacy organizations, such as the National Right to Life Association, and suggesting judges avoid formal membership in such associations).

The National Commission on Judicial Discipline and Removal, charged with reviewing issues related to the discipline and removal of federal judges, has recommended that public disclosure requirements under federal law be amended to require federal judges to certify that the judge does not hold membership prohibited by Canon 2C of the Code of Conduct for United States Judges or to list all organizations not exempted by Canon 2C of which the judge is a member. According to the National Commission, this self-reporting requirement would assist judges in compliance with Canon 2C of the Code of Conduct and increase public accountability, but also allow that "judges and their families . . . not be stripped of their privacy or made the victims of a standard whose meaning is avowedly contextual." *The Report of the National Commission on Judicial Discipline & Removal*, 152 F.R.D. 265 (1994).

Defining "Invidious Discrimination"

Generally, an organization discriminates invidiously if it arbitrarily excludes individuals from membership on the basis of race, sex, gender, religion, or national origin, ethnicity, or sexual orientation persons who would otherwise be eligible for admission. ABA Model Code of Judicial Conduct Rule 3.6 cmt. [2]. The term "invidious discrimination" is not defined in the Code, but Comment [2] provides guidelines to help determine when an organization engages in invidious discrimination, thus falling under the ban of Rule 3.6(A). The key test is a functional one: whether an excluded applicant (not possessing one of the listed characteristics) would otherwise be eligible for admission to membership. *See also In re Complaint of Judicial Misconduct*, No. C.C.D. 11-01, U.S. Jud. Conference Comm. on Judicial Conduct and Disability (2011) ("Typically, the inquiry is fact-specific and the answer depends on such factors as the organization's selection criteria, goals, size, and geographic location.").

In addition, the Comment explains that certain organizations practicing some forms of discrimination cannot be said to be practicing invidious or improper discrimination, either because the discrimination is based on rationales that are not socially harmful, or because members of the organization have a constitutional right to associate without governmental interference. Charles G. Geyh & W. William Hodes, *Reporters' Notes to the Model Code of Judicial Conduct* 65 (2009).

Some states have dropped the term "invidious discrimination." *See, e.g.*, Oregon Code of Judicial Conduct Rule 4.4 ("A judge shall not hold membership in an organization that the judge knows or should know is a discriminatory organization."); Texas Code of Judicial Conduct Canon 2C ("[a] judge shall not knowingly hold membership in any organization that practices discrimination prohibited by law").

Other states have further defined the term "invidious discrimination" in their Codes or elsewhere. *See, e.g.*, Ky. S. Ct. Rule 4.300, Code of Jud. Conduct Canon 2E (2003) ("Invidious discrimination includes any action by an organization that appears to regard some immutable individual trait, such as a person's race, gender, religion or national origin, as odious or inferior, which is used to justify arbitrary exclusion of persons possessing those traits from membership or participation in the organization. On the other hand, organizations dedicated to the preservation of religious, fraternal, sororal, spiritual, charitable, civic, or cultural values, which do not stigmatize any excluded persons as inferior and therefore unworthy of membership, are not considered to discriminate invidiously."); *cf.* Ind. Comm. on Jud. Qualifications Op. 1-94 (1994) ("invidious discrimination" is an arbitrary distinction made on illegitimate or offensive grounds; cites cases of invidious governmental discrimination, that is, where irrational classifications are not reasonably related to legitimate purposes and thus fail constitutional scrutiny).

The 1990 Code Committee restricted the categories of discrimination to race, sex, religion, and national origin in recognition of the fact that those categories are the only constitutionally protected categories. *See* Lisa L. Milord, *The Development of the ABA Judicial Code* 16 (1992). In 2007, however, the Code Committee expanded the list of prohibited bases of invidious discrimination to also include gender, ethnicity, and sexual orientation.

Immediate Resignation

The Commentary to Rule 3.6 provides that when a judge learns that an organization to which he or she belongs engages in invidious discrimination, the judge must resign immediately from the organization. This replaces commentary from the 1990 Code suggesting that as an alternative to immediate resignation, a judge might remain with the organization for one year, while making efforts to have the organization discontinue its discriminatory practices. This new comment makes it clear that immediate resignation is required in order to comply with Rule 3.6(A). Model Code of Judicial Conduct Rule 3.6 cmt. [3].

Not Applicable to Religious Organizations or the Military

The commentary to Rule 3.6 makes clear that while many religious organizations engage in some forms of discrimination, participation by a judge in any bona fide religious organization cannot be prohibited or punished by governmental authorities because of the constitutional guarantee of free exercise of religion. Similarly, although military organizations often engage in discrimination and sometimes discriminate on a basis that would be found invidious in other contexts, the drafting committee concluded that the practical difficulties involved in enforcing a ban on holding membership in a military organization and the need for uniform rules across the military justified an interpretation that service in state and national military does not violate Rule 3.6. Model Code of Judicial Conduct Rule 3.6 cmt. [4] and [5] and Charles G. Geyh & W. William Hodes, *Reporters' Notes to the Model Code of Judicial Conduct* 65 (2009). Some states had already taken this step, specifically exempting certain organizations from the general ban. Cal. Code of Jud. Ethics, Canon 2C Advisory Committee Commentary (2003) (exempts membership in religious and military organizations, and subject to Canon 4A, does not bar membership in nonprofit youth organizations); *In re Code of Judicial Conduct*, 643 So. 2d 1037 (Fla. 1994) (adding the following language to the Commentary: "This Canon is not intended to prohibit membership in religious and ethnic clubs, such as Knights of Columbus, Masons, B'nai B'rith, and Sons of Italy; civic organizations, such as Rotary, Kiwanis, and The Junior League; young people's organizations, such as Boy Scouts, Girl Scouts, Boy's Clubs, and Girl's Clubs; and charitable organizations, such as United Way and Red Cross"). *See also* Fla. Jud. Ethics Adv. Comm. Op. 2013-16 (judge may serve on board of scouting organization).

Restrictive Private Social Clubs

Rule 3.6's prohibition has been understood as targeting discriminatory private social clubs particularly. *See* Charles Gardner Geyh, James J. Alfini, Steven Lubet, & Jeffrey M. Shaman, *Judicial Conduct and Ethics*, § 10.05[4] at 10–27 (5th ed. 2013) ("The principal function of this provision is to bar membership in discriminatory social clubs, which previously had been the subject of much controversy. . . . [I]n a matter as sensitive to public perception as is judging, appearances and symbols take on an importance of their own. Minorities have every reason to mistrust judges who belong to discriminatory clubs"); *see also* Ind. Adv. Op. 1-94 (1994) (declining to create a list of "approved" or "disapproved" groups of lodges or fraternal organizations because practices vary from chapter to chapter; asserting that the rule is "aimed directly at country clubs, dining clubs, and service and professional organizations"); Ark. Jud. Ethics Adv. Comm. Op. 00-04 (2000) (citing the above quoted language of Ind. Comm'n on Jud. Qualifications Adv. Op. 1-94 with approval in assessing whether judge may serve on board of directors of country club, adding that "experience has taught us that discrimination takes subtle forms and caution is advisable"; reiterating notion that individual judge is in best position to determine whether organization complies with provision); *see generally* Wayne Doane, Note, *The Membership of Judges in Gender Discriminatory Private Clubs*, 12 Vt. L. Rev. 459 (1987) (distinguishing between acceptable "inclusive" private clubs where membership is restricted to persons sharing common religious, political cultural, and ethnic beliefs and the unacceptable "exclusive" clubs in which membership is restricted through the exclusion of persons with particular characteristics; concluding that governmental intrusion is justified in the context of judicial membership in gender discriminatory private clubs).

Commentators have been somewhat critical of the lack of clarity on the scope of the prohibition. *See, e.g.*, Leslie W. Abramson, *Canon 2 of the Code of Judicial Conduct*, 79 Marq. L. Rev. 949 (1996) (suggesting that the scope of Canon 2C requires further development because the criteria are indefinite, and there is a loophole in the rule that allows members of a judge's household to belong to a discriminatory organization); Randall T. Shepard, *Campaign Speech: Restraint and Liberty in Judicial Ethics*, 9 Geo. J. Legal Ethics 1059 (1996) (arguing that Canon 2C is based on paradigm of large city business clubs that historically exclude women; suggesting the rationale for protecting litigants' due process rights may be more attenuated in "the small town Elks Club" setting where wives of members may come and go at will and policy of admitting only men "may be more the result of inertia than the product of current sentiment").

Nonprofit Youth Organizations

A topic of considerable interest has been a judge's voluntary service in nonprofit youth organizations, such as the Boy Scouts or Girl Scouts, which restrict membership based on gender. At least one state has concluded that a judge may participate in membership or leadership of such organizations despite gender segregation policies. Ariz. Jud. Ethics Adv. Op. 94-07 (1994) (judge may be a member or leader of the Boys Scouts of America or the Girl Scouts of America because organization's membership practices can be justified under this analysis: "they (1) serve 'religious, ethnic, or cultural value of legitimate common interest to its members'; (2) are not generally regarded as repugnant in contemporary society; and (3) cause no harm to the excluded group or harm that is minimal and that is substantially outweighed by the group's legitimate interests"); *cf.* Ariz. Jud. Ethics Adv. Op. 94-13 (1994) (declining to state definitively whether Tucson Arizona Boys Chorus, limited to male singers of certain ages, and the Junior League of Tucson, with only female members, are invidiously discriminating organizations; the inquiry is fact-specific and burden of compliance falls to individual judge).

More recently, questions have arisen about the propriety of judicial involvement in these organizations because of the organizations' exclusion of gays and lesbians. The response to these questions has been divided. Some states have concluded that the position taken by the Boy Scouts of America in prohibiting membership and leadership based on sexual orientation does not bar judges from participating in volunteer work for the organization, particularly because the Code did not bar discrimination based on "sexual orientation." Ariz. Jud. Ethics Adv. Op. 00-05 (2000) ("sexual orientation" is "conspicuously absent" from Canon 2C and the Boy Scout's membership practices cannot be said to be "prohibited by law," given the Supreme Court's ruling supporting rejection of homosexual scoutmaster in *Boy Scouts of America v. Dale*, 530 U.S. 640 (2000); Del. Jud. Ethics Adv. Comm. Op. 2006-4 (2006) (judge may serve in leadership position with Boy Scouts of America (BSA), notwithstanding that the BSA maintains a policy of prohibiting homosexual scout leaders). Others have allowed participation with a caution about extensive involvement. Tex. Adv. Jud. Ethics Op. No. 158 (1993) (determining that a judge may serve as a District Chairman or District Commissioner of a local BSA organization that denies homosexuals and persons without religious principles from serving as leaders and as a member of the Knights of Columbus organization whose principles are against abortion; cautions that "in light of the controversy surrounding these issues the judge should consider Canon 2A before deciding how involved to become with any organization"); Wash. Ethics Adv. Comm. Op. 04-01 (2004) (judge should not participate in a leadership role in scouting activities as that participation may reflect adversely on the judge's impartiality and diminish the public confidence in the integrity and impartiality of the judiciary; judges who participate in Boy Scouts as a troop leader or other similar position should disqualify himself when doing so is appropriate pursuant to Canons 2 and 5). Still, other states recommend that judges steer clear of any involvement with these restrictive organizations because of the importance of eliminating the appearance of bias. *See generally* Jeff Bleich, *Fairness Required On and Off Bench*, Cal. Bar J. (Mar. 2003) (discussing resolution by San Francisco Superior Court, and currently under consideration by other courts, that duty not to cast doubt on impartiality toward gays and lesbians requires that judges not remain active in any social group, including the Boy Scouts, that declares gays or lesbians to be "unclean" and "not morally straight").

The 2007 Code added "sexual orientation" to the list of prohibited bases of invidious discrimination. Any states that adopt this language will have to determine whether it will affect their positions on judges' participation in youth organizations such as the Boy Scouts. The Commission received a large number of comments arguing that particular organizations did or did not practice invidious discrimination. However, the Commission decided not to cast any judgments in stone, because policies of an organization might change over time, as might the constitutional standard for judging whether an organization is sufficiently private to be immune from governmental regulation of its membership policies. Charles G. Geyh & W. William Hodes, *Reporters' Notes to the Model Code of Judicial Conduct* 65 (2009). For a discussion of Rule 3.6 and its impact on Boy Scout membership, *see* Sean V. Grindlay, Note, *May a Judge Be a Scoutmaster? Dale, White and the New Model Code of Judicial Conduct*, 5 Ave Maria L. Rev. 555 (2007) (asserting that, as applied to the Boy Scouts, Rule 3.6 would conflict with the right to freedom of association articulated in First Amendment jurisprudence and that overlooking any constitutional defects, the Rule should be rejected for policy reasons).

Dearth of Precedent

There is currently a paucity of case law interpreting the language of Rule 3.6. The only disciplinary case on point is *In re Complaint of Judicial Misconduct*, No. C.C.D. 11-01 (U.S. Jud. Conference Comm. on Judicial Conduct and Disability (2011)). In that matter, Judge George C. Paine, II, Chief Judge of the Bankruptcy Court for the Middle District of Tennessee was publicy reprimanded for maintaining his membership in Belle Meade Country Club. The Committee "easily" concluded that Belle Meade individuously discriminated against women and African-Americans because the club, although located in Nashville had no full club members of either. Additionally, under the club's rules, "Lady Members" who were the widows of full male members could not control, manage, vote, or hold office. The Committee on Judicial Conduct and Disability noted that Judge Paine had tried for 20 years to bring African-Americans into club membership, but explained that it "did not change the analysis" of the matter. Because Judge Paine was to retire at the end of 2011 and because the case presented matters of first impression, the Committee issued a reprimand as discipline.

Earlier cases that discuss prohibition on membership in organizations that practice invidious discrimination have done so merely in a footnote. *See, e.g., Curran v. Mount Diablo Council of the Boy Scouts of America*, 952 P2d 218, 227, n.10 (Cal. 1998) (in a civil rights challenge to the Boy Scout council's refusal to approve homosexual adult leader, the court received a letter "expressing concern" about a potential conflict of interest because of the court's adoption of Canon 2C of the Code; the court dismissed the allegation stating that "the court's adoption of the Code of Judicial Ethics provides no basis for questioning the propriety of the justices' participation in these cases"); *In re Hey*, 452 S.E. 2d 24, 32, n.11 (W. Va. Ct. App. 1994) (citing exceptions to the general ban on judges' membership in discriminatory organizations in a discussion of how the Canons are not insensitive to judge's free expression rights). One commentator has suggested that the reason for the dearth of precedents may be explained by lack of clarity regarding when and who can obtain relief for Canon 2C violations. Leslie W. Abramson, *Canon 2 of the Code of Judicial Conduct*, 79 Marq. L. Rev. 949 (1996).

USING BENEFITS OR FACILITIES OF ORGANIZATION THAT PRACTICES INVIDIOUS DISCRIMINATION

Rule 3.6(B) provides that a judge should not use the benefits or facilities of an organization if the judge knows or should know that the organization practices invidious discrimination on one or more of the bases identified in Rule 3.6(A). However, attendance at an isolated event in a facility of such an organization would not violate the Rule if the attendance could not reasonably be perceived as an endorsement of the organization's practices. Rule 3.6(B) focuses on the extent to which a judge actually uses the benefits or facilities provided by an organization. Building upon ideas found earlier in the Commentary to Canon 2C, this new Rule effectively provides that a judge cannot be the initiating party in scheduling an event or taking advantage of the facilities, but is permitted to attend an isolated event that has been scheduled or arranged by someone else, as long as it is clear that merely attending cannot reasonably be seen as endorsing the organization or its policies. During its deliberations, the Commission considered the example of a wedding reception held at a discriminatory club that the judge would not be permitted to join according to Rule 3.6(A): the judge may not schedule his or her *own* child's reception at the club, but would be permitted to attend the reception of a friend or relative's child. Charles G. Geyh & W. William Hodes, *Reporters' Notes to the Model Code of Judicial Conduct* 65–66 (2009).

RULE 3.7 PARTICIPATION IN EDUCATIONAL, RELIGIOUS, CHARITABLE, FRATERNAL, OR CIVIC ORGANIZATIONS AND ACTIVITIES

(A) Subject to the requirements of Rule 3.1, a judge may participate in activities sponsored by organizations or governmental entities concerned with the law, the legal system, or the administration of justice, and those sponsored by or on behalf of educational, religious, charitable, fraternal, or civic organizations not conducted for profit, including but not limited to the following activities:

(1) assisting such an organization or entity in planning related to fund-raising, and participating in the management and investment of the organization's or entity's funds;

(2) soliciting* contributions* for such an organization or entity, but only from members of the judge's family,* or from judges over whom the judge does not exercise supervisory or appellate authority;

(3) soliciting membership for such an organization or entity, even though the membership dues or fees generated may be used to support the objectives of the organization or entity, but only if the organization or entity is concerned with the law, the legal system, or the administration of justice;

(4) appearing or speaking at, receiving an award or other recognition at, being featured on the program of, and permitting his or her title to be used in connection with an event of such an organization or entity, but if the event serves a fund-raising purpose, the judge may participate only if the event concerns the law, the legal system, or the administration of justice;

(5) making recommendations to such a public or private fund-granting organization or entity in connection with its programs and activities, but only if the organization or entity is concerned with the law, the legal system, or the administration of justice; and

(6) serving as an officer, director, trustee, or nonlegal advisor of such an organization or entity, unless it is likely that the organization or entity:

(a) will be engaged in proceedings that would ordinarily come before the judge; or

(b) will frequently be engaged in adversary proceedings in the court of which the judge is a member, or in any court subject to the appellate jurisdiction of the court of which the judge is a member.

(B) A judge may encourage lawyers to provide pro bono publico legal services.

COMMENT

[1] The activities permitted by paragraph (A) generally include those sponsored by or undertaken on behalf of public or private not-for-profit educational institutions, and other not-for-profit organizations, including law-related, charitable, and other organizations.

[2] Even for law-related organizations, a judge should consider whether the membership and purposes of the organization, or the nature of the judge's

participation in or association with the organization, would conflict with the judge's obligation to refrain from activities that reflect adversely upon a judge's independence, integrity, and impartiality.

[3] Mere attendance at an event, whether or not the event serves a fund-raising purpose, does not constitute a violation of paragraph 4(A). It is also generally permissible for a judge to serve as an usher or a food server or preparer, or to perform similar functions, at fund-raising events sponsored by educational, religious, charitable, fraternal, or civic organizations. Such activities are not solicitation and do not present an element of coercion or abuse the prestige of judicial office.

[4] Identification of a judge's position in educational, religious, charitable, fraternal, or civic organizations on letterhead used for fund-raising or membership solicitation does not violate this Rule. The letterhead may list the judge's title or judicial office if comparable designations are used for other persons.

[5] In addition to appointing lawyers to serve as counsel for indigent parties in individual cases, a judge may promote broader access to justice by encouraging lawyers to participate in pro bono publico legal services, if in doing so the judge does not employ coercion, or abuse the prestige of judicial office. Such encouragement may take many forms, including providing lists of available programs, training lawyers to do pro bono publico legal work, and participating in events recognizing lawyers who have done pro bono publico work.

1990 CODE COMPARISON

Canon 4C(3) of the 1990 Code, on which Rule 3.7 is based, referred at the outset to service as an officer or a director of various not-for-profit organizations, and then used several subparagraphs to deal with activities in which such officers or directors engaged. The lead-in to Rule 3.7(A) establishes its coverage of essentially the same organizations—public and private, law-related and not law related—but then deals in subsequent subparagraphs with *all* activities related to those organizations, *including* service as an officer or a director. Charles G. Geyh & W. William Hodes, *Reporters' Notes to the Model Code of Judicial Conduct* 68–70 (2009).

Virtually, all the concepts in Canon 4C(3) have been retained, although some have been made more expansive or restrictive and some aspects of Canon 4C(3) were moved to Rule 3.1 because of their general applicability. *Id.* at 68.

Rule 3.7(A)(1) is substantially the same as the first clause of Canon 4C(3)(b)(i) of the 1990 Code. The difference is that the 1990 Code allowed these activities (assistance in planning fund-raising and management and investment of an organization's funds) *only* in connection with service as an officer, director, trustee, or nonlegal advisor, or the somewhat nebulous "as a member or otherwise." In the 2007 Code, these activities are permissible without more, if participation in the activities of the organization or entity itself is permissible.

Rule 3.7(A)(2) is substantially the same as the second clause of former Canon 4C(3)(b)(i), except that soliciting funds from family members was added as a permissible activity on the rationale that, as with solicitation of contributions from judges over whom a judge did not exercise supervisor or appellate authority, which was already permitted by the 1990 Code, the element of coercion is largely missing when judges solicit contributions from their own family members. *Id.* at 69.

Rule 3.7(A)(3) is based on some aspects of former Canon 4C(3)(b)(iii), but with other elements added or deleted or repositioned elsewhere in Canon 3. The basic idea of prohibiting a judge from soliciting membership in an organization where charging membership dues is essentially a fund-raising device is retained on the assumption that persons contacted will feel coerced into joining, or will attempt to curry favor with a sitting judge by joining. *Id.*

Rule 3.7(A)(4), which is a new provision to the Code, is based on Commentary to Canons 5B(2) and 5B(3) of the Code of Conduct for United States Judges, and reverses the thrust of Commentary to Canon 4C(3)(b) of the 1990 Model Code. The Code of Conduct for United States Judges provides that as a general matter, judges may *not* participate in the fund-raising activities of charitable and other civic organizations other than by attending, which is similar to Commentary in the 1990 Code. In context, however, the federal provision appears to be limited to non-law-related organizations and activities. The Commission adopted the same general stance in Rule 3.7(A)(4), but made the implicit exception explicit: a judge *is* permitted to be a featured speaker or participant at an event that has a fund-raising purpose, *but only if the organization or entity is a law-related one.* This is the reverse of the thrust of the 1990 Code. *Id.* at 70.

Rule 3.7(A)(5) is essentially the same as Canon 4C(3)(b)(ii) of the 1990 Code, except that the authority to make recommendations to fund-granting organizations and entities is not limited to officers, directors, and others directly associated with the organization or entity. This is consistent with the revised organization of Canon 3 generally, and Rule 3.7 specifically.

Rule 3.7(A)(6) is essentially identical to Canon 4C(3)(a) of the 1990 Code, but eliminates redundancy and makes explicit that service is allowed in both private organizations and public entities, whether or not they are law related, as long as the two caveats in subparagraphs (a) and (b) are satisfied.

Rule 3.7(B), encouraging judges to provide leadership in increasing *pro bono publico* lawyering, is new to the Code.

ANNOTATION

INTRODUCTION

Rule 3.7 defines the parameters of a judge's ability to participate in activities sponsored by organizations or governmental entities concerned with the law, the legal system, or the administration of justice, and those sponsored by or on behalf of nonprofit educational, religious, charitable, fraternal, or civic organizations. The introduction to the Rule notes that such participation is subject to the requirements of Rule 3.1 (Extrajudicial Activities in General). This is underlined in the Commentary, which states that a judge should consider whether the membership and purposes of the organization or the nature of the judge's participation in or association with it would conflict with the judge's obligation to refrain from activities that reflect adversely on the judge's independence, integrity, and impartiality. Model Code of Judicial Conduct Rule 3.7 cmt. [2].

ASSISTING IN PLANNING FOR FUND-RAISING AND MANAGING AND INVESTING FUNDS

Rule 3.7(A)(1) permits a judge to assist educational, religious, charitable, fraternal, or civic organizations in planning related to fund-raising and to take part in the management and investment of such an organization's funds, subject to the general restrictions on extrajudicial activities listed in Rule 3.1. *See* N.Y. Adv. Comm. on Jud. Ethics Op. 12-142 (2012) (judge who is president of religious organization may assist in planning and may attend organization's casino-themed fund-raising event).

SOLICITING CONTRIBUTIONS

Pursuant to Rule 3.7(A)(2), a judge may solicit contributions for a legal, educational, religious, charitable, fraternal, or civic organization, but only from members of the judge's family, or from judges over whom the judge does not exercise supervisory or appellate authority. The exception for family members was added to the Code in 2007 on the rationale that, as with solicitation of contributions from judges over whom a judge did not exercise supervisor or appellate authority, the element of coercion is largely missing when judges solicit contributions from their own family members. Family members include spouses, domestic partners, children, grandchildren, parents, grandparents, or other relatives or persons with whom a judge maintains a close relationship. "Contribution" is defined in the Code as "financial and in-kind contributions, such as goods, professional or volunteer services, advertising, and other types of assistance, which if obtained by the recipient otherwise, would require a financial expenditure." Model Code of Judicial Conduct, Terminology.

The restrictions on fund-raising in Rule 3.7(A)(2) address two concerns: that the person solicited will feel obligated to respond favorably because of the judge's position of influence or control or will expect future favors for their donations. *See* ABA Informal Op. 603 (1962); *see also* Charles Gardner Geyh, James J. Alfini, Steven Lubet, & Jeffrey M. Shaman, *Judicial Conduct and Ethics* § 9.04[2] at 9–16 (5th ed. 2013). These restrictions also reduce the possible appearance of impropriety or lack of impartiality that is implicit in fund-raising. E. Wayne Thode, *Reporter's Notes to the Code of Judicial Conduct* 77 (1973).

Most state courts and judicial ethics advisory committees have strictly applied restrictions on fund-raising, counseling against any "personal participation" in fund-raising even when participation is indirect, or bears no relationship to the judicial office, or cannot reasonably raise concerns about coercion or exploitation of the office or the appearance of impropriety. *See, e.g.*, Ala. Jud. Inquiry Comm'n Adv. Op. 00-768 (2000) (judge should not write letter to members of local bar association soliciting support for legal aid program; though proposed letter does not expressly ask for financial contributions, one objective of the letter clearly is to raise funds and/or services to offset reduction in public funding for the local legal aid office); Ariz. Jud. Ethics Adv. Comm. Op. 04-03 (2004) (judge may not solicit sponsorship funding for court-run symposium on mental health issues); Ark. Jud. Ethics Adv. Comm. Op. 2004-03 (2004) (judge may not personally solicit pledges from other members of Kiwanis even if the person solicited is not an attorney and lives outside the state); Fla. Jud. Ethics Adv. Comm. Op. 2012-04 (2012) (judge may not directly solict bar association for funds to produce brochure about perception of fairness in Florida's courts); Ill. Jud. Ethics Comm. Op. 99-1 (1990) (judge may not act as "celebrity bag person" for fund-raiser in which grocery store contributes 10 percent of sales to local charity); Md. Jud. Ethics Op. 2011-04 (2011) (judge may not serve as president of civic organization that focuses primarily on fund-raising for training paramedics, providing smoke detectors and automatic external defibrillators to community because of the active, although indirect, involvement of the president in fund-raising); Md. Jud. Ethics Op. 2005-11 (2005) (judge may serve as director of nonprofit corporation formed to solicit funds to provide incentives for participants in a local Drug Court provided judge's participation does not involve active or passive fund-raising activity); Mich. Comm. on Jud. Ethics Op. JI-125 (2001) (judge may not participate in fund-raiser called "Jail and Bail", where judge sets amount of money that constitutes a target amount for individual to pay or raise as "bail" paid to charity); Nev. Stand. Comm. on Jud. Ethics Op. JE12-009 (2012) (judge may not solicit cash, gift cards, or merchandise for incentives for participants in the court's drug court program); N.Y. Adv. Comm. on Jud. Ethics Op. 10-152 (2011) (judge may personally participate in annual walk that is fund-raiser but may not solicit contributions from others); N.C. Jud. Standards Comm'n Formal Op. 2010-07 (2010) (judge may not be listed as host or sponsor for fund-raising event because to do so would be "active assistance" in raising funds); S.C. Adv. Comm. on Stands. of Jud. Conduct Op. 16-2005 (2005) (judge may not serve as stewardship chair for church committee where one of his duties is to make personal contacts concerning a parishioner's giving); Utah Jud. Ethics Adv. Comm. Informal Op. 90-9 (1990) (judge may not participate in seminar sponsored by alumni association because proceeds will be used to fund other association activities); Wash. Ethics Adv. Comm. Op. 93-05 (1993) (judge may not appear as model at department store fashion show where some of the admission proceeds will be donated to charity). *But see* Neb. Jud. Ethics Adv. Comm. Op. 12-2 (2012) (judge's home, which he co-owns with wife, may be stop on garden walk organized to raise funds for local community theater when judge's name will not appear on materials related to the event and judge will not be present during garden walk); N.Y. Adv. Comm. on Jud. Ethics Op. 11-97 (2011) (judge may provide quote about benefits provided by not-for-profit organization in the organization's annual report because annual report would not be "designed or used primarily for fund-raising or promotional purposes").

Conduct that falls short of direct solicitation of funds but gives the appearance of fund-raising may also be prohibited under Rule 3.7(A)(2). *See, e.g.*, Fla. Jud. Ethics Adv. Comm. Op. 2000-31 (2000) (a judge's participation as chairperson for a "kickoff" event for a charitable organization, which was to be followed shortly thereafter by a fund-raising auction has been prohibited); Colo. Jud. Ethics Adv. Op. 2013-04 (2013) (judge may not contribute craft to auction for hospice organization); Colo. Jud. Ethics Adv. Bd. Op. 2012-01 (2012) (judge who is chairman of board for nonprofit may not sign grant request because signing such is the equivalent to fund-raising); S.C. Adv. Comm. on Stands. of Jud. Conduct Op. 22-2005 (2005) (judge may not serve as auctioneer at high school fund-raiser).

At least one jurisdiction has advised that, given the Code's directive to avoid the appearance of impropriety, Canon 1, and to maintain the highest standards of judicial and personal conduct, Preamble, a judge's participation in fund-raising activities should be evaluated by an objective, reasonable person standard. Therefore, a particular activity may be prohibited even if the judge believes that it would not influence others to donate funds, would not cause them to believe they could curry the judge's favor with their contributions, or would not affect the judge's impartiality or interfere with the proper performance of judicial duties. Ariz. Jud. Ethics Adv. Comm. Op. 00-06 (2000); *see also* (N.Y. Adv. Comm. on Jud. Ethics Op. 12-153 (2012) (judge may not allow bar association to create scholarship in judge's name even though judge's name will not be used in fund solicitation; the connection between the judge's name and the fund-raising creates appearance of impropriety).

Conversely, activity may be permitted if, under the circumstances, the judge's presence at a fund-raising event could not be perceived as a method of enticing individuals to contribute (*see, e.g.*, Ariz. Jud. Ethics Adv. Comm. Op. 04-04 (2004) (judge may be inducted into a school district's hall of fame during a fund-raising dinner for student scholarships if judge does not use his title and his attendance is not used to generate interest in the event)) or to adversely affect the judge's impartiality (Mich. Comm. on Jud. Ethics Op. JI-71 (1993) (judge may participate as model in fashion show where proceeds are allocated to charity, provided judge's participation does not detract from dignity of judicial office or interfere with judge's impartiality)).

A Comment to the Rule provides that "[i]t is . . . generally permissible for a judge to serve as an usher or a food server or preparer, or to perform similar functions at fund-raising events sponsored by educational, religious, charitable, fraternal, or civic organizations. Such activities are not solicitation and do not present an element of coercion or abuse the prestige of judicial office." Model Code of Judicial Conduct Rule 3.7 cmt. [3]. This Comment is designed to provide a safe harbor for minor and non-coercive activities undertaken in connection with an organization's or entity's fund-raising efforts. When a judge donates time to serve food or serve as an usher or other facilitator at an event, the dangers associated with direct solicitation of funds are not present. N.Y. Adv. Comm. on Jud. Ethics Op. 10-157 (2010) (judge may not distribute flyers asking persons to donate food or collect donations but may pack, load, and deliver food donations using judge's personal vehicle despite judicial license plate). The Rule does not give specific examples of situations involving handling of money, but also does not specifically exclude such activities. Whether such activities are appropriate depends on analysis of the overall situation of the overall event, and the significance of the judge's participation. As long as there is no coercion—even subtle and unstated coercion—and as long as the judge's position as a judge is not being exploited, the activity is permissible. Charles G. Geyh & W. William Hodes, *Reporters' Notes to the Model Code of Judicial Conduct* 71 (2009).

At least one jurisdiction, Indiana, has also advised that lesser degrees of participation in fund-raising are permissible so long as the activities do not cast doubt on the judge's capacity to act impartially, do not demean the judicial office, and do not interfere with the proper performance of judicial duties. Ind. Comm'n on Jud. Qualifications Adv. Op. 1-96 (1996); *see also* Tex. Comm. on Jud. Ethics Op. 237 (1999) (judges may participate in sports event with members of bar association even though event is fund-raiser and judges' participation is main attraction used in selling tickets to the event).

Pursuant to the exception in Rule 3.7(A)(2), a judge may solicit funds from family members and from other judges over whom the judge has no supervisory or appellate authority. *See, e.g.*, Fla. Jud. Ethics Adv. Comm. Op. 98-16 (1998) (chief judge, who exercises supervisory authority over all trial court judges within circuit and appellate authority over judges serving in county court may not personally solicit donations to homeless shelter from those judges); Mass. Comm. on Jud. Ethics Adv. Op. 04-2 (2004) (judge may not solicit funds for the private school on whose board he serves, except from members of his immediate family and from judges over whom he exercises no supervisory or appellate authority); Va. Jud. Ethics Adv. Comm. Op. 99-3 (1999) (retired judge may not solicit contributions for National Judicial College except from judge over whom judge does not exercise supervisory or appellate authority); Wash. Ethics Adv. Comm. Op. 06-07 (2006) (judge, acting as an individual and not identifying himself or herself as a judicial officer, may solicit pledges for charitable bike ride from family and friends who would have no occasion to appear before him); *but see* Nev. Stand. Comm. on Jud. Ethics Op. JE11-014 (2011) (judge may not solicit family member who is also court vendor for contributions to court symposium because concerns of perceived coercion and undermining judicial integrity are present).

Some states, including Illinois and New York, have rejected this exception. Other states have adopted the exception with different limitations. *See, e.g.*, R.I. Code of Jud. Conduct, Canon 4C(3)(b), cmt. (2007) (stating that "Canon 4 should not be read as proscribing participation in de minimis fund-raising activities so long as a judge is careful to avoid using the prestige of the office in the activity"); Wis. Code of Judicial Conduct SCR 60.05(3)(c)2.d cmt. (2006) (stating that "a judge may solicit other persons for membership in the organizations described above if neither those persons nor persons with whom they are affiliated are likely ever to appear before the court on which the judge serves").

Judge's Name on Organization's Letterhead

The Commission decided that letterhead including a judge's name and position, even when used for fund-raising or membership solicitation purposes, is not coercive and does not abuse the prestige of judicial office, as long as the judge is identified in the same way as other persons on the letterhead. Charles G. Geyh & W. William Hodes, *Reporters' Notes to the Model Code of Judicial Conduct* 71 (2009).

Therefore, the Commentary to Rule 3.7 provides that "[i]dentification of a judge's position in educational, religious, charitable, fraternal, or civic organization on letterhead used for fund-raising or membership solicitation does not violate this Rule." The Comment adds that "the letterhead may list the judge's title or judicial office if comparable designations are used for other persons." Model Code of Judicial Conduct Rule 3.7 cmt. [4]. *See, e.g.*, Alaska Comm'n on Jud. Conduct Formal Ethics Op. 019 (1994) (use of title and listing as member of board on stationary used for fund-raising not a violation of rules where it incidental to activity); Md. Jud. Ethics Op. 2011-17 (2011) (judge's name may appear on letterhead of nonprofit organization that provides pro bono legal services to indigent persons and invitation sent to lawyers asking them to join an alumni committee); Md. Jud. Ethics Op. 2008-06 (2008) (judge who is trustee of a college can used judicial title on invitation for outreach event for alumni who are lawyers in order to stimulate interest in the college and its career development efforts so long as the listing of the other outreach co-hosts includes their respective professional titles); N.M. Adv. Comm. on Code of Jud. Conduct Op. 13-03 (2013) (judge's name and biography may appear on website of organization for which he serves as a board member; presence of PayPal link, so that viewers may donate to group, does not "conflict with the Code"); N.Y. Adv. Comm. on Jud. Conduct Op. 11-136 (2011) (judge who is a member of the board of directors for a not-for-profit may permit his name to appear on organization's website which has boarder containing link to solicit donations); Nev. Stand. Comm. on Jud. Ethics & Election Prac. Op. 99-001 (1999) (letterhead used in letter soliciting lawyers to contribute to foundation as means of fulfilling their voluntary goal of providing pro bono legal services or monetary donations in lieu thereof was impermissible because it included the designation "Hon." next to judge's name but no similar designation next to other signatories' names); Wash. Ethics Adv. Comm. Op. 94-06 (1994) (judge may serve on board of directors and have name on stationary of nonprofit organization even though it may be used for fund-raising); Wyo. Jud. Ethics Adv. Comm. Op. 2012-02 (judge may serve on boards for environmental organization and hunting organization); U.S. Comm. on Codes of Conduct Adv. Op. No. 35 (1974, Rev. 1998) (if judge's name and title are included on charity's list of donors, it must be published in a manner similar to other contributors and without undue emphasis).

Some jurisdictions have not permitted a judge's name to appear on an organization's fund-raising letterhead regardless of whether the judge's designation is excluded. *See* Neb. Jud. Ethics Adv. Comm. Op. 07-03 (2007) (it is improper use of the office for judge's name and title to appear on a letter soliciting funds and where they are used without judge's authorization, judge must act immediately and decidedly in getting his name and title removed from solicitation materials); N.Y. Adv. Comm. on Jud. Ethics Op. 12-135 (2012) (judge's title may not appear in fund-raising communications for religious outreach trip); Okla. Jud. Ethics Op. 2006-1 (2006) (judge may not allow his or her name to be on the letterhead or stationery of a county leadership group who uses the stationery to solicit funds for worthwhile community projects; even though letterhead does not identify the listed members by profession or occupation, judges are well known in all counties); Pa. Jud. Ethics Comm. Informal Op. 7/31/00 (2000) (a judge's name may not appear on the letterhead of a letter soliciting funds); Tex. Adv. Comm. on Jud. Ethics Op. 131 (1989) (judges may serve on committee to restore courthouse, but may not allow their names to appear on letterhead used for fund-raising). Additionally, even if use of the judge's name on an organization's letterhead would not violate Rule 3.7, a judge may be advised not to permit such use of his or her name if it would create an appearance issue that could adversely reflect upon the integrity and independence of the judiciary. *See, e.g.*, N.M. Adv. Comm. on Code of Jud. Conduct Op. 07-08 (2007) (although nonprofit organization's use of judge's name on letterhead in fund-raising campaign likely did not violate

Rule 3.7, because judge is a family court judge and activities of the organization directly relate to parents and children involved in divorce and child custody issues some recipients of solicitation may seek contribute because of judge's prior relationship to the organization and some people may be involved, directly or indirectly, in cases that are, or may come, before judge; therefore, there is an appearance issue that can adversely reflect upon the integrity and independence of the judiciary).

Rule 3.1 prohibits the use of "court premises, staff, stationery, equipment, or other resources" for solicitations or any other activity on behalf of an educational, religious, charitable, fraternal or civic organization." So, although a judge's name and position may appear on letterhead used for fund-raising or membership solicitation, the court's stationery may not be used for such purposes. For additional discussion, see Raymond J. McKoski, *Ethical Considerations in the Use of Judicial Stationery for Private Purposes*, 112 Penn. St. L. Rev. 471 (2007).

Writing or Signing Fund-Raising Letters

Some states advise that a judge should not write or sign a fund-raising letter because that would be construed as bringing the judge into direct line for the solicitation of money. Ill. Jud. Ethics Comm. Op. 95-22 (1995) (though judge may serve as chair and allow his name on letterhead of bar association foundation, judge should not sign fund-raising letter); Neb. Jud. Ethics Adv. Comm. 02-3 (2002) (judge may not author a "recruiting letter" for the Nebraska State Bar Association's "One Hour Of Sharing" campaign to solicit bar members to contribute hours of service or cash contributions in lieu of services); Tex. Adv. Comm on Jud. Ethics Op. 196 (1996) (judge may not fund-raise among lawyers regardless of whether they are in or out of state for national program). A judge also may not use court stationery for a fund-raising letter, as it would lend the prestige of judicial office to solicit contributions for a charitable purpose. *See* Ariz. Jud. Ethics Adv. Comm. Op. 94-15 (1994) (use of judicial stationery to encourage contributions to charity involves the solicitation of funds and the use of prestige of judicial office to assist in the solicitation of funds); Wash. Ethics Adv. Comm. Op. 99-07(1999) (court personnel may not use court stationary to solicit contributions for charitable fund-raising event); *see also* Rule 1.3, Comment [1] ("[A] judge must not use judicial letterhead to gain advantage in conducting his or her personal business.").

Using Prestige of Judicial Office for Fund-Raising

Section 4C(3)(b)(iv) of the 1990 Code provided that a judge may not use or permit the use of the prestige of the judicial office for fund-raising solicitations. This provision was not carried forward to the 2007 Code. However, it is referred to in the Comment [3] to Rule 3.7, and in Rule 1.3 (Avoiding Abuse of the Prestige of Judicial Office).

Some states have found that a judge abuses the prestige of judicial office by engaging in fund-raising on or off the bench. For instance, a judge may not use the judicial position to encourage criminal defendants to donate to charity in lieu of paying a fine or other sentence. *See In re Shannon*, 637 N.W.2d 503 (Mich. 2002) (judge censured and suspended for advising defendants found guilty of traffic citations to purchase tickets for Detroit Fire and Police Field Day from police officer sitting in the courtroom; judge's conduct, whether well-intentioned or not, gave the appearance of using power of his position to solicit money from defendants for charitable cause); *In re Davis*, 946 P.2d 1033 (Nev. 1997) (judge's suggestion that criminal defendants contribute money to charities on a list prepared by judge in lieu of paying fines to the city violated Section 4C(3)(b)(iv)); Mich. Comm. on Jud. Ethics Op. JI-48 (1992) (sentencing judge may not give offenders the option of performing community service work or making monetary contribution to charity designated by judge); Fla. Jud. Ethics Adv. Comm. Op. 97-32 (1997) (judge may not advise jurors of option to donate jury service compensation to domestic violence shelter or organization specified by guardian ad litem program or to organization specificed by guardian ad litem program); Wash. Ethics Adv. Comm. Op. 95-18 (1995) (judge may not provide jurors with option of contributing their compensation to the city combined charities fund); *but see* Mich. Comm. on Jud. Ethics Op. JI-64 (1992) (judge may offer defendant, as an alternative to incarceration, the option of performing services or attending an organization's educational or rehabilitative program); Pa. Jud. Ethics Comm. Informal Op. 5/15/00 (2000) (judge may give proceeds of late fines to charity that provides free child care for parties who attend court because the sole purpose is to improve the administration of justice); Wash. Ethics Adv. Comm. Op. 99-10 (1999) (judge may give a lawyer the option to pay a bona fide monetary fine to either a pro bono program or civic or charitable organization of the lawyer's choice). Sylvia Shaz Shweder, Note, *Donating Debt to Society: Prosecutorial and Judicial Ethics of Plea Agreements and Sentences That Include Charitable Contributions*, 73 Fordham L. Rev. 377 (2004).

A judge also improperly uses judicial influence when he raises funds by selling items to people with whom the judge works and associates during work hours. *See, e.g., In re Arrigan*, 678 A.2d 446 (R.I. 1996) (judge publicly censured after he solicited lawyers, law firms and other judges to buy jewelry for a nonprofit organization, sold sweaters knit for benefit of another nonprofit organization from his chambers and sold raffle tickets to help sponsor memorial event).

Off the bench, a judge may not permit an organization to use the judge's position or title in an effort to raise funds. *See In re Brown*, 662 N.W.2d 733

(2003) (judge failed to take adequate steps to prevent her name from being used in fund-raising materials); *In re Coffey* (Neb. Comm'n on Jud. Qualifications 2006) (judge reprimanded for failing to take adequate measures to have his name and title removed from a fund-raising undertaking); Ark. Jud. Ethics Adv. Comm. Op. 1997-05 (1997) (judge may not be photographed and interviewed for use in school's capital campaign); Fla. Jud. Ethics Adv. Comm. Op. 2013-23 (2013) (judge should avoid being photographed with other attendees at a religious gathering if the judge knows or has reason to know that the photograph will be used for solicitation of members or donations); Mich. Comm. on Jud. Ethics Op. JI-115 (1997) (judge's attendance at testimonial dinner sponsored by political party where admission price exceeds reasonable cost of attendance would be exploiting judicial office); Neb. Jud. Ethics Adv. Comm. Op. 02-03 (2002) (judge may not provide supportive quotes for legal service's fund-raising pamphlet where the organization's request amounts to leveraging the judge's title and influence to solicit funds or pro bono legal services); Penn. Jud. Ethics Comm. of the Conference of State Trial Judges Op. 2011-1 (2011) ("judge may not permit an organization to capitalize on, or exploit, a judge's attendance at or participation in such events by advertising that fact or issuing invitations citing that attendance or participation in advance of the event. A judge who allows himself or herself to be used in this manner is engaged in a solicitation of funds"); S.C. Adv. Comm. on Stands. of Jud. Conduct, Op. 10-1995 (1995) (judge may not write letter of reference for organization in an effort to obtain funding); *but see* Fla. Jud. Ethics Adv. Comm. Op. 97-28 (1997) (judge may authorize his college alma mater to feature him in advertising campaign which is not used to generate funding, but which profiles successful alumni in order to inspire others to consider higher education); Ill. Jud. Ethics Comm. Op. 99-03 (1999) (judge's name may be included on list of donors to fund-raiser honoring retired public defender where list is not used for fund-raising); Nev. Stand. Comm. on Jud. Ethics and Election Prac. Op. JE 00-004 (2000) (Nevada's amended Section 4C(3)(b) permits judges to lend their names as hosts of proposed law-related reception to encourage membership in and donation of funds to support designated legal service organizations); S.C. Adv. Comm. on Stands. of Jud. Conduct Op. 11-2013 (2013) (judge may participate in dancing fund-raiser for religious organization, but judge has duty to ensure advertising for the event does not misuse the prestige of the office).

SOLICITING MEMBERSHIP

Rule 3.7(A)(3) permits a judge to solicit membership for an organization even though the membership dues or fees may be used to support the objectives of the organization or entity, that is, even if the membership solicitation serves a fund-raising purpose, but only if that organization or entity is concerned with the law, the legal system, or the administration of justice. This Rule relaxes the 1990 Code's restriction, which prohibited membership solicitation that is "essentially a fundraising mechanism" if fund-raising would not otherwise be acceptable in that setting. Charles Gardner Geyh, James J. Alfini, Steven Lubet, & Jeffrey M. Shaman, *Judicial Conduct and Ethics*, § 9.04[4] at 9–21 (5th ed. 2013). The rationale underlying the change is that solicitating membership in a law-related organization, such as a bar association or moot court society, would be perceived as more natural or more appropriate than soliciting membership in a fine arts society or a charity. This perception is related, at least indirectly, to the thematic requirement of avoiding abuse of the prestige of judicial office. A person who loves opera or is a dedicated member of an environmental protection organization, and who also happens to be a judge, should not use that position as an added reason for someone else to join the cause. On the other hand, it is not inappropriate for judges to use their positions as leaders in the legal community to increase membership in law-related organizations. Charles G. Geyh & W. William Hodes, *Reporters' Notes to the Model Code of Judicial Conduct* 69–70 (2009).

As noted earlier, when an organization sends out membership solicitation letters, the judge's position in the organization or entity may be stated and the letterhead may list the judge's title or office if comparable designations are used for other persons. Model Code of Judicial Conduct Rule 3.7 cmt. [4].

APPEARING, SPEAKING AT, OR RECEIVING AWARD AT AN EVENT

Rule 3.7(A)(4) makes an exception to the prohibition on judicial participation in fund-raising events by permitting a judge to speak or accept an award at a fund-raising event and be featured on the program and permit use of his or her title in connection with an organization's fund-raising event, so long as the organization or entity sponsoring the event concerns the law, the legal system, or the administration of justice. N.M. Adv. Comm. on Code of Jud. Conduct Op. 12-02 (2012) (judge may perform and judge state bar fund-raising event). This provision is new to the Code but is based on Commentary to Canons 5B(2) and (3) of the Code of Conduct for United States Judges, and reverses the Commentary to Canon 4C(3)(b), which permitted a judge to attend a fund-raising event but provided that a judge must not "be a speaker or guest of honor." The rationale for this change is that while it could be viewed as questionable for a judge to appear as a featured guest at the fund-raiser of an association unrelated to the legal field, it is natural and appropriate for judges to speak at law-related events, regardless of whether the event serves a fund-raising purpose.

Some commentators have suggested that the distinction drawn in 2007 Code is "open to question" because if the primary concern with judges serving as speakers at fund-raisers is the risk that donors would feel coerced to participate, then it would seem that risk is greater at law-related functions, where lawyers would feel pressured to attend for fear that they would offend the honoree before whom they may appear in the future. However, they note that Rule 3.7 is subject to the requirements of Rule 3.1, which prohibits a judge from engaging in any conduct "that would appear to a reasonable person to be coercive." Charles Gardner Geyh, James J. Alfini, Steven Lubet, & Jeffrey M. Shaman, *Judicial Conduct and Ethics*, § 9.04[5] at 9–23 (5th ed. 2013).

Judges have been and, pursuant to Rule 3.7(A)(4), likely will continue to be prohibited from speaking at, being honored by, or accepting an award from a nonlegal charitable organization during an event in which fund-raising will be conducted. *See* Conn. Comm. on Jud. Ethics Formal Adv. Op. JE 2013-28 (2013) (judge may not accept invitation to speak at Annual Hispana Leadership Summit); Fla. Jud. Ethics Adv. Comm. Op. 2011-03 (2011) (judge may not attend and accept award at Junior League fund-raising event and sending another in judge's stead to accept the award does not cure the violation because it "is the prestige of judicial office, not the actual appearance or charisma of the particular incumbent, that the Canons prohibit being put to use in service of private interests"); Fla. Jud. Ethics Adv. Comm. Op. 99-09 (1999) (judge may not receive an award and be inducted into a County Women's Hall of Fame at an annual luncheon where program advertisements have been sold to raise funds for the organization); Fla. Jud. Ethics Adv. Comm. Op. 98-10 (1998) (judge may be honored and receive award as long as event is not fund-raiser); Ill. Jud. Ethics Comm. Op. 01-04 (2001) (judge may not be a guest of honor at a civic organization's fund-raising event); Kan. Jud. Ethics Op. JE-147 (2006) (judge may not attend dinner during which he would be inducted into hall of fame and during which funds would be raised for business and economic education of youth because judge would be guest of honor); Mass. Comm. on Jud. Ethics Adv. Op. 03-1 (2003) (judge should not accept award from chamber of commerce where cost of reserving table at awards luncheon exceeds cost of tickets, luncheon is "sponsored by" a law firm, and chamber of commerce and its members regularly take one side on issues the state's courts); Neb. Jud. Ethics Adv. Comm. Op. 2007-1 (2007) (judge may not introduce the keynote speaker at an annual breakfast commemorating a historic legal opinion, because although the event is primarily commemorative, a fee is charged to attendees to cover the cost of the meal and excess funds are used for a scholarship fund for the benefit of a particular group); N.Y. Adv. Comm. on Jud. Ethics Op. 11-39 (2011) (judge may be honored at religious event if the event is not a fund-raiser); S.C. Adv. Comm. on Stands. of Jud. Conduct, Op. 07-2004 (2004) (part-time magistrate may serve not as the spokesperson for a cancer awareness event as it is a fund-raising event).

Comment [3] to Rule 3.7 states that "mere attendance at an event, whether or not the event serves a fund-raising purpose, does not constitute a violation of paragraph A(4)." Jurisdictions have also determined that receipt of an award or speaking at a nonlegal charitable organization event that is not a fund-raiser does not violate the Code. Fla. Jud. Ethics Adv. Op. 2012-24 (2012) (judge may speak at Girl Scouts' annual business meeting); N.Y. Adv. Comm. on Jud. Ethics Op. 12-112 (judge may attend and receive award at local newspaper event that does not involve fund-raising). However, if a judge is allowed to attend at no charge, it is likely that the organization intends to showcase the judge, which is prohibited as an improper use of the prestige of office. Pa. Jud. Ethics Comm. Informal Op. 2/5/99 (1999).

Attending Fund-Raising Events Advocating Particular Views on Legal Issues

As noted in the Commentary to Rule 3.7, "[m]ere attendance at an event, whether or not the event serves a fund-raising purpose, does not constitute a violation of paragraph (A)(4)." ABA Model Code of Judicial Conduct Rule 3.7 cmt. [3]. While judges are generally permitted to attend fund-raising events, more caution should be exercised when the hosting organization actively advocates positions or files amicus briefs on disputed legal issues. Ariz. Jud. Ethics Adv. Comm. Op. 00-06 (2000); Ind. Comm'n on Jud. Qualifications Adv. Op. 1-96 (1996) (if beneficiary or host of fund-raising event is a controversial group or connected with disputed social or legal issues, participation is probably inappropriate); W. Va. Jud. Investigation Comm'n Adv. Op. 4/24/97 (1997) (judge may not attend functions sponsored by victim assistance programs, sexual assault centers, family violence prevention programs, police agencies, or similar organizations that represent one interest in a particular area).

The key issue is whether, from an objective viewpoint, the judge's attendance at the fund-raiser may give the appearance that the judge is lending the prestige of the office to support a position that would impair the judge's impartiality. Fla. Jud. Ethics Adv. Comm. Op. 2013-18 (2013) (judge assigned to domestic violence division may not attend walk-a-thon to raise funds for domestic violence victims because judge's impartiality may be questioned); Cynthia Gray, *A Judge's Attendance at Social Events, Bar Association Functions, Civic and Charitable Functions, and Political Gatherings*, at 12–13 (paper prepared for American Judicature Society under grant from State Justice Institute, 1996, as revised, Aug., 1998); *see, e.g.*, Wash. Ethics Adv. Comm. Op. 96-16 (1996) (judge may attend "A Day of Remembrance" ceremony to honor victims of domestic violence, but should be sure that his or her mannerisms, actions, or speech do not cast doubt on impartiality).

MAKING RECOMMENDATIONS REGARDING PROGRAMS AND ACTIVITIES

Rule 3.7(A)(5) permits a judge to make recommendations to public and private fund-granting organizations on projects and programs concerning the law, the legal system, or the administration of justice. Fla. Jud. Ethics Adv. Comm. Op. 2011-06 (2011) (judge may make a recommendation for grant funding for courthouse childcare center operated by local YWCA because the "supervised childcare program, which aids the court system, certainly falls into this category"). This provision recognizes that many organizations seek the advice of judges about funding law-related projects and the belief that responses to such requests should not be precluded. E. Wayne Thode, *Reporter's Notes to the Code of Judicial Conduct* 77 (1973). However, such recommendations may be prohibited if they create an appearance of impartiality. *See, e.g.*, Fla. Jud. Ethics Adv. Comm. Op. 2002-09 (2002) (judge may not write letter to grant provider encouraging funding of nonprofit organization that provides advocates to domestic violence victims as cases proceed through court system; judge would be indirectly assisting litigants or witnesses who would appear in court and that could affect the perception of impartiality).

SERVING AS OFFICER, DIRECTOR, TRUSTEE, OR NONLEGAL ADVISOR

Rule 3.7(A)(6) of the 2007 Code permits a judge to serve as an "officer, director, trustee, or nonlegal advisor" for "organizations or governmental entities concerned with the law, the legal system, or the administration of justice," and "educational, religious, charitable, fraternal, or civic organizations not conducted for profit." *See, e.g.*, Ala. Jud. Inquiry Comm'n Adv. Op. 98-691 (1998) (judge may serve on Alabama Model Code on Domestic Violence Committee); Ark. Jud. Ethics Adv. Comm. Op. 94-01 (1994) (judge may serve on committee formed to promote passage of sales tax); Colo. Jud. Ethics Adv. Bd. Op. 2007-02 (2007) (judge may serve on the board of directors of a public charter school in a neighboring judicial district); Conn. Comm. on Judical Ethics Informal Op. 2013-01 (2013) (judge may serve on board of directors of an out-of-state homeowners' association with respect to property that the judge owns in that other state); Del. Jud. Ethics Adv. Comm. Op. 2012-1 (judge may serve as president of a charitable club but should exercise "elevated caution" regarding prohibition on fund-raising); Fla. Jud. Ethics Adv. Comm. Op. 2010-38 (judge may not serve on board of for-profit rehabilitation organization to which the judge orders misdemeanant defendants appearing before judge); Fla. Jud. Ethics Adv. Comm. Op. 2010-07 (2010) (judge sitting in criminal court may serve as board member for nonprofit organization that provides pre-trial services to juvenile court respondents); Fla. Jud. Ethics Adv. Comm. Op. 2002-17 (2002) (judge may assume presidency of nonprofit civic organization that provides cultural events and community outreach programs); Fla. Jud. Ethics Adv. Comm. Op. 98-6 (1998) (judge may continue as chairperson of mental health task force responsible for seeking funding to support a mental health facility); Ill. Jud. Ethics Comm. Op. 96-4 (1996) (judge may be president of a church, temple, or mosque); Md. Jud. Ethics Comm. Op. 2013-12 (2013) (Maryland state judge may serve as trustee for New Jersey nonprofit organized to provide access for low-income people to lawyers and courts because "organization involved in this request is based in New Jersey and there is no indication that it will carry on active business in Maryland, such that it might be involved in proceedings before the judge); Mass. Comm. on Jud. Ethics Adv. Op. 2010-2 (2010) (judge may serve on board of nonprofit that provides services to families involved in the court system in a county in which the judge does not preside); Neb. Jud. Ethics Adv. Comm. Op. 06-1 (2006) (newly appointed judge may continue to serve as a trustee on a charitable foundation, which does not solicit or accept donations and whose sole purpose is to donate to other charitable and nonprofit organizations): Nev. Stand. Comm. on Jud. Ethics and Election Practices Op. JE00-005 (2000) (family court domestic violence commissioner may participate in Domestic Fatality Review program intended to educate participants in performing professional duties in adjudicating such cases); Nev. Stand. Comm. on Jud. Ethics Op. JE13-005 (2013) (judge may serve on nonprofit health care improvement board); N. M. Adv. Comm. on Code of Jud. Conduct Op. 12-09 (judge may serve on board of limited liability company created for recreational ballooning); N.M. Adv. Comm. on Code of Jud. Conduct Op. 10-04 (2010) (judge may serve on board of drug court professionals association but only if participation does not cast doubt on judge's "ability to act impartially when those who reject an opportunity to participate in drug court come before" the judge and officers of the association do not regularly appear before the judge); N.Y. Adv. Comm. on Jud. Conduct Op. 12-177 (2012) (judge may serve as trustee of religious organization and on finance council); N.Y. Adv. Comm. on Judicial Conduct Op. 11-137 (2011) (judge may serve as officer of not-for-profit, appoint members to fund-raising committee, and keep track of membership and dues collected); N.C. Jud. Standards Comm'n Formal Op. 2010-06 (2010) (judge may not serve on board of hospital regardless of tax status because "a hospital, regardless of its tax status, is a business"); Okla. Jud. Ethics Op. 2007-4 (2007) (judge could serve as an officer and member of the board of directors of a private school); S.C. Adv. Comm. on Stands. of Jud. Conduct Op. 11-2005 (2005) (judge may serve on advisory board for youth court program that is designed as an alternative for children who misbehave in school and an educational tool for those interested in a career in law enforcement); Wash. Ethics Adv. Comm. Op. 93-06 (1993) (judge may serve on advisory committee of nonprofit organization that offers leadership training).

However, a judge may not serve in that capacity if it is likely that the organization or entity will be engaged in proceedings that would ordinarily come before the judge or will frequently be engaged in adversary proceedings in the court of which the judge is a member or in a court subject to the appellate jurisdiction of the court of which the judge is a member. *See, e.g.*, Colo. Jud. Ethics Adv. Bd. Op. 2005-03 (2005) (judge should not serve on board of directors of his or her homeowners' association where association is large and substantial, operates a sizeable budget and maintains significant cash reserves, and is engaged in substantial business-type contacts that might lead to or involve litigation); Ga. Jud. Qualifications Comm'n Op. 197 (1994) (upon taking the bench, judge should discontinue service on board of directors for state affiliate of the American Civil Liberties Union (ACLU) since the ACLU is frequently engaged in litigation in several courts); Ill. Jud. Ethics Comm. Op. 98-5 (1998) (judge may not serve on a board of directors of charitable organization that is involved in proceedings that regularly come before the court); Md. Jud. Ethics Op. 2008-05 (2008) (judge may not continue to serve as board member and in the future accept election as vice president, and eventually president, of charitable organization, which likely will appear in judge's court); Mass. Comm. on Jud. Ethics Adv. Op. 05-2 (2005) (judge may not serve on board of trustees of private, nonprofit hospital because hospital might frequently be engaged in adversary proceedings in the court on which the judge serves); N.M. Adv. Comm. on Code of Jud. Conduct Op. 07-09 (2007) (judge should not serve on board of nonprofit organization that contracts with county to serve public hospital that is likely to appear frequently before judge); Okla. Jud. Ethics Adv. Op. 2000-9 (2000) (judge's membership in organization that investigates incidents of child abuse and, where appropriate, aids in prosecution would violate spirit of Canon 4); S.C. Adv. Comm. on Stands. of Jud. Conduct, Op. 34-1996 (1996) (judge may not serve on board of directors of local bank as banks are frequently in court, and though judge presides primarily over criminal cases, there is possibility that bank could come before his court); W. Va. Jud. Investigation Comm'n Adv. Op. 10/7/94 (1994) (judge may not serve on board of directors of legal services organization or juvenile justice committee because they are regularly involved in adversary proceedings in court).

A judge may also be advised not to serve as an officer, director, trustee, or nonlegal advisor for an organization that does not appear in the judge's court but that is committed to causes that might affect cases that do come before the judge. Utah Jud. Ethics Adv. Comm. Informal Op. 07-4 (2007) (judge may not serve on the board of the National Alliance for the Mentally Ill (NAMI); although NAMI itself is not a frequent litigant before the judge's court, NAMI makes policy decisions that might have significance for the cases that come before the judge's court).

Even if a judge's extrajudicial service as an officer, director, or trustee is permitted under Rule 3.7(A)(6), a judge likely will need to regularly examine the activities of the organization to ensure that the judge's continued affiliation is appropriate. *See, e.g.*, Colo. Jud. Ethics Adv. Bd. Op. 2013-01 (judge may serve on board of crime victims assistance organization but must determine whether working on the board will lead to "disqualification-related limitations"); Fla. Jud. Ethics Adv. Comm. Op. 2013-06 (2013) (judge may serve on board of nonprofit that provides financial assistance to needy families who have been referred by law enforcement because board will make decisions independent of law enforcement agency and participation was not "so closely connected" to law enforcement agency "that the public would feel the two entities are alter egos of one another" and the that judge could not be impartial); Wash. Ethics Adv. Comm. Op. 13-1 (2013) (judge may serve on hospital board, but judge should monitor service to ensure that there is no confusion regarding the board's independence from the public hospital disctrict and to be mindful of disqualification issues); Wash. Ethics Adv. Comm. Op. 96-3 (1996) (judge may serve on board of crisis clinic but should periodically reexamine the activities of the board to determine that it is still proper to serve).

In addition to the restrictions within Rule 3.7(A)(6), a judge's service in a charitable or civic organization is subject to Rule 3.1, which imposes several restrictions on judge's extrajudicial activities. For instance, Rule 3.1 prohibits a judge from participating in extrajudicial activities that would lead to frequent disqualification of the judge or that would appear to a reasonable person to undermine the judge's independence, integrity, or impartiality. *See, e.g.*, Ariz. Jud. Ethics Adv. Comm. Op. 97-03 (1997) (judge may not serve as member of domestic violence commission; since commission exists to promote causes and espouse a particular point of view, judge's membership may give the appearance of favoritism and raise a question as to the judge's ability to preside fairly over certain cases); N.Y. Adv. Comm. on Jud. Ethics Op. 12-80 (2012) (judge who hears matters involving the court police department may not serve on board, which oversees career program for persons interested in law enforcement because judge's impartiality could reasonably be questioned).

ENCOURAGING LAWYERS TO PROVIDE PRO BONO SERVICES

Rule 3.7(B) permits a judge to encourage lawyers to provide pro bono legal services. As noted in the Commentary, this encouragement can take many forms, including providing lists of available programs, training lawyers to do pro bono work, and participating in events recognizing lawyers' pro bono work. In doing so, however, the judge should not employ coercion or abuse the prestige of judicial office. Model Code of Judicial Conduct Rule 3.7(B) cmt. [5]. This provision is consistent with the thrust of Rule 3.7(A). It was placed in a separate paragraph because paragraph (A) deals with a large variety of organizations and entities, with varied goals and programs, whereas paragraph (B) refers to specific activities, whether or not conducted in connection with a particular organization or entity. Charles G. Geyh & W. William Hodes, *Reporters' Notes to the Model Code of Judicial Conduct* 70–71 (2009). *See* Marla N. Greenstein, *Judges' Support for Pro Bono Legal Services*, 47 No. 4 Judges' J. 49 (2008).

Although Rule 3.7(B) is new to the 2007 Code, some ethics committees previously issued opinions regarding the types of activities judges may undertake to encourage pro bone activities by lawyers. Alaska Comm'n on Jud. Conduct Adv. Op. 2004-01 (2004) (advising about the types of activities judges may perform to help further pro bono participation by lawyers); Colo. Jud. Ethics Adv. Bd. Op. 2006-02 (2006) (judge may not participate in local legal service's call-a-lawyer program by providing pro bono advice to callers because doing so would constitute the practice of law but judge may engage in activities intended to encourage attorneys to perform pro bono services or act in an advisory capacity to the legal services pro bono program); Ky. Jud. Ethics Op. JE-107 (2005) (a judge may not, by personal letter, urge members of the local bar to donate time to a specific pro bono association on a free or reduced fee basis; a generic letter to the bar at large would be permissible so long as it does no reference any particular pro bono organization).

RULE 3.8 APPOINTMENTS TO FIDUCIARY POSITIONS

(A) A judge shall not accept appointment to serve in a fiduciary* position, such as executor, administrator, trustee, guardian, attorney in fact, or other personal representative, except for the estate, trust, or person of a member of the judge's family,* and then only if such service will not interfere with the proper performance of judicial duties.

(B) A judge shall not serve in a fiduciary position if the judge as fiduciary will likely be engaged in proceedings that would ordinarily come before the judge, or if the estate, trust, or ward becomes involved in adversary proceedings in the court on which the judge serves, or one under its appellate jurisdiction.

(C) A judge acting in a fiduciary capacity shall be subject to the same restrictions on engaging in financial activities that apply to a judge personally.

(D) If a person who is serving in a fiduciary position becomes a judge, he or she must comply with this Rule as soon as reasonably practicable, but in no event later than [one year] after becoming a judge.

COMMENT

[1] A judge should recognize that other restrictions imposed by this Code may conflict with a judge's obligations as a fiduciary; in such circumstances, a judge should resign as fiduciary. For example, serving as a fiduciary might require frequent disqualification of a judge under Rule 2.11 because a judge is deemed to have an economic interest in shares of stock held by a trust if the amount of stock held is more than de minimis.

1990 CODE COMPARISON

Rules 3.8(A), 3.8(B), and 3.8(C) are essentially identical to Canons 4E(1), 4E(2), and 4E(3) respectively with only minor stylistic revisions. Rule 3.8(D) is based on section F of the Application section and is new to the black letter text. It delineates when a newly elected or appointed judge, who is already serving in a fiduciary capacity, must comply with this Rule. The suggested outer limit is one year, but jurisdictions may choose some other time limit. The Commentary to the Rule is similar to the second paragraph of Commentary to Canon 4E and serves a reminder that in addition to the restrictions set forth in Rule 3.8, other provisions of the proposed Code may implicate the permissibility of serving in a fiduciary capacity. Charles G. Geyh & W. William Hodes, *Reporters' Notes to the Model Code of Judicial Conduct*, 72–73 (2009).

ANNOTATION

INTRODUCTION

The old Canons of Judicial Ethics gave judge's broad authority to serve as a fiduciary for family and non-family members, so long as the activity did not interfere with judicial duties. However, the drafters of the 1972 Model Code found that a party for whom the judge is acting as an executor, trustee, guardian, or other fiduciary may appear to have an advantage in a proceeding before a fellow judge. Therefore, the Committee decided that danger of the appearance of such an advantage was sufficiently real to justify severe limitations on fiduciary activities unless there are important countervailing considerations. E. Wayne Thode, *Reporter's Notes to Code of Judicial Conduct* 87–88 (1973).

This rationale has been carried through to Rule 3.8(A), which generally prohibits a judge from accepting an appointment to serve in a fiduciary position, such as executor, administrator, trustee, guardian, attorney in fact, or other personal representative. A judge may act in such capacity only for "a member of the judge's family," and then only if doing so will not interfere with the proper performance of judicial duties. Fla. Jud. Ethics Adv. Comm. Op. 2011-05 (2010) (judge may appear at mediation at contested probate proceeding as guardian of minor children). *See, e.g., In re O'Connor* (N.Y. Comm'n on Jud. Conduct 2013) (judge censured for continuing to serve as fiduciary in three matters after ascending to the bench and not disclosing on guardianship applications that he was a respondent in a foreclosure suit); *In re Cieminski*, 270 N.W.2d 321 (N.D. 1978) (judge censured for misconduct including handling personal checking accounts for individuals having difficulty managing finances, including the account of someone who was a party in a case before the judge; though judge was well-intentioned and did work without compensation, his action contravened Code); Ark. Jud. Ethics Adv. Comm. Op. 2004-05 (2004) (judge may not serve as trustee of life insurance trust); N.Y. Adv. Comm. on Jud. Ethics Op. 10-203(B) (2010) (judge may continue as trustee for trust that benefits judge's cousin); N.Y. Adv. Comm. on Jud. Ethics Op. 11-117 (2012) (judge may not continue to serve as successor co-trustee of testamentary trust of former partner's client); S.C. Adv. Comm. on Stands. of Jud. Conduct, Op. 07-2013 (2013) (judge may not serve as "tie breaker" vote between two executors or trustees on behalf of a family friend); S.C. Adv. Comm. on Stands. of Jud. Conduct Op. 14-2011 (2011) (judge may serve as executor of trust for close personal friend because "family" is defined term in Code and includes other person with whom the judge "maintains a close familial relationship"); S.C. Adv. Comm. on Stands. of Jud. Conduct Op. 11-2004 (2004) (assistant administrative judge may not act as the executor of the will of a non-family member); Wash. Ethics Adv. Comm. Op. 99-3 (1993) (judge may act as executor or trustee for first cousin, first cousin once removed, and spouse of that cousin as long as that service does not interfere with performance of judicial duties or reflect adversely on impartiality); W. Va. Jud. Investigation Comm'n Adv. Op. 1/5/93 (1993) (judge-elect may not continue to serve as executor of estate of non-family member after assuming office); W. Va. Jud. Investigation Comm'n Adv. Op. 2/19/96 (1996) (judge may not serve as trustee for charitable foundation that is not affiliated with judge's family).

A judge serving as administrator or executor for the estate of a family member, however, generally may not prepare and file the probate documents, as such activity constitutes the impermissible practice of law pursuant to Section 4G. Ill. Jud. Ethics Comm. Op. 97-10 (1997) (judge may serve as executor for mother's estate, but may not receive compensation); Wis. Sup. Ct. Rule Chap. 60.05(7) (permitting judges to represent without compensation the estate of a person with whom the judge maintains a close familial relationship as long as the estate remains uncontested).

In addition to the restrictions of Rule 3.8(A), Rule 3.8(B) provides that a judge may be prohibited from serving as a fiduciary if it is likely that in that capacity, the judge will be engaged in proceedings that would ordinarily come before his or her court. Similarly, a judge may not serve as a fiduciary if the estate, trust, or ward becomes involved in adversary proceedings in the court on which the judge serves or a court under its appellate jurisdiction. And, as noted in the Comment to the Rule, other restrictions in the Code may conflict with a judge's obligation as a fiduciary. For instance, serving as a fiduciary (even for a family member, which is generally permitted) might require frequent disqualification in violation of Rule 2.11 because a judge is deemed to have an economic interest in shares of stock held by a trust if the amount of stock is more than de minimis. Pursuant to Rule 3.8(C), when acting as a fiduciary, a judge must adhere to the same restrictions on financial activities that apply to the judge personally. (See Rule 3.11 for limits on financial activities.)

Rule 3.8(D) delineates when a newly elected or appointed judge who is already serving in a fiduciary capacity must comply with Rule 3.8. The suggested outer limit is one year, but jurisdictions may choose some other time limit. *See, e.g., In re Inquiry Concerning a Judge*, 566 S.E.2d 310 (Ga. 2002) (judge who resigned as guardian ten months after assuming bench complied with duties under the rule); Md. Jud. Ethics Op. 2013-22 (2013) (distinguishing between matters in which a judge is actively holding a fiduciary position and those in which the position is dormant and finding that new judge, who while a lawyer representing financial institutions was named as substitute trustee for many forclosure proceedings, did not violate Rule 3.8(d) by not resigning from dormant fiduciary positions; formal resignation when matters present themselves is consistent with the Rules); Nev. Stand. Comm. on Jud. Ethics Op. JE13-001 (2013) (judge has one year to remove self as trustee or successor trustee); N.Y. Adv. Comm. on Jud. Ethics Op. 10-169 (2010) (newly elected judge may perform the tasks necessary to terminate conservatorships); S.C. Adv. Comm. on Stands. of Jud. Conduct, Op. 21-2000 (2000) (new judge may not simply remain the fiduciary for one year, but can only remain the fiduciary for period of time that is necessary to avoid serious adverse consequences to the beneficiary of the fiduciary relationship and in no event, longer than one year).

"Close Familial Relationship"

A judge may serve as an executor, trustee, or guardian or other fiduciary position on behalf of a member of the judge's family, which according to the Code's Terminology section, includes the judge's spouse, domestic partner, child, grandchild, parent, grandparent, or other relative. A judge may also serve in a fiduciary capacity for a person with whom the judge maintains a "close familial relationship." ABA Model Code of Judicial Conduct, Terminology (defining "member of judge's family").

A "close familial relationship" may exist even when no bond of blood or marriage exists, and even when two unrelated persons have never cohabited. One court held that such a "close family relationship" exists when the relationship between two unrelated persons resembles a family relationship such as between spouses, parent and child, or siblings. The relationship must also be nurturing and possess some characteristics typical of traditional family relationship, that is, intimacy of address, recognition by others of close relationship, shared meals, frequent contact either by phone or in-person, shared holidays, shared family events, assistance with physical, medical, legal or emotional needs, and longevity. *In re Horgos*, 682 A.2d 447 (Pa. Ct. Jud. Disc. 1996); W. Va. Jud. Investigation Comm'n Adv. Op. 2/6/97 (1997) (newly appointed judge may continue to act as attorney in fact for 89-year-old person when judge has acted in that capacity for 15 years and has developed close familial relationship); *but see* Wash. Ethics Adv. Comm. Op. 87-07 (1987) (judge may not serve as uncompensated executor for close and longtime friend).

Compensation

A judge who is permitted to serve as a trustee for a family trust may be allowed to accept compensation for such service if the source of the compensation does not give the appearance of influencing the judge in the judge's judicial duties or otherwise give the appearance of impropriety. U.S. Comm. on Codes of Conduct Adv. Op. No. 96 (1999); *but see* Ill. Jud. Ethics Comm. Op. 97-10 (1997) (judge may serve as executor of his or her mother's estate but may not receive compensation). Any compensation received must be reported pursuant to Rule 3.14 (Reimbursement of Expenses and Waivers of Fees or Charges).

RULE 3.9 SERVICE AS ARBITRATOR OR MEDIATOR

A judge shall not act as an arbitrator or a mediator or perform other judicial functions apart from the judge's official duties unless expressly authorized by law.*

COMMENT

[1] This Rule does not prohibit a judge from participating in arbitration, mediation, or settlement conferences performed as part of assigned judicial duties. Rendering dispute resolution services apart from those duties, whether or not for economic gain, is prohibited unless it is expressly authorized by law.

1990 CODE COMPARISON

Rule 3.9 is based on Canon 4F of the 1990 Code. The only substantive change was to change the phrase "in a private capacity" to "apart from the judge's official duties." The prior language was deemed to be too narrow, because it might be read to permit a judge to provide dispute resolution services for another governmental entity, which the Commission considered inappropriate, despite considerable conflicting testimony, unless specifically authorized by law. Charles

G. Geyh & W. William Hodes, *Reporters' Notes to the Model Code of Judicial Conduct*, 73–74 (2009).

Annotation

Introduction

Pursuant to Rule 3.9, a judge may not serve as an arbitrator or mediator or otherwise perform judicial functions apart from the judge's official duties, unless expressly authorized by law. The Committee that drafted the 1972 Code of Judicial Conduct concluded that the potential dangers inherent in permitting judges to serve as arbitrators or mediators outweigh the public service and income supplementation values cited in support of permitting such service. Those dangers include the possibility that (1) arbitration proceedings could come before the court on which the judge sits, (2) the court could be drawn into social and political controversies in which a judge acted as an arbitrator, (3) the judicial office could be exploited in an effort to secure its dignity and prestige in support of an award, (4) judicial time could be diverted in a case in which a judge's fee would be thousands of dollars. E. Wayne Thode, *Reporter's Notes to the Code of Judicial Conduct* 89 (1973). Additionally, judges are appointed and paid to resolve disputes, and permitting the private practice of the same profession exploits the judicial office. Charles Gardner Geyh, James J. Alfini, Steven Lubet, & Jeffrey M. Shaman, *Judicial Conduct and Ethics* § 7.09 at 7–32 (5th ed. 2013).

Generally, jurisdictions have strictly applied this provision, advising judges to avoid serving as a mediator or arbitrator in a private capacity, regardless of the circumstances unless expressly permitted by law. *See, e.g.*, Colo. Jud. Ethics Adv. Bd. Op. 2006-09 (2006) (full-time judge who will be retiring soon should refrain from setting or hearing private mediations until after he retires as a judge); Del. Jud. Ethics Adv. Comm. Op. JPC 1985-2 (1985) (judge cannot serve as an arbitrator in conjunction with his part-time teaching of labor law in law school); Fla. Jud. Ethics Adv. Comm. Op. 2002-01 (2002) (prohibiting judge from privately mediating dissolution of friend's marriage); Ill. Jud. Ethics Comm. Op. 94-1 (1994) (advising that judge may not work as arbitrator after hours); Kan. Jud. Ethics Op. JE 153 (2007) (district magistrate judge may conduct mediation when assigned by Chief District Judge, pursuant to state statute); Nev. Stand. Comm. on Jud. Ethics and Election Prac. Op. JE01-001 (2001) (justice of the peace may not act as arbitrator binding or non-binding proceedings; "accepting appointments as a private arbitrator . . . has the clear capacity to distract the judge from the diligent performance of his or her judicial duties"); Okla. Jud. Ethics Op. 2006-2 (2006) (judge may not serve as a member of the dispute resolutions board of a sovereign Indian nation); Wis. Jud. Conduct Adv. Comm. Op. 01-3 (2001) (judge may not serve as member of state bar's fee arbitration panel). *But see* Fla. Jud. Ethics Adv. Comm. Op. 97-15

(1997) (allowing general master to engage in co-mediations required to become certified as family law mediator).

However, a judge may be permitted to complete an arbitration or mediation that was started prior to the judge's taking office. *See, e.g.*, W. Va. Jud. Investigation Comm'n Adv. Op. 8/18/95 (1995) (new judge may be permitted to rule on a substantially completed arbitration case that started before the judge took office if under the circumstances of the case: (1) the parties' rights to an expeditious decision would be jeopardized, (2) the parties would incur great additional expense, (3) an inordinate delay in the resolution of the matter would occur). Additionally, a judge may be permitted to serve on the board of directors of a nonprofit mediation organization. *Shake v. Ethics Comm. of the Ky. Judiciary*, 122 S.W.3d 577 (Ky. 2003) (rejecting argument that litigants might feel compelled to choose mediation if the judge sits on the board).

EXCEPTION FOR OFFICIAL DUTIES

A judge may participate in arbitration, mediation, or settlement conferences performed as part of his or her official duties. Model Code of Judicial Conduct Rule 3.9 cmt. [1]. *See, e.g.*, Pa. Jud. Ethics Comm. Informal Op. 3/18/99 (1999) (judge may act as an arbitrator if the judge is assigned by the court to conduct arbitration as part of his or her duties during regular working times for no additional compensation and an appeal is permitted only for a corrupt result); Utah Jud. Ethics Adv. Comm. Informal Op. 94-1 (1994) (judge's participation in uncompensated court annexed mediation or arbitration program does not constitute action "in a private capacity"). However, aside from this exception, a judge may not render dispute resolution services, whether or not for economic gain, unless expressly authorized by law. Model Code of Judicial Conduct Rule 3.9 cmt. [1]. Some states, including Oklahoma, do not provide an exception for official duties. Okla. Code of Jud. Conduct, Canon 4F (2006) ("A judge should not act as an arbitrator or mediator."); Okla. Jud. Ethics Op. 2000-4, 10 P.3d 898 (2000) (advising that administrative law judge could not act as mediator even when specific law permitted administrative law judge to do so because Canon 4F of Oklahoma Code of Judicial Conduct does not permit judicial participation in mediation established by governmental entity or created by statute).

RULE 3.10 PRACTICE OF LAW

A judge shall not practice law. A judge may act pro se and may, without compensation, give legal advice to and draft or review documents for a member of the judge's family,* but is prohibited from serving as the family member's lawyer in any forum.

COMMENT

[1] A judge may act pro se in all legal matters, including matters involving litigation and matters involving appearances before or other dealings with governmental bodies. A judge must not use the prestige of office to advance the judge's personal or family interests. See Rule 1.3.

1990 CODE COMPARISON

Rule 3.10 is essentially identical to Canon 4G of the 1990 Code, with language based on the second paragraph of Commentary to Canon 4G added as black letter text. The Comment to Rule 3.10 is based on the first paragraph of Commentary to Canon 4G. Rule 3.10's prohibition against "serving as the family member's lawyer in any forum" is a more narrow restriction than was "act[ing] as an advocate or negotiator. . .in a legal matter." The Commission took the view that in some informal settings, such as a dispute in a neighborhood association or a purely private and minor commercial dispute, a judge may serve as an "advocate" for a family member without becoming his or her lawyer and thus practicing law in violation of Rule 3.10. Charles G. Geyh & W. William Hodes, *Reporters' Notes to the Model Code of Judicial Conduct* 74–75 (2009).

ANNOTATION

INTRODUCTION

Rule 3.10 prohibits full-time judges from practicing law once they take the bench. *See, e.g., In re Fleischman*, 933 P.2d 563 (Ariz. 1997) (judge censured for negotiating contract for professional tennis player); *In re Henson*, 913 So. 2d 579 (Fla. 2005) (judge removed from office for misconduct including unauthorized practice of law while still a judge; judge agreed to represent criminal client, signed contract for representation, interviewed client, and took other actions in representing client prior to expiration of his term in office); *Miss. Comm'n on Jud. Performance v. Jenkins*, 725 So. 2d 163 (Miss. 1998) (judge violated provision by providing legal advice to corporation regarding the acquisition of property); *Cleveland Bar Assn. v. Katalinas*, 735 N.E.2d 432 (Ohio 2000) (lawyer disbarred for taking on legal separation and civil action while sitting as municipal court judge); *In re Piper*, 534 P.2d 159 (Or. 1975) (judge reprimanded for finishing work on estates undertaken while practicing law ten years earlier); Ariz. Jud. Ethics Adv. Comm. Op. 95-3 (1995) (judge may not handle pro bono cases as a lawyer); Ill. Jud. Ethics Comm. Op. 96-16 (1996) (judge may not act as advocate for rabbi in negotiations with synagogue); Nev. Stand. Comm. on Jud. Ethics, JE13-003 (2013) (judge may not act as legal advisor to political organization); Nev. Stand. Comm. on Jud. Ethics and Election Prac. JE06-019 (2006) (judge who assisted in preparing bylaws of homeowners' association prior to taking bench may not assist in amending them because that would constitute practicing law); S.C. Adv. Comm. on Stands. of Jud.

Conduct Op. 19-2000 (2000) (full time master-in-equity may not engage in the practice or law or accept appointments as special referee); *In re Broussard*, 900 So. 2d 814 (La. 2005) (non-lawyer justice of the peace's unauthorized practice of law, by preparing, notarizing, and filing or processing divorce pleadings in eight cases, had the potential to undermine the public's confidence in the integrity of the judiciary, in violation of provision of code of judicial conduct); *see generally* Annotation, *Propriety and Permissibility of Judge Engaging in Practice of Law*, 89 A.L.R.2d 886 (1963).

Some jurisdictions, including Georgia and West Virginia, have statutes that permit magistrates to practice law. *In re Inquiry Concerning a Judge*, 566 S.E.2d 310 (Ga. 2002) (citing Ga. Code Ann. § 15-10-22 (2007) in rejecting assertion that magistrate improperly practiced law); *W. Va. Inquiry Comm'n v. Allamong*, 252 S.E.2d 159 (W. Va. 1979) (holding that the provisions of Article VIII, Section 7 of state constitution, which permits attorneys who are magistrates to practice law except to the extent prohibited by the legislature, precludes court from prohibiting magistrates from practicing law under Canon 5F of Judicial Code).

THE "PRACTICE OF LAW"

The drafters of the 1972 Code contemplated defining the "practice of law," but decided that the definition should be left to common law development by each jurisdiction in light of its own decisions, ethics opinions, and local practices. E. Wayne Thode, *Reporter's Notes to the Code of Judicial Conduct* 90 (1973). Nor was a definition included in the 1990 or 2007 Codes. Activities that have been deemed to constitute the "practice of law" generally include those that are customarily performed from day to day in ordinary practice of members of the legal profession, even though they may also be performed, in part or in whole, by non-lawyers from time to time. *In re Fleischman*, 933 P.2d 563 (Ariz. 1997) (judge who acted as representative for corporation during contract renewal negotiations and advised corporation on contract being negotiated engaged in practice of law). W. Va. Jud. Investigation Comm'n Adv. Op. 6/14/95 (1995) (judge may not prepare tax returns for individuals who are not members of judge's family).

The practice of law may not be confined "to services by an attorney in a court of justice; it also includes any service of a legal nature rendered outside of courts and unrelated to matters pending in the courts. It is uniformly held that writing and interpreting wills, contracts, trust agreements, and the giving of legal advice in general constitute practicing law." *Jud. Disc. & Disability Comm'n v. Thompson*, 16 S.W.3d 212 (Ark. 2001) (newly elected judge engaged in "practice of law," rather than clerical activities, where he discussed with clients and obtained their approval of a release, dismissal motion, and dismissal order; faxed letter to co-counsel to confirm fee arrangement; sent cashier's check with a letter, written on judicial stationery, directing co-counsel to approve order of dismissal and giving her instructions on closing case). Ill. Jud. Ethics Comm. Op. 94-2 (1994) (legal counseling to any group, including social organizations, constitutes the practice of law); *but see* N.Y. Adv. Comm. on Jud. Ethics Op. 13-53 (2013) (judge may provide statement or sign affidavit related to case judge defended more than 20 years prior).

In addition to the ban on practicing law, judges may be prohibited from participating in activities that create the appearance of practicing law. *See* Nev. Stand. Comm. on Jud. Ethics and Election Practices Op. JE10-008 (2010) (judge's participation on committee drafting city ballot question "appear inextricably intertwined in the process of drafting the ballot language" and therefore raise Rule 3.10 issues); Utah Jud. Ethics Adv. Comm. Informal Op. 98-7 (1998) (judge may not issue title insurance through Attorney's Title because it creates the appearance that the judge is practicing law). Judges may also be prohibited from acting as a supervising attorney for law students or lawyers. *See* Wash. Ethics Adv. Comm. Op. 88-14 (1988) (judge may not be supervising lawyer for law students who act as negotiators in mandatory settlement negotiations for small claims cases); *but see Elane v. St. Bernard Hosp.*, 672 N.E.2d 820 (Ill. 1996) (legal responsibility of referring attorney under referral agreement, holding referring attorney responsible as if she were partner of receiving attorney, did not involve improper practice of law by referring attorney after she became judge); Ill. Jud. Ethics Comm. 94-16 (as mod. 1995) (judge may receive fee for referral made before becoming judge where fee based entirely upon making of referral and maintaining financial "legal responsibility").

Part-Time Judges

Rule 3.10 does not apply to part-time judges, so they may continue to practice law after taking the bench. However, a part-time judge who practices law must not do so in the court on which the judge serves or in any court subject to the appellate jurisdiction of the court on which the judge serves. A part-time judge should also not act as a lawyer in any proceeding or related proceeding in which he or she has served as a judge. Model Code of Judicial Conduct Application §§ III(B) and IV(B).

Part-time judges who practice law must adhere to the other sections of the Code that apply to them, including Rule 1.2 regarding impropriety and the appearance of impropriety and Rule 2.11(A)(3) regarding economic interests. *See, e.g., Miss. Comm'n on Jud. Performance v. Atkinson*, 645 So. 2d 1331 (Miss. 1994) (judge reprimanded for setting bail of accused while serving as part-time municipal judge and subsequently seeking reduction of bail while acting as lawyer representing accused); Ark. Jud. Ethics Adv. Comm. Op. 97-04 (1997) (part-time city judge's representation of city against chamber of commerce could create, in reasonable minds, perception that judge's ability to carry out judicial responsibilities with integrity, impartiality, and competence is impaired); N.Y. Adv. Comm. on Jud. Ethics Op. 94-71 (1994) (part-time judge who is a practicing attorney should disqualify himself where the police officer, appearing as arresting officer or witness, is current client of judge, or former client whose representation was within the past two years); Wash. Ethics Adv. Comm. Op. 93-20 (1993) (part-time judge may not serve as retained counsel for political party); *but see* Kan. Jud. Ethics Op. JE 49 (1994) (no appearance of impropriety or conflict of interest where part-time judge serves as city attorney for another city); *see generally* Gray and Biro, *An Ethics Guide for Part-time Lawyer Judges*, American Judicature Society (1999).

Some jurisdictions prohibit part-time judges from practicing criminal law on the grounds that it would create an appearance of impropriety. *See, e.g.*, Ark. Jud. Ethics Adv. Comm. Op. 2005-04 (2005) (part-time judge may not represent criminal defendants on felony charges in the same county in which the judge serves); N.Y. Adv. Comm. on Jud. Ethics Op. 228 (1972) (part-time judge with criminal jurisdiction cannot represent clients in criminal matters in his or her private practice); Utah Jud. Ethics Adv. Comm. Informal Op. 07-02 (2007) (part-time referee may not practice criminal law); *but see* Tenn. Jud. Ethics Comm. Adv. Op. 07-01 (2007) (part-time municipal court judge who has municipal ordinance jurisdiction only may practice criminal law in the same judicial circuit in which the part-time judge holds court).

Exceptions to Prohibition on Practice of Law

Appearing Pro Se

The prohibition against practicing law does not apply to a judge who is acting pro se. *See, e.g., U.S. v. Martinez*, 684 P.2d 509 (N.M. 1984) ("[r]epresenting one's self in a legal proceeding does not constitute practicing law."); Ill. Jud. Ethics Comm. Op. 98-4 (1998) (judge may appear pro se in appellate court in lawsuit seeking to enforce the provisions of judge's condominium agreement provided judge does not use prestige of office to advance his or her interests); N.Y. Adv. Comm. on Jud. Ethics Op. 12-41 (2012) (sitting judge may continue to commence or defend civil actions as a self represented litigant); *but see* Ky. Jud. Ethics Op. JE-32 (1981) (judge could not represent himself in collecting accounts due to former law practice). A judge acting pro se must ensure, however, that he or she is not indirectly representing the interest of others and must not use the prestige of the judicial office to advance the interests of the judge or the judge's family.

Advising Family Members

A judge may provide legal advice to and draft or review documents for a member of his or her family, so long as the judge does not receive compensation or serve as the family member's lawyer in any forum. *See, e.g.*, Mich. Comm. on Jud. Ethics Op. J-2 (1989) (judge may provide limited legal advice or counseling to son-in-law concerning real estate transaction, including drafting or reviewing documents, as long as judge does not receive compensation, function as advocate or negotiator, or make appearance as counsel).

A judge may not, however, represent a family member in a lawsuit or negotiate a legal matter with a third party on behalf of a family member. *See, e.g.*, *In re Kautz*, 149 So. 3d 681 (Fla. 2014) (judge reprimanded for appearing at hearing on behalf of sister); *In re Turner*, 76 So. 3d 898 (Fla. 2011) (judge removed from bench, in part, for representing mother in foreclosure when judge filed notice of appearance and negotitated with opposing counsel). *See also* Ariz. Jud. Ethics Adv. Comm. Op. 10-06 (2010) (judge may not represent spouse injuried in auto accident in negotiations with insurance company); Ill. Jud. Ethics Comm. Op. 95-19 (1995) (judge may not act on behalf of his son in son's dispute with insurance carrier); N.Y. Adv. Comm. on Jud. Ethics Op. 92-118 (1992) (full-time judge may not represent his or her daughter as a lawyer at real estate closing); Tex. Adv. Comm. on Jud. Ethics Op. 226 (1998) (if judge is sued individually, along with his or her spouse and a corporation that he or she and his or her spouse solely own, the judge may represent himself or herself, but cannot represent his or her spouse). A "member of the judge's family" includes "a spouse, domestic partner, child, grandchild, parent, grandparent, or other relative or person with whom the judge maintains a close familial relationship." Model Code of Judicial Conduct, Terminology (2007). However, some jurisdictions have advised that the exception permitting lawyers to advise family members does not extend to close personal friends of the judge. Pa. Jud. Ethics Comm. Informal Op. 10/4/01 (2001) (judge may not give legal advice to a close personal friend regarding criminal charges pending against the friend's child).

Service in the Military Reserves

Although not directly addressed by the Model Code, several jurisdictions have tackled the question of whether a judge's service in the judge advocate general corps violates the Code provision prohibiting judges from practicing law. Ala. Jud. Inquiry Comm'n Adv. Op. 03-820 (2003) (judge may serve on active duty as judge advocate general in the U.S. Army); Nev. Stand. Comm. on Jud. Ethics and Election Prac. JE 07-007 (2007) (a justice of the peace may serve in the Air Force Reserve as a judge advocate general and may be compensated as a reservist); Va. Jud. Ethics Adv. Comm. Op. 03-04 (amended 2004) (the duties of a Judge Advocate General's Corps (JAG) officer do not come within this concept of practicing law but the judge must be alert to the fact that certain types of legal assistance resemble the services provided by civilian attorneys and performing those duties may give the impression that the judge is practicing law and create an appearance of impropriety).

Some ethics committees advise that a judge may serve as a judge advocate if the judge's role is limited to performing those duties that do not resemble services provided by civilian attorneys. Alaska Comm'n on Jud. Conduct Adv. Op. 2007-01 (2007). The Alaska Commission advised that impermissible activities include serving as a recorder, legal advisor, or military defense counsel, or assisting military personnel in drafting personal legal documents such as wills or powers of attorney or advising in civil law areas such as consumer affairs and domestic relations. According to the Commission, such activities are similar in nature to what civilian attorneys perform and could lead to an appearance of improper advocacy on the part of the judge. The Commission advised that permissible activities include conducting training in the law of armed conflict, operations law, and international law, as well as teaching and training in these areas. *See also* Wash. Ethics Adv. Comm. Op. 04-08 (2004) (advising that a judge may serve as an officer of the Judge Advocate General's Corps but should not perform any services that resemble services provided by civilian attorneys for members of the military). Other committees permit judges to help prepare wills and other documents for military personnel. *See* Ill. Jud. Ethics Comm. Op. 97-8, 1997 WL 252765 (1997) (judge on military reserve duty with the JAG may give legal advice, serve on military courts, and help prepare wills, leases, or other documents for military personnel).

Winding Up Law Practice

Upon assuming the bench, a judge must cease representing clients and take appropriate steps to ensure that clients' interests are adequately protected. Winding up a law practice may involve selling a law practice, turning cases over to other lawyers, either inside or outside the firm, and ensuring that appearances are withdrawn. *See, e.g.*, Nev. Stand. Comm. on Jud. Ethics Ops. JE13-001(2013) (judge may sell former law practice, including good will; "sale must be for fixed sum rather than contingent on future success" in order to avoid appearance of impropriety); Nev. Stand. Comm. on Jud. Ethics JE13-002 (2013) (one-time cash sale of law practice does not create debtor-creditor relationship between lawyer and judge that would potentially lead to frequent disqualifiactions); N.Y. Adv. Comm. on Jud. Ethics Op. 89-38 (1989) (judge may not complete unfinished legal services performed for estate before assuming office; judge must turn over files and cooperate with new lawyer).

These winding-up activities do not constitute the practice of law. *See Stevens v. State*, 39 S.W.3d 758 (Ark. 2001) (mere filing of a motion to be relieved as counsel on the basis that one has been appointed to bench is not prohibited, but is rather a means of ensuring that the appellant is not abandoned without representation); N.Y. Adv. Comm. on Jud. Ethics Op. 95-12 (1992) (judge may supervise winding up of affairs of law practice including sending periodic bills to former clients and maintaining escrow account for processing fees earned before assuming the bench).

Judges may safeguard former clients by informing new counsel of past events or clarifying files, but may not offer advice as to the future conduct of the representation. Charles Gardner Geyh, James J. Alfini, Steven Lubet, & Jeffrey M. Shaman, *Judicial Conduct and Ethics* § 7.09[3] at 7–39 (5th ed. 2013); Fla. Jud. Ethics Adv. Comm. Op. 2013-11 (2013), citing Fla. Jud. Ethics Adv. Comm. Op. 05-19, ("discussion of pending cases with new counsel that would constitute the practice of law should take place during the process of closing the law practice, not after the judge takes office. After taking office, all further efforts on a former client's behalf should cease"); Nev. Stand. Comm. on Jud. Ethics Op. JE13-001 (2013) (judge's involvement should be "very limited" in transition to new counsel).

To avoid unnecessary conflicts of interest, a judge should diligently conclude matters related to his or her practice of law. *See* Mich. Comm. on Jud. Ethics Op. JI-89 (1994) (judge should not continue to use former firm's law library after assuming the bench); Okla. Jud. Ethics Op. 2010-1 (2010) (judge may not help former clients find successor counsel when the lawyer, to whom judge referred clients when judge assumed the bench, is retiring); *see generally* Goldstein, *Becoming a Judge: Problems with Leaving a Law Practice*, 69 Judicature 88 (1985) and Neb. Jud. Ethics Adv. Comm. Op. 07-2 (2007) (providing guidance for lawyers on how to wind up a law practice before taking the bench). Some jurisdictions expressly give new judges a specific period of time in which to wind up their law practices. *See, e.g.*, Tenn. Sup. Ct. Rule 10, Code of Judicial Conduct Canon 4G ("A newly elected or appointed judge can practice law only in an effort to wind up his or her practice ceasing to practice law as soon as reasonably possible and in no event longer than 180 days after assuming office.").

Legal Fees for Work Performed as Lawyer

The Model Code of Judicial Conduct does not directly address the question of whether a judge may receive fees for cases he or she worked on prior to becoming a judge but for which payment has not been made prior to taking the bench. However, a construction of the rules has led to the conclusion that after leaving a law practice to assume the bench, a judge may accept legal fees from his or her former firm or another lawyer, but the payment must be only for work completed prior to taking the bench. Ronald D. Rotunda & John S. Dzienkowski, *Legal Ethics: The Lawyer's Deskbook on Professional Responsibility* 1705 (2016); *see, e.g.*, N.Y. Adv. Comm. on Jud. Ethics Op. 95-12 (1995) (judge may maintain an escrow account for processing of fees earned prior to taking office even if fees are not payable for one or more years); Mass. Comm. on Jud. Ethics Adv. Op. 08-2 (2008) (new judge may receive legal fees for work already performed); Okla. Jud. Ethics Op. 2005-2 (2005) (judge may accept the payment of a fee owed by a former client four years after going on the bench and after the judge had specifically and formally forgiven all accounts receivable); Pa. Jud. Ethics Comm. Informal Op. 6/25a/01 (2001) (a judge-elect may receive legal fees from his former law firm after he is sworn in if the payment or share is fixed before he is sworn in). A judge may not receive any fees for matters that were not pending when the judge left the practice of law. *See* Pa. Jud. Ethics Comm. Informal Op. 10/14/99 (1999).

The fee may be paid to the judge over time as long as it is clear that the judge "is not sharing in profits of the firm earned after the judge's departure as distinguished from sharing in an amount representing the fair value of the judge's interest in fees to be collected in the future for work done before leaving the firm." Candice Goldstein, *Becoming a Judge: New Judge Must Cut Ties to Former Firm*, 6 No. 4 Judicial Conduct Reporter 1 (Winter 1985).

A judge must report any fees collected after taking office pursuant to Rule 3.15(A)(1). Additionally, a judge who is receiving payment from a former law firm for legal services provided prior to assuming judicial office is required to disqualify from cases in which the former firm is counsel for a party because "the judge's impartiality might reasonably be questioned," pursuant to Rule 2.11(A)(6). *See* Ohio Bd. of Commissioners on Grievances and Disc. Op. 2007-2 (2007); Ill. Jud. Ethics Comm. Op. 07-02 (2007) (judge receiving pension benefits from former law firm should ordinarily disqualify self from cases involving firm which may be submitted for remittal).

Contingent Fee Cases

Determining the appropriate payment in a contingent fee case can be more difficult. Generally, two approaches have been used to determine the amount the judge should be paid in such cases. At the time the judge takes the bench, he or she can estimate a percentage of compensation and enter into an agreement at that time with successor counsel or the judge can allow the new attorney to make the pro rata determination after the matter is completed. Either way, the fee must be reasonable and based on actual work performed by the judge before he or she took the bench. Charles Gardner Geyh, James J. Alfini, Steven Lubet, & Jeffrey M. Shaman, *Judicial Conduct and Ethics* § 7.09 at 7–39 (5th ed. 2013). *See also* ABA Comm. on Ethics and Prof'l Responsibility, Informal Op. 1215 (1972) (newly appointed judge was entitled to 30 percent contingent fee because fee was proportional to services performed on case prior to becoming judge); Fla. Jud. Ethics Adv. Comm. Op. 2013-04 (2013) (contingent "fees to be collected in the future must be calculated based upon legal services which the incoming judge performed on behalf of the client before taking office, and must satisfy the Rules

Regulating the Florida Bar's applicable requirements"); Ohio Bd. of Commissioners on Grievances and Disc. Op. 2007-2 (2007) (advising that in a contingent fee matter that is not completed before the judge takes the bench, the judge may accept compensation, once the contingency occurs, based upon quantum meruit for services performed prior to assuming judicial office); N. M. Adv. Comm. on Code of Judicial Conduct Op. 13-01 (2013) (while noting that winding down a large collection practice is difficult, judge must develop system for accepting fees earned prior to coming to the bench within five years of ascention, not 14 years, despite fact that some judgments are not being collected at this time); N. M. Adv. Comm. on Code of Judicial Conduct Op. 12-14 (2014) (best practice is for new judge and successor counsel to "agree to a fixed percentage" when the new judge transfers the case); (S.C. Adv. Comm. on Standards of Judicial Conduct Op. 12-2013 (2013) ("newly elected judge may receive reasonable remuneration for services actually rendered prior to taking the bench" but should recuse self in all matters in which the lawyer to whom the judge referred the matter appears); Tex. Adv. Comm. on Jud. Ethics Op. 293 (2007) (judge may receive referral fees after taking office for work performed and referrals made prior to taking office).

Presumably, if prior to taking the bench, a lawyer received a case and referred it to another lawyer without working on the case or supervising the other lawyer the amount of the fee would be trivial. Ronald D. Rotunda & John S. Dzienkowski, *Legal Ethics: The Lawyer's Deskbook on Professional Responsibility* 1707 (2016); *but see Elane v. St. Bernard Hosp.*, 672 N.E.2d 820 (Ill. 1996) (concluding that sitting judge could receive referral fee of 45 percent of attorney's fees for cases she referred to another lawyer a few weeks before assuming bench even though most of the work was done by the lawyer to whom cases were referred; court held that legal responsibility of referring attorney under referral agreement authorized by professional conduct rule, does not involve improper practice of law by referring attorney if he or she later becomes judge). For further discussion of this case, see Ronald D. Rotunda, *Judges as Ambulance Chasers*, Vol. 8, Issue 3 *The Professional Lawyer* 14 (ABA 1997).

A sitting judge may not receive a fee for simply referring a case to a lawyer, without having done any legal work. Allowing a fee for such a referral would be inconsistent with Rule 3.10, which would not permit a judge to receive compensation for actually working on the case. Tex. Adv. Comm. on Jud. Ethics Op. 255 (2000) (judge may not accept fee for referring a family member's "fen-phen" case to a lawyer); *see also* Mich. Comm. on Jud. Ethics Op. JI-45 (1991) (a full-time referee may not accept a referral fee for referring clients to a lawyer). *See also* ABA Formal Ethics Op. 474 (2016) ("A lawyer who refers a matter to another lawyer outside of the first lawyer's firm and divides a fee from the matter with the lawyer to whom the matter has been referred, has undertaken representation of the client.").

RULE 3.11 FINANCIAL, BUSINESS, OR REMUNERATIVE ACTIVITIES

(A) A judge may hold and manage investments of the judge and members of the judge's family.*

(B) A judge shall not serve as an officer, director, manager, general partner, advisor, or employee of any business entity except that a judge may manage or participate in:

(1) a business closely held by the judge or members of the judge's family; or

(2) a business entity primarily engaged in investment of the financial resources of the judge or members of the judge's family.

(C) A judge shall not engage in financial activities permitted under paragraphs (A) and (B) if they will:

(1) interfere with the proper performance of judicial duties;

(2) lead to frequent disqualification of the judge;

(3) involve the judge in frequent transactions or continuing business relationships with lawyers or other persons likely to come before the court on which the judge serves; or

(4) result in violation of other provisions of this Code.

COMMENT

[1] Judges are generally permitted to engage in financial activities, including managing real estate and other investments for themselves or for members of their families. Participation in these activities, like participation in other extrajudicial activities, is subject to the requirements of this Code. For example, it would be improper for a judge to spend so much time on business activities that it interferes with the performance of judicial duties. See Rule 2.1. Similarly, it would be improper for a judge to use his or her official title or appear in judicial robes in business advertising, or to conduct his or her business or financial affairs in such a way that disqualification is frequently required. See Rules 1.3 and 2.11.

[2] As soon as practicable without serious financial detriment, the judge must divest himself or herself of investments and other financial interests that might require frequent disqualification or otherwise violate this Rule.

1990 CODE COMPARISON

Rule 3.11(A) retains the core language of Canon 4D(2), but the lead-in phrase "subject to the requirements of this Code," which was reworded and moved to Rule 3.11(C)(4) to apply to Rules 3.11(A) and (B), and the catchall phrase "other remunerative activity" were deleted. The reference to "real estate" was deemed too specific for inclusion in the black letter text, and moved to Comment [1] as an example of the kinds of investments that a judge might hold or manage. Charles G. Geyh & W. William Hodes, *Reporters' Notes to the Model Code of Judicial Conduct* 76 (2009).

After long debate of the basic policy of Rule 3.11(B), the Commission retained the identical restrictions as were contained in Canon 4D(3) of the 1990 Code. *Id.* at 77–78.

Rule 3.11(C) is a new provision that gathers in one place some of the caveats about extrajudicial financial activities found throughout Canon 4D of the 1990 Code, while adding additional caveats. These caveats are meant to apply as restrictions on otherwise permissible activities. The specific language of Rule 3.11(C)(1) is taken from the fourth paragraph of the Commentary to Canon 4D(1) and the concept is also drawn in part from the second paragraph of the Commentary to Canon 4D(3): otherwise appropriate business activities (falling within the family business exception) would become improper if "participation requires significant time away from judicial duties." Rule 3.11(C)(2) is a paraphrase of Canon 4D(4), which requires a judge to minimize the number of cases in which he or she is disqualified. Rule 3.11(C)(3) is taken from Canon 4D(1)(b) and Rule 3.11(C)(4) is a catchall that makes some other caveats found in Canon 4D unnecessary. For example, the Canon 4D(1)(a) provision, "may reasonably be perceived to exploit the judge's judicial position," was not retained because of the prohibition against abusing the prestige of judicial office already found in Rule 1.3.

Comment [1] is largely new, but incorporates several aspects of the Commentary to Canon 4D, while Comment [2] is derived from the black letter text of Canon 4D(4).

ANNOTATION

MANAGING INVESTMENTS

Rule 3.11(A) permits a judge to hold and manage investments of the judge and the judge's family. *See, e.g.*, Fla. Jud. Ethics Adv. Comm. Op. 95-31 (1995) (judge may invest in new bank); Kan. Jud. Ethics Op. JE-19 (1987) (upon taking the bench, judge need not divest himself of 36-acre strip of land used for recreation purposes); Md. Jud. Ethics Comm. Op. 2013-17 (2013) (judicial appointee may make loan to personal friend). As noted in Comment [1] these activities may include management of real estate and other investments but participation in such activities is subject to other provisions of the Code. For instance, ownership of stock in a party appearing before the judge may be grounds for recusal under Rule 2.11(A)(3) if it is more than "de minimis" or under Rule 2.11(A) regardless of whether it is de minimis, if such ownership creates in reasonable minds an appearance of partiality. *See* Rule 2.11 and accompanying text.

Pursuant to Rule 3.11(A), passive investment, such as ownership of stocks, bonds, mutual funds, and other financial instruments is permitted. Such passive investment, which is common, will likely not raise questions regarding impropriety or interference with judicial duties. Charles Gardner Geyh, James J. Alfini, Steven Lubet, & Jeffrey M. Shaman, *Judicial Conduct and Ethics* § 7.03[1] at 7–6 (5th ed. 2013). However, if a judge's personal involvement in the management of investments becomes more active and time-consuming, it may interfere with the proper performance of judicial duties, in violation of Rule 3.11(C)(1). *In re Troy*, 306 N.E.2d 203 (Mass. 1974) (judge averaged three hours a day at the courthouse and spent remainder of time supervising business project) or increase the risk of impropriety or the appearance of impropriety in violation of Rule 1.2. *See, e.g., Miss. Comm'n on Jud. Performance v. Jenkins*, 725 So. 2d 162 (Miss. 1998) (removal from office warranted where judge's involvement in landfill management company included appearing on corporation's behalf before county board of supervisors, involving himself in lease negotiations between corporation and another party, and presiding over matters involving the company); *Ohio State Bar Assn. v. Reid*, 708 N.E.2d 193 (Ohio 1999) (appearing at zoning commission meetings to speak on behalf of real estate partnerships in which judge owned interest warranted public reprimand).

In addition, some states have statutes prohibiting involvement, including passive investment by public officials, in investments that are undignified or inherently corrupting, such as establishments that hold liquor or gambling licenses. A judge's failure to comply with such statutes could violate the judge's duty to comply with the law pursuant to Rule 1.1. In most disciplinary cases involving such activities, the judge's participation is more culpable than passive investment and often involves actual management of the business or attempts to conceal involvement in the business. Charles Gardner Geyh, James J. Alfini, Steven Lubet, & Jeffrey M. Shaman, *Judicial Conduct and Ethics* § 7.03[4] at 7–11 (5th ed. 2013). *See, e.g., In re Lawrence*, 335 N.W.2d 456 (Mich. 1983) (judge was shareholder in corporation that held liquor license in violation of Michigan statute and purported to sell his interest to his mother even though he maintained an active interest in corporation); *In re Yaccarino*, 502 A.2d 3 (N.J. 1985) (judge owned partnership interest in real estate occupied by bar, held beneficial interest in corporations that held liquor licenses and failed to disclose interest in these enterprises).

Serving as Officer, Director, Manager, General Partner, or Employee of a Business Entity

Rule 3.11(B) prohibits a judge from serving as an officer, director, manager, general partner, advisor, or employee of "any business entity" other than a closely held family business or a business "primarily engaged in investment of the financial resources of the judge or a member of the judge's family." *See, e.g.*, *In re Fleischman*, 933 P.2d 563 (Ariz. 1997) (judge violated provision by giving business advice to person or entity other than one closely held by the judge or members of the judge's family, even though advice was limited to one contract); *In re Johnson*, 683 So. 2d 1196 (La. 1996) (judge's management of business that provided telephone service to inmates under contract with sheriff after he became a judge warranted removal from office); *In re Imbriani*, 652 A.2d 1222 (N.J. 1995) (judge violated Canon by managing corporation's affairs); *In re Belk*, 691 S.E.2d 685 (N.C. 2010) (judge removed from office and disqualified from holding future office after refusing to resign from corporate board, from which judge earned more than $140,000 annually, despite advice from Judicial Standards Commission and Supreme Court denied judge's request to amend prohibition); Fla. Jud. Ethics Adv. Comm. Op. 97-35 (1997) (judge may not serve as part-time officer of corporation whose shares are predominantly owned by a non-family member); Mass. Comm. on Jud. Ethics Adv. Op. 95-2 (1995) (judge may not serve as officer of investment partnership that trades in publicly listed stock); Nev. Stand. Comm. on Jud. Ethics and Election Prac., JE08-001 (2008) (judge may not serve on an advisory board related to the construction of a commercial for-profit enterprise); Okla. Jud. Ethics Op. 2004-4 (2004) (upon taking bench judge must resign from board of directors for federal credit union); Pa. Jud. Ethics Comm. Informal Op. 8/28/00 (2000) (judge who is shareholder of bank may not serve as director on bank's board even though he recuses himself whenever bank is party).

Unlike Canon 4D(3), Rule 3.11(B)'s prohibition applies only to for-profit businesses, presumably permitting a judge to be actively involved in a nonprofit organizations so long as not prohibited by another provision of the code. Charles Gardner Geyh, James J. Alfini, Steven Lubet, & Jeffrey M. Shaman, *Judicial Conduct and Ethics* § 7.05 at 7–17 (5th ed. 2013).

The Commentary to the "Time for Compliance" provision of the Code (Application, Section VI) provides that if at the time of selection to the judiciary a new judge is engaged in a business activity he or she may continue in that activity for a reasonable period, but in no event, longer than a year. *See, e.g.*, *In re Disc. Proceedings Against Anderson*, 981 P.2d 426 (1999) (judge violated Canon by continuing to serve as president of three corporations for ten months after being sworn in as judge).

Family Business Exception

Under Rule 3.11(B), a judge may manage or participate in a closely held family business or a business entity primarily engaged in investment of the financial resources of the judge or members of the judge's family so long as the business entity does not (1) interfere with the proper performance of judicial duties, (2) lead to frequent disqualification of the judge, (3) involve the judge in frequent transactions or continuing relationships with people like to come before the court on which the judge serves, or (4) result in violation of other Code provisions. *See, e.g.*, Ariz. Jud. Ethics Adv. Comm. Op. 97-4 (1997) (judge may not be director or officer of corporation where only other shareholder is not family member); Okla. Jud. Ethics Op. 2003-4 (2003) (judge may not serve on board of directors of closely held corporation in which judge's family merely owns minority interest). The Code does not require that the family business predate the judgeship and nothing in the Code prevents a judge from initiating a business after taking the bench. Charles Gardner Geyh, James J. Alfini, Steven Lubet, & Jeffrey M. Shaman, *Judicial Conduct and Ethics* § 7.08[2] at 7–25 (5th ed. 2013).

When revising the Code, the Commission discussed the substantive point of Rule 3.11(B), which is to prohibit judges from engaging in off-bench remunerative activity, except in the case of closely held family businesses and investment of the judge's resources or those of the judge's family. This family business exception has been criticized as inconsistent with the rationale for the basic prohibition, that is avoiding the abuse of the prestige of the office and preventing a judge from taking too much time away from judicial activities. Two alternatives were considered, but not adopted. The first was to allow judges to engage in remunerative extrajudicial activities, as long as they did not interfere with the performance of judicial duties, lead to frequent disqualification, or otherwise violate the prohibitions found in Rule 3.11(C). The other was to eliminate the family business exception and require all judges to divest themselves of any interests in the family business when ascending the bench. The Commission elected to maintain the status quo of the 1990 Code. Charles G. Geyh & W. William Hodes, *Reporters' Notes to the Model Code of Judicial Conduct* 77–78 (2009).

The apparent purpose of the family business exception "is to ease judges' financial burdens." Charles Gardner Geyh, James J. Alfini, Steven Lubet, & Jeffrey M. Shaman, *Judicial Conduct and Ethics* § 7.08[2] at 7–26 (5th ed. 2013). *See also* Steven Lubet, *Regulation of Judges' Businesses and Financial Activities*, 37 Emory L.J. 34 (1988) ("drafters of the Code considered the family business exception to be an 'equitable and rational point at which to draw the line' between those business ventures that could be continued and those that had to be terminated"). However, some commentators argue that if the primary purpose of limiting judges' business activities is to avoid exploitation of the office, there is no real difference between a family business and any other kind of business. Charles Gardner Geyh, James J. Alfini, Steven Lubet, & Jeffrey M. Shaman, *Judicial Conduct and Ethics* § 7.08[2] at 7–26 (5th ed. 2013). ("If active involvement in business is subtly or apparently corrosive, which is otherwise the clear judgment of the Code, then it would seem that the principle ought to apply to closely held family business, not to mention sole proprietorships.") These commentators have also asserted that because of this "inescapable tension" between the no business rule and the broad family business exception, relatively few jurisdictions have adopted the family business exception. Charles Gardner Geyh, James J. Alfini, Steven Lubet, & Jeffrey M. Shaman, *Judicial Conduct and Ethics* § 7.08[2] at 7–26 (5th ed. 2013).

PROHIBITED FINANCIAL ACTIVITIES

Rule 3.11(C) prohibits judges from participating in four types of financial activities that would otherwise be permissible under subsections (A) and (B). First, it prohibits judges from financial activities that will "interfere with the proper performance of judicial duties." Second, a judge may not engage in financial activities that would lead to frequent disqualification of the judge. Third, the Rule prohibits financial activities that would involve the judge in frequent transactions or continuing business relationships with "lawyers or other persons likely to come before the court on which the judge serves." *See, e.g., In re Means*, 452 S.E.2d 696 (W. Va. 1994) (judge's presiding over marital dissolution case involving husband with whom judge shared financial interest in corporation violated predecessor to Rule 3.11(C)(3)); Ill. Jud. Ethics Comm. Op. 07-02 (2007) (judge who is receiving pension benefits from a former law firm is usually disqualified from presiding over cases where a party is represented by the firm); Pa. Jud. Ethics Comm. Informal Op. 3/22b/01 (2001) (judge may not engage in business of introducing a seller to state and local officials, where judge would receive commission for each sale); Tex. Adv. Comm. on Jud. Ethics Op. 228 (1998) (justice of the peace may not serve as member of board of directors of water supply corporation); *see generally* Steven Lubet, *Regulation of Judges' Business and Financial Activities*, 37 Emory L.J. 1 (1988). Lastly, a judge may not engage in financial activities that will result in violation of other Code provisions.

Interfering with Proper Performance of Judicial Duties

Rule 3.11(C)(1) prohibits a judge from engaging in financial activities that will interfere with the proper performance of judicial duties. For example, as noted in the Comment to the Rule, "it would be improper for a judge to spend so much time on business activities that it interferes with the performance of judicial duties. See Rule 2.1." Model Code of Judicial Conduct Rule 3.11 cmt. [1]. *See, e.g., In re Troy*, 306 N.E.2d 203 (Mass. 1974) (judge averaged three hours a day at the courthouse and spent remainder of time supervising business project); *In re Daley*, 82-CC-1 (Ill. Cts. Comm'n 1983) (judge submitted false reports stating that he was performing judicial duties during the time he was actually employed as a watchman on a construction project); *but see* S.C. Adv. Comm. on Stands. of Jud. Conduct Op. 13-2005 (2005) (magistrate judge may work part-time at a retail pharmacy so long as the part-time employment does not require significant time away from judicial duties).

Managing Financial Activities to Minimize Disqualification

Rule 3.11(C)(2) requires that a judge not engage in financial activities that would lead to frequent disqualification. *See, e.g., In re Yandell*, 772 P.2d 807 (Kan. 1989) (by taking out loans at six different financial institutions within the district, judge failed to manage financial interests to minimize number of cases in which he might be disqualified); Mich. Comm. on Jud. Ethics Op. JI-119 (1998) (judge may ethically participate in an "investment club" that has no lawyer members or that has lawyer members who *may* appear before judge; if lawyer members are *likely* to frequently come before judge, the judge should not seek membership or should terminate membership in club); Wash. Ethics Adv. Comm. Op. 93-4 (1993) (judge may not own real estate jointly with lawyer who regularly appears in judge's court because judge would have to be disqualified from all of lawyer's cases); *but see* Pa. Jud. Ethics Comm. Informal Op. 5/19/00 (2000) (judge may continue to own building with former law partner even though former partner has case that could be appealed to judge's court and a case judge previously worked on, where judge is member of judicial district with few judges).

A judge must divest himself or herself of investments and other financial interests that might require frequent disqualification as soon as the judge can do so without "serious financial detriment." Model Code of Judicial Conduct Rule 3.11 cmt. [2].

Business Dealings with Lawyers or Others Likely to Come before the Court

Rule 3.11(C)(3) requires judges to avoid financial activities that involve the judge in frequent transactions or continuing business relationships with lawyers and others who are likely to come before the judge or the court on which the judge serves. *See, e.g., In re Garcia* (Cal. Comm'n on Jud. Performance 2015) (judge resigned as part of stipulation with Commission and censured and barred from seeking or holding judicial office, violated rule when for four years after assuming the bench he accepted payments from former law firm based on contract to provide county with counsel secured while judge was lawyer at the firm); *In re McInnis*, 769 So. 2d 1186 (La. 2000) (justice of the peace may not serve as accountant for parish sheriff's office either as full-time employee or independent contractor); *In re Johnson*, 683 So. 2d 1196 (La. 1996) (judge's continuation and management of business that provided telephone service to inmates under contract with sheriff warranted removal from office);

In re Fuchsberg, 426 N.Y.S.2d 639 (N.Y. 1978) (judge's exchange of short-term government notes for long-term government bonds created a conflict since the judge knew cases challenging the legality of the bonds would soon come before the court on which he sat); *In re McKenzie* (Tenn. Ct. of the Judiciary 2010) (judge reprimanded for allowing lawyer who rented office space at building owned by judge to appear before judge); *cf.* N.M. Adv. Comm. on Code of Jud. Conduct Op. 06-06 (2006) (hearing officer should not enter into real estate contract for sale of home to attorney who appears in front of him where attorney would require owner financing because that would entail an ongoing financial relationship but may sell home to attorney with outside financing because that would be a single transaction); S.C. Adv. Comm. on Stands. of Jud. Conduct, Op. 9-2001 (2001) (a master-in-equity may not remain employed as title insurance agent because he or she handles title problems); Tex. Adv. Comm. on Jud. Ethics Op. 227 (1999) (judge must divest himself of interest in only title company in the county); Tex. Adv. Comm. on Jud. Ethics Op. 228 (1998) (justice of the peace may not serve on board of directors of water supply corporation whose customers are located in justice's district); Utah Informal Op. 05-1 (2005) (judge may not serve as president of a company that markets technology to correctional facilities); *but see* Mich. Comm. on Jud. Ethics Op. JI-119 (1998) (judge may participate in investment club that has lawyers who *may* appear before judge; but if members are likely to *frequently* come before judge, judge should not seek membership or should resign); S.C. Adv. Comm. on Stands. of Jud. Conduct, Op. 05-2008 (2008) (family court judge may serve on advisory board of bank since service will not interfere with judge's performance of his duties and it is unlikely that the bank would frequently appear before the judge); *see generally* Randall T. Shepard, *Judicial Professionalism and the Relations between Judges and Lawyers*, 14 Notre Dame J.L. Ethics & Pub. Pol'y 223 (2000) (discussing cases reprimanding judges for business relationships with lawyers).

Loans from Lawyers and Court Employees

The majority of cases on judges' acceptance of loans arise under the language of Rule 3.13, regarding judges' acceptance of gifts, loans, bequests, etc., but such conduct may also violate Rule 3.11(C)(3), when the judge accepts a loan from a person likely to come before the court on which the judge serves. *See, e.g., In re Drury*, 602 N.E.2d 1000 (Ind. 1992) (judge committed willful misconduct by soliciting, accepting and failing to report a $2,000 loan from lawyer practicing in his court; and once judge accepted loan, he should have disqualified himself from all cases involving lawyer's law firm); *Disc. Counsel v. Cox*, 770 N.E.2d 1007 (Ohio 2002) (judge suspended for receiving loans from lawyers who regularly practiced before him).

Renting or Leasing to or from Lawyers or Others Who Are Likely to Appear before Judge

In general, judges should neither rent property to nor lease property from a lawyer or someone else who regularly appears in the judge's court, because a landlord-tenant relationship is a "continuing business relationship" and would reflect adversely on the judge's impartiality. *See* Ala. Jud. Inquiry Comm'n Adv. Op. 97-660 (1997). Ariz. Jud. Ethics Adv. Comm. Op. 95-12 (1995) (judge may not rent office space to attorneys who regularly appear before the judge); S.C. Adv. Comm. on Stands. of Jud. Conduct, Op. 6-2006 (2006) (judge should not rent out a residence to a member of the Highway Patrol); Wisc. Jud. Conduct Adv. Comm. Op. 02-2 (2003) (newly elected judge may rent office to lawyer as part of law practice sale but for no more than a year); W. Va. Jud. Investigation Comm'n Adv. Op. 1/22/91 (1991) (judge who owns property rented to lawyers should sell property, refer cases of the tenant attorneys to other judges, or rent only to non-attorneys); Fla. Jud. Ethics Adv. Comm. Op. 97-33 (1997) (renting property to lawyers who appear before judge is prohibited even under a blind trust).

A judge may also need to avoid renting property from a lawyer whose partner appears in the judge's court, even though the lawyer does not. *See* W. Va. Jud. Investigation Comm'n Adv. Op. 6/22/93 (1993) (judge should not rent a residence from lawyer whose firm partner appears frequently in judge's court). However, a judge may be permitted to hear a case in which a party is represented by a lawyer who subleases space from the judge's lessee. *See, e.g.*, Nev. Stand. Comm. on Jud. Ethics Op. JE13-002 (2013) (judge's continued interest in a building leased to the state and housing the public defender would not lead to frequent disqualifications or create a continuing business interest with lawyers); Va. Jud. Ethics Adv. Comm. Op. 01-07 (2001) (where lawyer appearing in judge's court subleases from judge's former partner in building co-owned by judge, there are not transactions or on-going business between judge and sub lessee); Wisc. Jud. Conduct Adv. Comm. Op. 97-4 (1997) (judge not disqualified from cases involving lawyer who subleases office space from judge's lessee unless the judge knows that his financial interests could be substantially affected by outcome of proceeding or there are other additional circumstances causing judge's impartiality to be questioned); *but see* Kan. Jud. Ethics Op. JE 171 (2011) (disqualification provisions apply to judge who holds property in trust with tenants who sublease to lawyers appearing before judge).

Some jurisdictions permit landlord-tenant relationships between judges and lawyers, advising that such a relationship either does not exploit the judicial office or is not a financial dealing that involves a judge in frequent transactions with lawyers. Ky. Jud. Ethics Op. JE-7 (1980) (the routine, periodic payment of rent in the typical landlord-tenant relationship is generally not a financial dealing that involves judge in frequent transactions with lawyers); Wis. Jud. Conduct Adv. Comm. Op. 97-4 (1997) (judge may lease office space to lawyer as part of agreement between judge and lawyer for purchase of judge's law practice, but not for more than one year after taking office).

In other jurisdictions, a judge may lease property to or from a lawyer, provided that if the lawyer appears in the judge's courtroom, the judge discloses the landlord-tenant relationship and advises opposing counsel that the judge will recuse himself from the case unless recusal is waived. Md. Jud. Ethics Op. 2007-10 (2007) (when judge leases office space to lawyer who appears in judge's courtroom, judge must disclose nature of relationship so that parties have chance to object or waive their objections; if the parties do not waive disqualification, judge should recuse himself or herself unless there are compelling circumstances to the contrary); Okla. Jud. Ethics Op. 2000-1, 10 P.3d 893 (2000) (judge may lease office to attorney and must recuse upon request); Tex. Adv. Comm. on Jud. Ethics Op. 239 (1999) (judge may co-own and/or co-sign with her sister an office building leased to attorneys and may recuse when attorney-tenants appear); Wash. Ethics Adv. Comm. Op. 93-8 (1993) (landlord-tenant relationship alone does not reflect adversely on judge's impartiality, interfere with performance of judicial duties, exploit judicial position, or involve judge in frequent transactions with those coming before him; in appropriate circumstances disclosure of the landlord-tenant relationship should be made).

Violating Other Provisions of the Code

Rule 3.11(C)(4) is a catchall provision, which prohibits judges from engaging in financial transactions that are permitted under subsections (A) and (B) of the Rule, if they will violate other provisions of the Code. For instance, a judge may be prohibited from engaging in financial activities that would abuse the prestige of judicial office in violation of Rule 1.3.

Financial Activities That Abuse the Prestige of Judicial Office

Judges may not use their judicial office or the prestige of their office for financial gain. Exploitation of the office can take a variety of forms. For instance, a judge clearly exploits the office by conducting personal business out of his or her chambers. *See In re Davis*, 946 P.2d 1033 (Nev. 1997) (judge violated Code by storing antiques in courthouse, selling antiques to persons with whom he came in contact at the courthouse, and using court employees to move antiques); *see also In re Brown*, 512 S.E.2d 114 (S.C. 1999) (judge reprimanded for performing marriages for a fee and retaining the fees collected for personal use); Colo. Jud. Ethics Adv. Bd. Op. 2007-05 (2007) (judge may not advertise his or her availability to perform marriages as to do so would exploit the judicial office and give the appearance that the judge is using his or her position for personal benefit).

The mere nature of a judge's business may indicate exploitation of the judicial position. For example, a judge's operation of a loan broker business would reasonably justify suspicion that he is using the power or prestige of office to persuade or coerce others to patronize or contribute to the success of a private business venture. *Steinberg v. State Comm'n on Jud. Conduct*, 409 N.E.2d 1378 (N.Y. 1980). As noted previously, a judge should also not accept loans from court employees and others who work with the judge. *In re Doan*, 902 P.2d 272 (Cal. 1995) (judge violated Canon by obtaining loans from court clerk and police officer); *In re Davis*, 946 P.2d 1033 (Nev. 1997) (judge used his position to secure loans from court employees and refused to repay the loans when requested). A judge may also exploit his or her office by using court funds for his or her own personal use. *See, e.g., In re Douglas*, 382 A.2d 215 (Vt. 1977) (judge exploited his office when he retained for his own personal use excess money the court obtained when a newspaper discounted the court's probate notice fees).

Pursuant to Rules 3.1 and 3.12, judges may teach or lecture about the law and the legal system and may accept compensation for doing so. Judges may also be compensated for writing books and other publications on legal or non-legal subjects. However, financial benefits over and above the judicial salary, from the publication and sale of a book about the judge's own court, or from participation in a seminar on the same topic, may constitute exploiting the judicial position for financial gain. *See, e.g.*, U.S. Comm. on Codes of Conduct, Adv. Op. No. 87 (1992, revised 1998) (it is inappropriate for a judge to sell at CLE programs his or her expertise on the idiosyncrasies of practice before that particular court; when subject matter is that focused, judge may participate only if no compensation is accepted, and only if the sponsoring organization is a not-for-profit entity).

Pursuant to Rule 3.11(D)(4), in conjunction with Rule 1.3, judges should also discourage family members from engaging in business dealings that would reasonably appear to exploit the judge's judicial position. *See, e.g.*, W. Va. Jud. Investigation Comm'n Adv. Op. 6/30/97 (1997) (judge's wife is lawyer's landlord; opinion advised that judge should discourage wife from becoming involved in situations in which the judge is prohibited from becoming involved). The prohibition on such activities is necessary to avoid creating the appearance of exploitation of the office or favoritism and to reduce the potential for disqualification. *See, e.g., In re Wilkes*, 403 So. 2d 35 (La. 1981) (justice of the peace's collection of illegal fees from parties on whose behalf he had collected amounts due on open accounts and "N.S.F." checks reflected adversely on impartiality); *In re Rainaldi*, 727 P.2d 70 (N.M. 1986) (judge's ownership of "driving while intoxicated school" created appearance of impropriety and tended to reflect adversely on his impartiality; judge obtained direct financial gain from sentencing people to attend school).

Referring Cases to Lawyers

A judge may not refer or assign a case to a lawyer with whom the judge has financial ties. *See, e.g., In re Lawrence*, 335 N.W.2d 456 (Mich. 1983) (judge violated Canon by assigning indigent criminal cases to lawyers who were formerly associated with judge and who were paying judge for his interest in firm over a period of ten years); Ark. Jud. Ethics Adv. Comm. Op. 96-09 (1996) (once attorney becomes judge, he or she should never make a referral to any other attorneys for compensation). Such referrals would be seen as inappropriate by the general public and would create the strong likelihood that the judge's position would be exploited. Tex. Adv. Comm. on Jud. Ethics Op. 255 (2000) ("judges receiving money for referring business would not be seen as appropriate by the general public"). Similarly, a compensation arrangement that is contingent upon the acquiring firm's future success in attracting and retaining work from the former clients of a newly elected judge runs afoul of Code provision requiring judges not to engage in financial and business dealings that involve the judge in frequent transactions or continuing business relationships with lawyers or other persons likely to come before the court on which the judge serves. N.Y. Comm. on Professional Ethics Op. 699 (1998). See Rule 3.10 and accompanying text for a discussion of fees for cases judge worked on as lawyer and referred out after taking the bench.

Financial Activities That Cast Doubt on Impartiality

Rule 3.1(C) requires a judge to refrain from extrajudicial activities that would appear to a reasonable person to undermine the judge's independence, integrity, or impartiality. Judges may violate this provision, and Rule 3.11(C)(4), if they engage in financial and business dealings that reflect or appear to reflect bias or prejudice. For instance, if a judge enters into business deals with litigants who are or were recently before the judge, the judge's impartiality will be questioned. *Adams v. Comm'n on Jud. Performance*, 882 P.2d 358 (Cal. 1994) (bargain received by judge on a car purchased from car dealer whose case had been before judge, but was now on appeal, cast doubt on judge's capacity to act impartially); *In re Yandell*, 772 P.2d 807 (Kan. 1989) (judge's impartiality questioned in legal proceedings involving local financial institutions when judge had numerous insufficient funds checks and loan defaults with those institutions); *In re Yaccarino*, 502 A.2d 3 (N.J. 1985) (judge's attempt to purchase real estate that was an asset in a corporation dissolution action before the judge reflected adversely on judge's impartiality).

RULE 3.12 COMPENSATION FOR EXTRAJUDICIAL ACTIVITIES

A judge may accept reasonable compensation for extrajudicial activities permitted by this Code or other law* unless such acceptance would appear to a reasonable person to undermine the judge's independence,* integrity,* or impartiality.*

COMMENT

[1] A judge is permitted to accept honoraria, stipends, fees, wages, salaries, royalties, or other compensation for speaking, teaching, writing, and other extrajudicial activities, provided the compensation is reasonable and commensurate with the task performed. The judge should be mindful, however, that judicial duties must take precedence over other activities. See Rule 2.1.

[2] Compensation derived from extrajudicial activities may be subject to public reporting. See Rule 3.15.

1990 CODE COMPARISON

Rule 3.12 is based on Canon 4H(1), but only as it relates to compensation, not reimbursement of expenses, associated with extrajudicial activities or reporting. Reimbursement is now governed by Rule 3.14 while public reporting of compensation received for extrajudicial activities, as well as all other reporting requirements, is governed by Rule 3.15. Charles G. Geyh & W. William Hodes, *Reporters' Notes to the Model Code of Judicial Conduct* 78 (2009).

The language measuring the reasonableness of compensation by what a nonjudge would receive was deleted as unsound: if a judge were to be compensated for teaching a law school course on judicial ethics, or giving a lecture on evidentiary rulings, for example, the judge's services would in fact likely be more valuable than those of a nonjudge. Accordingly, the language in Canon 4H(1) about appearances was replaced by the language used throughout Canon 3 of the revised Code: "would appear to a reasonable person to undermine the judge's independence, integrity, or impartiality." *Id.* at 78–79.

Comment [1] is based on the text of Canon 4H(1)(a) and some of aspect of the Commentary to Canon 4H, but was substantially revised. Comment [2] is new and serves a cross-reference to the public reporting provisions in Rule 3.15.

ANNOTATION

Rule 3.12 provides that a judge may accept reasonable compensation for extrajudicial activities permitted by the Code or other law unless it would appear to a reasonable person to undermine the judge's independence, integrity, or impartiality. *See, e.g.*, Ariz. Jud. Ethics Adv. Comm. Op. 99-04 (1999) (judge may receive compensation for officiating high school sporting events);

Neb. Jud. Ethics Adv. Comm. Op. 04-2 (2004) (judge may retain gift or honorarium for performance of wedding ceremony if (1) the judge does not solicit his or her services in regard to performing the ceremony, (2) the ceremony is conducted outside normal court hours and without the use of publicly funded court resources, and (3) the compensation received by the judge is reasonable to the services rendered); Wash. Ethics Adv. Comm. Op. 93-28 (1993) (judge may serve as member of state bar association's Board of Bar Examiners and receive a small stipend); Nev. Stand. Comm. on Jud. Ethics and Election Practices Op. JE10-002 (2010) (judge may accept compensation for participation in education program sponsored by nonprofit organization); *but see* Okla. Jud. Ethics Op. 2004-3 (2004) (judge may not charge reasonable fee for performing wedding after court hours outside of courthouse because retention of such payment is exploitation of judicial office); *In re Ryan* (Wash. Comm'n on Jud. Conduct 2005) (judge may not receive compensation for weddings performed during regular court hours because judge should not receive compensation for private extrajudicial conduct when judge is on duty and being paid with public funds). Where the judge's extrajudicial activities violate the Code of Judicial Conduct, it is axiomatic that accepting compensation for such activities violates the Code, regardless of the amount of compensation. *In re Fleischman*, 933 P.2d 563 (Ariz. 1997) (judge publicly censured for representing corporation during contract renewal negotiations, serving as advisor to business entity, and receiving compensation and reimbursement for unauthorized extrajudicial activities). Compensation derived from extrajudicial activities may be subject to the reporting requirements of Rule 3.15. Model Code of Judicial Conduct Rule 3.12 cmt. [2]. See Rule 3.15 and accompanying text for discussion of requirements for reporting compensation for extrajudicial activities.

The source of the payment to the judge may raise a question of undue influence or of the judge's willingness and ability to be impartial. *See, e.g., In re Fleischman*, 933 P.2d 563 (Ariz. 1997) (judge violated predecessor to Rule 3.12 where income flowing directly to judge and his estate as result of business contract he negotiated while holding judicial office created appearance that performance of his judicial duties may have been influenced or compromised and gave obvious appearance of judicial impropriety).

Honoraria, Stipends, Fees, and Other Compensation

Judges frequently receive requests to speak at gatherings of legal, professional and other types of organizations. As noted in the Commentary, judges may accept honoraria for such engagements, so long as the compensation is reasonable and commensurate with the task performed. Model Code of Judicial Conduct Rule 3.12 cmt. [1]. *See, e.g.*, Ala. Jud. Inquiry Comm'n Adv. Op. 90-404 (1990) (judge may receive honorarium for delivering keynote address at medical society's annual banquet if compensation is not more that a person who is not a judge would receive); Ill. Jud. Ethics Comm. 96-26 (1996) (judge may accept an honorarium instead of compensation in pursuing his avocation of stage acting); N.Y. Adv. Comm. on Jud. Ethics 98-36 (1998) (judge may accept honorarium from American Pediatric Association for participating in seminar on law); Okla. Jud. Ethics Op. 2001-02 (2001) 73 P.3d 267 (judge may receive fee for delivering speech, regardless of whether the paying group is an organization pertaining to the law, the judiciary, or the government); *see generally* Note, *The Supreme Court's Indecent Proposal: Repealing the Honoraria Prohibition of the Ethics in Government Act of 1978*, 87 Cornell L. Rev. 1475 (2002).

As further noted in the Commentary, judges should be mindful that judicial duties take precedence over other activities. Model Code of Judicial Conduct Rule 3.12 cmt. [1]. Therefore, judges should not spend significant time away from their judicial duties to meet speaking or writing commitments for compensation. Judges must also ensure that the arrangement for reimbursement does not create a conflict of interest or the appearance that they are trading on their judicial position for personal advantage. *See, e.g.*, Ohio Bd. of Commissioners on Grievances and Disc., Op. 2006-3 (2006) (judge may teach six-hour course on adult protective services but may not accept compensation because compensation to a judge by another branch of government does not uphold the integrity, independence, and impartiality of the judiciary).

RULE 3.13 ACCEPTANCE AND REPORTING OF GIFTS, LOANS, BEQUESTS, BENEFITS, OR OTHER THINGS OF VALUE

(A) A judge shall not accept any gifts, loans, bequests, benefits, or other things of value, if acceptance is prohibited by law* or would appear to a reasonable person to undermine the judge's independence,* integrity,* or impartiality.*

(B) Unless otherwise prohibited by law, or by paragraph (A), a judge may accept the following without publicly reporting such acceptance:

(1) items with little intrinsic value, such as plaques, certificates, trophies, and greeting cards;

(2) gifts, loans, bequests, benefits, or other things of value from friends, relatives, or other persons, including lawyers, whose appearance or interest in a proceeding pending* or impending* before the judge would in any event require disqualification of the judge under Rule 2.11;

(3) ordinary social hospitality;

(4) commercial or financial opportunities and benefits, including special pricing and discounts, and loans from lending institutions in their regular course of business, if the same opportunities and benefits or loans are made available on the same terms to similarly situated persons who are not judges;

(5) rewards and prizes given to competitors or participants in random drawings, contests, or other events that are open to persons who are not judges;

(6) scholarships, fellowships, and similar benefits or awards, if they are available to similarly situated persons who are not judges, based upon the same terms and criteria;

(7) books, magazines, journals, audiovisual materials, and other resource materials supplied by publishers on a complimentary basis for official use; or

(8) gifts, awards, or benefits associated with the business, profession, or other separate activity of a spouse, a domestic partner,* or other family member of a judge residing in the judge's household,* but that incidentally benefit the judge.

(C) Unless otherwise prohibited by law or by paragraph (A), a judge may accept the following items, and must report such acceptance to the extent required by Rule 3.15:

(1) gifts incident to a public testimonial;

(2) invitations to the judge and the judge's spouse, domestic partner, or guest to attend without charge:

(a) an event associated with a bar-related function or other activity relating to the law, the legal system, or the administration of justice; or

(b) an event associated with any of the judge's educational, religious, charitable, fraternal or civic activities permitted by this Code, if the same invitation is offered to nonjudges who are engaged in similar ways in the activity as is the judge; and

(3) gifts, loans, bequests, benefits, or other things of value, if the source is a party or other person, including a lawyer, who has come or is likely to come before the judge, or whose interests have come or are likely to come before the judge.

COMMENT

[1] Whenever a judge accepts a gift or other thing of value without paying fair market value, there is a risk that the benefit might be viewed as intended to influence the judge's decision in a case. Rule 3.13 imposes restrictions upon the acceptance of such benefits, according to the magnitude of the risk. Paragraph (B) identifies circumstances in which the risk that the acceptance would appear to undermine the judge's independence, integrity, or impartiality is low, and explicitly provides that such items need not be publicly reported. As the value of the benefit or the likelihood that the source of the benefit will appear before the judge increases, the judge is either prohibited under paragraph (A) from accepting the gift, or required under paragraph (C) to publicly report it.

[2] Gift-giving between friends and relatives is a common occurrence, and ordinarily does not create an appearance of impropriety or cause reasonable persons to believe that the judge's independence, integrity, or impartiality has been compromised. In addition, when the appearance of friends or relatives in a case would require the judge's disqualification under Rule 2.11, there would be no opportunity for a gift to influence the judge's decision making. Paragraph (B)(2) places no restrictions upon the ability of a judge to accept gifts or other things of value from friends or relatives under these circumstances, and does not require public reporting.

[3] Businesses and financial institutions frequently make available special pricing, discounts, and other benefits, either in connection with a temporary promotion or for preferred customers, based upon longevity of the relationship, volume of business transacted, and other factors. A judge may freely accept such benefits if they are available to the general public, or if the judge qualifies for the special price or discount according to the same criteria as are applied to persons who are not judges. As an example, loans provided at generally prevailing interest rates are not gifts, but a judge could not accept a loan from a financial institution at below-market interest rates unless the same rate was being made available to the general public for a certain period of time or only to borrowers with specified qualifications that the judge also possesses.

[4] Rule 3.13 applies only to acceptance of gifts or other things of value by a judge. Nonetheless, if a gift or other benefit is given to the judge's spouse, domestic partner, or member of the judge's family residing in the judge's household, it may be viewed as an attempt to evade Rule 3.13 and influence the judge indirectly. Where the gift or benefit is being made primarily to such other persons, and the judge is merely an incidental beneficiary, this concern is reduced. A judge should, however, remind family and household members of the restrictions imposed upon judges, and urge them to take these restrictions into account when making decisions about accepting such gifts or benefits.

[5] Rule 3.13 does not apply to contributions to a judge's campaign for judicial office. Such contributions are governed by other Rules of this Code, including Rules 4.3 and 4.4.

1990 CODE COMPARISON

Rule 3.13 is based on Canon 4D(5), its subsections and related Commentary. Rule 3.13(A) expanded the universe of coverage to include "other things of value" and establishes a different organization and mode of analysis. Canon 4D(5) established a general prohibition against a judge accepting gifts or loans or similar items from anyone, then proceeded to make exceptions in subsections (a) through (h). Rule 3.13(A) also begins with a list of gifts and things of value that judges are prohibited from accepting. The subsequent provisions in Rule 3.13 permit acceptance of some items, sometimes accompanied by public reporting and sometimes not, but in each instance permission is granted only after it has been determined that acceptance has not already been barred by paragraph (A). This reflects the Commission's tiered approach to this subject matter. Paragraph (A) establishes a first tier of situations in which acceptance is not permitted at all; paragraph (B) deals with acceptance of items that are not problematic and do not require the transparency of public reporting; and paragraph (C) deals with items that do not warrant being banned, but must be reported to maintain the public's confidence in the judiciary. The dividing line between gifts and other items that cannot be accepted at all and those that may be accepted subject to the requirement of public reporting is when acceptance "would appear to a reasonable person to undermine the judge's independence, integrity, or impartiality." Charles G. Geyh & W. William Hodes, *Reporters' Notes to the Model Code of Judicial Conduct* 82–85 (2009).

Comments [1] through [3] are new to the Code. Comment [1] explains the three-tiered approach and its rationale. Comment [2] explains the classification in Rule 3.13 of gifts and other things of value given to a judge and provides the rationale for distinguishing between different types of gifts from this category of donor. Comment [3] provides the rationale for and gives examples of the principle that acceptance of benefits and other things of value that are generally available to nonjudges on the same basis as they are available to judges causes no ethical concerns. Accordingly, those items may be accepted, without public reporting. Comment [4] points out that while a code of judicial ethics cannot bind family members, and others, close to the judge, it is prudent for the judge to urge such individuals not to put the judge in a difficult position by accepting gifts and benefits that the judge could not. Comment [4] also explains the rationale for new Rule 3.13(B)(8), which does not require a judge to report gifts, awards, or benefits associated with a gift or benefit given to a family member because of the family member's business or other activities that benefits the judge incidentally. *Id.* Comment [5] paraphrases the first paragraph of the Commentary to Canon 4D(5).

ANNOTATION
INTRODUCTION

When a judge accepts a gift or other thing of value without paying fair market value, there is a risk that the benefit might be viewed as intended to influence the judge's decision in a case. Rule 3.13 imposes restrictions on a judge's acceptance of such benefits, according to the magnitude of risk. Paragraph (B) identifies circumstances in which the risk that a judge's acceptance would appear to undermine the judge's independence, integrity, or impartiality is low, and explicitly provides that such items need not be publicly reported. As the value of the benefit or the likelihood that the source of the benefit will appear before the judge increases, the judge is either prohibited under paragraph (A) from accepting the gift, or required under paragraph (C) to publicly report it. Model Code of Judicial Conduct Rule 3.13 cmt. [1].

GIFTS, BEQUESTS, FAVORS, LOANS, AND OTHER THINGS OF VALUE

Rule 3.13(A) prohibits a judge from accepting "any gifts, loans, bequests, benefits, or other things of value, if acceptance is prohibited by law or would appear to a reasonable person to undermine the judge's independence, integrity, or impartiality." The rationale for this general prohibition is to avoid the appearance of impropriety and possible actual impropriety created by a judge's acceptance of gifts, bequests, favors, or loans. E. Wayne Thode, *Reporter's Notes to Code of Judicial Conduct* 84 (1973). *See, e.g., In re Bonin*, 378 N.E. 2d 669 (Mass. 1978) (judge's receipt of leased car as a gift from former client created the appearance of impropriety even though former client had no cases pending in judge's court where judge subsequently appointed a key official in client's corporation to position in judge's office at higher than usual salary); *but see* S.C. Adv. Comm. on Stands. of Jud. Conduct Op. 04-2006 (2006) (family court judge may accept bequest from personal friend; since donor is deceased, neither she nor her estate will appear before the judge in the family court).

Gifts or favors from a party or lawyer who is appearing or has appeared in the judge's court are particularly troubling, and are likely to violate Rule 3.13(A), as well as the more general proscriptions against conduct that conveys the impression that a person or organization is in a position to influence the judge (Rule 2.4(C)) or erodes public confidence in the integrity or impartiality of the judiciary (Rule 1.2). *See, e.g., Adams v. Comm'n on Jud. Performance*, 882 P.2d 358 (Cal. 1994) (judge violated Code by accepting favorable price on automobile and discounts on auto repair from litigant in favor of whom the judge awarded substantial monetary judgment); *In re Terry*, 683 P.2d 42 (N.M. 1992) (judge's acceptance of favor from person appearing in his court warranted 30-day suspension); *In re Guerrero*, CJC No. 08-0797-CC, Tx. Comm'n on Jud. Conduct (2010) (judge who accepted premium Spurs basketball tickets from lawyers and bail-bondsmen who appeared in judge's courtroom could no longer be impartial); *In re Seraphim*, 294 N.W.2d 485 (Wis. 1980) (judge suspended for misconduct including accepting favorable car rental arrangement from dealership that appeared in judge's court); Wash. Ethics Adv. Comm. Op. 91-19 (1991) (acceptance of complimentary membership in social club would create the perception that the club and its members are in a position to influence the judge). *But see* Mass. Comm. on Jud. Ethics Adv. Op. 2013-1 (2013) (judge may accept gift of free legal services from lawyer who has never appeared, and likely will never appear, before judge). Rule 3.13 does not apply to contributions to a judge's campaign, which are governed by other Rules of the Code, including Rules 4.3 and 4.4. Model Code of Judicial Conduct Rule 3.13 cmt. [5].

Although the Code only applies to judges, a Comment to Rule 3.13 notes that gifts to a judge's spouse, domestic partner, or family member living in the judge's home can be seen as an attempt to circumvent the Rule and indirectly influence the judge. While the Comment notes that when such gifts are made primarily to the other person and the judge benefits only incidentally, the concern is reduced, the Comment advises judges to remind family and household members of the restrictions imposed on judges, and urge them to take these restrictions into account when making decisions about accepting such gifts or benefits. Model Code of Judicial Conduct Rule 3.13 cmt. [4].

A gift that is presented to all judges in a circuit may be more problematic than a gift to an individual judge as it may be seen as an attempt to curry favor or garner the prestige of the office. *See* Fla. Jud. Ethics Adv. Comm. Op. 97-27 (1997) (judge may not accept base commander's gift of an honorary membership in military officers' club that is offered to all judges in the circuit). When a gift is presented to a judge by an entity, such as a bar association, rather than by an individual lawyer, it is more likely to be deemed acceptable. *See* Ark. Jud. Ethics Adv. Comm. Op. 2000-10 (2000) (judge may accept gift of judicial robe from bar association); Fla. Jud. Ethics Adv. Comm. Op. 2001-10 (2001) (visiting judge may accept gift from bar association in appreciation of years spent presiding at courthouse).

ITEMS THAT MAY BE ACCEPTED WITHOUT PUBLIC REPORTING

Rule 3.13(B) establishes a "tier" of gifts and other things of value that a judge may accept without limitation and without public reporting. In the 1990 Code, the exceptions to the basic rule were set out serially, without further classification, and—except in the catchall provision of Canon 5D(5)(h)—without adverting to whether public reporting was a condition of acceptance. Paragraph (B) identifies circumstances in which the risk that the acceptance would appear to undermine the judge's independence, integrity, or impartiality is low, and explicitly provides that such items need not be reported.

Items with Little Intrinsic Value

Pursuant to Rule 3.13(B)(1), a judge may accept items with little intrinsic value, such as plaques, certificates, trophies, and greeting cards. A judge need not publicly report his or her acceptance of such items.

Gift, Loans, Bequests, Benefits, or Other Things of Value from Person Whose Appearance or Interest in Case Would Require Disqualification

Rule 3.13(B)(2) permits a judge to accept a gift, loan, bequest, benefit, or other thing of value from friends, relatives, or other persons, including lawyers, whose appearance or interest in a proceeding pending or impending before the judge would require the judge's disqualification under Rule 2.11. This provision is similar to Canon 4D(5)(e) of the 1990 Code. If a person's appearance or interest in a case pending or impending before a particular judge would require the disqualification of the judge, then any gift or favor from that person could not influence the judge—because by definition the judge would no longer be sitting on the case. Charles G. Geyh & W. William Hodes, *Reporters' Notes to the Model Code of Judicial Conduct* 84–85 (2009). For instance, a judge may accept pro bono legal services from his or her sibling in a case pending before another judge. The familial relationship and the client-lawyer relationship between the judge and his or her sibling would be grounds for disqualification regardless of the nature of the fee arrangement. Mich. Comm. on Jud. Ethics Op. JI-106 (1996) (judge may accept pro bono services from sibling on public policy issue pending before different judge). *See also* Kan. Jud. Ethics Op. JE 155 (2007) (judge and spouse may accept an invitation from former law partner to stay in Colorado condominium for a week without charge because former partner's appearance in case would require judge's disqualification); Okla. Jud. Ethics Op. 2013-1 (2013) (judge may accept gift of free camping, fishing, and hunting as well as cabin from family).

Ordinary Social Hospitality

Pursuant to Rule 3.13(B)(3), a judge may accept "ordinary social hospitality" without reporting such acceptance. The drafters of the 1972 Code determined that "judges should not be excluded from all social relationships with lawyers or persons who are likely to be litigants in his court." E. Wayne Thode, *Reporter's Notes to Code of Judicial Conduct* 84 (1973); *see also* Cal. Judges Ass'n Jud. Ethics Comm. Adv. Op. 43 (1994) ("[J]udges, like other members of society, must be able to extend common courtesies and social amenities to others, and be willing guests and willing hosts."). Therefore, pursuant to Rule 3.13(B)(3) and its predecessors in the 1972 and 1990 Codes, judges are permitted to accept "ordinary social hospitality," even from lawyers who appear before them. *See, e.g.*, Ill. Jud. Ethics Comm. Op. 93-12 (1993) (judge may attend golf outing as guest of lawyer who is social acquaintance even if lawyer or members of lawyer's firm have appeared or may appear in judge's court); N.Y. Adv. Comm. on Jud. Ethics Op. 95-99 (1995) (judge may attend golf outing as guest of lawyer who practices before judge provided lawyer is not on trial before judge at time of outing); Okla. Jud. Ethics Op. 2005-1 (2005) (judge may accept social invitations from former partners or associates or from social friends who are regularly on judge's docket, as long as it would not reasonably be construed as likely to carry the impression that such persons are in a special position to influence judge or interfere with judge's ability to perform duties of judicial office fairly and impartially).

"Ordinary Social Hospitality"

The 1972 Code drafting committee found the term "ordinary social hospitality" difficult to delineate and adopted a general standard that permits the scope of "permissible social hospitality" to "vary somewhat from place to place, depending on local customs and practices." The Committee also concluded that "there are common sense limits and that the standard is understandable and defensible; for example, the offer to a judge of a month at the mountain cabin of a lawyer friend who practices in the judge's court is clearly not ordinary social hospitality, and its acceptance is prohibited." E. Wayne Thode, *Reporter's Notes to Code of Judicial Conduct* 84–85 (1973); *see, e.g., In re Vaccaro*, 409 N.Y.S.2d 1009 (N.Y. Ct. Jud. 1977) (judge's spending weekend with wife as guest of a law firm is beyond permissible ordinary social hospitality). To allay criticism that the standard is too relaxed, the committee noted that the "impropriety and the appearance of impropriety" provisions of the Code are applicable to all of a judge's activities. "Each activity must be judged in light of the surrounding circumstances." E. Wayne Thode, *Reporter's Notes to Code of Judicial Conduct* 84–85 (1973).

Some jurisdictions have adopted a common sense approach and decide on a case-by-case basis whether or not a gift, bequest, favor or loan constitutes "ordinary social hospitality." A few states have defined "ordinary social hospitality," which may provide more definitive guidance to judges contemplating whether accepting a gift would be permissible. For instance, the Judicial Ethics Committee of the California Judges Association defined ordinary social hospitality as "that type of social event or other gift which is so common among people in the judge's community that no reasonable person would believe that (1) the donor was intending to or would obtain any advantage or (2) the donee would believe that the donor intended to obtain any advantage." Cal. Judges Ass'n Jud. Ethics Comm. Adv. Op. 43 (1994); *see also* Okla. Jud. Ethics Op. 2001-03 (2001) (using same definition).

The Illinois Supreme Court defined "ordinary social hospitality" as "those routine amenities, favors, and courtesies, which are normally exchanged between friends and acquaintances, and which would not create an appearance of impropriety to a reasonable, objective observer." *In re Corboy*, 528 N.E.2d 694 (Ill. 1988) (lawyers' gifts or loans of $1,000 to judge in court before which they or their associates practiced could not be deemed "ordinary social hospitality"); *see also In re Jones*, 532 N.E.2d 239 (Ill. 1988) ($15,000 loan did not constitute "ordinary social hospitality"). The test is objective, rather than subjective, the court said, and the touchstone is a careful consideration of social custom. The court suggested that the following factors be taken into consideration: (1) the monetary value of the gift; (2) the relationship, if any, between the judge and the donor/lender lawyer (3) the social practices and customs associated with gifts and loans; and (4) the particular circumstances surrounding the gifts and loans. *In re Corboy*, 528 N.E.2d 694 (Ill. 1988); *see also In re D'Angelo*, 533 N.E.2d 861 (Ill. 1988) (lawyer's payments for judges' car rentals worth hundreds or thousands of dollars are not, under any circumstances, "ordinary social hospitality"); *In re Haley*, 720 N.W.2d 246 (Mich. 2006) (holding that a "reasonable observer" would not conclude that "ordinary social hospitality" fairly describes a judge's acceptance of college football tickets from an attorney appearing before the judge).

Invitations to Law-Related Social Functions

Invitations to bar-related functions, such as dinners and receptions, where the sponsoring bar association pays the judge's expenses are generally permissible as ordinary social hospitality. Wash. Ethics Adv. Comm. Op. 91-08 (1991) (judge may attend bar association dinner at no expense to judge); *see also* Ariz. Jud. Ethics Adv. Comm. Op. 95-13 (1995) (judge's attendance at reception sponsored by private associations of attorney's who represent particular classes of litigants falls into exception for "ordinary social hospitality" as long as the event is not inappropriately extravagant); *cf*, N.Y. Adv. Comm. on Jud. Ethics Op. 87-15(c) (1987) (judge may attend a function of a bar association or other similar lawyers' association as a guest of that association, even if the function or affair is expensive). However, a judge's attendance at a dinner hosted by a lawyer to celebrate the satisfaction of a judgment in litigation over which the judge presided and acceptance of a free weekend stay at the resort condominium owned by a law firm whose interests regularly came before the judge do not fall into the "ordinary social hospitality" exception. *Adams v. Comm'n on Jud. Performance*, 897 P.2d 544 (Cal. 1995).

The Judicial Ethics Committee of the California Judges Association delineated factors that a judge should look at to determine whether an invitation to a social event would be deemed "ordinary social hospitality." According to the Committee, a judge should consider: (1) the cost of the event in the context of the community standards for similar events; (2) whether the benefits conferred are greater than that traditionally furnished at similar events sponsored by bar associations or similar groups; (3) whether the benefits are greater in value than that which the judge customarily provides his or her own guests; 4) whether the benefits conferred are usually exchanged only between friends or relatives, such as transportation, housing, or free admission to events that require a paid admission; 5) whether there is a history or expectation of reciprocal social hospitality, which is suggestive of ordinary social hospitality; 6) whether the event is a traditional occasion for social hospitality, such as a holiday party or the opening of an office; 7) whether the benefits received must be reported to any governmental entity. Cal. Judges Ass'n Jud. Ethics Comm. Adv. Op. 43 (1994). *See also* Okla. Jud. Ethics Op. 2005-1 (2005) (advising Oklahoma judiciary to take these factors into consideration).

Holiday Gifts and Parties

A judge's acceptance of gifts of nominal value from lawyers or court vendors during the holiday season have generally been permitted under the predecessor to Rule 3.13(B)(3). *See e.g.*, Okla. Jud. Ethics Op. 2001-3, 73 P.3d 268 (2001) (advising that gift package of homemade cookies at Christmas would not be perceived as an impropriety, but acceptance of larger gifts, such as season tickets to sporting events, free use of a vacation home, free vacation on a cruise ship, would not be proper); Wash. Ethics Adv. Comm. Op. 93-17 (1993) (judge may allow court employees under his control to accept gifts of nominal value, such as candy, from lawyers and court vendors during the holiday season); Wis. Jud. Conduct Adv. Comm. Op. 98-10R (1998) (judges and their staff may receive small, inexpensive holiday gifts of candy or food from lawyers); N.Y. Adv. Comm. on Jud. Ethics Op. 91-50 (1991) (judge may accept non-monetary gift of under $25 in value from a high school student, in appreciation for the extra time the judge has spent explaining the law to the student); *but see* Ariz. Jud. Ethics Adv. Comm. Op. 90-05 (1990) (judge and judge's staff may not accept Christmas gifts such as candy, gift baskets, etc., valued at between $5 and $30); Utah Jud. Ethics Adv. Comm. Informal Op. 89-6 (1989) (judge may not accept Christmas gifts from lawyers or parties likely to appear before judge, but court employees may accept gifts of nominal value).

Similarly, most jurisdictions permit judges to accept invitations to a law firm's holiday party, open house or summer picnic, provided such events are not extravagant and do not involve the awarding of expensive gifts. N.Y. Adv.

Comm. on Jud. Ethics Op. 87-12(a) (1987) (judge may attend firm's "ordinary" holiday party, which does not include a party at expensive restaurant, a cruise, or similar expensive and lavish affair); N.Y. Adv. Comm. on Jud. Ethics Op. 91-136 (1991) (judge may attend opening of lawyer's law office); Tex. Adv. Comm. on Jud. Ethics Op. 194 (1996) (judge may only accept gifts from friends but may attend ordinary holiday parties open to other court and judicial personnel); Wash. Ethics Adv. Comm. Op. 91-27 (1991) (judge may attend events sponsored by law firms or trade groups if the event does not cause judge's impartiality to be questioned); Wis. Jud. Conduct Adv. Comm. Op. 98-10R (1998) (judges and their staff may attend holiday party given by a law firm whose lawyers appear before the judge as long as cost does not exceed ordinary social hospitality).

COMMERCIAL OR FINANCIAL OPPORTUNITIES AND BENEFITS

Rule 3.13(B)(4) allows a judge to accept commercial or financial opportunities and benefits without reporting such acceptance. Commercial and financial opportunities and benefits may include special pricing and discounts, and loans from lending institutions in their regular course of business, if the same opportunities and benefits or loans are made available to similarly situated people who are not judges. *See In re McDonough*, 296 N.W.2d 648 (Minn. 1979) (judge's acceptance of preferential treatment from bank in the form of unsecured loan of over $20,000 and many uncharged overdrafts on wife's checking account did not violate Canon since there was no evidence that it was motivated by the unique fact of his judgeship or that other good "credit risks" could not receive similar treatment). The 1972 Drafting Committee was of the opinion that such a loan should not be prohibited, even though the lending institution may be a litigant in proceedings before the judge. The judge should not be forced to borrow money from persons or institutions not in the lending business, nor should he or she be forced to borrow money outside of his or her community. E. Wayne Thode, *Reporter's Notes to Code of Judicial Conduct* 84 (1973).

As noted in the Commentary to Rule 3.13, financial institutions frequently make available special pricing, discounts, and other benefits, either in connection with a temporary promotion or for preferred customers, based on longevity of the relationship, volume of business transacted, and other factors. A judge may accept such benefits if they are available to the general public or if the judge qualifies for the special price or discount according to the same criteria as are applied to persons who are not judges. For example, loans provided at generally prevailing interest rates are not gifts, but a judge could not accept a loan from a financial institution at below-market interest rates unless the same rate was being made available to the general public for a certain period of time or only to borrowers with specified qualifications that the judge also possesses. Model Code of Judicial Conduct Rule 3.13 cmt. [3].

Rewards and Prizes Given in Random Drawings, Contests, or Other Events Open to Persons Who Are Not Judges

Rule 3.13(B)(5) permits judges to accept, without public reporting, a reward or prize given in a random drawing, contest, or other event that is open to people who are not judges. This provision was added to the Code in 2007.

Scholarships, Fellowships, and Similar Benefits and Awards

Pursuant to Rule 3.13(B)(6), a judge may accept and need not report a scholarship, fellowship, and similar benefits or awards if they are available to other people who are similarly situated and who are not judges, based on the same criteria. *See, e.g.*, Ill. Jud. Ethics Comm. Op. 96-17 (1996) (judge who teaches part-time at private high school may request and accept a tuition waiver for his or her children, so long as it is offered on the same terms to nonjudges who teach at school); Mich. Comm. on Jud. Ethics Op. JI-75 (1993) (judge may accept scholarships or fellowships for professional development seminars provided that they are awarded on the same terms to nonjudicial applicants and do not reflect adversely on judge's impartiality).

Complimentary Books, Journals, and Other Resource Materials for Official Use

Rule 3.13(B)(7) permits judges to accept complimentary books, magazines, journals, audiovisual materials, and other resource material supplied by publishers for official use. *See, e.g.*, Ill. Jud. Ethics Comm. Op. 95-7 (1995) (judge may accept complimentary subscription of state law for official use); N.Y. Adv. Comm. on Jud. Ethics Op. 11-36 (2011) (judge may permit lawyer-lecturer at judicial education program to distribute free copies of lawyer's book to attendees); Wash. Ethics Adv. Comm. Op. 93-15 (1993) (appellate court may accept publisher's complimentary set of Washington Law in CD Rom format and judge may accept complimentary copy for home if it is for official use); *but see* Ariz. Jud. Ethics Adv. Comm. Op. 92-04 (1993) (judge may not accept complimentary legal publications from a publisher who is also a lawyer frequently appearing in judge's court).

Gift, Award, or Benefit Incident to the Business, Profession, or Other Separate Activity of a Spouse, Domestic Partner, or Other Family Member

Rule 3.13(B)(8) addresses gifts, awards, or benefits associated with the business, profession, or other separate activity of the judge's spouse, domestic partner, or other family member residing in the judge's household. A judge's family member may accept such a gift, award, or benefit, even if it incidentally benefits the judge and no report of such acceptance needs to be made. The Commission thought that it would not be reasonable to believe that a judge would be influenced by such items. Charles G. Geyh & W. William Hodes, *Reporters' Notes to the Model Code of Judicial Conduct* 85 (2009).

Commentary to the Rule, however, suggests that judges remind family and household members of the restrictions imposed on the judge, and urge them to take these restrictions into account when making decisions about accepting such gifts or benefits. Model Code of Judicial Conduct Rule 3.13 cmt. [4].

ITEMS JUDGE MAY ACCEPT BUT MUST REPORT

Rule 3.13(C) lists items that would not cause a reasonable person to believe that the judge's independence, integrity, or impartiality would be undermined, but are of sufficient concern that public reporting is required. Placement of these items in Rule 3.13(C), rather than paragraphs (A) or (B), represents the Commission's assessment of the level of concern that may attend the acceptance of various benefits. Charles G. Geyh & W. William Hodes, *Reporters' Notes to the Model Code of Judicial Conduct* 84 (2009).

GIFTS INCIDENT TO A PUBLIC TESTIMONIAL

Pursuant to Rule 3.13(C)(1) a judge may accept and must report a gift incident to a public testimonial. *See, e.g.*, Fla. Jud. Ethics Adv. Comm. Op. 95-19 (1995) (judge may accept complimentary tickets to the American Jewish Committee Dinner); Mich. Comm. on Jud. Ethics Op. JI-009 (1989) (judge may attend testimonial dinner in judge's honor).

INVITATIONS TO BAR OR LAW-RELATED FUNCTIONS

The Commentary to Rule 3.1 encourages judges to take part in activities of bar associations and other organizations that concern the law, the legal system, and the administration of justice. Rule 3.13(C)(2)(a) permits judges to accept invitations to the judge and the judge's spouse, domestic partner, or guest to attend without charge an event associated with a bar-related function or other activity relating to the law, the legal system or the administration of justice. *See, e.g., Petition of Wiley*, 671 A.2d 308 (R.I. 1996) (judge may attend meetings of professional associations as guest of organization or at his or her own expense); Fla. Jud. Ethics Adv. Comm. Op. 2013-12 (2013) (judge may attend legal aid gala at discounted rate offered to government lawyers); Fla. Jud. Ethics Adv. Comm. Op. 2000-20 (2000) (judge may attend law-related function where fees are waived for the judiciary); Maine Jud. Ethics Adv. Op. 10-1 (2010) (judge may attend Maine Trial Lawyers Association dinner honoring bar association members at reduced ticket price reflecting only the cost of the dinner); Wash. Ethics Adv. Comm. Op. 91-8 (1991) (judge and spouse may accept invitation to attend a bar-related dinner when the expenses will be paid by the bar association); Ill. Jud. Ethics

Comm. Op. 93-12 (1993) (judge may attend golf outing as honoree/guest of bar association as long as there is not appearance of improper influence). The Commission decided that the gift of a free ticket to attend a law-related event must be reported so that others might be able to assess whether the judge's association with a particular bar-related organization might appear to undermine the judge's independence, integrity, or impartiality. Charles G. Geyh & W. William Hodes, *Reporters' Notes to the Model Code of Judicial Conduct* 84 (2009).

Invitation to Event Associated with Judges' Civic Activities

Rule 3.13(C)(2)(b), which was new to the Code in 2007, provides that a judge may accept an invitation to the judge and the judge's spouse, domestic partner, or guest to attend an event that is associated with the judge's educational, religious, charitable, or civic activities, free of charge, as long as nonjudges who are also involved in such activities receive the same invitation. The Commission decided that if a judge is invited to attend, free of charge, an event sponsored by a non-law-related organization, the judge may not accept at all, unless equal treatment is given to nonjudges who are similarly engaged in the activity. If that condition is met, however, then the public reporting requirement should be sufficient to allay concerns about possible lack of impartiality. Charles G. Geyh & W. William Hodes, *Reporters' Notes to the Model Code of Judicial Conduct* 84 (2009).

Gifts, Loans, Bequests, or Other Things of Value from Person Who Has or Is Likely to Come before Judge

Rule 3.13(C)(3) provides that a judge may accept but must report any gifts, loans, bequests, benefits, or other things of value from a party or other person, including a lawyer, who has come or is likely to come before the judge, or whose interests have come or are likely to come before the judge. Rule 3.13(C)(3) addresses the same issue as Canon 4D(5)(h) of the 1990 Code, but according to a more discriminating analysis.

Under the 1990 Code, a judge cannot accept any gift or favor from a lawyer or party who has come or is likely to come before the judge. Many jurisdictions strictly enforced Section 4D(5)(h), advising judges not to accept gifts or loans, under almost any circumstances, from lawyers or others who have come or may come before the judge. *See, e.g., In re Luzzo*, 756 So. 2d 76 (Fla. 2000) (judge may not accept free tickets to professional baseball game from a law firm whose lawyers were appearing before the judge); *In re Free*, 158 So. 3d 711 (La. 2014) (judge suspended for 30 days without pay, in part, for accepting all-expenses-paid hunting trip from counsel who frequently appeared before judge immediately after that lawyer reached a $1 million settlement in a matter pending before the judge); *Disc. Counsel v. Lisotto*, 761 N.E.2d 1037 (Ohio

2002) (judge's misconduct, including his acceptance of tickets to professional football game from lawyer who appeared before him, warranted public reprimand); Ariz. Jud. Ethics Adv. Comm. Op. 92-04 (1994) (judge who presided over medical malpractice cases may not accept book on medical malpractice from a co-author who frequently argues before judge); Fla. Jud. Ethics Adv. Comm. Op. 2000-08 (2000) (judges and court employees may not accept gifts of money or certificates redeemable for money, goods, or services from lawyers, vendors, or other third parties who have come or are likely to come before the judge); Ill. Jud. Ethics Comm. Op. 93-6 (1993) (judge could accept free use of condominium from non-lawyer who has no cases pending before the judge and is unlikely to have any cases before the judge in the future); Ohio Bd. of Commissioners on Grievances and Disc. Op. 98-10 (1998) (judge may accept honorary country club membership as gift provided that donor country club is not a party who has come or is likely to come before judge or whose interests have come or are likely to come before judge); Tex. Adv. Comm. on Jud. Ethics Op. 215 (1997) (advising that judge and his family, who had suffered a catastrophic loss, were not permitted to accept gifts of money from any lawyers or parties who have come or might come before the court).

A gift that would otherwise have been permitted under Canon 4D might have been deemed to violate Section 4D(5)(h) where the donor is a lawyer who appears in the judge's court. *See, e.g.*, Ariz. Jud. Ethics Adv. Comm. Op. 93-05 (1993) (advising that although a judge may be permitted to accept resource materials supplied by publisher on a complimentary basis for official use, judge may not do so if publisher is also a lawyer frequently appearing in judge's court).

Under current Rule 3.13(C)(3) such gifts, loans, bequests, benefits, or other things of value may be accepted, if they have first passed the test of Rule 3.13 (A), as long as they are reported, which will give another party in litigation an opportunity to consider whether disqualification of the judge should be sought. Further, public reporting should effectively inhibit a judge from showing impartiality to a donor lawyer or the lawyer's client. Charles G. Geyh & W. William Hodes, *Reporters' Notes to the Model Code of Judicial Conduct* 82–84 (2009).

Loans between Judges and Lawyers

Loans between a judge and a lawyer practicing in the judge's court are particularly likely to create a perception of "justice for sale" and are generally prohibited. *In re Drury*, 602 N.E.2d 1000 (Ind. 1992) (judge removed for soliciting and accepting a $2,000 loan from a lawyer, failing to disclose it and continuing to preside over cases in which the lawyer appeared). A judge may be permitted to accept contributions to a defense fund from lawyers and other individuals, but only if the donors have not appeared before the judge and are unlikely to do so in the future. Fla. Jud. Ethics Adv. Comm. Op. 98-11 (1998) (judge may establish and maintain a fund to defend against charges of unethical behavior by the judicial qualifications commission but may not solicit contributions and must not accept contributions from a party or other person who has come or is likely to come or whose interest have come or are likely to come before the judge, including attorneys); Ill. Jud. Ethics Comm. Op. 97-14 (1997) (lawyers may contribute to a defense fund established for a judge charged with criminal offense as long as they have not practiced and are unlikely to practice before judge).

Permitting Former Law Firm to Host Party for Judge

Some state judicial ethics committees have advised that judges may permit their former law firm to host and pay for a party or reception to celebrate their ascendancy to the bench. The rationale is that upon taking the bench, the judge will be required to recuse himself or herself from cases involving his or her former firm and, therefore, the judge will not be accepting a gift or benefit from someone who "has come or is likely to come before the judge." *See, e.g.*, Fla. Jud. Ethics Adv. Comm. Op. 99-3 (1999) (former law firm of new judge may sponsor and pay for reception for new judge immediately following investiture because judge will recuse himself from cases handled by former firm); Ill. Jud. Ethics Op. 01-11 (2001) (judge may be feted at a post investiture party sponsored by former firm so long as disqualification requirements are strictly adhere to); Wash. Ethics Adv. Comm. Op. 95-05 (1995) (judge may permit his or her former firm to host reception following judge's swearing in ceremony provided judge reports it); U.S. Jud. Conf. Comm. on Codes of Conduct Adv. Op. 98 (2000) (no appearance of impropriety created when judge accepts benefit of reception upon investiture where donors are former firm, former clients, or colleagues because judge would likely have to recuse from cases involving such parties for a period of time following appointment); *but see* Md. Jud. Ethics Op. 2005-16 (2005) (judge may not allow former firm to pay for investiture party where judge has not been associated with firm for five years because occasion for recusal is minimal and the passage of time heightens the apprehension that the prestige of office is being used).

APPEARANCE OF UNDERMINING JUDGE'S INDEPENDENCE, INTEGRITY, OR IMPARTIALITY

Even if a judge's acceptance of a gift, favor or loan is otherwise acceptable pursuant to Rule 3.13(C) and the reporting requirement is satisfied, it may violate Rule 3.13(A), which prohibits acceptance if it would appear to undermine the judge's independence, integrity, or impartiality. *See, e.g., In re Bonin*, 378 N.E.2d 669 (Mass. 1978) (judge's receipt of leased car as gift from former client created the appearance of impropriety even though judge reported rental payments as gift and former client had no cases pending in judge's court where judge subsequently appointed a key official in client's corporation to position in judge's office at higher than usual salary); Wash. Ethics Adv. Comm. Op. 91-19 (1991) (acceptance of complimentary membership in social club would create the perception that the club and its members are in a position to influence the judge).

RULE 3.14 REIMBURSEMENT OF EXPENSES AND WAIVERS OF FEES OR CHARGES

(A) Unless otherwise prohibited by Rules 3.1 and 3.13(A) or other law,* a judge may accept reimbursement of necessary and reasonable expenses for travel, food, lodging, or other incidental expenses, or a waiver or partial waiver of fees or charges for registration, tuition, and similar items, from sources other than the judge's employing entity, if the expenses or charges are associated with the judge's participation in extrajudicial activities permitted by this Code.

(B) Reimbursement of expenses for necessary travel, food, lodging, or other incidental expenses shall be limited to the actual costs reasonably incurred by the judge and, when appropriate to the occasion, by the judge's spouse, domestic partner,* or guest.

(C) A judge who accepts reimbursement of expenses or waivers or partial waivers of fees or charges on behalf of the judge or the judge's spouse, domestic partner, or guest shall publicly report such acceptance as required by Rule 3.15.

COMMENT

[1] Educational, civic, religious, fraternal, and charitable organizations often sponsor meetings, seminars, symposia, dinners, awards ceremonies, and similar events. Judges are encouraged to attend educational programs, as both teachers and participants, in law-related and academic disciplines, in furtherance of their duty to remain competent in the law. Participation in a variety of other extrajudicial activity is also permitted and encouraged by this Code.

[2] Not infrequently, sponsoring organizations invite certain judges to attend seminars or other events on a fee-waived or partial-fee-waived basis, and sometimes include reimbursement for necessary travel, food, lodging, or other incidental expenses. A judge's decision whether to accept reimbursement of expenses or a waiver or partial waiver of fees or charges in connection with these or other extrajudicial activities must be based upon an assessment of all

the circumstances. The judge must undertake a reasonable inquiry to obtain the information necessary to make an informed judgment about whether acceptance would be consistent with the requirements of this Code.

[3] A judge must assure himself or herself that acceptance of reimbursement or fee waivers would not appear to a reasonable person to undermine the judge's independence, integrity, or impartiality. The factors that a judge should consider when deciding whether to accept reimbursement or a fee waiver for attendance at a particular activity include:

(a) whether the sponsor is an accredited educational institution or bar association rather than a trade association or a for-profit entity;

(b) whether the funding comes largely from numerous contributors rather than from a single entity and is earmarked for programs with specific content;

(c) whether the content is related or unrelated to the subject matter of litigation pending or impending before the judge, or to matters that are likely to come before the judge;

(d) whether the activity is primarily educational rather than recreational, and whether the costs of the event are reasonable and comparable to those associated with similar events sponsored by the judiciary, bar associations, or similar groups;

(e) whether information concerning the activity and its funding sources is available upon inquiry;

(f) whether the sponsor or source of funding is generally associated with particular parties or interests currently appearing or likely to appear in the judge's court, thus possibly requiring disqualification of the judge under Rule 2.11;

(g) whether differing viewpoints are presented; and

(h) whether a broad range of judicial and nonjudicial participants are invited, whether a large number of participants are invited, and whether the program is designed specifically for judges.

1990 Code Comparison

Rule 3.14(A) is derived from Canon 4H(1), except that it applies to reimbursement of expenses and waivers of fees or charges while the provisions relating to compensation have been moved to Rule 3.12. Rule 3.14(B) is essentially identical to Canon 4H(1)(b) of the 1990 Code, except that it applies to both reimbursements and waivers of fees and charges, and applies to an accompanying domestic partner as well as to a spouse or guest. Rule 3.14(C) is similar to the public reporting requirement set out in Canon 4H(2), except that it applies to reimbursements and waivers rather than compensation. Additionally, the actual mechanism for reporting is not contained in Rule 3.14(C) itself; the Rule instead cross-references Rule 3.15, which describes all the public reporting required by various Rules in Canon 3. Comments [1] through [3] to the Rule are new to the Code.

ANNOTATION

Rule 3.14(A) provides that, subject to Rules 3.1 and 3.13(A) and other law, a judge may accept reimbursement for necessary and reasonable expenses for travel, food, lodging, or other incidental expenses, or a waiver or partial waiver of fees or charges for registration, tuitions, and items, if they are associated with the judge's participation in extrajudicial activities permitted by the Code. Comment [1] to Rule 3.14 states that judges "are encouraged to attend educational programs, as both teachers and participants, in law-related and academic disciplines, in furtherance of their duty to remain competent in the law."

Although Rule 3.14 applies to events other than privately funded educational seminars, attendance at tuition-waived and expense-paid seminars and similar events has been a matter of public concern and media attention. The Commission heard testimony and received numerous comments about the need for more transparency regarding both the amount of fees waived or expenses reimbursed and the nature and sponsorship of the event attended on a cost-free or reduced-cost basis. The 1990 Code required the reporting of compensation, but not of reimbursement of expenses and waiver of fees. Rule 3.14 corrected that oversight. The factors listed in Comment [3] for the judge to consider in whether to accept a fee waiver or reimbursement are borrowed from revised Advisory Opinion 67 of the Committee on Codes of Conduct of the Judicial Conference of the United States. Charles G. Geyh & W. William Hodes, *Reporters' Notes to the Model Code of Judicial Conduct* 87–89 (2009).

In the Commission's view, judicial education of all kinds is of great value; it helps keep judges current on recent developments, alerts them to future trends, and exposes them to new ways of thinking about the law. Moreover, there was recognition that judicial budgets may not always be adequate to support educational opportunities for judges. For that reason, Rule 3.14, like Canon 4H(1), permits judges to accept reimbursement for reasonably necessary expenses associated with otherwise permissible extrajudicial activities, and further permits acceptance of waivers of otherwise applicable fees or charges. *Id.*

With regard to educational programs, such as seminars, when deciding whether to accept an invitation to attend on an expenses-paid or fee-waived basis, a judge has an affirmative duty to undertake a "reasonable inquiry" to obtain information necessary to make an informed decision about whether acceptance would violate the Code. Model Code of Judicial Conduct Rule 3.13 cmt. [2]. Comment 3 to the Rule list factors that a judge should consider when deciding to accept reimbursement or fee waiver for attendance at a particular event.

Those factors include: (1) whether the sponsor is an accredited educational institution or bar association rather than a trade association of for-profit entity; (2) whether the funding comes largely from numerous contributors rather than a single entity and is earmarked for programs with specific content; (3) whether the content is related or unrelated to the subject matter of litigation pending or impending before the judge, or to matters that are likely to come before the judge; (4) whether the activity is primarily educational rather than recreational, and whether the costs of the event are reasonable and comparable to those associated with similar events sponsored by the judiciary, bar associations, or similar groups; (5) whether the information concerning the activity and its funding sources is available upon inquiry; (6) whether the sponsor or source of funding is generally associated with particular parties or interests currently appearing or likely to appear in the judge's court, thus possibly requiring disqualification of the judge under Rule 2.11; (7) whether differing viewpoints are presented; and (8) whether a broad range of judicial and nonjudicial participants are invited, whether a large number of participants are invited, and whether the program is designed specifically for the judge. These factors are derived from U.S. Jud. Conf. Comm. on Codes of Conduct Adv. Op. 67 (2009).

As previously noted, Rule 3.14(A) is based on Canon 4H(1) of the 1990 Model Code. A critical aspect of Canon 4H(1) is that permission to accept benefits in connection with extrajudicial activities is conditioned upon the acceptance not giving the appearance of influencing the judge in the performance of judicial duties and not otherwise creating the appearance of impropriety. Rule 3.14 carries this condition forward, for both reimbursements and waivers of fees and charges, by cross-referencing Rules 3.1 and 3.13(A), making clear that a judge may not accept the proffered benefits if doing so would appear to a reasonable person to undermine the judge's independence, integrity, or impartiality, or if accepting would, for example, lead to frequent disqualification or otherwise interfere with the proper performance of the judge's judicial duties. *See, e.g.*, Neb. Jud. Ethics Adv. Comm. Op. 04-1 (2004) (judge may attend educational conference on domestic violence where curriculum is not primarily prosecutorial in nature, however, judge should not accept "tuition and expenses" being paid by domestic violence project or Department of Justice because acceptance of such payment could result in an appearance of partiality); N.Y. Adv. Comm. on Jud. Ethics Op. 13-136 (2013) (judge may attend education program sponsored by court, hosted by law school, with reimbursement of costs by law school from monies raised from alumni, law firms, and businesses); N.Y. Adv. Comm. on Jud. Ethics Op. 06-49 (2006) (judge may participate in mission to Israel sponsored by not-for-profit organization, and may accept reimbursement for cost of participating since sponsoring entity is a not-for-profit organization and is not likely to appear in judge's court).

Rule 3.14(B), like Canon 4H(1)(b), its predecessor in the 1990 Code, provides that the amount of expense reimbursement a judge may receive is limited to the "actual costs reasonably incurred by the judge and, when appropriate to the occasion, by the judge's spouse, domestic partner, or guest. *See, e.g.*, Ariz. Jud. Ethics Adv. Comm. Op. 00-02 (2000) (judge may participate in educational programs sponsored by private entities with certain limitations); Pa. Jud. Ethics Comm. Informal Op. 9/3/99 (1999) (judge may accept lodging, meals, and transportation expense for speaking at educational event); U.S. Jud. Conf. Comm. on Codes of Conduct Adv. Op. 67 (1980, reissued 1998) (judge may generally attend independently sponsored educational events at no cost or accept reimbursement for expenses).

Rule 3.14(C) requires that a judge publicly report acceptance of reimbursement of expense or a waiver or partial waiver of fees or charges on behalf of the judge or the judge's spouse, domestic partner, or guest. The Rule cross-references Rule 3.15, which delineates the reporting requirement.

RULE 3.15 REPORTING REQUIREMENTS

(A) A judge shall publicly report the amount or value of:

(1) compensation received for extrajudicial activities as permitted by Rule 3.12;

(2) gifts and other things of value as permitted by Rule 3.13(C), unless the value of such items, alone or in the aggregate with other items received from the same source in the same calendar year, does not exceed $[insert amount]; and

(3) reimbursement of expenses and waiver of fees or charges permitted by Rule 3.14(A), unless the amount of reimbursement or waiver, alone or in the aggregate with other reimbursements or waivers received from the same source in the same calendar year, does not exceed $[insert amount].

(B) When public reporting is required by paragraph (A), a judge shall report the date, place, and nature of the activity for which the judge received any compensation; the description of any gift, loan, bequest, benefit, or other thing of value accepted; and the source of reimbursement of expenses or waiver or partial waiver of fees or charges.

(C) The public report required by paragraph (A) shall be made at least annually, except that for reimbursement of expenses and waiver or partial waiver of fees or charges, the report shall be made within thirty days following the conclusion of the event or program.

(D) Reports made in compliance with this Rule shall be filed as public documents in the office of the clerk of the court on which the judge serves or other office designated by law,* and, when technically feasible, posted by the court or office personnel on the court's website.

1990 CODE COMPARISON

Rule 3.15 is based on Canon 4H(2). However, this provision is no longer limited to public reporting of compensation received for extrajudicial activities, but includes public reporting of gifts and other things of value accepted pursuant to Rule 3.13, and reimbursement of expenses and waiver or partial waiver of fees and charges accepted pursuant to Rule 3.14. The Rule deletes a 1990 Code provision on treatment of a spouse's compensation or income in community property states. It also abandons the 1990 Code's reporting threshold of $150 per item for reporting purposes in favor of an annual aggregate amount to be decided upon by each jurisdiction. Charles G. Geyh & W. William Hodes, *Reporters' Notes to the Model Code of Judicial Conduct* 90–91 (2009).

The requirement in Rule 3.15(C) of reporting no less frequently than annually is consistent with Canon 4H(2) of the 1990 Code. Reporting in connection with reimbursements and waivers of fees or charges, however, is required within 30 days of the underlying event, not on a calendar-based schedule. Rule 3.15(D) also tracks Canon 4H(2), except that it calls for posting on the appropriate website, when feasible, to facilitate public access. *Id.*

The requirement of disclosure of a judge's income and assets in some circumstances, found in Canon 4I of the 1990 Code, is already regulated by statute or court rule in most jurisdictions and was not included in the revised Code as unnecessary. *Id.*

ANNOTATION

REPORTING COMPENSATION RECEIVED FOR EXTRAJUDICIAL ACTIVITIES

Pursuant to Rule 3.15(A)(1), a judge must report the amount or value of compensation received for extrajudicial activities as permitted by Rule 3.12. *See, e.g., In re Disciplinary Proceedings Against Anderson*, 981 P.2d 426 (Wash. 1999) (judge removed for misconduct including failure to report vehicle loan payments made to him by friend as compensation for judge's efforts with respect to friend's purchase of business); Mich. Comm. on Jud. Ethics Op. CI-832 (1982) (judge should report the source and amount of rental income received from lawyers). A judge must report the date, place, and nature of any activity for which the judge received compensation, as well as the name of the payor and the amount of compensation received. Section 4D(5)(h) requires judges to report gifts over $150 in the same manner. *See, e.g.*, Ohio Bd. of Commissioners on Grievances and Disc. Op. 95-8 (1995) (where judge attends trial lawyer association's meeting at no charge, it must be reported if fee is over $150). However, the judge generally need not report gifts from his or her spouse, children, siblings, and close personal friends. The report must be made at least annually and filed as a public document with the office of the clerk of the court on which the judge presides or other office designated by a rule of court. Compensation or income of a spouse attributed to the judge by operation of community property law is not considered compensation and need not be reported. Rule 3.15(B) provides a list of what must be reported when reporting is required under paragraph (A). The judge must report the date, place, and nature of the activity for which the judge received compensation. Pursuant to Rule 3.13 (C), the report must be made at least annually, except for reimbursement of expenses and waiver or partial waiver of fees or charges, which must be reported with 30 days following the conclusion of the even.

REPORTING GIFTS

Rule 3.15(A)(2) requires that judges publicly report gifts and other things of value as permitted by Rule 3.13(C) unless the value alone or in the aggregate with other items received from the same source in the same calendar year does not exceed a certain amount, to be determined by each jurisdiction. The public report must describe the gift, loan, bequest, benefit, or other thing of value accepted, Rule 3.15(B), and must be made at least annually. Rule 3.15(C).

REPORTING REIMBURSEMENT OF EXPENSES AND WAIVER OF FEES OR CHARGES

Lastly, Rule 3.15(A)(3) requires a judge to publicly report reimbursement of expenses and waiver of fees or charges permitted by Rule 3.14(A), unless the amount alone or in the aggregate with other items received from the same source in the same calendar year does not exceed a certain amount, to be determined by each jurisdiction. Wyo. Jud. Ethics Adv. Comm. Op. 2012-01 (this rule requires judge to report accomodations, meals, and travel paid directly by another; judge should make a reasonable estimate of the value of items paid for directly or note that the value is unknown). According to Rule 3.15(B), the judge must report the source of the reimbursement or waiver or partial waiver and Rule 3.15(C) requires that the report be made within 30 days following the conclusion of the event or program.

ACCESSIBILITY OF PUBLIC REPORTS

Rule 3.15(D) directs that the reports required by Rule 3.15 be located in a central place and made accessible to the public to ensure transparency. When "technically feasible" reports must be posted on the court's website. Ordinarily, it is assumed that such posting will be to the court's official website, and will be done by court personnel according to a uniform format, rather than by each reporting judge individually. Charles G. Geyh & W. William Hodes, *Reporters' Notes to the Model Code of Judicial Conduct* 91 (2009).

CANON 4

A judge or candidate for judicial office shall not engage in political or campaign activity that is inconsistent with the independence, integrity, or impartiality of the judiciary.

1990 CODE COMPARISON

Canon 4 of the revised Code is derived from Canon 5 of the 1990 Code, as amended in 1997, 1999, and 2003, the last time in response to the decision of the United States Supreme Court in *Minnesota Republican Party v. White*, 536 U.S. 765 (2002), and other developments. Much of the black letter text and Commentary from Canon 5 was retained, although it has been thoroughly reorganized and streamlined. The reorganized Canon 4 differentiates more clearly between sitting judges who are and are not also judicial candidates and nonjudges who become candidates. Canon 4 continues to differentiate between judicial candidates running in public elections and those seeking appointment, and, within the former category, it further differentiates between partisan, nonpartisan, and retention elections. Charles G. Geyh & W. William Hodes, *Reporters' Notes to the Model Code of Judicial Conduct* 92 (2009).

In the Canon itself, the phrase "shall refrain from" was replaced by "shall not engage in," which more closely parallels the language of the other three Canons. "Political activity" was replaced with "political or campaign activity" to more accurately reflect the actual content of Canon 4. "Inappropriate activity" was replaced with "activity that is inconsistent with the independence, integrity, or impartiality of the judiciary" to make Canon 4 more consistent with the rest of the Code. Concern that the independence, integrity, or impartiality of the judiciary (including candidates who aspire to join the judiciary) will be compromised or undermined is a pervasive theme. *Id.*

ANNOTATION

INTRODUCTION

By assuming the bench, a judge does not completely lose the right to participate in the political process. Model Code of Judicial Conduct Rule 4.1 cmt. [6].

However, probably no area is more fraught with potential for ethical misconduct than judicial political conduct. *See* Roy A. Schotland, *New Challenges to States' Judicial Selection*, 95 Geo. L.J. 1077 (2007); Vincent R. Johnson, *The Ethical Foundations of American Judicial Independence*, 29 Fordham Urb. L. J. 1007, 1021 (2002) ("In general, the ethics rules on political activity are intended to distance judges and candidates from the pressures of politics. However, it is necessary to accommodate the reality that many judges must run for election and that political parties often play a role in judicial elections and appointments. Such accommodations undoubtedly cause the ethics rules to fall short of wholly separating judicial decision making from politics."); Shirley S. Abrahamson, *The Ballot and the Bench*, 76 N.Y.U. L. Rev. 973 (2001) (discussing advantages and criticisms of judicial elections); Stacie L. Sanders, Note, *Kissing Babies, Shaking Hands, and Campaign Contributions: Is This the Proper Role for the Kansas Judiciary?*, 34 Washburn L.J. 573 (1995); Kurt E. Scheuerman, Comment, *Rethinking Judicial Elections*, 72 Or. L. Rev. 459 (1993).

The starting point for analyzing judges' participation in the political process is Canon 4 of the Model Code, which states that "a judge or candidate for judicial office shall not engage in political or campaign activity that is inconsistent with the independence, integrity, or impartiality of the judiciary." The Canon goes on to define inappropriate political activity by outlining several proscribed statements and actions for judicial candidates. *See* discussion *infra*.

Most states that use some type of election to select their judges have adopted, at least in part, the 1990 version of the Model Code of Judicial Conduct. Thirty-two states and the District of Columbia have approved revised judicial codes based on the 2007 Model Code, and 14 others have committees reviewing the 2007 Model Code for possible adoption.

Many states have established specific procedures to help implement the political and campaign activity provisions in their Codes. These include creating campaign oversight committees and issuing advisory opinions. Several states, including Alabama, Georgia, New York, and Ohio, have created special committees to monitor unethical and unfair campaign practices in campaigns for judicial office. *See generally* Richard A. Dove, *Judicial Campaign Conduct: Rules, Education, and Enforcement*, 34 Loy. L.A. L. Rev. 1447 (2001).

Canon 4 generally applies to all incumbent judges and judicial candidates. *See, e.g.*, *In re Amended Canon 7 of Code of Judicial Conduct* (*In re Lyons*) 680 P.2d 601 (N.M. 1984) (magistrate who is running for district attorney must comply with judicial code provision requiring candidates for nonjudicial office to take leave without pay upon filing a statement of candidacy). Some individuals who exercise "quasi-judicial" power may also be subject to the Code of Judicial Conduct. *See, e.g.*, Nev. Off. of Atty. Gen. Op. 2002-26 (2002) (members of state commission on ethics exercise quasi-judicial powers and are, therefore, permitted to make campaign contributions, just as judges are under the judicial code); Tex. Adv. Comm. on Jud. Ethics Op. 193 (1996) (candidate for justice of the peace must comply with code of judicial conduct); W. Va. Jud. Investigatory Comm'n Adv. Op 11/3/95 (1995) (part-time family law master may attend a political party fund-raiser dinner because he is classified as continuing part-time judge, and is exempt from certain restrictions dealing with inappropriate political activity on the part of judges and judicial candidates). *But see* W. Va. Jud. Investigatory Comm'n Adv. Op. 2/26/86 (1986) (municipal judges and police judges not subject to judicial code).

Canon 4 does not apply to nonjudicial officers. *See Feltz v. Crabtree*, 370 S.E.2d 619 (W. Va. 1988) (although circuit clerk is part of judicial branch of government, clerk is not the kind of judicial officer contemplated by judicial code; circuit clerk does not exercise judicial power).

A successful judicial candidate, whether an incumbent or not, is subject to judicial discipline for his or her campaign conduct. *See, e.g.*, Fla. Jud. Ethics Adv. Comm. 98-25 (1998) (judge-elect bound by political restrictions in Code of Judicial Conduct and should comply with restrictions applicable to sitting judges who are not candidates); Fla. Jud. Ethics Adv. Comm. Op. 00-16 (2000) (judge-elect may not actively participate in nonjudicial campaigns before he is sworn into office as county judge; judge-elect no longer is private citizen and must curtail political involvement accordingly).

Even a lawyer, who is subject to merit selection, rather than election, may be subject to Canon 4 restrictions. In ABA Informal Op. 85-1513 (1985), a lawyer applied for an initial appointment to a then-existing judicial vacancy and was solicited to attend a political fund-raising event. The ABA Standing Committee on Ethics and Professional Responsibility stated that the political activity proscriptions of Canon 7A, in effect at the time, applied to candidates for judicial appointment under a merit selection plan, and prohibited the candidate from participating in political fund-raising. *See also* Alaska Bar Assn. Ethics Op. 85-1 (1985) (adopting Inf. Op. 85-1513 that judicial rules apply to lawyer judicial candidates).

RELATED FEDERAL PROVISION

Federal judges, including United States Circuit Judges, District Judges, Court of International Trade Judges, Court of Federal Claims Judges, Bankruptcy Judges, and Magistrate Judges, are governed by the Code of Conduct for United States Judges, which was initially adopted by the Judicial Conference on April 5, 1973, and which was substantially revised effective July 2009. The Judicial Conference of the United States did not adopt the overall organization and numbering format of the revised ABA Model Code, but it did combine former Canons 4, 5, and 6 into a single new Canon, along the lines of the Model Code's organization of these provisions. Andrew J. Lievense & Avern Cohn, *The Federal Judiciary and the ABA Model Code: The Parting of the Ways*, Just. Sys. J. (Jan. 1, 2007).

Canon 5A of the Code of Conduct for United States Judges provides that a judge should not (1) act as a leader or hold any office in a political organization; (2) make speeches for a political organization or candidate or publicly endorse or oppose a candidate for public office; or (3) solicit funds for, pay an assessment to, or make a contribution to a political organization or candidate, or attend or purchase a ticket for a dinner or other event sponsored by a political organization or candidate. Under Canon 5B, a federal judge should resign from office when he or she becomes a candidate either in a primary or in a general election for any office. Lastly, Canon 5C states that a "judge should not engage in any other political activity," provided, however, that this does not prevent a judge from engaging in the activities described in Canon 4, which permits a judge to engage in extrajudicial activities to improve the law, the legal system, and the administration of justice. *See* U.S. Jud. Conf. Comm. on Code of Cond. Adv. Op. 19 (*reaff'd* 2009) (judges should not retain memberships in political clubs); U.S. Jud. Conf. Comm. on Code of Cond. Adv. Op. 53 (reaff'd 2009) (regarding judge's disassociation from political involvement of a judge's spouse); U.S. Jud. Conf. Comm. on Code of Conduct Adv. Op. 92 (*reaff'd* 2009) (setting forth guidelines for judicial employees covered by Code of Conduct for Judicial Employees who are contemplating involvement in political activities).

RULE 4.1 POLITICAL AND CAMPAIGN ACTIVITIES OF JUDGES AND JUDICIAL CANDIDATES IN GENERAL

(A) Except as permitted by law,* or by Rules 4.2, 4.3, and 4.4, a judge or a judicial candidate* shall not:

(1) act as a leader in, or hold an office in, a political organization;*

(2) make speeches on behalf of a political organization;

(3) publicly endorse or oppose a candidate for any public office;

(4) solicit funds for, pay an assessment to, or make a contribution* to a political organization or a candidate for public office;

(5) attend or purchase tickets for dinners or other events sponsored by a political organization or a candidate for public office;

(6) publicly identify himself or herself as a candidate of a political organization;

(7) seek, accept, or use endorsements from a political organization;

(8) personally solicit* or accept campaign contributions other than through a campaign committee authorized by Rule 4.4;

(9) use or permit the use of campaign contributions for the private benefit of the judge, the candidate, or others;

(10) use court staff, facilities, or other court resources in a campaign for judicial office;

(11) knowingly,* or with reckless disregard for the truth, make any false or misleading statement;

(12) make any statement that would reasonably be expected to affect the outcome or impair the fairness of a matter pending* or impending* in any court; or

(13) in connection with cases, controversies, or issues that are likely to come before the court, make pledges, promises, or commitments that are inconsistent with the impartial* performance of the adjudicative duties of judicial office.

(B) A judge or judicial candidate shall take reasonable measures to ensure that other persons do not undertake, on behalf of the judge or judicial candidate, any activities prohibited under paragraph (A).

COMMENT

General Considerations

[1] Even when subject to public election, a judge plays a role different from that of a legislator or executive branch official. Rather than making decisions based upon the expressed views or preferences of the electorate, a judge makes decisions based on the law and the facts of every case. Therefore, in furtherance of this interest, judges and judicial candidates must, to the greatest extent possible, be free and appear to be free from political influence and political pressure. This Canon imposes narrowly tailored restrictions upon the political and campaign activities of all judges and judicial candidates, taking into account the various methods of selecting judges.

[2] When a person becomes a judicial candidate, this Canon becomes applicable to his or her conduct.

Participation in Political Activities

[3] Public confidence in the independence and impartiality of the judiciary is eroded if judges or judicial candidates are perceived to be subject to political influence. Although judges and judicial candidates may register to vote as members of a political party, they are prohibited by paragraph (A)(1) from assuming leadership roles in political organizations.

[4] Paragraphs (A)(2) and (A)(3) prohibit judges and judicial candidates from making speeches on behalf of political organizations or publicly endorsing or opposing candidates for public office, respectively, to prevent them from abusing the prestige of judicial office to advance the interests of others. See Rule 1.3. These Rules do not prohibit candidates from campaigning on their own behalf, or from endorsing or opposing candidates for the same judicial office for which they are running. See Rules 4.2(B)(2) and 4.2(B)(3).

[5] Although members of the families of judges and judicial candidates are free to engage in their own political activity, including running for public office, there is no "family exception" to the prohibition in paragraph (A)(3) against a judge or candidate publicly endorsing candidates for public office. A judge or judicial candidate must not become involved in, or publicly associated with, a family member's political activity or campaign for public office. To avoid public misunderstanding, judges and judicial candidates should take, and should urge members of their families to take, reasonable steps to avoid any implication that they endorse any family member's candidacy or other political activity.

[6] Judges and judicial candidates retain the right to participate in the political process as voters in both primary and general elections. For purposes of this Canon, participation in a caucus-type election procedure does not constitute public support for or endorsement of a political organization or candidate, and is not prohibited by paragraphs (A)(2) or (A)(3).

Statements and Comments Made during a Campaign for Judicial Office

[7] Judicial candidates must be scrupulously fair and accurate in all statements made by them and by their campaign committees. Paragraph (A)(11) obligates candidates and their committees to refrain from making statements that are false or misleading, or that omit facts necessary to make the communication considered as a whole not materially misleading.

[8] Judicial candidates are sometimes the subject of false, misleading, or unfair allegations made by opposing candidates, third parties, or the media. For example, false or misleading statements might be made regarding the identity, present position, experience, qualifications, or judicial rulings of a candidate. In other situations, false or misleading allegations may be made that bear upon a candidate's integrity or fitness for judicial office. As long as the candidate does

not violate paragraphs (A)(11), (A)(12), or (A)(13), the candidate may make a factually accurate public response. In addition, when an independent third party has made unwarranted attacks on a candidate's opponent, the candidate may disavow the attacks, and request the third party to cease and desist.

[9] Subject to paragraph (A)(12), a judicial candidate is permitted to respond directly to false, misleading, or unfair allegations made against him or her during a campaign, although it is preferable for someone else to respond if the allegations relate to a pending case.

[10] Paragraph (A)(12) prohibits judicial candidates from making comments that might impair the fairness of pending or impending judicial proceedings. This provision does not restrict arguments or statements to the court or jury by a lawyer who is a judicial candidate, or rulings, statements, or instructions by a judge that may appropriately affect the outcome of a matter.

Pledges, Promises, or Commitments Inconsistent with Impartial Performance of the Adjudicative Duties of Judicial Office

[11] The role of a judge is different from that of a legislator or executive branch official, even when the judge is subject to public election. Campaigns for judicial office must be conducted differently from campaigns for other offices. The narrowly drafted restrictions upon political and campaign activities of judicial candidates provided in Canon 4 allow candidates to conduct campaigns that provide voters with sufficient information to permit them to distinguish between candidates and make informed electoral choices.

[12] Paragraph (A)(13) makes applicable to both judges and judicial candidates the prohibition that applies to judges in Rule 2.10(B), relating to pledges, promises, or commitments that are inconsistent with the impartial performance of the adjudicative duties of judicial office.

[13] The making of a pledge, promise, or commitment is not dependent upon, or limited to, the use of any specific words or phrases; instead, the totality of the statement must be examined to determine if a reasonable person would believe that the candidate for judicial office has specifically undertaken to reach a particular result. Pledges, promises, or commitments must be contrasted with statements or announcements of personal views on legal, political, or other issues, which are not prohibited. When making such statements, a judge should acknowledge the overarching judicial obligation to apply and uphold the law, without regard to his or her personal views.

[14] A judicial candidate may make campaign promises related to judicial organization, administration, and court management, such as a promise to dispose of a backlog of cases, start court sessions on time, or avoid favoritism in appointments and hiring. A candidate may also pledge to take action outside

the courtroom, such as working toward an improved jury selection system, or advocating for more funds to improve the physical plant and amenities of the courthouse.

[15] Judicial candidates may receive questionnaires or requests for interviews from the media and from issue advocacy or other community organizations that seek to learn their views on disputed or controversial legal or political issues. Paragraph (A)(13) does not specifically address judicial responses to such inquiries. Depending upon the wording and format of such questionnaires, candidates' responses might be viewed as pledges, promises, or commitments to perform the adjudicative duties of office other than in an impartial way. To avoid violating paragraph (A)(13), therefore, candidates who respond to media and other inquiries should also give assurances that they will keep an open mind and will carry out their adjudicative duties faithfully and impartially, if elected. Candidates who do not respond may state their reasons for not responding, such as the danger that answering might be perceived by a reasonable person as undermining a successful candidate's independence or impartiality, or that it might lead to frequent disqualification. See Rule 2.11.

1990 Code Comparison

Most of Rule 4.1 and its Comments are either identical or virtually identical to provisions in Canon 5A and Canon 5C in the 1990 Code. Rule 4.1(B) combines in a single Rule, and greatly simplifies most provisions of Canon 5A(3)(a) and Canon 5A(3)(b). Some concepts that appeared in the black letter text in the 1990 Code have been moved to Comments, and some aspects of the Comments from 1990 have been incorporated into the new black letter text. There are three additional prohibitions, Rules 4.1(A)(6), (7), and (10). Charles G. Geyh & W. William Hodes, *Reporters' Notes to the Model Code of Judicial Conduct* 97–98 (2009).

Rule 4.1(A)(5) generally prohibits attending political organization functions. Rule 4.2(B)(4) permits an exception, but only during a candidate's candidacy and after a specific time.

Rule 4.1(A)(6), which states that "a judge or judicial candidate shall not publicly identify himself or herself as a candidate of a political organization," was added, but later Rules in Canon 4 create some exceptions. Rules 4.2(C)(1) and 4.2(C)(2) recognize that in partisan public elections for judicial office, judges must be permitted to communicate to voters the fact that they were nominated by a particular political organization or party. Rule 4.1(A)(7), which prohibits a judge or judicial candidate from seeking, accepting, or using endorsements from a political organization also is new, and is similar to Rule 4.1(A)(6) in terms of its relationship to other Rules in Canon 4. Charles G. Geyh & W. William Hodes, *Reporters' Notes to the Model Code of Judicial Conduct* 98–9 (2009).

Rule 4.1(A)(8) retains the language that prohibits a judge or candidate not to personally solicit campaign contributions. It was derived from the first two sentences of Canon 5C(2), but employs different terminology and applies only to solicitation of campaign contributions, not "publicly stated support." However, the 1990 Code's prohibition against personally soliciting publicly stated support was eliminated in favor of a prohibition against seeking support from political organizations, contained in subparagraph (A)(7). The Commission retained the provision permitting contributions to be accepted only through a duly established campaign committee, as provided for in Rule 4.4 on the theory that the solicitation of campaign funds in the judicial election context could justify restrictions greater than those permitted for lawyer advertising. *Id.*

Rule 4.1(A)(10), which prohibits use of official resources for a judge's campaign, is not substantially different from its counterpart in the 1990 Code. Pursuant to the Rule, judges are not permitted to use court staff, facilities, or other court resources in a campaign for judicial office.

In Rule 4.1(A)(11), "knowingly, or with reckless disregard for the truth, make any false or misleading statement" replaces 1990 Code language prohibiting judicial candidates from "knowingly misrepresenting the identity, qualifications, present position or other fact concerning the candidate or an opponent." The new language is borrowed from the law of libel and slander and fraudulent misrepresentation. Charles G. Geyh & W. William Hodes, *Reporters' Notes to the Model Code of Judicial Conduct* 99–100 (2009).

Rule 4.1(A)(12) adds a provision addressing statements that could affect the outcome or impair the fairness of pending or impending cases. The "pledges and promises" clause in the 1990 Code was substantively retained in Rule 4.1(A)(13). *Id.* at 100–02.

Rule 4.1(B) provides that no other person should take actions that are prohibited under any of the subparagraphs of Rule 4.1(A) on behalf of a judge or judicial candidate. Because the Code of Judicial Conduct reaches the conduct of only those who are judges or candidates for judicial office, Rule 4.1(B) requires that reasonable measures be taken by the judge or candidate to avoid improper assistance by others. In the 1990 Code, the problem of candidates taking prohibited actions through another was addressed separately for family members and for court employees and others under the control of the judge or judicial candidates.

New Comment [1] states that "judges and judicial candidates must, to the greatest extent possible, be free and appear to be free from political influence and political pressure." The Comment in effect serves as a preamble to Canon 4. Two key points are involved: that states have a compelling interest in the quality of their judiciary and in the regularity of the selection process; and that restrictions on political and campaign-related speech must be narrowly tailored and the least restrictive possible, even when serving such a compelling state interest.

New Comment [3] states that mere participation in electoral politics does not warrant a restriction, but assuming a leadership role would call into question the judge's or candidate's independence. Comment [4] is new, too, and states that although judicial candidates generally are not permitted to endorse other candidates (to avoid abusing the prestige of judicial office), they are nevertheless permitted to campaign on their own behalf. They also are permitted to campaign for other judicial candidates who are effectively running in the same race. Another new provision, Comment [5], states that judges and judicial candidates must take reasonable steps to ensure that the public does not receive the impression that a judge or judicial candidate is endorsing a family member's candidacy for political office.

Comment [10] to Rule 4.1 provides an important observation: statements that are legitimately designed to affect the outcome of a matter, such as arguments to a jury or instructions given by a court, are permissible provided that they do not impair the fairness of the proceeding. Comments [11] through [15], which describe what judges and nonjudge candidates may ethically say and not say, are consistent with *Minnesota Republican Party v. White.*

Comments [13] and [14] are completely new and address the making of pledges, promises, or commitments. They were added to encourage adoption of an appropriately narrow interpretation of the pledges and promises clause by disciplinary authorities and by judges and candidates assessing their own conduct. Comment [13] states that when making such statements, "a judge should acknowledge the overarching judicial obligation to apply and uphold the law, without regard to his or her personal views." Comment [14] allows judges or judicial candidates to makes campaign promises related to such matters as judicial organization, administration, and court management.

New Comment [15] addresses the widespread use of questionnaires, the responses to which could be viewed as pledges, promises, or commitments to perform the adjudicative duties of office other than in an impartial way. In recent years, questionnaires have become an important tool for issue advocacy and other citizen groups to determine judges' and judicial candidates' views concerning disputed or controversial legal or political issues. The Comment states that "candidates who respond to media and other inquiries should also give assurances that they will keep an open mind and will carry out their adjudicative duties faithfully and impartially, if elected." Judicial candidates also have the right to refuse to answer, with or without giving reasons, or to answer only in formats that are agreeable to them and are in compliance with Rule 4.1(A)(13).

ANNOTATION

Rule 4.1 seeks to define inappropriate political activity by setting forth proscribed activity for judges and judicial candidates, with a few exceptions. A "judicial candidate" is defined in the Terminology section of the Code as "any person, including a sitting judge, who is seeking selection for or retention in judicial office by election or appointment. A person becomes a candidate for judicial office as soon as he or she makes a public announcement of candidacy, declares or files as a candidate with the election or appointment authority, authorizes or, where permitted, engages in solicitation or acceptance of contributions or support, or is nominated for election or appointment to office." Taking a leave of absence, even without pay, does not relieve judges or judicial candidates of the obligation of refraining from prohibited partisan political activity. *See, e.g.*, Md. Jud. Ethics Comm. Op. 1986-03 (1986) (a "leave of absence" does not exempt one from judicial limitations). *See generally* Michael R. Dimino, Sr., *The Worst Way of Selecting Judges—Except All the Others That Have Been Tried*, 32 N. Ky. L. Rev. 267 (2005); Ryan L. Saunders, Note, *A Gorilla at the Dinner Table: Partisan Judicial Elections in the United States*, 25 Rev. Litig. 529 (Summer 2006).

"Political Activity" Defined

Judges and judicial candidates are prohibited from engaging in political activities, except as authorized by the codes and rules governing judicial conduct or other provisions of law. Further, judges and nonjudges who seek an elective judicial office may engage in political activity only during a prescribed "window period." *See* Nev. Stand. Comm. on Jud. Ethics and Election Pracs. Op. JE 03-005 (2003) (judicial candidate may not send out mailings announcing upcoming campaign event prior to commencement of 240-day judicial campaign season established in state code of judicial conduct); N.Y. Adv. Comm. on Jud. Ethics Op. 13-22 (2013) (judge may not participate in politically sponsored sporting event outside of applicable window period); Tex. Adv. Comm. on Jud. Ethics Op. 56 (1981) (judge may have fund-raising benefit in year when he is not up for election); W. Va. Jud. Investigatory Comm'n Adv. Op. 10/31/07 (2007) (judge who has filed appropriate pre-candidacy papers and has committee could begin campaigning in non-election year).

Defining the parameters of ethically permissible political activity in specific situations can be challenging. *See, e.g.*, *In re Braig*, 554 A.2d 493 (Pa. 1989) (de minimis activities of judge in nonpartisan selection of police commissioner were within exception allowing acts to improve law, the legal system, or the administration of justice); *In re Staples*, 719 P.2d 558 (Wash. 1986) (there are two reasons for limiting judicial political activity: to prevent the possibility that bias or the appearance of bias may result and to protect the esteem and dignity of the court. While these concerns are justified when considering partisan political activity, they do not exist when nonpartisan, civic-minded political activity is involved). Twelve years later, in considering disciplinary proceedings commenced against a justice of the Washington Supreme Court, a panel serving as justices pro tempore of the court found *Staples*' statement regarding partisan activity unhelpful because the prohibition on political activity "must be read in light of the directive in Canon 1 that judges act in furtherance of maintaining an impartial judiciary." *Matter of Disc. Proc. Against Sanders*, 955 P.2d 369 (Wash. 1998) ("The prohibition against engaging in other political activity cannot mean simply avoiding issues that divide neatly along traditional party lines. To do so would thwart efforts to fulfill the goals of Canon 1."). *See also* Colo. Jud. Ethics Adv. Bd. Op. 2008-04 (2008) (judges standing for retention may not appear on television program in which representative of League of Women Voters would ask them questions to help provide viewers with more information about whether or not judges should be retained; viewers might reasonably expect that judges are seeking approval vote and might therefore understand that judges are engaging in campaign activity); Del. Jud. Ethics Adv. Comm. Op. 2000-2 (2000) (judicial nominee who has not yet taken oath of office may participate in a Memorial Day Parade at the invitation of the Veterans of Foreign Wars as sitting judge would also be permitted to do so; though not yet bound by the Code, proper for judicial nominee to look to the Code for guidance); Fla. Sup. Ct. Jud. Ethics Adv. Comm. 2013-20 (2013) (judge may not be a member of SUNPAC, a political action committee); Ill. Jud. Ethics Comm. Op. 98-16 (1998) (judge who is campaigning for election cannot serve as deputy voter registrar; efforts to increase voter turnout in support of own candidacy constitutes political activity); Ind. Comm'n on Jud. Qualifications Adv. Op. 7-91 (1991) (judge may serve on precinct election board at voting polls); Ind. Comm'n on Jud. Qualifications Adv. Op. 8-90 (1990) (judge may act as voter registrar so long as activity does not become inappropriately political).

The New Jersey Supreme Court has held that not only partisan activities, but also any issue-oriented activity is impermissible under this Canon. *In re Randolph*, 502 A.2d 533, 539 (N.J. 1986) ("It has been traditional in New Jersey's judiciary to construe 'political activity' to include activity supporting or opposing different sides of social, political, and legislative issues."). *See generally* James R. Noseda, *Limiting Off-Bench Expression: Striking a Balance Between Accountability and Indifference*, 36 DePaul L. Rev. 519 (1987) (comparing the *Staples* and *Randolph* decisions, and noting that they represent disparate approaches to off-bench conduct; the *Staples* court trusts that the public's perception of an impartial jury is threatened only where a judge is involved in partisan politics, while the *Randolph* court is wary of any activity that might be remotely connected to politics or controversial political issues and grants little credit to the public's ability to evaluate the propriety of judicial off-bench conduct).

ACTING AS LEADER OR HOLDING OFFICE IN POLITICAL ORGANIZATION

Pursuant to Rule 4.1(A)(1), a judge or a candidate for judicial office shall not act as a leader or hold an office in a "political organization," except as authorized in Rules 4.2, 4.3, and 4.4. A "political organization" is defined in the Terminology section of the Code as "a political party or other group sponsored by or affiliated with a political party or candidate, the principal purpose of which is to further the election or appointment of candidates for political office." *See, e.g., Matter of Katic*, 549 N.E.2d 1039 (Ind. 1990) (judge violated Canon by deliberately and publicly acting as leader in the Democratic political party before and during primary elections); *Miss. Comm'n on Jud. Performance v. Peyton*, 555 So. 2d 1036 (Miss. 1990) (judge remained active in political party following election to bench, including serving as chair of Democratic Executive Committee, actively participating in party caucuses, serving as delegate at national convention, and attending several political meetings related to close friend's congressional campaign); *In re Maney*, 510 N.E.2d 312 (N.Y. 1987) (judge never really terminated intense political involvement after his election, but instead openly engaged in long-term struggle for control of local Democratic Party leadership and actively solicited support for his own faction among party members and assumed partisan stance in relatively public setting of party caucus); *In re Blauvelt*, 801 P.2d 235 (Wash. 1990) (judge serving as delegate to political party's county convention is "leader" within meaning of prohibition against judge acting as leader in political organization, even though judge does not have power over the party); Ga. Jud. Qualifications Comm'n Op. No. 208 (1996) (improper for judicial candidate to participate in and actually vote at meeting of county political party committee called to elect his replacement as committee chairman); Ill. Jud. Ethics. Comm. Op. 98-15 (1998) (candidate may not retain membership either in political party's central committee or on board of directors of nonprofit organization that, among other things, functions as political action committee); Ind. Comm'n on Jud. Qualification Adv. Op. 6-91 (1991) (judge may be member of political party editorial association that meets with politicians and newspaper editors of same political persuasion to discuss position on political issues that help formulate content of newspaper editorials so long as judge does not hold office in organization); Kan. Jud. Ethics Op. JE 66 (1996) (judicial candidate may not run for district judge and for precinct committee person at same election); Kan. Jud. Ethics Adv. Op. JE 51 (1994) (part-time judge may not serve as precinct committeeperson); Mich. Comm. on Jud. Ethics Op. JI-65 (1993) (judge may not serve on legislative affairs and political action committee whose mission is to support pro-business interests by promotion in media, before governmental bodies, and by supporting election of business-oriented candidates to partisan or nonpartisan offices); Mich. Comm. on Jud. Ethics Op. JI-22 (1990) (judge may not serve on board of directors of charitable fund-raising foundation to be established as separate entity with tax-exempt status by Democratic Party of county in honor of deceased political party leader); N.M. Adv. Comm. on the Code of Jud. Cond. Op. 09-02 (2009) (judge may not serve as delegate to a county political convention); N.M. Adv. Comm. on the Code of Jud. Cond. Op. 96-07 (1996) (judge not precluded from attending national party political convention when acting in non-official capacity; judge may not act as delegate or serve as alternate delegate); N.Y. Adv. Comm. on Jud. Ethics Op. 01-44 (2001) (nonjudge candidate for elective judicial office may not retain position of ward committee person of political party); Ohio Bd. of Commissioners on Grievances and Disc. Op. 98-08 (1998) (improper for full-time or part-time judge, full-time or part-time magistrate, or judge pro tempore to serve as member of state or county executive committee of political party or as member of county board of elections); Tex. Adv. Comm. on Jud. Ethics Op. 259 (2000) (judges may not serve as delegates to county, state, or national party conventions or on state Republican or Democrat executive committees); Utah Jud. Ethics Adv. Comm. Informal Op. 88-7 (1988) (judge or judge's spouse may not host or attend mass meeting because to do so would be to attend political gathering or act as leader in political organization); Wash. Ethics Adv. Comm. Op. 93-20 (1993) (judge may not serve as retained counsel for political party even if unpaid position); *but see* Ariz. Jud. Ethics Adv. Comm. Op. 94-14 (1994) (candidate for justice of peace not required to resign membership from school board, which is not a political organization); Fla. Comm. on Stands. of Cond. Governing Judges Op. 94-23 (1994) (nonjudge judicial candidate does not have to resign from the Nominating Council of Florida Public Service Commission if he or she will not actively participate on council during candidacy); Kan. Jud. Ethics Op. JE 110 (2002) (part-time municipal judge may serve as precinct committee member and accept a term as city council member if written in on ballot and elected without his or her consent); Kan. Jud. Ethics Op. JE 96 (2000) (judicial candidate may continue to serve on committee or commission concerned with issues of fact or law not involving law or courts; upon election, judge must resign); Kan. Jud. Ethics Adv. Op. JE 90 (1999) (newly appointed judge may complete present term on local school board, although better practice would be for judge to resign); Mich. Comm. on Jud. Ethics Op. JI-91 (1994) (candidate for judicial office, who is not currently judge, may continue to serve on township downtown developmental authority while campaigning); Tex. Adv. Comm. on Jud. Ethics Op. 51 (1980) (judge does not violate Canons by accepting position as treasurer for ad hoc political organization that confines itself to "get out the vote" program for all Democratic candidates); W. Va. Adv. Op. 8/2/07 (2007) (mental hygiene commissioner need not resign position in order to run for either circuit court judge or family court judge); W. Va. Adv. Op. 6/7/96 (1996) (no Canon requires advocate for domestic violence victims to resign that position upon becoming candidate for judicial office; but if elected, judicial officer may be required to recuse himself or herself from cases involving domestic violence issues in order to avoid appearance of partiality or reasonable questioning of impartiality).

This provision has been challenged as an unconstitutional restriction of judicial candidate's First Amendment right to free speech. In *Bauer v. Shepard*, 620 F.3d 704 (7th Cir. 2010), the Seventh Circuit Court of Appeals upheld the restriction, applying a balancing test and distinguishing between free speech rights in support of one's own election and conducting electoral activities on behalf of third parties. The court explained that states have a compelling interest in ensuring judges do not become "party bosses," participation in politics undermines the appearance of impropriety, and judges may not lend the prestige of their office to others. *Id.* at 711–12.

MAKING SPEECHES ON BEHALF OF POLITICAL ORGANIZATIONS

Rule 4.1(A)(2) prohibits judges or judicial candidates from making speeches on behalf of a political organization. *See, e.g.*, Alaska Comm'n on Jud. Cond. Formal Ethics Op. 011 (1991) (judges who give speeches on general legal issues at political party fund-raising events violate code of judicial conduct); Del. Jud. Ethics Adv. Comm. Op. 2005-3 (2005) (judge should not speak at or attend event organized by Republican Party honoring former attorney general; event is "political gathering"); Fla. Jud. Ethics Adv. Comm. Op. 93-07 (1993) (judge may not speak about court system at local women's Republican Club luncheon because judge is not currently candidate for election and is, therefore, ineligible to speak before political groups); Nev. Stand. Comm. on Jud. Ethics & Election Pracs. Op. JE 08-009 (2008) (candidate may not accept invitation to speak at event sponsored by political party when invitation states that only judicial candidates who are registered members of that party will be allowed to speak); Wash. Ethics Adv. Comm. Op. 96-01 (1996) (judge may not attend national convention of political party and address gathering even if judge's address is on nonpartisan topic).

The provision has been challenged as an unconstitutional infringement on judges and judicial candidates' First Amendment Rights. *See generally Bauer v. Shepard*, 620 F. 3d 704 (7th Cir. 2010); *Wolfson v. Concannon*, 811 F.3d 1176 (9th Cir. 2016). The Ninth Circuit upheld this provision in *Wolfson v. Concannon*, finding that the Arizona rule prohibiting judges and judicial candidates from making speeches on behalf of a political organization or a candidate for public office was not underinclusive. *Wolfson v. Concannon*, 811 F.3d 1176 (9th Cir. 2016). Applying the test articulated in the Supreme Court in *Williams–Yulee v.*

Fla. Bar, 575 U.S. ____, 135 S. Ct. 1656, 1664, 191 L. Ed. 2d 570 (2015), the Ninth Circuit held that the restriction was "squarely aimed at preventing conduct that could erode the judiciary's credibility," it had few exceptions, and it applied evenly to all judges and judicial candidates. *Wolfson v. Concannon*, 811 F.3d 1176 (9th Cir. 2016).

The Seventh Circuit Court of Appeals upheld this provision in *Bauer v. Shepard*, 620 F.3d 704 (7th Cir. 2010), finding that the Indiana Code did not violate the First Amendment rights of judicial candidates because it survived the balancing test used by the courts when analyzing a speech restriction of a government employee. The Court explained that a balancing approach was appropriate because this kind of electoral activity was to "assist other persons" not to support a judge's personal campaign for office.

State judicial ethics committees have found a number of exceptions to the general prohibition against making speeches on behalf of political organizations. The nature of the occasion may determine if the judge is speaking on behalf of the law, the legal system, or the administration of justice, which is permitted, or on behalf of a political party, which is not. *See* discussion of Comment [14] to Rule 4.1 *infra*. *See also* Ill. Jud. Ethics Comm. Op. 96-19 (1996) (judge may be featured as speaker at county Lincoln Day Dinner promoted by political party that is held after election only if event is community gathering rather than fund-raiser for political organization); Mich. Comm. on Jud. Ethics Op. JI-121 (1999) (judge may serve as moderator at forum on criminal justice initiatives conducted by political party provided (1) judge does not comment on pending or impending cases in court system, (2) judge does not take position on legislative initiative that would preclude judge from later presiding over case or controversy involving subject matter of forum, and (3) judge's participation in forum does not interfere with performance of judge's judicial duties); W. Va. Adv. Op. 11/3/95 (1995) (judicial officer may serve as moderator of debate between candidates for governor). The subject matter and context of the judge's speech may also be relevant factors; *see* Fla. Jud. Ethics Adv. Comm. Op. 94-27 (1994) (judge may speak at public meeting sponsored by organization closely associated with former third-party presidential candidate Ross Perot because talk would focus on functions of courts and related matters); Ill. Jud. Ethics Comm. Op. 94-17 (1994) (judges may speak publicly about local government issues, such as bond issues and school district tax referendums, so long as any such speech is not on behalf of a political organization). *Cf.* Cal. Judges Ass'n Jud. Ethics Comm. Adv. Op 46 (1997) (impossible to draw bright line between permissible and impermissible participation in organizations addressing issues involving social problems in community; opinion lists factors to be considered in determining whether judicial participation is appropriate).

PUBLICLY ENDORSING OR OPPOSING CANDIDATES FOR PUBLIC OFFICE

Pursuant to Rule 4.1(A)(3), judges or candidates for judicial office are prohibited from publicly endorsing or opposing another candidate for public office. However, Comment [4] states that these Rules do not prohibit candidates from campaigning on their own behalf or from endorsing or opposing candidates for the same judicial office for which they are running. *See, e.g., In re Katic*, 549 N.E.2d 1039 (Ind. 1990) (judge violated Canon by publicly opposing someone's candidacy for township trustee and making his position known to the media; judge also publicly encouraged candidacy of certain individuals and gave frequent interviews to newspapers in which he discussed his efforts to depose the township trustee); *In re Combs* (Ky. Jud. Cond. Comm. 2015) (judge suspended for 180 days in part for publicly endorsing or opposing a candidate when judge made calls to two people chastising them for having a political candidate's yard sign and called a third person to ask him to post a yard sign for a specific candidate); *In re Cohen* (Ky. Jud. Cond. Comm. 2014) (judge publicly reprimanded for violating prohibition against endorsing a candidate for public office when judge "liked" a Facebook post that endorsed a candidate); *In re Cacciatore* (N.Y. State Comm'n on Jud. Cond. Feb. 6, 1998) (justice endorsed certain candidates for mayor and trustee, criticized their opponents, and made statements on partisan political issues in campaign); *In re Decker* (N.Y. State Comm'n on Jud. Cond. 1994) (judge publicly supported county executive's campaign and criticized his opponent); *In Re Koon*, 580 S.E.2d 147 (S.C. 2003) (impermissible for part-time municipal court judge to participate in taped telephone message that solicited support for candidate for lieutenant governor); ABA Formal Ethics Op. 462 (2013) (when using electronic social media, judge should be aware that pushing a "like" button may be viewed as a political endorsement); ABA Informal Op. 1468 (1981) (improper under 1973 Code of Judicial Conduct for judge to publicly support or oppose election or re-election of another to court in same state; nor may judge participate in any public solicitation or partisan effort to recruit or oppose judicial candidate other than with his own candidacy); Ariz. Jud. Ethics Adv. Comm. Op. 10-01 (2010) (judge may not campaign on behalf of out-of-state candidate or national candidate); Ariz. Jud. Ethics Adv. Comm. Op. 08-01 (2008) (judicial candidate may not endorse other candidates for elective office, but may publish third-party endorsements); Ark. Jud. Ethics Adv. Comm. Op. 07-2 (2007) (judicial candidate may not honor commitment to chair fund-raising event for nonjudicial candidate made prior to announcing his or her candidacy); Cal. Judges Ass'n Jud. Ethics Comm. Adv. Op 57 (2006) (judge who was formerly district attorney may not comment on announced candidacy for that office of former colleague); Fla. Comm. on Standards of Conduct Governing Judges

Op. 90-3 (1990) (impermissible for sitting judge to support retention of another member of judiciary in merit retention election when that member is target of rejection campaign by head of another branch of government; judge may speak privately on behalf of judicial officer under attack but may not organize or serve on committee designed to support retention); Ind. Comm'n on Jud. Qualifications Adv. Op. 2-91 (1991) (judge should not appear in political candidate's campaign materials or in any way endorse candidate for public office); Kan. Jud. Ethics Op. JE 128 (2005) (judge may not write letter of recommendation or letter regarding qualifications of candidate to committee formed to select district magistrate judge); Kan. Jud. Ethics Op. JE 45 (1993) (judge prohibited from writing letter to President or members of Congress supporting or endorsing appointment of potential nominee to position in Justice Department or for federal judiciary); Md. Jud. Ethics Comm. Op. 2001-33 (2001) (judge may not attend political fund-raising event for judges of another court); Md. Jud. Ethics Comm. Op. 2001-10 (2001) (judicial candidate may not participate in joint fund-raiser for judge and register of wills); N.Y. Adv. Comm. on Jud. Ethics Op. 13-17 (2013) (judge may not sign petition purported to support change in law that reads as statement in support of state legislator); N.Y. Adv. Comm. on Jud. Ethics Op. 08-40 (2008) (judicial candidate should not engage in joint fund-raising activity with candidate for nonjudicial office); Ohio Bd. of Commissioners on Grievances and Disc. Op. 2002-13 (2002) (improper for magistrate to engage in campaign activities, such as going door-to-door to talk with people, going door-to-door to distribute campaign literature, placing yard signs, or participating in a telephone bank, on behalf of appointing judge who is seeking re-election); *In re Keys*, 671 N.E.2d 1124 (Ohio Comm'n of Judges 1996) (judicial candidates violated Canon by agreeing to have their names placed on invitation to fund-raiser for another candidate for public office as members of host committee); Tex. Adv. Comm. on Jud. Ethics Adv. Op. 267 (2000) (judge may not hire lawyer who is candidate for judicial office); Tex. Adv. Comm. on Jud. Ethics Adv. Op. 224 (1998) (justice of the peace and constables association may not endorse candidates for political office); Tex. Adv. Comm. on Jud. Ethics Adv. Op. 100 (1987) (two or more judges running for judicial office at same time may not jointly sponsor fund-raising event or have politically active group do so for them); W. Va. Adv. Op. 9/30/91 (1991) (improper for incumbent candidate to endorse another candidate for judicial office even if judge believes that election of latter would promote proper administration of justice; improper for judicial officer, whether or not candidate, to publicly oppose candidacy of lawyer for judicial office even if former believes that election of latter would be detrimental to proper administration of justice); *but see* Ala. Jud. Inquiry Comm'n Adv. Op. 00-755 (2000) (probate judge who is not running for re-election may publicly support candidate for position in upcoming election); Ky. Jud. Ethics

Op. JE-98 (2002) (judge or judicial candidate may attend fund-raiser for another candidate, but may not make contribution to another campaign); Nev. Stand. Comm. on Jud. Ethics and Election Pracs. Op. JE 07-013 (2007) (group of judges may issue joint invitations to potential supporters to attend joint function concerning their candidacy for election to their current positions, provided that judges exercise appropriate caution to avoid suggestion of endorsement by each judge of other participating judges); Okla. Jud. Ethics Op. 2006-3 (2006) (part-time municipal judge may act as chairperson of re-election committee of district judge) and *cf.* Ala. Jud. Inquiry Comm'n Adv. Op. 06-869 (2006) (judge or candidate for judicial office may serve on county committee for candidate for election to nonjudicial statewide office, but is strongly discouraged from doing so; certain of the activities, namely submitting names to another committee of possible campaign donors and volunteer workers and helping to organize fund-raising events, should be done in a personal capacity without any identification of the judicial position; certain other activities, namely making telephone calls on behalf of candidate and serving as host to candidate upon candidate's visit to county, are prohibited); Ala. Jud. Inquiry Comm'n Adv. Op. 93-493 (1993) (judge "strongly discouraged but not prohibited" from serving on and/or giving "general advice regarding political matters" to county committee formed to elect political candidate to the office of governor); Ariz. Jud. Ethics Adv. Comm. Op. 08-01 (2008) (judicial candidate may not endorse other candidates for elective office, but may publish third-party endorsements); Ill. Jud. Ethics Comm. Op. 01-07 (2001) (judge may provide letter of recommendation or serve as reference for person seeking appointment to township political organization's governing board).

A judge or judicial candidate may violate Rule 4.1(A)(3) by soliciting someone to run against another judge for office. *See* Fla. Comm. on Standards of Conduct Governing Judges Op. 82-8 (1982) (judge may not solicit lawyer to run against another judge).

Appearing on the same ballot as another candidate is not a public endorsement of that candidate. *See, e.g.*, Md. Jud. Ethics Comm. Op. 1985-04 (1985) (judicial candidate may appear on ticket with nonjudicial candidates); W. Va. Adv. Op. 2/18/00 (2000) (appearance of judicial candidate's name on same ballot as daughter who is running for county prosecutor does not violate prohibition against judicial candidate publicly endorsing or opposing any candidate for public office).

Washington and Montana draw a distinction in their rules between support of judicial and nonjudicial candidates. *See, e.g.*, Wash. Ethics Adv. Comm. Op. 93-09 (1993) (part-time judges may not publicly endorse candidate for prosecuting attorney as judges, as lawyers, or as private citizens); Wash. Ethics Adv. Comm. Op. 93-25 (1993) (judges holding offices filled by public election between competing candidates may attend political gatherings and speak to such gatherings on their own behalf or that of another judicial candidate; sitting judge may publicly endorse another sitting judge's candidacy in a contested election, which may include writing letters to local newspapers).

First Amendment Issues

State versions of Rule 4.1(A)(3)'s restriction on public endorsements by judges or judicial candidates of or in opposition to other candidates for public office have withstood constitutional challenge. *Wolfson v. Concannon*, 811 F.3d 1176 (9th Cir. 2016) (using strict scrutiny test, court finds Arizona rule prohibiting judges from opposing or endorsing another candidate for public office was "squarely aimed at preventing conduct that could erode the judiciary's credibility," it had few exceptions, and it applied evenly to all judges and judicial candidates); *Wersal v. Sexton*, 674 F. 3d 1010 (8th Cir. 2012) (using a strict scrutiny test, court upholds the Minnesota prohibition on publicly endorsing or publicly opposing another candidate for public office explaining that unlike the announce clause and the partisan-activities clause, the endorse clause is a narrowly tailored "restriction of speech for or against particular parties, rather than for or against particular issues" that advances the state's compelling goal of ensuring the appearance of impropriety); *Siefert v. Alexander*, 608 F.3d 974 (7th Cir. 2010) (using a balancing approach, court finds that state may prohibit government employees, including judges, from publicly endorsing or opposing other candidate's for public office to prevent the abuse of judicial office to "advance the interests of others"); *In re Code of Judicial Conduct*, 603 So. 2d 494 (Fla. 1992) (declaring Canon that prohibits judges from publicly endorsing candidate for public office constitutional).

Endorsing or Supporting Spouse's or Relative's Campaign

Restrictions on a judge's or judicial candidate's endorsement or support of a candidate apply even if the candidate is the judge's or judicial candidate's spouse or other relative. Rule 4.1(A) Comment [5] states that there is no "family exception" to the prohibition in Rule 4.1(A)(3), and that "judicial candidates should take, and should urge members of their families to take, reasonable steps to avoid any implication that they endorse any family member's candidacy or other political activity." Most of the cases and ethics opinions regarding family members' campaigns involve judges' or candidates' efforts to actively campaign for the relative or engage in other activity that indicates endorsement of or support for the relative's campaign. *See, e.g.*, *In re McGregor*, 614 So. 2d 1089 (Fla. 1993) (judge reprimanded for actively campaigning for wife in campaign for county clerk of court); *In re Turner*, 573 So. 2d 1 (Fla. 1990) (judge violated Canon by soliciting support for son's judicial campaign from local lawyers, asking supporters of son's opponent why they supported opponent, and soliciting fellow judges for guardian ad litem appointments for son); *In re Codispoti*, 438 S.E.2d 549 (W. Va. 1993) (judge was improperly involved in wife's judicial campaign); Ala. Jud. Inquiry Comm'n Adv. Op. 82-143 (1982) (judge may not allow his or her picture to be used in campaign of immediate family member); Cal. Judges Ass'n Jud. Ethics Comm. Adv. Op. 49 (2000) (judge should not publicly campaign on behalf of family member/candidate in any way); Fla. Comm. on Stands. of Cond. Governing Judges Op. 87-22 (1987) (judge may not do "leg work" for relative's campaign); La. Sup. Ct. Comm. on Jud. Ethics Adv. Op. 52 (1981) (judge may not solicit votes or contributions for family member's campaign through personal contact); Mass. Comm. on Jud. Ethics Adv. Op. 2003-8 (2003) (establishing guidelines with regard to judge with dependent son who wishes to run for public office); Mass. Comm. on Jud. Ethics Adv. Op. 99-16 (1999) (judge whose spouse is campaigning for U.S. Senate seat may not attend events designed to enhance electability of, to pay homage to, to rally support behind, or to raise funds for, particular candidate); Mich. Comm. on Jud. Ethics. Op. JI-30 (1990) (judge must not hand out campaign literature on behalf of nonjudicial candidate who is relative of judge or member of judge's household); N.M. Adv. Comm. on the Code of Jud. Cond. Op. 96-02 (1996) (judge may solicit signatures for spouse's nominating petition and assist spouse in door-to-door campaigning so long as judge does so as private person outside of his normal business hours); N.M. Adv. Comm. on the Code of Jud. Cond. Op. 96-01 (1996) (campaign literature of spouse or daughter of judge may state that candidate is related to judge but may not give indication of judge's office or use title in the campaign literature); N.Y. Adv. Comm. on Jud. Ethics Op. 06-147 (2007) (judge may march in parade so long as judge marches along with other dignitaries and judges in attendance rather than with campaigning spouse); Ohio Bd. of Commissioners on Grievances and Disc. Op. 2001-1 (2001) (when judge's spouse is candidate for elected public or judicial office, judge may appear in family picture and be listed by name with or without title "judge" in spouse's campaign literature but shall not be otherwise depicted in his or her official capacity; judge's inclusion in family picture and identification by name and title in spouse's campaign literature does not constitute "public endorsement"; judge may allow campaign signs promoting spouse's candidacy to be placed on real estate jointly owned by judge and spouse); Okla. Jud. Ethics Op. 2006-4 (2006) (court reporter who works for district court may not campaign for spouse who plans to run for associate district judge in that district); S.C. Adv. Comm. on Stands. of Jud. Cond. 09-2002 (2002) (judge may appear in family photo to be used in spouse's political campaign and may drive truck so that spouse can set out campaign signs); Tex. Adv. Comm. on Jud. Ethics Op. 295 (2009) (judge whose spouse is running for judicial office can appear in family photo or image in political advertising of spouse and be identified by name, but not title, as spouse of candidate for office; if inquiry is made to candidate at political event or interview, candidate may state occupation of spouse who is current judge); Vt. Jud. Ethics Comm. Op. 2728-10 (2004) (judge whose spouse is running for legislature may appear in family photograph if identified as family member and not as judge; judge may not accompany spouse to functions that are truly partisan in nature); Wash. Ethics Adv. Comm. Op. 02-02 (2002) (judge may appear in family photograph used in spouse's campaign so long as photograph does not identify judge as judge; judge may attend non-fund-raising campaign event for spouse provided that event is not sponsored by political organization or attended only by members of particular political organization; judge may not speak on behalf of spouse's candidacy); Wash. Ethics Adv. Comm. Op. 86-08 (1986) (judge does not violate code of judicial conduct when judge's spouse engages in political activities in their home if judge refrains from all participation in activities and is in no way identified with them); W. Va. Adv. Op. 2/18/00 (2000) (appearance of judicial candidate's name on same ballot as daughter who is running for county prosecutor does not violate prohibition against judicial candidate publicly endorsing or opposing any candidate for public office); W. Va. Adv. Op. 2/25/94 (1994) (judge whose spouse is candidate for prosecuting attorney may not be involved in fund-raising activities, volunteer manual labor, drive vehicle that displays campaign stickers, hand out campaign signs or posters, or deliver or pick up materials from printer or commercial advertiser at request of spouse or member of spouse's campaign committee). *Cf.* Del. Jud. Ethics. Adv. Comm. Op. 2008-3 (2008) (judicial intern whose spouse is candidate for political office can serve provided intern does not actively participate in political or campaign-related activity); Okla. Jud. Ethics Op. 2003-5 (2003) (municipal judge may retain office after judge's spouse is elected to city council; if, in future, spouse becomes mayor with right to appoint municipal judge, judge need not resign, but may not be reappointed by spouse). *See generally* Cynthia Gray, *When a Judge's Relative Is a Political Candidate*, Vol. 17, No. 3 Judicial Conduct Reporter (Fall 1995).

Some states advise that a judge may, with some restrictions, attend campaign fund-raisers and other campaign functions with his or her candidate spouse, while other states advise that such attendance may impermissibly suggest a public endorsement of the candidate. *Compare* Tex. Adv. Comm. on Jud. Ethics Op. 180 (1995) (judge whose spouse is candidate for elective office may attend campaign functions with spouse, but may not allow judge's name and title to be used in press releases or campaign literature identifying candidate as judge's spouse, may not be introduced by name and title as candidate's spouse, may not speak at public gatherings generally in support of spouse's candidacy) *with* Utah Jud. Ethics Adv. Comm. Informal Op. 89-15 (1989) (by attending public gatherings where judge's spouse is appearing as a candidate, the judge would be publicly endorsing a candidate for public office). *See also* Colo. Jud. Ethics Adv. Bd.

Op. 2005-05 (2005) (judge should refrain from attending all political events in support of spouse's candidacy and must avoid activities that could be perceived as constituting endorsement of candidate or using prestige of judicial office to benefit spouse; judge may allow photograph to be used in spouse's campaign literature as long as judge is not depicted as or identified as a judge); Fla. Jud. Ethics Adv. Comm. Op. 07-13 (2007) (judge, whose spouse plans to run for election to nonpartisan public office, may not attend spouse's nonpartisan "meet and greet" campaign gatherings at judge's home and at homes of friends and neighbors; judge may appear as candidate's spouse in family photograph to be used in spouse's campaign); Ill. Jud. Ethics Comm. Op. 96-12 (1996) (judge may buy tickets and attend political dinner with spouse who is candidate for sheriff); Kan. Jud. Ethics Op. JE 62 (1996) (judge may attend fund-raisers for wife, purchase tickets and attend functions of wife's political party, attend candidate forums and be introduced as wife's spouse, and appear in family photograph in wife's campaign material and television advertisements, so long as he is not identified as judge and does not solicit money); S.C. Adv. Comm. on Stands. of Jud. Cond. 14-2003 (2003) (judge may attend fund-raising and/or non-fund-raising activities of the spouse's political campaign, visit spouse's campaign office, attend spouse's announcement, appear in campaign advertisements and literature if not identified as judge, and be present on spouse's election night).

Displaying Signs or Bumper Stickers Publicly Endorsing Candidate for Public Office

Judges or judicial candidates who permit a candidate for public office to place a campaign sign outside their homes or offices publicly endorse that candidate for public office and engage in a prohibited political activity. *See, e.g., In re McCormick*, 639 N.W.2d 12 (Iowa 2002) (judge who allowed candidate for public office to place a sign in support of candidate outside judge's home publicly endorsed candidate for public office in violation of Canon); Neb. Jud. Ethics Adv. Comm. Op. 06-3 (2006) (inappropriate for clerk magistrate to place candidate signs in yard or to hand out campaign literature); Nev. Stand. Comm. on Jud. Ethics and Election Prac. JE 10-007 (2010) (judge may not display signs in support of political candidate on residential or other property); N.Y. Adv. Comm. on Jud. Ethics Op. 07-167 (2007) (judge whose law firm is primary lessee of space in office building should ask landlord to remove signs endorsing political candidates from property; judge may display campaign signs supporting own candidacy, including signs that also list other candidates for public office who make up slate of which judge is part, but must not publicly endorse any other candidate); W. Va. Adv. Op. 6/8/00 (2000) (senior status judge who has given his old signs to friend who in turn wishes to give signs to candidate should ensure that his name is covered so that it does not appear that judge is endorsing candidate);

W. Va. Adv. Op. 11/5/90 (1990) (judge who is not currently a candidate may not publicly endorse any candidate, judicial or nonjudicial, by displaying posters and billboards on private property).

Bumper stickers are generally treated similarly. *See, e.g.*, Del. Jud. Ethics Adv. Comm. Op. 2008-1 (2008) (judge may continue to serve during spouse's run for an elected seat in Delaware General Assembly; judge may not drive car that displays spouse's campaign sticker even if car is normally driven by spouse and even if title is in spouse's name); Ga. Jud. Qualifications Comm'n Op. No. 209 (1996) (improper for sitting judge to display bumper sticker on personal vehicle urging re-election of friend to judicial office and publicly stating that he is doing all he can to help his friend); Tex. Adv. Comm. on Jud. Ethics Op. 136 (1990) (a judge displaying a bumper sticker supporting a political candidate would violate at least the spirit of the judicial code because a judge cannot realistically separate the prestige of judicial office from the judge's personal affairs); *but see* N.Y. Adv. Comm. on Jud. Ethics Op. 06-94 (2006) (judge may drive car registered in spouse's name when it is necessary or particularly convenient even if the car displays bumper sticker supporting spouse's candidacy).

Advertisements in Support of Candidate for Public Office

A judge or judicial candidate may not support a candidate for office in print or recorded advertisements. *See In re Smith*, 449 So.2d 755 (Miss. 1984) (judge violated Canon by allowing political advertisement bearing his signature and stating his support for candidate for mayor to be published in local newspaper); *In re Crnkovich* (N.Y. State Comm'n on Jud. Cond. 2002) (judge disciplined for recording publicly broadcasted radio advertisement endorsing candidate for town court); *but see* Tex. Adv. Comm. on Jud. Ethics Op. 213 (1998) (as long as judge or judicial candidate does not participate in selection of candidates, he or she may contribute toward a publication in which political party, political action committee, specialty bar association, and/or individual endorse several candidates in one advertisement; however, two or more judges may not conduct joint campaign that includes mailed brochure and newspaper advertisement when campaign is funded totally by participating judges' campaigns and all funds are given to political party, which actually pays campaign expenditures; since the judicial candidates selected the candidates with whom they advertised, it is the opinion of the committee that this constitutes an impermissible endorsement); Kan. Jud. Ethics Op. JE 34 (1990) (political party may publish brochure containing picture and biographical data of all of party's candidates, including incumbent judge and five other candidates for judge in district; brochure, which will be printed and distributed by party at party's sole expense, does not constitute prohibited endorsement by judicial candidate of other candidates); Mich. Comm. on Jud. Ethics Op. JI-36 (1991) (judge or candidate may place advertisement in political party's advertisement book so long as content of advertisement does not constitute speech on behalf of political party or nonjudicial candidate or endorsement of candidate for nonjudicial office).

A judge or judicial candidate also may not purchase political advertisements on behalf of a candidate for office. *See, e.g., In re Steady*, 641 A.2d 117 (Vt. 1994) (judge violated Canon by purchasing paid political advertisement supporting various candidates for national, statewide, and local offices).

Membership in Organizations That Endorse Candidates

Although judges are permitted under Rule 3.7 to participate in activities concerned with the law, the legal system, or the administration of justice, or on behalf of an educational, religious, charitable, fraternal, or civic organization not conducted for profit, a judge is prohibited from maintaining a membership in an organization that endorses candidates for partisan political office. *See, e.g.*, Fla. Comm. on Stands. of Cond. Governing Judges Op. 01-15 (2001) (judge would violate Florida Canon 5A(1)(b) and other Canons by maintaining membership in a voluntary bar association that endorses judicial candidates); Fla. Comm. on Stands. of Cond. Governing Judges Op. 93-50 (1993) (judge's membership in County Political Women's Caucus is prohibited because, among other things, it is activist organization that recruits and supports candidates and lobbies for various laws); *cf. Siefert v. Alexander*, 608 F.3d 974, 982 (7th Cir. 2010) (Wisconsin Judicial Code prohibition on judge or judicial candidate from being a member of a political party violates the First Amendment because the state does not have a compelling interest in preventing candidates from announcing their views on legal or political issues, "let alone prohibiting them from announcing those views by proxy" through membership in a political organization); Wash. Ethics Adv. Comm. Op. 84-02 (1984) (judge may co-chair organization whose purpose is to foster and encourage election of women to public office but which does not endorse candidates for office).

Sending Letters

A judge may write a letter to a judicial council concerning the qualities and abilities of an applicant for a judicial position. The content of the letter should be limited to addressing those qualities about which the judge has direct knowledge and which relate to the criteria used by the council in evaluating the applicant. The judge may ethically permit the council to forward the letter to the governor, but should not send an unsolicited letter to the governor, whose role in the selection process is political. Alaska Comm'n on Jud. Cond. Adv. Op. 97-1 (1997).

A judge or judicial candidate may not endorse a candidate for public office by sending letters to potential voters in support of the candidate. *Disc. Counsel v. Capers*, 472 N.E.2d 1073 (Ohio 1984) (municipal judge reprimanded for signing and mailing to potential voters postcards issued by campaign committee supporting candidate for judge and also drafting, signing, and mailing letters supporting same candidate); *cf.* Nev. Stand. Comm. on Jud. Ethics & Election Pracs. Op. JE 98-006 (1998) (judge may submit letter of reference or recommendation for candidate for appointment to judicial office if formally requested to do so by appointing authority, but should not offer his or her recommendation, endorsement, or views on candidate for appointment to judicial office if judge has not been requested to provide such information by appointing authority).

A judge or judicial candidate may also be prohibited from sending letters to a newspaper in support of a candidate for office. *See, e.g., In re Cohen*, SC12-2244 (Fl. S. Ct. 2014) (judge reprimanded for writing letter to newspaper about state's attorney race); Alaska Bar Assn. Ethics Op. 88-5 (1988) (judge may not write letter to local newspapers supporting retention of judge who is being considered by voters for retention or rejection even if letter would not be on judicial stationery and would not identify writer as sitting judge); Ariz. Jud. Ethics Adv. Comm. Op. 96-6 (1996) (judge may not write letter to newspaper editorial board regarding qualifications of judicial candidate, even if a private communication); Ill. Jud. Ethics Comm. Op. 98-6 (1998) (judge may not write letter to the editor stating that candidate for elective judicial office is "qualified").

Developing Campaign Strategies

In some jurisdictions, a judge or judicial candidate is prohibited from assisting a candidate for public office to develop campaign strategies and identify campaign issues. *In re Inquiry Concerning a Judge, DeFoor*, 494 So. 2d 1121 (Fla. 1986) (judge improperly aided candidacies of two friends by developing campaign strategies, identifying campaign issues, privately lobbying members of local legal community, attempting to publicize circuit court statistics reflecting negatively upon the incumbent, and informing friends as to nature of certain pre-prepared questions to be used in public political forum that judge helped to organize); Tex. Adv. Comm. on Jud. Ethics Op. 14 (1976) (judge prohibited from meeting with and privately discussing political issues and political campaign strategy with candidate for elective public office other than his own; essence of Canon is to prevent judges from engaging in political activity other than that which is necessary and appropriate for their own election).

Signing Nominating Petitions

Several state judicial ethics committees have opined that signing a nomination petition of a candidate is not tantamount to an endorsement and is, therefore, permitted. *See, e.g.*, Ariz. Jud. Ethics Adv. Comm. Op. 96-07 (1996) ("[a] nominating petition does not contain a promise to vote for the nominee or any endorsement of the nominee. The restriction on the number of petitions that any given elector may sign appears to be a device to ensure the earnestness of signatories and does not imply an endorsement."); N.M. Adv. Comm. on the Code of Jud. Cond. Op. 96-01 (1996) (judge not precluded from signing or circulating nominating petition for judicial candidate so long as judge does not publicly endorse or oppose judicial candidate through news media or in campaign literature); N.Y. Adv. Comm. on Jud. Ethics Op. 89-89 (1989) (judge may sign nominating petition to place names of individuals on electoral ballot in any year, whether or not judge is standing for election in that year, and may, if election law permits, sign his or her own petition in year when judge is running for judicial office). *See also* Ill. Jud. Ethics Comm. Op. 98-02 (1998) (judge may sign and circulate nominating petitions of another judicial candidate when that judge also is candidate in same election); *Matter of Hotchkiss*, 327 N.W.2d 312 (Mich. 1982) (judge may purchase fund-raising tickets, make campaign contributions, and sign nominating petitions for candidate for nonjudicial office); Wis. Jud. Cond, Adv. Comm., Op. 00-2 (2001) ("A judge may sign nominating petition of partisan candidate, but should consider precise language of petition and whether it may be used for any purpose other than filing with appropriate public official.").

Some states, however, advise that signing a nominating petition is equivalent to a public endorsement and, therefore, not permitted. *See, e.g., Kan. Jud. Rev. v. Stout*, 196 P.3d 1162 (Kan. 2008) (judicial candidate violated Code when personally collecting signatures as same is "personally soliciting publicly stated support"); Conn. Comm. on Jud. Ethics Informal Op. 2013-36 (2013) (judicial official may not sign nominating petition; Connecticut law provides that signatories of the petition support the candidate); Fla. Comm. on Stands. of Cond. Governing Judges Op. 92-32 (1992) (even if judge does not refer to judge's office, petition does not indicate that signature is endorsement, and judge's sole purpose in signing petition is to allow petitioner to qualify for ballot without paying qualifying fee, judge may not sign petition for individual attempting to qualify for election to judicial or nonjudicial, partisan or nonpartisan office); Fla. Comm. on Stands. of Cond. Governing Judges Op. 84-8 (1984) (judge may not sign "minor party candidate petition" to be submitted to Florida electoral officials requesting that party candidates for President and Vice President of the United States be placed on Florida general election ballot); Mass. Comm. on Jud. Ethics Adv. Op. 1999-13 (1999) (signing a nomination paper constitutes a public endorsement of the candidate's placement on the ballot, and thus can be construed as a public endorsement of the candidate); Jud. Ethics Comm. of the Pa. Conf. of State Trial Judges Formal Op. 2001-1 (2001) (signing candidate's nomination petition prohibited because it is legal equivalent of public endorsement).

Voting in Primary Elections and Caucuses

Comment [6] to Rule 4.1 states that "[j]udges and judicial candidates retain the right to participate in the political process as voters in both primary and general elections" and "participation in a caucus-type election procedure does not constitute public support for or endorsement of political organization or candidate." Despite those statements, states seem to draw a distinction between primaries and caucuses, generally permitting participation in the former, but not the latter. *See* Colo. Jud. Ethics Adv. Bd. Op. 2008-02 (2008) (judge may not attend or participate in precinct caucus to determine presidential nominees for both major political parties; however, judge may vote in primary election); Neb. Jud. Ethics Adv. Comm. Op 08-1 (Feb. 8, 2008) (judge may not attend or participate in political party caucus held to elect delegates committed to certain presidential candidate in that political party); Utah Jud. Ethics Adv. Comm. Informal Op. 02-1 (2002) (judge may vote in primary election even when participation is conditioned on party affiliation); Wash. Ethics Adv. Comm. Op. 92-04 (1992) (judge may participate in presidential preference primary that does not require election participant to identify himself as member of political party). *See also* Commentary to Virginia Canons 2A and 5A, revised November 2, 2004 by the Virginia Supreme Court, specifically allowing judges to vote in "open primaries" and thereby effectively overruling prior Virginia Judicial Ethics Opinions 99-6 (1999) and 00-1 (2000).

Lending Home for Candidate Event

By lending his or her home for an event for a candidate running for public office, a judge or judicial candidate could be viewed as publicly endorsing the candidate. *See, e.g.*, Fla. Comm. on Stands. of Cond. Governing Judges Op. 87-22 (1987) (judge may not serve as hostess for husband's mayoral candidate event in home even if she does not solicit guests' vote or support); Kan. Jud. Ethics Op. JE 33 (1990) (judge allowing his or her home to be used to host "Meet the Candidate" party for governor during election year could be viewed as political endorsement); Mich. Comm. on Jud. Ethics Informal Op. CI-778 (1982) (judge offering his or her home for reception for partisan candidate for public office is tantamount to public endorsement); Nev. Stand. Comm. on Jud. Ethics and Election Prac. JE 10-005 (2010) (judge may not host "meet and greet" for another judicial candidate in judge's home); Tex. Adv. Comm. on Jud. Ethics Op. 284 (2001) (judge's spouse may not host fund-raiser for judicial candidate in judge's home); W. Va. Adv. Op. 1/12/00 (2000) (judicial election committee may not hold fund-raiser in home of candidate; even if candidate did not personally solicit or accept contributions, funds being raised in home would, at a minimum, create appearance of personal involvement). *But see* N.Y. Adv. Comm. on Jud. Ethics Op. 06-147 (2007) (although judge need not prohibit spouse from using joint marital home to host campaign-related meetings and/or fund-raising events in furtherance of spouse's own campaign for office, judge may not appear at such events); S.C. Adv. Comm. on Stands. of Jud. Cond. 14-2006 (2006) (judge's spouse may host party for political candidate at home of judge and judge's spouse); Wash. Ethics Adv. Comm. Op. 94-08 (1994) (judge may allow county bar association to have its annual picnic at judge's residence and bar association may invite all candidates for positions of superior court clerk and prosecutor to speak on behalf of their candidacy; however, judge should advise bar association that invitation must come from bar association and should identify site of picnic by address only to avoid possible misinterpretation that judge is endorsing nonjudicial candidates or engaging in partisan politics); W. Va. Adv. Op. 8/28/95 (1995) (judicial officer's spouse may have political fund-raiser in home in which judicial officer and spouse reside if judicial officer is careful not to become involved in raising funds for candidate or organization or endorsing any candidate and is careful to avoid any public endorsement of or public opposition to political candidate, and solicitation of funds for political organization or candidate).

Privately Expressing Views

The Model Code does not prohibit a judge or judicial candidate from privately expressing his or her views on judicial candidates or other candidates for public office. They must take appropriate steps, however, to ensure that their views do not become public, including managing privacy settings on electronic social media. ABA Formal Opinion 462 (2013).

See also Ariz. Jud. Ethics Adv. Comm. Op. 87-1 (1987) (incumbent judge may write letter of support to judicial nominating commission; incumbent judge may respond either orally or in writing to inquiries directed to him by members of judicial nominating commission; judge may respond to governor or communicate with governor regarding nominee for judicial appointment); Ill. Jud. Ethics Comm. Op. 99-8 (1999) (judge may, in confidential communication to bar association, express opinion regarding qualifications of fellow judge for retention or elective judicial office); Nev. Stand. Comm. on Jud. Ethics and Election Prac. Op. JE 98-006 (1998) (judge should use reasonable caution and restraint to ensure private endorsement does not become public); Tex. Adv. Comm. on Jud. Ethics Op. 222 (1998) (where judge's letter of recommendation to judicial nominating committee on behalf of applicant for appointment to judicial position would offer specific knowledge of personal and professional qualities pertinent to performance, judge is uniquely able to contribute insight to judicial process and thereby to administration of justice); Tex. Adv. Comm. on Jud. Ethics Op. 13 (1976) (district judge may introduce candidate for state legislature to his personal friends and recommend that such friends vote for candidate).

SOLICITING FUNDS FOR, PAYING AN ASSESSMENT TO, OR MAKING A CONTRIBUTION TO A POLITICAL ORGANIZATION OR A CANDIDATE FOR PUBLIC OFFICE

Rule 4.1(A)(4) prohibits a judge or a judicial candidate from soliciting funds for, paying an assessment to, or making a contribution to a political organization or a candidate for public office. *See, e.g., In re Sallee*, 579 N.E.2d 75 (Ind. 1991) (judge violated Canon by making a donation to a political candidate though purporting to do so on behalf of his wife); *In re Shea*, 815 So. 2d 813 (La. 2002) (municipal judge reprimanded for making contributions from excess campaign funds to candidates for public office); *In re Burke* (N.Y. Comm'n on Jud. Cond. 2014) (judge disciplined for political contributions made by the realty company judge owned); *In re Wright*, 329 S.E.2d 668 (N.C. 1985) (campaign contributions from judges made by checks payable to campaign committees of political candidates violate Canon); Alaska Comm'n on Jud. Cond. Adv. Op 2000-02 (2000) (judge may not contribute to any campaign fund for public office regardless of whether fund is aggregate fund or individual fund or whether fund supports retention of judicial candidate or exists for another elective purpose); Alaska Comm'n on Jud. Cond. Adv. Op. 98-3 (1998) (judge should not contribute to another judge's retention campaign fund); Ariz. Jud. Ethics Adv. Comm. Op. 78-02 (1978) (judge may not contribute to organization whose purpose is to advocate approval by voting public of ballot proposition seeking to increase legislative salaries; group is "political organization" within the meaning of the judicial code); *In re Schmidt* (Cal. Comm'n on Jud. Performance 1989) (judge made political contributions from his own campaign funds to nonjudicial candidates); Conn. Comm. on Jud. Ethics Informal Op. 2010-24 (2010) (judge prohibited from making contributions to federal, in-state, and out-of-state candidates); Del. Jud. Ethics Adv. Comm. Adv. Op. 1987-1 (1987) (newly appointed judge should ask candidate for political office to be relieved of judge's prior pledge to make campaign contribution); Fla. Comm. on Stands. of Cond. Governing Judges Op. 84-20 (1984) (judge may not make contribution to organization to promote the passage of local sales tax levy to finance new county justice facility because it is political organization); Fla Sup. Ct. Jud. Ethics Adv. Comm. 2013-20 (2013) (judge may not be a member of SUNPAC, a political action committee); Mich. Comm. on Ethics Op. JI-73 (1993) (judge may not participate in fund-raising for political party by calling bingo numbers, selling bingo cards, and handling money, even outside judicial campaign); *In re DeVaul* (N.Y. State Comm'n on Jud. Cond., 1985) (part-time justice's law firm, in which he had one-quarter interest, made seven contributions to campaigns in which judge was not candidate); Tex. Adv. Comm. on Jud. Ethics Op. 51 (1980) (although judge does not violate Canons by accepting position as treasurer for ad hoc political organization that confines itself to "get out the vote" program for all Democratic candidates, judge's actions after accepting office may cause judge to violate Canon that prohibits judges from soliciting funds for any political organization, or using or permitting the use of office for that purpose); W. Va. Adv. Op. 8/28/95 (1995) (judicial officer may not contribute to individual judicial officer's campaign); ABA Informal Op. 1400 (Nov. 18, 1977) (judge prohibited from making financial contribution to organizations such as National Women's Political Caucus, Women's Lobby, or the Women's Campaign Fund); ABA Informal Op. 1350 (1975) (inappropriate for judge to make financial contribution to campaign of colleague on his bench, whether or not the contribution was made to a political organization or simply to a candidate running for election).

The prohibition on campaign contributions has survived one constitutional challenge. *See In re Raab*, 793 N.E.2d 1287 (N.Y. 2003) (provision prohibiting judicial candidate from contributing funds to a political organization other than his own campaign did not violate First Amendment; rule was narrowly tailored to further compelling interests, such as preserving impartiality and independence of the judiciary and maintaining public confidence in state court system). *See also Wersal v. Sexton*, 674 F.3d 1010 (8th Cir. 2012) (sitting en banc, Appellate Court finds plaintiff's First Amendment challenge was not ripe).

Some jurisdictions have found some limited exceptions to the prohibition in Rule 4.1(A)(4). For instance, Illinois expressly permits judges to contribute to a political organization, which includes "a political party or other group, the principal purpose of which is to further the election or appointment of candidates to political office." Ill. Jud. Ethics Comm. Op. 94-6 (1994) (sitting associate judge who is not candidate may make political contribution to fellow associate judge who is running for circuit judge position). *See also* Kan. Jud. Ethics Op. JE 82 (1998) (judge may attend political reception for fellow judge who is up for election and contribute to fellow judge's campaign committee); Okla. Jud. Ethics Op. 2003-9 (2003) (part-time municipal court judge may make financial contribution to colleague running for office in partisan election); S.C. Adv. Comm. on Stands. of Jud. Cond. 2-2007 (2007) (probate judges are elected and thus may make contribution to political organization as allowed by judicial code); Tex. Adv. Comm. on Jud. Ethics Op. 231 (1998) (judge may be publicly thanked in political party state convention program for contributing to cost of dinner provided to young people who served as pages and sergeants-at-arms at state convention); Tex. Adv. Comm. on Jud. Ethics Op. 213 (1998) (judge or judicial candidate may contribute to political action committee or political party to pay for campaign publicity that includes only candidates who helped pay for advertisement); Tex. Comm. on Jud. Ethics. Adv. Op. 40 (1979) (judge does not violate Canons by making periodic and regular contributions to political party); Tex. Adv. Comm. on Jud. Ethics Op. 4 (1975) (judge permitted to make contribution to Democratic party); Wash. Ethics Adv. Comm. Op. 91-22 (1991) (Washington's Canon 7A(3) provides that a judge may solicit fellow members of judiciary for campaign contribution to third judge's contested judicial election campaign fund; judge may not, however, solicit members of the public for contributions to another judge's contested judicial election campaign).

Campaign funds can be used for some purposes, but not others. In Ohio, for example, a judicial candidate may use campaign funds to contribute to a political party or to attend events sponsored by a political party, so long as the funds are used to defray operating and maintenance costs of the party headquarters, to organize voter registration programs and get-out-the vote campaigns, to administer party fund-raising drives, to pay for advertisements sponsored jointly by two or more qualified political parties, to publicize a political party fund, to direct mail campaigns or other communications with registered voters of a party that are not related to any particular candidate or election, or to prepare reports required by law. A judge or judicial candidate may not use campaign funds to attend events sponsored by a political party if the funds are used to further the election or defeat of any particular candidate or to influence directly the outcome of any candidate or issue election, to pay party debts incurred as the result of any election, or to make a payment clearly in excess of the market value of that which is received for the payment. Ohio Bd. of Commissioners on Grievances and Disc. Op. 2003-8 (2003).

ATTENDING OR PURCHASING TICKETS FOR DINNERS OR OTHER EVENTS SPONSORED BY A POLITICAL ORGANIZATION OR A CANDIDATE FOR PUBLIC OFFICE

Judges and candidates for judicial office are generally prohibited from attending or purchasing tickets for dinners or other events sponsored by a political organization or a candidate for public office. *See Matter of Barrett*, 593 A.2d 529 (Del. Jud. 1991) (justice of the peace violated Canon by attending political fund-raising functions and distributing tickets for such functions to other court personnel); *In re Krause*, 141 So. 3d 1197 (Fla. 2014) (judge reprimanded for purchasing table at party fund-raiser); *In re Troy*, 306 N.E.2d 203 (Mass. 1973) (judge should not arrange and attend political gatherings or serve as toastmaster at testimonial for another candidate); *In re Martin*, 434 S.E.2d 262 (S.C. 1993) (improper for judge to sponsor and attend barbecue for state senate nominee, to appear in photo in endorsement for nominee's opponent, and to erect yard signs endorsing candidates); Conn. Comm. on Jud. Ethics Informal Op. 2009 07 (2009) (judge prohibited from attending political gathering/fund-raiser at which member of judge's family residing in judge's household is to receive award); Conn. Comm. on Jud. Ethics Informal Op. 2009-06 (2009) (judge prohibited from attending public event at which judge's friend plans to announce candidacy for political office); Del. Jud. Ethics Adv. Comm. Op. 2005-3 (2005) (judge may not attend steering committee event for political party to honor retired state attorney general; cost to attend event will include cost of meal plus contribution to a reputable charitable organization dedicated to relief for victims of Hurricane Katrina, and contribution to political party); Fla. Sup. Ct. Jud. Ethics Adv. Comm. Op. 12-03 (2012) (judge may not attend victory party for elected mayor); Fla. Sup. Ct. Jud. Ethics Adv. Comm. Op. 2009-07 (Apr. 9, 2009) (judge may not attend and receive award at event that is fund-raiser for organization that is primarily involved in education programs); Fla. Comm. on Stands. of Cond. Governing Judges Op. 94-42 (1994) (non-candidate judge may not attend political function for judicial candidate even if the judge does not speak, does not endorse any candidate, does not purchase ticket, and does not make contribution); Fla. Comm. on Stands. of Cond. Governing Judges Op. 88-9 (1988) (judge may not appear at partisan political meeting to discuss judicial system and need for new court building in judge's circuit); Mich. Comm. on Jud. Ethics Op. JI-115 (1997) (judge may not attend testimonial dinner sponsored by political party where price of admission exceeds reasonable cost of attendance); Ohio Bd. of Commissioners on Grievances and Disc. Op. 2003-8 (2003) (magistrate who is judicial candidate may use title "magistrate" when listed as contributor in dinner program of political party); Okla. Jud. Ethics Op. 2010-2 (2010) (judge may not attend political gathering in support of independent legislator); Utah Jud. Ethics Adv. Comm. Informal Op. 98-15 (1998) (inappropriate to act as master of ceremonies at "Meet the Candidates Night" sponsored by local Parent-Teacher Association); Wash Ethics Adv. Comm. Op. 11-02 (2011) (judge may not attend political party's fund-raising dinner to speak on veterans' court); Wash. Ethics Adv. Comm. Op. 02-03 (2002) (judicial officer may not attend a political party function to make an educational presentation about the law, the legal system, and the administration of justice); Wash. Ethics Adv. Comm. Op. 93-19 (1993) (discussing factors judges should consider regarding propriety of judges belonging to, participating in activities of, or attending different events of various types of organizations, including those that may be related to improvement of law, legal system, or administration of justice); ABA Informal Op. 867 (1965) (improper for judge to attend dinner meeting honoring U.S. Senator at which former Vice-President of United States is speaker; judge was invited to sit at speaker's table, and charged $50 a plate, a portion of which was to be used to further re-election candidacy of senator); *but see* Fla. Sup. Ct. Jud. Ethics Adv. Comm. Op. 13-20 (2013) (committee split on question of whether judge may attend dinner hosted by political action committee). *See generally* Cynthia Gray, *A Judge's Attendance at Social Events, Bar Association Functions, Civic and Charitable Functions, and Political Gatherings* (American Judicature Society 1996).

However, some states have permitted attendance. *See* Ill. Jud. Ethics Comm. Op. 01-09 (2001) (judge's mere attendance at a political gathering does not equate to a public endorsement, and a judge may attend a reception hosted by the judge's spouse in the home of the judge and spouse); Ill. Jud. Ethics Comm. Op. 94-21 (1994) (judge, whether or not candidate for election or retention, may attend political gathering and may be introduced at that gathering); Ill. Jud. Ethics Comm. Op. 93-12 (1993) (judge may attend a golf outing at the behest of a political candidate or office-holder and pay necessary fees or contributions; however, a judge should decline to attend such an event in the unusual circumstances where attendance would compromise the judge's ability to "uphold the integrity and independence of the judiciary"); Kan. Jud. Ethics Op. JE 82 (1998) (judge may attend political reception for fellow judge who is up for election and contribute to fellow judge's campaign committee); Nev. Stand. Comm. on Jud. Ethics and Election Prac. Op. JE 08-007 (2008) (judge may attend $500 per plate fund-raising luncheon held to support re-election of campaign incumbent judge); Tex. Comm. on Jud. Ethics Adv. Op. 162 (1993) (judge may indicate support for political party and attend political event). *Cf. In re Stoker*, 827 P.2d 986 (Wash. 1992) (county fair is not "political gathering" as contemplated by Canon of Code of Judicial Conduct prohibiting judges or judicial candidates from attending political gatherings except as authorized).

And, even where normally not permitted, exceptions have been made to allow attendance under certain circumstances. *See* Fla. Comm. on Stands. of Cond. Governing Judges Op. 77-15 (1977) (incumbent judge should not attend testimonial for announced political candidate or another judicial officer if testimonial is for purpose of raising funds for such candidate or is a purely political affair; judge may attend an appreciation or testimonial function for any person whether announced political candidate or not, if it is bona fide appreciation or testimonial function); Ind. Comm'n on Jud. Qualifications Adv. Op. 3-01 (2001) (judge who is not candidate for judicial office may not endorse political candidates or attend their fund-raisers and contribute to them; however, judge who serves for or is employed by judge who is candidate for judicial office may publicly endorse that judicial candidate and may purchase tickets for and attend fund-raisers for that judicial candidate); Mass. Comm. on Jud. Ethics Adv. Op. 1992-2 (1992) (judge may attend charitable fund-raiser "roast" of state senator); N.Y. Adv. Comm. on Jud. Ethics Op. 07-09 (2007) (judge who is currently candidate for judicial office may not be speaker or guest of honor at fund-raising event sponsored by political organization but may attend event, be introduced as judicial candidate, and briefly acknowledge introduction); S.C. Adv. Comm. on Stands. of Jud. Cond. 1-2007 (2007) (part-time municipal judge may join and attend meetings of political party, but full-time judge may not); *but see* Wash. Ethics Adv. Comm. Op. 90-11 (1990) (part-time judges may not attend and/or purchase tickets to political fund-raising event for local nonjudicial candidates).

Whether or not attendance is permitted may depend upon the way in which the fee for the event is allocated. *See, e.g., Shake v. Ethics Comm. of Kentucky Judiciary*, 122 S.W.3d 577 (Ky. 2003) (judge or judicial candidate may attend a fund-raiser for another judicial candidate and pay for the cost of the food and drink he or she consumes, but any amount above this is, under the Kentucky Code of Judicial Conduct, a "contribution" to the other candidate and therefore is prohibited); Fla. Comm. on Stands. of Cond. Governing Judges Op. 77-20 (1978) (judge may attend testimonial dinner for incumbent county commissioner if primary objective of the dinner is to honor distinguished public servant rather than to raise funds for re-election; $40 tickets were complimentary); Mass. Comm. on Jud. Ethics Adv. Op. 2001-15 (2001) (reception and dinner to honor mayor who has chosen not to run for re-election when his term expires is not "political party" dinner if sponsoring committee exists solely to produce event, but is such a dinner if that committee was mayor's campaign or political committee; the event is not "fund-raiser" if ticket price is designed solely to cover event's costs, but is "fund-raiser" if any part of ticket price is designed to cover costs of political activities in which mayor has engaged, is now engaging, or plans to engage in future).

In some jurisdictions, a judge may be permitted to attend a fund-raiser or similar event if the event is nonpartisan. *See, e.g.*, Cal. Judges Ass'n Jud. Ethics Comm. Adv. Op. 57 (2006) (judge may be moderator of candidates' forum so long as judge merely introduces candidates and is careful to maintain neutrality); Conn. Comm. Jud. Ethics Informal Op. 2012-21 (2012) (judge may attend small gathering at the home of a relative so that a retiring political official can thank the hosts and guests (other than the judicial official) for their prior support); Fla. Comm. on Stands. of Cond. Governing Judges Op. 96-17 (1996) (judge may serve as master of ceremonies at candidates' forum at local homeowners' association meeting because there is no partisan connection with the meeting); Fla. Comm. on Stands. of Cond. Governing Judges Op. 88-23 (1988) (judge may make contribution of $100 to nonpartisan entity to offset cost of an "old-fashioned campaign rally," nonpartisan political event in which the judge appears on behalf of his own candidacy); or if the judge's attendance does not constitute an endorsement of the candidate, Mich. Comm. on Jud. Ethics Op. JI-30 (1990) (judge may attend fund-raiser held for nonjudicial candidate and may participate in campaign activities that do not constitute public endorsement of nonjudicial candidate). *Cf.* Del. Jud. Ethics Adv. Comm. Op. 2007-1 (2007) (judge may attend but should not serve as auctioneer at Little League fund-raising event).

And then, of course, there is the inaugural ball exception. *See* Ark. Jud. Ethics Adv. Comm. Op. 92-05 (1992) (judges may purchase tickets to and attend inaugural ball for President Clinton, regardless of whether ball is considered celebration or political gathering and regardless of whether admission charge is used to defray costs of event, is given to charitable organization, or is used to support Democratic Party activities); Colo. Jud. Ethics Adv. Bd. Op. 2006-10 (2006) (judge may attend gubernatorial inauguration and related events); Fla. Comm. on Stands. of Cond. Governing Judges Op. 92-41 (1992) (judge may attend inaugural ball provided no funds are paid to political organization and attendance is not limited to members of one party); N.Y. Adv. Op. 10-06 (2010) (judge "may attend a swearing-in ceremony for any public official, as well as the ensuing reception, even if it is financed with unexpended campaign funds and/or sponsored by the official's political campaign committee); N.Y. Adv. Op. 97-145 (1997) (judge may not attend ball following inauguration where the $250 ticket price will be used to pay debts incurred by the candidate during the campaign); N.Y. Adv. Comm. on Jud. Ethics Op. 98-12 (1998) (judge may attend an inaugural ball for a mayor where any proceeds will go to a charitable organization and the event is not a political gathering); S.C. Adv. Comm. on Stands. of Jud. Cond. 02-1995 (2002) (judge may attend inaugural ball if any fee paid to attend covers only cost and will not be retained by any political party).

PUBLICLY IDENTIFYING ONESELF AS A CANDIDATE OF A POLITICAL ORGANIZATION

Pursuant to Rule 4.1(A)(6), a judge or candidate subject to public judicial election shall not publicly identify himself or herself as a candidate of a political organization. However, Rule 4.2(C)(1) provides an exception for judicial candidates in partisan public elections for a predetermined time span prior to the election. *See* Ariz. Jud. Ethics Adv. Comm. Op. 95-07 (1995) (candidate for superior court judge may indicate his or her political party affiliation when campaigning); Ind. Comm'n on Jud. Qualifications Adv. Op. 2-91 (1991) (elected judge permitted to join party ticket and campaign jointly with other candidates); Nev. Stand. Comm. on Jud. Ethics and Election Prac. Op. JE 08-009 (2008) (judicial candidate may place campaign materials at booth sponsored by political party when candidate knows that only judicial candidates who are members of that party will be allowed to do so); Nev. Stand. Comm. on Jud. Ethics and Election Prac. Op. JE 08-002 (2008) (judicial candidate may identify himself or herself as member of political party with respect to a request by the print or broadcast media, but not in his or her campaign literature); Nev. Stand. Comm. on Jud. Ethics and Election Prac. Op. JE 06-016 (2006) (judge or judicial candidate may not participate in parade as part of entry sponsored by political party, which entry is intended to represent that party's candidates for state and local office); N.M. Adv. Comm. on the Code of Jud. Cond. Op. 02-08 (2002) (judicial candidate may not provide political party with photograph under circumstances that indicate that photo will be used in advertisement that will reflect or imply candidate's affiliation with that party); Ohio Bd. of Commissioners on Grievances and Disc. Op. 2009-8 (2009) (from date of becoming candidate through day of primary, candidate may identify himself or herself in person and in advertising as member of or affiliated with political party. After day of primary, judicial candidate may in person, but not in advertising, identify himself or herself as member of or affiliated with political party); *cf.* Tex. Adv. Comm. on Jud. Ethics Op. 231 (1998) (because judges may indicate support for a political party, a judge's name may appear on list of contributors to a dinner sponsored by a political party).

The judicial codes in some states specifically prohibit announcing party affiliation. *See* Fla. Sup. Ct. Jud. Ethics Adv. Comm. Op. 02-13 (2002) (Canon 7(C)(3) of the Florida Code provides that a candidate "should refrain from commenting on the candidate's affiliation with any political party"); Fla. Sup. Ct. Jud. Ethics Adv. Comm. 12-13 (2012) (judge may not wear elephant or donkey jewelry if it would suggest or appear to suggest to a reasonable person the support of a political party); Nev. Stand. Comm. on Jud. Ethics and Election Prac. JE98-1 (1998) (pursuant to Canon 5C(1)(a)(ii), candidates for judicial office may privately identify themselves as members of a political party but should refrain from publicly announcing political party affiliation). *But see In re Stoker*, 827 P.2d 986 (Wash. 1992) (judicial candidate did not violate Canon that prohibits judges or candidates from identifying themselves as members of a political party by renting space at Democratic Committee booth at county fair, personally appearing at booth to campaign for re-election, and displaying campaign materials in both Democratic party and Republican party booths).

This provision has been challenged as an infringement on judicial candidates' First Amendment right to free speech. In *Carey v. Wolnitzek*, 614 F.3d 189 (6th Cir. 2010), the Sixth Circuit Court of Appeals applied the strict scrutiny test and struck down Kentucky's Code of Judicial Conduct Canon 5A(2), finding that while the state's goals of having an unbiased judiciary and "diminishing" the "reliance on political partics in judicial selection" were both compelling, the means used were not narrowly tailored. The court explained that prohibiting judicial candidates from announcing their party was effectively prohibiting candidates from "announcing their views on many issues at once" because a party affiliation and its platform was "a shorthand way of announcing one's views on many topics of the day." *Id.* at 202. As a result, the restriction suppressed too much speech. At the same time, the provision did not go far enough because discussion of a candidate's party affiliation was only prohibited "in any form of advertising or when speaking to a gathering." A candidate could discuss party affiliation in response to a question or in a "very small private informal" setting. The court noted, "That reality undermines the suggestion that a candidate deals a fatal blow to judicial impartiality by revealing her party affiliations." *Id.* at 201. *See also Republican Party of Minnesota v. White*, 416 F. 3d 738 (8th Cir. 2005).

Seeking, Accepting, or Using Endorsements from a Political Organization

The prohibition in Rule 4.1(A)(7) against seeking, accepting, or using endorsements from a political organization is new in the revised Code. The prohibition is grounded in judicial independence and the notion that judges are expected to interpret the laws impartially without regard to their personal political beliefs and prejudices and without being beholden to political organizations. In 2006, the South Dakota Special Committee on Judicial Election Campaign Intervention informed leadership of the state's political parties that South Dakota law and the state's code of judicial conduct prohibit political parties from providing an endorsement to candidates in judicial elections. *See also* Fla. Sup. Ct. Jud. Ethics Adv. Comm. Op. 98-19 (1998) (judicial candidate may not attend interview by political party for purpose of obtaining party's endorsement, nor may candidate send written campaign materials to political party in order to obtain endorsement); Neb. Jud. Ethics Adv. Comm. Op. 08-1 (2008) (judge may not attend political party caucus because participants publicly endorse candidate by simply standing or congregating with others favoring that candidate); *accord* Colo. Jud. Ethics Adv. Bd. Op. 2008-2 (2008) (judge may not participate in precinct caucus); Wash. Ethics Adv. Comm. Op. 08-1 (2008) (judge may not participate in a political party caucus); Utah Jud. Ethics Adv. Comm. Informal Op. 02-1 (2002) (judge may not attend political party caucus).

There have been states that have taken a different viewpoint. In New York, for instance, judicial candidates may seek and accept support and endorsement of a "wide variety of persons and entities, including labor unions, political parties, caucuses, political action committees, politicians and candidates for non-judicial office, and lawyers who appear before the court to which the candidate seeks election or re-election." New York State Advisory Committee on Judicial Ethics, *2009 New York Judicial Campaign Ethics Handbook*; Mich. Comm. on Jud. Ethics Op. JI-011 (1989) (nonpartisan judicial candidate's name may appear on reverse side of ticket for Democratic function as part of list of those endorsed by party for township office); Nev. Stand. Comm. on Jud. Ethics and Election Prac. Dec. JE 06-006 (2006) (judge or judicial candidate may place name on website of political party for the purpose of providing a link to website of judge or judicial candidate, at which site campaign materials are located); N.Y. Adv. Comm. on Jud. Ethics Op. 02-34 (2002) (judge may speak individually to members of party's county executive committee or to other party leaders about possible judicial candidacy even though window period is not in effect).

Florida allows an exception: a judicial candidate may accept an endorsement from a nonjudicial elected official who is not campaigning for election, but only if the partisan aspects of the official's position is not mentioned. *See* Fla. Sup. Ct. Jud. Ethics Adv. Comm. Op. 12-21 (2012), Fla. Sup. Ct.

Jud. Ethics Adv. Comm. Op. 12-18 (2012), and Fla. Sup. Ct. Jud. Ethics Adv. Comm. Op. 10-14 (2010).

In Ohio, throughout a judicial campaign, a judicial candidate may truthfully state in person or in advertising that he or she is "Endorsed by (or a nominee of) the Democratic Party" or "Democratic Party Endorsed (or nominee)" or "Endorsed by (or a nominee of) the Republican Party" or "Republican Party Endorsed (or nominee)"; provided that the phrase identifies which political party entity endorsed the candidate, for example, the county, state, or national Democratic or Republican Party. In regard to any other statement, the candidate may, through the day of the primary identify himself or herself in person and in advertising as a member of or affiliated with a political party. After the day of a primary, the candidate may in person, but not in advertising, identify himself or herself as a member of or affiliated with a political party. Ohio Bd. of Commissioners on Grievances and Disc., Op. 2009-8 (2009). *See generally* Kyle D. Cheek & Anthony Champagne, *Partisan Judicial Elections: Lessons from a Bellwether State*, 39 Willamette L. Rev. 4 (2003); Anthony Champagne, *Political Parties and Judicial Elections*, 34 Loy. L.A. L. Rev. 1411 (2001).

Personally Soliciting or Accepting Campaign Contributions Other than through a Campaign Committee

A judge or candidate for elective judicial office is prohibited from personally soliciting or accepting campaign contributions, though he or she may establish a committee to do so. *See In the Matter of Anderson*, 2013 Annual Report N.Y. Comm'n on Jud. Cond. 11 (2013) (judicial candidate censured for personally accepting loan from former employer); *In re Fadeley*, 802 P.2d 31 (Or. 1990) (judge violated Canon by sending letter to editor of a newspaper, which was published, requesting contributions to defray campaign expenses, participating in request for pledges to his campaign committee, and personally soliciting contributions from lawyers and businessmen he had asked to serve on his campaign finance committee); *In re Starcher*, 501 S.E.2d 772 (W. Va. 1998) (judicial candidate unambiguously precluded from personally soliciting publicly stated support; those activities must be conducted by candidate's committee); *In re Suder*, 398 S.E.2d 162 (W. Va. 1990) (magistrate violated Canon by personally accepting campaign contributions and failing to establish campaign committee); Ark. Jud. Ethics Adv. Comm. Op. 95-04 (1995) (judge shall not personally solicit or accept campaign contributions or personally solicit publicly stated support; Fla. Sup. Ct. Jud. Ethics Adv. Comm. Op 10-14 (2010) (judge may not encourage people thorough email or direct contact to attend a fund-raising event for the campaign); Fla. Sup. Ct. Jud. Ethics Adv. Comm. Op. 08-09 (2008) (judge's parents may not author and circulate letter to friends and acquaintances supporting their child's candidacy and soliciting campaign contributions; Kan. Jud. Ethics

Op. JE 118 (2004) (judge in elective district prohibited from e-mailing campaign letter to members of the local bar; however, judge's election committee may send out campaign literature).

Some states, however, have suggested exceptions to the prohibition. *See, e.g.*, Ariz. Jud. Ethics Adv. Comm. Op. 08-01 (2008) (subject to some limitations, judicial candidate may publicize political party affiliation, publicly associate with county and state political party organizations, speak and solicit support at political party events and functions, and use party telephone banks and volunteers to solicit donations and support); Fla. Comm. on Stands. of Cond. Governing Judges Op. 78-11 (1978) (judge may accept contributions from lawful sources toward the payment of his or her qualifying fee; because qualifying fee is necessary expenditure, whether or not active opposition develops, receipt of modest contributions, through committee, from friends, relatives, and others interested in maintenance of good judiciary, is not proscribed by Canons); Ky. Jud. Ethics Op. JE-114 (2006) (judicial candidate may accept unsolicited contributions from political parties); Tex. Adv. Comm. on Jud. Ethics Op. 55 (1981) (not unethical for judge to have fund-raising benefits to raise funds to pay for campaign expenses provided nature and type of benefit does not, in any manner, compromise judge in his integrity, his independence in judicial affairs, nor give appearance of impropriety); Wis. Jud. Cond. Adv. Comm. Op. 97-7 (1997) (judge can solicit campaign contributions from his or her spouse and other family members).

The ban against personal solicitation exists for two reasons: so that the party solicited will not feel "obligated" or "strong-armed" into feeling that a contribution is required; and if a contribution is made, the contributor will not appear to have "purchased" the candidate's favor. *See, e.g.*, *In re Sobel* (Nev. Comm. on Jud. Disc. 2005) (candidate unlawfully collected donations of $1,000 to $5,000 each from 39 attorneys and law firms while their cases were pending in his courtroom). Also, there is legitimate concern about a judge's impartiality when parties whose interests may come before a judge, or the lawyer who represents such parties, are known to have made contributions to the election campaigns of judicial candidates. However, as the Commentary acknowledges, the reality is that judicial candidates must raise funds to support their candidacies for election to judicial office. Therefore, a candidate is permitted to establish committees of responsible persons to engage in traditional campaign activities not prohibited by law such as advertising, mailings, running candidate forums, and soliciting and managing campaign funds. *See, e.g.*, Jud. Ethics Comm. of the Pa. Conf. of State Trial Judges Informal Op. 12/07/00 (2000) (candidate for retention may form a campaign committee that will solicit campaign funds from lawyers); *See generally* Roy Schotland, *Campaign Finance in Judicial Elections*, 34 Loyola L.A. L. Rev. 1489 (June 2001); Patrick M. McFadden, *Electing Justice: The Law and Ethics of Judicial Election Campaigns* (American Judicature Society 1990) (discussing law and ethics governing judicial election campaigns, including campaign finance and campaign advertising and other related judicial speech; author suggests re-examining codes of judicial conduct and offers specific recommendations regarding campaign fund-raising and campaign conduct).

Some states, such as Arkansas, advise that a judge may personally ask for support so long as when he or she does so, support is requested on an individual basis, rather than a request to a group, which would constitute soliciting publicly stated support. Ark. Jud. Ethics Adv. Comm. Op. 02-02 (2002) (judge may ask people on an individual basis and not as a group, such as at a social gathering, assembly, club or any other organization, whether organized formally or otherwise, to sign the judge's petition to have his name placed on the ballot; key is approaching people on an individual basis to ask them to sign the petition); Ark. Jud. Ethics Adv. Comm. Op. 95-04 (1995) (committee can prepare list of important individuals whom candidate may wish to contact personally, and candidate may then ask for their private support, but may not solicit publicly stated support); Neb. Jud. Ethics Adv. Comm. Op. 06-7 (2006) (current judge who wants to seek different judicial position may actively seek out support from lawyers who practice before judge and from non-lawyers who are acquaintances or friends). *But see In re Yacknin* (N.Y. State Comm'n on Jud. Cond. 2008) (judge solicited, from the bench, support from lawyer for judge's candidacy moments before judge presided over case involving lawyer's client); *In re Farrell* (N.Y. State Comm'n on Jud. Cond., 2004) (judge made numerous calls to party officials supporting re-election of county chair; judge's campaign committee made payment to political party committee that exceeded reasonable value of any services provided by committee to judge's election campaign).

Constitutional Challenges

The restriction on personal solicitation of funds has been challenged as a violation of the First Amendment. These challenges were successful in the Sixth, Eighth, Ninth, and Eleventh Circuits. *See Carey v. Wolnitzek*, 614 F.3d 189 (6th Cir. 2010); *Republican Party of Minnesota v. White*, 416 F.3d 738 (8th Cir. 2005); *Wolfson v. Concannon*, 750 F.3d 1145 (9th Cir. 2014), *superseded en banc*, 811 F.3d 1176 (9th Cir. 2016); *Weaver v. Bonner*, 309 F.3d 1312 (11th Cir. 2002).

In *Carey v. Wolnitzek*, 614 F.3d 189 (6th Cir. 2010), the Sixth Circuit Court of Appeals held that the Kentucky Code of Judicial Conduct's broad prohibition on solicitation, which extended to "all fundraising by the candidate, including in-person solicitations, group solicitations, telephone calls, and letters" was unconstitutional because it failed the strict scrutiny test. The court explained that while Kentucky's interest in an impartial judiciary and the "appearance and reality of a non-corrupt judiciary" is compelling, the means were not narrowly tailored. *Id.* at 204–5.

The court noted that the Kentucky Code prohibited both direct and indirect solicitation in the same way, but that indirect solicitation presents "little or no risk of undue pressure or the appearance of a quid pro quo." *Id.* at 205. Additionally, the Code allowed a member of a campaign committee to personally solicit lawyers who practiced before the candidate and allowed the candidate to write the contributor a thank-you letter. The court explained that this "suggests that the only interest at play is the impolitic interpersonal dynamics of a candidate's request for money, not the more corrosive reality of who gives and how much. If the purported risk addressed by the clause is that the judge or candidate will treat donors and non-donors differently, it is knowing who contributed and who balked that makes the difference, not who asked for the contribution." *Id.*

In *Republican Party of Minnesota v. White*, 416 F.3d 738 (8th Cir. 2005), the plaintiffs challenged Minnesota's ban on candidates soliciting contributions from large groups and soliciting contributions by fund-raising letters signed by the candidates. The Eighth Circuit found that the prohibition on these challenged types of solicitation were "barely tailored" to meet the goal of impartiality. Seven years later, in *Wersal v. Sexton*, 674 F.3d 1010 (8th Cir. 2012), the Eighth Circuit upheld a revised personal solicitation rule that prohibited judicial candidates from personally soliciting campaign funds from groups of fewer than 20 people. The court held that one-on-one campaign solicitations created a greater risk and appearance of a quid pro quo.

The Ninth Circuit, in *Wolfson v. Concannon*, 750 F.3d 1145 (9th Cir. 2014) *superseded en banc*, 811 F.3d 1176 (9th Cir. 2016), found that the Arizona prohibition on personal solicitation of campaign contributions was unconstitutional as applied to nonjudge candidates for judicial office because it failed the strict scrutiny test. The court held that the prohibition was both under and over inclusive because it "restricts speech that presents little to no risk of corruption or bias towards future litigants and is not narrowly tailored to serve those state interests." *Id.* at 1157. Agreeing with the holding in *Carey*, the Ninth Circuit wrote that indirect forms of solicitation like speeches to large groups and signed mass mailings do not risk undue pressure or create the appearance of a quid pro quo. The court also noted that unlike the Minnesota Code of Judicial Conduct, the Arizona Code does not prohibit a candidate's campaign committee from informing the candidate who contributed and how much. Therefore, the attempt to shield candidates from this information by prohibiting solicitation to ensure an unbiased judge was underinclusive. Citing the U.S. Supreme Court's finding in *Williams Yulee* discussed further on, however, the Ninth Circuit, sitting en banc, reheard *Wolfson* and held that Arizona had a compelling interest in maintaining public confidence in judicial integrity and that prohibiting judges from personally soliciting or accepting campaign contributions was a constitutional method for protecting this interest. *Wolfson v. Concannon*, 811 F.3d 1176 (9th Cir. 2016).

In *Weaver v. Bonner*, 309 F.3d 1312 (11th Cir. 2002), the Eleventh Circuit Court of Appeals struck down a provision of the Georgia Code of Judicial Conduct that prohibited judicial candidates from personally soliciting campaign contributions. The court held that the code provision violated the First Amendment because it was not narrowly tailored to serve Georgia's compelling interest in judicial impartiality. According to the court, the impartiality concerns, if any, are created by the state's decision to elect judges publicly, and the fact that judicial candidates require financial support and public endorsements to run successful campaigns does not suggest that they will be partial if they are elected. The court added, "even if there is a risk that judges will be tempted to rule a particular way because of contributions or endorsements, this risk is not significantly reduced by allowing the candidate's agent to seek these contributions and endorsements on the candidate's behalf, rather than the candidate seeking them himself. Successful candidates will feel beholden to the people who helped them get elected regardless of who did the soliciting of support. [Canon 5C(2)] thus fails strict scrutiny because it completely chills a candidate's speech on these topics while hardly advancing the state's interest in judicial impartiality at all." *Weaver v. Bonner*, 309 F.3d 1312, 1323 (11th Cir. 2002).

But, in *Siefert v. Alexander*, 608 F. 3d 974 (2010), the Seventh Circuit Court of Appeals analyzed the prohibition as a campaign finance restriction on contributions and applied the "closely drawn scrutiny" analysis. The court upheld the prohibition finding that it "is drawn closely enough to the state's interest in preserving impartiality and preventing corruption." *Id.* at 990. *See also Bauer v. Shepard*, 620 F.3d 704 (7th Cir. 2010); *Stretton v. Disc. Bd*, 944 F.2d 137 (3d Cir. 1991) (court found that prohibition on personal solicitation of campaign funds did not violate First Amendment); *In re Fadeley*, 802 P.2d 31 (Or. 1990) (prohibition against judge or judicial candidate personally soliciting campaign funds complies with First Amendment).

In 2015, the U.S. Supreme Court decided *Williams-Yulee v. Fla. Bar*, 575 U.S. ____, 135 S. Ct. 1656, 1664, 191 L. Ed. 2d 570 (2015). Addressing Florida's rule prohibiting judicial candidates from personally soliciting campaign contributions, the Supreme Court explained that the rule restricted the content of a candidate's speech and, therefore, would only survive a First Amendment challenge if it were "narrowly tailored to serve a compelling interest." *Williams-Yulee v. Florida Bar*, slip op. at 8 (Apr. 29, 2015).

The Court found that states have a compelling interest in protecting the integrity of the judiciary and maintaining the public's confidence in the judiciary. The Court explained that this interest extended beyond "preventing the appearance of corruption in legislative and executive elections" because "the role of judges differs from the role of politicians . . . a judge is not to follow the preferences of his supporters, or provide any special consideration to his campaign donors."

Id. at 10. Instead a judge is expected to be fair and independent. "[A] judge's personal solicitation could result (even unknowingly) in a possible temptation . . . which might lead him not to hold the balance nice, clear and true." *Id.* at 11 (internal citations omitted).

The Supreme Court rejected the appellant's argument that the prohibition on personal solicitation was unconstitutionally underinclusive because Florida's rules allow a candidate's campaign committee to solicit contributions and allow a candidate to write thank-you notes to contributors, both of which reduce the public's confidence in the integrity of the judiciary. The Court noted that in crafting judicial conduct rules, a state need not address all aspects of a problem in one rule. The Court also determined that the personal solicitation prohibition was not over-inclusive because, while the state's compelling interest in protecting the integrity of the judiciary "may be implicated to varying degrees in particular contexts," the interest is present whether the judicial candidate's personal solicitation is communicated through a mass mailing, a speech to 100 people, or when a "candidate tries to buttonhole" a potential donor. *Williams-Yulee v. Florida Bar*, slip op. at 11 (Apr. 29, 2015).

Finally, the Court found that neither recusal rules nor campaign contribution limits were a less restrictive means for protecting the state's compelling interest. The Court explained, "A rule requiring judges to recuse themselves from every case in which a lawyer or litigant made a campaign contribution would disable many jurisdictions." *Id.* at 19. Noting that Florida already had campaign contribution limits, the Court also found that even small donations create the appearance that "judges who personally solicit funds might improperly favor their campaign donors would remain." *Id.* at 20.

Appearance of Soliciting Contributions

A judge or judicial candidate may not in any way take part in the solicitation of campaign contributions. For instance, a candidate may not initiate a call to a potential campaign contributor and then turn over the phone to a campaign committee representative to make the actual solicitation. Such a solicitation method violates the Code because of the candidate's transparent attempt to avoid "personal" solicitation. Wis. Jud. Cond. Adv. Comm. Op. 97-7 (1997). Candidates may also be prohibited from activities that create the appearance of personal involvement in fund-raising. *See, e.g.*, W. Va. Adv. Op. 1/12/00 (2000) (judicial election committee may not hold fund-raiser in candidate's home because even if the candidate did not personally solicit or accept contributions, funds being raised in the home of the candidate would, at a minimum, create an appearance of personal involvement). A judge or judicial candidate may not host a website or Facebook page promoting the candidacy. The campaign committee should be responsible for the Internet presence. Fla. Sup. Ct. Jud. Ethics Adv. Comm.

Op. 10-28 (2010). Additionally, campaign contributions are sometimes made in the form of services. Therefore, the personal solicitation of services by a judicial candidate is also prohibited except for that solicitation necessary to begin and maintain a voluntary campaign committee. Wis. Jud. Cond. Adv. Comm., Op. 97-7 (1997).

Soliciting through Advertisements

Judges or judicial candidates are prohibited not only from in-person solicitation, but also from publishing or distributing print advertisements requesting campaign contributions. *See, e.g.*, Ga. Jud. Qualifications Comm'n Op. No. 210 (1996) (judge may not publish newspaper advertisement with the following language below his photo: "Paid for by Candidate," "Send Contributions to," "Committee to Elect (Name of Candidate)," "Address (Omitted)," "Phone No. (Omitted)"); W. Va. Adv. Op. 3/23/98 (1998) (judge may not distribute advertisement in which judge speaks in the first person describing his or her experiences and career history and which includes at the bottom the statement "Contributions May Be Made to Treasurer at Above Address" because such a statement gives the appearance that the judicial candidate is personally soliciting campaign contributions). *See also Justice at Stake Campaign, National Surveys of American Voters and State Judges, October 2001—January 2002*, (discussing how 9 in 10 voters, and 8 in 10 state judges, say they are quite concerned about special interest groups buying advertising to influence outcomes of judicial elections).

Acting as Campaign Treasurer

A judge or judicial candidate may be prohibited from serving as his or her own campaign treasurer. Kan. Jud. Ethics Adv. Op. JE 83 (1998) (candidate for district judge in elective district may not serve as campaign treasurer even if candidate will not solicit or accept campaign contributions of any type); Kan. Jud. Ethics Op. JE 65 (1996) (candidate for judicial office may not serve as own campaign treasurer); *but see* Fl. Jud. Ethics Adv. Comm. Op. 2012-17 (2012) (per state statute, candidate may act as treasurer for campaign; candidate may also deposit received donations into campaign account). The candidate's spouse may also be prohibited from filling the role of treasurer. *See* W. Va. Adv. Op. 12/28/99 (1999) (since a judicial candidate may not personally solicit funds and the candidate should encourage members of his or her family to adhere to the same standards of political conduct, a judicial candidate's wife is prohibited from serving as the candidate's campaign treasurer).

Accepting Contributions

Rule 4.1 provides that a judicial candidate may not "personally . . . accept campaign contributions." Some jurisdictions therefore advise candidates not to personally or directly accept campaign funds. *See, e.g.*, Wis. Jud. Cond. Adv. Comm. Op. 97-7 (1997) ("[a]ccording to the *American Heritage Dictionary* 'personally' means '. . . in person or without the intervention of another.' Thus, what is prohibited is the candidate's *personal* or direct solicitation of campaign funds and the *personal* or direct acceptance of campaign funds."). Kentucky has deleted the word "accept" from their Code, and therefore, while a candidate may not personally solicit campaign contributions, he or she may accept them. Ky. Jud. Ethics Op. JE-42 (1983) (candidate can accept both solicited and unsolicited gifts at any time, but may never solicit contributions; solicitation must be left to campaign committee).

Sending Thank-You Letters

Some jurisdictions permit judicial candidates to send thank-you letters to campaign contributors or express their gratitude in other ways. *See, e.g.*, Fla. Comm. on Stands. of Cond. Governing Judges Op. 77-22 (1978) (Canons do not prohibit a judge or candidate for judge from exercising the ordinary courtesies and manners of society that would anticipate thanks for support, and any note or statement of thanks would be in good taste); Ill. Jud. Ethics Comm. Op. 95-8 (1995) (judge may send a personally signed thank-you note to campaign contributors; however, campaign contributions of which a judge has knowledge made by lawyers and others who appear before the judge may be relevant to disqualification under Canon 3E); Kan. Jud. Ethics Op. JE 109 (2002) (judge in elective district may place thank-you advertisement in local newspapers); *but see* N.Y. Adv. Comm. on Jud. Ethics Op. 07-168 (2007) (part-time judge who is not candidate for judicial office may not send letter to local newspapers that includes expression of her gratitude to voters for electing her and discussing general development and activities of court); Wash. Ethics Adv. Comm. Op. 90-09 (1990) (improper for judge to send personal thank-you letter for contribution made to judge's campaign; judge's campaign committee may acknowledge contribution with thank-you letter on judge's behalf).

If a judge is permitted to send thank-you letters to campaign contributors, he or she should not print them on judicial stationery. Fla. Comm. on Stands. of Cond. Governing Judges Op. 92-02 (1992) (thank-you notes to campaign contributors should not be on judicial stationery, which is to be used for official business only, not for private purposes).

USING COURT STAFF, FACILITIES, OR OTHER COURT RESOURCES IN A CAMPAIGN FOR JUDICIAL OFFICE

Rule 4.1(A)(10), which was added to the Code in 2007, prohibits a judge or judicial candidate from using court staff, facilities, or other court resources in a campaign for judicial office. *See In re Grodman*, 2015 Ariz. LEXIS 319 (Ariz.

2015) (judge used court email to conduct campaign activities); *In re Cannizzaro*, 901 So. 2d 1035 (La. 2005) (judge permitted his minute clerk to plan and organize campaign fund-raising dinner); W. Va. Adv. Op. 2/28/92 (1992) (improper for incumbent who is candidate for judicial office to display campaign bumper sticker on his or her private automobile if vehicle were on court premises). *But see* Fla. Sup. Ct. Jud. Ethics Adv. Comm. Op. 08-11 (2008) (judge's campaign materials may include pictures of judge with jurors and/or complimentary letters from jurors so long as those jurors agree to the inclusion, and any such letters are unsolicited and not the product of official judicial business); Fla. Sup. Ct. Jud. Ethics Adv. Comm. Op. 97-34 (1998) (judge should strive to arrange campaign activities to be conducted outside regular courthouse hours; minor campaign related activities, such as brief telephone calls or minor emergency matters, may be permissible during regular office hours as long as conduct does not cast reasonable doubt on judge's capacity to act impartially as judge, demean judicial office, or interfere with proper performance of judicial duties).

KNOWINGLY OR WITH RECKLESS DISREGARD FOR THE TRUTH, MAKING ANY FALSE OR MISLEADING STATEMENTS

Rule 4.1(A)(11) states that a judge or judicial candidate shall not "knowingly, or with reckless disregard for the truth, make any false or misleading statement." *See generally In re Segal*, JC-14-0002 (Ariz. S. Ct. 2014) (judge censured for making false statements during judge's campaign about the state attorney general's investigation into judge); *In re Pendleton*, 870 N.W.2d 367 (Minn. 2015) (judge who knowingly made false statement about his residence address on his affidavit of candidacy was removed from office, agency not required to prove deceptive intent).

In the 1990 Code, judicial candidates were prohibited from "knowingly misrepresenting the identity, qualifications, present position, or other fact concerning the candidate or an opponent." *See In re Jud. Campaign Compl. Against Carr*, 658 N.E.2d 1158 (Ohio Comm. of Judges 1995), *aff'd*, 667 N.E.2d 956 (Ohio 1996) (judicial candidate does not act "knowingly" within meaning of judicial code merely by acting recklessly in making statement that is possibly false; judicial Canon will be violated only if candidate has knowledge of probable, and not just possible, falsity of his or her statements). The new language is borrowed from the law of libel and slander and fraudulent misrepresentation. Charles G. Geyh & W. William Hodes, *Reporters' Notes to the Model Code of Judicial Conduct*, 99–100 (2009). For a history of Canon 5A(3)(e), the 1990 counterpart to the 2007 provision, *see* Lisa L. Milord, *The Development of the ABA Judicial Code* 51 (1992).

Restrictions on knowingly making misrepresentations during a judicial election campaign have survived First Amendment challenges. *See Harper v. Disc.*

Counsel, 113 F.3d 1234 (6th Cir. 1992) (unpublished opinion) (finding that Ohio's restrictions on a judicial candidate's right to criticize the incumbent during an election, which only require that the criticism be truthful and accurate, are not overbroad); *Mahan v. Nev. Jud. Ethics & Election Pracs. Comm.*, 2000 WL 33937547 (D. Nev. 2000) (Nevada Canon 5A(3)(d)(ii), which prohibits knowing misrepresentations of identity, qualifications, present position or other facts, does not burden rights protected by First Amendment because it is quite clear what type of speech is prohibited); *In re Chmura*, 626 N.W.2d 876 (Mich. 2001) (judicial conduct rule that prohibits a judicial candidate from knowingly or recklessly using or participating in the use of any form of public communication that is false strikes a reasonable constitutional balance between the candidate's First Amendment rights and the state's interest in preserving the integrity of the judicial system); *In re Donohoe*, 580 P.2d 1093 (Wash. 1978) ("[W]e do not believe that the First Amendment protects one who utters a statement with knowledge of its falsity, even in the context of a judicial campaign. Such speech is not beneficial to the public and is generally harmful to the person against whom it is directed."). *See generally* James Sample, Lauren Jones, & Rachel Weiss, *The New Politics of Judicial Elections 2006: How 2006 Was the Most Threatening Year Yet to the Fairness and Impartiality of Our Courts—and How Americans are Fighting Back* (Justice At Stake 2006); Adam R. Long, *Keeping Mud Off The Bench: The First Amendment and Regulation of Candidates' False or Misleading Statements in Judicial Elections*, 51 Duke L.J. 787 (2001) (arguing that restrictions are constitutional); Alex Brauer & Tyng Loh, *Current Developments 2000–2001, Judicial Misconduct*, 14 Geo. J. Legal Ethics 963 (2001) (discussing tension between marketing aspect of political campaigns and standards of veracity to which judges are held by Model Code of Judicial Conduct); Robert C. Berness, *Norms of Judicial Behavior: Understanding Restrictions on Judicial Candidate Speech in the Age of Attack Politics*, 53 Rutgers L. Rev. 1027 (2001); Shaman, Lubet, & Alfini, Judicial Conduct and Ethics 386 (Lexis Law Publishing 2000) (candidates for judicial office held to high standard of accuracy in their public statements and conduct of their campaigns).

In Wisconsin, a television advertisement was broadcast by Justice Michael Gableman in his successful 2008 campaign to unseat incumbent Justice Louis Butler. A three sentence statement in the advertisement was found by three justices of the Wisconsin Supreme Court to be false, warranting discipline, such that it was not protected by the First Amendment. *Wisc. Jud. Comm'n v. Gableman*, 2010 WI 61. Three other justices concluded that the First Amendment protected the conduct of Justice Gableman and that the disciplinary matter should be dismissed. 2010 WI 62. (The Wisconsin Supreme Court was so divided on the issue that the second group of three demanded a separate citation for their opinion.) *See* Rebecca Love Kourlis, *America's Judicial Selection Wars*, 36 Human

Rights 5 (Winter 2009); Penny J. White, *"The Appeal" to the Masses,* 86 Denv. U. L. Rev. 251 (2008); George D. Brown, *Political Judges and Popular Justice: A Conservative Victory or a Conservative Dilemma?* 49 Wm. & Mary L. Rev. 1543 (2008).

Misleading Claim of Endorsement

A judge or candidate for judicial office violates Rule 4.1(A)(11) by falsely stating or implying that they have obtained the endorsement of a newspaper or group. *See In re Alley*, 699 So. 2d 1369 (Fla. 1997) (judge sent campaign mailers that included portion of newspaper editorial that falsely implied that judge, not her opponent, had been endorsed by newspaper); *Summe v. Jud. Retirement & Removal Comm'n*, 947 S.W.2d 42 (Ky. 1997) (judge's campaign literature gave false impression to voters that independent organization advocating child abuse issues supported judge); *Disc. Counsel v. Kaup*, 806 N.E.2d 513 (Ohio 2004) (judicial candidate put statement on placard that "Neighborhood Protection Council has endorsed Gary Kaup" and similar statements in campaign letter when in reality no entity called that ever existed); *Disc. Counsel v. Evans*, 733 N.E.2d 609 (Ohio 2000) (judicial candidate used television, radio, and print advertisements that stated that he was "Endorsed by Southern Ohio's Top Prosecutors and Sheriffs!", even though at time advertisements ran, only three of fourteen county prosecuting attorneys and five of fourteen sheriffs in appellate district had endorsed candidate); *In re Roberts*, 675 N.E.2d 84 (Ohio 1996) (candidate stated in literature that he was endorsed by "legal community" in district when, in fact, he had been endorsed by only one county bar association in seven-county district); *In re Elward*, 1 Ill. Cts. Comm'n 114 (1977) (circuit court judge published advertisements that were "materially misleading" in that he quoted only "truncated version" of bar association evaluation, thereby giving a false impression of support when association had actually found candidate unqualified; however, because numerous newspaper articles, editorials, and advertisements were published that had clearly stated that candidate had been found unqualified, courts commission found that "measured against this total mix" of information, candidate's advertisement did not create false impression); Fla. Sup. Ct. Jud. Ethics Adv. Comm. Op. 08-11 (2008) (judge's campaign materials may not include pictures of judge with fellow judges, but may include pictures with other officials, elected and non-elected, if materials include clear disclaimer that the persons depicted have not necessarily endorsed or decided to support the judge); N.Y. Adv. Comm. on Jud. Ethics Op. 12-114 (2012) (judicial candidate prohibited from using photograph of himself and elected public official from a different political party who has not endorsed candidate in campaign literature without consent of elected public official); Tex. Adv. Comm. on Jud. Ethics Op. 212 (1998) (judge or judicial candidate may not include in campaign literature photograph with recognized officeholder who has not endorsed the candidate in the race); Tex. Adv. Comm. on Jud. Ethics Op. 168 (1994) (judge may not use in his campaign advertising confidential, anonymous comments written by other judges who attended class that was taught by judge because judges who filled out evaluations may or may not be supportive of candidate).

Mailing Sample Ballots

Two or more judicial candidates may violate the Code of Judicial Conduct by sending out sample ballots that give the impression that each candidate endorses the others' candidacy. *See, e.g., In re Kay*, 508 So. 2d 329 (Fla. 1987) (judge's joining in venture and mailing sample ballots resembling official ballots gave appearance that partisan Democratic or Republican parties endorsed candidacy in nonpartisan race); *In re Pratt*, 508 So. 2d 8 (Fla. 1987) (candidate's participation, with other judicial candidates, in promoting and financing mailing of sample ballots that resembled official sample ballot, gave appearance that political parties endorsed candidacy and that each judicial candidate endorsed others).

Misrepresenting Current Position or Status

A judge or judicial candidate may violate Rule 4.1(A)(11) by using language in campaign materials that misrepresents his or her current position. This issue may arise when a nonjudge candidate gives the false impression that he or she is a judge or when a judge gives the false impression that he or she sits on the court that is the subject of the election. *See, e.g., In re Renke*, 933 So. 2d 482 (Fla. 2006) (judge's campaign brochure created impression candidate was running as an incumbent); *In re Jud. Campaign Compl. Against O'Toole*, 24 N.E.3d 1114 (Ohio 2014) (former judge who one year earlier was defeated in election, reprimanded for intentionally misrepresenting status in campaign materials for same office); *In re Jud. Campaign Compl. Against Emrich*, 669 N.E.2d 586 (Ohio Comm'n of Judges 1996) (candidate violated the Code of Judicial Conduct by knowingly misrepresenting his position on a billboard and on yard signs by using title "judge" without indicating that candidate sat in court different from one that was subject of campaign); Ariz. Jud. Ethics Adv. Comm. Op. 98-03 (1998) (candidate for judicial office who serves as part-time, judge pro tempore, may not use title "judge" in campaign literature without explaining limited nature of pro tempore position); Fla. Sup. Ct. Jud. Ethics Adv. Comm. Op. 08-13 (2008) (judicial candidate who has retired from circuit bench and enjoys senior status may not use title "judge" in campaign literature, media releases, printed ads, or other media venues); Fla. Sup. Ct. Jud. Ethics Adv. Comm. Op. 00-21 (2000) (candidate may not use website address of www.judgex.com ("x" denotes the judicial candidate's first name) even if website contains disclaimer that candidate is not judge); Florida Comm. on Stands. of Cond. Governing Judges Op. 84-17 (1984) (judicial candidate, a domestic relations commissioner, may not describe position in campaign literature as "judicial position," "limited jurisdiction family judge," or "judicial officer" because those terms are misleading and imply that candidate is judge); Ga. Jud. Qualifications Comm'n Op. 212 (1996) (inappropriate for a candidate for judicial office to use designation "judge" in political advertising if in fact the candidate does not presently hold a judicial position); Ga. Jud. Qualifications Comm'n Op. No. 211 (1996) (improper for judicial candidate to use designation "judge" in political advertising without clearly designating judicial position currently held by such candidate); Ill. Jud. Ethics Comm. Op. 98-3 (1998) (candidate who is not judge may not use word "judge" in advertising in way that would make people think he or she already was judge); Mich. Comm. on Jud. Ethics Inf. Op. CI-556 (1980) (candidate could not use slogan "A Judge for a Change" because it falsely suggested that candidate was incumbent judge); Tex. Adv. Comm. on Jud. Ethics Op. 195 (1996) (individual who resigned from county court at law bench to run for district court bench, and who is currently practicing law, may not use title "judge" in political advertisements; individual may not use election materials from previous campaigns for county bench races that say only "Vote for Judge __"); Tex. Adv. Comm. on Jud. Ethics Op. 193 (1996) (violation of code of judicial conduct for candidate for justice of the peace who is a former justice of the peace to imply in his political advertising that he is current justice of the peace); Tex. Adv. Comm. on Jud. Ethics Op. 159 (1993) (judge who runs for a nonjudicial political office may not use title "judge" as part of political advertising or in name of campaign committee; judge may describe in political literature past experience as judge, and use word "judge" in that connection).

Some leeway in language has been given in descriptions of the candidate's position. *See, e.g.*, Ariz. Jud. Ethics Adv. Comm. Op. 10-02 (2010) (sitting judge seeking another judicial position may use the title "judge" in campaign literature provided that the literature "clearly informs the public of the candidate's current position"); Fla. Sup. Ct. Jud. Ethics Adv. Comm. Op. 08-15 (2008) (candidate may use the title "administrative law judge" when describing candidate's years of service with division of administrative hearings, even though during portion of service title was "hearing officer"); Tex. Adv. Comm. on Jud. Ethics Op. 164 (1993) (municipal court judge running for justice of the peace may use title "judge" in campaign literature, campaign stationery, and press releases, and may use photograph wearing judicial robe in campaign literature and newspaper articles); Ark. Jud. Ethics Adv. Comm. Op. 02-03 (2002) (judicial candidate may describe himself in campaign materials, advertisements, and public statements as "judge" when he has served for past six years as part-time city judge, an appointive, rather than elective position).

A judicial candidate also may not use language such as "re-elect" or "keep" that falsely gives the impression that the candidate is an incumbent in the position for which he or she is running. *See Trujillo v. Essenpreis*, 00-1 (Nev. Stand. Comm. on Jud. Ethics and Election Prac. 2000) (candidate's campaign signs misrepresented him as incumbent); *DeLanoy v. Redmon*, 98-5 (Nev. Stand. Comm. on Jud. Ethics and Election Prac. 1998) (family court judge running for district court seat ran television commercial that urged voters to "re-elect" him to bench, a knowing misrepresentation because he was running for post on another court); Fla. Sup. Ct. Jud. Ethics Adv. Comm. Op. 02-07 (2002) (judge who is in contested election immediately after being appointed to the bench by governor may not use the word "re-elect" in campaign advertisements because it could give the false impression that the candidate was previously elected to this position; judge may use "retain"); Nev. Stand. Comm. on Jud. Ethics and Election Prac. Op. JE 08-006 (2008) (candidate may refer to his service as alternate municipal judge in campaign materials so long as materials do not refer to "retain" or "retention" or to "re-elect" or "re-election"; candidate may not wear judicial robe in campaign materials); Tex. Adv. Comm. on Jud. Ethics Op. 135 (1990) (judge, who sought re-election and was defeated, may not use words "re-elect" or "keep" on campaign material in subsequent campaign, against incumbent, for election to another court).

False impressions about a judicial candidate's current position can also arise when the candidate is pictured in campaign material wearing a judicial robe. *See, e.g.*, Nev. Stand. Comm. on Jud. Ethics and Election Prac. Op. JE 03-004 (2003) (full-time court master may not campaign for state district judge while wearing a judicial robe even if he or she clearly points out his or her judicial experience, because a judicial robe depicted in an advertisement has the potential to communicate a powerful message to the electorate); Nev. Stand. Comm. on Jud. Ethics and Election Prac. Op. JE 02-004 (2002) (candidate for election to judicial office who serves as unpaid part-time judge, may not appear in judicial robe in campaign advertising).

However, an incumbent judge who wears a robe in performing his or her judicial duties may be permitted to wear the robe in campaign advertisements. Fla. Sup. Ct. Jud. Ethics Adv. Comm. Op. 08-11 (2008); N.D. Jud. Ethics Adv. Comm. Op. 2016-2 (2016); ABA Informal Op. 1450 (1980) (no violation of the Code of Judicial Conduct when incumbent judge, in re-election campaign, allows use of photograph (including televised photograph) of himself wearing his judicial robe if photograph is otherwise proper and if he normally wears robe in performance of judicial duties).

If the judge is running for a position different from the one he or she currently holds, the judge should indicate his or her current position on the advertising materials. *See* Wash. Ethics Adv. Comm. Op. 88-03 (1988) (not improper for district court judge, who is running for superior court position, to be pictured in campaign literature in judicial robe as long as caption of picture indicates that judge is district court judge); Ohio Bd. of Commissioners on Grievances and Disc. Op. 2003-8 (2003) (magistrate who is judicial candidate may appear in robe in photograph used in campaign advertising if photograph has accurate label identifying judge as magistrate of court on which he or she serves); *But see In re Miller*, 759 A.2d 455 (Pa. Ct. Jud. Disc. 2000) (district judge running for position as common pleas judge did not inappropriately misrepresent his status to potential voters by wearing judicial robes and referring to himself as "judge" in advertisments).

A nonjudge candidate for judicial office may also violate the prohibition against making misleading statements by giving a false impression about the candidate's current employment position. *See, e.g.*, Fla. Sup. Ct. Jud. Ethics Adv. Comm. Op. 02-12 (2002) (assistant state attorney running for judicial office could not state: "Elect Prosecutor (name of candidate) for Circuit Judge" on candidate's campaign literature as use of term "prosecutor" misidentified candidate's current position). Making a false statement on a bar association screening committee questionnaire may also be a violation. *See In re Nocella*, 102 A.3d 422 (Penn. 2014) (judge, while attorney-candidate, lied repeatedly on candidate questionnaires about number of cases in which he was named as defendant).

Letterhead and Seal

A judge may be prohibited from using official judicial letterhead and state seal in campaign materials. W. Va. Adv. Op. 3/10/00 (2000) (judge may not use state seal on campaign material as all official judicial letterhead bears seal; use of seal would be confusing to public and give appearance that official letterhead was being used to further political campaign); W. Va. Adv. Op. 2/28/92 (1992) (improper for judicial officer to use state seal with his or her official title and courthouse address on campaign literature because it gives appearance of official stationery).

Misrepresenting Experience

A judge or judicial candidate may violate Rule 4.1(A)(11) by misrepresenting his or her judicial or legal experience. *See, e.g., In re Robertson*, JDDC 14-215 and 14-216 (Ark. Jud. Disc. & Disability Comm'n 2015) (candidate whose campaign materials titled her judge when she did not hold judicial office violated Rule 4.1(A)(11); *In Re Woodard*, 919 So. 2d 389 (Fla. 2006) (candidate misrepresented in campaign literature number of jury trials over which he presided); *In re Alley*, 699 So. 2d 1369 (Fla. 1997) (judge misrepresented her qualifications in newspaper advertisements by claiming to have circuit judicial experience when in fact her service was that of a general master); Fla. Sup. Ct. Jud. Ethics

Adv. Comm. Op. 00-27 (2000) (judicial candidate should not portray himself or herself trying a jury case, if in fact, the candidate did not have experience trying jury cases or trying a particular case or type of case that in fact the candidate had not tried); Fla. Sup. Ct. Jud. Ethics Adv. Comm. Op. 00-24 (2000) (non-incumbent candidate for judicial office who served as civil traffic hearing officer, parking ticket court hearing officer, and special master for juvenile smoking court and animal control violations may use phrase "quasi-judicial experience" in his or her campaign literature, but candidate must make specific reference to actual positions he or she has held so as not to mislead general public). *Cf.* Kan. Jud. Ethics Op. JE 64 (1996) (judicial candidate may reproduce and distribute previous public statements candidate or opponent have made and positions taken during tenure in different public offices); *but see* W. Va. Adv. Op. 4/18/00 (2000) (judicial candidate may continue to act as expert witness in field of insurance during his or her campaign; however, candidate is prohibited from using any position that he or she might take as expert witness to advance his or her campaign by publicizing opinion or using it in political way).

Making Slurs or Knowingly Misrepresenting Facts Concerning the Candidate or an Opponent

A judge or judicial candidate may violate Rule 4.1(A)(11) by making statements or running advertisements that include slurs or false statements of fact about an opponent. *See Doyle v. Jud. Retirement & Removal Comm'n*, 885 S.W.2d 917 (Ky. 1994) (judge made misrepresentation of fact in campaign advertisement that opponent had recently inherited $500,000); *In re Jud. Campaign Compl. Against Burick*, 705 N.E.2d 424 (Ohio Comm'n. of Judges 1999) (judicial candidate's advertisements stated that her opponent had been appointed by political bosses when in fact appointment was made by governor; candidate also misrepresented degree of union support); *In re Hopewell*, 507 N.W.2d 911 (S.D. 1993) (candidate labeled incumbent "judicial reactionary" and accused him of having "campaign treasury heavily laden with lavish contributions by politically influential lawyers and lobbyists, power brokers for liability risk insurance companies, . . ., environmental polluters and the heavy handed law enforcement establishment of this community"); *but see In re Baker*, 542 P.2d 701 (Kan. 1975) (candidate's campaign advertisement that made issue of opponent's health and suggested that because of candidate's good health it will not be necessary to import "outside" judges to hear cases in district if he is elected judge is not "misrepresentation" within Canon 5A(3)(d)(ii) even though, after such candidate is elected and takes office, "outside" judges would be used in certain cases due to disqualification of candidate). *See also* Fla. Comm. on Stands. of Cond. Governing Judges Op. 98-27 (1998) (violation of the Florida Code of Judicial Conduct to produce radio, television, or print advertising that reproduces negative or critical newspaper headlines, stories, opinions about candidate's opponent); Ill. Jud. Ethics Comm. Op. 03-01 (2003) (judge or candidate for judicial office should not make allegations about opponent's purported private sexual conduct absent likely criminal prosecution or judicial disciplinary violation); *In re Fortinberry* (Mich. Jud. Tenure Comm'n, 2005) (candidate made false allegations that opponent murdered his wife); *In re McMillan*, 797 So. 2d 560 (Fla. 2001) (candidate's statements gave false or misleading impression that his opponent asserted pressure on county sheriff not to support candidate and that opponent pressured law enforcement officers for preferential treatment for his children when they were arrested; candidate also issued campaign brochure that contained knowing and false attempt to attribute loss of funds and supposed defects in fines and court costs collection system to opponent and falsely claimed that opponent averaged only 14 hours a week on bench and frequently took off time from court); *Fine v. Lueck*, 98-6 (Nev. Stand. Comm. on Jud. Ethics and Election Prac. 1998) (candidate for family court judge placed newspaper advertisement stating that opponent, who recently was removed from office for misconduct but was appealing that ruling, had been "convicted" when in fact, there was no conviction and word "convicted" implied criminal action); *In re Kulkin* (N.Y. State Comm'n on Jud. Cond. 2006) (judicial candidate created false impression that opponent had refused to handle parking tickets and that such refusal resulted in $400,000 in delinquent fees); Tex. Adv. Comm. on Jud. Ethics Op. 169 (1994) (unethical for candidate for judicial office to state that his or her opponent had been "removed" as district judge when, in fact, opponent had not been removed but had been defeated for re-election).

Opponent's Lead

A judge or judicial candidate may violate Rule 4.1(A)(11) by falsely stating that he or she is leading an opponent in an election. *See In re Jack D. Wood*, 1982 WL 156141 (Ky. Jud. Retirement & Removal Comm'n, Unreported Order, 1982) (judge published campaign advertisement that indicated professional poll placed him ahead of his opponent when in fact no such poll had been conducted).

Opponent's Experience

A judge or candidate for judicial office may violate Rule 4.1(A)(11) by knowingly making false or misleading statements or distributing false or misleading campaign materials that indicate that his or her opponent lacks sufficient experience for the position. *See, e.g., In re Alley*, 699 So. 2d 1369 (Fla. 1997) (judge knowingly misrepresented qualifications of her opponent in newspaper advertisements by claiming that opponent had no circuit judicial experience when in fact she had extensive experience as a county judge who had been assigned to circuit court); *In re Morris*, 675 N.E.2d 580 (Ohio Comm'n of Judges 1997) (judge violated Canon by running television advertisement that aired opponent's remarks out of context to falsely convey to public that opponent, while serving as a judge, made critical remarks to small, troubled boy, who appeared in his courtroom); *In re Brigner*, 732 N.E.2d 994 (Ohio Comm'n of Judges 2000) (candidate's campaign committee distributed fund-raising letter that included misleading statements asserting that opponent "has never handled a divorce case" and was "a novice who lacks even one day of domestic relations experience"); *In re Jud. Campaign Compl. Against Carr*, 658 N.E.2d 1158 (Ohio Comm'n of Judges 1995), *aff'd*, 667 N.E.2d 956 (Ohio 1996) (candidate falsely claimed in letter to potential donors that opponent had never handled a single case in housing court as a lawyer).

Although judges or candidates for election or appointment to judicial office are prohibited from knowingly misrepresenting the identity, qualifications, present position or other facts concerning the candidate or an opponent, they may openly disagree with an opponent-incumbent's practices. For instance, in Florida Comm. on Stands. of Cond. Governing Judges Op. 84-18 (1984), the committee stated that a judicial candidate may openly disagree with an opponent-incumbent's practice of requiring a physical arrest of all persons charged, even first-time offenders, accused of minor offenses, and of threatening defendants with maximum sentences if they proceed to trial. It would not be unethical for the candidate to state that these practices are unfair and that, if elected, he would look closely at each case before issuing warrants for arrest in misdemeanor offenses. It also would not be unethical for the candidate to state that he generally would be in favor of using the summons power of the court to bring misdemeanor defendants to bar and that he would not threaten defendants for exercising their right to trial. Fla. Comm. on Stands. of Cond. Governing Judges Op. 84-18 (1984).

Opponent's Bar Rating

A judicial candidate may comment on an opponent's commission rating. N.Y. Adv. Comm. on Jud. Ethics Op. 09-162 (2009). A judge or judicial candidate may violate the Code of Judicial Conduct by misrepresenting the bar rating of his or her opponent. *See, e.g.*, Fla. Sup. Ct. Jud. Ethics. Adv. Comm. Op. 00-21 (2000) (non-incumbent candidate for judicial office may state that opponent ranks last among other county court judges in five of eight categories, but must disclose fact that rankings were based on responses of only 55 lawyers if failing to do so would likely mislead public as to incumbent's qualifications); Mich. Comm. on Jud. Ethics Op. JI-120 (1999) (misleading and unethical for judicial candidate to refer to opponent's rating by local bar association as "not recommended" in candidate's campaign literature when, in fact, bar association's actual rating of opponent is "qualified, but not recommended").

Misrepresenting Actions of Incumbent Judge While in Office

A judicial candidate may violate Rule 4.1(A)(11) by misrepresenting the incumbent's conduct while in office. For instance, a candidate committed a judicial ethics violation by trying to create a false impression in campaign flier that incumbent judge was causing needless delays and holding large numbers of cases under advisement despite candidate's knowledge to the contrary. *In re Nadeau*, 914 A.2d 714 (Me. 2007) (campaign advertisement stating that an opponent had been seen on video pulling a child from his grandparents' arms for forced visit with parent was a knowing misrepresentation in violation of the Code of Judicial Conduct Canon prohibiting judicial candidates from making knowing misrepresentations regarding their opponents; exchange of the child could not be seen on the tape, judge admitted that he had viewed the tape, and an objective viewing of the videotape showed that candidate's conduct was not inappropriate); *In re Bybee*, 716 N.E.2d 957 (Ind. 1999) (judicial candidate violated Canon by knowingly misrepresenting incumbent judge's judicial record in campaign brochure); *In re Jud. Campaign Compl. Against Kienzle*, 708 N.E.2d 800 (Ohio Comm'n of Judges 1999) (candidate falsely stated in campaign materials that opponent, the incumbent judge, had imposed $430,000 in taxes on county residents by issuing ruling that later was reversed on appeal and that he never would impose taxes on county residents contrary to law); Ga. Jud. Qualifications Comm'n Op. 213 (1996) (candidate ran television advertisement stating that incumbent reversed the conviction of man who repeatedly sexually assaulted his four-year-old son "on a technicality," but failed to disclose that the decision was by a 7-2 majority of the court, that cases, especially those on appeal, are frequently and properly decided on technical or procedural aspects of the law, and that the Georgia Supreme Court refused to hear an appeal of this decision by the State); Tex. Adv. Comm. on Jud. Ethics Op. 212 (1998) (judge or judicial candidate may not include in campaign literature statement criticizing the incumbent's previous decisions).

A judge or judicial candidate is not prohibited, however, from publicizing information about his or her opponent's business practices and dealings as gleaned from public records and newspaper articles so long as it is relevant to the qualifications for judicial office and it does not misrepresent the identity, qualifications, present position, or other fact concerning the opponent. Fla. Sup. Ct. Jud. Ethics Adv. Comm. Op. 02-13 (2002); Fla. Comm. on Stands. of Cond. Governing Judges Op. 00-23 (2000) (non-incumbent judicial candidate may ethically publish campaign advertisement that informs public that incumbent opponent entered into deferred retirement option program, that opponent is already officially in retired status with state retirement system, and that electing non-incumbent will not deprive incumbent of his/her retirement). *See also* Alicia Yager, *Complaint against Justice Gableman moves forward: Wisconsin*

Supreme Court will decide if campaign ad wrong, The Badger Herald (Dec. 4, 2009) (candidate ran advertisement, which insinuated that during his tenure as appellate state public defender, incumbent state Supreme Court justice "found a loophole" that allowed child molester to go free).

Correcting False Information

Rule 4.1(A)(11) states that judges and judicial candidates shall not "knowingly, or with reckless disregard for the truth, make any false or misleading statement." As noted in Comment [7] to Rule 4.1, the modern usage of the term "misleading" includes omitting facts necessary to make a communication, when considered as a whole, not misleading. Comment [8] to Rule 4.1 provides that judicial candidates who are the subject of false, misleading, or unfair allegations made by opposing candidates, third parties, or the media may make a factually accurate public response. The Comment further provides that, when an independent third party has made unwarranted attacks on a candidate's opponent, the candidate may disavow the attacks, and request the third party to cease and desist. Comment [9] states that a judicial candidate is permitted to respond directly to false, misleading, or unfair allegations made against him or her during a campaign, although it is preferable for someone else to respond if the allegations relate to a pending case. *See, e.g.*, Fla. Comm. on Stands. of Cond. Governing Judges Op. 96-24 (1996) (judicial candidate ethically may defend himself or herself publicly against opponent's false statements about him or her and may also address opponent's false statements concerning his own candidacy); Ga. Jud. Qualifications Comm'n Op. 207 (1996) (judge or candidate for judicial office may criticize performance of incumbent, but incumbent is not expected to remain silent in the face of criticism and may refer to his or her own record, court statistics or other facts); *but cf.* Neb. Ethics Adv. Comm. Op. 02-5 (2002) (advising Nebraska District Judges' Association to act with extreme caution in pursuing "public action" in response to "unjust criticism" of district judge). *See also* Citizens for Independent Courts, *Defending Justice: The Courts, Criticism, and Intimidation* in UNCERTAIN JUSTICE (The Constitution Project, 2000).

Attacks upon a judge's record and character may come from sources other than the judge's opponent. For instance, a Florida judge faced criticism after issuing a ruling in a highly publicized visitation case. Members of an organization distributed literature opposing the judge's re-election and appeared on a radio talk show threatening opposition to the judge's re-election. The Commission advised that a judge who receives active opposition and whose re-election may be opposed may, in accordance with the Canons, engage in all activities to the same extent a judge may with a named opponent. However, because the case was ongoing, the judge was proscribed from discussing its facts or merits. Fla. Comm. on Stands. of Cond. Governing Judges Op. 92-13 (1992). *See also* Colo.

Jud. Ethics Adv. Bd. Op. 2008-05 (2008) (judicial code states that judge who is candidate for retention should abstain from any campaign activity in connection with candidacy unless there is active opposition to retention; Board concluded that the numerous comments posted on the local newspaper's website recommending non-retention of the judge amounted to active opposition).

MAKING STATEMENTS THAT WOULD REASONABLY BE EXPECTED TO AFFECT THE OUTCOME OR IMPAIR THE FAIRNESS OF A MATTER PENDING OR IMPENDING IN ANY COURT

Rule 4.1(A)(12) states that judges and judicial candidates shall not "make any statement that would reasonably be expected to affect the outcome or impair the fairness of a matter pending or impending in any court." A judge is not prohibited from speaking publicly on matters that have been concluded and resolved. Col. Sup. Ct. Jud. Ethics Adv. Bd. Op. 2010-03 (2010) (judges may respond to questions raised about their participation in a concluded case, the disciplinary process and the stipulations the judges signed regarding their conduct in that case, and the dismissal of the civil suit brought against them based on the same facts).

A judicial candidate's public statement about a particular matter may be viewed as giving him or her a stake in the outcome of a case, and may in fact affect the outcome of a case. *See, e.g., In re Jud. Campaign Compl. Against Hein*, 706 N.E.2d 34 (Ohio Comm'n of Judges 1999) (candidate issued press release commenting on sentence imposed by his opponent in pending case and made improper statements labeling opponent as "liberal" and "soft on crime"); *In re Burick*, 705 N.E.2d 424 (Ohio Comm'n of Judges 1999) (judicial candidate made false and misleading statements regarding her opponent's sentencing in pending rape case); Fla. Sup. Ct. Jud. Ethics Adv. Comm. Op. 04-18 (2004) (judge who is candidate for re-election may not publicly comment on reasons for ruling on motion filed by judicial opponent in pending legal proceeding); Kan. Jud. Ethics Op. JE 163 (2008) (impermissible for judge to submit letter to editor of newspaper discussing issues regarding criminal code in response to editorial).

MAKING PLEDGES, PROMISES, OR COMMITMENTS THAT ARE INCONSISTENT WITH THE IMPARTIAL PERFORMANCE OF THE ADJUDICATIVE DUTIES OF JUDICIAL OFFICE

First Amendment Issues

In *Republican Party of Minnesota v. White*, 536 U.S. 765 (2002), the U.S. Supreme Court held in a 5–4 decision, authored by Justice Scalia, that "[t]he Minnesota Supreme Court's Canon of judicial conduct prohibiting candidates for judicial election from announcing their views on disputed legal and political issues violates the First Amendment." *White*, 536 U.S. at 788. The language ruled unconstitutional mirrored the "announce" clause of the 1972 version of the ABA Model Code of Judicial Conduct, which had been removed from the ABA Code in 1990 because of concerns about that clause's constitutionality.

As a content-based restriction on speech, the "announce" clause was subject to strict scrutiny, under which the respondents had the burden to prove that the clause was (1) narrowly tailored, to serve (2) a compelling state interest. According to the Court in *White*, the "announce" clause was not narrowly tailored to serve impartiality (or its appearance) in the traditional sense of the word, that is, as a lack of bias for or against either party to the proceeding, because it does not restrict speech for or against particular parties, but rather speech for or against particular issues. Secondly, the Court held that although "impartiality" in the sense of a lack of preconception in favor of or against a particular legal view may well be an interest served by the announce clause, pursuing this objective "is not a compelling state interest, since it is virtually impossible, and hardly desirable, to find a judge who does not have preconceptions about the law." *White*, 536 U.S. at 766. The Court explicitly declined to rule on the "pledges or promises" or the "commit" clauses. However, because both of those provisions and the "misrepresent clause" are, like the "announce clause," content-based restrictions on a candidate's speech, they would be subject to strict scrutiny if challenged in subsequent cases.

On remand from the Supreme Court, the federal appeals court struck down Minnesota's political activities Canons, which prohibited judges and judicial candidates from engaging in partisan political activity, but permitted them to speak at non-political party gatherings. *White*, 416 F.3d 738, 761–62 (8th Cir. 2005) (en banc), *cert. denied*, 546 U.S. 1157 (2006). The court also held that the state's solicitation clause, which prohibited judges and judicial candidates from personally soliciting campaign contributions (but allowed campaign committees to do so on behalf of the candidates), was unconstitutional to the extent that it prohibited candidates from signing solicitation letters and making campaign appeals before large groups. *Id.* at 763–66.

In light of the holding in *White*, the ABA Working Group on the First Amendment and Judicial Campaigns suggested several changes in the Model Code of Judicial Conduct with regard to judicial campaign speech. It carefully analyzed the "pledges or promises" clause, the "commit" clause, and the "misrepresent" clause of then-Canon 5A(3)(d) and arrived at a series of recommendations to accommodate the important interest of preserving judicial impartiality, integrity, and independence with the equally important concepts embodied in the First Amendment. The new wording of Canon 5A(3)(d) in the 1990 Code provided a clear enumeration of the restricted speech ("with respect to cases, controversies or issues that are likely to come before the court") and a clear statement of what is being protected by the restriction of this speech ("inconsistent with the impartial performance of the adjudicative duties of the office"). See *American Bar Association Standing Committee on Judicial Independence and the Standing Committee on Ethics and Professional Responsibility Report 105(B) to the House of Delegates* (August 2003) (detailing rationale for amendments). These amendments to Section 5(A)(d)(3) were adopted by the ABA House of Delegates in August 2003. *See American Bar Association Standing Committee on Judicial Independence and the Standing Committee on Ethics and Professional Responsibility Report 105(B) to the House of Delegates (August 2003)* (detailing rationale for amendments).

Restrictions on Judicial Campaign Speech After *White*

As noted above, in *White*, the Supreme Court declined to rule on the constitutionality of the "pledges or promises" and "commit" clauses of Canon 5A(3)(d). With regard to the "pledges or promises" clause, the Court stated that "this is a prohibition that is not challenged here and on which we express no view." *White*, 536 U.S. at 770. As to the "commit clause," the Court noted that at oral argument, respondents had argued that the limiting constructions placed upon Minnesota's announce clause by the Eighth Circuit, and adopted by the Minnesota Supreme Court, render the scope of the clause no broader than the 1990 Canon's "commit" clause. The Court then stated "[w]e do not know whether the announce clause (as interpreted by state authorities) and the 1990 ABA Canon are one in the same. No aspect of our constitutional analysis turns on this question." *Id.* at 773, n.5.

Given these statements, it remains an open question as to whether the campaign speech provisions of the 1990 ABA Model Code of Judicial Conduct are still viable. *See generally* Kelly Wayne Adams, *Walking the Tightrope: Maintaining an Independent Judiciary and Protecting Judicial Free Speech*, 50 S. Tex. L. Rev. 317 (2008); Mark S. Cady & Jess R. Phelps, *Preserving the Delicate Balance Between Judicial Accountability and Independence: Merit Selection in the Post-White World*, 17 Cornell J.L. & Pub. Pol'y 2 (2008); Jessica Gall. *Living with Republican Party of Minnesota v. White: The Birth and Death of Judicial Campaign Speech Restrictions*, 13 Comm. & Pol'y 97 (2008); James L. Gibson, *Campaigning for the Bench: The Corrosive Effects of Campaign Speech*, 42 Law & Soc'y Rev. 899 (2008); Nat Stern, *The Looming Collapse of Restrictions on Judicial Campaign Speech*, 38 Seton Hall L. Rev. 63 (2008); Kathleen M. Sullivan, *Republican Party v. Minnesota v. White: What Are the Alternatives?*, 21 Geo. J. Legal Ethics 1327 (2008); Roy Schotland, *Impacts of White*, 55 Drake L. Rev. 625 (2007); Thomas R. Phillips, *Free Speech for Judges and Fair Appeals for Litigants: Judicial Recusal in a Post-White World*, 55 Drake L. Rev. 691 (2007); Mary Eileen Weicher, *The Expansion of the First Amendment in Judicial Elections: Another Cause for Reform*, 38 Loy. U. Chi. L.J.

833 (2007); Matthew D. Besser, Note, *May I Be Recused? The Tension between Judicial Campaign Speech and Recusal after Republican Party of Minnesota v. White*, 64 Ohio St. L.J. 1197 (2003) (noting that the "commit" clause appears to be constitutional replacement for the "announce" clause, but adding that it is not clear how courts should apply it). *See also* Briffault, Richard, *Judicial Campaign Codes After Republican Party of Minnesota v. White*, 153 U. Pa. L. Rev. 181 (2004); Anca Cornis-Pop, *Republican Party of Minnesota v. White and the Announce Clause in Light of Theories of Judge and Voter Decisionmaking: with Strategic Judges and Rational Voters, the Supreme Court Was Right to Strike Down the Clause*, 40 Willamette L. Rev. 123 (2004); Brendan J. Doherty, *Stifled Speech and Judicial Campaigns: An Analysis of a Conflicted Legal Culture in Republican Party of Minnesota v. White*, 32 N. Ky. L. Rev. 305 (2005).

Shortly after the Supreme Court issued its opinion in *White*, a federal district court in New York struck all specific prohibitions on judicial political activity contained in Canon 5 of the New York Code of Judicial Conduct, which includes a "pledges or promises" clause, a "commit" clause, and a "misrepresent" clause, as a prior restraint on protected First Amendment activities. *Spargo v. New York State Comm'n on Jud. Cond.*, 244 F. Supp. 2d 72 (N.D.N.Y. 2003), *cert. denied*, 541 U.S. 1085 (2004). However, the U.S. Court of Appeals for the Second Circuit vacated the judgment and injunction of the district court and remanded the matter with instruction to the district court to abstain from exercising jurisdiction over the action. *Spargo v. New York State Comm'n on Jud. Cond.*, 351 F.3d 65 (2003) ("[i]t is to the State Commission on Judicial Conduct and the New York Court of Appeals that plaintiffs must make their arguments, and to which other interested parties must look, for further guidance and development of the law in the context of this controversy."). In another New York case, the New York Court of Appeals held that New York's judicial conduct rule prohibiting judicial candidates from making pledges or promises of conduct in office does not violate the First Amendment. The court found that New York's pledges or promises clause is "essential to maintaining impartiality and the appearance of impartiality in the state judiciary" and is "sufficiently circumscribed to withstand exacting scrutiny under the First Amendment." *In re Watson*, 794 N.E.2d 1 (N.Y. 2003).

The Seventh Circuit Court of Appeals, in *Bauer v. Shepard*, 620 F.3d 704 (7th Cir. 2010), held that Indiana's commitment clause was not overbroad. The Court explained that the provision only circumscribes statements that are "inconsistent with impartial adjudication" and not legal conclusions or those of "general stance." *See also Carey v. Wolnitzek*, 2012 WL 4597236 (Sept. 29, 2012) (Kentucky's pledges, promises, and commitment clause is neither overbroad nor vague); *Indiana Right to Life, Inc. v. Shepard*, 507 F.3d 545 (7th Cir. 2007) (Indiana's pledges or promises and commit clauses do not violate First Amendment); *North Dakota Family Alliance, Inc. v. Bader*, 361

F. Supp. 2d 1021 (D.N.D. 2005) (state's pledges or promises and commit clauses violate First Amendment because they forbid same types of speech as announce clause struck down in *White*); *Family Trust Found. of Ky. v. Wolnitzek*, 345 F. Supp. 2d 672 (E.D. Ky. 2004) (pledges or promises and commit clauses overbroad and insufficiently tailored to the interest of impartiality); *Smith v. Phillips*, 2002 WL 1870038 (W.D. Tex. 2002) (provision in Texas Code of Judicial Conduct that prohibited candidates from making "statements that indicate an opinion on any issue that may be subject to judicial interpretation by the office which is being sought" unconstitutional); *In re Kinsey*, 842 So. 2d 77 (Fla. 2003), *cert. denied*, 540 U.S. 825 (2003) (court upheld pledge or promise clause, commit clause, and the clause prohibiting false statements or misrepresentations about opponent).

Some states, such as Texas, have amended their Codes in light of *White*, while Kentucky and Georgia have issued statements that *White* did not directly impact provisions of their state codes. Missouri, Georgia, Ohio, Indiana, Kentucky, Tennessee, and Florida have issued a series of advisory opinions clarifying the implications of *White* for their judicial codes. *See, e.g.*, Ind. Comm'n on Jud. Qualifications Adv. Op. 1-02 (2002) ("[I]n light of the *White* opinion, the Commission is compelled to acknowledge that judicial candidates are permitted under the first amendment to state their general views about disputed social and legal issues," but "[a]s a judicial candidate makes more specific campaign statements relating to issues which may come before the court beyond, for example, the somewhat amorphous 'tough on crime' statement, or broad statements relating to the candidate's position on disputed social and legal issues, the candidate incurs the risk of violating the 'commitment' clause and/or the 'promises' clause."); Ohio Bd. of Commissioners on Grievances and Disc. Op. 02-008 (2002) (advising that judicial candidate are not prohibited from announcing views on disputed legal or political issues, but in so doing, the judge must abide by the restraints on judicial campaign speech within the Canon and stating that promising or pledging conduct in office [other than faithful and impartial performance of judicial duties] is not permitted; statements regarding substantive matters in specific cases pending before any judge are prohibited, as are statements that commit the judicial candidate with regard to cases or controversies that are likely to come before the court on which the judge serves or will serve); Tenn. Jud. Ethics Comm. Adv. Op. 05-03 (2005) ("The free speech rights of judicial candidates permit them to take positions on various matters, including disputed legal and social issues. However, in doing so, the candidate should be mindful . . . that some speech restrictions are indispensable to maintaining the integrity, impartiality, and independence of the judiciary and the state has a compelling interest in enforcing these restrictions. Accordingly, candidates should not make pledges, promises or commitments regarding pending or impending cases, specific classes of cases, specific litigants or classes of litigants, or specific propositions of law, that would reasonably lead to the conclusion that the candidate has prejudged a decision or ruling in cases that would fall within the scope of the pledge, promise or commitment."); W. Va. Adv. Op. 6/11/04 (2004) (judge may attend candidate's forum conducted by West Virginians for Life, but must not make comments on issues to be discussed).

Some commentators have asserted that *White* might have effectively closed the door on attempts to restrict candidate speech in judicial election campaigns. *See, e.g.*, Charles Gardner Geyh, *Why Judicial Elections Stink*, 64 Ohio St. L.J. 43, 69 (2003) ("Insofar as statements falling outside the scope of the pledges or promises clause are, by definition, non-promissory, it would appear that the future of restrictions on such statements, such as those imposed by ABA Canon 5A(d)(3)(ii) [the "commit" clause], is bleak."); Ronald D. Rotunda, *Judicial Campaigns in the Shadow of Republican Party of Minnesota v. White*, 14 No. 1 Prof. Law. 2 (2002) ("*White*, in short, casts a net that may catch far more than overly-restrictive judicial campaign restrictions. *White* may be a harbinger of what is to come in any challenges to other laws, regulations, or court rules that restrict free speech in the context of political campaigns."). Others have asserted that while states may continue to enforce the remaining provisions of the Code, "those provisions may be more narrowly interpreted following the decision in White." Cynthia Gray, *The States' Response to Republican Party of Minnesota v. White*, 86 Judicature 163 (2002); Plymouth Nelson, Note, *Don't Rock The Boat: Minnesota's Canon 5 Keeps Incumbents High and Dry While Voters Flounder in a Sea of Ignorance*, 28 Wm. Mitchell L. Rev. 1607 (2002). *See also* Robert A. Alsdorf, *The Sound of Silence: Thoughts of a Sitting Judge on the Problem of Free Speech and the Judiciary in a Democracy* 30 Hastings Const. L.Q. 197 (2003) (criticizing *White* and proposing a way in which the Court can address future judicial speech cases that is consistent with *White*, but would not permit the further erosion of the Canons of judicial ethics); Rachel Paine Caufield, *In the Wake of White: How States Are Responding to Republican Party of Minnesota v. White and How Judicial Elections Are Changing*, 38 Akron L. Rev. 625 (2005); Michael R. Dimino, *Pay No Attention to That Man Behind the Robe: Judicial Elections, The First Amendment, and Judges as Politicians*, 21 Yale L. & Pol'y Rev. 301 (2003); Sarah Frisque, Note, *Preventing Mudslinging in Chambers: Alternatives After the Demise of the Announce Clause in Republican Party of Minnesota v. White, 122 S. Ct. 2528* (2002), 26 Hamline L. Rev. 415 (2003); Katherine A. Moerke, *Must More Speech Be the Solution to Harmful Speech? Judicial Elections After Republican Party of Minnesota v. White*, 48 S.D. L. Rev. 262 (2002-03) (asserting that states can continue to regulate the more extreme judicial candidate speech through the remaining judicial code provisions); Marcia Coyle, *New Suits Foreseen on Judicial Elections*,

Nat'l L.J. (July 8, 2002); W. Bradley Wendel, *The Ideology of Judging and the First Amendment in Judicial Election Campaigns*, 43 S. Tex. L. Rev. 73 (2001).

General Statements

As made clear in Rule 4.1 Comment [13], judges and judicial candidates are not prohibited from making statements or announcements of personal views on legal, political, or other issues. *See, e.g.*, Fla. Sup. Ct. Jud. Ethics Adv. Comm. Op. 08-14 (2008) (candidate may sign Cuban American Bar Association judicial election campaign pledge committing candidate to diversity); Ga. Jud. Qualifications Comm'n Op. No. 214 (1996) (judicial candidate may use "conservative" in advertisements); N.M. Adv. Comm. on the Code of Jud. Cond. Op. 09-01 (2009) (district court judge may submit essay to national magazine on gay rights). However, when making such statements, "a judge should acknowledge the overarching judicial obligation to apply and uphold the law, without regard to his or her personal views." Rule 4.1 cmt. [13]. *See In re McMillan*, 797 So. 2d 560 (Fla. 2001) (judicial candidate violated Canon by making statement during campaign that he would "always have the heart of a prosecutor"); *In re Haan*, 676 N.E.2d 740 (Ind. 1997) (judicial candidate violated Canon by stating that, if elected, he would "stop suspending sentences" and "stop putting criminals on probation"); *In re Gridley*, 417 So. 2d 950, 954 (Fla. 1982); Ariz. Jud. Ethics Adv. Comm. Op. 08-01 (2008) (judicial candidate who publicly expresses views on legal and political issues may have to, after taking the bench, disqualify himself or herself from hearing cases that involve same issues on which he or she had commented depending on the extent to which remarks appeared to commit judge to a position, and whether judge made statements regarding intent to follow law regardless of personal beliefs); Kan. Jud. Ethics Op. JE 64 (1996) (judicial candidate may not make rhetorical reference to kind of judge he will or will not be, or who might or might not be willing to support him); Kan. Jud. Ethics Adv. Op. JE 97 (2000) (judge's newspaper article about underage drinking of alcoholic beverages would not create in reasonable minds perception that judge's ability to carry out judicial responsibilities with impartiality is impaired); Okla. Jud. Ethics Op. 2007-1 (2007) (judicial candidate may not state in campaign literature that he intended to "balance justice for victims and children too small to speak for themselves"; statement committed the candidate to favor certain parties in litigation).

Statements Relating to Administration of Justice

Comment [14] to Rule 4.1 states that a judge or judicial candidate may make campaign promises "related to judicial organization, administration, and court management, such as a promise to dispose of a backlog of cases, start court sessions on time, or avoid favoritism in appointments and hiring." A candidate also may "pledge to take action outside the courtroom, such as working toward an improved jury selection system, or advocating for more funds to improve the physical plant and amenities of the courthouse." *See, e.g., Ackerson v. Ky. Jud. Retirement & Removal Comm'n*, 776 F. Supp. 309 (W.D. Ky. 1991) (enjoining enforcement of Kentucky's "commit" and "pledges or promises" clauses as to comments on administrative matters); *In Matter of Staples*, 719 P.2d 558 (Wash. 1986) (superior court judge circulated petitions, made campaign speeches, organized a committee, and ran advertisements in the local papers in support of transferring the county seat from one town to another; in dismissing charges against the judge, the court stated this Canon exists "'because of the important and sometimes essential role of judges in legal reform.' If judges would have to remain silent, with their necessary expertise in matters of improving the law, then beneficial legal reform would be seriously impaired."); Ariz. Jud. Ethics Adv. Comm. Op. 96-08 (1996) (judge may participate in campaigns for or against initiatives concerning judicial reform; appear at partisan political events to speak for or against proposals that affect administration of justice; speak for or against such proposals at community meetings or organizations; assist in raising funds for organization devoted to improvement of legal system; and contribute to initiative, candidate, or media campaigns to support or oppose such proposals; judge may not participate in campaigns for or against political candidates who take positions affecting administration of justice); Ark. Jud. Ethics Adv. Op. 98-01 (1998) (permissible for judicial candidate to make specific campaign promises with respect to changing or improving court administration should he be elected; candidate may state general changes or improvements in court administration, but not specific terms, and may make general statements about ideas concerning rehabilitation and importance of education, public service, counseling, and strict rules of conduct with regard to those persons on probation); Colo. Jud. Ethics Adv. Bd. Op. 2008-06 (2008) (judges may be members of the Colorado District Judges' Association and may pay dues to Association knowing that dues will be used to hire lobbyist to advance member judges' interests as judges; judges may solicit membership dues from other judges over whom they do not have supervisory or appellate authority); Fla. Sup. Ct. Jud. Ethics Adv. Comm. Op. 09-19 (2009) (judge may publicly endorse quasi-legal organization's proclamation endorsing better cooperation in discovery process); Florida Sup. Ct. Jud. Ethics Adv. Comm. Op. 09-08 (2009) (judge may contact members of legislature on behalf of local Inn of Court to suggest passage or defeat of legislation relating to funding and duties of judiciary); Ga. Jud. Qualifications Comm'n Op. 115 (1988) (judge may not be member of advisory panel of "End Violence Now," organization concerned with police and court procedures for dealing with violence and with sentencing alternatives); Kan. Jud. Ethics Op. JE 137 (2006) (judge may contribute to coalition formed to educate legislature and citizens about advantages of merit-based judicial selection system and disadvantages of politically-based system); Kan. Jud. Ethics Op. JE 87 (1999) (judges may appear before local civic and religious groups to promote passage of sales tax for construction of new judicial center); Okla. Jud. Ethics Op. 2002-4 (2002) (judge may be involved in campaign organized by county commissioners to win passage of county-wide sales tax to finance construction of new county jail).

See also cases and opinions related to provision in 1990 Code permitting judges to participate in activities concerning the law, the legal system, and the administration of justice, *e.g.*, *In re Braig*, 554 A.2d 493 (Pa. 1989) (when judge learned that longtime friend with excellent credentials was interested in position of police commissioner, judge introduced candidate to state senator, who was also friend of the mayor; judge's conduct fell within the exception allowing political activity to improve the law, the legal system, or the administration of justice); Ala. Jud. Inquiry Comm'n Adv. Op. 07-885 (2007) (presiding circuit judge may not sign a letter to male leaders of his community encouraging them to join and support "Men Against Domestic Violence" and endorsing domestic violence manual for businesses' human resources departments); Cal. Judges Ass'n Jud. Ethics Comm. Adv. Op. 57 (2006) (judge may appear on local TV program sponsored by political party to discuss evolution in law relating to free speech, so long as no participants are identified by political affiliation); Colo. Jud. Ethics Adv. Bd. Op. 2009-03 (2009) (judge may not serve as volunteer on city bicycle advisory committee; work has no connection to law, legal system, or administration of justice); Colo. Jud. Ethics Adv. Bd. Op. 2006-08 (2006) (judge should not accept appointment to blue ribbon panel of public and private leaders charged with addressing how state can mitigate and adapt to climate change; work involves consulting with or providing recommendations to legislative and executive branches, which is unconnected with the law, the legal system, the administration of justice, or the role of the judiciary); Fla. Sup. Ct. Jud. Ethics Adv. Comm. Op. 09-11 (2009) (judge may not be member of judicial and legal education committee of domestic violence center); Fla. Sup. Ct. Jud. Ethics Adv. Comm. Op. 08-17 (2008) (judge may be speaker at fund-raiser dinner for drug court); Fla. Sup. Ct. Jud. Ethics Adv. Comm. Op. 07-20 (2007) (judge may not attend partisan ladies group monthly luncheon to address improvements in law, legal system and administration of justice in area of expediting permanency for children from foster care through adoption); Fla. Sup. Ct. Jud. Ethics Adv. Comm. Op. 08-01 (2008) (judge may serve on mortgage fraud task force established by city's mayor; judge may serve on university's regional planning council whose previous efforts were designed to raise profile of university in community and which is now trying to raise substantial funds so long as judge does not participate in fund-raising activities); Fla. Sup. Ct. Jud. Ethics Adv. Comm. Op. 07-07 (2007) (photograph of judge wearing judicial robe and identifying judge as judge may not be used on billboards and other campaign materials in public relations campaign conducted by county library system); Ill. Jud. Ethics Comm. Op. 07-05 (2007) (judge may appear at public hearing before mayor and city council, write letter to them, or have discussion with them for the purpose of giving recommendation for reduction in hours of liquor sales if recommendation is given to improve administration of justice); Kan. Jud. Ethics Op. JE 169 (2009) (judge may attend forum on diversity in the Kansas judiciary partially funded by Transparency and Integrity Fund of the Open Society Institute and League of Women Voters Education Fund); Kan. Jud. Ethics Adv. Op. JE 168 (2009) (judge may not attend presentation by nonprofit advocacy organization that offers services to DUI victims); Kan. Jud. Ethics Op. JE 158 (2007) (judges and retired judges may not participate in educational efforts regarding nonpartisan selection of district judges that would include speaking at functions during which brochure will be distributed that contains request for financial contribution); Kan. Jud. Ethics Op. JE 157 (2007) (judge may join group comprised of representatives of various agencies and offices in state who have role in offender registration laws); Kan. Jud. Ethics Op. JE 150 (2007) (judge may not be member of committee formed by school district to formulate student drug testing policy); Kan. Jud. Ethics Op. JE 149 (2007) (judge may serve as commissioner for the Department of Wildlife and Parks); Kan. Jud. Ethics Op. JE 146 (2007) (judges of judicial district may host dinner at their personal expense for state representatives and county commissioners so long as discussion are limited to issues concerning the improvement of the law, legal system, and administration of justice as well as matters of general local interest); Kan. Jud. Ethics Op. JE 111 (2003) (judge may serve on screening panel that will interview candidates and forward names to governor for consideration to fill judicial vacancy); Md. Jud. Ethics Comm. Op. 2007-11 (2008) (judge may not accept appointment as member of local management board charged with identifying needs of children, youth, and families; board directs funds and implements and evaluates programs, which are executive branch functions); Md. Jud. Ethics Comm. Op. 2004-24 (2004) (judge may be member of local drug and alcohol abuse counsel whose functions are advisory only); Mass. Comm. on Jud. Ethics Adv. Op. 97-1 (1997) (judge may contribute to Massachusetts Bar Foundation; funneling funds through intermediary greatly reduces likelihood of public perception that judge is supporting particular advocacy organization or cause); Neb. Jud. Ethics Adv. Comm. Op. 04-1 (2004) (judge may attend training conference concerning domestic violence issues where curriculum is not primarily prosecutorial in nature; judge may not accept funding from either local domestic violence project or through grant from Department of Justice, as each is partisan group whose interests will likely come before judge in future cases); Nev. Stand. Comm. on Jud. Ethics and Election Prac. JE 08-3 (2008) (judicial candidate who is not currently serving in judicial capacity may serve as officer of bar association); N.Y. Advisory Comm. on Jud. Ethics Op. 08-05 (2008) (judge may attend a "meet the candidates" event, and participate as audience member by distributing factual materials and questioning candidates for state legislature about judicial compensation); N.C. Jud. Standards Comm'n Formal Adv. Op. 2007-01 (2007) (judge may participate as member of interview committee/board as part of panel to interview candidates for position of city chief of police); S.C. Adv. Comm. on Stands. of Jud. Cond. 14-2009 (2009) (judge may provide information about judicial candidate to screening committee if requested); Va. Jud. Ethics Adv. Comm. Op. 01-4 (2001) (judge may lecture at police training academy regarding what is expected from officers in the courtroom and may teach about recent legal developments, provided that lecturing or teaching give no appearance that judge appears to be biased in favor of police); Wis. Jud. Cond. Adv. Comm., Op. 08-1 (2008) (non-candidate judge may not serve as greeter at election polling place, assist voters in determining proper voting district, direct them where to go if they need to register to vote, and give them "I voted" stickers when they leave); Wis. Jud. Cond. Adv. Comm. Op. 05-2 (2005) (judge may not serve as election official even if not a candidate). *See also* Colo. Jud. Ethics Adv. Bd. Op. 2007-07 (2007) (judge may not accept voting or non-voting board position on local community board that combines integrated services and legislative advocacy because such membership would involve legislative advocacy beyond matters to improve the law); Colo. Jud. Ethics Adv. Bd. Op. 2005-04 (2005) (although judge may not serve on governmental crime control commission, judge may, however, provide factual information to the commission to assist it in its policymaking efforts); Del. Jud. Ethics Adv. Comm. Adv. Op. 2006-7 (2006) (judge should not accept an appointment as chair of governor's consortium on Hispanic affairs); Wash. Ethics Adv. Comm. Op. 91-20 (1991) (judges may speak in support of or against referendum to stop salary increases for judges, but may not sign referendum to stop salary increases approved by salary commission; referendum involves salary increases for members of executive, legislative, and judicial branches of government, prohibited political activity under judicial code).

Responding to Questionnaires

Prior to *White*, questionnaires were not held in favor. *See* ABA Informal Op. 1487 (1982) ("It is ethically improper under the Model Code of Judicial Conduct for a judicial candidate to respond to a bar association questionnaire which seeks to elicit the candidate's views on highly charged and controversial issues, many of which are social and political, as well as legal."); Wash. Ethics Adv. Comm. Op. 92-16 (1992) (inappropriate for judicial candidate to answer questionnaire developed by families and friends of violent crime victims that asks whether candidate agrees or disagrees with statements regarding criminal sentencing and victim rights because the responses may reasonably give the impression that a judge is committed to acting in a certain way with respect to question that may come before the judge).

Since *White*, there has been an increased use of questionnaires, which special interest groups send to judicial candidates to ask them about their opinions on disputed political or legal issues such as whether *Roe v. Wade* was wrongly decided. For example, on July 19, 2002, the Alabama Judicial Inquiry Commission withdrew Alabama Judicial Inquiry Comm'n Adv. Op. 00-763 (2000), which had advised judicial candidates not to respond to a questionnaire from the Christian Coalition. In 2004, the Alaska Right to Life Political Action Committee challenged the constitutionality of the "pledges and promises" clause and the "commit" clause, maintaining that these restrictions chilled judicial candidates from responding to a questionnaire soliciting their views on various public issues, such as abortion and assisted suicide. In 2005, a federal district court struck down both provisions as violative of the First Amendment rights of the candidates. In 2007, the U.S. Court of Appeals for the Ninth Circuit vacated the district court's decision, ruling that the case was not ripe for review since there was no evidence that a judge would reasonably risk discipline by responding. *Alaska Right to Life Political Action Comm. v. Feldman*, 504 F.3d 840 (9th Cir. 2007). *See generally* Bert Brandenburg & Roy A. Schotland, *Justice in Peril: The Endangered Balance Between Impartial Courts and Judicial Election Campaigns*, 21 Geo. J. Legal Ethics 1229, 1244 (2008) (discussing rise of "push" questionnaires); Ari Shapiro, "Questionnaires Test Judge Candidates' Views," National Public Radio (Oct. 10, 2006); Bert Brandenburg, "Promissory Notes: How election-by questionnaire is threatening independent judges," (Oct. 15, 2005) ("In the wake of *White*, questionnaire answers are also helping determine which judicial candidates can tap into big money, powerful endorsements, and platoons of grass-roots support.").

For more on questionnaires, *see, e.g., Pa. Family Institute, Inc. v. Celluci*, 521 F. Supp. 2d 351 (E.D. Pa. 2007) (any speech by judicial candidate, short of a pledge, promise, or commitment to adjudicate particular result, would be permitted speech; thus, candidates may respond to questionnaires without fear of discipline); *Duwe v. Alexander*, 490 F. Supp. 2d 968 (W.D. Wis. 2007) (court enjoined enforcement of provision that required judges to recuse themselves if they had, while judge or candidate for judicial office, previously made statements that appeared to commit judge with respect to an issue in a proceeding; provision in Wisconsin Code that prohibited candidates from announcing views on disputed legal issues in responses to judicial questionnaires unconstitutional as applied to candidates who, based on provision, refused to respond to a questionnaire); *Kan. Jud. Rev. v. Stout*, 196 P.3d 1162 (Kan. 2008), *opinion vacated, appeal dismissed*, 562 F.3d 1240 (10th Cir. 2009) (judicial candidate permitted to answer questionnaire asking for views on disputed legal and political issues to the extent that questionnaire calls for personal views on disputed legal or political issues; candidate may not give responses that would bind candidate to resolution of particular case, controversy, or issue within particular controversy; Kansas Supreme Court later eliminated challenged portion of Kansas Code of Judicial Conduct prohibiting discussion by judicial candidate and constituents for purpose of soliciting public or contributions); Ariz. Jud. Ethics Adv. Comm. Op. 06-05 (2006) (under judicial Canon amended following *White*, judge may respond to political interest questionnaires and may publicly discuss personal opinion of an initiative measure or other political subject; however, taking a public position on disputed issue is inappropriate for noncampaigning judge because political activity by sitting judges does not serve important function of informing voters about their re-election campaigns and also suggests bias and predetermination of issues); Fla. Sup. Ct. Jud. Ethics Adv. Comm. Op. 06-18 (2006) (judicial candidate may respond to questionnaires that cover such subjects as same-sex marriage, parental notification, and school vouchers, and whether candidate agrees or disagrees with recent court decisions so long as candidate clearly indicates that answers do not constitute promise that candidate will rule certain way in a case; candidate clearly acknowledges obligation to follow binding legal precedent anywhere it exists; candidate does not appear to endorse any other individual who is likely to stand for election to or retention in any public office or any platform of a political party; and any commentary on past judicial decisions is analytical, informed, respectful, and dignified); Nev. Stand. Comm. on Jud. Ethics and Election Prac. Op. JE12-003 (2012) (judge prohibited from responding to issue-group, which submitted questionnaire asking judge to commit to working with the group on specific policies regarding workers' rights, predatory lending, and education); Okla. Jud. Ethics Op. 2010-5 (2010) (judicial candidate may respond to opinion questions on deferred, suspended, and reduced sentences, but should not respond that judge always or never uses such); *see generally* Note, *The Rule of Law in the Marketplace of Ideas: Pledges or Promises by Candidates for Judicial Election*, 122 Harv. L. Rev. 1511 (2009); Kelly Taylor, Note, *Silence at a Price? Judicial Questionnaires and the Independence of Alaska's Judiciary*, 25 Alaska L. Rev. 303 (2008).

Statements About Specific Issues or Parties

A judge or judicial candidate may violate Rule 4.1(A)(13) by making statements during a campaign that appear to commit the candidate with regard to specific issues or parties that are likely to come before the court. The main concern of the Rule is that judges' campaign speech not damage the public confidence in the impartiality of the judiciary in any cases, particularly those involving issues that arise in campaigns, such as crime, the death penalty, abortion, drunk driving and domestic abuse or those involving certain parties. *See* Fla. Comm. on Stands. of Cond. Governing Judges Op. 93-64 (1993) (impermissible for judge to advocate actively for handgun control, because it is a political issue not involving the administration of justice); *In re Ehlschide* (Ky. Jud. Retirement & Removal Comm'n Unreported Order, Apr. 9, 1982) (judge published campaign advertisements that implied that individual members of the United Mine Workers Union could expect favorable consideration in judge's court); *In re Birnbaum* (N.Y. State Comm'n on Jud. Cond. 1997) (candidate gave impression that he would favor tenants over landlords); Okla. Jud. Ethics Op. 2007-1 (2007) (judicial candidate may not state in campaign literature: "I believe justice requires a fair system for all, especially little children who may be too small or unable to speak for themselves," "Balance the scales of justice for victims"); Wash. Ethics Adv. Comm. Op. 89-11 (1989) (judge prohibited from speaking on merits of initiative intended to provide additional funds for children's services by means of tax increase as it does not relate to the law, the legal system, or the administration of justice). *See also* Fla. Comm. on Stands. of Cond. Governing Judges Op. 99-6 (1999) (retired judge eligible for recall to judicial service may not write to U.S. Senator with his views on impeachment trial of President of the United States; the impeachment trial of the President is a political issue not involving the "administration of justice"); Nev. Stand. Comm. on Jud. Ethics and Election Prac. Op. JE12-003 (2012) (judge prohibited from pledging to support specific policies regarding workers' rights, predatory lending, and education); Tex. Adv. Comm. on Jud. Ethics Op. 184 (1995) (judge or judicial candidate may list in political advertising endorsement of special interests groups with obvious political agenda, such as Texans Against Drunk Driving, Texans for Tort Reform, Texas Prosecutors Association, Texas Peace Officers Association, Texans for Law Enforcement, etc.; by listing the organizations, judge or candidate has made no statement indicating opinion on area subject to judicial interpretation).

With regard to some measures that are aimed at improving the law, the legal system or the administration of justice, a judge may be able to engage in certain activities, but not others. For instance, Arizona's Judicial Ethics Committee advised that a judge may help to draft proposed legislation that would permit doctors to prescribe drugs of all kinds for medical reasons and require drug users to undergo mandatory drug rehabilitation rather than incarceration, and may participate in debates about the propositions, but may not appear in television advertisement endorsing the ballot proposition. Ariz. Jud. Ethics Adv. Comm. Op. 96-09 (1996) (judge may not appear in television advertisement endorsing ballot proposition judge was involved in drafting. "[T]he code does not permit a judge to act as a spokesperson and advocate for others."); *see also* Colo. Jud. Ethics Adv. Bd. Op. 2006-07 (2006) (judge may make monetary contribution to group advocating for or against judicial term limit initiative so long as the group is not partisan political organization; judge may speak to civic groups about measure and write editorials opposing or promoting it. Such political activity is permissible because it implicates the law, the legal system, the administration of justice, and the role of the judiciary as an independent branch of government).

Constitutional Amendments

A judge may advocate for the passage of constitutional amendments designed to improve the law, the legal system, or the administration of justice. *See, e.g.*, Ark. Jud. Ethics Adv. Comm. Op. 94-04 (1994) (judge may take public stand on proposed constitutional amendment that would make judicial elections nonpartisan and would impose limits on judicial terms); Fla. Comm. on Stands. of Cond. Governing Judges Op. 98-14 (1998) (judge may speak, write, lecture, or teach electorate at public forums about issues concerning proposed constitutional amendments if they involve law and legal system but may not address partisan group regardless of the subject matter of the presentation; it is inappropriate for judicial circuit (as an entity) to publicly advocate position on any proposed constitutional amendments); Ky. Jud. Ethics Op. JE-97 (2002) (district court judges association may make financial contribution to Family Courts for Kentucky political issue committee for purpose of promoting state constitutional amendment); N.M. Adv. Comm. on the Code of Jud. Cond. Op. 08-1 (2008) (judge may publicly campaign against proposed constitutional amendment that would require that all candidates for municipal judge to be licensed to practice law in New Mexico by writing commentary for press, discussing matter at debates and elsewhere, appearing where it would be helpful to oppose amendment, and speaking against proposed amendment on radio); N.Y. Jud. Ethics Op. 09-244 (2010) (judge may publicly discuss need for constitutional convention and political reform); Ohio Bd. of Commissioners on Grievances and Disc. Op. 2002-03 (2002) (pursuant to Canon 2(A)(1), a judge may communicate to public his or her views in support of or opposition to proposed state constitutional amendment regarding drug treatment in lieu of incarceration, basing such support or opposition on judge's understanding of potential impact on courts, law, legal system, and administration of justice). *cf.* Ariz. Jud. Ethics Adv. Comm. Op. 96-09 (1996) (judge may not appear in television advertisement endorsing ballot proposition judge was involved in drafting. "[T]he code does not permit a judge to act as a spokesperson and advocate for others."); Wash. Ethics Adv. Comm. Op 13-02 (2013) (sitting judge may not advocate for the overturning of U.S. Supreme Court case and adoption of an amendment to the U.S. Constitution; nor may judge join a group with that purpose).

A judge may also be a member of a voluntary bar association that advocates the passage of a constitutional amendment designed to improve the law, the legal system or the administration of justice. Fla. Comm. on Stands. of Cond. Governing Judges Op. 98-31 (1998) (since judge may belong to a voluntary bar association, and it is permissible for a judge personally to advocate the passage of constitutional amendments designed to improve the law, the legal system or the administration of justice, then it is permissible for a judge to belong to a voluntary bar association that advocates the passage of such constitutional amendments).

Bond Campaigns

A judge may take a public stand in favor of, opposed to, or indifferent to a bond campaign that is related to the administration of justice. *See In re Chambliss*, 516 So. 2d 506 (Miss. 1987) (judge may speak in opposition to or in favor of bond issues where administration of justice is at stake, but otherwise may not participate in bond election); Ark. Jud. Ethics Adv. Comm. Op. 94-01 (1994) (judge may take a public stand in favor of, opposed to, or indifferent to an upcoming bond election in which county voters will decide whether to increase the sales tax to pay for a new courthouse and jail, and judge may be a member of a committee formed to promote passage of the sales tax, although there are limits on the judge's involvement in fund-raising); Kan. Jud. Ethics Op. JE 142 (2006) (judge may encourage voters to approve bond issue that will finance construction of new jail in judge's district); N.Y. Adv. Comm. on Jud. Ethics Op. 07-109 (2007) (judge may advocate for passage of bond resolution to fund new court facility by writing op-ed article for publication in local press, by speaking at public informational forums before vote, and by advocating publicly in favor of need for new court facility); Tex. Adv. Comm. on Jud. Ethics Op. 82 (1986) (judges may support a county bond election, designated a "law and order election," to fund an expanded and improved jail facility, a new county criminal courts building, and renovation and improvement of civil district and family courts facilities); Vt. Jud. Ethics Comm. Op. 2827-9 (2004) (judge may publicly endorse nonpartisan bond issue in home town); Wash. Ethics Adv. Comm. Op. 00-03 (2000) (judges may publicly support bond levy that will fund seismic retrofitting of courthouse); Wash. Ethics Adv. Comm. Op. 92-05 (1992) (judges may actively promote the passage of bond issue or levy for regional justice center that will provide additional jail space and superior court facilities).

A judge may, however, be prohibited from engaging in fund-raising activities on behalf of the passage of a bond issue or levy. *See* Wash. Ethics Adv. Comm. Op. 92-06 (1992) (judge may not solicit funds from other judges to promote bond issue campaign to construct new juvenile justice center); Wash. Ethics Adv. Comm. Op. 92-05 (1992) (judges may actively promote the passage of bond issue or levy for regional justice center that will provide additional jail space and superior court facilities; judges should not, however, engage in any fund-raising activities on behalf of passage of bond issue or levy). A judge also may not use court resources in bond campaign. *See* Wash. Ethics Adv. Comm. Op. 94-10 (1994) (judges may help organize campaign committee that will be responsible for conducting bond campaign for new juvenile court facility, but should not use public facilities such as stationery, postage, machines, equipment, use of state employees during working hours, vehicles, office space, and publications in these organization efforts).

Crime

Statements that convey the message that a judge or judicial candidate is predisposed to rule in a certain manner in criminal cases that may come before him or her as a judge violate Rules 4.1(A)(12) and (13). *See In re Kinsey*, 842 So.2d 77 (Fla. 2003) (by cloaking entire candidacy under umbrella of law enforcement and portraying herself as a pro-prosecution/pro-law enforcement judge while characterizing opponent as dismissing criminals and not holding them accountable, judge affirmatively conveyed message that it is permissible for judges to rule in predisposed manner in certain types of matters that may come before them; such statements convey false and misleading impression that judge's role is to combat crime, rather than to judge those who appear before court as criminal defendantsin fair and impartial manner); Ariz. Jud. Ethics Adv. Comm. Op. 96-12 (1996) (incumbent candidate for judicial office may not publicize endorsement of county sheriff if it would portray judge as pro law enforcement); *Hill v. Springgate*, Dec. 98-3 (Nev. Stand. Comm. on Jud. Ethics and Election Prac. 1998) (incumbent judge published campaign advertisement in English and Spanish that stated that she demanded personal accountability from those who commit crimes, that persons who drive after drinking or taking drugs will go to jail, that criminals who sell drugs to children will face the harshest sentences allowed by law, and that she would not allow "no contest" pleas in cases of rape or sexual abuse; the Nevada Committee stated that it did not believe that "these are innocuous statements of law or of mere administration of the court, but rather are promises to the voters to deal severely with those who commit these three classes of crimes"); N.Y. Adv. Comm. on Jud. Ethics Op. 07-136 (2007) (candidate may use a photograph taken with a relative, who is a state trooper in uniform, in campaign literature, so long as neither photograph nor context in which it appears suggests that candidate would support law enforcement interests over other parties that may appear before court); *In re Polito*, 1998 WL 939714 (N.Y. State Comm'n on Jud. Cond. 1998) (candidate ran graphic and sensational advertisements that portrayed him as judge who was biased against criminal defendants and made statements disparaging alternative sentences that appeared to commit him to imposing prison terms in every case and to rejecting other lawful criminal dispositions); ABA Informal Op. 1444 (1980) (judge may not utilize slogan

"A strict sentencing philosophy! A hard working man!" in re-election campaign materials because it can be viewed by voters as both campaign pledge of judicial conduct and also announcement of position on sentencing, which is disputed legal and political issue); *but see Hill v. Hardesty*, Amended Public Dec. 98-2 (Nevada Standing Comm. on Jud. Ethics & Election Prac. 1998) (judicial candidate did not violate Canon by running television advertisements that featured county sheriff in uniform, as well as other county-owned facilities, locations, and jail inmates).

A candidate's statement that he or she is an "experienced prosecutor" is permitted because an accurate discussion of qualifications is permissible, including prior positions held, even though someone reading the statement might conclude that a judge or judicial candidate who had been a prosecutor would be more likely to rule a particular way in certain types of cases. Tex. Adv. Comm. on Jud. Ethics Op. 212 (1998).

In some jurisdictions, a candidate for judicial office may be permitted to comment upon a general issue of public concern that touches upon the law, the legal system, and the administration of justice, such as gun control, so long as the candidate does not commit himself or herself to decide a case one way or another simply because he or she expressed an opinion on the issue. *See* Ill. Jud. Ethics. Comm. Op. 94-5 (1994) (judge who is candidate for higher judicial office may publish in a local newspaper an essay about crime and gun problems, the issues to be resolved in any specific cases the judge may have to hear would most likely be much more specific than the more general issue of society's tolerance of guns). However, making a general statement asserting that if elected, the candidate would do away with plea bargaining may violate the judicial code. *See generally* Vincent R. Johnson, *Ethical Campaigning for the Judiciary*, 29 Texas Tech L. Rev. 811 (1998) (examining scope of permissible campaign activity for Texas judicial candidates, including limitations on campaign speech).

"Tough on Crime"

A judicial candidate's statement that he or she will be "tough on crime" generally does not violate Rule 4.1. Tex. Adv. Comm. on Jud. Ethics Op. 212 (1998) ("tough on crime" statement would not violate the judicial code because pledges to be tough with criminals and tough on crime are of such an amorphous nature that they do not define any specific conduct), *See also In re Tully*, 90 CC 2 (Ill. Cts. Comm'n 1991) (statements to the effect that the candidate was "tough on crime" and "tough on taxes" were neither "pledges or promises of conduct in office" nor "statements on disputed legal or political issues"); Ariz. Jud. Ethics Adv. Comm. Op. 96-12 (1996) (an incumbent candidate for judicial office may obtain public support and publicized endorsements but may not utilize endorsements that cast doubt on independence and impartiality by suggesting that judge favors police or prosecution). *But see In re Watson*, 794 N.E.2d 1 (N.Y. 2003) (by advertising intention to be "tough" judge who would be tough on crime and by repeatedly stating intention to make city one that was "very unattractive" for criminal defendants who resided outside city, including statements concerning intended use of bail against defendants, and by urging police department employees to "put a real prosecutor on the bench," candidate created appearance that he would not be impartial as judge, would not judge cases on individual basis or upon merits, and would be biased against criminal defendants); W. Va. Adv. Op. issued Mar. 24, 2008 (judicial candidate should not advertise that judicial philosophy is that those who bring drugs for sale into jurisdiction should be dealt with harshly).

Similarly, a campaign statement that a candidate is a "law and order" candidate may also be permitted. *In re Shanley*, 774 N.E.2d 735 (N.Y. 2002) (finding that the phrase "law and order" candidate is "widely and indiscriminately used in everyday parlance and election campaigns" and is not a "'commit[ment]' or a 'pledge[ ] or promise[ ] of conduct in office'"); *but see In re Hafner*, 2000 WL 33172938 (N.Y. State Comm'n on Jud. Cond. 2000) (judicial candidate's advertisement stated "Are you tired of seeing career criminals get a 'slap' on the wrist? So am I . . . ." and "Soft judges make hard criminals!"; advertisement conveyed message that, if elected, candidate would treat criminal defendants more harshly than his opponent, the incumbent, had done and would deal harshly with all such defendants, rather than judge the merits of individual cases). *See generally* Joanna Cohn Weiss, Note, *Tough on Crime: How Campaigns for State Judiciary Violate Criminal Defendants' Due Process Rights*, 81 N.Y.U. L. Rev. 1101 (June 2006).

Death Penalty

A judge or judicial candidate may not make statements that would imply to a reasonable person that, as a judge, the candidate will use the death penalty regardless of the evidence presented during the mitigation phase of a trial and notwithstanding the statutory standards, a judge or jury must consider in determining the appropriateness of the death penalty. *See In re Jud. Campaign Compl. Against Burick*, 705 N.E.2d 422 (Ohio Comm'n of Judges 1999) (judicial candidate violated Canon by stating in advertisements that she "will be a tough Judge that supports the death penalty and isn't afraid to use it," and that she favored the death penalty for convicted murderers). A candidate may, however, be permitted to say that he or she will uphold the law with regard to the death penalty; Fla. Comm. on Stands. of Cond. Governing Judges Op. 94-26 (1994) (judicial candidate may ethically state the following regarding candidate's position on death penalty: "My sworn duty as a circuit judge will be to faithfully and impartially uphold the law and that duty may include ordering a person's execution in an appropriate case. If I am ever presiding over a case in which the death penalty is sought, and it is the legally appropriate punishment, I will impose it."). *See also* Mich. Comm. on Jud. Ethics Op. C-237 (1986) (candidate for judicial office may express opinion on ballot proposal that would allow capital punishment as a form of sentence, but care should be exercised to avoid identification with any partisan position); *but see* Wis. Jud. Cond. Adv. Comm. Op. 06-1 (2006) (impermissible for judge to publicly express personal opinion as to fairness, efficacy, and wisdom of death penalty that is subject of advisory referendum).

Drunk Driving Cases

A judicial candidate's statement that he or she will be tough on drunk drivers might violate Rule 4.1(A)(13). *See In re Kaiser*, 759 P.2d 392 (Wash. 1988) (candidate's campaign literature stating that candidate is "Toughest on Drunk Driving" singles out special class of defendants and suggests that DWI defendants' cases will be held to higher standard); *Brisebill v. Mersel*, Pub. Op. 00-3 (Nev. Stand. Comm. on Jud. Ethics and Election Prac. 2000) (candidate for justice of the peace's statements in television interview as to how he specifically would sentence all first time or repeat DUI offenders was pledge or promise of conduct in office that went beyond statement that he would faithfully and impartially perform duties of office).

Domestic Abuse Cases

A judicial candidate may violate Rule 4.1(A)(13) by making a pledge or promise to rule against defendants in certain types of domestic abuse cases. *See, e.g., Summe v. Jud. Retirement & Removal Comm'n*, 947 S.W.2d 42 (Ky. 1997) (letter by judicial candidate's supporter said that opponent allowed convicted child abuser to serve only 153 days and that "it is time to judge our judges" and "to stop repeated abuse instead of treating it" and concluded by encouraging voters to "join me in stopping the abuse and vote for a person who will let no one walk away before justice is served"; such a pledge to take a particular approach in deciding cases or a particular class of cases is prohibited); *In re Herrick*, 1998 WL 184273 (N.Y. State Comm'n on Jud. Cond. 1998) (candidate promised he would jail every person charged with violating protective order instead of judging merits of each case).

Abortion

A judge or judicial candidate may violate Rule 4.1(A)(13) by making a statement expressing an opinion on issues relating to abortion. *See In re La Cava*, (N.Y. State Comm'n on Jud. Cond. 1999) (judge seeking support in campaign for state supreme court wrote letter to Right-to-Life Party asserting, among other things, his "commitment to the sanctity of life from the moment of conception," his "strong moral opposition to the scourge of abortion and the termination of the lives of millions of human beings in the womb" and his "outrage[ ] by the continuation of the murderous and barbaric partial birth abortion procedure in this state"); Tex. Adv. Comm. on Jud. Ethics Op. 184 (1995) (judge or candidate may not make a statement declaring that he or she is pro-life or pro-choice because judge or candidate is clearly making a statement that indicates an opinion on an issue possibly subject to judicial interpretation; further, there is a strong implication of a promise of particular conduct in office other than the faithful performance of official duties; candidate may list in political advertising endorsement by Pro-Life Texans, or Texans for Choice, but may not state in advertisements, "I am the pro-choice/pro-life candidate").

Even attending an event sponsored by an organization that advocates a position on abortion may violate the Rule. Fla. Comm. on Stands. of Cond. Governing Judges Op. 96-10 (1996) (candidate's attendance at spring banquet held by local "Friends for Life" committee could be viewed as commitment to how he or she would rule regarding abortion issues; candidate may attend but should be careful not to give the appearance of adopting the Friends for Life's agenda).

ENSURING THAT OTHERS ADHERE TO SAME STANDARDS

Pursuant to Rule 4.1(B), a judge or judicial candidate shall take reasonable measures to ensure that other persons do not undertake, on behalf of the judge or judicial candidate, any activities prohibited under Rule 4.1(A). Canon 5A(3), the predecessor to Rule 4.1(B), contained a provision stating that a candidate for judicial office shall "maintain the dignity appropriate to the judicial office" during a judicial campaign. The Commission concluded that the provision was too amorphous and established too subjective a standard for use in a rule with potential disciplinary consequences, and eliminated it from the 2007 Code. Charles G. Geyh & W. William Hodes, *Reporters' Notes to the Model Code of Judicial Conduct* 102–03 (2009).

The "other persons" whom a judge might typically need to ensure do not undertake prohibited activities would include family members, employees, or appointees. *See, e.g.*, Fla. Jud. Ethics Adv. Comm. Op. 12-06 (2012) (judicial candidate must encourage spouse not to attend a political gathering wearing the candidate's campaign button); Fla. Comm. on Stands. of Cond. Governing Judges Op. 96-20 (1996) (candidate's campaign manager is forbidden from doing what candidate is prohibited from doing; therefore, campaign manager may not attend local Republican and Democratic meetings that are open to public); N.Y. Adv. Comm. on Jud. Ethics Op. 00-05 (2000) (judge's court attorney, who is judge's personal appointee, should not serve as treasurer of judge's re-election committee).

But despite the language of Rule 4.1(B), a candidate's family members are free to engage in their own political activity. *See* Rule 4.1(A) cmt. [5]. *See also In re Gaulkin*, 351 A.2d 740 (1976) (judge's nonjudicial spouse may engage in political activity but every precaution must be taken to ensure continued separation of judiciary from any involvement, either directly or indirectly, in political activities); Ariz. Jud. Ethics Adv. Comm. Op. 03-05 (2003) (judge's spouse or other family members may circulate nominating petitions for candidates, work on non-judge's political campaign, and hold office in political party or organization); Ark. Jud. Ethics Adv. Comm. Op. 02-06 (2002) (judge's wife may work either as paid employee or volunteer in political campaign of candidate seeking election to statewide office, however, spouse should make all efforts to avoid any suggestion or hint that judge is supportive of candidate); Fla. Sup. Ct. Jud. Ethics Adv. Comm. Op. 10-22 (2010) (judicial candidate's spouse may speak, host lunches, and campaign for the candidate however, candidate should encourage spouse to "adhere to the same standards of political conduct" as required for the candidate); Fla. Comm. on Stands. of Cond. Governing Judges Op. 98-3 (1998) (judicial candidate's spouse, who serves as member of state legislature, may accompany candidate to nonpartisan events while candidate is actively promoting campaign, mention candidate's campaign to other colleagues or constituents, answer questions about candidate's campaign, and attend nonpartisan legislative events and candidate's campaign events); Ill. Jud. Ethics Comm. Op. 06-02 (2006) (judge's spouse may engage in independent campaign activities in support of candidate for public office including soliciting funds, publicly endorsing candidate, displaying bumper sticker on vehicle jointly owned by spouse and judge and driven by spouse, and displaying campaign sign in yard of home jointly owned by spouse and judge; judicial candidate must encourage spouse to limit activities in support of judge's candidacy to those political activities in which judge is permitted to engage); Ill. Jud. Ethics Op. 03-06 (2003) (judge's spouse may circulate nominating petition for candidate for nonjudicial office); Ind. Comm'n on Jud. Qualifications Adv. Op. 2-93 (1993) (judicial spouses are not personally bound by Code of Judicial Conduct and its restrictions on political activities; although it is undesirable arrangement for judicial spouse to hold office in political party's central committee, arrangement in itself does not constitute Code violation); Kan. Jud. Ethics Op. JE 61 (1996) (judge's spouse may serve as campaign manager for congressional candidate in nonpartisan district); Mass. Comm. on Jud. Ethics Adv. Op. 98-4 (1998) (judge must disassociate himself from wife's and children's political activities, including avoiding being seen by those in attendance during political events hosting by spouse, not allowing political bumper stickers to be placed on vehicles registered to judge, and not allowing political signs to be placed on judge's lawn); Mass. Comm. on Jud. Ethics Adv. Op. 2005-8 (2005) (judge's daughter may not display campaign sign in front of judge's home in support of political campaign of judge's son); Mich. Comm. on Jud. Ethics Op. JI-47 (1992) (judge's spouse serving on campaign committee of nonjudicial candidate and appearing on campaign letterhead does not constitute the judge's public endorsement of that candidate);

N.Y. Adv. Comm. on Jud. Ethics Op. 08-168 (2008) (judge's spouse may serve as treasurer of political party committee so long as spouse does not state that he or she represents judge in that capacity); N.Y. Adv. Comm. on Jud. Ethics Op. 95-22 (1995) (judge's spouse may serve on campaign committee of candidate for office of district attorney); W. Va. Adv. Op. 11/8/93 (1993) (spouse of judicial officer may serve as member of county Democratic executive committee); *but see* Mich. Comm. on Jud. Ethics Op. JI-90 (1994) (judicial candidate may not appoint candidate's father-in-law to serve as candidate's campaign treasurer); W. Va. Adv. Op. 12/28/99 (1999) (because judicial candidate may not personally solicit funds, judicial candidate's wife is prohibited from serving as candidate's campaign treasurer; candidate's adult stepchild who is not residing in candidate's household may serve as candidate's re-election campaign committee treasurer). *See also* Judicial Conference of the United States, Committee on Codes of Conduct Adv. Op. 53 (Apr. 15, 1977, revised Apr. 11, 1983 and Jan. 16, 1998) (spouse's participation in politics will "undoubtedly increase the number of situations in which the judge will be obliged to recuse. This is especially true where the spouse is a candidate for elective office. We suggest that the judge make his or her spouse aware of such problems"). *See generally* Cynthia Gray, *An Ethics Guide for Judges and Their Families* (2001).

Spouse's Campaign Contributions

A judicial candidate's spouse may make a monetary contribution to a political candidate's campaign, but the money should come from the spouse and not from the judicial candidate. *See, e.g.*, Colo. Jud. Ethics Adv. Bd. Op. 2006-04 (2006) (to make clear that any contribution by judge's spouse to political candidate is not from judge, contribution should be made in spouse's name alone from spouse's separate bank account with no reference to judge or his judicial position); Kan. Adv. Op. JE-13 (1985) (if conduct of judge's spouse is independent so as not to impugn impartiality of judge or to give appearance of impropriety, spouse may make political contributions in his or her own name from his or her own business income maintained in separate account); Nebr. Ethics Adv. Op. 96-6 (1996) (if sole objective of Committee for an Independent Judiciary is to promote independence of judiciary, then contribution by judge and/or spouse from account that bears his name as joint tenant and that is composed of her contributions is not prohibited by judicial code; if objective of Committee is to support "candidate," then contribution from this account suggests political involvement by judge; contribution by spouse of her funds from separate account would not be inconsistent with Code); W. Va. Adv. Op. 8/28/95 (1995) (provided contributions are made from spouse's separate funds, preferably from separate account, judge's spouse may make financial contributions to political candidates).

In evaluating a spouse's political contribution, the committee for federal judges advises that the judge must play no role in the decision to contribute and must make "reasonable efforts to insure that the contribution is perceived as that of the spouse and not the judge, including, but not limited to, requiring that the contribution be made from a separate account over which the judge has no control." U.S. Compendium of Selected Opinions § 7.3(a) (1995).

Prohibited Activities on Behalf of Judge or Judicial Candidate by Others

Former Code Section 5(A)(3)(b) differentiated between employees and officials who serve at the pleasure of the judicial candidate and employees and officials who are subject to the candidate's direction and control, a distinction not retained in the 2007 Code. *See* Lisa L. Milord, *The Development of the ABA Judicial Code* 49–50 (1992). Rule 4.1(B) requires that reasonable measures be taken by the judge or judicial candidate to avoid improper assistance by others, including employees and officials who serve at the pleasure of the judge or judicial candidate. *See, e.g.,* W. Va. Adv. Op. 7/3/92 (1992) (incumbents who are candidates for judicial office are not permitted to request or require their employees to attend political functions and make speeches on their behalf; because of constitutional considerations, however, Canon cannot prohibit judicial employee from voluntarily and freely endorsing candidate for judicial office). *But see* Wash. Ethics Adv. Comm. Op. 86-09 (1986) (judge may accept unsolicited offer from court personnel who work in same court as judge sits to volunteer in judge's re-election campaign; court personnel who participate in judge's re-election campaign should be informed by the judge that they are required to adhere to the same standards of political conduct that apply to the judge); W. Va. Adv. Op. 3/8/00 (2000) (no prohibition against judicial officer who is candidate for re-election using staff for appearances in campaign commercials; staff would be appearing voluntarily and during their own time).

Political Activities by Employees or Others under the Judge's Control Not Done on Behalf of the Judge

Because the Code of Judicial Conduct reaches the conduct of only those who are judges or candidates for judicial office, political activities that are not done on behalf of a judge or judicial candidate by others under the control of the judge or judicial candidate are not covered. Nevertheless, questions often arise because of the perceived effect such activities may have on the administration of justice. *See generally Pruitt v. Kimbrough*, 536 F. Supp. 764 (D.C. Ind. 1982), *aff'd*, 705 F.2d 462 (7th Cir. 1983) (unethical for judges to permit court employees to actively engage in partisan politics). *See also* Ariz. Jud. Ethics Adv. Comm. Op. 92-13 (reissued Sept. 1, 1993) (court employees may run for public office if they resign their positions; prospective court employees must resign from elected public office if they wish to accept employment with court); Ind. Comm'n on Jud. Qualifications Adv. Op. 1-93 (1993) (pursuant to Indiana's Canon 5A(1)(f), elected judges may not allow their employees to run for or hold partisan elective office; the employees may run for elective office within their political parties, such as the office of precinct committee person, with the exception that they may not run for or hold office in a party's central committee); Nev. Stand. Comm. on Jud. Ethics and Election Prac. Op. JE 02-002 (2002) (district court employees may work as election polling center supervisors in response to directive from county manager if those employees are not subject to judge's direction and control; those employees are required to observe same standards of fidelity and diligence that apply to judge); N.M. Adv. Comm. on the Code of Jud. Cond. Op. 99-04 (1999) (judicial staff attorney not generally subject to same standards as judge under the Code but may not use her judicial position or position title in connection with her campaigning on behalf of judicial candidate-spouse); N.Y Adv. Comm. on Jud. Ethics Op. 07-189 (2007) (judge's personal appointee who is candidate for nonjudicial elective office may, as part of his or her own campaign, purchase tickets to fund-raisers and other political functions without regard to spending limits that apply to judge); Tex Comm. on Jud. Ethics Adv. Op. 145 (1992) (judge should not permit members of office staff to participate in political activities, such as publicly supporting candidate for election, acting as campaign manager, and fund-raising); W. Va. Adv. Op. 3/19/04 (2004) (probation officer's participation in campaign of gubernatorial candidate problematic); W. Va. Adv. Op. 3/15/04 (2004) (law clerks should consult their judge with respect to extent to which clerk may or may not become involved in political activity).

A distinction is sometimes drawn between the employees' on-duty or off-duty activities. *See, e.g.*, Fla. Comm. on Stands. of Cond. Governing Judges Op. 93-45 (1993) (employees subject to judge's direction or control may not be prohibited from engaging in partisan political activity during personal time providing such activity is conducted entirely independent of judge and without reference to judge or judge's office); Ind. Comm'n on Jud. Qualifications Adv. Op. 3-91 (1991) (advisory opinion in which commission stated that confidential court employees should not run for or hold partisan elective office does not apply to employees who run for or hold office on township boards); Ind. Comm'n on Jud. Qualifications Adv. Op. 1-90 (1990) (judge must prohibit employees subject to judge's direction and control from engaging in partisan campaign activity while on duty, specifically displaying buttons, posters, and bumper stickers; employees may participate in political activity during off-duty hours); Neb. Jud. Ethics Adv. Comm. Op. 98-3 (1998) (under Canon 3C(2), judges should direct their staff to scrupulously avoid any political activity or manifestation of political activity during working hours; staff should not be allowed to display any items referencing political parties or candidates in the workplace, staff should be required to refrain from identifying themselves by reference to their employment or position when they are engaged in political activity, and staff must avoid any conduct that would suggest bias or prejudice by the court or that would support an inference that the judge is condoning or approving the political party, candidate, or activity); Wash. Ethics Adv. Comm. Op. 99-01 (1999) (judge's law clerk may run for city council, which is a local, nonpartisan elected office, but law clerk may not use prestige of judicial office to benefit campaign; clerk may not engage in any activities related to campaign, and if elected, to performance of city council position responsibilities while at work and may not use state resources at any time in this undertaking).

Also see the discussion under Rule 2.12. Rule 2.12(A), which provides that a "judge shall require court staff, court officials, and others subject to the judge's direction and control to act in a manner consistent with the judge's obligation under this Code." Rule 2.12(B) states that "[a] judge with supervisory authority for the performance of other judges shall take reasonable measures to ensure that those judges properly discharge their judicial responsibilities, including the prompt disposition of matters before them." Some jurisdictions address the issue of employees' political activities during work hours under similar provisions.

RETIRED JUDGES

The Code of Judicial Conduct does not prohibit retired judges who are not performing judicial functions from endorsing political candidates. *See, e.g., McDonald v. Ethics Comm. of the Ky. Judiciary*, 3 S.W.3d 740 (Ky. 1999) (Kentucky Judicial Ethics Committee opinion prohibiting retired judges from endorsing political candidates if they subjectively intended to accept future appointments as special judges was unconstitutional restriction on free speech; although state had compelling interest in protecting integrity and independence of its judiciary, retired judges, who were not performing judicial functions, did not jeopardize judicial integrity by making endorsements). Kan. Jud. Ethics Op. JE 99 (2000) (retired judge may actively supporting candidate for judicial office; if judge accepts any judicial assignment, code's prohibitions would apply); W. Va. Adv. Op. 4/14/00 (2000) (retired judicial officer who is not admitted to senior status and whose son is candidate for judicial office is not required to comply with judicial code; only retired senior-status judges are required to comply); *cf.* Ark. Jud. Ethics Adv. Comm. Op. 94-06 (1994) (retired judge who receives retirement pay may participate in campaign of candidate who is running for judge to same extent and with same limitations as any other lawyer whether or not retired judge is subject to recall to service).

However, retired judges who themselves are candidates may be subject to certain restrictions. *See, e.g.*, Fla. Sup. Ct. Jud. Ethics Adv. Comm. Op. 2008-10

(2008) (retired judicial candidate may not use title "judge," "former judge," or "retired judge" or wear a robe in campaign literature, media releases, printed ads, or other media venues. Candidate's campaign may reproduce news articles that include editorials addressing candidate as "judge" or "honorable" and that include photographs of candidate prior to retirement, in robe, and seated on bench).

RULE 4.2 POLITICAL AND CAMPAIGN ACTIVITIES OF JUDICIAL CANDIDATES IN PUBLIC ELECTIONS

(A) A judicial candidate* in a partisan, nonpartisan, or retention public election* shall:

(1) act at all times in a manner consistent with the independence,* integrity,* and impartiality* of the judiciary;

(2) comply with all applicable election, election campaign, and election campaign fund-raising laws and regulations of this jurisdiction;

(3) review and approve the content of all campaign statements and materials produced by the candidate or his or her campaign committee, as authorized by Rule 4.4, before their dissemination; and

(4) take reasonable measures to ensure that other persons do not undertake on behalf of the candidate activities, other than those described in Rule 4.4, that the candidate is prohibited from doing by Rule 4.1.

(B) A candidate for elective judicial office may, unless prohibited by law,* and not earlier than [insert amount of time] before the first applicable primary election, caucus, or general or retention election:

(1) establish a campaign committee pursuant to the provisions of Rule 4.4;

(2) speak on behalf of his or her candidacy through any medium, including, but not limited to, advertisements, websites, or other campaign literature;

(3) publicly endorse or oppose candidates for the same judicial office for which he or she is running;

(4) attend or purchase tickets for dinners or other events sponsored by a political organization* or a candidate for public office;

(5) seek, accept, or use endorsements from any person or organization other than a partisan political organization; and

(6) contribute to a political organization or candidate for public office, but not more than $[insert amount] to any one organization or candidate.

(C) A judicial candidate in a partisan public election may, unless prohibited by law, and not earlier than [insert amount of time] before the first applicable primary election, caucus, or general election:

(1) identify himself or herself as a candidate of a political organization; and

(2) seek, accept, and use endorsements of a political organization.

COMMENT

[1] Paragraphs (B) and (C) permit judicial candidates in public elections to engage in some political and campaign activities otherwise prohibited by Rule 4.1. Candidates may not engage in these activities earlier than [insert amount of time] before the first applicable electoral event, such as a caucus or a primary election.

[2] Despite paragraphs (B) and (C), judicial candidates for public election remain subject to many of the provisions of Rule 4.1. For example, a candidate continues to be prohibited from soliciting funds for a political organization, knowingly making false or misleading statements during a campaign, or making certain promises, pledges, or commitments related to future adjudicative duties. See Rule 4.1(A), paragraphs (4), (11), and (13).

[3] In partisan public elections for judicial office, a candidate may be nominated by, affiliated with, or otherwise publicly identified or associated with a political organization, including a political party. This relationship may be maintained throughout the period of the public campaign, and may include use of political party or similar designations on campaign literature and on the ballot.

[4] In nonpartisan public elections or retention elections, paragraph (B)(5) prohibits a candidate from seeking, accepting, or using nominations or endorsements from a partisan political organization.

[5] Judicial candidates are permitted to attend or purchase tickets for dinners and other events sponsored by political organizations.

[6] For purposes of paragraph (B)(3), candidates are considered to be running for the same judicial office if they are competing for a single judgeship or if several judgeships on the same court are to be filled as a result of the election. In endorsing or opposing another candidate for a position on the same court, a judicial candidate must abide by the same rules governing campaign conduct and speech as apply to the candidate's own campaign.

[7] Although judicial candidates in nonpartisan public elections are prohibited from running on a ticket or slate associated with a political organization, they may group themselves into slates or other alliances to conduct their campaigns more effectively. Candidates who have grouped themselves together are considered to be running for the same judicial office if they satisfy the conditions described in Comment [6].

1990 CODE COMPARISON

Rule 4.2 is derived from the specific regulation of campaign activity included in Canon 5C, with the exception of provisions concerning campaign committees, which are treated in Rule 4.4. The 1990 Code did not advert to the distinction between partisan and nonpartisan or retention elections. Charles G. Geyh & W. William Hodes, *Reporters' Notes to the Model Code of Judicial Conduct* 105 (2009). For a discussion of Canon 5C under the 1990 Code, *see* Lisa L. Milord, *The Development of the ABA Judicial Code* 52–55 (1992). By distinguishing between the three modes of public elections—artisan, nonpartisan, or retention—Rule 4.2(A) sets up the possibility of applying further restrictions and permissive provisions to all three modes or to some designated subset, as required. The Rule adds some restrictions on the activity of judicial candidates that do not appear in Rule 4.1, makes exceptions to some of the restrictions set out in Rule 4.1, and then makes further exceptions that apply only to judicial candidates in partisan elections. Geyh & Hodes at 105.

The 1990 Code allowed judicial candidates to solicit endorsements, "publicly stated support," only through campaign committees. Rule 4.2(B)(5) permits candidates to solicit such support on their own, but not from partisan political organizations. *Id.* at 108.

Rule 4.2(B)(6) is similar to Canon 5C(1)(a)(iii), but establishes dollar limitations (to be supplied by each jurisdiction) on the contributions that can be made.

Rule 4.2(C) and its two subparagraphs permit only candidates in partisan elections to identify themselves as candidates of political organizations and to seek such organizations' endorsements. Canon 5C(1)(a)(ii) had permitted the first of these two activities for candidates in both partisan and nonpartisan elections.

Rule 4.2(B) identifies a time period prior to the relevant primary or election, during which certain activities that would or might otherwise be prohibited by Rule 4.1(A) are permitted. Although the creation of this time period is not new, its use in this Rule is to disconnect the status of being a judicial candidate from being permitted to engage in the activities of a candidate. With the time period in place, the judge can continue to call himself or herself a candidate for ten years, but can raise campaign funds only after the time period has been satisfied, typically one year before the first primary.

Rule 4.2(B)(6) allows all candidates for judicial office to make contributions to political organizations or other candidates for public office, but only during the time period determined by the jurisdiction.

Rule 4.2(C) permits judicial candidates in partisan public elections to identify themselves as candidates of a political organization and to accept endorsements from political organizations.

ANNOTATION

Revised Canon 4 establishes standards for the political and campaign conduct of judges and judicial candidates, like Canon 5 of the 1990 Model Code. The key to understanding Canon 4 is to keep in mind that Rule 4.1 applies to all judges and all judicial candidates, whereas Rule 4.2 applies only to judicial candidates running in partisan, nonpartisan, or retention public elections. Further, Rule 4.2 adds some restrictions on the activity of judicial candidates that do not appear in Rule 4.1, makes exceptions to some of the restrictions set out in Rule 4.1, and then makes further exceptions that apply only to judicial candidates in partisan elections. Charles G. Geyh & W. William Hodes, *Reporters' Notes to the Model Code of Judicial Conduct* 105 (2009).

The additional requirements imposed upon all judicial candidates for elective office are largely new, but are consistent with or implicit in their antecedents in Canon 5 of the 1990 Code, as well as other provisions of Canon 4 of the 2007 Code. *See generally* Ark. Jud. Ethics Adv. Comm. Op. 95-04 (1995) (noting specific acts that may or may not be done by the candidate or the candidate's campaign committee under the state counterpart to Canon 5C); Ind. Comm'n on Jud. Qualifications Adv. Op. 1-93 (1993) (describing permissible acts pursuant to Canon 5 of 1993 Indiana Code of Judicial Conduct). *See generally* Hon. Hans A. Linde, *The Judge as Political Candidate*, 40 Clev. St. L. Rev. 1 (1992); J. Scott Gary, Comment, *Ethical Conduct in a Judicial Campaign: Is Campaigning an Ethical Activity?* 57 Wash. L. Rev. 119 (1981).

ACTING IN A MANNER CONSISTENT WITH THE INDEPENDENCE, INTEGRITY, AND IMPARTIALITY OF THE JUDICIARY

Rule 4.2(A)(1) is based upon parts of former Canon 5A(3). Section 5A(3)(a) was added to the Code to require a high standard of conduct of nonjudge candidates as well as of judges who are candidates and thereby remove an inequality in the conduct of campaigns for judicial office. Lisa L. Milord, *The Development of the ABA Judicial Code* 49 (1992).

Rule 4.2 (A)(1) requires that candidates for judicial office "act at all times in a manner consistent with the independence, integrity, and impartiality of the judiciary." A variety of misconduct may fall under this provision. *See, e.g., In re Grodman*, 2015 Ariz. LEXIS 319 (Ariz. 2015) (judge violated Rule 4.2(A)(1) when he campaigned during court hours); *In re Schwartz*, 174 So. 3d 987 (Fla. 2015) (judge who asked store owner who displayed judge's campaign opponent's sign in window to also display judge's sign and lost her temper, swore at the store owner, and threated to sue the owner when the owner refused, violated the rule); *In re Davis*, Ind. S. Ct. Order No. 24S00-1210-JD-610 (May 7, 2013) (judicial candidate violated Rule 4.2(A)(1) when she made false and misleading statements about incumbent-opponent's character and judicial conduct); *In re Bybee*, 716 N.E.2d 957 (Ind. 1999) (judicial candidate violated Canon by knowingly misrepresenting incumbent judge's judicial record in campaign brochure); *In re Boles*, 555 N.E.2d 1284 (Ind. 1990) (judge engaged in serious misconduct when, during an ongoing, acrimonious political dispute with county commissioners, judge posted notices around courthouse accusing commissioners of violating open meetings law, and spent $59 of his own money on a calendar advertisement printed and distributed by the county sheriff's department that contained a large eyeball and the statement "Always watching—J.V. Boles," referring to judge's desire to portray himself to voters as the "taxpayers' hero"); *Disc. Counsel v. Evans*, 733 N.E.2d 609 (Ohio 2000) (judicial candidate's lack of close supervision of campaign activities, failure to report contributions by township for use of township garage for producing signs and value of labor of inmates and welfare workers, and exaggeration of his endorsements during primary campaign violated judicial disciplinary rule requiring judicial candidate to maintain the dignity appropriate to judicial office); Ariz. Jud. Ethics Adv. Comm. Op. 96-12 (1996) (an incumbent candidate for judicial office may obtain public support and publicized endorsements but may not utilize endorsements that cast doubt on independence and impartiality by suggesting that judge favors police or prosecution); Fla. Comm. on Stands. of Cond. Governing Judges Op. 97-34 (1998) (judge should strive to arrange campaign activities to be conducted outside regular courthouse hours; minor campaign related activities, such as brief telephone calls or minor emergency matters, during regular office hours may be permissible as long as conduct does not cast reasonable doubt on judge's capacity to act impartially as judge, demean judicial office, or interfere with proper performance of judicial duties); Ill. Jud. Ethics Comm. Op. 03-01 (2003) (judge or candidate for judicial office should not make allegations about opponent's purported private sexual conduct absent likely criminal prosecution or judicial disciplinary violation); *In Re Davis* (Tex. State Comm'n on Jud. Cond. 2008). (judge allowed grand jury he had appointed to be influenced by political supporter seeking indictments against political opponents; judge requested court of inquiry to investigate political opponent.); W. Va. Adv. Op. 4/18/00 (2000) (judicial candidate may continue to act as expert witness in field of insurance during his or her campaign; however, candidate is prohibited from using any position that he or she might take as expert witness to advance his or her campaign by publicizing opinion or using it in political way). *See also* Ariz. Jud. Ethics Adv. Comm. Op. 04-02 (2004) (incumbent judges required to recuse themselves in cases filed by announced opponents in judicial elections; judge not disqualified when defeated political opponent of judge represents party in post-election proceeding before that judge).

COMPLYING WITH ELECTION, ELECTION CAMPAIGN, AND ELECTION CAMPAIGN FUND-RAISING LAWS AND REGULATIONS

In furtherance of public interest in an independent judiciary, judicial candidates must, to the greatest extent possible, be free and appear to be free from political influence and political pressure. Concerned with inappropriate politicization of the judiciary, the ABA has, over the years, approved amendments to the Model Code of Judicial Conduct addressing judicial electoral reform issues and judicial independence concerns. In August 1999, Sections 5C(3) and 5C(4) were added to the Code, imposing contribution limits and disclosure standards on judges who must campaign for office. Specific dollar limits and time frames are to be set by each adopting jurisdiction. *See American Bar Association Ad Hoc Committee on Judicial Campaign Finance, Standing Committee on Ethics and Professional Responsibility, the Judicial Division and Special Committee on Judicial Independence 123 to the House of Delegates* (August 1999).

Caperton v. A.T. Massey Coal Co.

According to a February 2009 poll conducted for Justice at Stake, 85 percent of respondents believe judges should not hear cases in which a litigant spent $50,000 or more to help elect them. In recent years, as special interest spending has soared nationally in state court races, there have been increased calls for judicial disqualification in cases that might pose ethical conflicts. *See, e.g., City of Las Vegas Downtown Redevelopment Agency v. Eighth Judicial Dist. Court ex rel. County of Clark*, 5 P.3d 1059 (Nev. 2000) (campaign contributions to judge by casinos that stood to benefit from outcome of eminent domain action did not constitute proper grounds for judge's disqualification; contributions were not extraordinary in amount, and without more, constituted only an insignificant interest that did not raise reasonable question as to judge's impartiality).

In *Caperton v. A.T. Massey Coal Company, Inc*, 129 S. Ct. 2252 (2009), *rev'd on remand*, 225 W. Va. 128 (W. Va. 2009), the Court ruled that elected judges must step aside from cases when large campaign contributions from interested parties create the appearance of bias. In *Caperton*, a West Virginia high court judge declined to recuse himself from hearing the appeal of a $50 million judgment against A.T. Massey Coal Company despite the fact that its owner contributed at least $3 million to a pair of committees that ran advertisements attacking the judge's opponent. The judge twice rejected motions that he recuse himself because the company owner's extraordinary financial support for the judge's campaign created a constitutionally unacceptable appearance of impropriety. In a lengthy concurrence posted on the court's website, the judge stated that due process requires recusal only when a judge has a direct, personal, substantial, pecuniary interest in the case before him.

After a West Virginia jury found Massey Coal Co. liable for fraudulent misrepresentation, concealment, and tortious interference with existing contractual relations and awarded Caperton $50 million in damages, West Virginia held its 2004 judicial elections. Knowing that the West Virginia Supreme Court of Appeals would consider the appeal, Don Blankenship, Massey's chairman and principal officer, supported Brent Benjamin rather than Justice Warren McGraw, the incumbent justice seeking re-election. He contributed the $1,000 statutory maximum to Benjamin's campaign committee and donated almost $2.5 million to "And for the Sake of the Kids," a Section 527 political organization that opposed McGraw. Benjamin won by fewer than 50,000 votes. Justice Benjamin denied the motions by Caperton to disqualify him based on the conflict caused by Blankenship's campaign involvement. The court voted 3–2 to reverse the $50 million verdict.

By a 5–4 vote, the Supreme Court stated that the Due Process Clause incorporates the common-law rule requiring recusal when a judge has a direct, personal, substantial, pecuniary interest in a case. Additionally, recusal is required where the probability of actual bias on the part of the judge or decision maker is too high to be constitutionally tolerable. Because the objective standards implementing the Due Process Clause do not require proof of actual bias, the Court did not question the judge's subjective findings of impartiality and propriety and did not determine whether there was actual bias. Rather, it defined the central question as being whether, "under a realistic appraisal of psychological tendencies and human weakness," whether the interest "poses such a risk of actual bias or prejudgment that the practice must be forbidden if the guarantee of due process is to be adequately implemented." *Id.* at 2263. citing *Withrow v. Larkin*, 421 U.S. 35, 47 (1975). According to the Court, there is a serious risk of actual bias when a person with a personal stake in a particular case has a significant and disproportionate influence in placing the judge on the case by raising funds or directing the judge's election campaign when the case is pending or imminent. "Just as no man is allowed to be a judge in his own cause, similar fears of bias can arise when — without the consent of the other parties — a man chooses the judge in his own cause." *Id.* at 2256.

Further, regarding the proper inquiry, said the Court, is focus on "the contribution's relative size in comparison to the total amount contributed to the campaign, the total amount spent in the election, and the apparent effect of the contribution on the outcome," not whether the contributions were a necessary and sufficient cause of victory.

On remand from the U.S. Supreme Court, the West Virginia Supreme Court voted 4–1 to overturn the award for Caperton and remanded the case to the circuit court to enter an order of dismissal with prejudice. Lawrence Messina, *For 3rd time, W. Va. Supreme Court finds in favor of Massey*, The Associated Press (Nov. 2, 2009). *See generally* Opinion, *Honest Justice*, New York Times (June 8, 2009) (last visited on Mar. 24, 2010); Bob Bauer, *Kennedy's Problem in Caperton v. Massey and the Unfortunate Solution He Chose* (last visited on Mar. 24, 2010); Stephen M. Hoersting, *The Caperton Caper and the Kennedy Conundrum*, 2009 Cato Sup. Ct. Rev. 319 (2009); Pamela S. Karlan, *Electing Judges, Judging Elections, and the Lessons of Caperton*, 123 Harv. L. Rev. 80 (2009); Lawrence Lessig, *What Everybody Knows and What Too Few Accept*, 123 Harv. L. Rev. 104 (2009); Donald R. Lundberg, *Dancin' with Them What Brung Ya: Electing Appellate Judges*, 52 Res Gestae 31 (2009); Molly McLucas, *The Need for Effective Recusal Standards for an Elected Judiciary*, 42 Loy. L. Rev. 671 (2009); Tuan Samahon, *Caperton and Judicial Disqualification in Nevada*, 17 Nev. Law 28 (Jan. 2009); Penny J. White, *Relinquished Responsibilities*, 123 Harv. L. Rev. 129 (2009); Jess Bravin & Kris Maher, *Justices Set new Standard for Recusals*, Wall Street Journal, June 9, 2009, at A-3; Kate David & Jennifer S. Greenlief, *Juicy Enough for Grisham, But Does It Have Any Bite?*, Houston Lawyer (Sept./Oct. 2009); Dee Hall, *Can Our Elected Judges Be Neutral? Campaign Contributions from Special Interest Groups Can Create an "Appearance of Conflict of Interest" Some Say*, Wis. St. J., April 9, 2007, at A1; David Ingram, *Congress Set to Take Aim at Judicial Recusals*, The National Law Journal, November 2, 2009 (last visited on Mar. 24, 2010); Wade Kolb, III, 2009 Supreme Court Case Commentary, *Caperton V. Massey: The Due Process Implications of Contributions to Judicial Campaigns*, 4 Duke J. Const. L. & Pub. Pol'y Sidebar 315 (Mar. 18, 2009); John A. Meiser, Notes, *The (Non) Problem of a Limited Due Process Right to Judicial Disqualification*, 84 Notre Dame L. Rev. 1799 (Apr. 2009); Kevin C. Newsom, Marc James Ayers, *A Brave New World of Judicial Recusal?*, 70 Ala. Law. 368 (Sept. 2009); Christian W. Peck, Zogby International (commissioned by The Committee for Economic Development), *Attitudes and Views of American Business Leaders on State Judicial Elections and Political Contributions to Judges* (May 2007) (last visited on Mar. 24, 2010); Stuart Banner, Note, *Disqualifying Elected Judges from Cases Involving Campaign Contributors*, 40 Stan. L. Rev. 449 (1988).

One of the first states to reconsider its recusal provisions in response to *Caperton* was Wisconsin, which approved rules stating that endorsements, campaign contributions, and independently run advertisements do not by themselves require judges to recuse themselves. *See* Patrick Marley, *State High Court Says Campaign Donations Can't Force Recusals*, Milwaukee

Journal Sentinel (Oct. 28, 2009); Alex De Grand, *Recusal not required on account of campaign contribution, independent expenditure of party to proceedings* (Oct. 28, 2009); Ryan J. Foley, *Wisconsin High Court: Donations Don't Require Recusals*, Associated Press (Oct. 29, 2009). On November 25, 2009, the Michigan Supreme Court approved an amendment to Rule 2.003 of the Michigan Court Rules that states that disqualification of a judge may be warranted if the judge, based on objective and reasonable perceptions, has a serious risk of actual bias impacting the due process rights of a party as enunciated in *Caperton. See also* Justice at Stake, *JAS Lauds New Judicial Rules in Michigan* (Nov. 6, 2009) (last visited on Mar. 24, 2010); Bert Brandenburg, *The Future of Recusal: A Tale of Two States*, American Constitution Society (Nov. 17, 2009).

REVIEWING AND APPROVING CONTENT OF CAMPAIGN STATEMENTS

Rule 4.2(A)(3) requires judicial candidates to personally approve the contents of campaign literature and other materials, which gives fuller effect to the Rule 4.1(A)(11) prohibition against making false or misleading statements in a campaign. Charles G. Geyh & W. William Hodes, *Reporters' Notes to the Model Code of Judicial Conduct* 106 (2009). *See* Ark. Jud. Ethics Adv. Comm. Op. 2009-04 (2009) (candidate has personal responsibility to review and approve content of all campaign statements and material produced by candidate's campaign committee and to ensure they are consistent with code); *In re Hildebrandt*, 675 N.E.2d 889 (Ohio Comm'n of Judges), *appeal dismissed*, 679 N.E.2d 7 (Ohio 1997) (judge violated Canon by running advertisements that were designed to mislead the public with regard to his opponent's voting record on the death penalty while in Congress and his service as public official; judge failed to verify personally content of advertisements, especially after he was informed of incorrect statements).

In response to negative campaigning, several states and municipalitics have "fair campaign acts," which contain a statement of fair campaign practices in which candidates for elected office, including judges, promise to conduct their campaigns without the use of false statements and scurrilous attacks on opponents. Many of these acts are voluntary and provide neither an enforcement mechanism nor a private cause of action. Some candidates for judicial office choose to sign on to Florida's Voluntary Code of Fair Campaign Practices, which states in part that all candidates will take personal responsibility for approving or disavowing the substance of attacks on opponents that may come from third parties supporting the judicial candidate. *See generally* Cleveland Ferguson, III, *The Politics of Ethics and Elections: Can Negative Campaign Advertising Be Regulated in Florida?*, 24 Fla. St. U. L. Rev. 463, 485–86 (1997).

PERMISSIBLE ACTIVITY UNDER RULE 4.2

Although Rule 4.2(B) and (C) permit judicial candidates in public elections to engage in some political and campaign activities otherwise prohibited by Rule 4.1, the candidates remain subject to many of the provisions of Rule 4.1. *See, e.g., In re Alley*, 699 So. 2d 1369 (Fla. 1997) (judicial candidate may not inject party politics into nonpartisan election); Fla. Sup. Ct. Jud. Ethics Adv. Comm. Op. 08-16 (2008) (judicial candidate may not hire partisan political candidate or executive officer of partisan political committee running for different office to be judicial candidate's campaign manager/consultant).

Establishing a Campaign Committee

Though Rule 4.2 applies only to judicial candidates in public elections, the rule may also impact candidates for appointed judicial office. *See* Tenn. Jud. Ethics Comm. Adv. Op. 00-01 (2000) (if candidate for judicial appointment is also, by definition, candidate for judicial election, he or she may form committee to solicit and accept contributions limited to use in candidate's election campaign; any contributions accepted may not be used in furtherance of the person's candidacy for judicial appointment).

Speaking on Behalf of Candidacy

Pursuant to Rule 4.2(B)(2), a judicial candidate may speak on behalf of his or her candidacy through any medium. Naturally, this includes speaking in-person. *See, e.g.*, Fla. Sup. Ct. Jud. Ethics Adv. Comm. Op. 10-30 (2010) (judicial candidate may attend and distribute literature at nonpartisan "meet-the-candidates" event that is not a fund-raiser); Fla. Comm. on Stands. of Cond. Governing Judges Op. 02-11 (2002) (candidate may attend political party meeting, hand out campaign literature, and speak with audience); Fla. Comm. on Stands. of Cond. Governing Judges Op. 96-11 (1996) (judicial candidate may attend a partisan political function in order to meet people, have alternative petitions signed, and make a speech on behalf of his or her candidacy as long as the function is not a fund-raiser and the other candidates for the office are also invited); Fla. Comm. on Stands. of Cond. Governing Judges Op. 88-16 (1988) (county judge who has announced candidacy for circuit judgeship is not prohibited from being present at private homes to meet people); N.M. Adv. Comm. on the Code of Jud. Cond. Op. 12-07 (2012) (judicial candidate may host political party's central committee for the purpose of introducing self and seeking votes for ballot position); N.Y. Adv. Comm. on Jud. Ethics Op. 12-129(A)-(G) (judge who is candidate may host a free "meet and greet," serve refreshments to attendees, and speak with attendees); Wash. Ethics Adv. Comm. 13-06 (2013) (judge or judicial candidate may attend political forum sponsored by political action committee with membership of DUI lawyers).

Appearing in Media Advertisements in Support of Candidacy

Media advertisements may include those on television and in print. *See, e.g.,* Fla. Comm. on Stands. of Cond. Governing Judges Op. 84-10 (1984) (announced candidate for circuit judge may run television commercials that state that candidate is certified by state bar as civil trial lawyer). *See also* Nev. Stand. Comm. on Jud. Ethics and Election Prac. Op. 06-008 (2006) (candidate in judicial election who is not serving in judicial capacity on full or part-time basis may continue to publish weekly newspaper column and appear in media advertisements, neither of which directly support candidacy). *But see* Fl. Sup. Ct. Jud. Ethics. Adv. Comm. Op. 2010-18 (2010) (judge may not use photograph that depicts judge accepting an award with members of the Supreme Court looking on because joint picture implies endorsement that Supreme Court justices may not make).

Posting on Websites

Candidates for judicial election may establish a campaign website and post articles and editorials regarding the campaign. *See* Fla. Sup. Ct. Jud. Ethics Adv. Comm. Op. 10-28 (2010) (campaign committee may host website and Facebook page supporting candidate); Fla. Sup. Ct. Jud. Ethics Adv. Comm. Op. 10-21 (2010) (website may contain "contribute" button); Fla. Comm. on Stands. of Cond. Governing Judges Op. 08-11 (2008) (judge's campaign website may make reference to, and facilitate, giving of financial and other support to judge's re-election effort only if website is created and maintained by committee of responsible persons organized for purpose of assisting judge's re-election efforts); Fla. Comm. on Stands. of Cond. Governing Judges Op. 00-22 (2000) (judicial candidate may post on internet campaign website newspaper articles and editorials regarding campaign); Fla. Comm. on Stands. of Cond. Governing Judges Op. 99-26 (1999) (judge may establish web page to prepare for upcoming election campaign and to provide general information to public).

Electronic Social Media

Candidates, through their campaign committees, may use electronic social media to raise campaign money and provide information about the candidate. ABA Formal Op. 462 (2013). Viewers may be allowed to "like" the judge's page "if the campaign is not required to accept or reject a request." *See also* N.D. Jud. Ethics Adv. Comm. Op. 2016-2 (2016). *Cf.* Fla. Sup. Ct. Jud. Ethics Adv. Comm. Op. 09-20 (2009) (judge may not "friend" lawyers who appear before the judge because it conveys to others the impression that these lawyer "friends" are in a special position to influence the judge); Fla. Sup. Ct. Jud. Ethics Adv. Comm. Op. 10-05 (2010) (Op. 09-20 not applicable to nonjudge judicial candidate). Judges and their campaigns may tweet campaign messages. Fla. Sup. Ct. Jud. Ethics Adv. Comm. Op. 13-14 (2013) (best practice would be to allow the campaign manager to tweet messages because while the simple act of a tweeting does not necessarily raise issues, the fact that Twitter allows the judge to block followers, favorite certain tweets, and create a list of followers, raises concerns; specifically, the Committee noted that these features could convey impression that a person who a judge lists or retweets as a favorite is "in a special position to influence the judge").

Distributing Campaign Literature

A judicial candidate may, when a candidate for election, distribute pamphlets and other promotional campaign literature supporting his or her candidacy, except as prohibited by law. *See* Fla. Comm. on Stands. of Cond. Governing Judges Op. 94-24 (1994) (sitting judge who will be up for re-election may mail press release and photograph to local newspapers for purpose of announcing his or her candidacy); Ky. Jud. Ethics Op. JE-114 (2006) (judicial candidate may distribute yard signs and other campaign literature to political parties and public officials who request them); *but cf.* Nev. Stand. Comm. on Jud. Ethics and Election Prac. Op. JE 98-005 (1998) (candidate may not place campaign materials at booth sponsored by political party at the state fair because it would create danger that members of public will associate judge with philosophy of that political party and assume that judge is publicly identifying himself or herself as member of that political organization). *See also* Mich. Comm. on Jud. Ethics Op. JI-93 (1994) (judicial candidate may distribute personal campaign literature at event held for nonjudicial candidate, but may not reciprocate in kind by affording an opportunity for distribution of nonjudicial candidate's campaign materials at event given for judicial candidate); Tex. Adv. Comm. on Jud. Ethics Op. 170 (1994) (judges running for re-election may not hand out campaign material for candidates of own political party along with own material and recommend to people that they vote for those candidates).

Publicly Endorsing or Opposing Other Candidates for the Same Judicial Office

Pursuant to Rule 4.2(B)(3), a candidate may, unless prohibited by law, publicly endorse or oppose candidates for the same judicial office for which he or she is running. *See generally* Ill. Jud. Ethics Comm. Op. 94-11 (1994) (judge who is running for circuit court position may publicly endorse other candidates for circuit court judge as well as candidate for any other office; in addition, judge who is running for retention is candidate for public election and can publicly support or oppose other candidate including candidates for judicial election and other judges running for retention); Mich. Comm. on Jud. Ethics Op. JI-11 (1989) (inclusion of name of judicial candidate in third party's communication with nonjudicial candidates does not constitute public endorsement of nonjudicial candidate by judge and does not in itself constitute improper conduct by judge); W. Va. Adv. Op. 3/28/02 (2002) (candidate for judge may be listed on campaign materials along with names of other candidates for elected public office and may appear in promotions of party ticket; candidates for judge may not, however, campaign, travel and visit potential voters with another candidate for either judicial or nonjudicial office); ABA Informal Op. 1468 (1981) (judge may not participate in any public solicitation or partisan effort to recruit or oppose judicial candidate other than with own candidacy). *But see* Nev. Stand. Comm. on Jud. Ethics and Election Prac. JE 10-005 (2010) (judge may not host "meet and greet" for another judicial candidate in judge's home because it would constitute a prohibited endorsement of the candidate); Tex. Adv. Comm. on Jud. Ethics Op. 130 (1989) (judge's public endorsement of candidate for public office violates code of judicial conduct because "such an endorsement tends to diminish public confidence in the independence and impartiality of the judiciary and may give the appearance of involvement in partisan interests and of judicial concern about public clamor or criticism, and because such an endorsement of necessity involves the use of the prestige of the judge and the prestige of his office"); Tex. Adv. Comm. on Jud. Ethics Op. 92 (1987) (part-time municipal judge may not publicly endorse judicial or nonjudicial candidates for political office); *In Re Krouse*, CJC No. 4560-F-117 (Wash. State Comm'n on Jud. Cond. 2005) (candidate attended political function for nonjudicial candidate and personally contributed money to that candidate's election campaign; candidate also questioned lawyer in his courtroom, immediately after court hearing, for apparently supporting former opponent). *Cf.* N.Y. Adv. Comm. on Jud. Ethics Op. 08-42 (2008) (lawyer who is nonjudge candidate for elective judicial office may accept employment from another candidate or from political party as election law expert so long as formal attorney-client relationship exists, his actions are clearly identifiable as those of lawyer representing client, and not as partisan political activity; and lawyer is fairly compensated for legal services to avoid the perception that he is making an improper contribution to the political party or candidate); ABA Informal Decision C-744 (1964) (lawyer intending to run for judicial office against incumbent judge, who seeks re-election, may, "with propriety," publicly criticize judge for not operating on a full-time basis, as long as lawyer's criticism is "on a high level plane" and within bounds of truth).

Attending or Purchasing Tickets for Dinners or Other Events Sponsored by a Political Organization or a Candidate for Public Office

Rule 4.2(B)(4) specifically permits a judicial candidate in a public election to attend and purchase tickets for political functions, such as dinners or campaign rallies, beginning at an established time prior to the election. Such activity is prohibited at all other times by Rule 4.1(A)(5) for both judges and candidates. The Rule 4.2(B)(4) exception applies to judicial candidates running in partisan, nonpartisan, and retention elections, but not to candidates seeking appointment.

Many jurisdictions provide that a candidate for elective judicial office may not attend a campaign event at which admission tickets are sold or place certain restrictions on attendance unrelated to the timing of the event because the appearance would amount to the judicial officer participating indirectly in the solicitation of funds. *See* Fla. Comm. on Stands. of Cond. Governing Judges Op. 02-08 (2002) (judicial candidate may not attend political meeting to socialize and greet participants even though candidate does not speak); Fla. Comm. on Stands. of Cond. Governing Judges Op. 00-26 (2000) (judicial candidate, invited along with all other judicial candidates in circuit, may not attend informal function as guest of political party for sole purpose of socializing and talking one-on-one to other guests); Fla. Comm. on Stands. of Cond. Governing Judges Op. 96-19 (1996) (judicial candidate may attend political rally sponsored by local civic organization where all candidates are invited and allowed to speak, there is no fund-raising involved, and all the fees must are spent to defray the cost of the rally); Fla. Comm. on Stands. of Cond. Governing Judges Op. 00-12 (2000) (candidate for re-election to judicial office, having no active opposition, may attend political forum hosted by national Hispanic Republican Assembly if all candidates for that office, if any, have been invited and forum is not fund-raiser); Fla. Sup. Ct. Jud. Ethics Adv. Comm. Op. 10-19 (2010) (although Tea Party Patriot's group is a political party, judge may attend and speak at event if it is not a fund-raiser, other candidates for the judge's position are invited, and the presentation topics are limited to those allowed under the Florida Code); N.Y. Adv. Comm. on Jud. Ethics Op. 07-64 (2007) (candidate who has already purchased tickets to politically sponsored function to be held during candidate's window period but is unable to attend due to actual conflict may send bona fide campaign representatives to attend on candidate's behalf but must instruct them about the limitations on campaign speech and conduct that they should observe when speaking on the judge's behalf at the function); N.Y. Adv. Comm. on Jud. Ethics Op. 12-129(A)-(G) (2012) (candidate may attend politically sponsored golf outing subject to rule's limitation on price and number of tickets purchased); Okla. Jud. Ethics Op. 2002-9 (2002) (judge or judicial candidate may purchase tickets for political party annual dinner for purpose of campaigning on his/her behalf so long as the cost of ticket covers only reasonable cost of event apportioned on individual basis to candidate and would not enlarge coffers of party to advance its agenda); Wash. Ethics Adv. Comm. Op. 00-10 (2000) (judicial candidate may attend event that is put on by candidate's campaign where attendees are asked only to pay to defray cost of putting on event); Wash. Ethics Adv. Comm. Op 95-24 (1995) (candidate may not attend a campaign event at which admission tickets are sold; candidate may attend campaign fund-raising event where admission fee is not charged, but fund-raising should take place out of presence of the candidate by having candidate either make appearance before there is any solicitation for contributions or by having solicitation take place in location at which candidate is not present); Wash. Ethics Adv. Comm. Op 90-13 (1990) (candidate may not attend dinner where tickets are either pre-sold or sold at door by candidate or others on candidate's behalf, but campaign committee may sponsor fund-raising dinner for which tickets are either pre-sold or sold at the door if the candidate did not attend the dinner; if there is no admission charge in addition to cost of dinner, candidate could attend dinner provided candidate did not participate in any fund-raising activities and left dinner before donations are solicited); *but see* Ga. Jud. Qualifications Comm'n Op. 205 (1996) (judicial candidates may attend political gatherings such as fish fries for which tickets have been sold by candidate's campaign committee and may speak to such gatherings on their own behalf without any mention or solicitation of funds); Nev. Stand. Comm. on Jud. Ethics and Election Prac. Op. JE12-001 (2012) (judge may attend and speak at event sponsored by political organization). *Cf.* Fla. Comm. on Stands. of Cond. Governing Judges Op. 00-22 (2000) (judicial candidate may attend and distribute campaign materials at National Rifle Association (NRA) fund-raiser; NRA is neither "political party" nor "political organization" as that term is defined in state code of judicial conduct).

Seeking, Accepting, or Using Endorsements from Any Person or Organization Other than a Partisan Political Organization

Rule 4.2(B)(5) allows a candidate for elective judicial office to seek, accept, or use endorsements other than from a partisan political organization within the applicable time frame. However, some other restrictions may be placed on the permissible activity. *See, e.g.*, Fla. Sup. Ct. Ethics Adv. Comm. Op. 13-21 (2013) (judge may accept the unsolicited endorsement of a lawyer who is not a candidate for office but also endorses another judicial candidate in another race); Fla. Sup. Ct. Jud. Ethics Adv. Comm. Op. 10-14 (2010) (judicial candidate may accept endorsements from nonjudicial elected official provided the endorsement is from the individual, not the individual's party, the official is not also campaigning for re-election, and the individual does not mention party affiliation); Fla. Sup. Ct. Jud. Ethics Adv. Comm. Op. 08-02 (2008) (incumbent judge campaigning for re-election must disclose support of local state attorney, sheriff, and defense lawyers); Ga. Jud. Qualifications Comm'n Op. No. 205 (1996) (while public support may be sought from lawyer, bar associations, civic clubs, private interest groups, and the like by a duly established campaign committee, neither an incumbent judge nor a candidate for judicial office may personally ask any such individual or group for permission to place the supporter's name in any form of campaign literature or media advertisement).

Contributing to a Political Organization or Candidate for Public Office

Rule 4.2(B)(6) allows a judicial candidate to contribute to a political organization or candidate for public office, but not more than an amount specified by each jurisdiction for any one organization or candidate. *See, e.g.*, Ariz. Jud. Ethics Adv. Comm. Op. 08-01 (2008) (judicial candidate may make contributions to political organizations, including his or her own campaign committee, provided that contributions conform to standard in judicial code); Kan. Jud. Ethics Op. JE 106 (2001) (judicial candidate, subject to election, may contribute to his or her political party, subject to any limitations that may be provided by law); Mich. Comm. on Jud. Ethics Op. JI-105 (1997) (judge or judicial candidate may make general contribution to political action committee; no ethics provision prohibits group of judges, or judges' organization, from making contributions to political action committees under the same conditions permitted to individual judges); W. Va. Adv. Op. 9/1/00 (2000) (judge may donate, subject to adherence to appropriate election laws, space for political party headquarters); W. Va. Adv. Op. 8/28/95 (1995) (judicial officer may contribute to county political party executive committee if committee meets definition of political organization under state code, but contribution may not be restricted for use only in fellow judicial officer's campaign); *cf. In re Stoker*, 827 P.2d 986 (Wash. 1992) (payment by judge's campaign committee to political party for use of its booth at county fair is not "political contribution" prohibited by code of judicial conduct); Alaska Comm'n on Jud. Cond. Adv. Op. 97-2 (1997) (judges may contribute to charitable organizations that also engage in some political activities if those organizations are primarily engaged in non-political charitable work); Fla. Sup. Ct. Jud. Ethics Adv. Comm. Op. 08-07 (2008) (judge may anonymously contribute financially to defray campaign costs of candidate for seat on state university's student government; activity does not raise concerns addressed by Canon 7A(1)(e) and is more closely analogous to donation to fund-raising activity).

Identifying Himself or Herself as a Candidate of a Political Organization

Rule 4.2(C)(1) permits judicial candidates in partisan elections to identify themselves as candidates of political organizations beginning a specified amount of time prior to the election period. *See* N.Y. Adv. Comm. on Jud.

Ethics Op. 12-84/12-95(B)-(G) (judicial candidate may include a link from his/her campaign website to a political organization's website that contains information promoting the judicial candidate's campaign). *See also* discussion under Rule 4.1(A)(6).

Seeking, Accepting, or Using Endorsements from Any Person or Organization Other than a Partisan Political Organization

Rule 4.2(C)(2) permits judicial candidates in partisan elections to seek, accept, and use endorsements of a political organization beginning a specified amount of time prior to the election period. *See* Fla. Sup. Ct. Jud. Ethics Adv. Comm. Op. 08-12 (2008) (candidate for election to judicial office may receive and publish endorsement for election from senior assistant county attorney who is additionally employed by municipality as independent contractor); Fla. Sup. Ct. Jud. Ethics Adv. Comm. Op. 08-02 (2008) (insufficient disclosure for incumbent candidate to send out mass mailing to local bar members stating that judge is being supported by local state attorney, sheriff, and defense lawyers; not improper to announce these relationships in open court). *Cf.* N.Y. Adv. Comm. on Jud. Ethics Op. 09-40 (2009) (judge may apply to political party's judicial screening panel outside the window period to determine qualifications for particular judicial office at time when there are no actual, known vacancies for such office provided there is good-faith reason to believe there will be vacancy later in same election cycle, judicial screening panel process is available to all potential candidates, and panel is official screening panel, such as standing panel of existing political party).

However, in some jurisdictions, a candidate for judicial office may not take action that would suggest that the candidate is endorsed by a partisan political party or is running on the same slate as another candidate. *See, e.g.*, Fla. Sup. Ct. Jud. Ethics Adv. Comm. Op. 04-29 (2004) (judicial candidates running for different judicial seats prohibited from mailing their individual campaign brochures in single envelope notwithstanding written disclaimer that judicial candidates were not endorsing each other).

RULE 4.3 ACTIVITIES OF CANDIDATES FOR APPOINTIVE JUDICIAL OFFICE

A candidate for appointment to judicial office may:

(A) communicate with the appointing or confirming authority, including any selection, screening, or nominating commission or similar agency; and

(B) seek endorsements for the appointment from any person or organization other than a partisan political organization.

COMMENT

[1] When seeking support or endorsement, or when communicating directly with an appointing or confirming authority, a candidate for appointive judicial office must not make any pledges, promises, or commitments that are inconsistent with the impartial performance of the adjudicative duties of the office. See Rule 4.1(A)(13).

1990 CODE COMPARISON

Rule 4.3(A) includes a stylistic and a small substantive change from comparable provisions in the 1990 Code found in Canon 5B(2)(a). Stylistically, "other agency designated to screen candidates" was replaced with "any selection, screening, or nominating commission or similar agency," which is intended to be more comprehensive. The substantive change was to make reference to a "confirming authority," in addition to an "appointing authority." Charles G. Geyh & W. William Hodes, *Reporters' Notes to the Model Code of Judicial Conduct* 110 (2009).

According to the Reporters' Notes, the reference to "confirming authorities" may be to the United States Senate when sitting to confirm or reject presidential nominations of federal judges. Some state jurisdictions have a similar confirmation process that allows candidates for judicial appointment to state their qualifications and views to confirming agencies as well as to nominating and screening agencies. *Id.*

Unlike the 1990 Code, which permitted seeking support only from organizations that "regularly" made recommendations to appointing authorities, and only from those individuals who had been invited by the appointing or confirming authority to provide information to them, Rule 4.3(B) permits a candidate for appointment to judicial office to seek endorsements from any person or organization, thus relaxing the restrictions on organizations or individuals from whom a candidate for appointive judicial office can seek support. Rule 4.3 thus helps to ensure that sources of informed comments that might have been overlooked have the opportunity to contribute their recommendations concerning candidates for appointment. For a history of Canon 5B(2) see Lisa L. Milord, *The Development of the ABA Judicial Code* 52 (1992).

New Comment [1] specifically reminds candidates for appointment to judicial office that they may not make improper pledges or promises about particular results to be reached in future cases, and may not make recklessly false or misleading statements in connection with the appointment process. Charles G. Geyh & W. William Hodes, *Reporters' Notes to the Model Code of Judicial Conduct* 110 (2009).

ANNOTATION

Rule 4.3 is devoted to candidates seeking appointment to judicial office. Unlike Rule 4.2, Rule 4.3 contains no exceptions to the prohibitions of Rule 4.1, but it does affirmatively permit certain activities. *See, e.g.*, Neb. Jud. Ethics Adv. Comm. Op. 94-1 (1994) (candidates for appointment to judicial office are permitted to seek support or endorsements from individuals other than, and in addition to, the individuals the nominating commission requests candidates to name in their application papers).

Although seeking endorsements for the appointed position is permitted, there may be limitations placed upon the process. *See, e.g.*, Kan. Jud. Ethics Op. JE 141 (2006) (judge seeking district court appointment may not ask lawyer who has appeared or may appear before judge for letter of support to nominating commission); Fla. Comm. on Stands. of Cond. Governing Judges Op. 93-13 (1993) (sitting judge who is judicial nominating commission nominee for appointment by governor to another judicial office is prohibited from appearing before partisan political group along with other nominees for appointment to be interviewed so that partisan political group may make recommendation to governor); Joanna M. Shepherd, *Are Appointed Judges Strategic Too?*, 58 Duke L.J. 1589 (Apr. 2009) (analyzing whether appointed judges vote strategically to avoid reappointment denials).

Even a lawyer who is subject to merit selection, rather than election, may be subject to Canon 4 restrictions. In ABA Informal Op. 85-1513 (1985), a lawyer applied for an initial appointment to a then-existing judicial vacancy and was solicited to attend a political fund-raising event. The ABA Standing Committee on Ethics and Professional Responsibility stated that the political activity proscriptions of Canon 7A, in effect at the time, applied to candidates for judicial appointment under a merit selection plan, and prohibited the candidate from participating in political fund-raising. *See also* Alaska Bar Ass'n Ethics Op. 85-1 (1985) (adopting ABA Informal Op. 85-1513).

RULE 4.4 CAMPAIGN COMMITTEES

(A) A judicial candidate* subject to public election* may establish a campaign committee to manage and conduct a campaign for the candidate, subject to the provisions of this Code. The candidate is responsible for ensuring that his or her campaign committee complies with applicable provisions of this Code and other applicable law.*

(B) A judicial candidate subject to public election shall direct his or her campaign committee:

(1) to solicit and accept only such campaign contributions* as are reasonable, in any event not to exceed, in the aggregate,* $[insert amount] from any individual or $[insert amount] from any entity or organization;

(2) not to solicit or accept contributions for a candidate's current campaign more than [insert amount of time] before the applicable primary election, caucus, or

general or retention election, nor more than [insert number] days after the last election in which the candidate participated; and

(3) to comply with all applicable statutory requirements for disclosure and divestiture of campaign contributions, and to file with [name of appropriate regulatory authority] a report stating the name, address, occupation, and employer of each person who has made campaign contributions to the committee in an aggregate value exceeding $[insert amount]. The report must be filed within [insert number] days following an election, or within such other period as is provided by law.

COMMENT

[1] Judicial candidates are prohibited from personally soliciting campaign contributions or personally accepting campaign contributions. See Rule 4.1(A)(8). This Rule recognizes that in many jurisdictions, judicial candidates must raise campaign funds to support their candidacies, and permits candidates, other than candidates for appointive judicial office, to establish campaign committees to solicit and accept reasonable financial contributions or in-kind contributions.

[2] Campaign committees may solicit and accept campaign contributions, manage the expenditure of campaign funds, and generally conduct campaigns. Candidates are responsible for compliance with the requirements of election law and other applicable law, and for the activities of their campaign committees.

[3] At the start of a campaign, the candidate must instruct the campaign committee to solicit or accept only such contributions as are reasonable in amount, appropriate under the circumstances, and in conformity with applicable law. Although lawyers and others who might appear before a successful candidate for judicial office are permitted to make campaign contributions, the candidate should instruct his or her campaign committee to be especially cautious in connection with such contributions, so they do not create grounds for disqualification if the candidate is elected to judicial office. See Rule 2.11.

1990 CODE COMPARISON

Rule 4.4 and its Comment are essentially the same as Canon 5C of the 1990 Code. Rule 4.4(A) combines aspects of the second sentence of Canon 5C(2), part of Canon 5C(4), and some of the Commentary following Canon 5C(2). Rule 4.4(B)(1) combines and recasts material from both Canon 5C(2) and Canon 5C(3). Rule 4.4(B)(2) is essentially the same as the fifth sentence of Canon 5C(2), but with additional language citing compliance with any applicable laws relating to divestiture of campaign funds subsequent to the campaign. Rule 4.4(A) makes explicit what was implicit or assumed in former Canon 5: candidates are responsible for the actions of their campaign committees. Charles G. Geyh & W. William Hodes, *Reporters' Notes to the Model Code of Judicial Conduct* 112 (2009).

Rule 4.4(B)(1) requires that campaign contributions be "reasonable" in amount and imposes aggregate dollar limits per campaign for individuals and organizations making donations. Each jurisdiction sets its own limit. In Rule 4.4(B)(2), the Commission added the word "current" before the word "campaign," and left it to each jurisdiction to determine how long after an election a candidate may solicit contributions to pay off campaign expenses. *Id.* at 112–13.

Rule 4.4(B)(3) is based upon Canon 5C(4), but includes an entirely new reference to divestiture of campaign funds. The Rule recognizes that many jurisdictions already have provisions in their general election and campaign finance laws regarding disclosure and divestiture of campaign funds, and defers to local law in setting the specific details. Rule 4.4(B)(3) requires candidates to direct their campaign committees to learn about and comply with whatever local regulations are in place. *Id.* at 113.

ANNOTATION

CAMPAIGN COMMITTEES

A judicial candidate who wants to engage in traditional campaign activities must, pursuant to Rules 4.2(B) and 4.4, establish a campaign committee to do so. *See, e.g., Simes v. Ark. Judicial Discipline & Disability Comm'n*, 247 S.W.3d 876 (Ark. 2007) (provision that forbids judges from soliciting campaign contributions except through campaign committees narrowly tailored to the state's interests in judicial impartiality and open-mindedness); *In re Cannizzaro*, No. 05-O-0524 (La. Sup. Ct. Comm. on Judicial Ethics, 2005) (judge failed to use campaign committee to solicit and accept contributions); *In re Suder*, 398 S.E.2d 162 (W. Va. 1992) (judge's failure to form a committee to solicit or accept funds violates Canon); N.M. Adv. Comm. on the Code of Jud. Cond. Op. 10-02 (2010) (New Mexico Code "is mandatory in its language requiring judicial candidates to establish campaign committees").

It has been suggested, however, that a candidate who is self-funding his or her campaign is not required to establish a campaign committee. *See* N.Y. Adv. Comm. on Jud. Ethics Op. 08-43 (2008) (candidate for election to judicial office who finances his/her entire campaign with personal funds and neither solicits nor accepts any campaign contributions from any source is not ethically required to form campaign committee); W. Va. Adv. Op. 12/28/07 (2007). *But see* W. Va. Adv. Op. 1/12/00 (2000) (judicial candidate is required to have campaign committee if candidate wishes to conduct traditional campaign activities such as mailings, brochures, media advertisements, and other such activity even though candidate will personally finance such activities).

The restrictions in the Rule cannot be circumvented by calling a campaign committee something else. Okla. Jud. Ethics Adv. Panel Op. 2008-02 (2008) (lawyer who intends to become candidate for judicial office at next election cycle may not establish political action committee as opposed to "candidate committee" in excess of one year before filing period for purpose of soliciting support and campaign contributions).

A campaign committee may conduct a campaign through advertisements, brochures, mailings, candidate forums, and other means not prohibited by law. Fla. Sup. Ct. Jud. Ethics Adv. Comm. Op. 10-28 (2010) (campaign committee may host website and Facebook page supporting candidate).

The committee may also obtain public statements of support for the candidate, accept and solicit reasonable contributions, and manage the expenditure of campaign funds. *See, e.g.*, Fla. Sup. Ct. Jud. Ethics Adv. Comm. Op. 10-21 (2010) (candidate's committee's website may contain "contribute" button); Fla. Sup. Ct. Jud. Ethics Adv. Comm. Op. 00-19 (2000) (candidate for appointment to judicial office, who also is candidate for election to judicial office, may raise funds through campaign committee); Ga. Jud. Qualifications Comm'n Op. 205 (1996) (candidates may personally establish campaign committees to seek public expressions of support or other form of written endorsement); Ill. Jud. Ethics Comm. Op. 96-1 (1996) (judicial candidate or family member is not prohibited from signing campaign fund checks to pay campaign expenses); W. Va. Adv. Op. 12/2/02 (2002) (fund-raiser to be held to pay off campaign debts would be in compliance with judicial code so long as fund-raiser was conducted by candidate's campaign committee; fact that idea for fund-raiser was initiated by lawyers or that campaign debts were those of candidate and candidate's parent would not affect result); W. Va. Adv. Op. 9/28/01 (2001) (judge and unsuccessful candidate for higher judicial office must form a committee in order to solicit funds to retire campaign debt); W. Va. Adv. Op. 9/23/96 (1996) (candidate for judicial office may establish committee or responsible person to accept campaign contributions, but may not personally accept campaign contributions). *See also* Ark. Jud. Ethics Advisory Comm. Op. 95-04 (1995) (setting forth guidelines regarding what a judicial candidate's campaign committee is ethically permitted to do including: preparing list of important individuals in the district, contacting those individuals on behalf of the candidate and asking for publicly stated support; soliciting names for newspaper advertisements, volunteers to make phone calls to the community, and signatures on widely distributed post cards; seeking publicly stated support from an organization or a well-known individual or public figure, soliciting funds within time periods set forth in the code).

A judicial candidate may select a public official, elected in a partisan campaign, to head his or her campaign committee provided that "neither the candidate nor the campaign committee . . . make any reference to the official's public office or political affiliation in any official campaign materials, filings, press releases or similar information disseminated to the public." Ky. Jud. Ethics Op. JE-124 (2013). *See generally* David B. Koch, *Futures Trading in Judicial Election*, Washington Bar Ass'n Bar News (June 2000); Roy Schotland, *Elective Judges Campaign Financing: Are State Judges' Robes the Emperor's Clothes of American Democracy?* 2 J.L. & Pol'y 57 (1985).

An individual who is simultaneously a candidate for appointive judicial office and a candidate for elective judicial office may form a committee to solicit or accept funds for his or her candidacy for election to that same office. *See* Tenn. Jud. Ethics Comm. Adv. Op. 00-01 (2000) (advising that to "interpret the applicable judicial Canons to prohibit a candidate for appointment from forming committees to solicit contributions for the foreseeable election campaign would place the judicial appointee at an unfair disadvantage and on unequal footings with those candidates not seeking appointment").

Time Limitations on Pre-Election Fund-Raising

Rule 4.4 applies to "current" campaigns, meaning that the time window for a campaign committee to solicit funds applies to each campaign separately. To prevent candidates from engaging in too early a buildup of campaign funds, each jurisdiction should establish the point in time at which contributions may be solicited and accepted. Some states have adopted more restrictive limitations on pre-election fund-raising. *See* Okla. Jud. Ethics Op. 2008-2 (2008) (lawyer who intends to become candidate for judicial office at next election cycle may not establish "political action committee" as opposed to a "candidate committee" in excess of one year before filing period, for the purpose of soliciting support and campaign contributions; state judicial code provides that candidate may establish committee of responsible persons to perform these acts on candidate's behalf no earlier than 90 days before election filing period); S.D. Code of Judicial Conduct, Canon 5C(2) (providing that a "candidate's campaign committee may solicit contributions for the candidate's campaign no earlier than January first of the election year").

A judge or judicial candidate may form a campaign committee before the fund-raising period begins. *See* Mich. Comm. on Jud. Ethics. Op. JI-74 (1993) (candidate may form and register a campaign committee prior to its 180-day fund-raising period); Ohio Bd. of Commissioners on Grievances and Disc. Op. 97-06 (1997) (incumbent judge may form campaign committee prior to time period for soliciting and receiving funds; by forming such committee, the incumbent judge becomes a "judicial candidate" subject to any restrictions placed on "judicial candidates").

A candidate's committee may also be permitted to accept personal contributions from the candidate and unsolicited contributions before the fund-raising period begins, but may be restricted in expending those unsolicited funds. *See* Mich. Comm. on Jud. Ethics Op. JI-74 (1993) (committee may use the personal contributions made by the candidate prior to 180-day fund-raising period begins, but may expend unsolicited contributions only within fund-raising period); *but see* Ohio Bd. of Commissioners on Grievances and Disc. Op. 97-06 (1997) (because there is no express prohibition in Canon 7, an incumbent judge's judicial campaign committee may expend retained campaign funds outside the Canon 7C(4) time period for soliciting and receiving campaign funds). *See also* Nev. Stand. Comm. on Jud. Ethics and Election Prac. Op. JE 08-005 (2008) (judicial candidate may solicit and receive contributions for re-election campaign at a time when it may not yet be possible to determine whether candidate will or will not be opposed).

Constitutionality of Time Restrictions

In *O'Toole v. O'Connor*, the Sixth Circuit Court of Appeals upheld the dismissal of a judicial candidate campaign committee's motion for a preliminary injunction to enjoin enforcement of time restrictions on judicial campaign fund-raising. *O'Toole v. O'Connor*, 802 F.3d 783 (6th Cir. 2015). The plaintiff challenged Ohio Code of Judicial Conduct Rule 4.4(E), claiming it violated "both the First Amendment and the Equal Protection Clause of the Fourteenth Amendment . . . by unconstitutionally restricting campaign committees' core political speech" and "by treating judicial campaign committees differently than other political organizations." *Id.* at 788–89.

Citing *Williams-Yulee v. Fla. Bar*, 575 U.S. ____, 135 S. Ct. 1656, 1664, 191 L. Ed. 2d 570 (2015), the Sixth Circuit found that a state's compelling interest in judicial impartiality, integrity, and independence extended beyond a judge's direct solicitation of campaign funds to solicitations conducted by judicial campaign committees. *O'Toole*, 802 F.3d at 789. The Court also rejected plaintiff's argument that the prohibition could have been more narrowly drawn. The Court, again citing *Williams-Yulee*, held that narrow tailoring need not be perfect tailoring and that plaintiff failed to show that the rule was unconstitutionally overbroad in violation of the First Amendment. *Id.* at 791. The Sixth Circuit also rejected plaintiff's argument that the time restriction for fund-raising violated the Equal Protection Clause of the Fourteenth Amendment because, in part, it "impermissibly treats judicial campaign committees differently than political action committees and other political organizations that are not subject to comparable restrictions." *O'Toole v. O'Connor*, 802 F.3d at 791. The Court rejected the argument, noting the unique nature of judicial campaigns allows states to regulate judicial campaigns differently than campaigns for political office.

One federal district court has held that Florida's Code of Judicial Conduct provision, which prohibits supporters from soliciting the public for contributions to judicial campaigns earlier than one year prior to election, violates the rights of expression guaranteed by the First Amendment. *Zeller v. The Florida Bar*, 909 F. Supp. 1518 (N.D. Fla. 1995); *cf. State v. Alaska Civil Liberties Union*, 978 P.2d 597 (Alaska 1999), *cert. denied*, 528 U.S. 1153 (2000) (statutory ban on pre-election campaign contributions to candidate for state and local elections was invalid, but ban on post-election contributions was valid).

Time Limitations on Post-Election Fund-Raising

Rule 4.4(B)(2) leaves it to each jurisdiction to determine how long after an election a candidate may solicit contributions to pay off campaign expenses. *See, e.g.*, N.Y. Ct. Rules §§ 100.0(Q) and 100.5(A)(5) (judicial candidates who do not run in the general election can raise funds for six months after the primary, convention, caucus, or meeting, while candidates who run in the general election may raise funds for six months after the general election); N.Y. Adv. Comm. on Jud. Ethics Op. 97-41 (1997) (judge may attend fund-raising event held on judge's behalf within six-month window following general election that resulted in judge's re-election); Ohio Code of Judicial Conduct Canons 7C(4)(a), (b) and (c) (expressly providing that candidates who participate in the general election may raise funds until 120 days after the general election; a defeated or withdrawn judicial candidate must end fund-raising at the earlier of the time the campaign debt is paid off or 120 days after the defeat or withdrawal); Tex. Adv. Comm. on Jud. Ethics Op. 176 (1995) (judge or judicial candidate may solicit and accept contributions later than 120 days after general election). *See also* Kan. Jud. Ethics Op. JE 68 (1996) (campaign committee may solicit funds for 90 days after election even though candidate was unopposed; contributions received after general election may be used to pay expenses and indebtedness incurred in earlier primary election); Jud. Ethics Comm. of the Pa. Conf. of State Trial Judges Formal Op. 2002-1 (2002) (judicial candidate who has withdrawn candidacy must end fund-raising when campaign debt has been extinguished or by December 31 of election year, whichever occurs first).

Some jurisdictions measure the ending time for fund-raising from the number of days after the last election in which the judicial candidate participates during the election year, and do not expressly address withdrawn candidates. *See, e.g.*, Alabama Canons of Judicial Ethics, Canon 7B(4)(b) (120 days); Nebraska Code of Judicial Conduct, Canon 5C(2) (30 days); North Dakota Code of Judicial Conduct, Canon 5C(2) (90 days); South Dakota Code of Judicial Conduct, Canon 5C(2) (December 31st of the election year); Washington Code of Judicial Conduct, Canon 7B(2) (60 days) (proposed new Washington Code of Judicial Conduct Rule 4.4(B)(2) would allow acceptance of contributions after the election "only as permitted by law." The Kentucky Code of Judicial Conduct prohibits any fund-raising after the general election. Kentucky Rules of the Supreme Court 4.300, Code of Judicial Conduct, Canon 5B(2). Louisiana permits post-election fund-raising only for the purpose of extinguishing campaign debt resulting from that election. Louisiana Code of Judicial Conduct, Canon 7D(3).

Solicitation versus Acceptance of Campaign Funds

Tennessee's Judicial Ethics Committee advises that that the 90-day limitation applies only to the *solicitation* of political campaign funds for a judicial candidate. According to the Committee, there is no time limitation on the *acceptance* of political campaign funds under the Canon. Therefore, even if the 90-day time limit has passed, a candidate's campaign committee may accept campaign funds that were solicited within 90 days after the election and may accept any unsolicited campaign funds. Tenn. Jud. Ethics Comm. Adv. Op. 01-01 (2001).

Unopposed Candidates

In states that retain the "active opposition" language, judicial candidates who are running unopposed are not prohibited from setting up a campaign committee to solicit campaign contributions. *See, e.g.*, Fla. Comm. on Stands. of Cond. Governing Judges Op. 76-15 (1976) (candidate for judicial office, either incumbent or not, may solicit or accept campaign contributions through campaign committee before he or she has active and announced opposition; reference to "active opposition" does not limit or otherwise prohibit candidate for judicial office from soliciting or accepting campaign contributions as long as judicial candidate complies with Canons and campaign reporting laws). *See also* Ark. Jud. Ethics Adv. Comm. Op. 96-02 (1996) (candidate for judicial office who is unopposed in primary election may, pursuant to Arkansas Canon 5C(2), solicit contributions for 45 days after filing deadline for party candidates or filing deadline for independent candidates, whichever is later); N.M. Adv. Comm. on the Code of Jud. Cond. Op. 06-05 (2006) (unopposed magistrate judge's campaign may engage in fund-raising to retire the outstanding debt of campaign). A candidate who is running unopposed and who is not campaigning is not required to establish a campaign committee. *See* W. Va. Adv. Ops. 3/8/00 & 3/13/00 (2000) (unopposed judicial candidate who does not intend to engage in campaigning is not required to establish campaign committee or hire treasurer).

Excess Funds

Some states have judicial code provisions for disposition of excess campaign funds. *See* Arkansas Code of Judicial Conduct Rule 4.4(C) ("Any campaign fund surplus shall be returned to the contributors or turned over to the State Treasurer as provided by law."); Ark. Jud. Ethics Adv. Op. 93-04 (1993) (violation of judicial code for judicial campaign surplus fund to exist); Michigan Code of Judicial Conduct, Canon 7B(2)(f) ("[A]ny candidate or committee having funds remaining after payment of all campaign expenses shall either return such funds to the contributors thereof or donate the funds to the client security fund of the State Bar of Michigan, not later than January 1 following the election."); Nevada Code of Judicial Conduct Rule 4.2(A)(6) ("If elected to judicial office, a candidate who received contributions that were not spent or committed for expenditure as a result of the campaign may dispose of the money" by returning the unspent money to contributors; donating the money to the general fund of the state, county, or city relating to the judge's office; using the money in the judge's next election or for the payment of other expenses related to the judge's public office or the judge's previous campaigns for judicial office; or donating the money to any tax-exempt nonprofit entity, including a nonprofit state or local bar association, the Administrative Office of the Courts or any foundation entrusted with the distribution of Interest on Lawyer's Trust Accounts funds. Any other disposition of the money is prohibited); Nev. Stand. Comm. on Jud. Ethics and Election Prac. Op. JE11-004 (2011) (excess campaign funds may be used to pay bona fide costs incurred to travel and attend conferences, reach out to voters, attend meetings and charitable events); New Mexico Code of Judicial Conduct Rule 21-404B ("A candidate for judicial office in either a partisan, nonpartisan, or retention election who has unused campaign funds remaining after election, and after all expenses of the campaign and election have been paid, shall refund the remaining funds pro rata to the campaign contributors, or donate the funds to a charitable organization, or to the State of New Mexico, as the candidate may choose, within thirty (30) days after the date the election results are certified.").

New York has allowed for other limited uses of the funds. N.Y. Adv. Comm. on Jud. Ethics Op. 12-129 (A)-(G) (2012) (nonjudge candidate may use unexpended campaign funds to host modest event to thank campaign volunteers); N.Y. Adv. Comm. on Jud. Ethics Op. 12-95(A) (2012) (unexpended campaign funds totaling less than $1,000 may be treated as de minimis, not returned to donors on pro rata basis, but used for any lawful non-political purpose connected with judicial office); N.Y Adv. Comm. on Jud. Ethics Op. 07-187 (2007) (recently elected judge may retain small portion of unexpended campaign funds to pay for tickets to political events that judge will attend during window period and for modest victory reception to be held during window period and may return remainder to donors on pro rata basis before window period expires; at end of window period, campaign treasurer must return any remaining unexpended campaign funds to judge's donors on pro rata basis); *but see* W. Va. Adv. Op. 9/19/08 (2008) (impermissible for judge to donate excess campaign funds to county or state Democratic Executive Committee because judicial code provides that a "candidate shall not use or permit the use of campaign contributions for the private benefit of the candidate or others").

A candidate who receives a refund due to an overcharge for campaign services after the time period for soliciting funds has expired may be permitted to apply the late-arriving refund to an unsatisfied campaign debt. Mich. Comm. on Jud. Ethics Op. JI-63 (1992) (refund on a paid expense is not a "campaign fund").

SUPPORT AND CONTRIBUTIONS FROM LAWYERS

Rule 4.4 Comment [3] states that "[a]lthough lawyers and others who might appear before a successful candidate for judicial office are permitted to make campaign contributions, the candidate should instruct his or her campaign committee to be especially cautious in connection with such contributions, so they do not create grounds for disqualification if the candidate is elected to judicial office." Most of the ethics opinions addressing this issue involve the permissibility, under lawyer ethics rules, of lawyers endorsing judicial candidates. *See, e.g.,* Conn. Bar Ass'n Comm. on Prof. Ethics Op. 13 (1988) (lawyers may speak on radio on behalf of judicial candidate and run newspaper advertisement on behalf of candidate containing list of lawyers, identified as such, endorsing candidate); ABA Informal Op. 948 (1966) (county bar association would not violate Canons of Ethics by conducting poll wherein members of bar are asked to express opinion as to whether incumbent judge or incumbent county attorney is or is not qualified to hold office); ABA Informal Op. 841 (1965) (local bar association may endorse candidate for appointment to federal bench; not improper for association to poll its members to determine their opinion as to qualifications of prospective appointees). *See also* ABA Informal Op. 817 (1965) (judicial candidate may announce that he has support of X number of former local bar association presidents or that he is endorsed by X number of lawyers whose names are listed). With regard to a lawyer's endorsement of judicial candidate, ABA Formal Opinion 189 (1938) states the following:

> Lawyers are better able than laymen to appraise accurately the qualifications of candidates for judicial office. It is proper that they should make that appraisal known to the voters in a proper and dignified manner. A lawyer may with propriety endorse a candidate for judicial office and seek like endorsement from other lawyers. But the lawyer who endorses a judicial candidate or seeks that endorsement from other lawyers should be actuated by a sincere belief in the superior qualifications of the candidate for judicial service and not by personal or selfish motives; and a lawyer should not use or attempt to use the power or prestige of the judicial office to secure such endorsement.

In addition to endorsements, a judicial candidate's campaign committee is permitted to solicit and accept "reasonable campaign contributions" from lawyers. *See, e.g.*, Ohio Bd. of Commissioners on Grievances and Disc., Op. 90-24 (1990) (judge's campaign committee may solicit campaign contributions from lawyers); Wash. Ethics Adv. Comm. Op. 86-17 (1986) (campaign committees are not prohibited from soliciting campaign contributions and public support from lawyers or others); *cf.* Fla. Sup. Ct. Comm. on Stands. of Cond. Governing Judges Op. 82-10 (1982) (unopposed judge may accept unsolicited campaign contributions from lawyers); Michigan Code of Judicial Conduct, Canon 7B(2)(c) (providing that campaign committees "may solicit public support from lawyers," but "are prohibited from soliciting campaign contributions from lawyers in excess of $100 per lawyer").

A judicial candidate may not, however, personally solicit a contribution from a lawyer. *See In re Lantz*, 402 So. 2d 1144 (Fla. 1981) (judge reprimanded for misconduct including directly soliciting election support from member of bar); *In re Hotchkiss*, 327 N.W.2d 312 (Mich. 1982) (judge who was candidate for re-election improperly solicited campaign contribution from lawyer and his law firm over telephone); *In re Tennant*, 516 S.E.2d 496 (W. Va. 1999) (candidate for magistrate violated Canon by personally soliciting campaign contributions from two lawyers). *See generally* James J. Alfini and Terrence J. Brooks, *Ethical Constraints on Judicial Election Campaigns: A Review and Critique of Canon 7*, 77 Ky. L. J. 671 (1989) (describing situation in which judges preside over cases in which parties are represented by counsel who have contributed in varying amounts to judicial campaigns); Mark Andrew Grannis, Note, *Safeguarding the Litigant's Constitutional Right to a Fair and Impartial Forum: A Due Process Approach to Improprieties Arising from Judicial Campaign Contributions from Lawyers*, 86 Mich. L. Rev. 382, 406–10 (1987) (suggesting recusal for judges who receive contributions from lawyers). *Cf.* Michelle L. Bullard, Comment, *Collier v. Griffith: Determining Whether Tennessee State Court Judges Should Recuse Themselves from Cases Which Involve Attorneys in Leadership Positions in Their Campaigns for Re-election*, 23 Memphis St. U. L. Rev. 741 (1993).

Lawyers and law firms contributing to judicial candidates must be sure to adhere to applicable lawyer conduct rules. *See In re Lidov*, 544 N.E.2d 294 (Ill. 1989) (making campaign contribution in form of loan directly to trial judge constituted violation of disciplinary rule of state code of professional responsibility); Darcie Cobden, Comment, *"Ms. Placed" Presumptions in the Texas Election Code: Texas Legislature Tightening the Old Ball and Chain on Political Contributions Made by the Spouses of Lawyers*, 50 S. Tex. L. Rev. 529 (2009). *See also* ABA Informal Op. 1281 (1973) (proper for lawyers to participate in or contribute financial assistance to bi-partisan citizens' action committee whose purpose is to support election of competent and qualified judges and lawyers to the bench); ABA Comm. on Prof'l Ethics & Grievances, Formal Op. 226 (1941) (lawyer may contribute to campaign of judge or lawyer, who is seeking judicial office, before whom lawyer is likely to appear if candidate is elected; preferably, contribution should be made to campaign committee rather than candidate). In 2002, the ABA adopted Model Rule of Professional Conduct 7.6, which prohibits lawyers and law firms from making political contributions to obtain government legal engagements or appointments by judges. *See generally Annotated Model Rules of Professional Conduct* 636 (8th ed. 2015) (explaining background and purpose of rule); *A Legislative History: The Development of the ABA Model Rules of Professional Conduct 1982–2013* 825 (2013).

CONTRIBUTIONS FROM LAWYERS CREATING APPEARANCE OF IMPARTIALITY REQUIRING RECUSAL

In 2005–06, 44 percent of the contributions to state high court candidates came from business groups, and 21 percent came from lawyers. *See The New Politics of Judicial Elections 2006* (Justice at Stake Campaign 2007). A number of courts have held that a campaign contribution from a lawyer who appears before a judge or from that lawyer's client generally does not raise a question as to the judge's impartiality requiring recusal. *See Ex parte Kenneth D. McLeod, Sr., Family Ltd. Partnership XV*, 725 So. 2d 271 (Ala. 1998) (since there is no evidence of bias on trial judge's part, court finds request for a new trial on the basis of a party's campaign contribution to the judge "borders on the frivolous"); *Lueg v. Lueg*, 976 S.W.2d 308 (Tex. App. 1998) ("Texas courts repeatedly have rejected the notion that a judge's acceptance of campaign contributions from lawyers creates bias necessitating recusal, or even an appearance of impropriety."); Ill. Jud. Ethics Comm. Op. 93-11 (1993) (judge is not obliged to disqualify himself or herself from proceeding because lawyer or party was campaign contributor); Wash. Ethics Adv. Comm. Op. 96-15 (1996) (judge may ask attorney general to serve as honorary co-chair of judge's re-election committee and may list name and title of attorney general on campaign letterhead); Wash. Ethics Adv. Comm. Op. 88-7 (1988) (judge may hear matters presented by lawyer who has formed campaign committee for judge's candidacy for another judicial position if there is disclosure of relationship and lawyers and parties, independently of judge's participation, all agree in writing or on record that campaign relationship is immaterial). *See generally* Bradley A. Siciliano, Note, *Attorney Contributions in Judicial Campaigns: Creating the Appearance of Impropriety*, 20 Hofstra L. Rev. 217 (1991); Stuart Banner, Note, *Disqualifying Elected Judges from Cases Involving Campaign Contributors*, 40 Stan. L. Rev. 449 (1988); Mark Andrew Grannis, Note, *Safe Guarding the Litigant's Constitutional Right to a Fair and Impartial Forum: A Due Process Approach to Improprieties Arising from Judicial Campaign Contributions from Lawyers*,

86 Mich. L. Rev. 382 (1987) (suggesting that recusal is an inadequate remedy in the context of judicial campaign contributions from lawyers and that preventing improper influence, by severely limiting lawyers' contributions to judicial candidates, is the best way for states with elected judiciaries to ensure the impartiality of their judges).

At least one state, Mississippi, provides that "[a] party may file a motion to recuse a judge based on the fact that an opposing party or counsel of record for that party is a major donor to the election campaign of such judge." Mississippi Code of Judicial Conduct, Canon 3E(2). Earlier proposed language, now withdrawn, would have made recusal mandatory in cases involving a major donor. The Mississippi code defines a "major donor" as a donor "who or which has, in the judge's most recent election campaign, made a contribution to the judge's campaign of (a) more than $2,000 if the judge is a justice of the Supreme Court or judge of the Court of Appeals, or (b) more than $1,000 if the judge is a judge of a court other than the Supreme Court or the Court of Appeals."

Some courts and state ethics committees encourage judges to disclose to all parties when they are aware that a party or a party's lawyer has contributed to their campaigns, particularly if the contribution is extraordinary in amount. *See, e.g.*, Nev. Stand. Comm. on Jud. Ethics and Election Prac. Op. JE 02-001 (2002) (when contribution is extraordinary in amount, disclosure should be made and judge should determine if recusal is required).

CONTRIBUTIONS FROM POLITICAL PARTIES

A judge may accept a campaign contribution from a political party. Nev. Stand. Comm. on Jud. Ethics and Election Prac. Op. 12-008 (2012).

USING CAMPAIGN CONTRIBUTIONS FOR PRIVATE BENEFIT OF CANDIDATE OR OTHERS

Permitted expenditures must be "directly attributable to the election campaign." Fla. Comm. on Stands. of Cond. Governing Judges Op. 88-13a (1988) (campaign contributions may be used for payment of qualifying fee, expenses incurred in traveling to state capitol for filing of qualifying documents if such documents are delivered in person, and for reimbursement of campaign related gas consumption, hotel, and meal costs and travel expenses of candidate's spouse if candidate determines that the presence of his or her spouse is essential to the candidacy). *See also* N.Y. Adv. Comm. on Jud. Ethics Op. 97-80, 1997 WL 1133748 (1997) (judge who is up for re-election should not participate in campaign bank account maintained by political organization in which contributions received by organization on behalf of judge are mingled with contributions received on behalf of other judicial and nonjudicial candidates). However, a campaign committee may be permitted to reimburse a judicial candidate for personal funds expended for campaign-related expenses from funds raised during the campaign. N.Y. Adv. Comm. on Jud. Ethics Op. 98-132, 1998 WL 1674741 (1998).

LIMITATIONS ON AMOUNT OF CAMPAIGN CONTRIBUTIONS

Canon 5C(3), which was added to the Code in 1999, stated that "[a] candidate shall instruct his or her campaign committee(s) at the start of the campaign not to accept campaign contributions for any election that exceed, in the aggregate, [$] from an individual or [$] from an entity. This limitation is in addition to the limitations provided in Section 5C(2)." *See* ABA *Ad Hoc Committee on Judicial Campaign Finance, Standing Committee on Ethics and Professional Responsibility, ABA Judicial Division, ABA Special Committee on Judicial Independence Report 123 to the House of Delegates* (ABA Annual Meeting, Atlanta, Georgia, Aug. 9–10, 1999). Rule 4.4(B)(1) is essentially the same as Canon 5C(3), but also includes an element from Canon 5C(2). The Rule requires that campaign contributions be "reasonable" in amount (to avoid a suggestion of undue influence) and imposes aggregate dollar limits (per campaign) for individuals and organizations making donations; the specific limits to be set in each jurisdiction.

Some states have imposed limitations on campaign contributions either by limiting the amount of contributions from individuals, groups, or committees to any single candidate or by limiting the amount of aggregate contributions from an individual or entity to all candidates in an election. For example, Alaska permits a political party to contribute to a judge seeking retention an amount not to exceed $5,000 per year. Alaska Stat. § 15.13.070 (2002). Arkansas, California, Connecticut, and Kansas limit contributions to committees or political parties by using a combination of approaches, including limits on how much an individual may give to a political party or political action committee (PAC); a corporation, union or organization may give to a political party or PAC; a political party may give to another political party or PAC; and a PAC may give to another PAC or political party.

CAMPAIGN COMMITTEE DISCLOSURE REPORTS

Rule 4.4(B)(3) requires judicial candidates subject to public election to comply with all applicable statutory requirements for disclosure and divestiture of campaign contributions, and to file with the appropriate regulatory authority a report stating the name, address, occupation, and employer of each person who made campaign contributions to the committee in an aggregate value exceeding a specified amount. The provision contains a blank for the time period by which the report must be filed, as required by the particular jurisdiction. Most states also have statutes requiring judges to file a statement disclosing the names and addresses of campaign contributors and the amount of each contribution made. *See, e.g.*, Ala. Code § 12-24-2 (2003); Ariz. Rev. Stat. Ann. § 16-916 (2003). *Cf.* Wash. Ethics Adv. Comm. Op. 88-07 (1988) (judge may hear matters presented by lawyer who has formed campaign committee for judge's candidacy for another judicial position if there is disclosure of campaign relationship and lawyers and parties, independently of judge's participation, all agree in writing or on record that campaign relationship is immaterial). *See generally* Geoffrey P. Miller, *Bad Judges*, 83 Tex. L. Rev. 431, 474 (2004) (arguing that one method of systematic reform for dealing with bad judges is to increase public disclosure about judges); Ian Ayres, *The Donation Booth: Mandating Donor Anonymity to Disrupt the Market for Political Influence*, 50 Stan. L. Rev. 837, 844 (1998) (public disclosure produces very little deterrent benefit); Maura A. Schoshinski, Note, *Towards an Independent, Fair, and Competent Judiciary: An Argument for Improving Judicial Elections*, 7 Geo. J. Legal Ethics 839 (1994) (advocating in favor of requiring actual and complete public disclosure of all aspects of campaign financing, and establishing election monitors and watch groups who also can encourage voluntary limits on spending and advise on disqualification).

RULE 4.5 ACTIVITIES OF JUDGES WHO BECOME CANDIDATES FOR NONJUDICIAL OFFICE

(A) Upon becoming a candidate for a nonjudicial elective office, a judge shall resign from judicial office, unless permitted by law* to continue to hold judicial office.

(B) Upon becoming a candidate for a nonjudicial appointive office, a judge is not required to resign from judicial office, provided that the judge complies with the other provisions of this Code.

COMMENT

[1] In campaigns for nonjudicial elective public office, candidates may make pledges, promises, or commitments related to positions they would take and ways they would act if elected to office. Although appropriate in nonjudicial campaigns, this manner of campaigning is inconsistent with the role of a judge, who must remain fair and impartial to all who come before him or her. The potential for misuse of the judicial office, and the political promises that the judge would be compelled to make in the course of campaigning for nonjudicial elective office, together dictate that a judge who wishes to run for such an office must resign upon becoming a candidate.

[2] The "resign-to-run" rule set forth in paragraph (A) ensures that a judge cannot use the judicial office to promote his or her candidacy, and prevents post-campaign retaliation from the judge in the event the judge is defeated in the

election. When a judge is seeking appointive nonjudicial office, however, the dangers are not sufficient to warrant imposing the resign-to-run rule.

1990 Code Comparison

Rule 4.5 is largely derived from Canon 5A(2) and addresses the situation of a sitting judge who becomes a candidate for a nonjudicial office. In Rule 4.5(A), the Commission retained the traditional resign-to-run rule, with only minor revisions for style and clarity. The new Rule makes it explicit that the Rule applies to elective nonjudicial offices only. The special exemption that had appeared in the 1990 Code allowing judges to campaign for election to a state constitutional convention was eliminated, because of the rarity with which that situation occurs and because such service is easily captured in the Rule's language allowing that which is "permitted by law." Rule 4.5(B) makes it clear that, if a judge becomes a candidate for appointment to a nonjudicial office, the judge is not required to resign from judicial office as a general proposition. Charles G. Geyh & W. William Hodes, *Reporters' Notes to the Model Code of Judicial Conduct* 114 (2009).

Two new Comments were added to explain the rationale for applying the resign-to-run rule to elective nonjudicial offices, but not to appointive ones. Comments [1] and [2] explain that the resign-to-run rule is compelling only when elective nonjudicial offices are at stake. The danger that a candidate for an appointive nonjudicial office would be tempted to make pledges and promises incompatible with the obligations of judicial office is almost nonexistent, as is the danger that a judge who remained on the bench after a failed attempt to gain another office would use the judicial office to engage in retaliation. *Id.*

Additionally, because a sitting judge may become a candidate for an appointive nonjudicial office merely by being considered by an executive branch officer for appointment, the Commission concluded that it was unwarranted to require automatic resignation from the bench. Mandatory resignation would be especially harsh when an executive branch officer is considering several nominees for the same position, or when the confirmation process, if any, is lengthy, of uncertain outcome, or both. *Id.* at 115.

Annotation

Resigning to Run for Nonjudicial Elective Office

Rule 4.5(A) continues the resign-to-run requirement of Canon 5A(2) in the 1990 Code, with only minor revisions for style and clarity. The Reporter's Notes to the 1972 Model Code state that the drafting committee included this resignation requirement in order to avoid "the appearance of impropriety or of trading on the prestige and dignity of the judicial office," and because of the "fear of involving the court in political controversy." E. Wayne Thode, *Reporter's Notes to Code of Judicial Conduct* 97 (1973). *See, e.g., In re Freeman*, 995 So. 2d 1197 (La. 2008) (justice of the peace failed to resign his office when he became a candidate for the elected nonjudicial office of police juror); *In re Dunleavy*, 838 A.2d 338 (Me. 2003), *cert. denied*, 541 U.S. 960 (2004) (judge violated Canon 5A(2) when he chose to run for the state senate without resigning position as probate judge; however, discipline was not warranted because judge had not engaged in a pattern of unethical behavior and apparently acted in good faith and with an honest belief that the Code provisions at issue were both superseded by statute and unconstitutional); *Miss. Comm'n on Jud. Performance v. Haltom*, 681 So. 2d 1332 (Miss. 1996) (judge violated Canon by failing to resign as municipal judge while running for a board of supervisors, a nonjudicial office); *In re Buckson*, 610 A.2d 203 (Del. 1992) (judge sought endorsement of his party convention for nomination for office of Governor without first resigning his judicial office); *In re Peagler*, 401 S.E.2d 416 (S.C. 1991) (judge's action in continuing to serve as probate judge throughout primary and general elections when he was candidate for office of county supervisor warranted public reprimand); *In re Pressentin*, 406 N.W.2d 779 (Wis. 1987) (judge impermissibly campaigned for position of county supervisor while holding judicial office); Arkansas Jud. Ethics Op. 2008-01 (2008) (nothing in state judicial ethics code prohibits candidate from serving as city attorney for one city and district judge for another, but candidate must resign from judicial office to run for elective office); Fla. Comm. on Stands. of Cond. Governing Judges Op. 96-5 (1996) (traffic magistrate cannot ethically continue to serve in office while seeking election as sheriff); Ga. Jud. Qualifications Comm'n Op. No. 233 (2000) (dual service as part-time judge and member of the general assembly prohibited); Kan. Jud. Ethics Op. JE 120 (2004) (part-time municipal judge, serving as register of deeds, must resign when upon becoming candidate for re-election); Mich. Comm. on Jud. Ethics Op. JI-59 (1992) (friend of court referee is required to resign as referee prior to becoming candidate for city council); Mich. Comm. on Jud. Ethics Op. JI-10 (1989) (full-time, non-lawyer judicial district court administrator-magistrate is "judge" for purposes of code of judicial conduct and may not simultaneously hold judicial office and elected township clerk position); N.Y. Adv. Comm. on Judicial Ethics Op. 10-207 (2011) (judge must resign seat before running for commissioner of the fire district); Neb. Jud. Ethics Adv. Comm. Op. 02-1 (2002) (clerk magistrate may not be candidate for election to nonjudicial office (clerk of the district court) while remaining clerk magistrate); Nev. Stand. Comm. on Jud. Ethics and Election Prac. Op. 11-015 (2010) (judge may not retain judicial office after becoming candidate for district attorney); Nev. Stand. Comm. on Jud. Ethics and Election Prac. Op. JE 98-001 (2000) (elected, nonpartisan municipal judge may not run for and serve, if elected, as nonpartisan, non-paid Regent of University of Nevada system); N.M. Adv. Comm. on the Code of Jud. Cond. Op. 01-10 (2002) (part-time municipal judge must resign upon filing of statement of candidacy for nonjudicial office); *In re Vosburgh* (N.Y. State Comm'n on Jud. Cond. 1991) (judge should not run for or serve on school board); Wash. Ethics Adv. Comm. Op. 85-08 (1985) (improper for part-time municipal court judge to continue in judicial position while candidate for school board even though school district is outside municipality where judge sits); W. Va. Adv. Op. 3/15/04 (2004) (magistrate assistant bound by same limitations as magistrate when it comes to political activity and thus would be required to resign to run for a nonpartisan position on board of education); W. Va. Adv. Op. 2/25/94 (1994) (family law master is prohibited from retaining that judicial office while running for election to nonjudicial office of county commissioner); *cf.* Kan. Jud. Ethics Op. JE 110 (2002) (part-time municipal judge contemplating term as city council member need not resign if written in on ballot; judge not "candidate"); Kan. Jud. Ethics Op. JE 56 (1995) (full-time municipal court judge may finish term as member of local board of education, but upon again becoming candidate for that position, must resign from judgeship); Tex. Comm. on Jud. Ethics Adv. Op. 235 (1998) (permissible for master over mental health cases in statutory county court to remain as president of county women's political caucus; and/or remain as chair of mayor's commission on status of women).

Constitutional Challenges

The resign-to-run rule has been challenged as unconstitutional. In *Morial v. Judiciary Comm'n of the State of La.*, 565 F.2d 295 (5th Cir. 1977), *cert. denied*, 435 U.S. 1013 (1978) the court upheld a Louisiana statute and Canon of judicial conduct that required that a judge resign his/her position prior to becoming a candidate for nonjudicial office. *See also Adams v. Sup. Ct. of Penn.*, 502 F. Supp. 1282 (D.C. Pa. 1980) (state law requiring justice of the peace to resign from office when he or she becomes candidate either in party primary or in a general election for nonjudicial office not unconstitutional).

Canon 5A(2) in the 1990 Code was interpreted to apply only to *elective* nonjudicial offices; the 2007 Code language and the accompanying Comments make that explicit. The 1990 Code made an exception concerning state constitutional conventions, because, according to Thode, the Committee "believed that a judge should not be prevented from being a candidate for or a delegate to a state constitutional convention if he is otherwise permitted by law to do so." E. Wayne Thode, *Reporter's Notes to Code of Judicial Conduct* 97 (1973). That provision was deleted from the 2007 Code because of the rarity with which that situation occurs and because such service is easily captured in the Rule's language allowing that which is "permitted by law."

NOT REQUIRED TO RESIGN TO BE CANDIDATE FOR NONJUDICIAL APPOINTIVE OFFICE

If a judge becomes a candidate for appointment to a nonjudicial office, the judge is not required to resign from judicial office. Comments [1] and [2] to Rule 4.5 state that when a judge is seeking appointive nonjudicial office, the dangers are not sufficient to warrant imposing the resign-to-run rule. The danger that a candidate for an appointive nonjudicial office would be tempted to make pledges and promises incompatible with the obligations of judicial office is small, as is the danger that a judge who remained on the bench after a failed attempt to gain another office would use the judicial office to engage in retaliation. *See* Ill. Jud. Ethics Comm. Op. 94-14 (1994) (sitting judge may be applicant for appointment to nonjudicial office (part-time public defender) by fellow judges in same circuit); Ohio Bd. of Commissioners on Grievances and Disc. Op. 98-6 (1998) (judge is not required to resign from judicial office to become candidate for appointment by county central committee to fill office of prosecuting attorney when vacancy occurs).

Additionally, because a sitting judge may become a candidate for an appointive nonjudicial office merely by being considered by an executive branch officer for appointment, the Commission concluded that it was unwarranted to require automatic resignation from the bench. Mandatory resignation would be especially harsh when an executive branch officer is considering several nominees for the same position, or when the confirmation process, if any, is lengthy, of uncertain outcome, or both. Rule 4.5(B) requires that, even though a judge who is a candidate for appointive nonjudicial office can remain on the bench, the judge must continue to abide by all applicable provisions of the Code.

JUDGES NEED NOT RESIGN WHEN SEEKING ANOTHER JUDICIAL POSITION

Rule 4.5 deals only with judges who are seeking nonjudicial positions. The Code does not put restrictions on judges who are seeking another judicial position. *See, e.g.*, Kan. Jud. Ethics Op. JE 117 (2004) (judge may retain office of municipal judge while running for magistrate judgeship); Tenn. Jud. Ethics Comm. Adv. Op. 03-04 (2003) (general sessions judge may retain office upon becoming a candidate for a state court judgeship). *But see* Ark. Jud. Ethics Adv. Comm. Op. 2008-02 (2008) (circuit court judge must resign before running for county judge, position that public generally views as county executive and that is not under the auspices of administrative office of courts).

Appendix A

Judicial Ethics Committee

A. The [chief judge of the highest court of the jurisdiction] shall appoint a Judicial Ethics Committee consisting of [nine] members. [Five] members shall be judges; [two] members shall be non-judge lawyers; and [two] members shall be public members. Of the judicial members, one member shall be appointed from each of [the highest court, the intermediate levels of courts, and the trial courts]. The remaining judicial members shall be judges appointed from any of the above courts, but not from the [highest court of the jurisdiction]. The [chief judge] shall designate one of the members as chairperson. Members shall serve three-year terms; terms shall be staggered; and no individual shall serve for more than two consecutive terms.

B. The Judicial Ethics Committee so established shall have the authority to:
   (1) by the concurrence of a majority of its members, express its opinion on proper judicial conduct with respect to the provisions of [the code of judicial conduct adopted by the jurisdiction and any other specified sections of law of the jurisdiction regarding the judiciary, such as financial reporting requirements], either on its own initiative, at the request of a judge or candidate for judicial office, or at the request of a court or an agency charged with the administration of judicial discipline in the jurisdiction, provided that an opinion may not be issued on a matter that is pending before a court or before such an agency except on request of the court or agency;
   (2) make recommendations to [the highest court of the jurisdiction] for amendment of the Code of Judicial Conduct for the jurisdiction]; and

(3) adopt rules relating to the procedures to be used in expressing opinions, including rules to assure a timely response to inquiries.

C. A judge or candidate for judicial office as defined in the Terminology section of this Code who has requested and relied upon an opinion may not be disciplined for conduct conforming to that opinion.

D. An opinion issued pursuant to this rule shall be filed with the [appropriate official of the judicial conference of the jurisdiction]. Such an opinion is confidential and not public information, unless [the highest court of the jurisdiction] directs otherwise. However, the [appropriate official of the judicial conference of the jurisdiction] shall cause an edited version of each opinion to be prepared, in which the identity and geographic location of the person who has requested the opinion; the specific court involved; and the identity of other individuals, organizations, or groups mentioned in the opinion are not disclosed. Opinions so edited shall be published periodically in the manner [the appropriate official of the judicial conference of the jurisdiction] deems proper.

Appendix B

ABA Model Code of Judicial Conduct Correlation Tables

1990 Code to 2007 Code

1990 Code	2007 Code
Preamble	Preamble and Scope
Terminology	Terminology
Canon 1	Canon 1 (partial)
Canon 1A	Preamble [1]
Canon 2	Canon 1 (partial) and Rule 1.2 (partial)
Canon 2A	Rules 1.1 and 1.2 (partial)
Canon 2B	Rules 1.3, 2.4(B) and (C), 3.1(E) and 3.3
Canon 2C	Rule 3.6(A)
Canon 3	Canon 2
Judicial Duties in General	
Canon 3A	Rule 2.1
Adjudicative Responsibilities	
Canon 3B(1)	Rule 2.7
Canon 3B(2)	Rules 2.2 (partial), 2.4(A) and 2.5(A) (partial)
Canon 3B(3)	Rule 2.8(A)
Canon 3B(4)	Rule 2.8(B)
Canon 3B(5)	Rule 2.3(A) and (B)
Canon 3B(6)	Rule 2.3(C) and (D)
Canon 3B(7)	Rules 2.6(A) and 2.9(A)
Canon 3B(7)(a)	Rule 2.9(A)(1)
Canon 3B(7)(a)(i)	Rule 2.9(A)(1)(a)

1990 CODE	2007 CODE
Canon 3B(7)(a)(ii)	Rule 2.9(A)(1)(b)
Canon 3B(7)(b)	Rule 2.9(A)(2)
Canon 3B(7)(c)	Rule 2.9(A)(3)
Canon 3B(7)(d)	Rule 2.9(A)(4)
Canon 3B(7)(e)	Rule 2.9(A)(5)
Canon 3B(8)	Rule 2.2 (partial)
Canon 3B(9)	Rule 2.10(A), (C) and (D)
Canon 3B(10)	Rule 2.10(B)
Canon 3B(11)	Rule 2.8(C)
Canon 3B(12)	Rule 3.5
Administrative Responsibilities	
Canon 3C(1)	Rule 2.5(A) and (B)
Canon 3C(2)	Rule 2.12(A)
Canon 3C(3)	Rule 2.12(B)
Canon 3C(4)	Rule 2.13(A), (A)(1), (A)(2) and (C)
Canon 3C(5)	Rule 2.13(B)
Canon 3C(5)(a)	Rule 2.13(B)(1)
Canon 3C(5)(b)	Rule 2.13(B)(2)
Canon 3C(5)(c)	Rule 2.13(B)(3)
Disciplinary Responsibilities	
Canon 3D(1)	Rule 2.15(A) and (B)
Canon 3D(2)	Rule 2.15(C) and (D)
Canon 3D(3)	Deleted (See REC to Rule 2.15)
Disqualification	
Canon 3E(1)	Rule 2.11(A)
Canon 3E(1)(a)	Rule 2.11(A)(1)
Canon 3E(1)(b)	Rule 2.11(A)(6), (A)(6)(a) and (A)(6)(c)
Canon 3E(1)(c)	Rule 2.11(A)(3)
Canon 3E(1)(d)	Rule 2.11(A)(2)
Canon 3E(1)(d)(i)	Rule 2.11(A)(2)(a)
Canon 3E(1)(d)(ii)	Rule 2.11(A)(2)(b)
Canon 3E(1)(d)(iii)	Rule 2.11(A)(2)(c)
Canon 3E(1)(d)(iv)	Rule 2.11(A)(2)(d)
Canon 3E(1)(e)	Rule 2.11(A)(4)
Canon 3E(1)(f)	Rule 2.11(A)(5)
Canon 3E(2)	Rule 2.11(B)

1990 CODE	2007 CODE
Remittal of Disqualification	
Canon 3F	Rule 2.11(C)
Canon 4	Canon 3
Extrajudicial Activities in General	
Canon 4A	Rule 3.1
Canon 4A(1)	Rule 3.1(C)
Canon 4A(2)	Deleted
Canon 4A(3)	Rule 3.1(A)
Avocational Activities	
Canon 4B	Deleted (See REC to Comment [1] of Rule 3.1)
Governmental, Civic, or Charitable Activities	
Canon 4C(1)	Rules 3.2 and 3.2(A) and (C)
Canon 4C(2)	Rule 3.4
Canon 4C(3)	Rule 3.7(A)
Canon 4C(3)(a)	Rule 3.7(A)(6)
Canon 4C(3)(a)(i)	Rule 3.7(A)(6)(a)
Canon 4C(3)(a)(ii)	Rule 3.7(A)(6)(b)
Canon 4C(3)(b)(i)	Rule 3.7(A)(1) and (2)
Canon 4C(3)(b)(ii)	Rule 3.7(A)(5)
Canon 4C(3)(b)(iii)	Rule 3.7(A)(3)
Canon 4C(3)(b)(iv)	Deleted
Financial Activities	
Canon 4D(1)	Rule 3.11(C)
Canon 4D(1)(a)	Deleted (See REC to Rule 3.11)
Canon 4D(1)(b)	Rule 3.11(C)(3)
Canon 4D(2)	Rule 3.11(A)
Canon 4D(3)	Rule 3.11(B)
Canon 4D(3)(a)	Rule 3.11(B)(1)
Canon 4D(3)(b)	Rule 3.11(B)(2)
Canon 4D(4)	Rule 3.11(C)(2)
Canon 4D(5)	Rule 3.13(A), (B) and (C)
Canon 4D(5)(a)	Rule 3.13(B)(7), (C)(1), (C)(2) and (C)(2)(a)
Canon 4D(5)(b)	Rule 3.13(B)(8)
Canon 4D(5)(c)	Rule 3.13(B)(3)

1990 CODE	2007 CODE
Canon 4D(5)(d)	Rule 3.13 Comment [2]
Canon 4D(5)(e)	Rule 3.13(B)(2)
Canon 4D(5)(f)	Rule 3.13(B)(4)
Canon 4D(5)(g)	Rule 3.13(B)(6)
Canon 4D(5)(h)	Rule 3.13(C)(3)
Fiduciary Activities	
Canon 4E(1)	Rule 3.8(A)
Canon 4E(2)	Rule 3.8(B)
Canon 4E(3)	Rule 3.8(C)
Service as Arbitrator or Mediator	
Canon 4F	Rule 3.9
Practice of Law	
Canon 4G	Rule 3.10
Compensation, Reimbursement, and Reporting	
Canon 4H(1)	Rules 3.12 (partial) and 3.14(A)
Canon 4H(1)(a)	Rule 3.12 (partial)
Canon 4H(1)(b)	Rule 3.14(B)
Canon 4H(2)	Rules 3.14(C) and 3.15
Canon 4I	Deleted (See REC to Rule 3.15)
Canon 5	Canon 4
All Judges and Candidates	
Canon 5A(1)	Rule 4.1(A)
Canon 5A(1)(a)	Rule 4.1(A)(1)
Canon 5A(1)(b)	Rule 4.1(A)(3)
Canon 5A(1)(c)	Rule 4.1(A)(2)
Canon 5A(1)(d)	Deleted (See REC to Rule 4.1)
Canon 5A(1)(e)	Rule 4.1(A)(4) and (5)
Canon 5A(2)	Rule 4.5(A)
Canon 5A(3)(a)	Rule 4.2(A)(1)
Canon 5A(3)(b)	Rule 4.1(B)
Canon 5A(3)(c)	Rule 4.2(A)(4)
Canon 5A(3)(d)	Rule 4.1(A)(13) (partial)
Canon 5A(3)(d)(i)	Rule 4.1(A)(13) (partial)
Canon 5A(3)(d)(ii)	Rule 4.1(A)(11)
Canon 5A(3)(e)	Rule 4.1 Comments [8] and [9]

1990 CODE	**2007 CODE**
Candidates Seeking Appointment to Judicial or Other Governmental Office	
Canon 5B	Rule 4.3
Canon 5B(1)	Deleted
Canon 5B(2)	Deleted
Canon 5B(2)(a)(i)	Rule 4.3(A)
Canon 5B(2)(a)(ii)	Rule 4.3(B)
Canon 5B(2)(a)(iii)	Deleted
Canon 5B(2)(b)	Deleted
Judges and Candidates Subject to Public Election	
Canon 5C(1)	Rule 4.2(A) and (C)
Canon 5C(1)(a)(i)	Rule 4.2(B)(4)
Canon 5C(1)(a)(ii)	Rule 4.2(C)(1)
Canon 5C(1)(a)(iii)	Rule 4.2(B)(6)
Canon 5C(1)(b)(i)	Rule 4.2(B)(2) (partial)
Canon 5C(1)(b)(ii)	Rule 4.2(B)(2) (partial)
Canon 5C(1)(b)(iii)	Rule 4.2(B)(2) (partial)
Canon 5C(1)(b)(iv)	Rule 4.2(B)(3)
Canon 5C(2)	Rules 4.1(A)(8) and (9), 4.2(B) and (B)(1) and 4.4(A), (B), (B)(1) (partial) and (B)(2)
Canon 5C(3)	Rule 4.4(B)(1) (partial)
Canon 5C(4)	Rule 4.4(B)(3)
Canon 5C(5)	Rule 4.2(B)(3)
Incumbent Judges	
Canon 5D	Deleted
Applicability	
Canon 5E	Deleted
APPLICATION	**APPLICATION**

2007 CODE TO 1990 CODE

2007 CODE	1990 CODE
PREAMBLE	Preamble (partial) and Canon 1A
SCOPE	Preamble (partial)
TERMINOLOGY	Terminology
APPLICATION	Application
CANON 1	Canons 1 and 2
Compliance with the Law	
Rule 1.1	Canon 2A (partial)
Promoting Confidence in the Judiciary	
Rule 1.2	Canons 2 and 2A (partial)
Avoiding Abuse of the Prestige of Judicial Office	
Rule 1.3	Canon 2B (partial)
CANON 2	Canon 3
Giving Precedence to the Duties of Judicial Office	
Rule 2.1	Canon 3A
Impartiality and Fairness	
Rule 2.2	Canons 3B(2) (partial) and 3B(8)
Bias, Prejudice, and Harassment	
Rule 2.3(A)	Canon 3B(5) (partial)
Rule 2.3(B)	Canon 3B(5) (partial)
Rule 2.3(C)	Canon 3B(6) (partial)
Rule 2.3(D)	Canon 3B(6) (partial)
External Influences on Judicial Conduct	
Rule 2.4(A)	Canon 3B(2) (partial)
Rule 2.4(B)	Canon 2B (partial)
Rule 2.4(C)	Canon 2B (partial)
Competence, Diligence, and Cooperation	
Rule 2.5(A)	Canons 3B(2) (partial) and 3C(1) (partial)
Rule 2.5(B)	Canon 3C(1) (partial)
Ensuring the Right to Be Heard	
Rule 2.6(A)	Canon 3B(7) (partial)
Rule 2.6(B)	Canon 3B(8) Commentary

2007 CODE	1990 CODE
Responsibility to Decide	
Rule 2.7	Canon 3B(1)
Decorum, Demeanor, and Communication with Jurors	
Rule 2.8(A)	Canon 3B(3)
Rule 2.8(B)	Canon 3B(4)
Rule 2.8(C)	Canon 3B(11)
Ex Parte Communication	
Rule 2.9(A)	Canon 3B(7) (partial)
Rule 2.9(A)(1)	Canon 3B(7)(a)
Rule 2.9(A)(1)(a)	Canon 3B(7)(a)(i)
Rule 2.9(A)(1)(b)	Canon 3B(7)(a)(ii)
Rule 2.9(A)(2)	Canon 3B(7)(b)
Rule 2.9(A)(3)	Canon 3B(7)(c)
Rule 2.9(A)(4)	Canon 3B(7)(d)
Rule 2.9(A)(5)	Canon 3B(7)(e)
Rule 2.9(B)	New
Rule 2.9(C)	Canon 3B(7) Commentary
Rule 2.9(D)	Canon 3B(7) Commentary
Judicial Statements on Pending and Impending Cases	
Rule 2.10(A)	Canon 3B(9) (partial)
Rule 2.10(B)	Canon 3B(10)
Rule 2.10(C)	Canon 3B(9)(partial)
Rule 2.10(D)	Canon 3B(9) (partial)
Rule 2.10(E)	New
Disqualification	
Rule 2.11(A)	Canon 3E(1)
Rule 2.11(A)(1)	Canon 3E(1)(a)
Rule 2.11(A)(2)	Canon 3E(1)(d)
Rule 2.11(A)(2)(a)	Canon 3E(1)(d)(i)
Rule 2.11(A)(2)(b)	Canon 3E(1)(d)(ii)
Rule 2.11(A)(2)(c)	Canon 3E(1)(d)(iii)
Rule 2.11(A)(2)(d)	Canon 3E(1)(d)(iv)
Rule 2.11(A)(3)	Canon 3E(1)(c)
Rule 2.11(A)(4)	Canon 3E(1)(e)
Rule 2.11(A)(5)	Canon 3E(1)(f)

2007 CODE	1990 CODE
Rule 2.11(A)(6)	Canon 3E(1)(b) (partial)
Rule 2.11(A)(6)(a)	Canon 3E(1)(b) (partial)
Rule 2.11(A)(6)(b)	Canon 3E(1)(b) Commentary
Rule 2.11(A)(6)(c)	Canon 3E(1)(b) (partial)
Rule 2.11(A)(6)(d)	New
Rule 2.11(B)	Canon 3E(2)
Rule 2.11(C)	Canon 3F
Supervisory Duties	
Rule 2.12(A)	Canon 3C(2)
Rule 2.12(B)	Canon 3C(3)
Administrative Appointments	
Rule 2.13(A)	Canon 3C(4) (partial)
Rule 2.13(A)(1)	Canon 3C(4) (partial)
Rule 2.13(A)(2)	Canon 3C(4) (partial)
Rule 2.13(B)	Canon 3C(5)
Rule 2.13(B)(1)	Canon 3C(5)(a)
Rule 2.13(B)(2)	Canon 3C(5)(b)
Rule 2.13(B)(3)	Canon 3C(5)(c)
Rule 2.13(C)	Canon 3C(4) (partial)
Disability and Impairment	
Rule 2.14	New
Responding to Judicial and Lawyer Misconduct	
Rule 2.15(A)	Canon 3D(1) (partial)
Rule 2.15(B)	Canon 3D(1) (partial)
Rule 2.15(C)	Canon 3D(2) (partial)
Rule 2.15(D)	Canon 3D(2) (partial)
Cooperation with Disciplinary Authorities	
Rule 2.16(A)	New
Rule 2.16(B)	New
CANON 3	Canon 4
Extrajudicial Activities in General	
Rule 3.1	Canon 4A
Rule 3.1(A)	Canon 4A(3)
Rule 3.1(B)	New (but derived from Canon 4(A)(3)

2007 CODE	**1990 CODE**
Rule 3.1(C)	Canon 4A(1)
Rule 3.1(D)	New
Rule 3.1(E)	Canon 2B (partial)

Appearances before Governmental Bodies and Consultation with Government Officials

Rule 3.2	Canon 4C(1) (partial)
Rule 3.2(A)	Canon 4C(1) (partial)
Rule 3.2(B)	New
Rule 3.2(C)	Canon 4C(1) (partial)

Testifying as a Character Witness

Rule 3.3	Canon 2B (partial)

Appointments to Governmental Positions

Rule 3.4	Canon 4C(2)

Use of Nonpublic Information

Rule 3.5	Canon 3B(12)

Affiliation with Discriminatory Organizations

Rule 3.6(A)	Canon 2C
Rule 3.6(B)	Canon 2C Commentary

Participation in Educational, Religious, Charitable, Fraternal, or Civic Organizations and Activities

Rule 3.7(A)	Canon 4C(3)
Rule 3.7(A)(1)	Canon 4C(3)(b)(i) (partial)
Rule 3.7(A)(2)	Canon 4C(3)(b)(i) (partial)
Rule 3.7(A)(3)	Canon 4C(3)(b)(iii)
Rule 3.7(A)(4)	New
Rule 3.7(A)(5)	Canon 4C(3)(b)(ii)
Rule 3.7(A)(6)	Canon 4C(3)(a)
Rule 3.7(A)(6)(a)	Canon 4C(3)(a)(i)
Rule 3.7(A)(6)(b)	Canon 4C(3)(a)(ii)
Rule 3.7(B)	New

Appointments to Fiduciary Positions

Rule 3.8(A)	Canon 4E(1)
Rule 3.8(B)	Canon 4E(2)

2007 Code	**1990 Code**
Rule 3.8(C)	Canon 4E(3)
Rule 3.8(D)	Canon 4E Commentary

Service as Arbitrator or Mediator

Rule 3.9	Canon 4F

Practice of Law

Rule 3.10	Canon 4G

Financial, Business, or Remunerative Activities

Rule 3.11(A)	Canon 4D(2)
Rule 3.11(B)	Canon 4D(3)
Rule 3.11(B)(1)	Canon 4D(3)(a)
Rule 3.11(B)(2)	Canon 4D(3)(b)
Rule 3.11(C)	Canon 4D(1)
Rule 3.11(C)(1)	Canon 4D(1) Commentary
Rule 3.11(C)(2)	Canon 4D(4)
Rule 3.11(C)(3)	Canon 4D(1)(b)
Rule 3.11(C)(4)	New

Compensation for Extrajudicial Activities

Rule 3.12	Canons 4H(1) (partial) and 4H(1)(a)

Acceptance and Reporting of Gifts, Loans, Bequests, Benefits, or Other Things of Value

Rule 3.13(A)	Canon 4D(5) (partial)
Rule 3.13(B)	Canon 4D(5) (partial)
Rule 3.13(B)(1)	Canon 4D(5)(h) (partial)
Rule 3.13(B)(2)	Canon 4D(5)(e)
Rule 3.13(B)(3)	Canon 4D(5)(c)
Rule 3.13(B)(4)	Canon 4D(5)(f)
Rule 3.13(B)(5)	New
Rule 3.13(B)(6)	Canon 4D(5)(g)
Rule 3.13(B)(7)	Canon 4D(5)(a) (partial)
Rule 3.13(B)(8)	Canon 4D(5)(b)
Rule 3.13(C)	Canon 4D(5) (partial)
Rule 3.13(C)(1)	Canon 4D(5)(a) (partial)
Rule 3.13(C)(2)	Canon 4D(5)(a) (partial)
Rule 3.13(C)(2)(a)	Canon 4D(5)(a) (partial)
Rule 3.13(C)(2)(b)	New
Rule 3.13(C)(3)	Canon 4D(5)(h)

2007 CODE	**1990 CODE**

Reimbursement of Expenses and Waivers of Fees or Charges

Rule 3.14(A)	Canon 4H(1) (partial)
Rule 3.14(B)	Canon 4H(1)(b)
Rule 3.14(C)	Canon 4H(2)

Reporting Requirements

Rule 3.15(A)	Canon 4H(2) (partial)
Rule 3.15(A)(1)	Canon 4H(2) (partial)
Rule 3.15(A)(2)	Canon 4H(2) (partial)
Rule 3.15(A)(3)	Canon 4H(2) (partial
Rule 3.15(B)	Canon 4H(2) (partial)
Rule 3.15(C)	Canon 4H(2) (partial)
Rule 3.15(D)	Canon 4H(2) (partial)
CANON 4	Canon 5

Political and Campaign Activities of Judges and Judicial Candidates in General

Rule 4.1(A)	Canon 5A(1)
Rule 4.1(A)(1)	Canon 5A(1)(a)
Rule 4.1(A)(2)	Canon 5A(1)(c)
Rule 4.1(A)(3)	Canon 5A(1)(b)
Rule 4.1(A)(4)	Canon 5A(1)(e) (partial)
Rule 4.1(A)(5)	Canon 5A(1)(e) (partial)
Rule 4.1(A)(6)	New
Rule 4.1(A)(7)	New
Rulc 4.1(A)(8)	Canon 5C(2) (partial)
Rule 4.1(A)(9)	Canon 5C(2) (partial)
Rule 4.1(A)(10)	New
Rule 4.1(A)(11)	Canon 5A(3)(d)(ii)
Rule 4.1(A)(12)	Canon 3B(9) (partial)
Rule 4.1(A)(13)	Canon 5A(3)(d) and (d)(i)
Rule 4.1(B)	Canon 5A(3)(b)

Political and Campaign Activities of Judicial Candidates in Public Elections

Rule 4.2(A)	Canon 5C(1)
Rule 4.2(A)(1)	Canon 5A(3)(a)
Rule 4.2(A)(2)	New
Rule 4.2(A)(3)	New

2007 CODE	1990 CODE
Rule 4.2(A)(4)	Canon 5A(3)(c)
Rule 4.2(B)	Canon 5C(2) (partial)
Rule 4.2(B)(1)	Canon 5C(2) (partial)
Rule 4.2(B)(2)	Canons 5C(1)(b)(i)–(iii)
Rule 4.2(B)(3)	Canon 5C(1)(b)(iv)
Rule 4.2(B)(4)	Canon 5C(1)(a)(i)
Rule 4.2(B)(5)	New
Rule 4.2(B)(6)	Canon 5C(1)(a)(iii)
Rule 4.2(C)	Canon 5C(1)
Rule 4.2(C)(1)	Canon 5C(1)(a)(ii)
Rule 4.2(C)(2)	New

Activities of Candidates for Appointive Judicial Office

Rule 4.3	Canon 5B
Rule 4.3(A)	Canon 5B(2)(a)(i)
Rule 4.3(B)	Canon 5B(2)(a)(ii)

Campaign Committees

Rule 4.4(A)	Canon 5C(2) (partial)
Rule 4.4(B)	Canon 5C(2) (partial)
Rule 4.4(B)(1)	Canons 5C(2) (partial) and 5C(3)
Rule 4.4(B)(2)	Canon 5C(2) (partial)
Rule 4.4(B)(3)	Canon 5C(4)

Activities of Judges Who Become Candidates for Nonjudicial Office

Rule 4.5(A)	Canon 5A(2)
Rule 4.5(B)	New (but implicit in and derived from Canon 5A(2))

TABLE OF CASES

B

Barr, *In re*, 13 S.W.3d 525 (Tex. Special Review Tribunal 1998), 4, 164, 165, 176, 178, 186, 187, 188

Barrett v. City of Margate, 743 So. 2d 1160 (Fla. App. 1999), 129

Barrett, *In re*, 512 A.2d 1030 (Me. 1986), 150

Barrett, *In re*, 593 A.2d 529 (Del. Jud. 1991), 71, 508

Barrows, *In re*, 917 A.2d 490 (Vt. 2007), 299

Barton, People v., 121 P.3d 224 (Colo. App. 2004), 277

Bass, *In re*, 2013-31 (Ga. Jud. Qualifications Comm'n 2013), 43

Batiste, *In re* (Ala. Ct. of the Judiciary 2013), 61

Battle v. Thornton, 646 A.2d 315 (D.C. 1994), 384

Bauer v. Memorial Hospital, 879 N.E.2d 478 (Ill. App. 5th Dist. 2007), 209

Bauer v. Shepard, 620 F.3d 704 (7th Cir. 2010), 491, 492, 519, 538

Bauer, *In re*, 818 N.E.2d 1113 (N.Y. 2004), 114, 116

Baugh, *In re*, 334 P.3d 352 (Mont. 2014), 71

Bayer, State v., 656 N.E.2d 1314 (Ohio App. 1995), 54

Bearse, *In re*, 15-17 (Minn. Bd. on Jud. Standards 2015), 225

Beckham, *In re*, 620 S.E.2d 69 (S.C. 2005), 91, 140

Beckum v. State, 917 So. 2d 808 (Miss. App. 2005), 293

Belk, *In re*, 691 S.E.2d 685 (N.C. 2010), 441

Bell v. State, 655 N.E.2d 129 (Ind. App. 1995), 203

Bell, *In re*, 11-4565 (Tenn. Ct. of the Judiciary 2012), 32

Bell, *In re*, 344 S.W.2d 304 (Tenn. 2011), 149

Bell, *In re*, 373 A.2d 232 (D.C. 1977), 308

Bell, *In re*, 894 S.W.2d 119 (Tex. Spec. Ct. Rev. 1995), 65, 119, 151

BellSouth Corp., *In re*, 334 F.3d 941 (11th Cir. 2003), 303, 313

Belton v. U.S., 581 A.2d 1205 (D.C. 1990), 206

Benge, *In re*, 24 So. 3d 822 (La. 2009), 143

Bennett, *In re*, 267 N.W.2d 914 (Mich. 1978), 170, 177

Bennington, *In re*, 24 N.E.3d 958 (Ind. 2015), 120

Benoit, *In re*, 487 A.2d 1158 (Me. 1985), 108, 110, 113, 114, 116

Benoit, *In re*, 523 A.2d 1381 (Me. 1987), 225, 226, 229, 231

Berrigan, Cmmw. v., 472 A.2d 1099 (Pa. Super. 1984), 285

Berry v. Berry, 765 So. 2d 855 (Fla. Dist. Ct. App. 2000), 263, 333

Best, *In re*, 719 So. 2d 432 (La. 1998), 64, 165, 171, 178

Biddle, People v., 180 P.3d 461 (Colo. 2007), 49

Bigby v. Drekte, 402 F.3d 551 (5th Cir. 2005), 303

Bilal, State v., 893 P.2d 674 (Wash. App. 1995), 303

Billips v. Commw., 630 S.E.2d 340 (Va. 2006), 243

Binkoski, *In re*, 515 S.E.2d 828 (W. Va. 1999), 28

Birano, State v., 126 P.3d 357 (Haw. 2006), 218

Birnbaum, *In re* (N.Y. State Comm'n on Jud. Cond. 1997), 548

Bishop, Miss. Comm'n on Jud. Performance v., 761 So. 2d 195 (Miss. 2000), 84

Bissell, *In re*, 429 S.E.2d 731 (N.C. 1993), 65, 180, 296

Blackburne, *In re*, 851 N.E.2d 1175 (N.Y. 2006), 35

Blackman, *In re*, 591 A.2d 1339 (N.J. 1991), 70

Blackman, *In re*, JDDC 09-345 and 10-361 (Ark. Jud. Disc. & Disability Comm'n 2014), 110

Blaisdell v. City of Rochester, 609 A.2d 388 (N.H. 1992), 68, 315, 333, 334, 335

Blakeney, Miss. Comm'n on Jud. Performance v., 848 So. 2d 824 (Miss. 2003), 31

Bland v. Graves, 650 N.E.2d 117 (Ohio App. 1994), 213

Blauvelt, *In re*, 801 P.2d 235 (Wash. 1990), 489

Block, *In re*, 816 N.W.2d 362 (Iowa 2012), 27

Bobo, U.S. v., 395 F. Supp. 2d 1116 (N.D. Ala. 2004), 272, 274, 279, 317

Boese, *In re*, 410 S.E.2d 282 (W. Va. 1991), 139

Boland, Miss. Comm'n on Jud. Performance v., 975 So. 2d 882 (Miss. 2008), 41

Bole v. Nationwide Ins. Co., 379 A.2d 1346 (Pa. 1977), 265

Boles, *In re*, 555 N.E.2d 1284 (Ind. 1990), 105, 136, 565

Bonelli v. Bonelli, 570 A.2d 189 (Conn. 1990), 258, 260

Bonin, *In re*, 378 N.E.2d 669 (Mass. 1978), 456, 467

Boone, *In re*, 2009-117 (Md. Comm'n on Jud. Disabilities 2011), 27

Boothe, *In re*, 110 So. 3d 1002 (La. 2013), 203, 299

Boston's Children First, *In re*, 244 F.3d 164 (1st Cir. 2001), 229, 247

Bowen, Miss. Comm'n on Jud. Performance v., 123 So. 3d 381 (Miss. 2013), 277

Bowers, *In re*, 721 So. 2d 875 (La. 1998), 36, 57, 164, 170, 177, 183

Boy Scouts of America v. Dale, 530 U.S. 640 (2000), 400

Boyd v. State, 581 A.2d 1 (Md. 1990), 288, 308

C

E

Eads, *In re*, 362 N.W.2d 541 (Iowa 1985), 170
Eagen, *In re*, 814 A.2d 304 (Pa. Ct. Jud. Disc. 2002), 32–33
Earls v. Earls, 2001 WL 504905 (Tenn. Ct. App. 2001), 66
Easterling, *In re* (Ky. Jud. Conduct Comm'n 2015), 170
Eastmoore, *In re*, 504 So. 2d 756 (Fla. 1987), 179
Eastside Baptist Church v. Vicinanza, 603 S.E.2d 681 (Ga. App. 2004), 307
Edens, *In re*, 226 S.E.2d 5 (N.C. 1976), 157
Edgar v. K.L., 93 F.3d 256 (7th Cir. 1996), 221
Edwards, *In re* (Cal. Comm'n on Jud. Performance 2012), 31
Edwards, *In re*, 12-075 (N.C. Jud. Standards Comm'n 2012), 149–150
Edwards, *In re*, 492 N.E.2d 124 (N.Y. 1986), 122
Edwards, *In re*, 694 N.E.2d 701 (Ind. 1998), 77, 272, 293, 334
Ehlschide, *In re* (Ky. Jud. Retirement & Removal Comm'n Unreported Order, Apr. 9, 1982), 548
Eiler, *In re*, 236 P.3d 873 (Wash. 2010), 182
Elane v. St. Bernard Hosp., 672 N.E.2d 820 (Ill. 1996), 431, 437
Eldridge v. Eldridge, 137 S.W.3d 1 (Tenn. Ct. App. 2002), 74
Elizabeth S., *In re*, 698 N.W.2d 252 (Neb. App. 2005), 218
Ellender, *In re*, 16 So. 3d 351 (La. 2009), 164
Ellender, *In re*, 889 So. 2d 225 (La. 2004), 39, 71
Ellis, People v., 658 N.W.2d 142 (Mich. 2003), 117, 118
Ellis, State v., 889 A.2d 1 (N.H. 2005), 293
Ellison, State v., 140 P.3d 899 (Ariz. 2006), 288
Elliston, *In re*, 789 S.W.2d 469 (Mo. 1990), 57, 170, 173, 174, 179, 181
Elloie, *In re*, 921 So. 2d 882 (La. 2006), 109
Elum, Disc. Counsel v., 979 N.E.2d 289 (Ohio 2012), 35
Elward, *In re*, 1 Ill. Cts. Comm'n 114 (1977), 525
Emanuel, *In re*, 755 So. 2d 862 (La. 1999), 152, 153, 155
Emanuel, State v., 768 P.2d 196 (Ariz. Ct. App. 1989), 219
Emmanuel, Miss. Comm'n on Jud. Performance v., 688 So. 2d 222 (Miss. 1996), 120
Empson, *In re*, 562 N.W.2d 817 (Neb. 1997), 45, 49, 133, 181, 187, 188

F

G

H

J

K

M

N

O

P

Q

R

S

Sallee, *In re*, 579 N.E.2d 75 (Ind. 1991), 506

Samay, *In re*, 764 A.2d 398 (N.J. 2001), 84, 86

Sanders, *Ex parte*, 659 So. 2d 1036 (Ala. Crim. App. 1995), 291

Sanders, *In re*, 564 S.E.2d 670 (S.C. 2002), 124, 148

Sanders, *In re* Disc. Proc. Against, 145 P.3d 1208 (Wash. 2006), 40

Sanders, Miss. Comm'n on Jud. Performance v., 708 So. 2d 866 (Miss. 1998), 60, 121

Sanders, Miss. Comm'n on Jud. Performance v., 749 So. 2d 1062 (Miss. 1999), 116

Sanjines v. Sanjines, 1998 WL 761849 (Tenn. Ct. App. 1998), 75

Sansone v. Garvey, Schubert & Barer, 71 P.3d 124 (Or. App. 2003), 385

Santini, *In re*, 597 A.2d 1388 (N.J. 1991), 142

Santoya, *In re* (Tex. Comm'n on Jud. Conduct 2006), 112

Sargeant, Disc. Counsel v., 889 N.E.2d 96 (Ohio 2008), 147, 149

Sargent County Bank v. Wentworth, 500 N.W.2d 862 (N.D. 1993), 262

Sauce, *In re*, 561 N.E.2d 751 (Ind. 1990), 57

Saucedo, *In re* (Cal. Comm'n on Jud. Performance 2015), 38

Savani v. Savani, 403 S.E.2d 900 (N.C. App. 1991), 258

SCA Services, Inc. v. Morgan, 557 F.2d 110 (7th Cir. 1977), 316

Scales, State v., 933 P.2d 737 (Kan. 1997), 203

Scarlett, *In re*, No. 10-209 (N.C. Jud. Standards Comm'n 2011), 56

Schapiro, *In re*, 845 So. 2d 170 (Fla. 2003), 55, 173, 177

Schatz, *In re*, 845 N.W.2d 273 (Neb. 2014), 88

Scheehle v. Justices of the Sup. Ct. of the St. of Ariz., 120 P.3d 1092 (Ariz. 2005), 249, 298, 299

Schenck, *In re*, 870 P.2d 185 (Or. 1994), 231, 233, 367

Schenck, *In re* Conduct of, 870 P.2d 185 (Or. 1994), 79, 231–232, 296

Schenck, *In re* Conduct of, 879 P.2d 863 (Or. 1994), 208

Schiff, *In re*, 635 N.E.2d 286 (N.Y. 1994), 51, 175

Schildknecht, *In re*, CJC 14-1080-DI & 15-0002-DI (Tex. Comm'n on Jud. Conduct 2015), 129

Schmidt, *In re* (Cal. Comm'n on Jud. Performance 1989), 506

Schupper v. People, 157 P.3d 516 (Colo. 2007), 272

Schwartz v. Hosp. of Univ. of Pa., 1992 WL 102864 (E.D. Pa. 1992), 261

T

U

V

W

Weeks, *In re*, 658 P.2d 174 (Ariz. 1983), 150

Weinberger v. Equifax, Inc., State *ex rel.*, 557 F.2d 456 (5th Cir. 1997), 314

Weinberger v. Equifax, Inc., U.S. *ex rel.*, 557 F.2d 456 (5th Cir. 1977), 274, 316

Weinstock v. Holden, 995 S.W.2d 408 (Mo. 1999), 248

Weithman, *In re*, 34 N.E.3d 865 (Ohio 2015), 171

Wells, Miss. Comm'n on Jud. Performance v., 794 So. 2d 1030 (Miss. 2001), 30, 35, 112

Wenger v. Comm'n on Jud. Performance, 630 P.2d 954 (Cal. 1981), 226

Wersal v. Sexton, 674 F.3d 1010 (8th Cir. 2012), 496, 507, 518

Westbrook v. State, 29 S.W.3d 103 (Tex. Crim. App. 2000), 200

Westra, *In re* (Cal. Comm'n on Jud. Performance 2007), 172

Whitaker, *In re*, 948 So. 2d 1067 (La. 2007), 91

White v. Jud. Inquiry & Rev. Bd. of Penn., 744 F. Supp. 658 (E.D. Pa. 1990), 144

White v. SunTrust Bank, 538 S.E.2d 889 (Ga. Ct. App. 2000), 74, 281, 333

White, *In re*, 499 S.E.2d 813 (S.C. 1998), 46

White, *In re* Complaint Against, 651 N.W.2d 551 (Neb. 2002), 31–32, 42, 196, 197, 198, 228, 232, 236

Whitten, Miss. Comm'n on Jud. Performance v., 687 So. 2d 744 (Miss. 1997), 39

Whittey, State v., 821 A.2d 1086 (N.H. 2003), 291

Wilder, *In re*, 516 S.E.2d 927 (S.C. 1999), 65, 116, 132, 140

Wiley, *In re*, 844 N.W.2d 1 (Mich. 2014), 61

Wilkerson, Miss. Comm'n on Jud. Performance v., 876 So. 2d 1006 (Miss. 2004), 40, 78, 130, 367

Wilkes, *In re*, 403 So. 2d 35 (La. 1981), 448

Wilkinson, *In re*, 678 A.2d 1257 (Vt. 1996), 385

Wilks v. Israel, 627 F.2d 32 (7th Cir. 1980), 303

Will, U.S. v., 449 U.S. 200 (1980), 248

Willard, Miss. Comm'n on Jud. Performance v., 788 So. 2d 736 (Miss. 2001), 47

Williams & Connolly, L.L.P. v. P.E.T.A., 643 S.E.2d 136 (Va. 2007), 203

Williams v. Farmers Ins. Group, Inc., 720 P.2d 598 (Colo. App. 1985), 215, 216

Williams v. Pennsylvania, 579 U.S. ___ (June 9, 2016), 292

Williams v. Reed, 6 S.W.3d 916 (Mo. Ct. App. 1999), 284, 320

Williams-Yulee v. Fla. Bar, 575 U.S. ____, 135 S. Ct. 1656, 191 L. Ed. 2d 570 (2015), 3, 491–492, 518, 519, 584

Y

Z

INDEX

F

W

Y